CONIECTANEA BIBLICA • NEW TESTAMENT SERIES 39

CB

CONIECTANEA BIBLICA

NEW TESTAMENT SERIES 39

Present editors:
Birger Olsson (Lund) and Kari Syreeni (Uppsala)

The Ancient Synagogue From Its Origins until 200 C.E.

Papers Presented at an International Conference at Lund University, October 14–17, 2001

Edited by
Birger Olsson and Magnus Zetterholm

Almqvist & Wiksell International • Stockholm
2003

Abstract

Olsson, Birger and Zetterholm, Magnus, eds. The Ancient Synagogue From Its Origins until 200 C.E.: Papers Presented at an International Conference at Lund University, October 14–17, 2001. Coniectanea Biblica. New Testament Series 39. xviii + 571 pp. ISBN 91-22-02028-4.

This conference volume is structured by the five research areas of the Lund synagogue project "The Ancient Synagogue: Birthplace of Two World Religions," funded by The Bank of Sweden Tercentenary Foundations, and by its time limit up to ca 200 C.E. The aim of the conference was to give an opportunity for young, emerging scholars to interact with some of the most prominent and established scholars of the field.

Lee I. Levine, in his opening paper, carefully defines the results and the main problems of the synagogue research of today, and the main papers contribute to five central themes: the origins of the synagogue (J. F. Strange, A. Runesson, P. Richardson), the life in the Diaspora synagogues (C. Claussen, M. Zetterholm, J. Lieu), the languages of the synagogue (E. Tov, G. Walser, J. Watt), the worship of the synagogue (R. Kimelman, I. von Görtz-Wrisberg, D. K. Falk) and the hermeneutics of the synagogue (K. Hedner Zetterholm, P. V. M. Flesher). Introductions and evaluations of the contributions to these areas and a discussion about the synagogue at ancient Ostia are included.

Old positions are refined and discussed, new hypotheses are presented. Persian colonial strategy is the beginning of the synagogue in Palestine; local temples developed into synagogues in Egypt; a special variety of Greek, formed by the Pentateuch in Greek, was used by Jews and Christians; a Palestinian Targum was used already at the end of the second century; the separation into two competing groups, Judaism and Christianity, is an "inner-Christian" process in a synagogue context among Jesus-believing Jews and Jesus-believing non-Jews.

The summarizing presentation and discussion of results and problems, the broad approach to the ancient synagogue as such, the combination of several methods, the use of theories and models, new definitions, new hypotheses, new insights, new combinations of older results and new questions make the conference volume a challenging contribution to the investigation of the ancient synagogue today.

Keywords

Antioch incident, archeology, benediction, blessing, Christianity, church, divine sovereignty, festival of Shavuot, Greek, Hebrew, house synagogues, imperial cult, Josephus, Judaism, Laban, language pragmatism, liturgy, Masada, midrash, origin, Ostia, Pentateuchal, Persian imperial politics, Philo, Qumran, Second Temple, separation, Septuagint, synagogue, Targum, voluntary associations, worship

Published with the aid of a grant from
The Bank of Sweden Tercentenary Foundations

ISBN 91-22-02028-4
© Birger Olsson, Magnus Zetterholm, and the authors
Published by Almqvist & Wiksell International, Stockholm
Printed at Studentlitteratur, Lund 2003

Contents

List of Figures and Tables	viii
List of Contributors	xi
Preface	xiv
Publications of the Synagogue Project	xvi

1 The First Century C.E. Synagogue in Historical Perspective 1
   Lee I. Levine

Part I • The Origins of the Synagogue

2 The Origins of the Synagogue: An Introduction 27
   Birger Olsson

3 Archaeology and Ancient Synagogues
   up to about 200 C.E. 37
   James F. Strange

4 Persian Imperial Politics, the Beginnings of
   Public Torah Readings, and the Origins
   of the Synagogue 63
   Anders Runesson

5 An Architectural Case for Synagogues as Associations 90
   Peter Richardson

6 The Origins of the Synagogue: An Evaluation 118
   Donald D. Binder

7 The Origins of the Synagogue: An Evaluation 132
   Birger Olsson

Part II • The Life in the Diaspora Synagogues

8 The Life in the Diaspora Synagogues: An Introduction 141
   Bengt Holmberg

9	Meeting, Community, Synagogue—Different Frameworks of Ancient Jewish Congregations in the Diaspora *Carsten Claussen*	144
10	A Covenant for Gentiles? Covenantal Nomism and the Incident at Antioch *Magnus Zetterholm*	168
11	The Synagogue and the Separation of the Christians *Judith Lieu*	189
12	The Life in the Diaspora Synagogues: An Evaluation *Mark D. Nanos*	208
13	The Life in the Diaspora Synagogues: An Evaluation *Bengt Holmberg*	219

Part III • The Languages of the Synagogue

14	The Languages of the Synagogue: An Introduction *Jerker Blomqvist*	235
15	The Text of the Hebrew/Aramaic and Greek Bible Used in the Ancient Synagogues *Emanuel Tov*	237
16	The Greek of the Ancient Synagogue *Georg Walser*	260
17	Language Pragmatism in a Multilingual Religious Community *Jonathan Watt*	277
18	The Languages of the Synagogue: An Evaluation *Staffan Wahlgren*	298
19	The Languages of the Synagogue: An Evaluation *Jerker Blomqvist*	303

Part IV • The Worship of the Synagogue

20	The Worship of the Synagogue: An Introduction *Sten Hidal*	315
21	Again Blessing Formulae and Divine Sovereignty in Rabbinic Liturgy *Reuven Kimelman*	320

22 No Second Temple—No Shavuot? *The Book of*   376
    Jubilees as a Case Study
    Irene von Görtz-Wrisberg

23 Qumran and the Synagogue Liturgy   404
    Daniel K. Falk

24 The Worship of the Synagogue: An Evaluation   435
    Håkan Ulfgard

Part V • The Hermeneutics of the Synagogue

25 The Hermeneutics of the Synagogue: An Introduction   449
    Birger Olsson

26 The Attempted Murder by Laban the Aramean: Rabbinic   453
    Hermeneutics and the Emergence of an Ideology
    Karin Hedner Zetterholm

27 The Literary Legacy of the Priests? The Pentateuchal   467
    Targums of Israel in their Social and Linguistic Context
    Paul V. M. Flesher

28 The Hermeneutics of the Synagogue: An Evaluation   509
    Bruce Chilton

Part VI • The Synagogue of Ancient Ostia and the Jews of Rome

29 Current Views on the Synagogue of Ostia Antica and
    the Jews of Rome and Ostia   521
    Dieter Mitternacht

Figures and Tables

Figures

3.1	The synagogue at Qiryat Sefer	38
3.2	Plan of the Gamla synagogue	41
3.3	Silhouette of the Gamla synagogue	43
3.4	Viewshed analysis of the Gamla synagogue	44
3.5	The synagogue at el-Khirbe	47
3.6	The synagogue at Khirbet Samara	48
3.7	Plan of the synagogue at Sha'alvim	49
3.8	Plan of the Masada synagogue	52
3.9	The Jericho synagogue	53
3.10	A possible synagogue ark	54
3.11	Interior of Capernaum I synagogue	55
3.12	Plan of the Byzantine synagogue at Capernaum	58
4.1	The relation between the two types of synagogues	69
4.2	Status of legitimacy and authority range	79
4.3	The development of public torah reading and teaching	82
5.1	Plan of the Ostia synagogue	98
5.2	Entrance area of the Ostia synagogue	99
5.3	Area G of the Ostia synagogue	100
5.4	Area G of the Ostia synagogue, to the south	100
5.5	The west side of area D of the Ostia synagogue	101
5.6	The Ostia synagogue's torah niche	102
5.7	Plan of Ostia's Association of the Housebuilders	103
5.8	Central courtyard of the Housebuilders' Association	104

5.9	One of the suite of four triclinia east of the central courtyard in the Housebuilders' Association building	105
27.1	Standard view of the relationships between the Pentateuchal Targums	472
27.2	Development of the relationships between the Pentateuchal Targums during the second century C.E.	487
27.3	Location of expansions in the Palestinian Targums	495
27.4	Development of the relationship between the Pentateuchal Targums from first to the fourth century C.E., or later	497
29.1	Isometric drawing of the Ostia synagogue in its fourth century state	534
29.2	The restored northern wall of area D (Ostia)	537
29.3	The synagogue at Ostia: second half of the first century C.E.	538
29.4	The eastern wall of one of the two *tepidaria* in the *Terme del Foro* (Ostia)	539
29.5	The rough bedding course on the inside of the wall between A and G (Ostia)	540
29.6	Wall structure on the wall between A and G (Ostia)	541
29.7	Erosion in the marble slab surface (Ostia)	543
29.8	Navalia and temple construction at the Tiber mouth	547
29.9	Reconstruction of the harbor basin and the Navalia with temple	548
29.10	Map of the Quarter outside the Porta Marina	550

Tables

4.1	Synagogue terms and their distribution	66
4.2	Categorization of public buildings	83
5.1	Comparison of Palestine and Diaspora Synagogues	92–3
16.1	Position of the principal verb in relation to the conjunctions in the whole corpus	265

16.2	Relative frequency of examples with no words between the conjunction and the principal verb in the whole corpus	266
16.3	Relative frequency of examples with no words between the conjunction and the principal verb in the whole corpus	267
16.4	Mean of LXX-indexes	269

Contributors

Donald D. Binder, Rector, Historic Pohick Episcopal Church, Virginia, USA

Jerker Blomqvist, Professor of Greek Language and Literature, Department of Classics and Semitics, Lund University, Sweden

Bruce Chilton, Bernard Iddings Bell Professor of Religion, Bard College, New York, USA

Carsten Claussen, Lecturer in New Testament, Protestant Theological Faculty, University of Munich, Germany. He is at present a visiting scholar and lecturer at Princeton Theological Seminary, New Jersey, USA

Daniel K. Falk, Assistant Professor of Ancient Judaism and Biblical Studies, Department of Religious Studies, University of Oregon, Oregon, USA

Paul V. M. Flesher, Associate Professor of Religious Studies, Religious Studies Program, University of Wyoming, Wyoming, USA

Irene von Görtz-Wrisberg, Doctoral Student in Old Testament Studies, Centre for Theology and Religious Studies, Lund University, Sweden

Karin Hedner Zetterholm, Lecturer in Jewish Studies, Centre for Theology and Religious Studies, Lund University, Sweden

Sten Hidal, Professor of Old Testament Studies, Centre for Theology and Religious Studies, Lund University, Sweden

Bengt Holmberg, Professor of New Testament Studies, Centre for Theology and Religious Studies, Lund University, Sweden

Reuven Kimelman, Associate Professor of Classical Rabbinic Literature, Department of Near Eastern and Judaic Studies, Brandeis University, Massachusetts, USA

Lee I. Levine, Professor of Jewish History and Archeology, Institute of Archeology, The Hebrew University of Jerusalem, Israel

Judith Lieu, Professor of New Testament Studies, Department of Theology and Religious Studies, King's College, London, England

Dieter Mitternacht, Research Fellow in New Testament Studies, Centre for Theology and Religious Studies, Lund University, Sweden

Mark D. Nanos, Ph.D., Independent Scholar, Kansas City, Missouri, USA

Birger Olsson, Professor of New Testament Studies, Centre for Theology and Religious Studies, Lund University, Sweden

Peter Richardson, Professor Emeritus in the Department for the Study of Religion, University of Toronto, Canada

Anders Runesson, Assistant Professor of Early Christianity, Department of Religious Studies, McMaster University, Canada

James F. Strange, Distinguished University Professor, Department of Religious Studies, College of Arts and Sciences, University of South Florida, Florida, USA

Emanuel Tov, Professor of Bible, Institute of Jewish Studies, The Hebrew University of Jerusalem, Israel

Håkan Ulfgard, Associate Professor of New Testament Studies, Department of Religion and Culture, Linköping University, Sweden

Staffan Wahlgren, Associate Professor in Classical Philology at the Norwegian University of Science and Technology, Trondheim, Norway

Georg Walser, Research Fellow in Greek, Department of Classics and Semitics, Lund University, Sweden

Jonathan Watt, Assistant Professor of Biblical Studies, Department of Biblical Studies, Christian Ministries, and Philosophy, Geneva College, Pennsylvania, USA

Magnus Zetterholm, Lecturer in New Testament Studies, Centre for Theology and Religious Studies, Lund University, Sweden

Preface

THE INTENSE DEBATE FROM the early 1990's about the origins and development of the ancient synagogue was one of the motivating factors behind the synagogue project at Lund University. Professor Birger Olsson made the first bibliographical studies in 1995 at *The Pontifical Biblical Institute* in Rome, and in March, 1997 the project started with funding from *The Bank of Sweden Tercentenary Foundation*. The research team included, five doctoral students, one research fellow, and five professors as supervisors from four departments: Biblical Studies, Jewish Studies, Classical Studies and Semitic Studies.

The scope of the project was limited to the period prior to the year 200 C.E. There were strong arguments for extending the period up to the eighth century, but in the end it was decided that this would have rendered the project too unwieldy. The normal procedure, of course, is to make 70 C.E. the *terminus ad quem*, but the chronological limits we have chosen gave us a somewhat different historical perspective. It allowed us to take into account three large collections of texts, namely, the Dead Sea Scrolls, the New Testament, and the Mishnah, as well as the Septuagint, Philo and Josephus. These texts, along with the Hebrew Bible, Targums and other Jewish literature, Jewish-Christian Greek writings, various documents, inscriptions and archaeological finds constitute the primary source material for the project's investigations.

In order to insure that the project has the breadth that the research climate requires today, we divided the investigation into five research areas:

1) An historical analysis of the synagogue's origin, development and history up to 200 C.E. based on a fresh study of available material in light of new methodological considerations.

2) A sociological analysis of the synagogue in its social, economic, religious, cultural and political contexts.

3) A linguistic analysis of the languages employed in the synagogue in primarily Greek-speaking areas.
4) A liturgical, ideological analysis of the synagogue's "services" in broad terms.
5) A hermeneutical, ideological analysis that employs Targum studies to elucidate the comprehensive interpretation of sacred writings and religious traditions that took place in the synagogue.

Within each area of research a doctoral dissertation was to be produced that would be highly focused in its area of study. In addition, the five areas of study could be analyzed in other works and articles, as well as in the project's concluding conference. The project was finished this year and its major publications in English are listed below.

An international conference was planned as an important part of the project. We invited scholars in leading positions within the different areas of research. Together with the doctoral students, many of these experts read papers at the conference, others made critical evaluations of the different contributions and all took part in a very intensive interdisciplinary discussion about the various aspects of the ancient synagogue. We wish to thank all those who contributed to this important event.

We also wish to express our thanks to *The Bank of Sweden Tercentenary Foundation* which has funded the project as a whole, including the conference, and also provided funds for publishing this volume. Thanks also to *Société Royale des Lettres de Lund* and to *Signe and Oscar Krook's Foundation* for contributions to the conference. We are also indebted to B.A. Janet Runeson and Dr. Carole Gillis who have contributed ideas for linguistic improvements in some of the papers. To you, and to all who have in different ways helped make this volume possible, we express our deepest gratitude.

Birger Olsson, Magnus Zetterholm
Lund, August 2003

Publications of the Synagogue Project

Bengtsson, P. Å., *Passover in Targum Pseudo-Jonathan Genesis. The Connection of Early Biblical Events with Passover in Targum Pseudo-Jonathan in a Synagogue.* Almqvist & Wiksell International: Stockholm, 2001.

—, "Semitic Inscriptions in Rome." Pages 151–66 in *The Synagogue of Ancient Ostia and the Jews of Rome: Interdisciplinary Studies.* Edited by B. Olsson et al. Stockholm: Paul Åströms förlag, 2001.

Brandt, O. "The Quarter Surrounding the Syangogue at Ostia." Pages 19–28 in *The Synagogue of Ancient Ostia and the Jews of Rome: Interdisciplinary Studies.* Edited by B. Olsson et al. Stockholm: Paul Åströms förlag, 2001.

Görtz-Wrisberg, I. von, "A Sabbath Service in Ostia: What Do We Know about the Ancient Synagogal Service?" Pages 167–202 in *The Synagogue of Ancient Ostia and the Jews of Rome: Interdisciplinary Studies.* Edited by B. Olsson et al. Stockholm: Paul Åströms förlag, 2001.

Hedner Zetterholm, K., "The Jewish Communities of Ancient Rome." Pages 131–40 in *The Synagogue of Ancient Ostia and the Jews of Rome: Interdisciplinary Studies.* Edited by B. Olsson et al. Stockholm: Paul Åströms förlag, 2001.

—, *Portrait of a Villain. Laban the Aramean in Rabbinic Literature.* Peeters: Leuven 2002.

Hidal, S., "The Jews as the Roman Authors Saw Them." Pages 141–4 in *The Synagogue of Ancient Ostia and the Jews of Rome: Interdisciplinary Studies.* Edited by B. Olsson et al. Stockholm: Paul Åströms förlag, 2001.

Olsson, B. "Introduction." Pages 11–16 in *The Synagogue of Ancient Ostia and the Jews of Rome: Interdisciplinary Studies*. Edited by B. Olsson et al. Stockholm: Paul Åströms förlag, 2001.

Olsson, B., D. Mitternacht, and O. Brand, eds., *The Synagogue of Ancient Ostia and the Jews of Rome*. Stockholm: Paul Åströms Förlag, 2001.

Olsson, B., and M. Zetterholm, eds. *The Ancient Synagogue from Its Origins until 200 C.E. Papers Presented at an International Conference at Lund University, 14-17 October, 2001*. Almqvist & Wiksell International: Stockholm, 2003.

Runesson, A., "The Oldest Original Synagogue Building in the Diaspora. A Response to L. Michael White," *HTR* 92 (1999): 409–33.

—, "The Synagogue at Ancient Ostia: The Building and its History From the First to the Fifth Century." Pages 29–99 in *The Synagogue of Ancient Ostia and the Jews of Rome: Interdisciplinary Studies*. Edited by B. Olsson et al. Stockholm: Paul Åströms förlag, 2001.

—, "Water and Worship: Ostia and the Ritual Bath in the Diaspora Synagogue." Pages 115–129 in *The Synagogue of Ancient Ostia and the Jews of Rome: Interdisciplinary Studies*. Edited by B. Olsson et al. Stockholm: Paul Åströms förlag, 2001.

—, "A Monumental Synagogue from the First Century: The Case of Ostia," *JSJ* 33 (2002): 171–220.

—, *The Origins of the Synagogue. A Socio-Historical Study*. Almqvist & Wiksell International: Stockholm, 2001.

Walser, G. "The Greek of the Jews in Ancient Rome." Pages 145–50 in *The Synagogue of Ancient Ostia and the Jews of Rome: Interdisciplinary Studies*. Edited by B. Olsson et al. Stockholm: Paul Åströms förlag, 2001.

—, *The Greek of the Ancient Synagogue. An Investigation on the Greek of the Septuagint, Pseudepigrapha and the New Testament* Almqvist & Wiksell International: Stockholm, 2001.

—, "A Peculiar Word Order Rule for the Septuagint and for Cognate Texts." Pages 499–511 in *X Congress of the International Organization for Septuagint and Cognate Studies, Oslo, 1998*. Edited by B. A. Taylor. Atlanta: Society of Biblical Literature, 2001.

Zetterholm, M. "A Struggle Among Brothers: An Interpretation of the Relations Between Jews and Christians in Ostia." Pages 101–13 in *The Synagogue of Ancient Ostia and the Jews of Rome: Interdisciplinary Studies*. Edited by B. Olsson et al. Stockholm: Paul Åströms förlag, 2001.

—, *The Formation of Christianity in Antioch: A Social-Scientific Approach to the Separation between Judaism and Christianity*. London: Routledge, 2003.

Forthcoming

Görtz-Wrisberg, I. von, *Shavuot. A Festival of Manifold Meanings According to the Ancient Sources*. Stockholm: Almqvist and Wiksell International, 2004.

Mitternacht, D. and B. Olsson, *The Ancient Synagogue. A Bibliography*.

Runesson, A. and B. Olsson, *The Ancient Synagogue. A Sourcebook*.

1
The First Century C.E. Synagogue in Historical Perspective

Lee I. Levine

IT IS A GREAT HONOR for me, and I am sure that I speak for everyone gathered here, to participate in this conference. It is a fitting tribute to Lund University generally and to the dedicated efforts of Professor Birger Olsson in particular. Over the last five or so years, the Faculty of Theology under his leadership has succeeded in initiating a most ambitious synagogue project, attracting students of exceptionally high caliber; now, with the project reaching successful completion, it has produced a large number of seminal doctoral dissertations regarding the ancient synagogue. These studies contribute significantly to our understanding of the formative stages of what became a pivotal Jewish communal institution. This impressive conference has been convened through the efforts of Professor Olsson in celebration of this project's denouement. It brings together scholars who have contributed significantly to the field of synagogue studies over the last few decades, many of whom are responsible for the rich trove of creative suggestions and insights that have become an important part of the scholarly literature regarding the early synagogue.

The timeframe of this conference, from the institution's beginnings until 200 C.E., is understandable though, admittedly, somewhat frustrating. Given the fact that the overwhelming bulk of information regarding the synagogue stems from Late Antiquity (third to seventh centuries), both in terms of archaeological remains (including the architectural, artistic, and epigraphic dimensions) and literary sources (especially the abundance of data found in rabbinic literature), the exclusion of this material from our deliberations would appear to ignore a large corpus of data that might provide a solid basis for understanding the ancient synagogue. However, it is also true that the synagogue of Late Antiquity was not necessarily the same institution that it was in the first centuries C.E. Throughout this period, the synagogue was far from a fixed institution, continuing to evolve architecturally and religiously; what was true of the fourth and fifth centuries was often not applicable several hundred years earlier. One has but to compare the synagogue of first-century Gamla or Masada with that of sixth-century Bet Alpha, or that of first-century Delos with the Sardis building of Late Antiquity, to recognize the enormous changes that had taken place in the interim. The later synagogue is suffused, inter alia, with Jewish symbols and elements of holiness in its orientation, internal plan, and art, all of which were absent in the first century. For the later synagogue buildings, the primary architectural model was the Byzantine Christian basilica, while for the Gamla and Masada buildings, it was very likely the Hellenistic *bouleuterion*.[1]

Even within the confines of the first century C.E., the synagogue was far from being a monolithic or isomorphic institution. It is at this time that it emerges full-blown on history's stage, appearing throughout much of the Roman Empire, both in Judaea and the Diaspora, as the central Jewish communal institution. The growth of Judaea's Jewish population, the appearance of far-flung Diaspora communities, and the destruction of the temple and Jerusalem in the year 70 all contributed to the enhancement of the synagogue's role in Jewish life, although the pace and nature of this newfound status varied from place to place. Before 70, for example, geographical proximity to Jerusalem was an important factor in the synagogue's development for Jews living in Judaea, while local influences from the surrounding non-Jewish cultures were always of central importance for Diaspora Jews.

Areas of Scholarly Consensus and Disagreement

We will begin by briefly rehearsing those issues regarding the first-century synagogue that I presume are generally agreed upon by scholars, bearing in mind that, given the vast amount of scholarly material being published of late, there will always be exceptions. We will then note certain points of disagreement and proceed to discuss a number of cen-

---

[1] See Levine, *Ancient Synagogue*, passim.

tral issues and methodological challenges that lie at the heart of any attempt to understand this institution at the beginning of our era.

There are at least three commonly shared assumptions in the study of the first-century synagogue:

1. The synagogue was a central institution, and most often the definitive one, in every Jewish community; indeed, it regularly appears to have been the most prominent, identifiable Jewish public building. Recognition of distinguished individuals, Jewish or non-Jewish, by the Jewish community was often recorded within the synagogue (as at Cyrene in North Africa and Acmonia in Asia Minor), and at times recognition of the community's standing and importance by the ruling authorities found expression in the local synagogue (e.g., in Antioch). The Jews also used this venue to express their loyalty to the ruling powers, as evidenced by the dedicatory inscriptions to Ptolemy and his wife Berenice in Egyptian *proseuchai*, the inscriptions and trophies in honor of Augustus in a central Alexandrian synagogue (as mentioned by Philo), or the naming of synagogues in Rome after Imperial officials (such as Augustus and Agrippa). Moreover, attacks on the local Jewish community often resulted in the desecration of synagogues, as was the case at Dor, Caesarea, and Alexandria, and the efforts to curtail Jewish communal activities in a number of Asia Minor cities, according to some of the edicts preserved especially by Josephus (*A.J.* 14 and 16), seem to have often targeted the local synagogue.[2]
2. Given the fact that the Jews constituted both an ethnic and religious group, the synagogue from the outset catered to a varied communal and religious agenda, for which a great deal of evidence exists. The synagogue's liturgical functions are recorded in Luke-Acts, Josephus, and Philo, while the range of its communal functions is alluded to by Josephus and in epigraphic data.
3. There is widespread recognition in scholarly circles of the existence of both diachronic and synchronic dimensions in the synagogue's makeup and of the need to factor in these components for a full understanding of the institution's origins and its

[2] Ibid., 74–123.

overall profile. On the one hand, the synagogue cannot be understood without recognizing its Jewish dimension that was rooted in Second Temple Judaism; on the other hand, the institution should not be divorced from its Greco-Roman moorings and the various non-Jewish social, religious, and architectural models that impacted upon it.

Having said that, some areas of disagreement emerge when the above-noted points of agreement are explored in greater depth:

1. Granted the synagogue's communal and religious dimensions, can one speak of the primary raison d'être of the institution? Assuming that both these facets were integral to the essence of the institution, can it be determined if one was fundamental and the other ancillary in differing circumstances? Might a synagogue's primary function be reflected in the name it was given by a community, especially with regard to the two most widespread terms, *proseuche* and *synagoge*? One might well assume that very fundamental differences existed between them, one name having a more distinct religious profile (*proseuche*), the other a more neutral, communal one (*synagoge*).
2. Given the fact that both synchronic and diachronic dimensions find expression within the synagogue, can we determine which of these was more decisive in shaping the first-century institution? Was it essentially Jewish, having evolved from earlier Judaean models and thus reflecting a strong continuity with the past (diachronic)? Alternatively, was the synagogue in essence a Greco-Roman institution shaped primarily by similar settings found in its non-Jewish surroundings, and did it function in similar ways when serving a Jewish constituency (synchronic)? Assuming a diachronic approach, can the synagogue's roots and inspiration be traced to the Jerusalem temple,[3] or to some other communal institution that preceded it in an earlier period, such as the city-gate?[4] If, however, one assumes that the synagogue was primarily indebted to synchronic influences, was it a Jewish

---

[3] Kasher, "Synagogues," 205–20; Strange, "Art and Archaeology," 75–6; "Ancient Texts," 27–45; and especially, Binder, *Into the Temple Courts*.
[4] Levine, *Ancient Synagogue*, 26–31.

version of a Greco-Roman voluntary association[5] or of a Greco-Roman temple?[6] Moreover, when making such comparisons, are we relating to all aspects of the synagogue (architectural, liturgical, communal, etc.), or only to certain ones?

3. Then there is the question of uniformity vs. diversity. Was there only one type of synagogue institution throughout the Jewish world? In Judaea? In the Diaspora? Did all synagogues have monolithic religious and communal dimensions? If not, what determined the differences between them? If local influences were crucial in shaping the synagogue's physical appearance and functioning, did these change in different historical settings? For example, were the manumission ceremonies typical of the Bosphorus region only, or were local patriotic sentiments unique to the synagogues of Egypt and Rome?

4. Finally, one of the most debated issues in early synagogue studies revolves around the question of origins. When and where did the synagogue first emerge? How did it then evolve and spread? Is it possible to pinpoint the origin of this institution, shrouded as it is in mystery, to one particular place or one specific time?

Exploring several of the above points in greater depth will not only allow us to focus on some of the fundamental issues in synagogue studies, but will also afford us the opportunity to hone in on a number of basic methodological differences among scholars. We will begin by focusing on the sources at our disposal and then turn to what we know about the first-century synagogue on the basis of these sources.

Sources of Information

Our information derives from three types of sources: literary material, archaeological finds, and inscriptions.[7]

---

[5] Richardson, "Early Synagogues," 90–109.
[6] Flesher, "Prolegomenon," 121–53.
[7] See Levine, *Ancient Synagogue*, 42–159; Binder, *Into the Temple Courts*, passim; Claussen, *Versammlung*, 49–81.

In the first century C.E., Philo refers to the Egyptian *proseuche* on several dozen occasions. In his historical writings, he speaks of Alexandrian buildings that were ravaged in the pogroms of 38 C.E., and in other works he takes note of the religious activities in the synagogue on the Sabbath, highlighting the role of the Torah-reading ceremony. His description of the Therapeutae and Essenes and their religious practices, including Sabbath gatherings, is of particular value.

Josephus takes note of synagogues (that is, in Dor, Caesarea, and Tiberias) in the context of his historical narratives, *Bellum judaicum*, *Vita*, and *Antiquitates judaicae*, and also in his apologetic work, *Contra Apionem*. Many of these references are to the synagogues of Judaea, but he also refers to Diaspora institutions on a number of occasions, especially in the Roman edicts preserved in books 14 and 16 of *Antiquitates judaicae*; these documents constitute a particularly rich mine of information on the Diaspora synagogue and its functions.[8]

The New Testament preserves a number of traditions in the gospels about Jesus' activity in several first-century Galilean synagogues. This institution plays a key role in Luke's account, not only in his gospel but also in the Acts of the Apostles. His descriptions of Jesus' participation in the Sabbath morning services in Nazareth, as well as Paul's in Asia Minor, are far and away the most valuable descriptions in this regard.

Rabbinic literature makes reference to first-century synagogues in several early third-century collections. Several focus on pre-70 Jerusalem, but one, undoubtedly the richest of all, furnishes a surprisingly detailed description of a monumental first-century synagogue in Alexandria.

Only one reference in the Dead Sea scrolls seems to refer to a place of worship. The term "house of prostration" is probably a designation for the place where the communal Qumran liturgy was conducted on a daily basis.

The archaeological evidence for first-century synagogues is relatively meager. Only two buildings in the Diaspora, Delos and Ostia, have been dated to the first century.[9] For Judaea, the picture is somewhat

---

[8] Pucci Ben Zeev, *Jewish Rights*.
[9] Kraabel, "Diaspora Synagogue," 477–510; and the recently published Olsson, Mitternacht, and Brandt, *Synagogue of Ancient Ostia*. On the debate between Runesson and White regarding a first- or second-century date for the earliest stage of the Ostia synagogue building, see Runesson, "Oldest Synagogue," 409–33; White, "Reading," 435–64.

fuller and, interestingly, the list has grown steadily in the last decade. The buildings at Gamla, Masada, and Herodium have long been regarded as early synagogues, although suggestions that the buildings at Capernaum, Chorazim, Magdala, and Jericho are synagogues have met with greater skepticism. Recently, communal buildings found at three sites in western Judaea's coastal plain (Qiryat Sefer, Modi'in, and Kh. 'Etri) have opened up a new chapter in the study of the Judaean synagogue in the first and early second centuries C.E.

It may legitimately be asked, on what basis are such structures identified as synagogues? The answer has to do with our understanding of the first-century synagogue generally and that in Judaea specifically. In our opinion, they served first and foremost as communal buildings that included a religious dimension. At this stage in its development, however, the synagogue building bore no expression of its religious dimension, either architectural, artistic, or epigraphical. Several synagogue buildings, in Judaea at least, seem to have been modeled, as noted, after Hellenistic communal institutions such as the *bouleuterion* or *ecclesiasterion*. As has been indicated elsewhere, the first-century synagogue was where all communal affairs were addressed.[10] The name *synagoge* is thus most appropriate for such an institution, indicating a place for gathering with no overt religious connotations. In short, the synagogue at this time can be identified as the largest, and often the only, public building in a Jewish town or village.[11]

The epigraphic evidence for the first-century synagogue is particularly valuable.[12] For Judaea, we have only the well-known monumental Theodotus inscription from Jerusalem. For the Diaspora, however, there is more extensive epigraphic evidence from numerous regions around the Mediterranean, and this material is more readily available than ever before thanks to the efforts of W. Horbury and D. Noy.[13] Some sixteen inscriptions and four papyri come from Hellenistic–early

---

[10] Levine, *Ancient Synagogue*, 128–34.
[11] This, of course applies to areas of Jewish population in Judaea. For the Diaspora, other criteria need to be invoked as, for example, an orientation toward Jerusalem (Ostia), the use of Jewish symbols (non-existent for this period), or the use of Jewishly identifiable terms in inscriptions (Cyrene, Bosphorus).
[12] We will also make reference to several papyri from Egypt that refer to the local synagogue.
[13] Horbury and Noy, *Jewish Inscriptions of Graeco-Roman Egypt*; Noy, *Jewish Inscriptions of Western Europe*; as well as the classic work of Frey, *Corpus inscriptionum iudaicarum*.

Roman Egypt, three monumental inscriptions from Cyrene to Egypt's west, almost two dozen from Rome,[14] another five from Delos, one from Asia Minor, and nine (several dating to the early second century) from the Bosphorus region. The diversity of even this small amount of material is striking: Some inscriptions are major communal documents (Cyrene); some are brief contracts of manumission which mention the community as well (Bosphorus); others are short dedicatory declarations, either of individuals (Delos, Acmonia, Egypt) or a community (Egypt); and still others are epitaphs noting synagogue affiliation (Rome).

For certain locales, this epigraphic evidence is all that we have, for others additional types of evidence are available as well, and the combinations vary widely. Epigraphic evidence is our sole source for Cyrene and the Bosphorus Kingdom, literary and epigraphic testimony exist for Egypt, Asia Minor, and Rome, while archaeological, epigraphic, and limited literary material are available for Delos and Italy; only literary evidence exists for Syria.

Thus, the relative paucity of evidence is important to bear in mind when dealing with issues regarding the first-century synagogue. All told, literary references to the synagogue in the New Testament, Josephus, Philo, and elsewhere number no more than three score (depending on how one counts the parallel accounts in the New Testament and Josephus) for the entire Jewish world! Archaeological material is likewise meager, especially when compared to the enormous quantity dating from Late Antiquity. As noted, only about a half-dozen buildings can be securely identified as a synagogue building and dated to the first century, and only a modest number of inscriptions and papyri exist for Egypt, Cyrene, Delos, Rome, Asia Minor, and the Bosphorus Kingdom. Thus, any kind of theorizing about the first-century synagogue—its origin, essence, functions, and possible derivation—should be done with much caution and with an awareness that any suggestions must remain tentative, at best.

---

[14] Richardson, "Augustan-Era Synagogues," 17–29.

Methodological Dispositions

In utilizing the above sources for study of the first-century synagogue, one ought to be fully aware of the nature of the various types of sources at our disposal as well as of the particular sources themselves. For example, we have noted above that many studies seek to define the essence of the Diaspora synagogue, and the questions posed above become pivotal; granting the presence of both religious and communal dimensions, which of these was more central to the synagogue's basic raison d'être? Was the Jewish component more determinant of the synagogue's character than one derived from the Greco-Roman world?

Two interrelated factors often play a decisive role in shaping a response to the above questions—which of the above-noted types of evidence we choose to emphasize, and the components of the synagogue we wish to highlight. Regarding the first issue, the archaeological evidence, and literary sources offer very different emphases on the nature of the synagogue. The archaeological material (building plans, architecture, inscriptions, and orientation) tends to highlight the communal dimension of the building and offers no evidence relating to its religious character. There is no art bearing a clear religious message (as, for example, the Binding of Isaac later on), no inscriptions speaking of "a holy congregation," and no distinct orientation toward Jerusalem (Ostia perhaps excepted), all of which were to become quite prominent in synagogue buildings of Late Antiquity. The archaeological evidence at the Gamla synagogue, for example, appears to indicate a communal building par excellence; the only component that might possibly reflect some sort of religious concern is a *miqveh* (ritual bath) located outside the main hall. However, even here, the *miqveh*'s date is unclear, some suggesting that it was added only on the eve of the Jewish revolt of 66, many decades after the building was erected and just a few months before the synagogue and town were destroyed.[15]

In contradistinction to the archaeological material, most literary sources tend to underscore the religious component of the synagogue—the Torah-reading on Sabbaths and other religious practices. This dimension forms the almost exclusive focus of evidence in the

---

[15] Exceptions to the above claim regarding the secular character of the first-century synagogue can be found in those Diaspora inscriptions that refer to a *proseuche* (prayer house) when describing the institution, a term that clearly points to a religious dimension.

New Testament and rabbinic literature, and is dominant in Philo and Josephus as well, although the latter, in quoting Imperial edicts, also notes a number of communal, non-liturgical, aspects. The question, therefore, is whether we choose to rely primarily on these written sources for a comprehensive picture of the first-century synagogue, under the assumption that they reflect the basic functions of the synagogue; alternatively, should we posit that these sources, given their particular proclivities and interests, are intent on zeroing in on the religious component, and that this narrow focus tends to distort the overall picture of the institution? Among the major challenges in the study of the first-century synagogue, then, is how to factor in the diverse nature of these very different kinds of sources, and how to integrate this seemingly contrasting evidence.[16]

A second factor to be considered involves not just the sources themselves, but also the choice of subject matter. If one decides to focus on liturgy, e.g., the Torah-reading, then ipso facto the Jewish and religious components are brought to the fore. If, however, one chooses to deal with the architecture, inscriptions, official titles, or certain kinds of institutional activities (such as community meals), then the communal dimension, along with the larger Greco-Roman context, comes more prominently into play.

Between Rome and Jerusalem

The synagogue's dependence on outside sources of inspiration for much of what falls under the category of material culture (architecture, art, and epigraphy) should come as no surprise. Thus, it is important to bear in mind that the Jews never had an independent architectural, artistic, or even institutional model for the synagogue. The nature of the Jews' material culture, and very often their other socio-religious frameworks as well, has always involved some sort of borrowing from contemporary models. A visit to the Museum of the Diaspora in Tel Aviv University vividly demonstrates the fact that there were always large-

---

[16] It is also noteworthy that archaeological remains tend to highlight the heterogeneity among synagogues while literary sources tend to generalize and thus homogenize synagogue-related traits. This holds true for the first century C.E. as it does for Late Antiquity.

scale adoption and adaptation of architectural and artistic models in each and every historical context in which Jewish communities found themselves throughout history. Instructive in this vein is the analysis by A. Silverstein of the transformation of the Reform synagogue in the United States during the nineteenth and twentieth centuries in light of the changes and newly-evolving models within American society generally, not only in the architectural sphere, but in religious and communal areas as well.[17]

Of late, synagogue studies have been enriched by P. Richardson's and P. V. M. Flesher's probing inquiries regarding which Greco-Roman model may have influenced the form and functioning of the first-century synagogue. The former suggests the *collegia* or voluntary associations, the latter the Greco-Roman temple.[18] Whatever the merit of these specific suggestions, the larger question is whether any outside model, no matter how much light it may shed on the synagogue in its institutional trappings and as a physical entity, can fully explain this institution's workings. Might it not be the case that Jewish communities not only used these non-Jewish models selectively but, in doing so, also integrated them with traditions and practices inherited from earlier generations? A Jewish community was an entity no less ethnic than religious in essence and, as such, its common history, origins, customs, culture, and aspirations served to bind it together. When one combines an ethnic base and a well-defined religious component, the bonds forged—internally and with other communities—can be formidable.

The synagogue's continuity from earlier Jewish precedents is far from simple, given the fact that many of these communities may not have existed for much time beforehand. What we seem to be dealing with in the first century, and I would suggest that this applies to the situation in Judaea as well as the Diaspora, is an institution in the midst of a process of self-definition. In a sense, it was a cultural construct of the Hellenistic and Roman eras, continually undergoing revision and development. By viewing the synagogue in such a manner, its dynamic and diverse nature assumes center stage; it was constantly reinventing itself as outside influences shaped the direction and supplied the tools used by Jewish communities to promote their interests and answer their needs.

---

[17] Silverstein, *Alternatives*.
[18] See above, nn. 5 and 6.

The Complexities of the Early Synagogue

To demonstrate some of the challenges in defining the different components of first-century synagogue life, we will examine three different examples from the Diaspora: the Egyptian *proseuche*, an inscription from Cyrene, and the Dura Europos synagogue.

The evidence from Egypt is quantitatively significant, and acquires added importance owing to the fact that it is the earliest material available regarding the ancient synagogue. It is precisely because of its chronological precedence that a number of scholars have posited that this institution, in fact, originated there. This view is supported by the fact that the Egyptian *proseuche* was heavily influenced by its Ptolemaic surroundings, particularly those of local temples, and is expressed by the following features:

1. The exclusive use of Greek in inscriptions and papyri;
2. Dedicating synagogues to Ptolemaic rulers;
3. Utilizing the word *proseuche* for the synagogue, a term well known in pagan contexts as well;
4. The presence in local synagogue contexts of an exedra, gateway, or groves;
5. The status of the synagogue as an "inviolate" place (ἄσυλος);
6. The use of a common pagan designation for God, the Most High God (θεὸς ὕψιστος), as in Delos;
7. Referring to the *proseuche* as a sacred place or sacred precinct;
8. The name of a synagogue attendant (νακόρος);
9. Use of the synagogue as a communal archive or a place of meeting for local associations;
10. The presence of statues in a number of synagogues.[19]

It has even been suggested by J. G. Griffiths that the Per Ankh annex to the local Egyptian temple, where prayer and the reading of sacred

---

[19] For references to the above phenomena, see Levine, *Ancient Synagogue*, 75–82. This topic has also been treated by M. Hengel, "Proseuche und Synagoge," 157–84; Dion, "Synagogues et temples," 45–75.

texts took place, was the immediate model for the creation of the Jewish *proseuche*.[20]

Yet with all the borrowing, the Jewish community managed to set very clear limits. Ptolemaic *proseuchae* were not dedicated "to" Ptolemy, but "on behalf of" the king. Thus, the Jews found a way to honor the ruler, as was customary in Egypt, without compromising their religious sensitivities. The Jewish place of worship was not identical to the pagan sanctuary or any other place of sacrifice; rather, it was a *proseuche*, a place for prayer and communal study. If the Tosefta account is in any way reliable historically (*t. Sukkah* 4, 6), it would seem that this large Alexandrian synagogue building was modeled, at least in part, after the Jerusalem temple.[21] The full expression of the unique Jewish component of this institution rests in the religious rituals that transpired therein on Sabbaths and holidays (see below).

A first-century synagogue from Cyrene, which is referred to, interestingly enough, as an amphitheater, has produced three monumental inscriptions.[22] One inscription, from 24–25 C.E., records the decision of the community (here called *politeuma*) and its leaders (referred to as *archontes*) to honor a Roman official, Marcus Tittius son of Sextus from the tribe of Aemilia, who had apparently been supportive of the Jewish community as well as the city's citizens generally. This recognition, which was publicly announced in the synagogue on the Festival of Tabernacles (Sukkot), included praising him and awarding him a crown of olive branches and a woolen fillet at each (Sabbath?) assembly and New Moon. The decision was recorded on a stele of Parian marble set up in the amphitheater and was endorsed by the community by a majority casting white stones.

Both communal and religious components of the local Jewish community are easily detectable in this inscription. It is recorded that the ceremony took place at the initiative of the local Jewish community, which also decided whom to honor. All the days and events noted for the various convocations are Jewish: Sukkot, the New Moon, and probably the Sabbath are intended. Thus, these two components of the community's life—the communal and the religious—are inextricably intertwined.

---

[20] Griffiths, "Egypt," 1–15. For a critique of this suggestion, see Levine, "First-Century Synagogue."
[21] Levine, *Ancient Synagogue*, 84–9.
[22] Ibid., 89–96; Binder, *Into the Temple Courts*, 257–63

Yet, while the commemoration was organized by and for the local community, Greco-Roman influences are distinctly present as well. The community's leadership bore official titles and personal names of Greek origin, as did the organizational framework of the community itself (*politeuma*). Moreover, the means of expressing this recognition was taken straight out of Greco-Roman etiquette—a crown of olive branches and a fillet, a prominently displayed inscription, and the voting process—much as similar events within Jewish communities today are carried out under the influence of accepted patterns drawn from Western culture.

The awarding of a crown and a fillet merits further comment. Such displays of gratitude and praise were time-honored patterns in Greco-Roman society. Similar ceremonies are documented in Classical Greece and attested throughout the Roman Empire. This Cyrene Jewish community apparently had little compunction in adopting such a procedure for its purposes, however with one striking difference: Whereas in Roman society such ceremonies were usually repeated only annually, it appears that, for whatever reason, the Jewish community decided to make this award, at the very least, a monthly (on each New Moon), and perhaps even weekly, event.[23]

The third example, the Dura Europos synagogue, derives from the upper limits of the conference's purview, and slightly beyond it. This is a very special and sui generis synagogue building, dating from the first half of the third century C.E., which is generally regarded as the best-preserved ancient synagogue whose walls contain a stunning display of Jewish art featuring biblical scenes. Nothing remotely similar is known in synagogues (or elsewhere) prior to the third century or, for that matter, afterwards.

The Dura synagogue building was heavily influenced by its immediate surroundings. It is eminently clear that those responsible for the building and its decorations adapted local architectural and artistic models, neatly fitting the institution into patterns typical of the city.[24] Theories abound as to whether Greco-Roman, Parthian, or Syrian-Mesopotamian artistic traditions stand behind this building's artwork.

---

[23] My thanks to Professor Charles H. Cosgrove for calling my attention to this fact on the basis of F. W. Danker's study, *Benefactor: Epigraphic Study of a Graeco-Roman and New Testament Semantic Field* (St. Louis, MO: Clayton, 1982), which, unfortunately, I have not been able to consult personally.

[24] See Wharton, *Refiguring*, 23–63.

Nevertheless, it is perfectly clear that the local Jewish community was profoundly influenced by its urban milieu in the ways it chose to organize and decorate its synagogue complex and sanctuary. Frescoed registers on the synagogue walls, decorated ceiling tiles, the delineation of a sacred area by an *aedicula*, the placement of a courtyard before the sanctuary, and the addition of a series of rooms for communal purposes all follow a pattern of temple structures common to Dura's sixteen other holy sites.[25]

Linguistically as well, the local community was well integrated into the cultural milieu of Dura. Some of the nineteen Greek and twenty-two Aramaic inscriptions found there are dedicatory in nature, while others serve to identify figures and scenes depicted in the frescoes. The ten Iranian graffiti are enigmatic, possibly documenting a series of visits to the synagogue by foreigners from the East.[26] In short, given the architectural, artistic, and epigraphic evidence regarding this synagogue and its surroundings, one can safely say than no other site known to date is more illustrative of the adaptability of a Diaspora community to its immediate social, religious, and cultural environment than that of Dura.

The realization of the broader contextual factor that we have noted in Egypt, Cyrene, and Dura must be balanced by the recognition that this same community was first and foremost committed to its survival as a self-contained and clearly-identified Jewish entity. Together with their efforts to adopt and adapt, Dura's Jews strove to preserve their uniqueness and cohesiveness in the face of the city's pluralistic and diverse social and religious setting in the late second and third centuries. Thus, the well-attested *aedicula* that had served many temples in Dura was introduced into the synagogue sanctuary as well, but here it was intended to house Torah scrolls and not the statue of a pagan god. The division of frescoed walls into a series of registers, often three in number, each depicting scenes relating to the cult, was likewise common at Dura.[27] Although the pagan temples usually depicted processions of worshippers and priests bringing sacrifices and gifts to the god, only the local Mithraeum, displaying several scenes from the life of Mithras and the nearby church featuring scattered episodes in the life of Jesus, are somewhat similar to the synagogue frescoes. The latter contained a

---

[25] Downey, *Mesopotamian Religious Architecture*.
[26] Kraeling, *Excavations*, 261–317.
[27] Perkins, *Art of Dura-Europos*.

spectacularly diverse and rich collection of scenes from the Hebrew Bible presented in a most innovative and intriguing fashion. In contrast to others, the Jews chose to give vivid expression to their common heritage as recorded in their sacred text. Furthermore, the names and titles of the synagogue's officials, along with remains of a prayer in Hebrew (the Blessing after Meals), also reflect a congregation that shared much with other Jewish communities, not only in the types of leaders but also in its forms of liturgical expression.

Heterogeneity and Homogeneity

The above examples should serve as a warning against positing one general, all-inclusive model—architectural or functional—for ancient synagogues in the Roman world. The Jews of the Hellenistic and early Roman Diaspora arrived at their new places of residence with a gamut of basic communal needs, not the least of which, of course, was a religious component. Many of these needs were endemic to any Jewish community and undoubtedly existed in earlier periods as well. Others emerged from their new circumstances and surroundings, and resembled other religious-ethnic communities in the Greco-Roman era. This phenomenon is well attested in Jewish history generally; wherever Jews found themselves, they created the mechanisms that would allow them to function on a local level. In seeking the most appropriate models by which to address these communal concerns, they quite naturally adopted those institutional frameworks at hand, those with which they felt most comfortable. The particular models, and the consequent form the synagogue took in different locales, were thus varied.

Given the historical reality of the Hellenistic-Roman Diaspora, Jewish communities now found themselves living in dramatically new social surroundings without the benefit of having brought with them a fixed or fully-developed communal institution. As a result, diversity among them was very much in evidence. What we know of the manumissions in the Bosphorus Kingdom, the awards granted by the Cyrene *politeuma*, the naming of synagogues after officials in Rome, the dedication of an Egyptian *proseuche* to the Ptolemaic royal family, the pagan benefactress of Acmonia who donated a building to the Jewish community, the sanctity of the Antioch synagogue with its collection of temple vessels, and the concentration of *Theos Hypsistos* inscriptions along with lamps decorated with pagan motifs in Delos[28] are, in each and every instance, *sui generis* the first-century synagogue map. No two synagogues come close to replicating each other.

What, then, united these various synagogues, stretching over farflung geographical areas, in urban and rural contexts, in West and East? First and foremost, these buildings served communities having a unique cluster of religious and ethnic commitments.[29] Their monotheistic faith focused on the God of Israel, a series of foundational beliefs (e.g., the sanctity of the Torah, of Jerusalem and its temple, the concept of chosenness), a range of customs and practices that set them apart from other groups, and a yearly cycle of festivals and rites of passage from birth to death—all these and more provided a significant measure of commonality that bound these communities together, each within itself and perhaps between one another (although we have preciously little information about this last point), and certainly to Jerusalem and its temple. The extent of this commonality is well reflected in the dozens of Roman edicts, referred to above, that record a comparable series of rights and privileges enjoyed by Jewish communities in different parts of the Roman East.[30]

The degree of uniformity among the synagogues of the empire is likewise reflected in the names used by Jews for this institution. The terms *synagoge* and *proseuche* are almost universal; other names were invoked (*sabbateion, didaskaleion, templum, hieron,* amphitheater, etc.) on only rare occasion.[31] Although it is quite likely that each name conveyed a unique feature of the institution in the eyes of that particular community (e.g., *hieron*—a holy place [Antioch]; *didaskaleion*—an institution for learning [Alexandria]; *sabbateion*—a place for Sabbath gatherings [Asia Minor], etc.), there can be little doubt that the cluster of activities

---

[28] On the worship of *Theos Hypsistos* in antiquity among Jews and pagans, see Mitchell, "Cult of Theos Hypsistos," 81–148.

[29] The latter, ethnic, component would include an attachment and loyalty to Jerusalem and its Temple, as expressed through pilgrimage and the half-sheqel donation. See Levine, *Jerusalem,* chap. 6.

[30] See Pucci Ben Zeev, *Jewish Rights,* 374–7. These rights include exemptions from taxes in a sabbatical year, exemptions from military service and providing soldiers with winter quarters, the right to follow Jewish customs and laws (including the provision of required foods), the right to assemble, follow Jewish cultic practices, enjoy organizational and judicial autonomy, and the community's right to have its own premises. See also in this regard: Barclay, *Jews,* 399–444.

[31] See Binder, *Into the Temple Courts,* 91–154; Claussen, *Versammlung,* 113–45.

encompassed by these different edifices was quite similar. The fact that over ninety percent of the buildings noted in our sources are called either *synagoge* or *proseuche* indicates a commonality among Jewish communities throughout the Roman world. It should be remembered, nevertheless, that the difference between these two terms is noteworthy. Clearly, prayer played a central role in some Diaspora communities; in others, presumably, less so.

The terms used for synagogue leadership, though far from abundant for this period, also indicate some sort of uniformity.[32] The primary title at this time seems to have been *archisynagogos*, and it appears in connection with Jerusalem (the Theodotus inscription), the Galilee (Mark 5:22 and parallels), and Asia Minor (Acts 13:15; the Acmonia inscription). The title *"archon"* is also invoked, but often refers to a communal leader generally, with no necessary affiliation (which may have, in fact, existed) to the local synagogue.

The common thread among the different synagogues throughout the Empire is particularly evident with regard to the religious sphere. The centrality of the Torah-reading service, for instance, is widely attested:

> He [Moses] appointed the Law to be the most excellent and necessary form of instruction, ordaining, not that it should be heard once for all or twice or on several occasions, but that every week men should desert their other occupations and assemble to listen to the Law and to obtain a thorough and accurate knowledge of it, a practice which all other legislators seem to have neglected (Josephus, *C. Ap.* 2.175).

> He [Augustus] knew therefore that they have houses of prayer (*proseuchae*) and meet together in them, particularly on the sacred Sabbaths when they receive as a body training in their ancestral philosophy (Philo, *Legat.* 156).

> He required them to assemble in the same place on these seventh days, and, sitting together in a respectful and orderly manner, hear the laws read so that none should be ignorant of them (Philo, *Hypoth.* 7.12).

---

[32] Levine, *Ancient Synagogue*, 387–404; Binder, *Into the Temple Courts*, 34–52.

For Moses of old time has in every city those that preach him, being read in the synagogues every Sabbath day (Acts 15:21).

These sweeping references refer to Jewish communities generally, yet a number of sources relate to the centrality of the Torah service in specific locales. The Theodotus inscription notes this activity for Jerusalem, rabbinic literature for Alexandria (*t. Sukkah* 4, 6), the New Testament for Nazareth and Asia Minor (Luke 4:16–22; Acts 13:14–15), and Philo for Alexandria and the Essenes of Judaea (*Hypoth.* 7, 12; *Prob.* 81–2).

By the first century, a weekly ceremony featuring the communal reading and study of holy texts had become a universal liturgical practice, unique to the Jewish world; no such form of worship was known in paganism. True enough, certain mystery cults in the Hellenistic-Roman world produced sacred texts that were read on occasion. However, it was indeed sui generis for an entire community to devote regular occasions to such activity. This, it appears, is the context within which to understand the above-quoted sources, and while the tone of Josephus and Philo may have been self-laudatory, it is not without cause. They were indeed trumpeting a form of worship that set the Jewish community apart from the surrounding cultures.

In addition, other elements of first-century liturgy also seem to have been shared by Jewish communities in different geographical locations. The sermon, other forms of Sabbath morning instruction, the recitation of prophetic readings (*haftarah*), and possibly *targum* may have been well-known features in the first century.[33]

In light of the above, it appears that certain questions at times posed vis-à-vis the first-century synagogue may miss the mark. The issue is not whether the early synagogue was more a Jewish institution (that may have been defined and practiced in different locales) or a Greco-Roman one, nor whether it was fundamentally more communal than religious, or vice versa. Jewish communities everywhere faced these dichotomies, and the subsequent responses varied. Resolution of these alternatives lay with each individual community as it charted its path, whether in the Diaspora or in Judaea. To the best of our knowledge, there was no higher authority, either pre- or post-70, that might have been able to impose one pattern or another on these synagogues. Therefore, it was

---

[33] Levine, *Ancient Synagogue*, 142–51.

each community's decision how to integrate the contextual factors with its particular needs, or vice versa, namely how to satisfy its communal requirements within the context of one or another local model. How this challenge was handled is, by and large, beyond what our sources enable us to know; what we can be sure of, however, is that the resultant character of each community (its practices and its physical setting) was unique and depended upon its constituency and particular social and cultural context, although its inherited tradition (or "common Judaism," however that was understood) also had a crucial role in shaping this institution. The nature of this process as well as its ultimate expression clearly differed from locale to locale.[34]

On a broader scale, the synagogue as the pivotal institution served as a bellwether for a given community. The Jewish community was attacked and honored via the synagogue, its rights and privileges invariably found expression in and through this institution, and the community itself often chose to honor its own members and others within its walls. As the quintessential Jewish institution, it reflected the major cultural and social currents within the wider community. It is often assumed that Diaspora Jews were either headed toward assimilation or ensconced in their secluded communities. However, neither of these extremes reflects the majority of Jews. Rather, there was an ongoing drive for acculturation while, at the same time, a striving to maintain a strong identification with Judaism and the Jewish people. The synagogue not only reflected this dual goal by its very existence, but in no small measure also provided the means for the community to achieve its goals, individually and collectively. The survival of the Jewish people in the first half millennium of our era is due largely to the synagogue institution that facilitated Jewish particularism and universality. Together with the *polis* context, the inclusiveness of which allowed the synagogue to flourish on the local scene, as it did other religious, ethnic, and socioeconomic associations,[35] the synagogue served as the institution that fostered integration and exclusivity, a Janus-type posture that looked inward and outward at one and the same time.

---

[34] See also the discussion of many of the same issues by Barclay (*Jews,* passim), who, however, concentrates on specific cases (individuals, literary works, and historical incidents) and not on the community as a whole. The study of contemporary synagogues as communal institutions helps fill that void.
[35] Rajak, "Synagogue," 164–6.

There is little question that a great deal of ferment characterizes the study of the synagogue in the first centuries. One might be kind and describe the state of these synagogue studies as flourishing, dynamic, and creative. Alternatively, one could be less generous and describe the situation as being in a fluid, even muddled, state, concerning which all sorts of theories—from the interesting to the bizarre—are espoused. Yet, it is precisely the large number of theories, ofttimes conflicting, that alerts us to the problems and challenges of this topic. Thus, we are especially grateful to our hosts here at Lund University, who have provided this opportunity to meet, listen to one another, engage in scholarly discourse, assert, defend, challenge, and respond, and all within a congenial setting. We all share a common goal: to understand more fully the how and whys of this revolutionary Jewish institution that played such a central role not only in nascent Christianity but also in Judaism of the post-temple era, and indeed right up to our own day.

Bibliography

Barclay, J. M. G., *Jews in the Mediterranean Diaspora From Alexander to Trajan (323 BCE–117 CE)*. Edinburgh: T&T Clark, 1996.

Binder, D. D., *Into the Temple Courts: The Place of the Synagogues in the Second Temple Period*. Atlanta: Scholars Press, 1999.

Claussen, C., *Versammlung, Gemeinde, Synagoge: Das hellenistisch-jüdische Umfeld der frühchristlichen Gemeinden*. Göttingen: Vandenhoeck & Ruprecht, 2002.

Danker, F. W., *Benefactor: Epigraphic Study of a Graeco-Roman and New Testament Semantic Field*. St. Louis: Clayton, 1982.

Dion, P. E., "Synagogues et temples dans l'Égypte hellénistique," *Science et esprit* 29 (1977): 45–75.

Downey, S. B., *Mesopotamian Religious Architecture: Alexander through the Parthians*. Princeton: Princeton University Press, 1988.

Flesher P. V. M., "Prolegomenon to a Theory of Early Synagogue Development." Pages 121–53 in *Judaism in Late Antiquity*, Vol. 4. Edited by A. J. Avery-Peck and J. Neusner. Leiden: Brill, 2001.

Frey, J.-B. *Corpvs Inscriptionvm Jvdaicarvm.* 2 vols. Rome: Pontificio Istituto di Archaeologia Cristiana, 1936–52 (reprint; New York: KTAV, 1975).

Griffiths, J. G., "Egypt and the Rise of the Synagogue," *JTS* 38 (1987): 1–15 (reprinted in: Urman and Flesher, *Ancient Synagogues,* I, 3–16).

Hengel, M., "Proseuche und Synagoge: Jüdische Gemeinde, Gotteshaus und Gottesdienst in der Diaspora und in Palästina." Pages 157–84 in *Tradition und Glaube: Das frühe Christentum in seiner Umwelt.* Edited by G. Jeremias *et al.* Göttingen: Vandenhoeck & Ruprecht, 1971.

Horbury, W., and D. Noy, *Jewish Inscriptions of Graeco-Roman Egypt.* Cambridge: Cambridge University Press, 1992.

Kasher, A., "Synagogues as 'Houses of Prayer' and 'Holy Places' in the Jewish Communities of Hellenistic and Roman Egypt." Pages 205–20 in *Ancient Synagogues: Historical Analysis and Archaeological Discovery.* Edited by D. Urman and P. V. M. Flesher. Leiden: Brill, 1995.

Kraabel, A. T., "The Diaspora Synagogue: Archaeological and Epigraphic Evidence since Sukenik." Pages 477–510 in *ANRW* II, 19.1. Edited by H. Temporini and W. Haase. Berlin: de Gruyter, 1979.

Kraeling, C., *The Excavations at Dura-Europos,* VIII, Part I: *The Synagogue.* New Haven: Yale University Press, 1956 (reprint; New York: KTAV, 1979).

Levine, L. I., *The Ancient Synagogue: The First Thousand Years.* New Haven: Yale University Press, 2000.

—, *Jerusalem: Portrait of the City in the Second Temple Period (538 BCE – 70 CE).* Philadelphia: Jewish Publication Society, 2002.

—, "The First-Century Synagogue: Critical Reassessments and Assessments of the Critical." In *The Archaeology of Difference: Gender, Ethnicity, Class and the 'Other' in Antiquity. Studies in Honor of Eric M. Meyers.* Edited by D. Edwards and C. T. McCollough (in press).

Mitchell, S., "The Cult of Theos Hypsistos between Pagans, Jews, and Christians." Pages 81–148 in *Pagan Monotheism in Late*

Antiquity. Edited by P. Athanassiadi and M. Frede. Oxford: Clarendon, 1999.

Noy, D., *Jewish Inscriptions of Western Europe*. 2 vols. Cambridge: Cambridge University Press, 1993–95.

Olsson, B., Mitternacht, D., and O. Brandt, eds. *The Synagogue of Ancient Ostia and the Jews of Rome: Interdisciplinary Studies*. Stockholm: Paul Åström, 2001.

Perkins, A., *Art of Dura-Europos*. Oxford: Clarendon, 1973.

Pucci Ben Zeev, M., *Jewish Rights in the Roman World: The Greek and Roman Documents Quoted by Josephus Flavius*. Tübingen: Mohr Siebeck, 1998.

Rajak, T., "The Synagogue within the Greco-Roman City." Pages 161–73 in *Jews, Christians and Polytheists in the Ancient Synagogue: Cultural Interaction during the Greco-Roman Period*. Edited by S. Fine. London: Routledge, 1999.

Richardson, P., "Early Synagogues as *Collegia* in the Diaspora and Palestine," Pages 90–109 in *Voluntary Associations in the Graeco-Roman World*. Edited by J. S. Kloppenborg and S. G. Wilson. London: Routledge, 1996.

—, "Augustan-Era Synagogues in Rome." Pages 17–29 in *Judaism and Christianity in First-Century Rome*. Edited by K. P. Donfried and P. Richardson. Grand Rapids: Eerdmans, 1998.

Runesson, A., "The Oldest Synagogue Building in the Diaspora: A Response to L. M. White," *HTR* 92 (1999): 409–33.

Silverstein, A., *Alternatives to Assimilation: The Response of Reform Judaism to American Culture, 1840-1930*. Hanover: Brandeis University Press, 1994.

Strange, J. F., "The Art and Archaeology of Ancient Judaism." Pages 64–114 in *Judaism in Late Antiquity, I: The Literary and Archaeological Sources*. Edited by J. Neusner. Leiden: Brill, 1995.

—, "Ancient Texts, Archaeology as Text, and the Problem of the First-Century Synagogue." Pages 27–45 in *Evolution of the Synagogue: Problems and Progress*. Edited by H. C. Kee and L. H. Cohick. Harrisburg: Trinity Press, 1999.

Urman, D. and P. V. M Flesher, eds. *Ancient Synagogues: Historical Analysis and Archaeological Discovery*. Leiden: Brill, 1995.

Wharton, A. J., *Refiguring the Post Classical City: Dura Europos, Jerash, Jerusalem, and Ravenna.* Cambridge: Cambridge University Press, 1995.

White, L. M., "Reading the Ostia Synagogue: A Reply to A. Runesson," *HTR* 92 (1999): 435–64.

Part I

The Origins of the Synagogue

2
The Origins of the Synagogue: An Introduction

Birger Olsson

LEE LEVINE HAS, IN FORM and content, given us a brilliant opening to this conference, also to this section on the origins of the synagogue. Surveying the key problems of the synagogue research of today, he emphasizes both where we agree (the central position of the ancient synagogue, the combination of communal and religious functions, the integration of Jewish and Greco-Roman elements) and where we disagree (mainly, where on the scale we position ourselves with regard to communal vs. religious, synchronic (= Greco-Roman) vs. diachronic (= Jewish),[1] and uniformity vs. diversity.

The sources of explicit information about the synagogue up to ca. 200 C.E., literary material, archaeological finds, and inscriptions, are very meager. Therefore, any kind of theorizing about the first-century synagogue, about its origin, essence, functions, and possible derivation, should, with the words of Levine, "be done with much caution and with an awareness that any suggestions must remain tentative, at best."[2]

The different opinions, according to Levine, mostly depend on two interrelated factors: what types of evidence we choose to emphasize, and what components of the synagogue we wish to highlight. He himself highlights both the diversity and the uniformity in a harmonizing way. Every local community formed their synagogue in their own context. The institution fostered both integration and exclusivity, both heterogeneity and homogeneity. The question cannot be "whether the early

---

[1] The use of "synchronic" and "diachronic" in this context may be misleading, because the Jewish and the Greco-Roman dimensions are both synchronic and diachronic.

[2] Levine, "First Century C.E. Synagogue," 8.

synagogue was more a Jewish . . . or Graeco-Roman institution, nor whether it was fundamentally more communal than religious, or vice versa."[3] What we seem to be dealing with in the first century "is an institution in the midst of a process of self-definition. . . . It was constantly reinventing itself as outside influences shaped the direction and supplied the tools used by Jewish communities to promote their interests and answer their needs."[4] I am not sure that this comprehensive solution functions as a challenge for future studies.

The question of origins is mentioned by Levine as one of the most debated issues "in early synagogue studies." I think that the question is still very relevant and of great current interest.[5] It is also one of the essential issues of our synagogue project: When, how, and why did the synagogue come into existence? What changes took place in the first phase of its existence? There are still several answers to these questions.

Synagogue Research During the 90's

Synagogue research has change very much during the last 10–15 years and our project in Lund "The Ancient Synagogue: Birthplace of Two World Religions," is a part of this process.[6] We all know the strong consensus from the last century, based primarily on information from the New Testament, on an anachronistic use of rabbinical material, and on general common sense arguments: the synagogue as the center for Jewish piety in New Testament times, a complement or a rival to the temple, having its roots in the exile, developed during the Hellenistic period, dominated by Pharisees. Synagogues were built in the Diaspora as soon as a region had a sufficiently large Jewish population. In Palestine the Galilean synagogues from the first century B.C.E. and later were completely destroyed by the Romans during the two Jewish wars, and thus archaeological finds from this period are rare. Beginning in the third century, synagogues again began to be constructed, often on sites where there had formerly been a synagogue. Although the synagogue

---

[3] Ibid., 20.
[4] Ibid., 11.
[5] I cannot agree with Levine when he with reference to the city gate as the origin of the synagogue says: "The question of where and when it began becomes superfluous," see Levine, "First-Century Synagogue," 29.
[6] A short presentation of the project is to be found in Olsson, "Introduction."

could be used as a school, a guest house, a council room or a courtroom, its primary purpose was to provide a locale for regular worship meetings, including Shema, benedictions, prayers such as the Amidah, text readings according to a fixed order and sermons.

No synagogue scholar of today will defend this traditional reconstruction, which was still the dominating one fifteen years ago.[7] The situation has changed very much during the last decade. We could refer to many articles and monographs, in alphabetical order: Atkinson 1997, Barclay 1997, Binder (1997) 1999, Bloedhorn, H. and G. Hüttenmeister 1999, Claussen 1999 (2002), Cohen 1997, Fine (ed) 1996, Flesher 1995 (1989), Grabbe 1995, Hachlili 1997, van der Horst 1999, Kee 1990, 1994, 1995, 2000, Kloppenborg 2000, Levine 1987, 1992, 1993, 1996, 2000, 2001, McKay 1994, 1998, Meyers 1996, Oster 1993, Richardson 1996, 1998, Sanders 1992, Strange 1995, 1997, 1999, 2001, Urman and Flesher 1995, White 1997, and others.[8]

At the SNTS conference in Cambridge 1988, H.C. Kee read his paper on "The Transformation of the Synagogue after 70 CE: Its Import for Early Christianity," published in *New Testament Studies* 1990, a "remarkably ill-informed and often incoherent" article according to E. P. Sanders,[9] but it started an intense debate which has not yet come to an end. As background for his article, he ten years later mentioned J. Neusner's general criticism of scholars' use of rabbinic sources and M. White's hypothesis of a development of the synagogue from "housing meetings in private homes or general purpose public halls."[10] There was a process of adaptation from informal gathering place to a site of more formal religious gatherings. After analyzing the meanings of the word *synagoge* and the archaeological evidence for early synagogues he drew the conclusion that we have no buildings especially for religious gatherings before the third and fourth centuries, and then they are often reconstructions of private houses.

The reactions against Kee's article were strong, especially against his way of dating the Theodotus inscription, but a new debate arose lasting one decade on the use of sources in synagogue research and the need for

---

[7] See the summarizing articles in *Le Monde de la Bible*, 1989.
[8] It is easy to find bibliographical information about these contributions in the bibliographies of this volume or in the comprehensive bibliography in Levine, *Ancient Synagogue*.
[9] Sanders, *Jewish Law*, 341, n. 29.
[10] Kee, "Introduction," 1–2.

clear definitions. The use of models and theories, however, was discussed very little. H. McKay, who in her work on the Sabbath and the synagogue had come to the same conclusions as Kee, tried to summarize and evaluate the debate in an article in 1998: "Ancient Synagogues: The Continuing Dialectic Between Two Major Views." She rightly notes that "it is the first century CE that provides the key focus of the controversy," and that the sometimes inflammatory debate may reflect ideological backgrounds.[11] But I am not sure that McKay's way of taking two main positions can move the synagogue research forward. It may have relevance for the first part of the 90's, from McKay's point of view, but not for the complex situation at the end of the decade.

There is, according to McKay, a traditional, or "optimistic," or "maximalist" position which is very much connected to the old consensus, and an opposing, or "skeptical," or "minimalist" position, which "holds that the synagogue did not reach a form of more or less recognizable consistency with that of the present day, until the third and fourth centuries CE."[12] Her definition of "synagogue" very much depends on "the synagogue, *as we know it today*." When she lists the conflicting assumptions between the two positions, five of them are related to the synagogue as a separate building, two of them to the use of sources and one to a distinction between religious factors on the one hand and social, political and economic factors on the other hand. Further investigations require more precise definitions of what we mean by "synagogue" and by "religious." Both Kee's and McKay's definitions seem to depend too much on concepts from our own time.

The Situation as of 2001

Looking at the monographs which have been published during the last two or three years, we find no consensus about the ancient synagogue. The traditional consensus is not there anymore. The debate will continue.

Kee is still arguing for a late date for the ancient synagogue.[13] His call for a very thorough and methodologically stringent use of different

---

[11] McKay, "Ancient Synagogues," 104.
[12] Ibid., 106.
[13] See Kee, "Defining."

The Origins of the Synagogue: An Introduction

sources has been heard, and if we want to date, for example, the Theodotus inscription, the first century is the more probable suggestion.[14] But the question of definitions is not yet solved. And what explicit information from non-Christian *sources* do we have about a process of adaptation from an informal gathering place to a site of more formal religious gatherings?

L. Levine's *opus magnum*, published three years ago (2000), is a brilliant handbook, which summarizes and integrates all the material we now have about the first thousand years of the history of the synagogue. His main thesis may be formulated as follows: the ancient synagogue is a communal institution with a religious dimension with roots in Hellenistic times in the gatherings at the city gate and its many functions. It remained first and foremost a communal framework down to the end of antiquity. It was always a multifunctional institution answering the many needs of the entire community. The religious component was from the beginning very small with the reading and teaching of the Torah at its center, the earliest and the most characteristic form of Jewish worship. Communal prayer became a part of the synagogue activities first in the Diaspora and regular communal prayer developed in post-70 Roman Palestine in order to fill the vacuum created by the destruction of the temple.

D. Binder, in his dissertation from 1997, published in 1999, accepts the theory of city gate as the beginning of the synagogue, but notes that in Jerusalem the functions of the city gate were moved to the temple courts. He has made a very thorough investigation of all the sources from the first century. Even Kee should be satisfied with his impressive analysis of all sources. It is, according to Binder, the dynamic relations to the Jerusalem temple that create the ancient synagogue. I quote: "The synagogues in both Palestine and the Diaspora served as subsidiary sacred precincts that extended spatially the sacrality of the Temple shrine and allowed Jews everywhere participation within the central cult."[15] He tries to show that the functions of the synagogues paralleled those of the temple precincts in many respects. There was only one difference: the sacrifices. "The offering of prayers and the reading of sacred scriptures served as a form of sacrifice for those worshiping in the synagogues."[16] Levine has reacted very strongly against Binder's main thesis

---

[14] See the convincing arguments in Kloppenborg, "Dating."
[15] Binder, *Temple Courts*, 32.
[16] Ibid., 450.

of the synagogues as patterned after the temple: "The evidence is just not there and what is invoked is speculative and forced, at best. Despite his efforts, it must be concluded that everything about these two institutions was different."[17]

C. Claussen has written the latest dissertation about the ancient synagogue, as far as I know, defended in Munich in 1999 and published in 2002. Claussen's view of the origin of the synagogue is reminiscent of Kee and White in many respects, and even of Richardson, but he emphasizes much more a development from the Jewish homes and a long period of small house synagogues. "Der hohe Rang häuslichen Glaubenslebens ist im Judentum kaum zu überschätzen."[18] Every Jewish family had the potentiality of most functions which you find later on in a synagogue congregation. The reference to the functions of the city gate does not explain the religious dimension. The central question for Claussen, however, is what model do we have for the early Christian congregation, the typical German question about *praeparatio evangelica*. And his answer is:

1. Die jüdischen Synagogen des 1.Jh.s n.Chr. sind in ihrer weit überwiegenden Zahl als kleine Haussynagogen zu denken. Die jüdischen Versammlungen dieser Zeit wurden in Privathäusern abgehalten.

2. Grössere Synagogegebäude sind zwar auch vor 70 n.Chr. sowohl für die Diaspora als auch für Israel eindeutig belegbar. Sie stellen jedoch quantitativ die Ausnahme dar.

3. Das frühe Christentum formierte sich ebenso wie das Judentum in kleinen Hausgemeinden im privaten Rahmen. Insofern erscheint es uns sehr wahrscheinlich , die jüdische Haussynagoge, wenn auch ohne ganz scharfe formale Abgrenzungsmöglichkeit zu Hausversammlungen der heidnischen Kulte, als konkretes Modell für christliche Hausgemeinden von Jerusalem bis Rom anzusehen.[19]

---

[17] Levine, "First-Century Synagogue," 27
[18] Claussen, *Versamlung,* 298.
[19] Ibid., 304.

The Origins of the Synagogue: An Introduction

The latest book on the ancient synagogue is a disappointment, part 3, vol. 4 of *Judaism in Late Antiquity, Where We Stand: Issues and Debates in Ancient Judaism, The Special Problem of the Synagogue*, edited by A. Avery-Peck and J. Neusner (2001). The individual contributions on limited problems could be good, but there is no effort at all to present "where we stand" in synagogue research today.[20] With regard to the question of our first section the comprehensive article by P. V. M. Flesher is of great interest: "Prolegomenon to a Theory of Early Synagogue Development."

Flesher sees the origin of the synagogue in the Diaspora; in the minority situation of the Jews during the second century B.C.E. The synagogue of medieval times later on descended from the synagogue formed in Galilee and Golan after the destruction of the Jerusalem temple in 70. In the Greco-Roman world the synagogue was regarded as a temple, defined as a monument of common identity. The synagogue building "is a symbolic display created by the group to represent itself, its needs, and its achievements".[21] The synagogue gave the Jews a religious, ethnic, and political identity within the Roman Empire. Flesher gives many examples of the extensive integration of Jewish and non-Jewish elements in the synagogue and its activities.

After two centuries the synagogues entered Jerusalem from the Diaspora. They shaped themselves to the dominant temple culture and were not regarded as temples any more. As far as we know, they remained an institution for Jews coming from abroad and never became a native institution. The situation in Galilee was another one. The synagogues lost their strong relations to Greco-Roman temples and the Jerusalem temple and were transformed into "a native cultural and religious institution." Galilee and Golan had (1) Jewish communities that were linked to (2) synagogue buildings that interacted with a (3) Jewish culture in which the synagogue was the main institution. . . . Here in the north, first-century Jewish culture was based on the notion of synagogues as the main religious institution, at least locally."[22] The Galilean synagogue developed after the destruction of the Jerusalem temple in 70 and became the mother of the synagogues of the late antiquity and medieval times.

---

[20] The book is a part of *Handbook of Oriental Studies* (Abt. 1, Bd. 55). The reader expects more of a handbook!
[21] Flesher, "Prolegomenon," 141.
[22] Ibid., 148.

The most important purpose of our synagogue conference in Lund has been to invite the main actors on the arena of synagogue research for the reading of papers and to create a constructive discussion between them and together with members of our project, especially our doctoral students, and some other scholars. James Strange, Anders Runesson, Peter Richardson and Donald Binder will make special contributions to this first section. Strange, like Binder, emphasizes the role of the temple courts in Jerusalem as formative for the early synagogues, but as an archaeologist he is more interested in an analysis of the interior space of the synagogue buildings and its relations to the functions of these rooms.[23] Runesson has written his dissertation about the question of the origins [24] and also analysed all the material we have about the synagogue at ancient Ostia.[25] He argues for an origin of the Palestine synagogues in Persian colonial strategies and finds quite another development of the synagogues in the Diaspora. Richardson has presented another hypothesis about the ancient synagogue: it originated in the Diaspora; the clearest analogy for synagogues was the Greco-Roman association.[26] The exchange of different opinions on the origins of the synagogue in the same room will prepare the ground for good and constructive discussions in this first section of our conference.

Bibliography

Avery-Peck, A. J. and J. Neusner, eds. *Judaism in Late Antiquity, Part Three, Where We Stand: Issues and Debates in Ancient Judaism, Vol. Four, The Special Problem of the Synagogue*. Leiden: Brill, 2001.

Binder, D. D., *Into the Temple Courts: The Place of the Synagogues in the Second Temple Period*. Atlanta: Scholars Press, 1999.

Claussen, C., *Geminde und Synagoge. Studien zum hellenistisch-jüdischen Umfeld der frühchristlichen Geminden*. Diss München 1999. Revi-

---

[23] See the articles by Strange listed in the bibliography.
[24] The dissertation was published two months after the conference, *The Origins of the Synagogue: A Socio-Historical Study*.
[25] Runesson, "Ostia." In 1999 he discussed the results with White in *HTR*; see Runesson, "Oldest Original Building" and White, "Ostia Synagogue." A second response by Runesson was published in another periodical; see Runesson, "Monumental Synagogue". White was invited to the conference, but was unable to come.
[26] Richardson, "Early Synagogues" and "Synagogues in Rome."

sed and printed as *Versammlung, Gemeinde, Synagoge: Das hellenistisch-jüdische Umfeld der frühchristlichen Gemeinden*. Göttingen: Vandenhoeck & Ruprecht, 2002.

Flescher, P. V. M., "Prolegomenon to a Theory of Early Synagogue Development." Pages 121–54 in *Judaism in Late Antiquity, Part Three, Where We Stand: Issues and Debates in Ancient Judaism, Vol. Four, The Special Problem of the Synagogue*. Edited by A. J. Avery-Peck and J. Neusner. Leiden: Brill, 2001.

Kee, H. C., "The Transformation of the Synagogue after 70 CE: Its Impact for Early Christianity." *NTS* 36 (1990): 1–24.

—, "Introduction." Pages 1–3 in *Evolution of the Synagogue: Problems and Progress*. Edited by H. C. Kee and L. H Cohick. Harrisburg: Trinity International Press, 1999.

—, "Defining the First-Century C.E. Synagogue." Pages 7–26 in *Evolution of the Synagogue: Problems and Progress*. Edited by H. C. Kee and L. H. Cohick. Harrisburg: Trinity International Press, 2000.

Kee. H. C. and L. H. Cohick, eds, *Evolution of the Synagogue: Problems and Progress*. Harrisburg: Trinity International Press, 2000.

Kloppenborg Verbin, J. S., "Dating Theodotus (*CIJ* II 1404)." *JJS* 51 (2000): 243–80.

Levine, L. I., *The Ancient Synagogue: The First Thousand Years*. New Haven: Yale University Press, 2000.

—, "The First-Century Synagogue: New Perspectives." *STK* 77 (2001): 22–30.

—, The First Century C.E. Synagogue in Historical Perspective. In this volume.

McKay, H. A., "Ancient Synagogues: The Continuing Dialectic Between Two Major Views." *Currents in Research: Biblical Studies* 6 (1998): 103–42.

Olsson, B., "Introduction." Pages 13–17 in *The Synagogue of Ancient Ostia and the Jews of Rome: Interdisciplinary Studies*. Edited by Olsson, B., D. Mitternacht and O. Brandt. Stockholm: Paul Åström, 2001.

Richardson, P., "Early Synagogues as *Collegia* in the Diaspora and Palestine." Pages 90–109 in *Voluntary Associations in the Graeco-Roman World*. Edited by J. S. Kloppenborg and S. G. Wilson. London: Routledge, 1996.

—, "Augustan-Era Synagogues in Rome." Pages 17–29 in *Judaism and*

Christianity in First-Century Rome. Edited by K. Donfried and P. Richardson. Grand Rapids: Eerdmans, 1998

Sanders, E. P., *Jewish Law from Jesus to the Mishna: Five Studies.* London: SCM Press, 1990.

Strange, J. F., "The Art and Archaeology of Ancient Judaism." Pages 64–114 in *Judaism in Late Antiquity.* Vol 1. Edited by J. Neusner. Leiden: Brill, 1995.

—, "Ancient Texts, Archaeology as Text, and the Problem of the First Century Synagogue." Pages 27–45 in *Evolution of the Synagogue: Problems and Progress.* Edited by H. C. Kee and L. H. Cohick. Harrisburg: Trinity International Press, 2000.

—, "Synagogue as Metaphor." Pages 93–120 in *Judaism in Late Antiquity, Part Three, Where We Stand: Issues and Debates in Ancient Judaism, Vol. Four, The Special Problem of the Synagogue.* Edited by A. J. Avery-Peck and J. Neusner. Leiden: Brill, 2001.

Runesson, A., "The Oldest Original Synagogue Building in the Dispora: A Response to L. Michael White." *HTR* 92 (1999): 409–33.

—, "The Synagogue at Ancient Ostia: The Building and Its History from the First to the Fifth Century." Pages 29–99 in *The Synagogue of Ancient Ostia and the Jews of Rome: Interdisciplinary Studies.* Edited by Olsson, B., D. Mitternacht and O. Brandt. Stockholm: Paul Åström, 2001.

—, *The Origins of the Synagogue: A Socio-Historical Study.* Stockholm: Almqvist & Wiksell, 2001.

—, "A Monumental Synagogue from the First Century: The Case of Ostia." *JSJ* 33 (2002): 171–220.

White, L. M., "Reading the Ostia Synagogue: A Reply to A. Runesson." *HTR* 92 (1999): 435–64.

3
Archaeology and Ancient Synagogues up to about 200 C.E.

James F. Strange

ARCHAEOLOGY HAS CHANGED IN the fifty years or so that synagogue archaeology has taken place. No longer are excavations dominated solely by architectural or history of art concerns, though almost all inferences drawn about the uses of buildings are architectural arguments, and most publications about mosaic floors ask history of art questions.[1] Rather many excavators now gather and record data about the history of use and renovation of a building, detailed data about decoration, but also about abandonment and the re-use by others, re-occupation by transients after abandonment, and so forth. Furthermore, some excavators ask not only what the coins were, but precisely where they were found so that they can examine patterns of dropped coins. From the patterns of lost coins and other small artifacts such as beads, one may infer behavioral patterns within buildings.

The most recent synagogue excavations yield more data than the old excavators thought possible. This is because of the use of more meticulous recording and excavation methods. Not only may one record the characteristics of the soil eroded into a building after abandonment, but one may examine the pollen trapped in these soil layers to infer changing vegetation during synagogue use and disuse. The taking, recording, and interpretation of pollen samples, merely to name one theoretical example, may place a building in an environmental history that once was simply not available.[2]

---

[1] For example see Roussin, "Zodiac," 83–96.
[2] A recent example is Longstaff and Tristram, "Palynology," 151–62.

On the other hand there are limitations in our data. Some of the most recent excavations remain unpublished in final form (Nabratein[3] and Qiryat Sefer[4]) or are too recent to be published (Modi'in[5]). In other cases the original excavator has died and others have taken up the task of publishing from notes and daily logs, but without the aid of the ones who directed or conducted the excavations. This means that sometimes later interpretations do not cohere with preliminary reports, as in the case of Hammath-Tiberias.[6]

The earliest putative synagogue sites so far excavated in Israel, the West Bank, and the Golan Heights are Capernaum I, Gamla, Herodium, Masada, Qiryat Sefer, Jericho and Modi'in. This list stands, even if one doubts that some of the buildings are synagogues, for reasons which will be argued below.

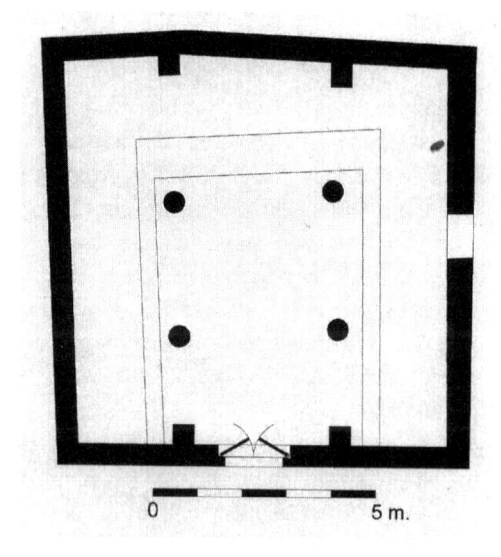

Figure 3.1 The synagogue at Qiryat Sefer. Adapted from Magen 1999.

The announcement of the excavations at Qiryat Sefer described a small building which resembles the synagogues of Herodium and

---

[3] Meyers, "Nabratein," 85–7.
[4] Magen and Sirkis, "Qiryat Sefer," 25–32.
[5] Cox, "Rescue Excavation."
[6] Compare Dothan, *Hammath Tiberias*, and the works cited on p. 75, nn. 17–19.

Masada, though it has a side entrance. According to the notice, the building stood in the center of the ancient settlement. Furthermore inside the building four benches surrounded the central hall. There was one row of four columns on each side. Craftsmen plastered the interior walls in antiquity, and then painters decorated them with shades of red, orange and white. The pottery, coins and signs of fire on the site suggested that the Romans destroyed the synagogue in the early second century. Most importantly for the purposes of this article, A. Onn, Director of the excavation on behalf of the IAA, disclosed that the synagogue is similar in plan to those found at Gamla, Masada and Herodion.[7]

Evidence for Early Synagogues in Ancient Palestine

It seems clear to me that there is little reason to deny that the structures at Capernaum, Gamla, Masada, Herodium, Jericho, Qiryat Sefer, and Modi'in are "synagogues" for reasons that will become clear below.[8] By "synagogues" I mean a building devoted to the declamation of Torah on certain occasions, notably on Sabbaths and festivals. It may well be that they were also used for other purposes such as community meetings, instruction of children, informal gatherings, sacred meals, and the like. The main argument, articulated below, is that these buildings reveal a single plan and resemble in plan and furniture later buildings excavated in Israel and known to be synagogues because of inscriptions, Jewish art, and Jewish icons.[9]

Almost all buildings identified as synagogues in Israel exhibit a kind of standard plan. This plan is so regular that it virtually amounts to a signature for its function. The regular plan also reveals intentionality on the part of the builders. In this template, derived from examination of the putative synagogue buildings listed above, the builders marked

---

[7] See n. 4.
[8] The leading contender for the theory that there are no first century synagogue buildings at all is Kee, " Transformation," 1–24. A response appears in Oster, "Anachronism, " 178–208; Kee, "Defining" 481–500. A similar scepticism also appears in McKay, "Ancient Synagogues," 103–42.
[9] Levine, " Nature" 425–448; Hachlili, "Origin," 34–47. For a more skeptical view see van der Horst, "Sabbath Worship," 18–43. For the latest exhaustive study see Runesson, *Origins*.

interior floor space by walkways on three or all four walls with benches between the walls and the columniation. The result of such a design is that participants had to look between the columns to see what was going on. Although this feature is known from Nabatean mortuary temples, it is otherwise virtually unknown in the Roman world.[10]

The seven possible synagogue buildings at Capernaum, Masada, Gamla, Masada, Herodium, Jericho, Qiryat Sefer, and Modi'in all follow this template, though not all plans are identical to one another. They have more in common than not.[11] It is to these commonalities that we now turn in detail.

> 1. These buildings organize the interior space in a similar manner, namely by nesting the walls, benches, aisles or walkways, columns, and the innermost rectangle of space.[12] That is, the central space is a rectangular floor with no mosaic, but either simply a dirt floor or paved with plaster or squared paving stones. Columns surround this space on two and sometimes four sides. If the columns surround four sides, then the columns which stand at the intersections of two rows at right angles in at least one case (Gamla) are "corner columns" or "double columns," even "heart-shaped columns" in imitation of a Roman architectural pattern. An aisle or walkway surrounds three or four sides of the internal rectangle of space. The walkway is always paved. Ranges of benches surround the aisles on two, three, or four sides. The benches nest against the walls. There may be one, two, or three or more benches arranged in ascending or descending ranks.

---

[10] Strange, "Art and Archaeology," 64–114 and "Ancient Texts," 27–45.

[11] *Contra* Ovadiah and Michaeli, "Observations," 234–41. On Nabatean Mortuary Temples as a model for the synagogue see Foerster, "Architectural Models," 45–8. For a rejoinder see Ovadiah and Michaeli, "Observations," 240.

[12] This pattern or template continues until the 6th century C.E. as the majority pattern. Other patterns include the broadhouses of Estemo'a and Susiya and the Samaritan synagogues with no internal columns. Magen, "Samaritan Synagogues," 66–90. For more bibliography see n. 20 below. Parenthetically, that the Sepphoris synagogue only exhibits one row of columns calls into question its identification as a synagogue.

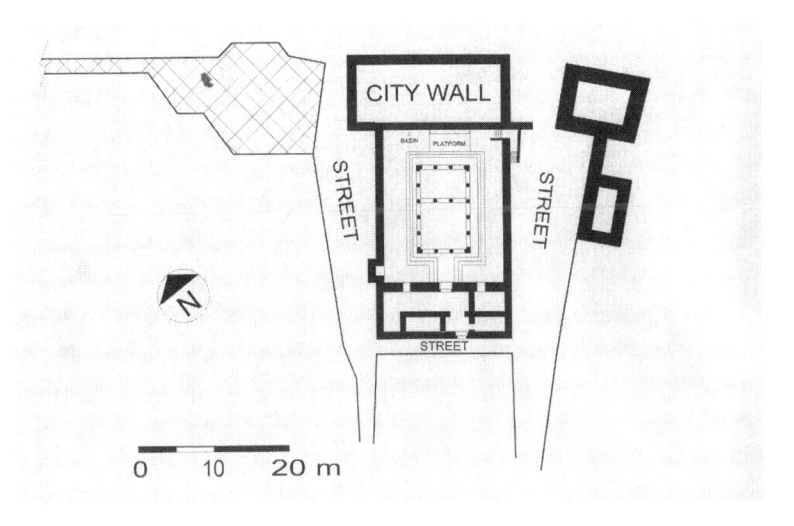

Archaeology and Ancient Synagogues up to 200 C.E.

Figure 3.2 Plan of the Gamla synagogue.

2. One may enter at the level of the innermost rectangular floor, or at the level of the top-most bench, depending on the design and placement of the door. To move from entry level to the top bench or landing to the floor (or sometimes from entry level at the floor to the top rank of benches), one must walk on the benches as steps. There is no separate staircase to lead the worshiper from floor to highest bench or the other way around.[13]

3. Perhaps the most curious feature of the interior is that those seated on the benches must look through a balustrade of columns to see what is going on centrally. This circumstance is also found in the Diaspora synagogue at Priene in Greece.

4. The "Jewishness" of these structures is not given by building elements or decorations, unless we count the palm tree on the lintels at Gamla as Jewish decorations. Generally speaking one

---

[13] R. Simeon ben 'Azai (about second century C.E., but preserved in a much later context), said, "Descend from your place two or three steps and sit down. It is better that you should be told 'ascend' than 'descend.'" (ʾ*Abot R. Nat.* 25.4). Matt 23:6 mentions πρωτοκαθεδρίας or "best seats" in synagogues. Josephus knows the idea of preferred seating and refers to, for instance, in *B.J.* 2.25 where Gaius sat in preferred seating: Γάιον πρώτως εκάθισεν.

understands the structures to be Jewish because they stand in a Jewish town or village.

5. Although parts of these buildings resemble structures in the Roman Empire, their total organization is novel. For example, one might consider a Council Chamber (*bouleuterion*) as a progenitor of this synagogue space.[14] This is because *bouleuteria* were built with concentric, square ranges of benches for seating and a central, rectangular space, presumably for the leader or speaker. One may also think of a basilica as the natural parent of the synagogue, and many scholars do. The parade example of a basilica as synagogue is found at Sardis, though the synagogue at Meiron is also a fine example.[15] As a matter of fact we cannot help but notice and it occurs many times in the literature that Late Roman and Byzantine synagogues are most commonly identified as basilicas. Late Roman and Byzantine baslica synagogues organize inner space by dividing it into a nave and three aisles by columns (one aisle on either side of the nave and one across the back).[16] Often the builders placed the principal entrances at the narrow end of the building. Yet neither in a Council Chamber nor in a Roman basilica is one required to stand or sit in the aisles and look between the columns to watch business, a ritual, or a spectacle carried on centrally. Rather, one stands in the nave within the space of the ritual or spectacle in either of these two types of buildings.

6. In any case, in terms of ancient architecture these seven buildings appear to be a type of basilica or at the very least a building with an interior colonnade. This does not mean there is no variation between them. It simply means that they are all roofed halls featuring a rectangle of columns around the central space so as to divide the space into a central area surrounded by

---

[14] Foerster, "Architectural Models," 45–8.

[15] Meyers, Strange and Meyers, *Excavations*.

[16] Note that fourth century churches, in comparison, organize inner space into a nave and *two* aisles leading from entrance to the sacred area in back. (Occasionally there are four rows of columns, that is, two on each side of the nave). This is no accident. The Christian architects are following another template. See Strange, *Emergence*. For a case study in a specific basilica church in Rome see Visser, *Geometry*, 54–6.

a walkways between the columns and the outside walls.[17] Double columns ("heart-shaped columns") mark the corners of the columniation in at least one instance. Double columns in any period inform the eye from inside the columniation that there is a corner between two rows of columns. One can also think of the corner columns as corner markers.

7. The builders of basilicas and of most synagogues arranged for light to enter the structure through second stories over the central space. Windows let in light through a clerestory. The columns support the clerestory walls above. The area within the columns, then, would be relatively more brightly lit by the sun than would the walking spaces or aisles outside the columns.

8. The roof of such a building yields a distinctive silhouette. That is, the roof over the aisles is one story lower than the roof over the central space, which is about twice as high as the side aisles. In all seven cases the silhouette of the putative synagogues would be noteworthy and would call attention to itself.

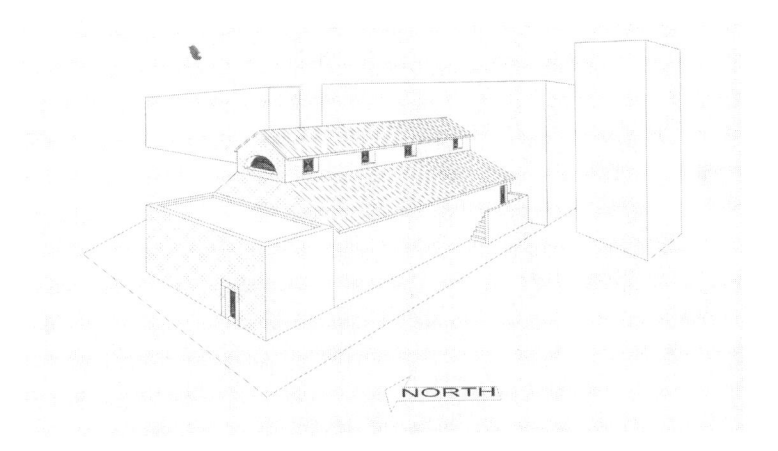

Figure 3.3   Silhouette of the Gamla synagogue.

9. In all seven cases those who sit or stand on the benches have their attention directed to the central space. The row of columns in front of each observer limits vision. In fact, if it were crowded, it would be quite difficult to gain a vantage that

[17] Robertson, *Architecture*, 267–71; MacDonald, *Architecture*, 53.

is not blocked by a column. Analysis of the lines of sight in these seven buildings from the benches suggests that the interior space was better constructed for hearing than for seeing.[18] This suggests that these buildings were built with audition in mind, not vision. This circumstance happens to fit the conclusion from Jewish sources that the one unvarying ritual associated with the ancient synagogue is declamation of Torah. J. Neusner has said:

> [T]he synagogue represents the occasion at which ten or more Israelite males assemble and so embody Israel, and provides for the declamation of the Torah to Israel . . . It is a place made holy by Israel's presence and activity, anywhere Israel assembles, and the presence is for the activity of hearing the Torah proclaimed.[19]

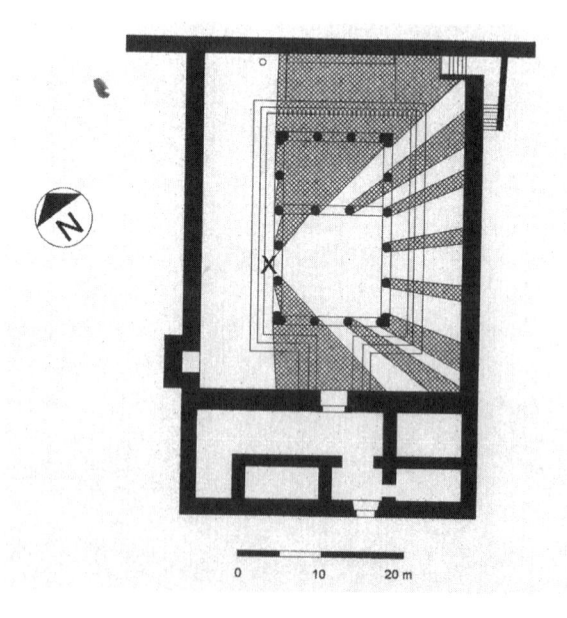

Figure 3.4 Viewshed analysis of the Gamla synagogue.

---

[18] Strange, "Synagogue as Metaphor," 120, fig. 7.
[19] Neusner, "Tractate Megillah," 407–31.

The resemblance of these seven buildings to one another extends to structures in the Diaspora, notably at Sardis, Ostia, and Priene.[20] The commonality between them also suggests strongly that their builders shared a mental template for this space. Another way to put this is that these seven buildings and their successors refer to or stand for something else. The builders knew some structure that was of such enormous social and religious moment that it impressed them with the extraordinary idea of arranging seating between the columns and the walls.

The most obvious source of this idea is the Temple Mount in Jerusalem, but specifically, those areas where one expects to hear reading of Torah.[21] This narrows our view to one of the perimeter porticos of the temple mount or one of the interior courts. Josephus says that porches with columns surrounded the Court of Women.[22] We may speculate that the Court of Israel and the Court of the Priests featured similar porches, since populations needed to be able to view the slaughter and sacrifices out of the weather. Porches or cloisters (στόα) resemble the internal space of the majority of Galilean and Judean synagogues from the first to the sixth centuries C.E. Although we know little of benches for seating inside the colonnades on the temple mount,[23] the architectural similarities of the buildings of Capernaum,

---

[20] The proposal that a first or second century synagogue existed in the Crimea offers another opportunity to test the hypothesis of the constancy of the floorplan abroad. See MacLennan, "Search," 44–51, 69.

[21] Noticed as early as 1983 by Friedman, "Unexplained Features," 35–42 and by the present author independently in 1995, see n. 10. Binder, *Temple Courts*. See also Branham, "Vicarious Sacrality," 319–45.

[22] "The western part of this court had no gate at all, but the wall was built entire on that side. But then the cloisters which were betwixt the gates extended from the wall inward, before the chambers ["treasuries" as in Mark 12:41]; for they were supported by very fine and large pillars. These cloisters were single, and, excepting their magnitude, were in no way inferior to those of the lower court." (τὸ δὲ πρὸς δύσιν μέρος οὐκ εἶχε πύλην, ἀλλὰ διηνεκὲς ἐδεδόμητο ταύτῃ τὸ τεῖχος. αἱ στοαὶ δὲ μεταξὺ τῶν πυλῶν ἀπὸ τοῦ τείχους ἔνδον ἐστραμμέναι πρὸ τῶν γαζοφυλακίων σφόδρα μὲν καλοῖς καὶ μεγάλοις ἀνείχοντο κίοσιν, ἦσαν δ' ἁπλαῖ, καὶ πλὴν τοῦ μεγέθους τῶν κάτω κατ' οὐδὲν ἀπελείποντο), *B.J.* 5.200.

[23] We have references to Jesus "seated" in the temple in Matt 26:55, Mark 12:41 "He sat down opposite the treasury." (Καὶ καθίσας κατέναντι τοῦ γαζοφυλακίου), Luke 2:46 (as a boy) and John 8:2. In the pericope of the woman take in adultery in John 8:1–11, Jesus is presented as seated in an unpaved area, for he stoops down and writes "in the earth" twice (εἰς τὴν γῆν vv. 6 and 8). The accusers stood the

Masada, Gamla, Masada, Herodium, Jericho, Qiryat Sefer, and Modi'in to porches on the Temple Mount strongly suggest that the late Hellenistic to Early Roman synagogue in Israel was a Jewish invention based upon the porches or colonnaded spaces of the Temple.[24] This hypothesis still applies whether these halls were sometimes used for ritual purposes and sometimes for non-ritual purposes, such as community meetings.

Samaritan Synagogues in Palestine

In order to strengthen our case that the synagogues of Judea and Galilee represent a type, we need a contrasting type. Since Judaism and Samaritanism seem to have developed separate paths by the first century, it seems appropriate to examine the case of Samaritan synagogues. We hypothesize that, since Samaritanism is self-consciously separate from the Judaism of the period, their synagogues should follow a different template in all periods.

In fact, the excavations of Y. Magen in Samaria, specifically in the region of Nablus (ancient Neapolis), have revealed several third to fifth century synagogues. These include those excavated at Khirbet Samara (Deir Srôr), El-Khirbe near Sebastiya, Hazzan Ya'aqov at Shechem, Khirbet Majdal (Zur Nathan), and Kafr Fahma.[25] Several scholars have discussed these, but no one has noticed that the Samaritan synagogues do not follow the template of the preceding section. Their mosaic floors, when they exist, in fact show beautiful designs with many of the same motifs found in mosaic floors in Judea and Galilee.[26] The differences between Jewish synagogues and Samaritan synagogues lie in other features of their plans.

The builders of the certainly identified Samaritan synagogues near Nablus did not define the rectangle of central space by columns around

---

woman "in the middle" (ἐν μέσῳ), which must mean in the middle of a court, because in v. 9 the woman still stood "in the middle" after the crowd left.
[24] Binder, *Temple Courts*, 169.
[25] Magen, "Samaritan Synagogues," 1424–7 and "Samaritan Synagogues," (*Qadmoniot* 25), 66–90. For the English version see, Manns and Alliata, *Early Christianity in Context*, 193–230.
[26] Pummer, "Samaritan Synagogue," 118–60. See also Pummer, "Samaritan Material," 139–51.

two, three, or four sides. Although the walls, benches, and central rectangle of mosaic floor are nested, there is no row of columns between which the observer must look to see what transpires in the middle. Otherwise, the mosaic floor in the central area displays two menorahs, the lulav, ethrog, and incense shovel, exactly as in Late Roman synagogues elsewhere in Palestine.

In the case of the El-Khirbe synagogue, the entrance on the narrow, east side leads one through an opening in the three benches on four sides directly to the central rectangle. There is no columniation to obscure the view. The interior space is about 12 x 8.3 meters *in toto*.[27]

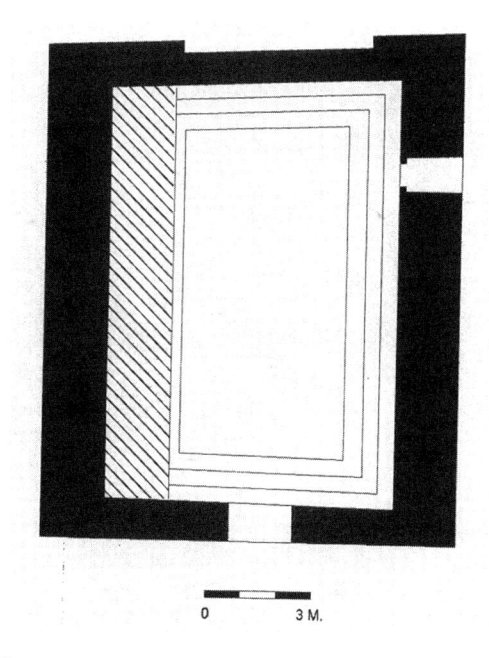

Figure 3.5 The synagogue at El-Khirbe. Adapted from Magen 1993.

Likewise the published plan of the synagogue of Khirbet Samara (Deir Srôr) shows benches around four sides, rather like those at Gamla. The benches are interrupted by a doorway for access to the inner rectangle of mosaic, which is *not* surrounded on two, three, or four sides

---

[27] Magen, "Samaritan Synagogues," n. 25, figs. 3–4.

by columns. Indeed, the only columns found are outside in the porch on the north side. The total interior space was about 15 x 8.5 meters.[28]

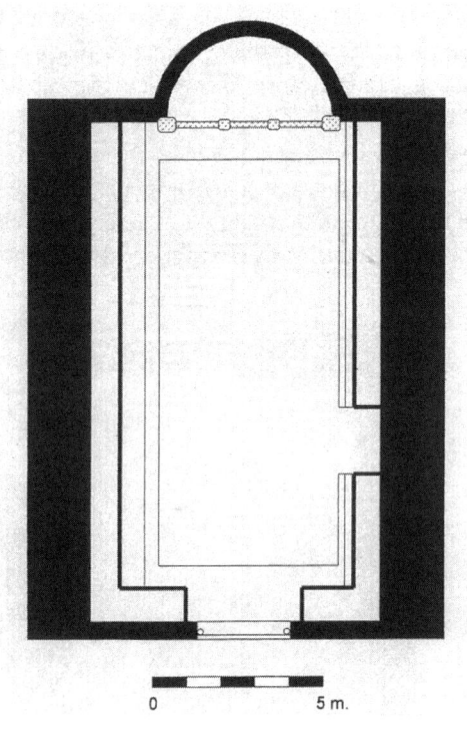

Figure 3.6   The synagogue at Khirbet Samara. Adapted from Magen 1993.

Magen publishes another putative synagogue from Zur Nathan (Khirbet Majdal) which he dates to the 4th or 5th century C.E. However, this building fits the pattern of a square building with external apse and two stylobates to hold up columns, rather like the synagogue at Ma'on.[29] Magen cites the find of Jewish symbols in rooms *north* of the hall. He mentions "a millstone ornamented with a seven-branched Menorah and a fragment of a marble chancel screen, [which] may be

---

[28] Ibid., 205, fig. 17. Another possible synagogue appears in fig. 45 on p. 224, a fragment of a Crusader building with an apse on the east end, but incorporating earlier masonry on its south side. This room also has no interior columns and appears to measure about 4.8 x 11.2 meters.
[29] Ibid., 222, fig. 42. Barag, "Ma'on (Nirim)," 944–6.

Archaeology and Ancient Synagogues up to 200 C.E.

attributed to the Samaritan builders of the synagogue."[30] Since the context is a Byzantine monastery, it is prudent to await further evidence from this site.

A third example for which we have some evidence for the plan is the Samaritan synagogue of Sha'alvim (Salbit, Selbit, Selebi), a site in the Shephelah. This synagogue was first reported in the *Survey of Western Palestine,* vol. III, and then excavated by E. L. Sukenik in 1949, who identified the site as Samaritan on the basis of a Samaritan inscription.[31] The plan and some few added details were published by R. Reich in 1994, because Sukenik did not publish the plan.[32]

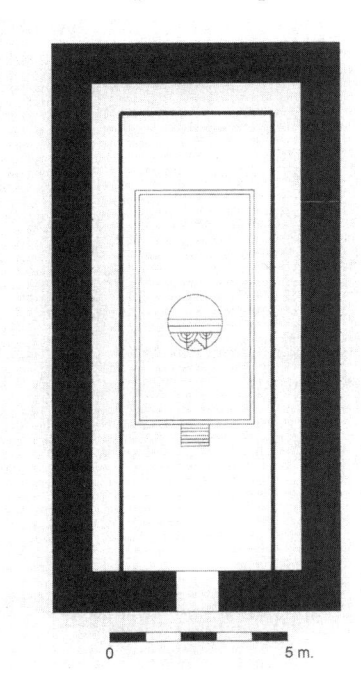

Figure 3.7   Plan of the synagogue at Sha'alvim. Adapted from Reich 1994.

[30] Magen, "Samaritan Synagogues," 222. The drawing (no photograph) of the Greek inscription in the mosaic floor of the putative prayer hall is rather curiously rendered, but may begin with "Be remembered...," though only MNHΣ is preserved, though there seems to be room for more. Magen gives two different translations on p. 232 and in the caption to fig.43 on p. 223.
[31] Conder and Kitchener *Survey,* 52, 157. Sukenik, " Samaritan Synagogue" 25–30, Pls. XIV–XVI.
[32] Reich, "Plan," 216–27.

The building is a rectangle 15 x 8.05 meters oriented on Mt. Gerizim.[33] Reich reports that the interior space was 13.4 x 6.0 meters. It is worth noting that the interior measurements of the two other Samaritan synagogues discussed above were 12 x 8.3 meters and 15 x 8.5 meters. The three are quite similar in size and layout. Reich is of the opinion that there were no columns on the interior, as it is very easy to span six meters. He noted that Barag thought that the interior resembled a basilica with columns to form a nave and two aisles.[34] However, between the inner face of the side wall and the black band that marks the outline of the inner mosaic only about one meter of space remains for columns and a walkway on either side of the presumed columns. This is too little space, given that synagogue columns are about 50 cm. in diameter, which means that the walking space on either side of the row of columns would only amount to 25 cm. It seems that Reich is right.

It is quite arresting that the builders built interior space in at least these three instances with no columns. It is as though they sought to build their synagogues from a template alternative to that in use in Galilee and in Judea. The implication of this alternative arrangement is to support a hypothesis that the nesting of walls, benches, walk-ways, columns, and interior space is a marker for "Judaism" while a similar nesting, but with no columns, is a marker for "Samaritanism," at least in ancient Judea. In any case the configuration of space in these three Samaritan synagogues is firmly suggestive. It will take further excavation to confirm the hypothesis.

Analysis of Space in Seven Putative Synagogues

It now seems appropriate to examine the mental template of a synagogue inferred from seven Golani, Galilean, and Judean but not Samaritan first-century structures. We describe the "type" as a structure resembling a Roman basilica more than any other building, but with the benches arranged along the walls between the walls and the aisles. The purpose of this analysis is heuristic, mainly to discover how the space would work for declamation of Torah in the first two centuries.

---

[33] Ibid., 228.
[34] Barag, "Shaalbim," 1338.

That is, can we connect this template with the synagogue as envisioned in Mishnah Megilla, even though it is not described architecturally?

First, we observe that these seven structures invite us into a rectangular floor plan. Columns surround the central space, and benches and walk-ways (or aisles) surround the columns. The benches stood against the exterior walls. The roof is like that of a basilica, either with a sloping roof over each aisle and a peaked roof over the central rectangle or with a flat roof over both areas. Either way the silhouette of the building is distinctive and calls attention to itself among mainly one-storied, flat-roofed houses. There may be a slightly raised platform at the narrow end opposite an entrance, as at Gamla, but this is not necessary for this analysis. It is also the case that one may enter on the narrow end or in the broad side of the building. The analysis is similar in either case.

I have argued elsewhere that the synagogue stands in a metaphorical relationship to the religion that produced it. The synagogue, in that case, "stands for" this religious reality. It provides ways of giving form to certain abstract, religious ideas. The synagogue brings to expression or presents the religious system of the congregation or its understanding of the world.[35]

The builders did not always place these synagogues on the highest point of the city, as legislated by *t. Meg.* 3:23. Gamla's emplotment consists of streets on three sides (or squares on two sides and a narrow street on one side), which isolate the building. It is also built against the city wall, which ties it to a municipal structure rather than to a domestic building. The other buildings, like Masada, on the other hand, are not isolated. They nestle among other buildings or, in the case of Masada, are built within the casemate wall.

In terms of ancient architecture, the buildings' roofs were surely constructed with a clerestory because of the columns. This roofing gave these buildings a distinctive silhouette. The area within the columns, then, would be significantly more brightly lit by the sun than would the walking space outside the columns.

The tall silhouette of these buildings signal that they are not houses or domestic spaces. This would agree with an assumption of *m. Meg.* 3:3, which suggests that people may have taken short cuts through destroyed synagogues, but it is (later) forbidden. In other words, the

---

[35] Strange, " Synagogue as Metaphor," n. 13 above.

citizen can recognize a synagogue as a synagogue and not take the forbidden short-cut through it. The space is visually distinctive, and what is allowed in domestic spaces is not allowed for synagogues.

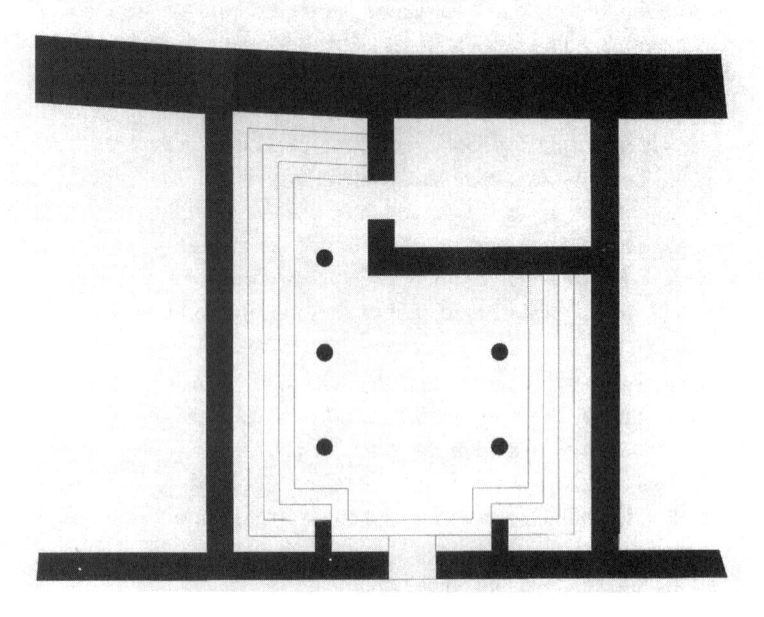

Figure 3.8   Plan of the Masada synagogue.

If we turn to the interior spaces of these structures with their columns and benches, we notice that the interior space is more or less symmetric about its long axis. A niche near a corner in the case of Jericho and Gamla highlights the lack of symmetry about the short axis. The symmetry about the long axis draws attention to an imaginary line from the middle of the narrow side to the opposite wall. It seems likely that the main activities within the hall would take place along this line.

It is important to notice that, as one enters through an entrance on the long axis and through the narrow wall, he or she does not walk the length of the hall on the long axis. The row of columns all around forms an architectural marker or boundary for the central space.

The ranks of benches introduce the literal notions of higher and lower, which may in fact operate as metaphors for higher and lower in desirability if not in rank. Of course it is also possible that social rank played a role in the seating arrangement, as was the case in Roman theaters. After walking into the rectangle of space between the columns and the benches, one must *ascend* to stand or sit (in the case of Gamla, Herodium, Masada, Qiryat Sefer), unless one chooses to keep one's seat on the first rank of benches. One must decide whether to stay on the floor or ascend to a higher bench. One must also decide which one of the four sides to occupy. It is possible, of course, that participants simply sat near their friends or relied upon tradition.

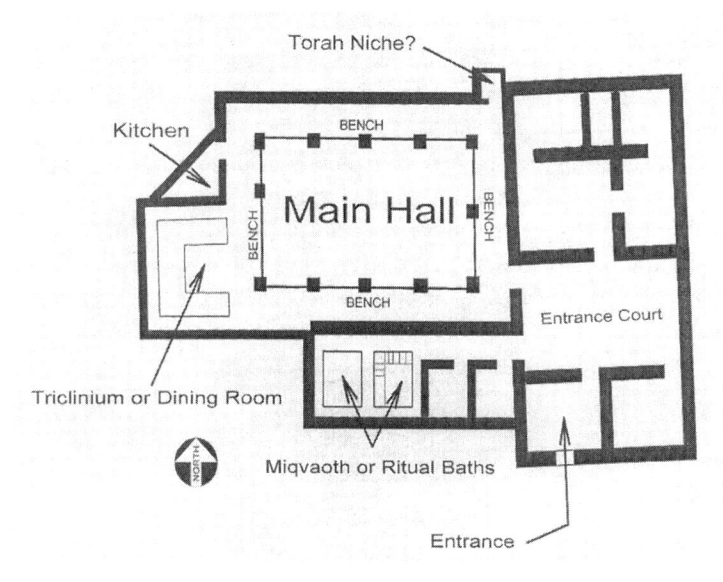

Figure 3.9 The Jericho synagogue. Adapted from Netzer 1998.

Furthermore the columniation draws our eyes down the length of the space, but also upward to the clerestory, which is lighted. Using sun models it is possible to show that, at these latitudes, the light coming in through the clerestory wall near noon in the summer would ordinarily illuminate the central area. If the sun were low enough, as for example during winter, it would illuminate part of the wall on the north side of the meridian.

Analysis of the line of sight or "viewshed" suggests that the interior space is better suited for hearing or listening than for sight. Nearly 50 per cent of the space on the opposite side of the hall is obscured by the row of columns nearest the viewer.

The most desirable seats were those not behind columns and with the best view. This may be at the lowest rank in order to be near the action. A saying of Jesus in Mark 12:38–39 gives the reader the idea of favored seating: "Beware of the scribes, who wish to walk about in robes and be greeted in the markets and yearn for the first seats (πρωτοκαθεδρίας) in the synagogues and the first couch in banquets." It is tempting to place these "first seats" opposite a main entrance on the long axis and atop the highest bench, or even on the lowest, as in theaters.

This restricted visual situation suggests that the ritual of Torah reading, for in the case of Torah declamation, hearing and listening are at issue, not watching someone read.

If the building is built so that Torah may be declaimed, then it follows that there must be at least one Torah scroll present. If there is a Torah scroll, is there an ark for the scroll? The literary sources seem to assume the presence of an ark or some kind of repository for scrolls.[36] This is true of *m. Meg.* 3:1 and following, where the ark is mentioned many times.

Figure 3.10 A possible synagogue ark. Reconstruction courtesy of The Virtual Bible, Inc.

[36] In Luke 4:17, the scroll simply appears, so that we have no idea how it got into the space: ἐπεδόθη αὐτῷ βιβλίον' Ἡσαΐου: "The scroll (little book) of Isaiah was given to him." In v. 20 we discover that it was an attendant who gave it to him, for Jesus gave it *back*: ἀποδοὺς τῷ ὑπηρέτῃ ἐκάθισεν. "Giving [it] back to the attendant he sat down." We do not know where the attendant got it.

Not only does the Mishnah mention the ark, but it uses a stereotypical phrase for the behavior or ritual appropriate to the ark; namely, one "passes before the ark" (to lead in worship or lead the *Amidah*). Even if one objects that these texts are late (ca. 200 C.E.), it is clear that there is a developed ritual behavior and a ritual piece of furniture associated with the synagogue. If the ark exists around 200 C.E., it is because it fulfills a ritual need. If that need exists in the first century, then it seems reasonable that the ark also existed then.

We reason about the presence of an ark as follows: if one sets aside space for reading of Torah, then one needs a Torah scroll at hand. It is simplest to store the Torah scroll within the hall, perhaps in a chest or container of some sort. If we read as a real practice the legislation of the sages about ending a Torah reading with a lection from a prophet (*m. Meg.* 3:4, 6), then we expect scrolls of the prophets to be present as well. The more scrolls we need, the larger our chest or container must be. Furthermore, because of the number of representations of arks on early Roman gold glass, for example, it seems reasonable to hypothesize that a special container called an "ark" would in fact be present. In other words, Jewish art depicts a real object.[37]

Figure 3.11 Interior of Capernaum I synagogue, showing reconstructed ark. Reconstruction courtesy of The Virtual Bible, Inc.

---

[37] Considering how religion operates with its artifacts, the chances are that any chest devoted to holding Torah scrolls would exhibit the finest workmanship and materials. See Renfrew and Bahn, *Archaeology*, 391.

In terms of the present analysis, where was the ark? Some have hypothesized that the niches in the walls at Gamla and at Jericho were for an ark. Ancient depictions of the ark show the ark standing in a central place opposite the main entrance on the long axis. If this applies to these seven buildings, then, when the ark was in use, the ark would stand on the narrow end opposite the main entrance.

Finally, we may also deduce a simple hypothesis that those involved in Torah reading (as many as seven men according to *m. Meg.* 3:4) sat at the highest rank of the benches (not necessarily the highest bench) when they were not reading. This would be the evident place also for the translator (*m. Meg.* 3:6 and more often) and for an attendant (Luke 4:20).

Our analysis has yielded several ways of understanding the putative synagogues of Capernaum, Gamla, Herodium, Masada, Qiryat Sefer, Jericho, and Modi'in. First we see that these buildings are nested among other buildings, but they have distinctive silhouettes as compared to domestic structures. Such a silhouette alerts the citizenry to its distinctive status and function.

The vestibule shields or hides the synagogue hall from the street in the two cases where that feature is available. That is, the vestibule deadens the sounds of the street and expunges outside sights. Thus the vestibule eases the visitor into the environment of the prayer hall without a sudden transition.

Lighting plays a role, as the brightest area would likely be innermost rectangle of space surrounded by the columns. There would be less lighting on the benches and in the aisles.

We discover that the buildings contain within them the idea of higher and lower, of higher rank and lower rank, or more desirable seats and less desirable seats. This may suggest that the society which uses the synagogue is stratified in terms of rank. It also suggests that high-ranking or most desirable space can be reserved for those who play a central role in Torah reading, the central idea of the synagogue according to *Mishnah Megilla*, and a situation known by Josephus.

We discover that the presence of a Torah scroll and other scrolls, as revealed in the ancient literature, suggests that an ark was present, which makes sense of those representations of arks in Jewish art. We can even deduce the likely position of the ark at the narrow end of the building. This position lies on the long axis opposite the main entrance and on a special, high platform built for it and the readers, for the translator, and perhaps even for an attendant, if he is different from the translator. Unfortunately we do not know when such a feature appeared for the first time.

Not all of these ideas are equally probably represented, but all of them are best understood as testable hypotheses. That is, we need to examine further examples of possible first century buildings in future archaeology and discover whether they tend to cohere with this pattern. It is certainly true that the buildings at Gamla, Masada, possibly Capernaum (first building), Herodium, Jericho, Qiryat Sefer, and Modi'in exhibit the nesting of walls, walkways, columns, and central space. All seven contain the idea of higher and lower, and therefore potentially of rank. The new building at Jericho exhibits a vestibule with apparently the same functions as the one at Gamla. It also has a niche near the corner, as at Gamla.

Conclusions

We are now in a position to suggest that both the ancient Jewish sources, comparison with the remains of Samaritan synagogues in Samaria, and analysis of interior space in seven putative synagogues suggest that (1) The builders of first century synagogues in the Golan, Galilee, and Judea followed a kind of cultural template in building synagogues. (2) These buildings were first and foremost appropriate for hearing declamation of Torah rather than for watching a spectacle (including a liturgy), unless one deliberately moved off the benches. It is not so much that one could not see a dialogue or other performance in the innermost space, but it would be far easier to hear it. (3) The architectural similarities of the buildings of Capernaum, Masada, Gamla, Masada, Herodium, Jericho, Qiryat Sefer, and Modi'in to porches on the Temple Mount strongly suggest that the late Hellenistic to Early Roman synagogue in Israel was a Jewish invention based upon the porches or colonnaded spaces of the Temple. (4) This template did not extend to Samaritan synagogues, though the data base is slimmer in that case. Yet the buildings at El-Khirbe, Khirbet Samara, and Sha'alvim reveal an alternative form and regularity of plan that suggests that the Samaritans are following an alternative convention. In other words, the data as it now stands tends to support the hypothesis that these halls were built according to two kinds of templates in the minds of the builders.

If so, then we should expect to find more examples of simple halls with nested walls, benches, aisles, columns, and central space. Furthermore we should expect to find more Samaritan synagogues with no interior columns at all. We will be far less hesitant about calling them synagogues, and we will give them their due, namely, as inventions of ancient Jews and Samaritans in an ancient land.

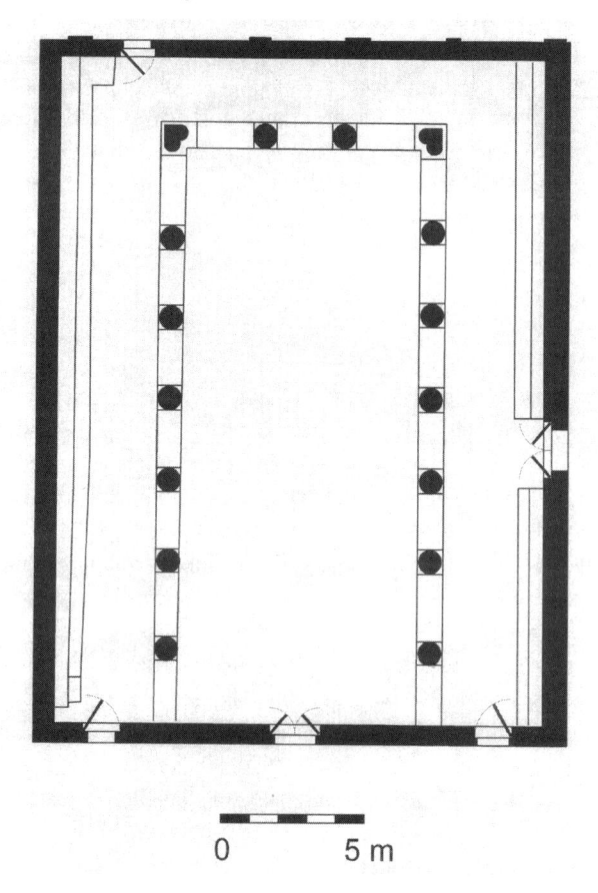

Figure 3.12 Plan of the Byzantine synagogue at Capernaum.

Bibliography

Barag, D., "Ma'on (Nirim)." Pages 944–6 in vol. 3 of *The New Encyclopedia of Archaeological Excavations in the Holy Land*. Edited by E. Stern. Jerusalem: Israel Exploration Society, 1993.

—, "Shaalbim." Page 1338 in vol. 4 of *The New Encyclopedia of Archaeological Excavations in the Holy Land*. Edited by Ephraim Stern. 4 vols. Jerusalem: Israel Exploration Society and Carta, 1993.

Binder, D. D., *Into the Temple Courts: The Place of the Synagogues in the Second Temple Period*. Atlanta: Society for Biblical Literature, 1999.

Branham, J. R., "Vicarious Sacrality: Temple Space in Ancient Synagogues." Pages 319–45 in vol. 2 of *Ancient Synagogues: Historical Analysis and Archaeological Discovery*. Edited by D. Urman and Paul V. M. Flesher. Leiden, New York: Brill, 1995.

Conder, C. R., and H. H. Kitchener, *Survey of Western Palestine*. London: Palestine Exploration Fund, 1883.

Cox, V., "IAA Rescue Excavation at Modi'in Uncovers Hasmonean period Jewish Settlement and Artifacts," http://www.bibleinterp.com/articles/Modi'in.htm, 2000. (Oct. 1, 2001)

Dothan, M., *Hammath Tiberias*. Jerusalem: Israel Exploration Society, 1983.

Foerster, G., "Architectural Models of the Greco-Roman Period and the Origin of The 'Galilean' Synagogue." Pages 45–8 in *Ancient Synagogues Revealed*. Edited by L. I. Levine. Jerusalem: Israel Exploration Society, 1982.

Friedman, T., "Some Unexplained Features of Ancient Synagogues," *Conservative Judaism* 36 (1983): 35–42.

Hachlili, R., "The Origin of the Synagogue: A Re-assessment," *JSJ* 28 (1997): 34–47.

Horst, van der, P. W., "Was de synagoge voor 70 een plaats van eredienst op sabbat?" *Bijdragen* 69 (1999): 125–46.

—, "Was the Synagogue a Place of Sabbath Worship before 70 CE?" Pages 18–43 in *Jews, Christians, and Polytheists in the Ancient Synagogue: Cultural Interaction during the Graeco-Roman Period.* Edited by Steven Fine. London: Routledge, 1999.

Kee, H. C., "The Transformation of the Synagogue after 70 C.E.: Its Import for Early Christianity," *NTS* 36 (1990): 1–24.

—, "Defining the First-Century CE Synagogue: Problems and Progress," *NTS* 41 (1995): 481–500.

Levine, L. I., "The Nature and Origin of the Palestinian Synagogue Reconsidered," *JBL* 115 (1996): 425–48.

—, *The Ancient synagogue: The First Thousand Years.* New Haven: Yale University Press, 2000.

Longstaff, T. R. W., and T. C. Hussey, "Palynology and Cultural Process: An Exercise in the New Archaeology." Pages 151–62 in *Archaeology and the Galilee: Texts and Contexts in the Greco-Roman and Byzantine Periods.* Edited by D. R., Edwards and C. T. McCollough. Atlanta: Scholars Press, 1997.

MacDonald, W. L., *The Architecture of the Roman Empire. Vol. 1: An Introductory Study.* New Haven and London: Yale University Press, 1982.

MacLennan, R. S., "In Search of the Jewish Diaspora, A First-Century Synagogue in Crimea?" *BAR* 22 (1996): 44–51, 69.

Magen, Y., "Samaritan Synagogues," *Qadmoniot* 25 (1992): 66–90 (Hebrew).

—, "Samaritan Synagogues." Pages 1424–7 in vol. 4 of *The New Encyclopedia of Archaeological Excavations in the Holy Land.* Edited by E. Stern. 4 vols. New York: Simon & Schuster, 1993.

—, "Samaritan Synagogues." Pages 193–230 in *Early Christianity in Context: Monuments and Documents.* Edited by F. Manns and E. Alliata. Jerusalem: Franciscan Printing Press, 1993.

Magen, Y. and E. Sirkis. "Qiryat Sefer: A Jewish Village and Synagogue of the Second Temple Period." *Qadmoniot* 33 (1999): 25–32 (in Hebrew).

Manns, F., and E. Alliata, eds. *Early Christianity in Context: Monuments and Documents.* Jerusalem: Franciscan, 1993.

McKay, H. A., "Ancient Synagogues: The Continuing Dialectic between Two Major Views." *Currents in Research: Biblical Studies* 6 (1998): 103–42.

Meyers, E. M., "Nabratein." Pages 85–7 in vol. 4 of *The Oxford Encyclopedia of Archaeology in the Near East*. Edited by Eric M. Meyers. Oxford: Oxford University Press, 1997.

Meyers, E. M., J. F. Strange, and C. L. Meyers, *Excavations at Ancient Meiron, Upper Galilee, Israel, 1971–72, 1974–75, 1977*. Cambridge: American Schools of Oriental Research, 1981.

Neusner, J., "Tractate Megillah." Pages 407–31 in vol. 2 of *The Halakhah: An Encyclopaedia of the Law of Judaism*. Edited by J. Neusner, A. J. Avery-Peck, and W. S. Green. Leiden: Brill, 2000.

Netzer, E., "Le Scoperte sotto il Palazzo di Erode." *Archeo* 14 (1998): 33.

Oster, R. E., "Supposed Anachronism in Luke-Acts' Use of *synagôgê*: A Rejoinder to H.C. Kee." *NTS* 39 (1993): 178–208

Ovadiah, A., and T. Michaeli, "Observations on the Origin of the Architectural Plan of Ancient Synagogues." *JJS* 38 (1987): 234–241.

Pummer, R., "The Samaritan Material Remains and Archaeology." Pages 139–51 in *The Samaritans*. Edited by Alan D. Crown. Tübingen: Mohr Siebeck, 1989.

—, "Samaritan Synagogues and Jewish Synagogues: Similarities and Differences." Pages 118–60 in *Jews, Christians, and Polytheists in the Ancient Synagogue: Cultural Interaction during the Greco-Roman Period*. Edited by Steven Fine. London: Routledge, 1999.

Renfrew, C., and P. Bahn, *Archaeology: Theories, Methods, and Practice*. New York: Thames and Hudson, 1996

Runesson, A., *The Origins of the Synagogue: A Socio-Historical Study*. Stockholm: Almqvist & Wiksell, 2001.

Reich, R., "The Plan of the Samaritan Synagogue at Sha'alvim." *IEJ* 44 (1994): 216–27.

Robertson, D. S., *Greek and Roman Architecture*. 2nd ed. Cambridge: Cambridge University Press, 1943

Roussin, L. A., "The Zodiac in Synagogue Decoration." Pages 83–96 in *Archaeology and the Galilee: Texts and Contexts in the Greco-Roman and Byzantine Periods.* Edited by D. R. Edwards and C. T. McCollough. Atlanta: Scholars Press, 1997.

Strange, J. F., "The Art and Archaeology of Ancient Judaism." Pages 64–114 of vol. 1 in *Judaism in Late Antiquity.* Edited by J. Neusner. Leiden: Brill, 1995.

—, "Ancient Texts, Archaeology as Text, and the Problem of the First Century Synagogue." Pages 27–45 in *Evolution of the Synagogue: Problems and Progress.* Edited by H. C. Kee and L. H. Cohick. Harrisburg: Trinity Press International, 1999.

—, "Synagogue as Metaphor," Pages 93–120 in vol. 4 of *Judaism in Late Antiquity, Part Three, Where We Stand: Issues & Debates in Ancient Judaism, The Special Problem of the Synagogue.* Edited by A. Avery-Peck and J. Neusner. Leiden: Brill, 2001.

Strange, J. R., *The Emergence of the Christian Basilica in the Fourth Century.* International Studies in Formative Christianity and Judaism. Edited by J. Neusner et al. Binghamton: Global Binghamton University, 2000.

Sukenik, E. L., "The Samaritan Synagogue at Salbit, Preliminary Report." *Bulletin, Louis M. Rabinowitz Fund for the Exploration of Ancient Synagogues* I (1949) 25–30, Pls. XIV–XVI.

Visser, Margaret, *The Geometry of Love: Space, Time, Mystery, and Meaning in an Ordinary Church.* New York: North Point Press, 2000.

4
Persian Imperial Politics, the Beginnings of Public Torah Readings, and the Origins of the Synagogue

Anders Runesson

THE QUEST FOR THE ORIGINS of the synagogue is as old as modern history writing itself. Already in the 16th century when old views ascribing the institution to Moses where challenged by Sigonius (1583), who thought that the synagogue originated in the Babylonian exile, there was a debate among scholars which was not resolved until Vitringa's magisterial work appeared in 1696.[1] From this time until the 1970s, the opinion of most scholars was that the synagogue originated in the Babylonian exile as a replacement for the lost sacrificial cult.[2] However, the lack of evidence supporting this theory have been pointed out by several scholars during the 19th and 20th centuries, especially in the last third of the latter one, with the result that it is no longer possible to maintain this consensus.[3]

Today, the trend is to date the synagogue coevally with the earliest sources mentioning synagogue terms, that is, the Hellenistic period. It is

---

[1] Sigonius, *De republica*, 89–90; Grotius, *Annotata*, 173; Vitringa, *De synagoga*, 271–428, where Vitringa's criticism of Grotius is found on pp. 308–14.
[2] Moore, *Judaism*, vol. 1, 283; Baron, *Jewish Community*, vol. 1, 61–2; Rowley, *Worship*, 224; Nicholson, *Preaching*, 134–5; Wigoder, *Story*, 9. Most recently, the same view has been voiced by Livingstone, "Synagogue," 1567–8.
[3] I have analysed the history of research in some detail in Runesson, *Origins*, 67–168.

from this time that the first evidence of *proseuchai* in Egypt is dated.[4] Indeed, some authors argue that synagogue origins should not be dated before the Early Roman period.[5]

It should be noted that the assumption underlying the first proposal (the Hellenistic period) is basically two-fold: first, it is assumed that the earliest sources mentioning the institution by name must be contemporary with its earliest existence. Second, the term *proseuche* is assumed to indicate an institution similar to the synagogue.

Further, it should also be noted that scholars proposing that the synagogue originated in the Roman period do so only on the basis of certain limiting definitions of "synagogue" as, for example, a "formal" or "central" or "distinctive" or "rabbinic" institution, or as a "characteristically stylized structure" *et cetera*.[6] This indicates an increasing awareness that the search for the origins of the synagogue depends on how "synagogue" is defined.

Therefore, I shall begin by defining some aspects of the synagogue. Then, after having sketched the main characteristics of the first century synagogue, this institution's origins will be sought and its development described. As will be clear, pursuing this goal requires taking one main feature of the first century synagogue and tracing this particular aspect to its origins before dealing with the other aspects of the institution.

Defining "Synagogue"

It is not possible to isolate and focus on synagogue terms in the search for the origins of the institution, since an institution may exist before it is given the specific name under which it is recognised in later times. Instead, we should describe the synagogue through a four-fold definition corresponding to what we know about it from the ancient sources:

1) Liturgical activities

---

[4] The foremost proponent of the Egyptian theory is Griffiths, "Egypt;" see also Flesher, "Palestinian Synagogues," 28. Note, however, that it is by no means sure that the term *proseuche* should be understood as a "synagogue term" in this early period. See, e.g., Gutmann, "Scholarly Assumption." See also the discussion in Runesson, *Origins*, 429–36.

[5] E.g., Hoenig, "Ancient City-Square," 452; Kee, "Transformation;" White, *Building*, 161; Hachlili, "Origin," 46.

[6] See n. 5 above.

2) Non-liturgical activities
3) Spatial aspects
4) Institutional aspects.

These four aspects of the synagogue constitute a pattern with the help of which we can isolate and analyse different parts of the institution. Liturgical aspects refer to rituals performed as independent acts in relation to God, while non-liturgical activities include, for example, court proceedings. I am deliberately avoiding the term "secular" or "social" since all ritual acts are social acts, and further, no clear distinction can be made between secular and religious activities in ancient societies.[7] "Spatial" refers to the place where these activities were performed and the institutional aspect includes leadership patterns and hierarchies, indicating a certain level of institutionalisation.

In previous research, the different parts of this four-fold definition of synagogue have been studied separately, but seldom has an attempt been made to bring all the aspects together in an attempt to determine when the synagogue originated. This is what we shall try to do here.[8]

Nature and Activities of the Synagogue

While it is not possible to limit the search for synagogue origins to the investigation of institutions designated by synagogue terms, such terms must nevertheless be taken into account in the initial work analyzing the institution(s) behind the terms. Thus, the activities that we connect with the synagogue around the first century were performed in assemblies/buildings designated by the following names:[9]

---

[7] Note, e.g., that non-liturgical proceedings most often include religious rituals. However, I have reserved the word "liturgy" for ritual complexes performed independently as acts between gods and human beings.

[8] The following discussion is, by necessity, rather brief; for a detailed analysis, see Runesson, *Origins*, 237–400.

[9] Apart from *universitas*, εὔχειον (both from the second century C.E.), *templum*, *proseucha* (both early second century C.E.), κατοικία, λαός (second or third century C.E.), and בית הכנסת (attested in written sources first in the second century C.E.), all terms come from sources dating to the first century C.E. or earlier. Other terms for assembly/community occur in later sources, e.g., ἔθνος in an inscription from third century C.E. Smyrna (*CIJ* 741).

Building	Area	Source	Assembly/ Community	Area	Source
συναγωγή	Palestine/ Diaspora	B.J. 2.285/ CJZC 72 (I.5)	συναγωγή	Palestine/ Diaspora	Pss.Sol. 10:7/ CIRB 71
συναγώγιον	Diaspora	Somn. 2.127	συναγώγιον	Diaspora	Legat. 311
σαββατεῖον	Diaspora	A.J. 16.164	σύνοδος	Diaspora	CPJ 138
σεμνεῖον	Diaspora	Contempl. 32[10]	πολίτευμα	Diaspora	CJZC 70
διδασκαλεῖον	Diaspora	Spec. 2.62	universitas	Diaspora	Cod. Just. 1.9,1[11]
ἀμφιθέατρον	Diaspora	CJZC 70			
προσευχή	Palestine/ Diaspora	Vit. 277/ JIGRE 117	οἱ Ἰουδαῖοι	Diaspora	JIGRE 22[12]
εὐχεῖον	Diaspora	CPJ 432	ἐκκλησία	Palestine/ Diaspora	Jdt 6:16/Acts 11:26[13]
προσευκτήριον	Diaspora	Mos. 2.216	λαός	Diaspora	CIJ 776[14]
οἶκος/οἴκημα	Palestine/ Diaspora	Vit. 277/ DF 33	κατοικία	Diaspora	CIJ 775
τόπος	Diaspora	A.J. 14.260	συμφοίτησις	Diaspora	Legat. 316
ἱερὸς τόπος	Palestine	Prob. 81	בית התורה	Palestine	CD 20.2:10–13
ἱερὸς περίβολος	Diaspora	JIGRE 9[15]			
ἱερόν	Palestine/ Diaspora	B.J. 7.144; B.J. 7.45			
templum	Diaspora	Tacitus *Hist* 5.5.4			
proseucha	Diaspora	Juvenal *Sat* 3.296			
בית מועד	Palestine	1QM 3.4			
בית הכנסת	Palestine	m. Meg. 3:3			

Table 4.1 Synagogue terms and their distribution. In the column "source" only one example of each area mentioned is given though in most cases there are several occurrences in the ancient material (inscriptions, papyri, literary texts).

The geographical distribution of institutions known by any of the names mentioned in Table 4.1 confirms ancient testimonies to the fact that the "synagogue" by the first century C.E. was a widespread phe-

---

[10] For σεμνεῖον as a "synagogue" term, see Binder, *Temple Courts*, 149–51. The same term was also used for the private cell of each house of the members of the Therapeutae.

[11] This reference dates to 213 C.E. However, if Ghislanzoni's restoration of the Gaius Julius Justus inscription (*JIWE*, vol. 1 No. 18) is correct, *universitas* is witnessed already in the second century C.E. (Noy has *synagoga*. Cf. Runesson, "Synagogue," 88–9)

[12] Οἱ Ἰουδαῖοι refers to the local community in Schediá, and not the people as a whole. Cf. Claussen, *Versammlung*, 146.

[13] The Jesus believing ἐκκλησία in Antioch was, as other "synagogues" were, within the frames of the civic rights of the Jews in the Roman Empire. It is important not to impose an anachronistic view on Jesus-believing Jews as not belonging to the Jewish people and not sharing their status in this early period. For a discussion, see Zetterholm, *Formation*, 6, 91–6.

[14] Λαός refers to the local community, and not, as the common usage is, to the people as a whole. Cf. Claussen, *Versammlung*, 146–7.

[15] The reading ἱερὸς περίβολος, though partly a reconstruction, is very probable. For the same expression, see also Philo, *Flacc.* 48.

nomenon.[16] The sources reveal that the institutions had a formal leadership (the institutional aspect). It is also clear that there were public buildings adapted for assemblies of the kind described in the sources, such as those at Gamla, Masada, Herodion, Kiryat Sefer, Qumran, and, I would argue, Capernaum and Jericho.[17] Further, both liturgical and non-liturgical activities were performed in institutions with these names.[18]

The activity which is mentioned most often and which is emphasised as characteristic of institutions named in synagogue terms is, however, torah reading.[19] As it happens, public torah reading and teaching are also the activities which can claim the longest uninterrupted continuity in the history of the synagogue, from the earliest sources connecting it with institutions designated by synagogue terms until the present day. It is further an activity unique to the Jews in pre-Christian antiquity.

For these reasons, in searching for synagogue origins it is a good strategy to focus on public torah readings and trace them as far back in

---

[16] See, e.g., Philo, *Flacc.* 45–6; *Spec.* 2.62; Acts 15:21.
[17] See Runesson, *Origins*, 174–89, 350–70.
[18] "Synagogues" were places where judicial proceedings took place (e.g., Mark 13:9). They also functioned as council halls (*CJZC* 70), archives (apart from copies of the torah, Josephus, *B.J.* 2.291, records of manumissions were kept in these buildings; *CIRB*, 70), and treasuries (Philo, *Spec.* 1.77–8; Josephus, *A.J.* 16.164; cf. Matt 6:2). Travellers could find shelter in at least some of them (*CIJ* 1404). Further, "synagogues" were places where manumissions took place (*CIRB* 71–3, 985, 1123, 1127; Levinskaya, *Diaspora Setting*, 236–9). An often-cited example of political meetings in a *proseuche* is the Tiberias incident recounted by Josephus, *Vita* 277–82, 290–303. Liturgical activities included torah readings (see below), prayers (e.g., Josephus, *A.J.* 14.260; *Vita* 295; *C. Ap.* 1.209; Philo, *Spec.* 3.171; Matt 6:5), public fasts (e.g., *Vita* 290); communal meals (*A.J.* 14.216). For an overview of non-liturgical activities, see Levine, "Formative Years," 14–15. Cf. more recent and comprehensive treatments in Binder, *Temple Courts*, 389–450; Levine, *Ancient Synagogue*, 124–59.
[19] The following sources mention torah reading, teaching or the presence of torah scrolls in a "synagogue:" Philo, *Somn.* 2.127; *Opif.* 128; *Hypoth.* 7.11–13; *Legat.* 156, 157, 311–13; *Mos.* 2.215–16; *Spec.* 2.60–2; *Contempl.* 30–1 (cf. 28); *Prob.* 80–3; Josephus, *B.J.* 2.289–92; *A.J.* 16.43–5, 164; *C. Ap.* 2.175; Mark 1:21, 39; 6:2; Matt 4:23; 9:35; 13:54; Luke 4:15, 16–30, 31–3, 44; 6:6; 13:10; Acts 9:20; 13:5, 14–16; 14:1; 15:21; 17:2–3, 10–11, 17; 18:4–6, 26; 19:8; John 6:59; 18:20; *CIJ* 1404. Cf. 1 Tim 4:13. Note that when teaching is mentioned without readings in connection with a "synagogue," readings or quotations from the torah may nevertheless be assumed, since there was hardly more than one copy of the law in each "synagogue;" cf. Acts 17:3.

time as we can. None of the other activities has these advantages: explicit evidence for communal, set prayers is younger than the earliest sources mentioning synagogue terms. And as to non-liturgical activities, such as judicial and administrative functions, these activities existed in relation to non-Jewish temples as well. Indeed, if we focus on non-liturgical activities, the search for synagogue origins becomes meaningless since such activities belong to every developed society: we would end up with answers which cannot explain the unique institution of the synagogue as it appeared in the first century. Since the origin and development of the synagogue in the Diaspora differed significantly from the course of events in Palestine, I shall limit the present investigation to the Palestinian synagogue. The origins of the Diaspora synagogue are treated in detail elsewhere.[20]

Before proceeding back in time, it is important to note that institutions designated by synagogue terms in the first century were of two basic types. On the one hand, we have the village assemblies, often mentioned in the Gospels. These were official and public, open to anyone. They dealt with the affairs of certain geographical areas, including administrative and judicial matters, and performed torah-reading rituals on the Sabbath.

On the other hand, there were assemblies of certain communities which were open primarily to members and sympathisers. Such semi-public, non-official institutions were also designated by synagogue terms, as is shown by Philo in his description of the synagogue of the Essenes.[21] Also, the Theodotos inscription is an example of this type of semi-public synagogue: this was an assembly house for torah readings for a certain group, open especially for pilgrims to Jerusalem—it was not the official administrative centre of Jerusalem. Another example of a semi-public synagogue is the "synagogue of the Freedmen" in Acts 6:9.[22] While the public assemblies were held in public architecture only,

---

[20] Runesson, *Origins*, 401–76.
[21] *Prob.* 81–2.
[22] "Then some of those who belonged to the synagogue of the Freedmen (as it was called), Cyrenians, Alexandrians, and others of those from Cilicia and Asia, stood up and argued with Stephen." Josephus also recounts that two law-teachers ("sophists"), Judas and Matthias, held lectures on torah which were attended by many people: *B.J.* 1.648–9. Such assemblies were appearently open to sympathisers in the same way that the assemblies held by Jesus and his followers were. Both should be defined as non-official "synagogues."

such semi-public synagogues could make use of both public and private buildings.[23]

Apart from the fact that these two types of synagogues both included torah reading and studying, they had one more thing in common, and that was their independence from any supra-local, overarching authority structure controlling the ideological aspect of the institutions. In other words, neither the Jerusalem authorities nor the Pharisees controlled the official, public synagogues of the land, and we have no evidence that, for example, the Essene communities, or any other non-official semi-public synagogue (such as the Jesus movement or the Pharisees), were controlled from a supra-local level. The social position of the two institutions may be summarized in the following figure.

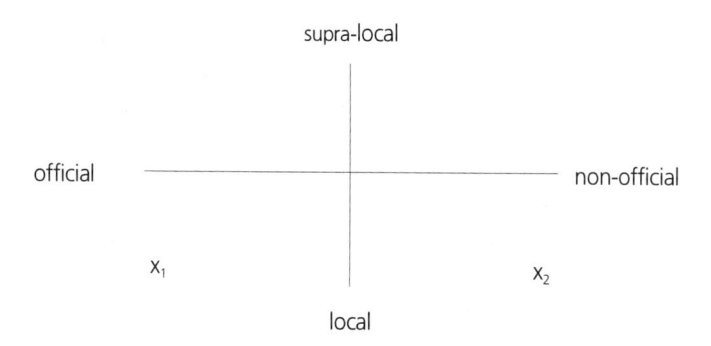

Figure 4.1 The relation between the two types of synagogues in first century Palestine as defined by status of legitimacy (official—non-official) and authority range (local—supra-local). x_1 = public synagogues; x_2 = semi-public synagogues.

The quest for the origins of the synagogue must thus be two-fold, distinguishing between public and semi-public synagogues. Having these definitions and distinctions in mind, and focussing on public torah readings, we shall begin with the former, attempting to explain when, where, how, and why the synagogues of the first century came into existence.

---

[23] Cf. Acts 5:42.

The Earliest Synagogue in the Land of Israel

When analyzing the Hebrew Bible documents which refer to the earliest public torah-reading rituals from a redaction-critical perspective, it soon becomes clear that all references to such readings belong to late, mostly Deuteronomistic redactions.[24] The Deuteronomistic history, into which Deuteronomy was incorporated, was redacted in the early Persian period to include stories retrojecting public readings of the law into the early history of Israel. Deuteronomy itself, the document which more than any other text in the Hebrew Bible emphasises the knowledge of torah among the people,[25] was most likely written during the reign of Darius (522–486 B.C.E.).[26]

The conclusion from this is that while we know of no custom of public reading of law prior to the Persian period, certain groups belonging to this period had a need to portray this custom as ancient and attribute it to the great heroes of their people (Moses, Joshua, Josiah). This strategy of legitimisation is so obvious that it makes us ask for the reasons behind it. The basic question is this: why did torah knowledge among ordinary people become important for the leading strata of Yehudite society during this time? In order to answer this question it is necessary to understand the situation in Persian Yehud from an international, imperial perspective.[27]

From the beginning, the colonial strategy of Cyrus (557–530 B.C.E.) was to minimise administrative changes in the nations he conquered, making it easy for these nations to adapt to their new status as provinces.[28] Furthermore, as the Cyrus Cylinder tells us, he allowed exiled people to return to their home countries and he restored local cults in his empire.[29] This earned him the goodwill of many ancient peoples, including the exiled Judahites.[30]

---

[24] See, e.g., Exod 24:7; Deut 31:11; Josh 8:34; 2 Kgs 23:1–3. For the dating of these and other texts from the Hebrew Bible discussed below, see Runesson, *Origins*, 245–258.
[25] E.g., Deut 4:40; 7:11–12; 10:12–13; 12:1; 16:12; 26:16–19; 32:46.
[26] For a post-exilic date for Deuteronomy, see also Hölscher, "Ursprung;" Hoffmann, *Reform*; Davies, *Scribes*, 93–9.
[27] Cf. Berquist, *Judaism*, 241.
[28] See Cook, *Persian Empire*, 41.
[29] Cyrus, *Cyl.* II. 26–30, 34–35 (*ANET*, 315–16).
[30] Isa 44:28; 45:1, 13; 2 Chr 36:22–3. See also Stern, "Social History," 70.

His policy with regard to local cults was followed by his successors, but not until Darius' reign were major administrative reforms consolidating the empire enforced. In his effort to stabilise the situation in conquered territories and enhance his control, he reformed local administration, installed new governors and codified local laws. The most extensive evidence for this colonial strategy comes from Egypt, but it is likely that the same reforms were enforced in Babylonia as well. Darius became know as the "law-giver."[31]

It is from this perspective that we should understand the situation in Yehud when the emphasis on common knowledge of the law suddenly became so prominent.[32] Despite permission from Cyrus, the temple had not been rebuilt, and social cohesion had not been achieved: in short, the creation of Yehud as a secondary state was still in its infancy.[33] Under Darius' reign, administration was reformed, the temple constructed, cult centralisation implemented and the laws, most likely in the form of Deuteronomy, were codified. This was an attempt to create effective, functioning structures and a unifying national identity, modifying the symbolic universe of the inhabitants of Yehud to include the status of the land as a province with (limited) self-government.[34] This served to maintain the status quo with the support of state ideology.

Such a strategy, which coincided with the interests of the leading strata in Yehud, the gola community in Jerusalem, concerned all inhabitants of the land and thus all inhabitants must be instructed in the laws and traditions of the society, as emphasised in Deuteronomy and the Deuteronomistic redactions of other documents.

One of the means to achieve this goal was the establishment of the institution of reading the law publicly in the administrative and cultic centre of the province, that is, the Jerusalem temple. This was done in relation to sukkoth on a seven-year cycle (the *haqhel* ceremony): Deut

---

[31] See, e.g., Olmstead, "Lawgiver." The laws of Egypt were collected and codified over a period of 21 years as recorded in the Demotic chronicle: Reich, "Codification," cf. Blenkinsopp, "Udjahorresnet," 412; Yamauchi, *Persia*, 150, n. 107.

[32] For a more detailed discussion, see Runesson, *Origins*, 259–83.

[33] For the concept of "secondary state" as distinct from "pristine state," see Fried, "State", especially p. 37; Price, "State Formation." In contrast to the pristine state, the development of a secondary state is heavily dependent on another (colonial) state.

[34] For such local, limited, self government as a Persian colonial strategy, see also Frei and Koch, *Reichsorganisation*, 110.

31:9–13. We know little, or nothing about other such strategies: while the administrative reforms of Darius affected local administrative centres in Yehud, we have no sources telling us about public torah-reading rituals in such local centres at this early time. Such evidence emerges only with Ezra-Nehemiah.

The accounts of public reading and teaching of torah in the books of Ezra and Nehemiah in fact provides us with important information of such readings and their development during a period of about 50 to 100 years.

Following Japhet and others, the books of Ezra-Nehemiah should not be dated together with Chronicles.[35] Instead, the former should be placed somewhere in the late Persian period, ca. 400–375 BCE,[36] while the latter dates to the Early Hellenistic period, towards the end of the fourth century or slightly later.[37] As to the historical period described in Ezra and Nehemiah, we have to proceed back in time to around the middle of the fifth century B.C.E., that is, under the rule of Artaxerxes I (465–423 B.C.E.).[38]

Hoglund has argued convincingly that the missions of Ezra and Nehemiah are to be seen as measures taken by this Artaxerxes to secure dominance in the region in the wake of the Egyptian revolt, which involved the Delian league and continuous Greek naval operations in the eastern Mediterranean.[39] If the decisive Egyptian victory at Papremis is

---

[35] Japhet, "Common Authorship"; Williamson, *Israel*, 37–59.

[36] Japhet, "Sheshbazzar," 89, n. 55. Albertz, *History*, vol. 2, 545, dates Ezra-Nehemiah to around 350 B.C.E.

[37] Japhet, *Chronicles*, 23–8. Albertz, *History*, vol. 2, 545, dates Chronicles somewhere between 330–250 B.C.E. Williamson, *Israel*, 83–6, advocates a late Persian date for Chronicles as does Grabbe, *Judaism*, 50, but this is less probable. We shall return to Chronicles below.

[38] Though Ezra 4:7 and 7:1 do not explicitly mention which Artaxerxes they refer to, it is most likely the first king with that name who is meant: see Williamson, *Ezra, Nehemiah*, xxxix–xliv. Thus, Ezra's mission began in 458 B.C.E. Nehemiah was governor in Yehud 445–432 B.C.E.

[39] Hoglund, *Imperial Administration*, 207–40. Cf. Blenkinsopp, "Udjahorresnet," 420; Albertz, *History*, vol 2, 445–6. Grabbe, "Mission," has brought attention to several problems in the description of the mission of Ezra in Ezra-Nehemiah, including criticism of the similarities between this mission and the mission of Udjahorresnet (294–7), pointing to, e.g., the different periods in which these people were active as well as the difference in importance between a nation like Egypt and a small province like Yehud. However, the chronological difference is no real problem since Darius' policy and strategies were retained by his immediate successors.

to be dated around 459 B.C.E.,[40] the arrival of Ezra in Jerusalem in 458 B.C.E. as well as the later mission of Nehemiah, who fortified Jerusalem and accomplished economic and social reforms,[41] is set within the context of Persian strategy to counteract hostile Egyptian and Greek activities.[42] This shows that Persian strategic thinking involved a broad spectrum of steps combining military, economic and social aspects to form a massive response to such major unrest in the empire as the Egyptian revolt, including Greek interference. However, we shall limit our discussion here to socio-religious reforms and how they relate to the use of public reading of law as a political strategy.

It seems clear that what we are dealing with in the time of Ezra is the enforcement of a new legal order, evidenced not the least by the appointment of (new) "magistrates and judges who may judge all the people in the province Beyond the River" (Ezra 7:25).[43] The "law of your God" mentioned by Artaxerxes in the decree given to Ezra is probably to be identified with Deuteronomy,[44] known in Yehud from

---

Further, from a strategic military and socio-political perspective it is not possible to isolate and differentiate provinces as Grabbe does: a small province like Yehud may have had considerable strategic importance necessitating imperial action. While details in the narrative of Ezra-Nehemiah may indeed be the object of discussion, the basic similarities between strategic action taken by the Persians in different parts of their Empire in response to different situations can hardly be discarded. Most recently Janzen, "Mission," has contributed with a valuable discussion of Ezra and his mission. However, Janzen, like Grabbe, requires too specific agreement between Ezra's work and extra-Biblical sources, resulting in the downplaying of the specifics of each political and military situation. As a result, Janzen does not succeed in establishing a credible motive behind the actions of Ezra as described in the narrative, especially the public reading of torah. Instead, Hoglund's analysis, which takes into account the international political scene, provides a historical setting explaining the work of Ezra and Nehemiah as intimately related to colonial and military strategies.

[40] Cook, *Persian Empire*, 168.
[41] When Nehemiah took office in 445, the unrest in the region was still not settled permanently.
[42] Hoglund, *Imperial Administration*, 90–6, 226. See also Cook, *Persian Empire*, 127–8 for a discussion of the events.
[43] Regarding the authenticity of Artaxerxes' decree, see Widengren, "Persian Period," 496–8; Williamson, *Ezra*, 98–105; Hoglund, *Imperial Administration*, 227; cf. Grabbe, *Judaism*, 32–6.
[44] The contents of the book of the law read by Ezra have been the object of considerable debate, opinions ranging from a smaller collection of legal materials, the priestly code or Deuteronomistic laws to the Pentateuch. For relevant literature, see Yamauchi, *Persia*, 257–8.

the time of Darius.[45] Thus Ezra's achievement was not the completion of a collection of laws which he then promulgated, but rather an authoritative interpretation and enforcement of an already existing corpus of traditions created through public readings and teachings. The question is, then, which kind of imperial strategies it was that promoted the method of public readings of torah in order to accomplish the desired political, social and religious goals.

Hoglund has shown that one of the most important themes in Ezra and Nehemiah, the issue of intermarriage, is to be understood against the background of the imperial mechanism of dependent population and ethnic collectivisation.[46] This imperial strategy served to control well-defined ethnic collectives which, being dependent on the imperial power for their existences in an allotted land, could be removed from their home countries and re-located in other lands, maintaining their administrative identity.[47] In analogy with this, the exiles returning to Yehud did so not because of any legal claims or rights to the territory, but solely on the basis of the benevolence of the empire, thus being dependent on the Persian king for their continuous residence in the land. Quoting Hoglund:

> Such systems of allocating territories to dependent populations will work as long as the imperial system is capable of maintaining some clarity as to who is allowed

---

[45] As presupposed by Ezra 7:25. See Albertz, *History*, vol. 2, 470; cf. Rendtorff, "Noch einmal," 90. Ezra's mission was not the imposition of a new law code on the people, but the enforcement of a certain social reform programme ideologically motivated by reinterpretations of an already existing law (cf. Neh 8:7–8).

[46] Hoglund, *Imperial Administration*, 236–40. Essential to note here is the social function of marriage to regulate the transferring of property and status from one group to another: "By circumscribing the options available in marriage outside of the group, all property, kinship-related rights and status remain within a closed community." (p. 237.) See also Hoglund, "Achaemenid Context," 65–8. Intermarriage also involves other social and religious aspects as shown by Smith-Christopher, "Mixed Marriage," and Eskenazi and Judd, "Marriage," both drawing heavily on modern sociological parallels. For a recent study of intermarriage in the genealogy of 1 Chr 2:3–8:40 as compared to and contrasted with the Ezra-Nehemiah material, see Knoppers, "Intermarriage," especially 28–30.

[47] Hoglund, *Imperial Administration*, 237, mentions an example from cuneiform texts from the reign of Cambyses where Egyptian groups were said to be living in various Mesopotamian cities, governed by local assemblies of Egyptians. See also Hoglund, "Achaemenid Context," 66.

access to a particular region and who is not. Intermarriage among various groups would tend to smudge the demarcation between the groups. . . . When a territory is imperilled and it becomes essential to administrative control to have a clear sense of who is allowed to function in a region and who is not, one could anticipate imperial efforts to control the mechanisms of assimilation. This scenario accords well with the efforts by Ezra and Nehemiah to prohibit intermarriage.[48]

The prohibition of intermarriage, which was innovatively theologised by the author of Ezra and Nehemiah,[49] was thus a means to achieve a larger goal, namely, to nip the possibility of loose ethnic boundaries in the bud that the Empire could strengthen its control.[50] As the prevention of assimilation was the overarching goal, several other measures included in the missions of Ezra and Nehemiah should be understood—from an imperial perspective—as means towards the same end: the emphasis on the centralised cult in the Jerusalem temple and regulations regarding its personnel and ritual performances (Ezra 7:15–20; Neh 10:32–39); the reforms of festivals (Neh 8:13–18) and the emphasis on the keeping of the Sabbath (Neh 10:31; 13:15–22); and, finally, the focus on a common history (Neh 9:6–37; cf. 9:2). All these aspects should be seen together with the prohibition of intermarriage (Ezra 10:7–44; Neh 10:28–30; 13:1–3, 23–30) as working towards the interests of the Persian imperial government as well as those of their appointed leaders and the priesthood in Jerusalem.[51]

---

[48] Hoglund, *Imperial Administration*, 239. *Pace* Blenkinsopp, "Udjahorresnet," 420–1, who suggests that the issue of divorce from foreign women was precisely the point at which Ezra went beyond his commission; this act would have led to the termination of his mandate.

[49] Ezra 9:1–10:44. See Cohen, *Beginnings*, 241–62, especially 243–4, 249, 261; Hoglund, *Imperial Administration*, 231–3; Knoppers, "Intermarriage", 29. Note that the modified understanding of the prohibition presupposes the existence of Deuteronomy as accepted, codified law.

[50] The situation in Persian Yehud thus differed markedly from the monarchic period as to the need for a well-defined ethnic identity; cf. Albertz, *History*, vol. 2, 449.

[51] Needless to say, "common" people had no primary interest in such reforms, which is also shown from their way of life before the arrival of Ezra as described in Ezra-Nehemiah. These were reforms officially dictated and implemented from "above." Contrary to the intents of the author, this is also shown by the rather

All reforms find support in written and interpreted torah. While these laws and traditions were compiled and authored in the period of Darius and was known to officials active in Yehud, it is clear from the information concerning the installation of new judicial and other officials that a decisive change occurred in the time of Ezra.[52] Further, the period of Ezra and Nehemiah brought with it an explicit effort to read aloud and teach the laws and traditions of Yehud to its inhabitants (Ezra 7:25; Neh 8:1–12). As part of the enforcement of a clearly defined ethnic identity initiated by the Persian rulers and implemented by local officials, these readings and teaching had to be performed publicly by official authorities.

In order to accomplish such thoroughgoing reforms, it would be necessary to undertake decisive action, with a maximum of legitimising strategies balanced by threats supported by imperial force (cf. Ezra 7:26; 10:8). It would also be necessary to make sure that all the people affected, not only leading officials, be included in the program and informed of the consequences of not obeying. Therefore, not only torah itself but also the public reading and teaching of torah ("the law of God:" Neh 8:8; "the law of Moses:" Ezra 7:6; Neh 8:1) receive a central position in the implementation of the reforms. In modern sociological terminology, these readings and teachings were meant to modify and adapt the symbolic universe of the people and so ensure a socially and religiously unified population within the ideological confines supported by the Persian king. It may therefore be anticipated that much effort was to be made in promulgating the traditions constructing the renewed self-definition of the people of Yehud.[53]

In sum, the public reading and teaching of torah described several times in Nehemiah originally belonged within the context of socio-religious reforms performed as a response to the risk of social unrest in relation to the major upheavals in the western part of the Persian Empire. The first public reading was performed in the water gate of Jeru-

---

forced information provided in Neh 8:1 that the initiative for the public reading of the torah at the Water gate came from the people who assembled at the square in front of that gate.

[52] See Hoglund, *Imperial Administration*, 236.

[53] Cf. the conclusion by Balentine, "Politics," 143: "The Biblical vision of a community centered on torah and temple, for all its theological merit, was to a large extent the result of Yehud's willingness to concede its limitations and to adjust its religious ideals to the realities of life in the Persian Empire."

salem as stated in Neh 8:1, but it is extremely unlikely that similar readings were not also performed locally in other cities. It is interesting to note here that the temple was not chosen as the place for the readings in the description in Neh 8. The city gates were the local administrative centres of the land and as such the public places where readings could be performed.

This is further supported by the likelihood that Neh 8:1–8 is a late text stemming from the time of the author, written about 50 to 100 years later than the events described. The detailed description of the liturgy in Neh 8:1–8 most likely reflects contemporary customs in the first half of the fourth century B.C.E., the story explaining how this reading custom came into being, assuring this practice legitimacy from historical authorities (legitimacy through authorisation).[54]

It is likely, however, that the original liturgy was similar to that described in the text for two reasons: 1) on the level of performance, rituals are extremely conservative and are likely to have remained constant, not the least since, in our case, the liturgy was imposed from religious and political authorities; 2) the elaborate legitimising structure of the liturgy (Ezra the priest and scribe as reader, the wooden podium, the authorities sitting beside him, the ritual opening of the scroll, the blessings, the shifting posture of the people present and their response, and the authoritative expounding of what was read by religious authorities, that is, the Levites) shows the need for symbolic and ideological support both for the reforms and for the performance of the rituals themselves. This is an indication that the ritual complex is young and established in a certain social context as described earlier.

As we have seen in relation to the earlier public reading at sukkoth, it is necessary to connect such rituals to the cycle of nature. Often, regularly repeated feasts or fasting are used for such purposes. If this is not done, ideologically motivated rituals such as these public readings of law run the risk of failing to become fully integrated in the ritual system of

---

[54] Cf. Kellermann, *Nehemiah*, 30; Pohlmann, *Studien*, 136. See also Smitten, *Esra*, 38–47. The elaborate description of the liturgy in Neh 8:1–12 is also noted by Fishbane, *Interpretation*, 113, as a sign that it had been in use for some time when the passage was written down. However, Fishbane does not discuss the date of the sources separately from the time for the editing of the book. Instead he assumes that the pericope describes the time of Ezra and must, consequently, ascribe the development of the liturgy to the exile. This is, however, very unlikely.

the people.⁵⁵ Therefore, having demonstrated that public reading rituals performed according to the pattern of Neh 8 were repeated over time and in different geographical locations, it remains to establish how and in which contexts these readings were performed.

A clue is, in fact, given in Neh 9:1–5, which describes a liturgy for fasting into which public reading of torah has been incorporated. Fast liturgies could be ritual responses to situations of crisis, but they could also follow the cycle of nature as shown by Zech 7:3, 5; 8:9.

While the ritual described in Neh 9:1–5 is used by the author as a springboard for the theological message of the following prayer (Neh 9:6–37), leading in turn to the written agreement to reform society signed by all official leaders (Neh 9:38–10:40), the ritual itself, on the level of performance, reflect beyond doubt actual practice during the time of the author.

Nehemiah 9:1–5 thus shows that by the mid-fourth century reading rituals were incorporated into fast liturgies.⁵⁶ Furthermore, the liturgy described in this passage is a response to a situation of crisis. This means that the liturgy itself most likely originated in another ritual context and was now well established and could be described as used in order to handle a crisis. The best explanation for the continuity between the constitutive liturgy of Ezra in the mid-fifth century and the ritual of crisis some 50 to 100 years later is that when the readings were spread and repeated in the cities of Yehud, they were tied to cycle of nature rituals.

Such strategy has already been seen in relation to Sukkoth (Deut 31:9–13; Neh 8:18), but most likely a shorter interval was used in relation to the thoroughgoing social reforms of Ezra and Nehemiah. Other public cycle of nature rituals were probably used as vehicles for torah readings, rituals that could be performed outside Jerusalem. It is quite

---

⁵⁵ This conclusion builds on anthropological analysis of rituals: for a full discussion see Runesson, *Origins*, 44–60.

⁵⁶ Williamson, *Ezra*, 311, refers to Jer 36 to show that readings in a similar context (public fasting) were not unheard of at this time. However, the story of how Baruch reads the scroll with the words of Jeremiah in the Jerusalem temple is to be referred to the category of prophetic oracles given in public space (oral or in writing), and is not compatible with official reading of official law in public space. Further, the reading in Neh 9:1–5 is set within a liturgy while Jer 36:1–10 tells how Jeremiah (and Baruch) used the opportunity of a public assembly to promulgate their own message.

possible that the former fasting days, transformed into feasts of joy in the period of Darius and mentioned in Zech 7:3, 5; 8:19, could have been used to proclaim the law to the people gathered. It is also possible, however, that any other day or feast when people gathered for some reason could have been used for such purpose.

Relating the conclusions reached hitherto to the institution of the synagogue, the following can be said. The non-liturgical activities of the local administrative and judicial centres of Yehud were thoroughly reformed, or perhaps we may even say created, during the reign of Darius and may thus be said to constitute the beginnings of the institution into which the public torah-reading rituals were incorporated. However, while the non-liturgical activities performed in these local centres were the same as those performed in the later, first century synagogue, these activities cannot by themselves constitute the criterion for when the synagogue originated, since, as we have said earlier, any developed society had such institutions. If this were the only criterion, we would not be able to say when the unique institution of the synagogue originated.

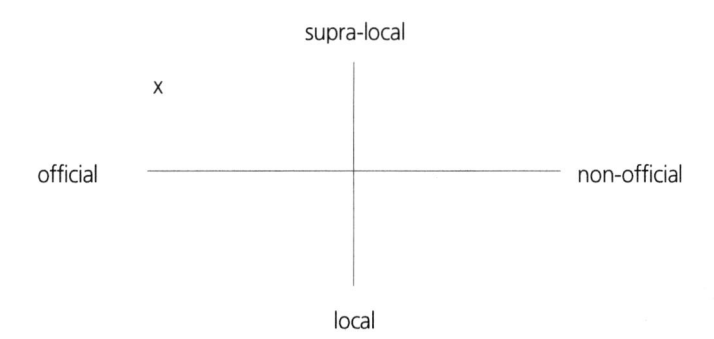

```
                    supra-local
                        |
         x              |
                        |
official  ──────────────┼────────────── non-official
                        |
                        |
                        |
                      local
```

Figure 4.2   Status of legitimacy and authority range of the earliest public torah-reading and teaching institution.

Instead, the unique activity of the synagogue, the torah reading and teaching, must be made the primary criterion. This phenomenon was introduced in the middle of the fifth century. Its liturgical setting was prayers and blessings. It continued since torah reading was incorporated into, among other rituals, fasting liturgies, which included such rituals. The spatial setting was the city gates and other public places in the regions of Yehud. Since the ideological message was connected to socio-religious reforms initiated by the authorities in Jerusalem and the Persian ruler, the torah-reading and teaching ritual was performed by government-approved officials and controlled from the capital. Thus, as to the sphere of authority (authority range), the original synagogue institution, dated to around 450 B.C.E., was different from the public synagogue of the first century:

Having thus explained and dated the origins of the public synagogue, it remains to trace its continuity and development into Hellenistic times. Unfortunately, space will allow only a short discussion: for a full presentation I refer the reader to my earlier study, *The Origins of the Synagogue*.

The Changing Nature of the Synagogue

We have explicit evidence for the continuity of public torah reading and teaching into the Hellenistic period.

The author of Chronicles has left us a pericope revealing a situation similar to that described previously in relation to the Persian period, but dated towards the end of the fourth century.[57] In his idealised portrait of King Jehoshaphat, the chronicler ascribes several reforms to this monarch. For our purposes the most important of these reforms is the sending of officials, Levites and priests, to the cities of Judea to teach torah to the people (2 Chr 17:7–9).[58]

The purpose behind the insertion of this pericope seems to be to mediate the message that knowledge of torah among the people as a whole, together with military arrangements (2 Chr 17:1–5) and judicial administration (cf. 2 Chr 19:4–11), is an important part of the maintenance of society and ensures protection from external enemies (2 Chr 17:10). The general knowledge of torah[59] is thus equated with the tem-

---

[57] For the dating of 1–2 Chr to this period, see above, n. 31.

[58] For the date of this pericope in the late fourth to early third centuries B.C.E., see Japhet, *Chronicles*, 749. See also Blenkinsopp, *Wisdom*, 16, 137. A similar view is held by Welten, *Geschichte*, 184–5; North, "The Chronicler", 377; Knoppers, "Reform," 508, n. 26.

[59] Dillard, *2 Chronicles*, 134, believes that the Pentateuch is referred to in this passage, but cf. Blenkinsopp, *Wisdom*, 138, who argues on the basis of a comparison with 2 Chr 25:4 and Deut 24:16 that only Deuteronomy is meant. For our purposes this matters little: the important thing is that public reading of law is reported to have occurred.

ple cult in Jerusalem, so important for the chronicler,[60] as a means to uphold a good society, one that God approves of, and thereby ensuring well-being for the nation. We may thus say that general knowledge of torah among the people was part of the symbolic universe of the chronicler and his contemporaries;[61] this led to a positive appreciation of teaching it publicly in local places. This development in religious worldview compared to that of the sixth century could hardly have taken place without continuity in public readings of torah, from the reforms under Darius and the significant development during the reign of Artaxerxes I.

Second Chronicles 17:7–9 describes the teaching of torah as a mission carried out by itinerant representatives of the Jerusalem authorities, thereby ensuring a uniform understanding of torah in all of Judea in compliance with official views on political and religious issues. This description of travelling teachers is an attempt to retroject contemporary customs of reading and teaching rituals back in time. This means a double gain for the author: Jehoshaphat receives further glory through the connection with a custom perceived positively at the time of the chronicler. At the same time, the reading and teaching of torah in local cities at the time of the chronicler receives the legitimacy of being an old monarchic custom.[62]

While we note that torah teaching is performed by non-priests for the first time, its interpretation is still in the hands of the Jerusalem authorities. It is not until sometime in the period of stability and prosperity in the third century B.C.E. that we find that torah is the focus also in non-official institutions, such as the οἶκος παιδείας of Ben Sira (Sir 51:23; the Hebrew original reading בית מדרש).[63]

This educational institution was run privately and represented a certain interpretative community.[64] The "house of instruction" was most

---

[60] See, e.g., Japhet, *Ideology*, especially 222–47.
[61] Cf. Japhet, *Ideology*, 514: "The Chronicler's account of history is subordinate to a particular world-view."
[62] This serves the purpose of emphasising the continuity between monarchic and post-monarchic times, a purpose witnessed in several other instances in Chronicles.
[63] Cf. Crenshaw, *Education*, 271. For the view that this verse belonged to the original composition, see Byrskog, *Teacher*, 67–8.
[64] For the view that Ben Sira's school was private, see Crenshaw, *Education*, 111–12.

likely a building (οἶκος) with appropriate equipment, such as benches.[65] This specific building was probably not private, but public since designation, form, and function may be expected to be related to each other. It seems, therefore, that by the third to second centuries B.C.E., apart from public assemblies,[66] separate institutions had developed that could be described as "houses of learning" and which used non-private space for their activities.[67] It is very likely, however, that other institutions similar to Ben Sira's had developed and that some of these did not gather in public but private buildings.

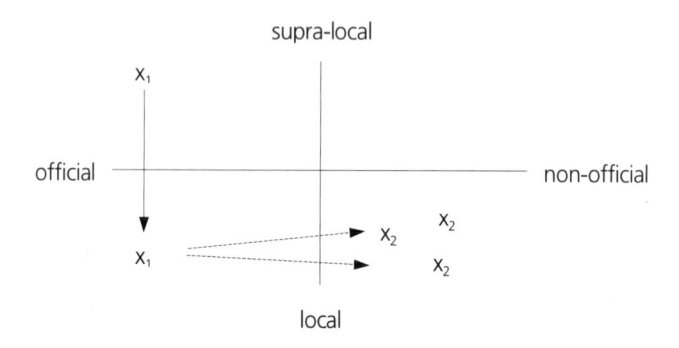

Figure 4.3 The development of the institution of public torah reading and teaching in the Early Hellenistic period. x_1 = public assemblies, x_2 = semi-public assemblies.

Thus, in the latter part of the Hellenistic period, due to the political stability and the prosperity during the third century B.C.E., as well as the increasing general acknowledgement of the holy status of the torah and the codification of several traditions in the collection we know as the Pentateuch, the state authorities had loosened the control of the inter-

---

[65] For the interpretation of ἐν οἴκῳ παιδείας as referring to a building, see Byrskog, *Teacher*, 69.

[66] Public, national and local assemblies are witnessed in Sir 15:5; 21:17; 23:24; 31:11; 33:19; 38:33; 39:10; 44:15. It seems that the common Greek usage of the word ἐκκλεσία, denoting either all citizens of a democratic city state, or the meetings of such states where decisions were taken concerning state matters, is to guide the definition of the Palestinian institution mentioned here. Note, however, that Sir 24:23 speaks about local assemblies (συναγωγαί), which may be understood as extensions of the national assemblies: these assemblies are understood by Ben Sira as the heirs of the "book of the covenant."

[67] Cf. Urman, "House," 241, n. 67.

pretation of torah in local public assemblies. This development, that is, the decentralisation of authority and reduction in authority range was also connected with the growth of the scribal class. This, together with the influx of Hellenistic organisational forms, the so-called voluntary associations, the *thiasoi*, provided the necessary conditions for the development of non-official institutions. From this time on we find several such semi-public synagogues. The origins of the semi-public synagogue should thus be dated to the third to second centuries B.C.E. The development of the synagogue as defined by status of legitimacy and authority range could thus be summarised graphically as in Figure 4.3.

In sum, while the non-liturgical activities of the public synagogues remained the same, the institutional aspect developed as we now find the first evidence of non-priestly reading and teaching of torah in the Hellenistic period. This development continued into later times, as shown by Luke 4:16–30. If we relate these conclusions to the development of the spatial aspect, it is interesting to note that no architectural features may be singled out that differentiate between the public and the semi-public synagogue. Such a differentiation can only be made on the basis of the location of the building and other similar external criteria. Thus, categorising some examples of early, excavated, public buildings including a second century C.E. example, the following picture emerges.

Buildings for public assemblies	Buildings for semi-public assemblies
Gamla	Jericho
Capernaum I	Qumran
Kiryat Sefer	Masada
Nabratein	Herodion

Table 4.2   Public buildings categorized after the type of assembly which probably took place in them.

Conclusions

Summing up, we have seen that the recent trend in synagogue studies that dates the institution to the Hellenistic or Roman period cannot be maintained. On the other hand, the increasing awareness that any theory about synagogue origins must carefully define how "synagogue" is understood and which criteria are used in the investigation constitutes a decisive step forward in the scholarly discussion. The present investigation has attempted to continue on this path and present an explanation of when and why the Palestinian synagogue originated.

We have come to the conclusion that a distinction must be made between public and semi-public synagogues. The origins of the public institution can be traced back to the middle of the fifth century B.C.E. At that time public torah readings were introduced in local administrative centres in Yehud as a political strategy in support of radical social reforms. Being joined to existing cycle of nature rituals, these reading and teaching liturgies were repeatedly enacted and became part of the ritual system of Judaism.

Our search for the first semi-public synagogues, institutions completely disconnected from state authorities and interests, takes us well into the Hellenistic period. In addition to internal political factors, a decisive aspect of this development was the influence from Hellenistic organisational forms, the *thiasoi*. This development was crucial for the formation of later Jewish sects and denominations, such as Pharisaism and the Jesus movement.

Bibliography

Albertz, R., *A History of Israelite Religion in the Old Testament Period: From the Exile to the Maccabees.* Vol. 2. London: SCM Press, 1994.

Balentine, S. E., "The Politics of Religion in the Persian Period." Pages 129–46 in *After the Exile: Essays in Honour of Rex Mason.* Edited by J. Barton and D. J. Reimer. Macon: Mercer University Press, 1996.

Baron, S. W., *The Jewish Community: Its History and Structure To the American Revolution.* 3 vols. Philadelphia: The Jewish Publication Society of America, 1942.

Berquist, J. L., *Judaism in Persia's Shadow: A Social and Historical Approach.* Minneapolis: Fortress Press, 1995.

Binder, D. D., *Into the Temple Courts: The Place of the Synagogues in the Second Temple Period.* Atlanta: Society of Biblical Literature, 1999.

Blenkinsopp, J., "The Mission of Udjahorresnet and those of Ezra and Nehemiah." *JBL* 106 (1987): 409–421.

—, *Wisdom and Law in the Old Testament: The Ordering of Life in Israel and Early Judaism*. Oxford: Oxford University Press, 1995.

Byrskog, S., *Jesus the Only Teacher: Didactive Authority and Transmission in Ancient Israel, Ancient Judaism, and the Matthean Community*. Lund: Almqvist & Wiksell, 1994.

Claussen, C., *Versammlung, Gemeinde, Synagoge: Das hellenistisch-jüdische Umfeld der frühchristlichen Gemeinden*. Göttingen: Vandenhoeck & Ruprecht, 2002.

Cohen, S. J. D. *The Beginnings of Jewishness: Boundaries, Varieties, Uncertainties*. Berkeley: University of California Press.

Cook, J. M., *The Persian Empire*. London: Dent, 1983.

Crenshaw, J. L., *Education in Ancient Israel: Across the Deadening Silence*. New York: Doubleday, 1998.

Davies, P. R., *Scribes and Schools: The Canonisation of the Hebrew Scriptures*. Louisville: Westminster John Knox Press, 1998.

Dillard, R. B., *2 Chronicles.*. Waco: Word Books, 1987.

Eskenazi, T. C., and E. P. Judd, "Marriage to a Stranger in Ezra 9–10." Pages 265–85 in *Second Temple Studies, 2: Temple Community in the Persian Period*. Edited by Ph. R. Davies. Sheffield: JSOT Press, 1994.

Fishbane, M., *Biblical Interpretation in Ancient Israel*. Oxford: Clarendon Press, 1985.

Flesher, P. V. M., "Palestinian Synagogues Before 70 C.E.: A Review of the Evidence." Pages 27–39 in *Ancient Synagogues: Historical Analysis and Archaeological Discovery*. Edited by D. Urman et al. Leiden: Brill, 1995.

Frei, P., and K. Koch, *Reichsidee und Reichsorganisation im Perserreich*. 2nd ed. Göttingen: Vandenhoek, 1996.

Fried, M. H., "The State, the Chicken, and the Egg: Or, What Came First?" Pages 35–47 in *Origins of the State: The Anthropology of Political Evolution*. Edited by R. Cohen *et al*. Philadelphia: Institute for the Study of Human Issues, 1978.

Grabbe, L. L., *Judaism From Cyrus to Hadrian*. London: SCM Press, 1994.

—, "What was Ezra's Mission?" Pages 286–99 in *Second Temple Studies, 2: Temple Community in the Persian Period.* Edited by Ph. R. Davies. Sheffield: JSOT Press, 1994.

Griffiths, J. G., "Egypt and the Rise of the Synagogue." Pages 3–16 in *Ancient Synagogues: Historical Analysis and Archaeological Discovery.* Edited by D. Urman et al. Leiden: Brill, 1995.

Grotius, H., *Annotata ad Vetus Testamentum.* Vol. 1. Paris: Johannes Blaev, 1644.

Gutmann, J., "Ancient Synagogues: Archaeological Fact and Scholarly Assumption." *Bulletin of the Asia Institute* 9 (1997): 226–7.

Hachlili, R., "The Origin of the Synagogue: A Re-Assessment." *JSJ* 28 (1997): 34–47.

Hoenig, S. B., "The Ancient City-Square: The Forerunner of the Synagogue." Pages 448–76 in *ANRW* II.19.1. Edited by W. Haase. Berlin: de Gruyter, 1979.

Hoffmann, H.-D., *Reform und Reformen: Untersuchungen zu einem Grundthema der deuteronomistischen Geschichtsschreibung.* Zürich: Theologischer Verlag, 1980.

Hoglund, K. G., "The Achaemenid Context." Pages 54–72 in *Second Temple Studies 1: The Persian Period.* Edited by P. R. Davies. Sheffield: JSOT Press, 1991.

—, *Achaemenid Imperial Administration in Syria-Palestine and the Missions of Ezra and Nehemiah.* Atlanta: Scholars Press, 1992.

Hölscher, G., "Komposition und Ursprung des Deuteronomiums." *ZAW* 40 (1922): 161–255.

Janzen, D., "The 'Mission' of Ezra and the Persian-Period Temple Community." *JBL* 119 (2000): 619–43.

Japhet, S., "The Supposed Common Authorship of Chronicles and Ezra-Nehemiah Investigated Anew." *VT* 18 (1968): 330–71.

—, "Sheshbazzar and Zerubbabel." *ZAW* 94 (1982): 66–98.

—, *1 and 2 Chronicles: A Commentary.* London: SCM Press, 1992.

—, *The Ideology of the Book of Chronicles and its Place in Biblical Thought.* 2nd ed. Frankfurt am Main: Peter Lang, 1997.

Kee, H. C., "The Transformation of the Synagogue after 70 C.E.: Its Import for Early Christianity." *NTS* 36 (1990): 1–24.

Kellerman, U., *Nehemia: Quellen Überlieferung und Geschichte*. Berlin: Alfred Töpelmann, 1967.

Knoppers, G. N., "Reform and Regression: The Chronicler's Presentation of Jehoshaphat." *Biblica* 72 (1991): 500–24.

—, "Intermarriage, Social Complexity, and Ethnic Diversity in the Genealogy of Judah." *JBL* 120 (2001): 15–30.

Levine, L. I., "The Second Temple Synagogue: The Formative Years." Pages 7–31 in *The Synagogue in Late Antiquity*. Edited by L. I. Levine. Philadelphia: The American Schools of Oriental Research, 1987.

—, *The Ancient Synagogue: The First Thousand Years*. New Haven: Yale University Press, 2000.

Levinskaya, I., *The Book of Acts in Its Diaspora Setting. Vol. 5, The Book of Acts in Its First Century Setting*. Grand Rapids: Eerdmans, 1996.

Livingstone, E. A., ed. *The Oxford Dictionary of the Christian Church*. 3rd ed. Oxford: Oxford University Press, 1997.

Moore, G. F., *Judaism in the First Centuries of the Christian Era: The Age of the Tannaim*. 3 vols. Cambridge: Harvard University Press, 1927–1930.

Nicholson, E. W., *Preaching to the Exiles: A Study of the Prose Tradition in the Book of Jeremiah*. Oxford: Blackwell, 1970.

North, R., "The Chronicler: 1–2 Chronicles, Ezra, Nehemiah." Pages 362–398 in *The New Jerome Biblical Commentary*. Edited by R. E. Brown et al. London: Geoffrey Chapman, 1990.

Olmstead, A. T., "Darius as Lawgiver." *AJSL* 51 (1934–1935): 247–9.

Pohlmann, K.-F., *Studien zum dritten Esra: ein Beitrag zur Frage nach dem ursprünglichen Schluss des chronistischen Geschichtswerkes*. Göttingen: Vandenhoeck und Ruprecht, 1970.

Price, B. J., "Secondary State Formation: An Explanatory Model." Pages 161–86 in *Origins of the State: The Anthropology of Political Evolution*. Edited by R. E. Cohen *et al*. Philadelphia: Institute for the Study of Human Issues, 1978.

Reich, N. J., "The Codification of Egyptian Laws by Darius and the Origin of the 'Demotic Chronicle'." *Mizraim* 1 (1933): 178–85.

Rendtorff, R., "Noch einmal: Esra und das 'Gesetz'." *ZAW* 111 (1999): 89–91.

Rowley, H. H., *Worship in Ancient Israel. Its Forms and Meaning.* London: SPCK, 1967.

Runesson, A., *The Origins of the Synagogue: A Socio-Historical Study.* Stockholm: Almquist & Wiksell, 2001.

—, "The Synagogue at Ancient Ostia: The Building and Its History from the First to the Fifth Century." Pages 29–99 in *The Synagogue of Ancient Ostia and the Jews of Rome: Interdisciplinary Studies.* Edited by B. Olsson, D. Mitternacht and O. Brandt. Stockholm: Paul Åströms Förlag, 2001.

Sigonius, C., *De republica Hebraeorum libri VII.* Coloniae 1583.

Smith-Christopher, D. L., "The Mixed Marriage Crisis in Ezra 9–10 and Nehemiah 13: A Study of the Sociology of the Post-Exilic Judean Community." Pages 243–65 in *Second Temple Studies, 2: Temple Community in the Persian Period.* Edited by Ph. R. Davies. Sheffield: JSOT Press, 1994.

Smitten, W. T. in der, *Esra : Quellen, Überlieferung und Geschichte.* Assen: Gorcum, 1973.

Stern, E., "The Persian Empire and the Political and Social History of Palestine in the Persian Period." Pages 70–87 in *The Cambridge History of Judaism.* Edited by W. D. Davies *et al.* Cambridge: Cambridge University Press, 1984.

Urman, D., "The House of Assembly and the House of Study: Are They One and the Same?" Pages 232–55 in *Ancient Synagogues: Historical Analysis and Archaeological Discovery.* Edited by D. Urman et al. Leiden: Brill, 1995.

Vitringa, C., *De synagoga vetere libri tres.* Franequeræ: Typis & impensis Johannis Gyzelaar, 1696.

Welten, P., *Geschichte und Geschichtsdarstellung in den Chronikbüchern.* Neukirchen: Vluyn, 1973.

White, L. M., *The Social Origins of Christian Architecture. Building God's House in the Roman World: Architectural Adaptation Among Pagans, Jews, and Christians.*. Vol 1. Valley Forge: Trinity Press, 1996 [1990].

Widengren, G., "The Persian Period." Pages 489–538 in *Israelite and Judean History*. Edited by J. H. Hayes and J. M. Miller. London: SCM Press, 1977.

Wigoder, G., *The Story of the Synagogue: A Diaspora Museum Book*. London: Weinfeld and Nicolson, 1986.

Williamson, H. G. M., *Israel in the Books of Chronicles*. Cambridge: Cambridge University Press, 1977.

—, *Ezra, Nehemiah*. Waco: Word Books, 1985.

Yamauchi, E. M., *Persia and the Bible*. Grand Rapids: Baker Book House, 1990.

Zetterholm, M., *The Formation of Christianity in Antioch: A Social-Scientific Approach to the Separation between Judaism and Christianity*. London: Routledge, 2003.

5
An Architectural Case for Synagogues as Associations

Peter Richardson

ANCIENT SYNAGOGUES WERE COMPLEX social organizations; they found architectural expression, especially in the Diaspora, in similarly complex ways. Though my concern in this chapter is architectural and comparative, not social, political, communal, theological, or liturgical, still the architectural questions are relevant to broader issues, for ancient buildings, like modern ones, both shaped behavior and were shaped by the actions and functions carried on within. I am here amplifying an earlier hypothesis about "synagogue origins" as associations.[1] Since this view may seem counter-intuitive, let me say explicitly that synagogues might be modeled architecturally on association buildings without needing to be viewed politically as associations or to operate internally exactly like associations, though in fact I think the similarities are very close.[2] Explanations of origins of ancient building forms depend upon inference; the most cogent hypothesis will usually be the more general as against the more narrowly focused. I argue that the strongest and most general hypothesis derives from associations;[3] to make the case, I concentrate on early buildings in the Diaspora, with only a brief glance at the homeland.

---

[1] Richardson, "Early Synagogues"; Richardson and Heuchan, "Jewish Voluntary associations"; Richardson, "Building an Association."
[2] Much of what follows is in dialogue with Levine, *Ancient Synagogue*; "First-Century Synagogue." For history of research, Runesson, *Origins*, chap. 2; in his terms I use a "spatial" approach.
[3] Uncertainty about synagogue origins is like uncertainty about the origin of Roman public baths. Baths did not originate at one moment, nor was there a simple linear development. There was neither a single building where the distinctive Roman form of baths originated nor a simple developmental process that eventually

Synagogues' origins did not lie in a historical crisis or specific challenge but were the result of lengthy experimentation with building forms learned first in the Diaspora.[4] Evidence—as distinct from theoretical or causative explanations—for the architectural origins of synagogues is found in a combination of literary, archaeological and epigraphic information, though the sources fail to answer directly questions of analogy or origins. There is room for uncertainty and speculation. Nevertheless, the case is strong for claiming that associations were models for synagogues; cumulative lines of evidence converge on association buildings in a Diaspora setting. In making this case, however, it is a serious difficulty that we lack studies of voluntary association buildings as a group, partly because there is imprecision in the category "associations," partly due to difficulty in identifying association buildings, and partly a result of associations' relatively lowly place on scholarly agenda.[5]

Distribution and Dating of Evidence

The list below summarizes the evidence for synagogue buildings constructed before about 100 C.E., categorized as either Palestinian or Diaspora (though it is debatable how to list Dor and Caesarea).[6] Each building stands separately to emphasize the relationship of Diaspora and Palestinian evidence.[7]

---

resulted in the bath. The form combined various influences from Greek practices, Campanian preferences, and practical or experiential considerations of bathing. Fagan, "Genesis of the Roman Public Bath."
[4] Levine, *Ancient Synagogues,* 33: "the emergence of the Judean synagogue was not the outcome of any specific event or crisis, but rather a gradual development."
[5] Richardson, "Building an Association," surveys briefly some of the evidence.
[6] I ignore that Jewish temples were sometimes referred to as *proseuchai,* alongside a wider group of Yahwistic temples outside Israel; Runesson, *Origins,* 409–22; 429–36.
[7] Earlier table in Richardson, "Architectural Transitions"; see also Grabbe, "Synagogues in Pre-70 Palestine."

Diaspora Site			Palestine Site		
Location	*Evidence*	*Date*	*Location*	*Evidence*	*Date*
North Africa			**Judea**		
Schedia	ins	246–221 B.C.E.	Jerusalem: Theodotos	ins	1st c. C.E.
Arsinöe/ Crcodilo-polis	ins	246–221 B.C.E.	Jerusalem: Freedmen	NT	1st c. C.E.
Fayum	ins	11 May 218 B.C.E.	Qumran	arch/lit	1st c. B.C.E.
Athribis	ins	180–145 B.C.E.	Jericho	arch	70–50 B.C.E.
Nitriai	ins	144–116 B.C.E.	Herodium	arch	60s C.E.
Xenephyris	ins	144–116 B.C.E.	Masada	arch	60s C.E.
Alexandria	ins	2nd c. B.C.E.	Modi'n	arch	1st c. C.E.
Alexandria	Philo	1st c. C.E.	Qiryat Sefer	arch	1st–2nd c. C.E.
Uncertain location	ins	c. 130 or 40 B.C.E.	Horvat 'Ethri	arch	1st c. C.E.
Leontopolis	ins/lit	mid 2nd c. B.C.E.	**Galilee**		
Therapeutae	Philo	1st c. B.C.E.?	Tiberias	Jos	1st c. C.E.
Naucratis	ins	30 B.C.E.–14 C.E.	Capernaum	NT/arch?	1st c. C.E.?
Uncertain location	ins	1st c. C.E.	Nazareth	NT	1st c. C.E.
Berenice	ins	Late 1st c. B.C.E.	**Gaulanitis**		
Black Sea			Gamla I	arch	1st c. C.E.
Panticapaea	ins	81 C.E.	Gamla II?	arch	1st c. C.E.
Chersonesus	ins	1st c. C.E.	Coast Cities		
Phanagoria	ins	16 c. C.E.	Dor (Diaspora?)	Jos	1st c. C.E.
Gorgippia	ins	1st c. C.E.	Caesarea	Jos/NT/ arch?	1st c. C.E.
Syria			**Uncertain**		
Damascus	NT/Jos	2nd–1st c. B.C.E.	Migdal	arch	
Antioch-on-Orontes	Jos	2nd c. B.C.E.	Cana	arch	
Greece & Asia					
Ephesus	Jos/NT	1st c. B.C.E.			
Halicarn-assus	Jos	1st c. B.C.E.			
Sardis	Jos/arch?	1st c. B.C.E.			
Delos-Judean	arch/ins	2nd c. B.C.E.			
Delos-Samaritan	ins	2nd c. B.C.E.			
Salamis	NT	1st c. C.E.?			
Pisidian Antioch	NT	1st c. C.E.?			
Iconium	NT	1st c. C.E.?			
Thessalonica	NT	1st c. C.E.?			
Beroea	NT	1st c. C.E.?			
Athens	NT	1st c. C.E.?			
Corinth	NT	1st c. C.E.?			
Philippi	NT	1st c. C.E.?			
Laodicea	unc				
Tralles	unc				
Miletus	unc				

Italy		
Ostia	ins/arch	1st c. C.E.
Rome: Augustesians	ins	1st c. B.C.E.
Rome: Agrippesians	ins	1st c. B.C.E.
Rome: Volumnians	ins	1st c. B.C.E.
Rome: Hebrews	ins	1st c. B.C.E.
Rome: Herodians	ins	1st c. B.C.E.?
Marano-Campania	ins	1st c. C.E.

Table 5.1 Comparison of Palestine and Diaspora synagogues to end 1st century.

Diaspora/Palestine Comparison

Not all the above locations are certain. Some, implied by literary allusions (Acts, Josephus' decrees), should be accepted only with caution;[8] yet the literary evidence for widespread distribution of synagogues is important. I emphasize several points from the table. (1) The Diaspora evidence (40+ synagogues) strongly outweighs the Palestinian evidence (about 15 synagogues, even when Caesarea, Dor and Tiberias, with their strong Hellenistic and Roman influences, are included). (2) About 20 Diaspora buildings (mostly based on relatively precise inscriptional evidence) precede the first century CE, compared with one or two Judean structures (Qumran and Jericho, both debated). (3) There is only one reliable early inscription from Palestine against more than twenty inscriptions from the Diaspora, though in almost all inscriptional cases no relevant building has been found. The Jewish Diaspora followed the Roman "epigraphic habit" in marking their buildings but this habit was less consistently followed in Palestine. (4) Nevertheless, there are eight excavated buildings in the homeland, against two in the

---

[8] Josephus records 23 decrees in *A.J.* 14.188–264 and seven in *A.J.* 16.162–73. Six plausibly presuppose buildings: Sardis (three times), Delos, Ephesus, and Halicarnassus. Other allusions may also suggest the presence of a building: thus, references to performing sacred rites at Alexandria, Laodicea, Tralles (twice), Miletus; allusions to Jewish "superstitions" (Delos, Sardis, Ephesus (twice), Alexandria) may likewise presuppose cultic activity in a building:

Diaspora.[9] This imbalance is attributable to two factors: in Palestinian villages and towns the synagogue stands out as the sole public building and Israeli archaeologists have focused attention on such structures, whereas in larger Diaspora centers they go unnoticed. (5) The evidence is complex and varied in both settings, with overlapping inscriptional, literary, and archaeological data; the juxtaposition of material and literary evidence provides a relatively coherent picture of early synagogues.

Architectural Comparison

Though in many cases we can only guess at size and form, these nearly sixty synagogues covered a range of building types. Some may have been basilical (Tiberias, Alexandria); many were simple meeting places (Gamla, Masada); some were house adaptations (Jericho, and later Priene, Dura); some were complex structures (Delos, Ostia, Jerusalem, Qumran). The later classic architectural form of the synagogue was the basilica, a Roman form despite its Greek name (*basilikos*). Use of the term should be limited to structures with basilical features: for a large assembly, usually beside a public open space, with interior columns usually arranged in a rectangle that supported a clerestory roof, with one or more apses and platform. Synagogues apparently used this form long before Constantine popularized its use for churches, so the common claim that Jewish synagogues copied Christian basilicas needs qualification.

Alongside the basilical form for synagogues two other forms developed. The simple "meeting place" was important, not only for synagogues but also for other religious communities and associations.[10] And the "house synagogue," as M. White has shown, was an important strategy.[11] In various communities and associations (e.g., Christianity, Mithraism), houses of wealthy patrons were converted as community meeting places in a strategy that nicely suited an age of benefactions and patronal activity. These adaptations had a common architectural character: the modifications were usually modest and without external visibility unless they included raised roofs, inscribed lintels, or extensions.

---

[9] Recent excavations at Khirbet Qana may have added one more 1st–2nd c. C.E. synagogue; the putative identification needs to be confirmed by further work.
[10] For initial comments on this problem, Richardson, "Architectural Transitions"; see also White, *Social Origins* 1: chaps 2 and 5; Snyder, *Ante Pacem*, chap. 5.
[11] White, *Social Origins*; Blue, "Acts and the House Church."

Terminology

The terminology used of Jewish public buildings varied by region, period, and type of evidence. Outsiders preferred some terms; Jews may have preferred others (as the North African and Bosporan inscriptional evidence suggests). The range is wide: *proseuche, synagoge, synagogion, synodos, collegium, thiasos, sabbateion, politeuma, therapeutai, amphitheatron, hieron*, and so on.[12] The preferred Jewish terms were *proseuchê* and *synagoge*, terms utilized by other associations also, but occasionally Jews used terms preferred by non-Jews: *synodos, thiasos*, and *therapeutai*. In the early period *proseuchê* was the commonest term, but by the first century C.E. *synagoge* was being used, initially as a term for the community but soon as a building term.[13]

Josephus illustrates the overlap in terminology between associations and Jewish communities (*A.J.* 14.215; associated with Parium and Delos). He claims to have seen an inscription of Julius Caesar's forbidding "religious societies to assemble *[thiasous synagesthai]* in the city, but these people [Jews] alone he did not forbid to do so or to collect contributions of money or to hold common meals. Similarly do I forbid other religious assemblies *[allous thiasous]* to assemble and feast in accordance with their native customs and ordinances *[ta patria ethe kai nomima synagesthai te kai estiasthai]*." Since "other *thiasoi*" had been forbidden to meet, Caesar's treatment of Judaism was in one sense *sui generis*, but the group's general classification was among *thiasoi*. Josephus, following Caesar, used a term for Jews that he deemed appropriate, just as he described Jewish practices and obligations appropriately. The *synagoge* was not a unique category in first-century C.E. Roman society but viewed as part of a larger classification, *thiasoi*.

Architectural Details

Some inscriptional and literary descriptions allude to architectural details, details that suggest that some early synagogue buildings were carefully articulated complexes. From Egyptian inscriptions we find: *exedra*, gateway *(pylon)*, *peribolos*, appurtenances, and gardens. Jose-

---

[12] Table in Runesson, *Origins*, 171–3.
[13] The important inscription *CJZC* 72 from Berenice in Cyrenaica (55 C.E.) uses *synagôgê* twice, in line 3 of the community and in line 5 of the building. In the Bosporan Kingdom, *proseuchê* tends to be used of the building and *synagôgê* of the community: Levinskaya, *Diaspora Setting*, 105–16 on *synodos* and *thiasos*, appendix 3.

phus's decrees refer to: dining room (*triclinium* for common meals), facilities for observing rites, sacrifice, courtroom, and library. The Theodotos inscription mentions: facilities for assembly, reading, teaching, rooms, hostel, and water installations.[14] This inscriptional evidence from Egypt, Asia Minor and Judea confirms that prior to 100 C.E. synagogues commonly had complex architectural forms; it coheres with archaeological evidence from Delos and Ostia. Some synagogues at least had sophisticated design features.

If we include Qumran and Jericho as synagogues, a roughly analogous picture in some cases emerges for Judea. But in ordinary towns and villages, however, such as Gamla and Kiryat Sefer, public buildings were simpler multi-purpose structures that provided for a range of functions, without architecturally differentiated spaces. Thus, the literary and epigraphic records imply that Diaspora buildings were relatively more complex architecturally and at an earlier period. These design details of buildings align synagogues with association buildings, as we shall see.

Diaspora Synagogues in Context

Associations in the Greek and Roman worlds typically had a meeting room, *triclinium*, and a variety of other ancillary spaces.[15] Their architectural forms and the forms used by synagogues were relatively similar. The most instructive sites to demonstrate these analogies are Ostia, Delos, and Priene, all with relevant comparanda. At Ostia many associations were found inside the city and a synagogue outside the city near the ancient shoreline. On Delos a synagogue was found on the east side of the island while most other associations were found on the west. At Priene, three houses almost beside each other were converted to the worship of Cybele, the hero-cult of Alexander, and (later) a Jewish synagogue. In each case, the Jewish building had close analogies to nearby associations.

---

[14] Kloppenborg Verbin, "Dating Theodotos," who concludes, contra Kee, that it "attests a synagogue building in Jerusalem, probably constructed in the early first century C.E. . . . It confirms that *synagōgē* was used of buildings not only in Egypt and Cyrenaica but also in Roman Palestine" (277).

[15] Richardson, "Building an Association."

Regrettably, the absence of an inventory of association buildings makes comparisons difficult. We know association buildings best in cases of gradual decline in the cities' fortunes and where a large percentage of the city has been excavated (Ostia, Delos, and Priene), or where large numbers of inscriptions have been recovered (Ephesus).[16] But we need an analysis of the strategies used in locating, constructing, adapting, embellishing, and identifying association buildings, including those religious groups of the ancient world that were perceived as associations. Was there implied rivalry or even overt competition among associations, that vied for the attention of the citizens?[17] Comparative analysis of association buildings would shed light on the conditions under which Judaism and early Christianity operated.

Ostia

About 60 associations or collegia are known archaeologically at Ostia,[18] some rather impressive and complex. The distribution of cultic, trade, and civic associations follows no simple pattern, though they tend to be in secondary locations on main streets.[19] Some wealthy associations built their own structures, some met in temples; wherever they met their activities included assemblies, worship, banquets, and provision of water.

---

[16] Philip Harland, "Associations and Empire"; Richardson, "Building an Association; 60 associations in Ephesus are known from inscriptions, 41 trade associations and 19 cultic associations..

[17] The Canadian Society of Biblical Studies seminar on "religious rivalries" has dealt with related questions for many years. See Donaldson, *Caesarea Maritima*; Vaage, *Christians, Jews and Pagans*; Ascough, *Sardis and Smyrna*.

[18] Hermansen, *Ostia*, 55, puts the number at "close to forty"; his lists (56–9; 239–41) show 59 guilds, not all identifiable on the ground. Unpublished inscriptions add only one to that number (59–60).

[19] Meiggs, *Roman Ostia*, 382, fig. 27, shows the distribution of the "Ostian cults." Guild seats are shown at the Ostia website http://www.ncl.ac.uk/ostia/.

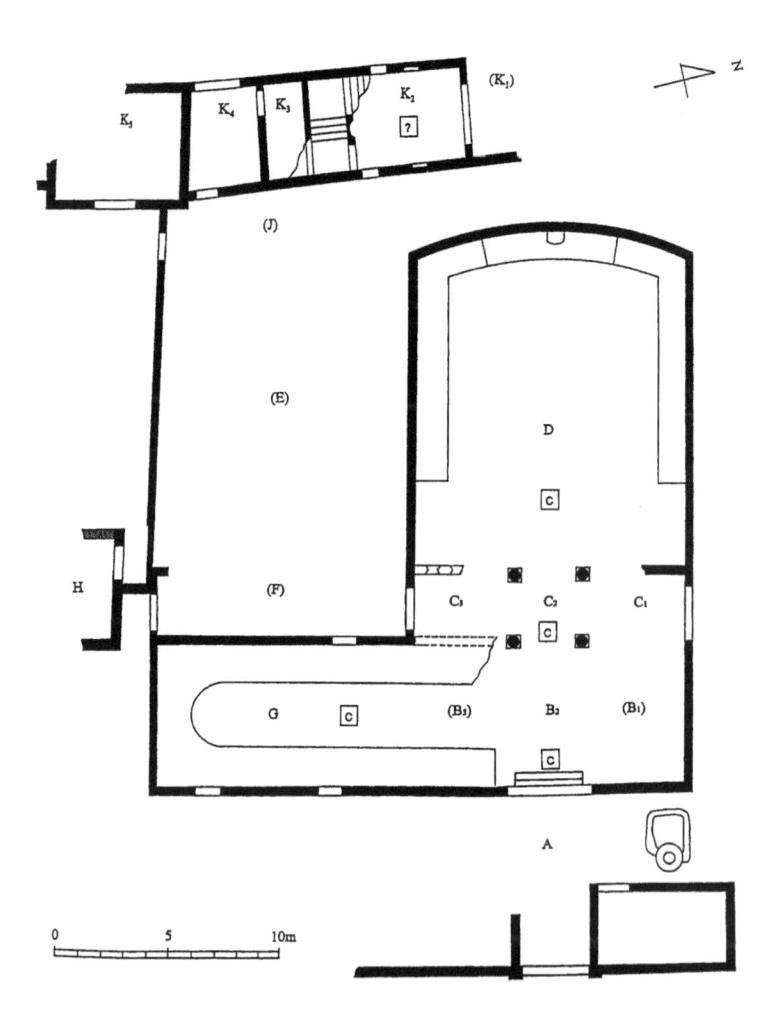

Figure 5.1 Plan of the Ostia synagogue in the late-first century C.E., according to the investigations of the Lund research team. Courtesy of Anders Runesson.

The synagogue at Ostia (see Runesson in this volume),[20] according to the Lund analysis, was a purpose-built building from the latter part of

---

[20] Olsson, Mitternacht and Brandt, *Synagogue of Ancient Ostia*; Binder, *Temple Courts*, 322–6.

An Architectural Case for Synagogues as Associations

the first century C.E.[21] The synagogue's design—a complex structure, with provision for assembly, banqueting, worship, and a water supply—aligns it closely with other Ostian associations. The earliest plan included a *triclinium* (in the area subsequently utilized as a kitchen), assembly room, and cistern. The assembly had a gently curved west wall with benches on three sides and a *bema* at the center of the curved wall. The *triclinium* had benches on three sides of a narrow room, in the standard form but with relatively little space between the bench fronts. At this early stage, the synagogue lacked the later monumental torah niche and the additional room on the southwest later used as the *triclinium*.

Figure 5.2   Entrance area (A on the plan) on the east side of the synagogue; the door leads to area B, to the left is area G, and the assembly hall (area D with its later torah niche *(aedicula)* is to the right. Originally area G was a *triclinium* but in later stages it became a kitchen. Photo by Peter Richardson.

---

[21] Runesson, "Oldest Original Synagogue Building," supporting the view of the excavator, Maria Floriano Squarciapino; *per contra*, White, "Reading the Ostia Synagogue."

Figure 5.3 Area G, originally a *triclinium* but in its present state a kitchen, looking north. On the left are the later *aedicula* and walls defining area F, a later large *triclinium*. Photo by Peter Richardson.

Figure 5.4 Area G, to the south. Photo by Peter Richardson.

An Architectural Case for Synagogues as Associations

Figure 5.5 The west side of area D, the assembly room, looking north, with curved wall and *bema*. Photo by Peter Richardson.

Some issues are still being debated.[22] Was the area originally residential? Was the synagogue adapted from a private house? How prominent was it initially? When did it begin to function as a synagogue? But it is certain that when it began to be used as a Jewish communal building it would have been viewed by Ostians as being in the same architectural idiom as other associations. Its most noticeable difference from others—though as Bona Dea shows, not unique—was that it stood outside the city.

---

[22] White began a five-year project in 2001 to answer such questions.

Figure 5.6 The Ostia synagogue's torah niche *(aedicula)*, inserted at a later stage at the east end of the assembly room. Photo by Peter Richardson.

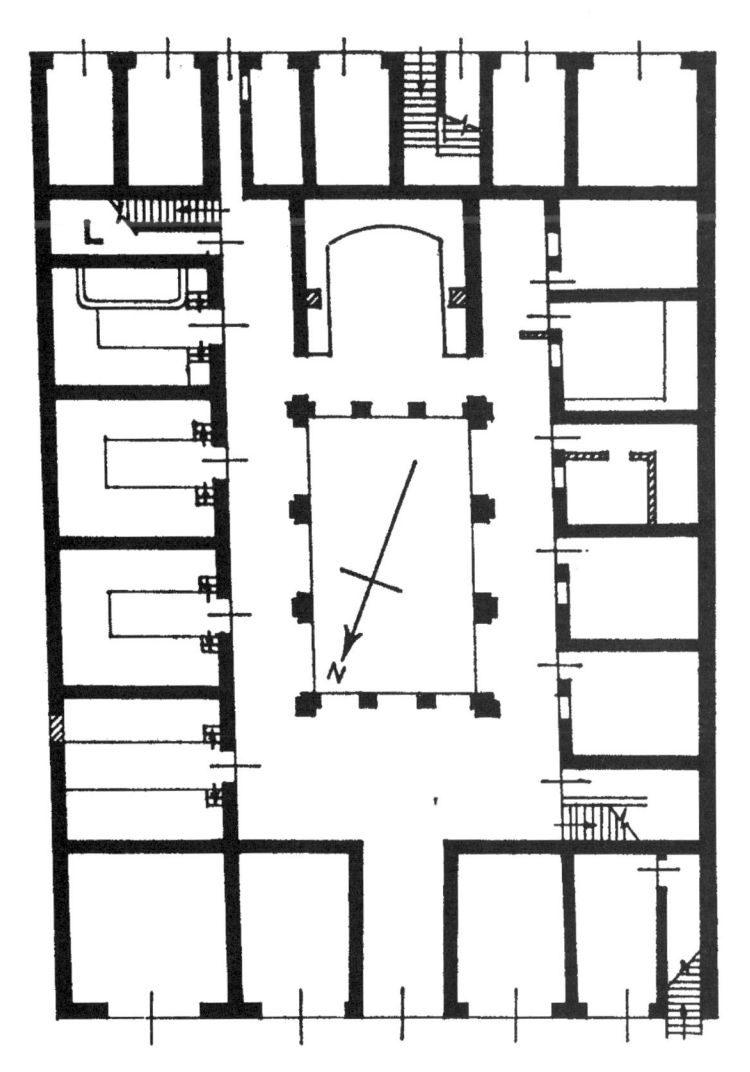

An Architectural Case for Synagogues as Associations

Figure 5.7 Plan of Ostia's Association of the Housebuilders (Caseggiato dei triclinic [I,XII,1] after Meiggs.

The shape of the synagogue's meeting room was repeated in the shape of the curved bench in the *tablinum* of the House builders' guild *(Caseggiato dei Triclini)*, and the *triclinium* was similar to three of its four *triclinia*. The building was originally constructed early in the reign of Hadrian; an inscription on a statue base dedicated to Septimius

Severus identifies this association as for the *fabri tignuari*.[23] The guild building was designed around a central courtyard that gave it "an aristocratic air,"[24] though the upper floor and roof were carried on utilitarian brick piers. Ten shops faced the streets, four on the north and six on the south. Four stairwells served rooms on the upper floor(s). Four *triclinia* on the east opened into the courtyard, matched by four other rooms on the west.[25] The *tablinum*, with its gently curved "bench" that partly mimics the arrangement in the synagogue, was centered on the south side of the courtyard opposite the main door (because the synagogue did not lack for space it was not designed around a courtyard). A public latrine (*forica*) was introduced into two shops at the southeast corner in the fourth century C.E.[26] The House builders association may have had another "guild temple" on the eastern decumanus—the *Tempio collegiale*—to express their loyalty to Pertinax, and if so the *Caseggiato dei Triclini* was used for guild affairs.[27]

Figure 5.8 Central courtyard of the Housebuilders' Association building, looking from the entrance to the shrine room, with its curved low podium. The doors to the *triclinia* are on the left. Courtesy Philip Harland.

---

[23] Meiggs, *Roman Ostia*, 547 (cf. 543, 140), dated by the brick stamps.
[24] Ibid., 244. Plans in Hermansen, *Ostia*, fig 12; Meiggs, *Roman Ostia*, fig. 8.
[25] Hermansen, *Ostia*, 75, suggests the triclinia were added later and that banquets earlier took place in the colonnade.
[26] Meiggs, *Roman Ostia*, 551 and plate IX b.
[27] Hermansen, *Ostia*, 64 and fig 33.

An Architectural Case for Synagogues as Associations

Associations in Ostia did not hew to one line only. With different organizations it is understandable that they constructed a variety of facilities in response to their needs.[28] The Ostia synagogue's analogies with one of the wealthiest of all the associations—the House builders' guild—made it fit comfortably within the typology of Ostian association buildings.

Figure 5.9   One of the suite of four *triclinia* (dining rooms) east of the central courtyard in the Housebuilders' Association building, looking east. There are resemblances between this and the synagogue *triclinia*. Courtesy Philip Harland.

---

[28] Meiggs, *Roman Ostia*, 317–21, on organization, offices, wealth, and firefighting role.

Delos

For a century-and-a-half Delos was an independent polis; Rome made it a free port (166 B.C.E.), challenging the dominance of Rhodes.[29] Numerous communities of Italians and easterners—for example, Phoenicians, Egyptians, Jews, and Samaritans— established themselves on the island during the late-second/early-first century B.C.E.[30] But Delos declined after two sackings (Mithradates VI, 88 B.C.E.; pirates, 69 B.C.E.), and its commercial opportunities were assumed by Corinth (re-founded 44 B.C.E.). More than 24 associations are known on Delos, primarily from inscriptions; most foreign cults were on the higher ground below Mount Kynthos, though some foreign associations such as the Poseidoniasts of Berytos, were in the city by the sacred harbor.

Four Jewish inscriptions were found inside a building on the northeast coast identified as a synagogue (GD 80).[31] A fifth inscription was found in an insula (GD 79),[32] between it and the stadium and gymnasium (GD 76, 77, 78).[33] Two other clearly Samaritan inscriptions were discovered in 1979–80 about 90 m north of the synagogue.[34] Were there one or two synagogues? The epigraphic evidence is ambiguous.[35] McLean argues for only a Samaritan synagogue, based on the certain reading of the more recently found inscriptions;[36] White believes there were two buildings.[37] It seems likelier that the building remains are Jewish and that the Samaritan synagogue has yet to be found.

---

[29] Excavations began in 1873; H. Holleaux excavated the most significant areas in 1904–14.

[30] McLean, "Place of Cult," 186–90.

[31] Excavated 1912–13; Plassart, "Synagogue juive."

[32] McLean, "Place of Cult,"189. Four inscriptions refer to "God most high" (*theos hypsistos*), none refers to Jews or Judeans, and the fifth one (bearing the name Lysimachos, who appears on one of the other four) refers to the *proseuchê*,.

[33] Herod Antipas or Herod Philip was honored by "the Athenian people and those living on the island" (Delos) in an inscription (*OGIS* 417) found in front of the Temple of Apollo. Three fragments of an inscription—found on Syros but probably originating on Delos—referred to "King Herod"; the inscription was likely associated with the *xystos* near the synagogue finds. Richardson, *Herod*, 205–6, 209.

[34] Bruneau, "Juiverie délienne"; one inscription has *proseuchê*, both have *Israêlitai* and *Argarizein* ("Mount Gerizim"); texts and translations conveniently in White, "Delos Synagogue Revisited," 139–41.

[35] Llewelyn, "An Association of Samaritans in Delos," in Llewelyn, *New Documents*, 148–51.

[36] McLean, "Place of Cult"; Kraabel, "Samaritan Diaspora."

[37] White, *Social Origins*, 2:335 n. 81, "another building."

The remains comprise a suite of rooms on the west with a peristyle courtyard on the east, though its eastern portico, if it had one, has now fallen into the sea.[38] The suite of rooms may have been part of a larger (unexcavated) structure. One large benched meeting hall was subdivided into two rooms in one of the renovation phases, at which time the central of three doors was blocked up.[39] In the subdivided form, a *thronos* occupied a central position among the benches on the west wall of the northern room, opposite what was now the main door into the meeting room. There were also benches in the northwest corner of the courtyard's *stoa*. South of the meeting room(s) was a complex of six rooms, one of which had a large cistern partly under the southern half of the meeting room.

White claims that the building was a conversion into a synagogue from a second-century B.C.E. house, through two renovation stages in the early first century B.C.E.[40] Binder and Runesson, argue for a purpose-built building (possibly originally a non-Jewish association, which was taken over by Jews after 88 B.C.E.)[41] on the basis of its similarity in plan and scale to the building of the Poseidoniasts of Berytos.[42] The scale of the peristyle columns, and meeting hall are consistent with a purpose-built building (the column drums were 45–55 cm in diameter, and thus about 3.60 to 4.60 m. high, plus about 1 m. entablature; White). The disagreements, while important, need not concern us, since the main point is that the synagogue was closely analogous to the Poseidoniasts' building, in just the same way as the synagogue in Ostia was analogous to the House Builders' guild. This point stands independent of the debate over house-synagogue adaptation versus purpose-built synagogue.

Priene

To solidify the point about synagogues and associations, I draw in one later example. Priene was re-founded on a new site (c. 350 B.C.E.) after

---

[38] White, "Delos synagogue revisited," 147–52; McLean, "Place of cult," 191–6.

[39] I had not noticed the similarity between its renovated form and my schematic drawing of the Therapeutae's assembly room; see Runesson, *Origins*, 187 n. 79 (Richardson, "Philo and Eusebius" fig 6).

[40] White, *Social Origins*, 2:332–9; "Delos synagogue revisited," 147–51.

[41] Binder, *Temple Courts*, 299–316; Runesson, *Origins*, 185–7.

[42] Mazur, *Jewry in Greece*, 15–24, who denies it was a synagogue; cf. Binder, *Temple Courts*, 315–16.

an earlier (still unidentified) site was abandoned, due to silting up of the Meander River.[43] By the time of Augustus the new harbor also became unusable as the silting continued. Little is known of Priene's subsequent history. Its gradual deterioration and abandonment meant that Priene survived relatively intact, like Ostia, with little Roman overbuilding, so the urban design is still an exceptional example of a Hippodamian plan molded over a sloping topography. Many Hellenistic civic buildings and houses survive. Three houses on the south side of Westthorstrasse (West Gate Street) along the city wall were adapted to meet the needs of three cultic associations, illustrating clearly the strategy that White has illuminated:[44] one dedicated to Cybele (ignored here), another for the hero cult of Alexander, and a third for the Jewish community. All were originally houses, adapted for associational needs at various periods.

The House of Alexander was the earliest to be converted to association use. Wiegand and Schrader referred to it as an *hieros oikos*, adapted from a typical Hellenistic private house with courtyard and smaller rooms surrounding it.[45] In its renovated state (soon after Alexander's death?) it included a sanctuary 9.2 x 19.0 m., with three columns down the middle and a podium in the northeast corner. Parts of two tables were discovered, one in front of the podium and another in the room northeast of the courtyard. The door to the courtyard, whose left doorpost was discovered with an inscription that none shall enter the "holy sanctuary" except those wearing white clothing, was from a lane on the west.[46] Between the courtyard and the sanctuary was a porch with three statue bases in a row. Portions of two statues of Alexander were found, and elsewhere another inscription was found referring to restorations in 140 B.C.E. to the sacred place devoted to Alexander. The adaptations were carried out in a somewhat slipshod manner, for much of the east wall simply utilizes the wall of the house to the east (details in Murray).

---

[43] Excavations began in 1895, under Karl Humann's direction. Reports in Wiegand and Schrader, *Priene*.
[44] White, *Social Origins*, 325–32; see also Murray, "Religious coexistence," in Ascough, *Sardis and Smyrna*; I draw from Murray's draft.
[45] Wiegand and Schrader, *Priene*, 172–3.
[46] Schede, *Ruinen*, 101.

The synagogue was the latest of the three adaptations. There has been little discussion of the building's dating[47] or of the history of the Jewish community in Priene and how that history connected with overall urban developments. White's suggested three stages of adaptation may well be correct, but there is still a need for precision on the timing of those stages and the house's architectural history, as White points out.

The renovations turned the Hellenistic courtyard into a monumentalized meeting hall, with a new door from the west lane into a new porch area (built over some earlier small rooms that had opened off the lane), all axially related to a new niche on the east built in space borrowed from the neighboring house. The original *oecus* (living room) and *prostas* (vestibule) became ancillary spaces, with a new entrance directly into the *oecus*, though the excavation reports are unclear if there was a direct connection from this suite of rooms into the meeting hall. New stylobates were constructed in the meeting hall, the north one slightly splayed, and with one column drum still roughly in place. A bench ran along a new north wall of the meeting hall. Beside the niche were a small basin, a tall rectangular stele (2.20 m high) decorated with a *menorah* (fallen, but still in place), a broken slab (0.52 x 0.60 m) with a relief of two peacocks and a *lulav* (neither of the latter pieces have been properly studied).[48]

While the synagogue project was not as large as the renovation of Alexander's house, it was similar in several major respects: it took over an earlier Hellenistic house so that domestic functions disappeared, it created a new entrance, it inserted a major meeting hall with new columns and roof, it provided a new liturgical area: in Alexander's house with a small podium and table and possibly a sacrificial area with statues of Alexander nearby; in the synagogue with a small niche and basin and two *menorah* reliefs.

Three of the oldest synagogues in the Diaspora show that synagogues were constructed on the same lines as association buildings. The three differed from each other, underscoring that there was no single model

---

[47] Wiegand and Schrader, *Priene*, 480, call it a *Hauskirche* from the 4th–5th centuries C.E. It has since been redated to the 2nd–3rd centuries C.E. and identified as a synagogue (e.g., White, *Social Origins* 2: 329–30).
[48] Another relief of a menorah was found in the Byzantine church near the theatre, though it is sometimes incorrectly associated with the synagogue: Kraabel, "Diaspora Synagogue"; Trebilco, *Asia Minor*, 55.

for synagogues, just as there was no single association model. Without a common model, each followed near at hand association practice to find an appropriate solution for the Jewish community's needs.

Levine on Associations

Levine recently considered three possible explanations of synagogue origins: his own preferred city-gate, the Jerusalem temple, and association buildings.[49] With respect to associations he argues (1) that Roman authorities used words such as *thiasoi* or *collegia* or *synodoi* without precision; (2) that Jewish communities were not simply associations because they had a "far greater range of activities" and legal "rights" than associations; (3) that Jewish communities were not voluntary.

These points are essentially correct and show how Jewish communities can be differentiated from Greek and Roman associations. But they do not subvert the claim that associations were models for synagogues, for the variety among associations is wide enough that—architecturally, organizationally, and behaviorally—synagogues fell naturally within the limits of associations. Levine's big book deals more extensively with these issues;[50] he notes the bearing of voluntary associations on the analysis of synagogues, saying, amongst other things:

> Synagogues shifted gradually from communal centers with religious components to houses of worship with communal activities (pp. 2–4).
>
> Sometimes *proseuchai* incorporated associations, so that in Egypt we find a *synodos*, burial society, Sambathic association, and other professional associations (pp. 80–1, 87, 129, 368).[51] The same is true in Aphrodisias and possibly in Miletus, where the theatre had seats for "Godfearers of the Jews" beside an association of *philaugustoi*.
>
> Josephus' decrees describe activities that complement and sometimes dovetail with the epigraphic linguistic evidence.[52] Levine emphasizes

---

[49] Levine, "First-Century Synagogue," referring in part to Richardson, "Early Synagogues."
[50] Levine, *Ancient Synagogue*.
[51] Griffiths, "Egypt."
[52] Richardson, *Herod*, 264–70.

that Jews "freely borrowed different frameworks from their surroundings, with models ranging from the *politeuma* [e.g., Berenice, pp. 89–96] and *collegium*, through the *synodos, koinon* and *thiasos*" (p. 121, cf. pp. 106–7). He considers this a "high degree of Hellenization," though it might be merely a case of the synagogue adopting forms and models from the local culture.

Synagogue functions—both in Judea and Diaspora (pp. 124–5)—were analogous to those of associations: professional and social groups, benevolent societies, manumissions, dining and kitchens, courts, charity, study, library, residence, incubation (pp. 368–85). Synagogues were "not sui generis."

Thus, the synagogue "clearly borrowed much from Greco-Roman associations (*thiasos, koinon, collegia,* etc.)," yet "no analogy does justice to the unique role of this institution" (p. 159). "Diaspora synagogues functioned, and indeed were often referred to, as associations; they followed one of several Greco-Roman models" (p. 589).

Levine grants most of what this chapter claims, that the clearest analogy for synagogues—whether one thinks of architecture, functions, organization, popular perceptions, or legal status—was the association. Since associations developed in the Greek and Roman world, Judaism, I suggest, first learned from this model in the Diaspora. Levine draws back from this obvious conclusion, on the grounds that synagogues had more functions and were more complex, so could not be contained entirely by an associational model. Though he rejects *sui generis* arguments, in the end he seems to make a *sui generis* argument for synagogues. But if the difference is merely one of degree, it seems proper to include synagogues within the general classification associations. The institution of the synagogue emerged out of that broad category of social and religious groups called associations, and the clear architectural similarities of their buildings reinforce that relationship.

Judea

A brief addendum on Judea. The majority of early Palestinian synagogues were simple communal meeting halls: Gamla, Masada, Herodium, Qiryat Sefer, Modi'in, and Horvat 'Ethri. Three cases, however, were more nearly analogous to complex Diaspora buildings:

Jerusalem, Qumran, and Jericho. All three pose difficulties. The Theodotos inscription from Jerusalem is wonderfully descriptive, but without archaeological remains all that can be said is it had assembly hall for reading and teaching, chambers and water installation as an inn.

Our knowledge of Qumran comes from the archaeological investigation of buildings, but no final report has yet been produced, though parts of the notebooks and photographs have been published.[53] The debates over meeting rooms and anything that might be called a "synagogue" are intense. If the Qumran group was an association, like the Therapeutae in Egypt,[54] it was appropriate that it should have communal spaces: dining and pantry (rooms 77, 86, 89), kitchen (rooms 41, 38), benched meeting room (room 4), work areas, living areas, and water installations for ritual purity. The likeliest allocation of meeting spaces is dining (77), meeting (30) and council rooms (4).

The recently excavated building at Jericho has been published in limited detail to date. It was a complex structure, adapted from a house, with *triclinium*, kitchen, meeting hall, *mikveh*, entrance, and other rooms. If Netzer is correct that this was a synagogue, it is another example of an early Judean synagogue that broke away from the simple meeting hall structure of the majority.

The above examples are suggestive: the Jerusalem synagogue met the needs of foreign visitors (*tois chrezousin apo xenes*); the Qumran complex was for a group voluntarily assembled in the desert awaiting God's future decisive acts; the Jericho synagogue was set in the context of late-Hellenistic elite palaces. All were early, and all three seem to have drawn their architectural inspiration from traditions other than those that later led to the more common simple meeting halls.

Note two other considerations. (a) Caesarea Maritima,[55] Dor, and Tiberias all had synagogues from the late-Hellenistic/early-Roman periods. All three were in contact with the wider Roman world and might have natural affinities with synagogues elsewhere. Lack of information about them prohibits their effective use in such discussions. (b) Recent study of Samaritan synagogues suggests a distribution both geographically and chronologically similar to Judean synagogues, possibly with a

---

[53] Humbert and Chambon, *Fouilles*.
[54] Richardson, "Philo and Eusebius."
[55] Richardson, "Religion and Urbanism."

similar range of types.[56] Future histories of synagogues in the eastern Mediterranean need to take this parallel information into account; in general it reinforces the above conclusion. With enough data, we might eventually construct a stemma of developments that bridged disjunctions between Diaspora and Palestine, between Judean and Samaritan synagogues.

Conclusion

I have located Jewish synagogues architecturally in the context of the eastern Mediterranean in a setting of Roman tolerance of Jewish communities. Jewish communal buildings fitted comfortably within the range of *synodoi*, *thiasoi*, and *collegia* in that Diaspora world. While Jewish communities might form a discrete subgroup among other associations, they adopted architectural forms that were part of a common vocabulary of buildings from the same period and met a variety of communal needs, like other associations.

The range of evidence for studying synagogues forces us methodologically to use logic, inference, intuition, and even speculation. But we must still begin with the evidence—archaeological, epigraphic and literary—not with hypothetical or theoretical constructs. Can one reasonably follow evidence towards a conclusion on origins? I think so. The literary and epigraphic evidence demonstrates early and widespread distribution of Jewish public buildings in the Diaspora. This creates a presumption, a hypothesis, a relatively simple explanation, but not proof, that synagogues originated in the Diaspora. Other hypotheses are possible, but they must posit either long silences or complex processes of which we have no evidence. Beyond the competing proposal, a more complex process of development is possible, which might include two discrete processes, one leading to simple meeting room synagogues, another leading to more highly articulated synagogues.[57] Still, chronological priority and weight of evidence falls clearly on the side of the Diaspora and within the context of associations.

---

[56] Pummer, "Samaritan Synagogues."
[57] Runesson, *Origins*, holds a variant on this view.

Bibliography

Ascough, R., ed. *Religious Rivalries and the Struggle for Success in Sardis and Smyrna.* Waterloo: Wilfrid Laurier University Press, forthcoming.

Binder, D. D., *Into the Temple Courts: The Place of the Synagogues in the Second Temple Period.* Atlanta: Society of Biblical Literature, 1999.

Blue, B., "Acts and the House Church." Pages 119–222 in *Graeco-Roman Setting.* Edited by D. W. J. Gill and C. Gempf. Vol. 2 of *The Book of Acts in its First Century Setting.* Edited by B. W. Winter. Grand Rapids: Eerdmans, 1994.

Bruneau, P. and J. Ducat. *Guide de Délos.* 3rd ed. Athens: École française d'Athènes, 1983.

Bruneau, P., "'Les Israélites de Délos' et la Juiverie délienne." *Bulletin de Corresondance hellénique* 106 (1982): 465–504.

Donaldson, T. L., ed. *Religious Rivalries and the Struggle for Success in Caesarea Maritima.* Waterloo: Wilfrid Laurier University Press, 2000.

Fagan, G. G., "The Genesis of the Roman Public Bath: Recent Approaches and New Directions." *AJA* 105 (2001): 403–26.

Grabbe, L. L., "Synagogues in Pre-70 Palestine." Pages 17–26 in *Ancient Synagogues: Historical Analysis and Archaeological Discovery.* Edited by D. Urman and P. V. M. Flesher. Leiden: Brill, 1995.

Griffiths, J. G., "Egypt and the Rise of the Synagogue." Pages 3–16 in *Ancient Synagogues: Historical Analysis and Archaeological Discovery.* Edited by D. Urman and P. V. M. Flesher. Leiden: Brill, 1995.

Harland, P., "Associations and Empire: A Socio-Historical Study of Voluntary Associations in Ephesus (I–II CE)," unpublished paper, University of Toronto, 1995.

Hermansen, G., *Ostia: Aspects of Roman City Life.* Edmonton: University of Alberta Press 1982.

Humbert, J-B. and A. Chambon. *Les Fouilles de Khirbet Qumran et de Aïn Feshkha.* Göttingen: Vandenhoeck und Ruprecht, 1994.

Kloppenborg, J. S., "Dating Theodotos (CIJ ii.1404)." *JJS* 51 (2000): 243–80.

Kraabel, A. T., "The Diaspora Synagogue: Archaeological and Epigraphic Evidence since Sukenik. Pages 447–510 in *ANRW*, II.19.1. Edited by H. Temporini and W. Haase. Berlin: de Gruyter, 1979

Levine, L. I., *The Ancient Synagogue: The First Thousand Years*. New Haven/London: Yale University Press, 2000.

—, "The First-Century Synagogue: New Perspectives." *STK* 77 (2001): 22–30.

Levinskaya, I., *Diaspora Setting*. Vol. 5 of *The Book of Acts in its First Century Settting*. Edited by B. W. Winter. Grand Rapids: Eerdmans, 1996.

Llewelyn, S. R., *New Documents Illustrating Early Christianity, Volume 8*. Eerdmans: Grand Rapids, 1998.

McLean, B. H., "The Place of Cult in Voluntary Associations and Christian Churches on Delos." Pages 186–225 in *Voluntary Associations in the Graeco-Roman World*. Edited by J. S. Kloppenborg and S. G. Wilson. London: Routledge, 1996.

Mazur, B. D., *Studies on Jewry in Greece*. Athens: Hestia, 1935.

Meiggs, R., *Roman Ostia*. Oxford: Clarendon: 1960.

Murray. M., "Was There Religious Coexistence or Competition in Ancient Priene?" In *Religious Rivalries and the Struggle for Success in Sardis and Smyrna*. Edited by R. Ascough. Waterloo: Wilfrid Laurier University Press, 2003.

Olsson, B., D. Mitternacht and O. Brandt, eds. *The Synagogue of Ancient Ostia and the Jews of Rome*. Stockholm: Paul Åström, 2001.

Plassart, A., "La synagogue juive de Délos." Pages 201–15 in *Mélanges Holleaux: Receuil de mémoires concernant l'antiquité grecque offert à Maurice Holleaux*. Paris: Auguste Picard, 1913.

Pummer, R., "Samaritan Synagogues and Jewish Synagogues: Similarities and Differences." Pages 118–60 in *Jews, Christians, and Polytheists in the Ancient Synagogue*. Edited by S. Fine. London: Routledge, 1999.

Richardson, P., *Herod, King of the Jews and Friend of the Romans*. Minneapolis: Fortress, 1999.

—, "Early Synagogues as *Collegia* in the Diaspora and Palestine." Pages 90–109 in *Voluntary Associations in the Graeco-Roman World*. Edited by J. S. Kloppenborg and S. G. Wilson. London: Routledge, 1996.

—, "Building a synodos . . . and a place of their own." Pages 36–56 in *Models of Ministry: Community Formation in the New Testament, the Ante-Nicene Fathers, and the Church Today*. Edited by R. N. Longenecker. Peabody: Hendrickson, 2002.

—, "Architectural Transitions from Synagogues to House Churches." Pages 373–89 in *Common Life in the Early Church. Essays Honoring Graydon F. Snyder*. Edited by J. V. Hills *et al.* Harrisburg: Trinity Press, 1998.

—, "Augustan-Era Synagogues in Rome." Pages 17–29 in *Judaism and Christianity in First-Century Rome*. Edited by K. Donfried and P. Richardson. Grand Rapids: Eerdmans, 1998.

—, "Archaeological Evidence for Religion and Urbanism in Caesarea Maritima." Pages 11–34 in *Religious Rivalries and the Struggle for Success in Caesarea Maritima*. Edited by T. L. Donaldson. Waterloo: Wilfrid Laurier University Press, 2000.

—, "Philo and Eusebius on Monasteries and Monasticism." Pages 334–59 in *Origins and Method: Towards a New Understanding of Judaism and Christianity*. Edited by B. H. McLean. Sheffield: Sheffield Academic Press, 1993.

Richardson, P., and V. Heuchan., "Jewish Voluntary Associations in Egypt and the Roles of Women." Pages 226–51 in *Voluntary Associations in the Graeco-Roman World*. Edited by J. S. Kloppenborg and S. G. Wilson. London: Routledge, 1996.

Runesson, A., "The Oldest Original Synagogue Building in the Diaspora: A Response to L. Michael White." *HTR* 92 (1999): 409–33.

—, *The Origins of the Synagogue: A Socio-Historical Study*. Stockholm: Almqvist & Wiksell, 2001.

Schede, M., *Die Ruinen von Priene*. Berlin: de Gruyter, 1964 [1934].

Snyder, G. F., *Ante Pacem: Archaeological Evidence of Church Life before Constantine*. Mercer University Press, 1991.

Talmon, S., *The World of Qumran From Within: Collected Studies*. Jerusalem: Magness, 1989.

Trebilco, P. R., *Jewish Communities in Asia Minor*. Cambridge: Cambridge University Press, 1991.

White, L. M., "The Delos Synagogue Revisited: Recent Fieldwork in the Graeco-Roman Diaspora." *HTR* 80 (1987): 133–60.

—, "Reading the Ostia Synagogue: A Reply to A. Runesson." *HTR* 92 (1999): 435–64.

—, *The Social Origins of Christian Architecture*. 2 vols.; Valley Forge: Trinity Press International, 1997.

Urman, D., and P. V. M. Flesher, eds. *Ancient Synagogues*. 2 vols; Leiden: Brill, 1995.

Vaage, L., ed. *Religious Rivalries in the Early Roman Empire (and the Rise of Christianity)*. Waterloo: Wilfrid Laurier University Press, forthcoming.

Wiegand, T., and H. Schrader. *Priene: Ergebnisse der Ausgrabungen und Untersuchungen in den Jahren 1895–1898*. Berlin: Georg Reimer, 1904.

6
The Origins of the Synagogue: An Evaluation

Donald D. Binder

IT IS MY GREAT HONOR and privilege to present the first response to three thoughtful and stimulating papers that each probed the possible origins of the synagogues, a topic with which I have been enthusiastically engaged now for several years—not only in my writings, but also in my authorship and day-to-day management of an Internet site that has served as a clearing house for new information and ideas relating to synagogues of the Second Temple period.[1]

Yet because each essay has come at this topic from such disparate starting points and, to some degree, by using different subsets of data, I see my task as being not simply an evaluative one, but one that endeavors to bring these three viewpoints more into conversation with each other.

Along the way, I hope to throw a little fuel on the fire by playing the role of the *provocateur*, if for no other reason than to invite us to re-examine some of the presuppositions that may have been undergirding these and other recent studies on the earliest synagogues. In the ensuing discussion, it is my hope that, while we all may not reach a full agreement with each other, we might achieve a consensus on at least some points and thus lay the groundwork for future progress in this subfield.

The first paper presented, that of James Strange, focused primarily on the earliest architectural evidence from Palestine. Through an analysis of seven synagogue remains—those of Gamla, Masada, Herodium, Capernaum I, Jericho, Kiryat Sefer and Modi'in—Strange

---

[1] See Binder, *Temple Courts*; "Second Temple Synagogues," Online: http://faculty.smu.edu/dbinder.

concludes that the earliest Palestinian synagogues constituted a type of basilica. But this type of basilica he views as uniquely Jewish in its incorporation of benches along the walls, sometimes with intervening aisles, and in its separation of the assembly from the central hall through the placement of rows of columns between the two. Proposing a clerestory roofing over the hall's central rectangle, Strange notes that this area would have been better lit than the surrounding area encompassing the benches. Nevertheless, because of the intervening columns, the hall was clearly designed for hearing rather than for seeing.

From the early literary evidence which outlines a religious function for the synagogues, particularly that of the reading and explication of Torah, Strange infers that the inspiration for this basilica type was the courts of the Second Temple, which were not only similarly arranged but also a place where Torah reading took place. Finally, his emphasis upon the Torah-reading aspect of the synagogue leads him to propose that the earliest synagogues, like their Late Roman and Byzantine period counterparts, also contained an ark.

While I obviously sympathize with Strange's comparison between the earliest synagogues and the temple courts,[2] I believe that the link between the two can be even more firmly made. This can be done first of all by observing that a clerestory roofing for the earliest synagogues is by no means a foregone conclusion. Here, we must recall that the oldest extant basilica—the basilica at Pompeii, which dates to the late second century B.C.E.—clearly did *not* have clerestory roofing. Indeed, although there is some debate on the matter, the leading view is that the interior plaza of the building was open to the air.[3] This also may have been so with several of the earliest synagogues, particularly those at Masada and Herodium. Along these lines, Josephus quotes Apion as characterizing Jerusalem synagogues *(proseuchai)* as being "open to the air" and does not challenge him on this point (*C. Ap.* 2.10–12). If this were in fact the case, then the architectural resemblance between the earliest synagogues and the temple courts is even more striking.

The absence of a roof over the central plaza in both the more common type of early basilica and the subtype of the Palestinian synagogue would further hint at their origins in the sacred precincts

---

[2] This was one of the main conclusions of my study, which itself drew partially on Strange's work in this area. See Binder, *Temple Courts,* 222–6.
[3] See Robertson, *Greek and Roman Architecture,* 267–9; Binder, *Temple Courts,* 222–6.

marked by the Greek rectangular stoa.[4] If so, this is yet another point of intersection between the temple courts and the Palestinian synagogues, for the former was clearly influenced by the introduction of this architectural style during the Hellenistic period.[5]

From the side of the Jerusalem temple, elsewhere I have argued that seating along the inner walls of the temple courts is suggested both by a comparison with similar courts of contemporary temples in Southern Syria and Nabatea, which did have benches along the walls, and by the description of such seating in the idealized temple of the *Temple Scroll* (11QT 37.8–10).[6]

In another area, although I would agree with Strange that the arrangement of the early synagogues facilitated audition, including the reading and explication of Torah, I would also want to add that the synagogue was not just the place for Torah reading, but also for public prayer. Despite H. McKay's recent attempts to argue otherwise, the early evidence clearly attests this function, as can be seen, for instance,

---

[4] See Owens, *City*, *passim*; Coulton, *Architectural Development*, 174–5 and *passim*.

[5] It is interesting to note, for example, that the LXX of Ezek 40:17–19 and 42:3 mentions the presence of *stoas* around Ezekiel's temple—a detail missing from the Hebrew text. Likewise, Josephus' description of the rebuilding of the temple under Zerubbabel mentions the presence of *stoas* (*A.J.* 11.108; cf. *B.J.* 5:200–6), even though their presence is not mentioned in either of his sources (Ezra 6:18, 1 Esdr 7:9; cf. also *A.J.* 9.237 with 2 Chr 27:3 and 2 Kgs 15:35). Even the idealized temple of the Essenes envisions *stoas* within the inner courts (11QT 37.9), demonstrating the impact of Hellenistic architectural ideas within Palestine during this period.

[6] Binder, *Temple Courts*, 218–26. See also Richardson, "Law and Piety," 351, which argues that Herod had a hand in building not only the Jerusalem temple, but also the temple of Baal Shamim in southern Syria, where there was seating along the inside perimeter of its forecourts. The original connection between the courts of the Nabatean temples and the Galilean synagogues was made in Foerster, "Architectural Models," 47–8, though Foerster himself sees only parallels between these courts and the Galilean synagogues of the Late Roman and Byzantine periods. He prefers instead to find the origins of the earliest Palestinian synagogues in the *pronaoi* of the temples of Atargatis, Artemis and Tyche at Dura-Europos (idem, "Synagogues at Masada and Herodium, 28–9; ibid., 9–11). For a critique of this latter position, see Ma'oz, "Synagogue of Gamla," 41; Ovadiah and Michaeli, "Observations," 238–40; Chiat, "First-Century Synagogue Architecture," 49–60. I agree with the critiques of the Dura-Europos proposal, but find Foerster's other suggestion apt for not only the later Galilean-style synagogues, but also the earliest Palestinian synagogues—albeit by way of the courts of the similarly constructed Jerusalem temple.

in Josephus' description of a public prayer service in the synagogue at Tiberias (*Vita* 290–295).[7] This additional cultic function further ties the temple to the synagogues, since not only were individual prayers offered in the temple courts, but the Levites also continuously chanted the psalms in their very midst as the sacrifices were being offered on the altar.[8]

Finally, I will observe that Strange's emphasis on Torah reading as the key synagogue function may have led him astray in his proposal of a Torah ark in even the earliest synagogues. Here, such an appointment is totally unattested in the Second Temple period evidence. Moreover, it is difficult to envision a wooden ark in the area he proposes in any of the remains under discussion. Based on this lack of evidence, it seems more likely to me that the ark was added only *after* the destruction of the temple both as a memorial to the lost central shrine and as a result of the further accentuation of Torah study in the synagogues by the surviving Pharisaic leaders.[9]

In contrast to Strange's focus on architectural data, Anders Runesson bases his conclusions largely on an analysis of literary and epigraphic

---

[7] See McKay, *Sabbath and Synagogue*; "New Moon or Sabbath?". Somewhat less radically, several scholars have recently maintained that communal prayer was not a feature of *Palestinian* synagogues prior to 70 C.E. (aside from that exercised in the Essene synagogues): Levine, *Ancient Synagogue*, 155–8; "Synagogues," 1421; "Second Temple Synagogue," 19–20; Fine, *This Holy Place*, 31–3; Fine and Meyers, "Synagogues," 118; Fleisher, "Beginnings." For more comprehensive rebuttals to these positions, see Binder, *Temple Courts*, 404–15; Horst, "Place of Sabbath Worship Before 70 CE?"; Runesson, *Origins*, 342–50.

[8] See, e.g., Josephus, *A.J.* 9.269, 11.80, 20.217–18; Philo, *Spec.* 1.272; Sir 50:14–21. These accounts of spoken prayer and hymnody in the temple courts belie the sometimes seen view that temple ritual was held in silence (e.g., Levine, "First-Century Synagogue," 27). Such a characterization accepts too uncritically the highly stylized account of *Let. Aris.* 92–6, which goes to great lengths to impress upon a Gentile audience the reverence of temple worship. See Binder, *Temple Courts*, 404–6.

[9] The custom of the Second Temple period appears to be that Torah scrolls and other sacred scriptures were kept in niches that may have been covered with a drape. Such niches can be seen in the remains at Gamla, Masada, Jericho and (perhaps) Delos. In the Ostia synagogue, the late-second century addition of an ark, followed by its replacement with a monumental aedicula in the fourth century, presents graphically the rising reverence exhibited toward the Torah within Jewish sacred space. See Binder, *Temple Courts*, 162–79 (Gamla and Masada), 297–317 (Delos), 322–36 (Ostia); Netzer, "Synagogue from the Hasmonean Period" (Jericho).

evidence. Still, Runesson, like Strange, singles out Torah reading as the distinctive and central function of the oldest synagogues, at least in Palestine. This allows him to trace back the earliest references to public Torah reading to the fifth century, when the post-exilic priestly leadership sought to enforce a degree of religious uniformity and social cohesion on the returning exiles.

He sees this tight control as being relaxed during the relatively more prosperous times of the early Hellenistic period, a time when the homeland also saw the introduction of the Diaspora-style synagogues, which were not subject to this degree of central control. Their appearance also perhaps inspired the evolution of the "semi-public" synagogues in Palestine, that is, sectarian congregations which parted company radically with the central authorities in Jerusalem.

It is difficult for me to criticize Runesson's reconstruction very forcefully, since I have myself argued along these same lines, though certainly not with as much detail nor with as many fine-points.[10]

I will take issue, however, with his view that a loosening of central authority resulted from the prosperity and political stability of Palestine during the third century B.C.E. This is simply contradicted by what we know about that century, namely, that it saw Palestine ravaged by five wars fought largely on its soil between the competing Ptolemaic and Seleucid dynasties. The following century was even more chaotic, being fraught with high-priestly succession battles and guerilla warfare brought on by the repressive measures of Antiochus Epiphanes. Consequently, it is more likely that any decentralization in the early Hellenistic period resulted not from the self-confident stability of the Jerusalem authorities, but rather from their disintegration.[11]

---

[10] See Binder, *Temple Courts*, 204–26, 482–4.

[11] While historical sources for third-century Palestine are admittedly sparse, the ongoing conflicts between the Seleucid and Ptolemaic monarchies during this period almost certainly made life in Palestine far from prosperous for Jews other than wealthy tax farmers such as Tobias, whose example obviously cannot be generalized to the larger population. In addition, Josephus alludes to the rising power of the Samaritans during this century, noting how they aggressively seized Jewish lands and took many Jews as slaves (*A.J.* 12.6.1). Unless one dismisses this passage as pure anti-Samaritan polemic—a view that hardly seems warranted from the matter-of-fact tone of the segment—then the Jewish-Samaritan turmoil mentioned highlights even further the tensions within Palestine in the third century. Generally on this period, see Gafni, "Historical Background," 1–16.

Drawing off my earlier comments on Strange's essay, I would also want to add that the early Hellenistic period contributed significant architectural innovations relevant to our discussion, such as the introduction of colonnades to the temple courts and the movement of local public assemblies from the city gates to open city squares and finally into specialized synagogue buildings.[12]

Lastly, I would want to observe that at least some of the sectarian groups that Runesson classifies as maintaining semi-public synagogues, while in reality being local and non-official, nevertheless envisioned themselves as eventually supplanting the existing order and becoming supra-local and official. Thus we have the Essenes' manifesto of revolution in the *Temple* and *War Scrolls* and their early delineation of sacred space at Qumran. Likewise, Christian assemblies quickly moved out of private homes and into sacred, synagogue-like basilicas following the Edict of Milan. Sectarian synagogues therefore frequently appear to have internal ambitions for authority that external circumstances have sublimated, forcing them to take temporary, survival measures, more as a matter of expediency than of preference.[13]

The last paper, that of Peter Richardson, returns to the architectural emphasis of the first, but in this case, the discussion stresses not the Palestinian evidence, but that of the Diaspora. This arises from Richardson's belief that synagogues originated outside of Palestine, a case he makes through his table comparing the evidence from the two areas.[14]

---

[12] Thus my view for the development of the Palestinian synagogues maintains *not* that they sprang directly from the temple courts; rather my position essentially integrates Levine's theories on the synagogues' city gate origins with Strange's insights about the architectural influence of the temple courts on the earliest Palestinian buildings, adding the potentially intermediate stage of the city squares as places of assembly (see Binder, *Temple Courts*, 204–26). For an accurate reading of my position, see Runesson, *Origins*, 94–7, 163–8. For Levine and Strange's views, see Levine, "Nature and Origins"; Strange, "First Century Galilee,"; "Ancient Texts."

[13] See Binder, *Temple Courts*, 451–68, 498–500.

[14] Because the sections in Richardson's essay dealing specifically with Ostia, Delos, Priene and Judea were not included in the paper presented at the conference, but added later, they are not addressed in the text of my response, which preserves my original remarks given at Lund. While the additions significantly increase the substance of Richardson's initial discourse, they do not, I believe, blunt the force of my original criticism, since the added material covers sites we both have largely treated elsewhere. Moreover, the revisions do not grapple at all with the

Yet because the Diaspora encompassed territories vastly greater than the land of Palestine, the arguments he makes through this table are more convincing when they focus on the difference in the quality of the data, rather than that of their quantity. Specifically, the early Egyptian evidence is particularly compelling in making the case that the first synagogue *buildings* were constructed in the Diaspora.[15]

Here, the architectural aspect of the synagogue seems paramount to Richardson, leading me to suspect that he would place little stock in Runesson's use of fifth-century literary allusions to national and local

---

fundamental question of the sacrality of the early synagogues, nor with their potential relationships with the temples at Jerusalem or Gerizim. For my treatment of three of the four added topics, see Binder, *Temple Courts*, 322–36 (Ostia), 297–317 (Delos), and 155–226 (Judea). Since the Priene synagogue probably dates to III-IV C.E., I would disagree with Richardson's grouping of it with the earliest phases of the synagogues at Ostia (I C.E.) and Delos (II-I B.C.E.), as the former comes from a later era, one post-dating the destruction of the Jerusalem temple and one in which Christian innovations may have exerted an architectural influence.

[15] A few comments on the contents of Table 5.1 in Richardson's essay. For Palestine, I have elsewhere argued that the structure at Migdal was a spring house in all phases (*Temple Courts*, 193–6). Also, given the lack of consensus regarding the identification of the structures at Modi'in, Kiryat Sefer, Jericho and Horvat 'Ethri, these should probably also be moved to the "Uncertain" category (as should the "Gamla II" reference), pending further investigation and argumentation. The claim by Alexander Onn of a synagogue in Shuafat could also be added there (see ibid., 196–7). For the Diaspora, the structure listed as being from the Fayum is mentioned not in an inscription, but a papyrus fragment (*CPJ* 1.129) originating from the village of Alexandou-Nesos in that district. Similarly, unless the reference is to a separate structure, the synagogue at Arsinoë-Crocodilopolis is attested by not only an inscription, but also a papyrus reference (*CPJ* 1.134). In addition to the inscriptions at Berenice, both literary and epigraphic evidence attest the presence of a synagogue in Cyrene in the first century B.C.E. (ibid., 256–7). On the other hand, I am not aware of any published inscriptions referencing a first-century synagogue in Chersonesus (for a recent review, see Edwards, "Jews and Christians at Ancient Chersonesus"). Finally, all of the inscriptions mentioned in the table as originating from Rome date later than indicated, namely, from II–IV CE (See Noy, *Jewish Inscriptions of Western Europe* [*JIWE*], vol. 2, nos. 96, 169, 189, 194, 542, 547 [Augustesians], 130, 170, 549, 562 [Agrippesians], 100, 163, 167, 577 [Volumnians], 2, 33, 578, 579 [Hebrews], 292 [Herodians], 288, 560, 577 [Campesians]). Currently, only one inscription from Rome dates to I C.E. (*JIWE* 2.602, using the term *proseucha*). Mention could also be made of the literary evidence for synagogues in Rome in the first century CE (Philo, *Legat*. 155–7; Josephus, *A.J.* 14.213–16). For more detailed discussions of the various attestations, see Binder, *Temple Courts*, 91–341; Levine, *Ancient Synagogue*, 42–123.

assemblies to argue for a Palestinian origin of the synagogues, just as he does not find compelling Lee Levine's similar conclusions, which draw not only on these same allusions, but also on archaeological analyses of the ancient city gates. If so, one must here question his willingness to accept readily the idea that the earliest Diaspora synagogues evolved out of meetings in private homes when there is absolutely no direct evidence to that effect during the Second Temple period, while at the same time being reluctant to admit literary evidence that clearly attests early national and local assemblies in Palestine.[16]

Yet if this double standard is dropped and the Palestinian literary evidence taken more seriously, it suggests not a linear movement of the synagogues from the Diaspora into Palestine, as Richardson seems to propose, but two independent trajectories that intersect at various points in time and space.

One of those intersections appears to be architectural form. And here I was glad to see the agreement between Strange and Richardson that the classic architectural form of the synagogue, at least in its latest stage of evolution, was the basilica. What I missed in Richardson's presentation, and would hope to hear in our subsequent discussion period, is his view of Strange's now well-known position linking synagogue architecture to that of the temple courts.[17]

I would appreciate this discussion not only from an architectural standpoint, but also from a socio-religious one. I say this because Richardson was quite clear about his rejection of any link between the synagogues and the temple, a position I myself have championed. This has truly puzzled me, for in print I have essentially agreed with his view that Diaspora synagogues constituted *collegia*. To be sure, I have haggled with him over legal definitions; but more or less I have come down with him on the same side.[18]

Yet in his paper he did not pick up the gauntlet I threw down for him in those same writings: namely, to take his comparison between the synagogues and the *collegia* to its logical conclusion by admitting that

---

[16] For an examination of the difficulties inherent in recent claims regarding the possible origins of the synagogues in private houses, see Binder, *Temple Courts*, 200–4, 228–9, 297–317, 322–41.

[17] Strange's view has previously been presented in Strange, "First Century Galilee"; idem, "Ancient Texts." It has also been drawn upon in Binder, *Temple Courts*, 222–6.

[18] See ibid., 35–7, 229–33.

the sacred, cultic nature of the latter is also characteristic of the former. Here again, I detect a double standard. For while I doubt that Richardson would object to the view that an Ephesian *collegium* in Syria would have some cultic connection with and loyalty to the temple of Artemis in the mother city, he appears reluctant to consider such a connection between Jewish *collegia* and the temple of their homeland.[19] Likewise, while he would probably admit to the sacred, cultic character of pagan *collegia*, he is silent on this aspect of the synagogue, despite clear architectural markers to this effect, such as the presence of nearby *mikvaoth* or their frequent placement near bodies of water.[20] I therefore

---

[19] Elsewhere, for instance, when citing examples of pagan *collegia* (*scholae*), Richardson refers to Mithraea and to the Athenian Bakcheion with its "decorated altar built for the worship of Dionysus" ("Early Synagogues," 97). Conversely, synagogues are characterized as "unsophisticated" liturgically with "no feature . . . modeled on the Jerusalem temple, its character, divisions, or motifs" (ibid., 103). Likewise, Richardson concludes that the arrangement of the benches within the early synagogues evince a social entity that was totally unlike that of the temple hierarchy: one that was "democratic" and analogous to "the 'puritan' and left-wing streams of reformed Christianity" (ibid., 102), an analysis that overlooks the *thronos* of the Delos synagogue, the separated single benches in the synagogues at Gamla and Masada, and the numerous literary and epigraphic references to various synagogue offices (see Binder, *Temple Courts*, 343–71). Along similar lines, it is interesting to note that the Samaritan synagogue inscriptions from Delos make explicit mention of the connection to the cultic site on Mount Gerizim, referring to the dedicators as "the Israelites on Delos who make first-fruit offerings to the temple on Mt. Gerizim." The Samaritans apparently did this to distinguish themselves from the Jews on the island, whose synagogue presumably held similar connections with its central cultic site in Jerusalem, as literary evidence indicates was true for synagogues throughout the Diaspora. See ibid., 471–4.

[20] *Mikvaoth* are associated with the synagogues at Gamla, Herodium, Masada, Jerusalem (*CIJ* 2.1404, l. 7), Qumran and (if it is accepted as a synagogue) Jericho. The synagogues at Capernaum, Arsinoë-Crocodilopolis (*CPJ* 1.134), Philippi (Acts 16:13), Delos, and Ostia were built near bodies of water (the latter two also had water basins outside their entrances, while the Gamla synagogue had one near an upper bench). With respect to these, archaeologist Renfrew mentions the following criterion among his archaeological indicators of ritual: "Concepts of cleanliness and pollution may be reflected in the facilities (e.g., pools or basins of water) and maintenance of the sacred area" ("Archaeology of Religion," 51). Another archaeological marker indicating the sacrality of the synagogues can be found in the Egyptian inscriptions which dedicate either the entire building or portions thereof to the Jewish Deity. Of these, Fraser writes, "in most instances the [Jewish] dedication is indistinguishable from a pagan equivalent save for the substitution of the term 'synagogue' for 'the shrine' or 'the temple' and by the name of the

would be interested in hearing his explanation of why he allows for so many other apt comparisons between the synagogues and the *collegia*, but seems to disallow these.

This leads me to conclude my response by playing the promised role of the *provocateur* and suggesting that the resistance to a temple-synagogue connection that I have seen in some of my colleagues may be indicative of a confessionally linked anti-temple bias. That is to say, many of us here directly or indirectly derive personal meaning from the teachings that have emanated from the synagogue. With this at stake, there may be at work an unconscious tendency to insulate this institution from one whose emphasis on animal sacrifice seems barbaric, whose patriarchal and hereditary leadership style appears chauvinistic, and whose ethnic and gender gradations strike us as unenlightened. Yet if these inner prescriptive sentiments lead us to overlook or dismiss evidence that is vital for fulfilling our descriptive task, then we do our profession a disservice.

It is my hope that, while acknowledging that the topic of this conference may hold deep, personal meaning for many of us, we can nevertheless enter the field of evidence with all the dispassion of an ancient historian approaching a now-defunct pagan religion—one with little connection to his or her current belief system.

If we can do this, we may in the process unearth something quite foreign from our present experiences. Still, through exercise of this

---

dedicating party" (*Ptolemaic Alexandria*, 1.283). Indeed, one of these inscriptions (*JIGRE* 9 = *CIJ* 2.1433) refers to the synagogue as being encompassed by a sacred precinct (*hieros peribolos*; cf. Philo, *Flacc.* 48). In a similar vein, votive dedications were found in the synagogue at Delos, while the manumission inscriptions from the Bosporus synagogues indicate that release rituals took place there—ceremonies that otherwise were conducted in pagan temples. Cultic meals are attested for the early synagogues in the literary evidence (e.g., Josephus, *A.J.* 14.213–16), a function indicated in the communal dining facilities in the synagogues at Ostia (phase 1), Qumran, Jericho (if accepted) and the Theodotus synagogue in Jerusalem (*CIJ* 2.1404, ll. 6–7). Finally, even the subtle combination of the palm branch and rosette found in the lintel of the Gamla synagogue finds parallels among the remains of Herod's temple, which otherwise contained no overt religious imagery (for photographs of these images from the Temple Mount excavations, see Mazar, "Archaeological Excavations," 28–9; Ben-Dov, *Shadow*, 138–9; for literary attestations of these motifs in the temple, see both the MT and LXX of 1 Kgs 6:29, 32, 25; Ezek 40:16, 22, 26, 31, 34; 41:18, 19, 20, 25, 26). Thus, even holding strictly to Richardson's approach of examining only architectural markers, the sacrality of these buildings is strongly suggested.

discipline, we may be surprised to discover something quite new, not only about our ancestors, but also about ourselves.

Bibliography

Ben-Dov, M., *In the Shadow of the Temple.* New York: Harper and Row, 1985.

Binder, D. D., *Into the Temple Courts: The Place of the Synagogues in the Second Temple Period.* Atlanta: Society of Biblical Literature, 1999.

—, "Second Temple Synagogues." Online: http://faculty.smu.edu/dbinder.

Chiat, M. J., "First-Century Synagogue Architecture: Methodological Problems." Pages 49–60 in *Ancient Synagogues: The State of Research.* Edited by J. Gutmann. Chico, California: Scholars Press, 1981.

Coulton, J. J., *The Architectural Development of the Greek Stoa.* Oxford: Clarendon Press, 1976.

Edwards, D. R., "Jews and Christians at Ancient Chersonesus." Pages 158–73 in *Evolution of the Synagogue: Problems and Progress.* Edited by H. C. Kee and L. H. Cohick. Harrisburg: Trinity Press, 1999.

Fine, S., *This Holy Place. On the Sanctity of the Synagogue during the Greco-Roman Period.* Edited by G. E. Sterling. Notre Dame, Indiana: University of Notre Dame Press, 1998.

Fine, S. and E. M. Meyers., "Synagogues." Pages 118–23 in *The Oxford Encyclopedia of Archaeology in the Near East* Vol. 5. Edited by E. M. Meyers. Oxford: Oxford University Press, 1996.

Fleisher, E., "On the Beginnings of Obligatory Jewish Prayer." *Tarviz* 59 (1990): 397–441. Hebrew.

Foerster, G., "The Synagogues at Masada and Herodion." *Journal of Jewish Art* 3–4 (1977): 6–11.

—, "Architectural Models of the Greco-Roman Period and the Origin of The 'Galilean' Synagogue." Pages 45–8 in *Ancient Synagogues Revealed.* Edited by L. I. Levine. Jerusalem: Israel Exploration Society, 1982.

—, "The Synagogues at Masada and Herodium." Pages 24–9 in *Ancient Synagogues Revealed.* Edited by L. I. Levine. Jerusalem: Israel Exploration Society, 1982.

Fraser, P. M., *Ptolemaic Alexandria.* 3 vols. Oxford: Clarendon Press, 1972.

Frey, J-B., *Corpus inscriptionum judaicarum.* 2 vols. Rome: Poniticio Instituto di Archeologia Christiana, 1936–52.

Gafni, I., "The Historical Background." Pages 1–31 in *Jewish Writings of the Second Temple Period.* Edited by M. E. Stone. Philadelphia: Fortress Press, 1984.

Horbury, W. and D. Noy., *Jewish Inscriptions of Graeco-Roman Egypt: With an Index of the Jewish Inscriptions of Egypt and Cyrenaica.* Cambridge: Cambridge University Press, 1992.

Horst, P. W. van der, "Was the Synagogue a Place of Sabbath Worship Before 70 CE?" Pages 18–43 in *Jews, Christians, and Polytheists in the Ancient Syngogue: Cultural Interaction during the Greco-Roman Period.* Edited by S. Fine. London: Routledge, 1999.

Levine, L. I., "The Second Temple Synagogue: The Formative Years." Pages 7–31 in *The Synagogue in Late Antiquity.* Edited by L. I. Levine. Philadelphia: American Schools of Oriental Research, 1987.

—, "Synagogues." Pages 1421–4 in *The New Encyclopedia of Archaeological Excavations in the Holy Land.* Vol. 4. Edited by E. Stern. Jerusalem: Israel Exploration Society & Carta; New York: Simon and Schuster, 1993.

—, "The Nature and Origin of the Palestinian Synagogue Reconsidered." *JBL* 115 (1996): 425–48.

—, *The Ancient Synagogue: The First Thousand Years.* New Haven: Yale University Press, 2000.

—, "The First-Century Synagogue: New Perspectives." *STK* 77 (2001): 22–30.

Ma'oz, Z., "The Synagogue of Gamla and the Typology of Second-Temple Synagogues." Pages 35–41 in *Ancient Synagogues Revealed.* Edited by L. I. Levine. Jerusalem: Israel Exploration Society, 1982

Mazar, B., "The Archaeological Excavations near the Temple Mount." Pages 25–51 in *Jerusalem Revealed: Archaeology in the Holy City, 1968–1974*. Edited by Yigael Yadin. Jerusalem: Israel Exploration Society, 1975.

McKay, H. A., "New Moon or Sabbath?" Pages 12–27 in *The Sabbath in Jewish and Christian Traditions*. Edited by T. C. Eskenazi, D. J. Harrington and W. H. Shea. New York: Crossroads, 1991.

—, *Sabbath and Synagogue: The Question of Sabbath Worship in Ancient Judaism*. Religions in the Graeco-Roman World, vol. 122. Leiden; New York: Brill, 1994.

Netzer, E., "A Synagogue from the Hasmonean Period Recently Exposed in the Western Plain of Jericho." *IEJ* 49 (1999): 203–21.

Noy, D., *Jewish Inscriptions of Western Europe*. 2 vols. Cambridge; New York: Cambridge University Press, 1993–95.

Ovadiah, A., and T. Michaeli. "Observations on the Origin of the Architectural Plan of Ancient Synagogues." *JJS* 38 (1987): 234–41.

Owens, E. J. *The City in the Greek and Roman World*. London: Routledge, 1991.

Renfrew, C., "The Archaeology of Religion." Pages 47–54 in *The Ancient Mind: Elements of Cognitive Archaeology*. Edited by C. Renfrew and E. B. W. Zubrow. Cambridge: Cambridge University Press, 1994.

Richardson, P., "Law and Piety in Herod's Architecture." *SR* 15, no. 3 (1986): 347–60.

—, "Early Synagogues as Collegia in the Diaspora and Palestine." Pages 90–109 in *Voluntary Associations*. Edited by J. S. Kloppenborg and S. G. Wilson. London: Routledge, 1996.

Robertson, D.S., *Greek and Roman Architecture*. 2nd ed. Cambridge: Cambridge University Press, 1969.

Runesson, A., *The Origins of the Synagogue: A Socio–Historical Study*. Stockholm: Almqvist & Wiksell, 2001.

Strange, J. F., "First Century Galilee from Archaeology and from the Texts." Pages 39–48 in *Archaeology and the Galilee: Texts and Contexts in Graeco-Roman and Byzantine Periods*. Edited by D. R. Edwards and C. T. McCollough. Atlanta: Scholars Press, 1997.

—, "Ancient Texts, Archaeology as Text, and the Problem of the First-Century Synagogue." Pages 27–45 in *Evolution of the Synagogue: Problems and Progress*. Edited by H. C. Kee and L. H. Cohick. Harrisburg: Trinity Press International, 1999.

Tcherikover, V. A., and A. Fuks, eds. *Corpus Papyrorum Judaicarum*. 3 vols. Cambridge: Harvard University Press, 1957–64.

7
The Origins of the Synagogue: An Evaluation

Birger Olsson

IN HIS EVALUATION D. D. BINDER has shortly characterized the three contributions and added more information on some points and criticized others from the perspectives of his own work on the ancient synagogue. The relations between the temple courts in Jerusalem and the synagogues have been strengthened and an inclusion of both Palestine and the Diaspora in an analysis of the origin of the synagogue has been required. The different opinions may be a good example of the remark of L. I. Levine in his opening paper that two interrelated factors often play a decisive role in synagogue research: what types of evidence we choose to emphasize and what components of the synagogue we wish to highlight.

As a background of my short comments I want to summarize some of the results of our project.[1] The unique character of the project is, as I see it, its limitation in time up to 200 C.E. and its emphasis on a broad analysis of the ancient synagogue (five research areas) and on the importance of definitions and theories. The main results are the following ones:

1. A critical analysis of all relevant sources and a conscious use of theories and models demonstrate that there were many synagogues in the ancient world at the beginning of our era. The attempts in the 90s, especially by some American scholars, to date the synagogue as institution and building in Palestine to ca. 200

---

[1] Three monographs from the project have not yet been published: a dissertation about Shavuot and a source-book and a bibliography about the ancient synagogue up to 200 C. E.

C.E. and find early synagogues only in the Diaspora have not been proven to lead to any valid results.

2. The material and the research about the ancient synagogue seem to require a broad and dynamic definition of "synagogue" including four basic dimensions: the synagogue as an institution, the synagogue as a liturgical activity, the synagogue as a non-liturgical activity and the synagogue as a place/building where these activities take place.[2] All four dimensions must be included in investigations of the origins and developments of the synagogue. The history of the synagogue research very clearly shows that definitions strongly influence our way of describing the ancient synagogue.

3. There are different types of synagogues in the "early" antiquity, communal synagogues, association synagogues and temple synagogues. In Judah and Galilee there were public gatherings at the city gate, in the city square or in special buildings characterized by both non-liturgical and liturgical activities, especially by the reading and teaching of the Torah (the synagogue in Gamla as a good example). There were also semi-public gatherings of certain groups, formally similar to the Graeco-Roman associations (Theodotos' synagogue in Jerusalem as a good example). And in Egypt B.C.E. we find developments from local temples to synagogues which the non-Jewish environment regarded as temples or associations.

4. Every type of synagogue has its own history. The communal synagogue in Palestine has its roots in the Persian time when the Persian occupation strategy required that the ingenious laws should be read and taught to the people in the colonies, also in the province of Yehud. In Hellenistic time it became legally possible to found associations. Political instability, Hellenization, individualization and canonization of the Holy Scriptures resulted in different religious groups who had their own gatherings in semi-public synagogues. Synagogues in Egypt had their roots in local Jewish temples. In all these cases we find a clear influence from outside: political strategies of the Persian empire, Hellenistic modes of life, Greco-Roman temples and the *collegia* institutions

---

[2] See the discussion in Runesson, *Origins,* 29–37, and his survey of the research on the origin of the synagogue, 67–168.

in the Antiquity. This way of describing the origins of the ancient synagogue combine several competing theories of synagogue research today and see them as parts of a long history of different types of synagogues.

5. All published material and little more about the synagogue at the ancient Ostia has once again been thoroughly analysed and seen in a wider context. The opinion of the excavator that the first-century building is a synagogue from the very beginning is verified. A common American hypothesis that the synagogues begun as prayer meetings in homes and later on in rebuilt private houses cannot get any support from Ostia (or Delos). The two Diaspora synagogues from the time period of the project that have been excavated show many similarities with the *collegia* houses of their times.

6. The reading and teaching of the Torah stands out as the most unique and most continuous activity of the ancient synagogue. These books were translated into Greek in Egypt in the second century B.C.E. An investigation of some qualities in this translation (word order, use of participles, use of conjunctives etc.) compared with Jewish and Christian writings demonstrates a special variety of Greek for such forms and contents we have in the Torah. From this I draw the conclusion that the Septuagint had a strong position in the Jewish Diaspora—and a position even in Palestine—and was read and taught in the Diaspora synagogues during a long time.

7. If the public or semi-public reading and teaching of the Torah was the central activity of the early synagogues, what conclusions could we draw from that with regard to the study of the targums? The text read in Palestine synagogue had to be translated from Hebrew to Aramaic for many centuries before 200 C.E. So the production of targums are early, even if the final versions are late. The results of the project support an earlier date for the production of the targums. The targums ought to say a lot of the hermeneutic principles that characterized even the earlier synagogues. The early translations of the Hebrew text into Greek and Aramaic are, therefore, important sources for studying both Judaism and Christianity.

8. In general the studies within the project have revealed a very strong social complexity and a manifold of activities within the ancient synagogues which cry for new investigations of different kinds. Later formative periods of Judaism and Christianity seem to have simplified the history of the first two centuries of our era.

9. The different types of synagogues have a important role in the development of Judaism and Christianity as two world religions. There is a hypothesis by M. Zetterholm that the separation into two competing groups is an "inner-Christian" process in a synagogue context, a process among Jesus-believing Jews and Jesus-believing non-Jews. According another hypothesis by A. Runesson world-wide Judaism and Christianity have their roots in Pharisaic and Christian association synagogues in the second and third centuries. The problems related to "the parting of the way" have partly got a continuation in a new project called "Christian identity—the first hundred years", led by B. Holmberg and sponsored by the Bank of Sweden Tercentenary Foundation.

10. The project is methodologically characterized by common critical analysis of the limited material we have and by a use of modern theories and models, a combination that is not so dominating in synagogue research. The sociological approaches are most prominent with their theories and models from social science and a socio-linguistic theory for language studies. A narratological analysis of Targum texts verified and deepened results that had been reached by common historical, philological methods.

This combination of several methods, the broad approach to the ancient synagogue as such, new definitions, new insights, new combinations of older results and new questions have partly confused the present synagogue research. With regard to the question of this section, the origins of the synagogue, I want to add the following:

We are all waiting for new material and new funds. Since 1997, when the project started, new buildings in Kiryat Sefer, Jericho and other places have been excavated and been presented as synagogues. If we now "expect to find more examples of simple halls with nested walls, benches, aisles, columns, and central space"[3] we may find some of them. We see more, if we know what we are looking for. The communal

---

[3] Strange, "Archeology and Ancient Synagogues," 58.

synagogue in Judah and Galilee was the main public building of the town or village and often the largest building too.

The discussion of definitions and methods must continue. The material is so meagre that we cannot reduce our analysis to what the sources are explicitly saying. As Runesson I think we cannot limit ourselves mainly to one dimension of the ancient synagogue, the architectural one, as P. Richardson and even Strange do. Runesson is also using both sources and different models for his historical reconstruction, more in his dissertation than in the conference paper. I am not sure, as Richardson, that "we must still begin with the evidence—archaeological, epigraphic and literary—not with hypothetical or theoretical constructs."[4] The important thing is not where we begin but how we combine source analysis and models/theories. All use of sources is connected to theoretical premises or general models of different kind. There has during the last decade been a clear tendency to concentrate the analysis to what the sources are explicitly saying.[5] This is important in the present situation, but the methods must be broadened to include a conscious use of sociological, political, psychological, ritual and other models/theories. In such a perspective I would once again examine the complicated use of Biblical sources in Runesson's reconstruction of the development up to the first century B.C.E.

The origin of the synagogue is a long and complicated history. We have to use the plural form, the origins, and not the singular one, the origin. Richardson, who most clearly suggest one origin of the synagogue in the Diaspora, opens at the end of his paper for "a more complex process of development". The material we have clearly speak for such a complexity and cannot be put together in one linear development. The papers of this section invite us to investigate more thoroughly what kind of influences there are between the development of different types of synagogues, especially between developments in Palestine and the Diaspora.

The role of Greco-Roman *collegia* in the history of the synagogue is very much emphasized by Richardson: Synagogues originated in the Diaspora and within the context of associations. But could we say that the association of the antiquity is the *origin* of the synagogue? The soci-

---

[4] Richardson, "Architectural Case," 113.
[5] See the thoroughly analyses by Binder, *Temple Courts,* and Claussen, *Versamlung,* and also such a excellent presentation of the sources as Barclay, *Jews.*

ety provided, as I see it, the association as a legal and institutional form for different kinds of synagogues, and in this way the associations very much influenced the ancient synagogue in the Diaspora and also in Palestine with regard to architecture, legal status and activities. If the synagogue has old roots in Judah and Galilee, the reading and teaching of the Torah is of importance also for the development of synagogues in the Diaspora. In Egypt local temples seem to have developed into synagogues, in other places, as in Delos, Jewish associations were rebuilt in order to function as meeting room for reading and teaching the Torah.

The near relation between the Jerusalem temple and the early synagogues is central for both Strange and Binder. But I have a similar question here: Is the temple in Jerusalem the *origin* of the synagogue? Were activities and architecture of the Jerusalem temple courts moved to other places where Jews wanted to come together? Or are there only some parallels between the temple courts and early synagogues? Runesson argues that the architectural design of first-century synagogues in Palestine, so beautifully described by Strange, can be explained by their function as public buildings.[6] Even if I agree with Runesson in his view of different developments of different types of synagogues I can see influences from the temple courts in early synagogues. Both the function as public buildings and similarities to the Jerusalem temple have formed ancient synagogues.

The time limitation of the project has been discussed a lot. Strange and Richardson look for evidence before about 100 C.E. What about the second century in the history of the ancient synagogue? The year 70 C.E. is often taken as a *terminus ad quem* in synagogue research. Our pragmatic choice of 200 C.E. gives a somewhat different historical perspective and a clear limitation of the primary source material for the project. The destruction of the temple seems not to be so important for the history of ancient synagogue as almost everybody suppose. What happened during the second century? We find no good answers in the papers of this conference, nor in our project. Maybe, the most important result of the Lund synagogue project is new investigations, including a thoroughly analysis of the second century.

---

[6] Runesson, *Origins,* 363.

Bibliography

Barclay, J. M. G., *Jews in the Mediterranean Diaspora: From Alexander to Trajan (323 BCE – 117 CE)*. Edinburgh: T & T Clark, 1996.

Binder, D. D., *Into the Temple Courts: The Place of the Synagogues in the Second Temple Period*. Atlanta: Scolars Press, 1999.

Claussen, C., *Versammlung, Gemeinde, Synagoge: Das hellenistisch-jüdische Umfeld der frühchristlichen Gemeinden*. Göttingen: Vandenhoeck & Ruprecht, 2002.

Strange, J. F., "Archaeology and Ancient Synagogues up to about 200 C.E." In this volume.

Richardson, P., "An Architectural Case for Synagogues as Associations." In this volume.

Runesson, A., *The Origins of the Synagogue: A Socio-Historical Study*. Stockholm: Almqvist & Wiksell, 2001.

Part II

The Life in the Diaspora Synagogues

8
The Life in the Diaspora Synagogue: An Introduction

Bengt Holmberg

A MOMENT'S REFLECTION WILL MAKE one realize that "the Diaspora Synagogue" is a designation for several different realities. The term could refer to a certain type of building, or to assemblies of small and large Jewish groups in- and outside such buildings, or, as it frequently does, to all Jews living outside the Holy Land in ancient times. A heading like the one above might then be taken to signify an intent to describe the life of several million people living around the Mediterranean and in the Near East—a project so vast that it obviously is intractable.

Actually, the conference that resulted in this book had a more modest aim. In this section, the contributors should discuss neither the archaeology, the art, the worship, the language, nor the kind of teaching and exposition of scripture that could be found in Diaspora Jewish assemblies and their buildings. They should rather try to grapple with one or more aspects of the social reality of the congregations that built and used synagogues in the Diaspora. These often functioned as ethnic minority milieus, interacting in interesting ways with the larger society of which they were part.

In the research project that culminated in the October 2001 Conference, this section of work aimed at investigating and understanding the data about the ancient Diaspora synagogue communities especially from a *sociological* point of view. The synagogue (community) in a sociological perspective could be described as a social, economic, pedagogic, religious, cultural, and political institution. A very large number of questions could be asked about this institution, such as: "What do we know about the people who in different ways made up the synagogue's social network? Is there a relation between Jewish demography and the existence of synagogues, or are more factors than the size of the local Jewish population involved? How were Jewish groups in the Diaspora related to the surrounding society during the period we are considering? What did their internal relations and organization look like, and how did that change over time? Which types of synagogal activities answered the individual and collective needs of Jews living in a non-Jewish majority culture? What were the mechanisms of religious and cultural socialization that took place in synagogues?" The limitations of our research did not lie in the questions that could be asked but in the scarcity of materials preserved from that period in history, and in the need to select among researchable materials and questions.

As indicated by the title of the project behind the conference (and this book), "The Ancient Synagogue: Birthplace of Two World Religions", the project participants wanted to focus especially on the internal relations within Jewish congregations that were affected by the new messianic ("Christian")[1] preaching coming from Jerusalem, resulting in internal conflict and eventually in the splitting of these communities. The pattern of association and competitive conflict that marks the relation between Christian and non-Christian Jewish groups in the Diaspora is of special importance in a project that wants to investigate the common root of what later became two separate religions. Not unreasonably, Magnus Zetterholm (who published a doctoral dissertation as part of the project) analyzed especially the social mechanisms that effected a separation between the two originally intra-Jewish groups in a specific Diaspora location, namely, Syrian Antioch. A part of this analysis is found in his contribution to this volume.

This essay is flanked by two essays, which focus more on matters of definition in relation to historical realities. Carsten Claussen gives an overview of the state of synagogue research that brings in a number of historical facts into the picture, such as the terminology used for this institution, its probable origin, its legal situation in the Roman Empire and how it was organized. Judith Lieu gives a trenchant analysis of how the term "synagogue" has been (mis)used in much historical research as some kind of parallel entity to "church", and shows very clearly that the

---

[1] "Christian" designates a Jewish or non-Jewish person or group who believes that Jesus of Nazareth was God's Messiah to Israel, cf. Acts 11:26.

relation between early Christians and Jewish communities was never a clean and total break, nor even a uniformly increasing separation.

9
Meeting, Community, Synagogue—Different Frameworks of Ancient Jewish Congregations in the Diaspora

Carsten Claussen

JUDAISM IN THE DIASPORA is by no means something marginal in the study of ancient Judaism. During the first century C.E. there were about five to six million Jews living in the Diaspora compared to perhaps between 2,5 and 2,8 million in Palestine before 70 C.E.[1] For many generations of Jews the land they inhabited in the Diaspora had been "accounted by them to be their fatherland in which they were born and reared" as Philo says.[2] If one wants to describe any kind of Jewish life in the Diaspora—religious and social—there could hardly be a better topic than to look at what eventually became known as "the synagogue."[3]

We shall start our study with searching for a working definition. What are we talking about when using terms like Jewish meeting, community, or synagogue? Then we shall go back to the very beginning of the phenomenon: when and where did synagogues first arise? Trying to find our way through this history, we shall look for the names that were given to synagogues. Some of these names will lead us to the functions of these places. Among the exterior conditions, which allow Jewish communities to organize their own business is the matter of a legal

---

[1] For an overview and a discussion of the numbers cf. Noethlichs, *Judentum*, 10. See also Barclay, *Jews,* for a study of the ancient Jewish Diaspora.
[2] Philo, *Flacc.* 47.
[3] A more detailed treatment of the topic can be found in my doctoral dissertation, see Claussen, *Versammlung*.

framework that might encourage or hinder day-to-day activities. When and where were Jews allowed to meet in order to look after their own communal and religious affairs? The archaeological findings will point us to the question of what synagogue buildings looked like. Considering synagogues as communities of people, we shall then address the question of how they were organized. What role did women play in these settings? Finally, we shall try to answer the question of what held together the Jewish Diaspora synagogues.

Searching for a Definition

Sometimes talking about ancient *synagogues* is blurred by anachronistic concepts of what a synagogue might have been. Far too quickly many commentators and scholars assume they know exactly what it looked like when Jesus, Peter or Paul walked into a synagogue in Nazareth, Capernaum or Philippi, perhaps with the pictures of the white synagogue in Capernaum in mind. However, as we all know, this is a fourth- to fifth-century C.E. synagogue. While some scholars nevertheless believe that the white synagogue in Capernaum may tell us something about Jewish life in the first century C.E., in many ways our knowledge may be better symbolized by the blackness of the basalt stone underneath the building's limestone walls.[4]

In choosing the title for this study I wanted us not to narrow down too quickly what we are looking for and not to pretend knowing all the answers before we start.

So, what we are looking for is a place of religious meetings and deliberations, as well as one, which provides for other communal needs of a Jewish community up to the time of 200 C.E. If we look at the embryonic stages of the synagogue, we must take into account that "early formative stages simply were not worthy of comment at the time."[5] Therefore we have to be prepared to read between the lines of ancient sources and look for evidence for plausible reconstructions. Not much more can be expected from a time from which we have inherited so lit-

---

[4] Cf. Hüttenmeister, *Synagogen*, 260–70; Charlesworth, *Millenium Guide*, 70–4 (with a photo of the synagogue); Claussen, *Versammlung*, 180f.
[5] Levine, *Synagogue*, 19.

tle evidence. Thus how far do we get asking for the earliest evidence of what later was called a synagogue?

The Origins of the Synagogue

Despite the numerous archaeological findings and the many literary sources that talk of synagogues we still do not know where the institution came from.[6] However, this lack of a clear understanding shall not prevent us from looking for historically plausible theories. Thus we shall approach this question from three different angles: What were the historical circumstances that provided a plausible background for the origin of the synagogue? Where does the earliest unambiguous evidence lead us? What kind of original context demanded the functions that were later on performed by synagogues?

Many ancient references that we have to early synagogues all make the same assumption as S. Krauss puts it: "In the spirit of a later time an epoch of Israel without synagogues was just unthinkable."[7] This understanding is mirrored in Acts 15:21: "For in every city, for generations past, Moses has had those who proclaim him, for he has been read aloud every Sabbath in the synagogues."[8] The rabbinic interpretations of 2 Kgs 25:9 and Jer 52:13 show a similar tendency of projecting the origin of the synagogue back into biblical times. The burning of the houses of Jerusalem in 586 B.C.E. is interpreted as the destruction of synagogues. Although this account is of little, if any, historical value, it is remarkable that private houses are identified with synagogues,[9] for the

---

[6] For very recent and extensive treatments of the question see Binder, *Temple*, 204–26; Levine, *Synagogue*, 19–41; Runesson, *Origins*; Claussen, *Versammlung*, 151–65.
[7] Krauss, *Altertümer*, 34, (transl. mine).
[8] Transl. *NRSV*. Cf. Krauss, *Altertümer*, 44.
[9] *y. Meg.* 3:1 (73d, 27ff.): "What is the law concerning the sale of a synagogue for the purchase of a schoolhouse? A statement of R. Joshua b. Levi implies that it is permitted to do so. For R. Joshua b. Levi said: 'And he burned the house of the Lord, and the king's house and all the houses of Jerusalem every great house he burned down' (2 Kings 25:9; Jer 52:13). 'The house of the Lord' refers to the Temple. 'And the king's house' refers to the palace of Zedekiah. 'And all the houses of Jerusalem' refers to the 480 synagogues that were in Jerusalem" (trans. Neusner, *Talmud*, 91).

rabbis normally made a very sharp distinction between private dwellings and sacred places.[10]

The cornerstone of very early biblical evidence for supposed synagogues is the phrase מִקְדָּשׁ מְעַט in Ezek 11:16. This phrase[11] has been interpreted as referring to "house of assembly (בֵּית הַכְּנֶסֶת)" and "house of study (בֵּית הַמִּדְרָשׁ)."[12]

For quite some time and until only a couple of decades ago the majority of scholars agreed that synagogues originated in the Babylonian exile. Of course this theory is in many ways quite plausible. After the catastrophe of 587/6 B.C.E., far away from Jerusalem without the focal point of the temple, there must have been a need to establish some kind of meeting for religious purposes, that is, local gatherings where communal prayers may be offered and psalms sung.[13]

However, as we do not have any early epigraphical, papyrological or other archaeological material, a Babylonian origin of the synagogue must be dismissed for the time being.

The earliest archaeological evidence that we have for the existence of a προσευχή appears in two Greek inscriptions that date from the reign of Ptolemy III. Euergetes (reigned 246–221 B.C.E.). Altogether sixteen inscriptions and four papyri mention or seem to imply the existence of synagogues in Egypt between the third century B.C.E. and the early second century C.E.[14] The dedicatory inscriptions witness to a common Egyptian practice: synagogue buildings were dedicated to the royal

---

[10] Cf. *m. Meg.* 3:3.

[11] Cf. the even less convincing allusions in Ezek 8:1; 14:1; 20:1. The elders sitting before the prophet show a practice of consultation but hardly any institutionalized setting.

[12] Cf. *Tg. Ps.-J.* Ezek 11:16; *b. Meg.* 29a. For a discussion of the relationship between בֵּית הַכְּנֶסֶת and בֵּית הַמִּדְרָשׁ see Urman, "House of Assembly," 232–55.

[13] Cf. the earlier article of Hüttenmeister and Hengel, "Synagoge," 327–32, esp. 327 with Hüttenmeister's rejection of this theory in Hüttenmeister, "'Synagoge'" 163: "Die These, die Synagoge sei im babylonischen Exil entstanden, welche noch vor einem Jahrzehnt vorherrschend war, muß heute als überholt angesehen werden."

[14] *JIGRE* 22.117 (246–221 B.C.E.); *JIGRE* 24.25.125 (140–116 B.C.E.); *JIGRE* 13.27.28 (2nd or 1st century B.C.E.); *JIGRE* 126 (1st or 2nd century C.E.); *JIGRE* 9 (2nd century B.C.E.?); *JIGRE* 20 (late Ptolemaic or Roman; perhaps not Jewish); *JIGRE* 105 (restored; mid-2nd century B.C.E.–early 2nd century C.E.); *CPJ* I 129 (218 B.C.E.); *CPJ* I 134 (late 2nd century B.C.E.); *CPJ* I 138 (second half of 1st century B.C.E.?); *CPJ* II 432 (113 C.E.). In addition to these *JIGRE* 16.17.127.129 may imply a synagogue.

family as a sign of expressing loyalty and gratitude as well as of dependence on them.

As early as 1971 M. Hengel argued for a Hellenistic Egyptian origin of the synagogue.[15] He builds his argument upon the evidence provided by the inscriptions mentioned above and tries to understand Egyptian synagogues in terms of a Jewish form of the Hellenistic religious association, which was prevalent in Ptolemaic Egypt.

However, up to the present date no ancient synagogue building has been discovered in Egypt. This places tight restrictions on any further attempt to reconstruct an Egyptian origin on the basis of architectural or functional parallels to what we know about pagan temples in the same area.[16]

Summing up the hard evidence, we must conclude that we can only trace back the origins of the Jewish synagogues to third century B.C.E. Ptolemaic Egypt. However, this does not address the question of possible forerunners of synagogues according to their multiple functions.

As we shall argue in detail later, first-century synagogues may best be viewed as a kind of community center for a rather broad variety of functions. It would almost be impossible to make a clear distinction between their religious and their communal activities.

If one looks for a place in the ancient city that may have served some of the functions of the synagogue before this institution actually came into being, then the city-gate has often been suggested as a model.[17] As the focal point of communal life it served a broad variety of mercantile, juridical, military and police functions and was a common place in the whole ancient near east. It is well attested in biblical and non-biblical literature and also through archaeological evidence.[18] Thus especially for the development in Palestine the city-gate may well be seen as a synagogue forerunner.

---

[15] Hengel, "Proseuche," 157–84. As Levine, *Synagogue*, 24 notices, Hengel thus follows the line of argument proposed earlier by Bousset, Gressmann, Friedländer, and others.

[16] Griffiths, "Egypt," 3–16, claims links between Egyptian and Jewish institutions. However, the evidence for this seems far too limited.

[17] See Levine, *Synagogue*, 27–31. Cf. Hoenig, "City-Square," 448–76. For a very important discussion and critique of Hoenig's confusing the Greco-Roman town square and the Near Eastern city-gate and on his rather free use of latter rabbinic material see Levine, *Synagogue*, 27, n. 29.

[18] Claussen, *Versammlung*, 156–8.

The Diaspora, however, shows a broad range of different settings. A situation like that of the huge Jewish *politeuma* in Alexandria[19] is by no means common for other places and regions. It needs to be stressed that Jews in the Diaspora must not be viewed as an urban minority of traders and businessmen.[20] In Asia Minor until the middle of the second century C.E., the Jews we know of were almost entirely working as farmers or craftsmen.[21] The early Jewish settlers in Asia Minor are reported to have received land for wine growing.[22] Many Jews in that area lived in the countryside.[23] For them there must have been types of religious or communal gatherings, which were far less institutionalized than the synagogues that may have existed in the provincial capitals. This brings us back to a sociological setting which is far older and more basic than a Jewish synagogue: the family.

Already during the Babylonian Exile piety within the family became the backbone of a new system of faith and community. It is very important to notice that this concept of ancient families must not be confused with any modern European or North-American disposition of a nuclear family.[24] Excavations of city dwellings provide evidence that rural families consisted of ten members whereas in the countryside one may expect up to thirty members. Aside from its nucleus, members of the grandparents' generation, sons with their in-laws and offspring, unmarried women and servants were part of it.[25]

As the family was the place where especially the father taught his children this setting was of pivotal importance for the preservation and passing on of the faith, history, law, and other traditions. Thus it is hardly possible to overestimate the family in its private dwellings as the original and still most important place for the transmission of practice and beliefs within Judaism. This emphasis can already be found in Deut 11:19: "Teach them (*sc.* the words of God) to your children, talking about them when you are at home and when you are away, when you

---

[19] *Ep. Arist.* 310; Josephus, *A.J.* 12.108. Philo, *Flacc.* 43 gives the number of one million Jews for Egypt, which may, however, be an exaggeration.

[20] Cf. the criticism by Ameling, "Gemeinden," 31.

[21] See, however, a Jewish medical doctor in Ephesus in *Inschriften der griechischen Städte Kleinasiens* 15.1677.

[22] Josephus, *A.J.* 12.151.

[23] Cf. Mitchell, *Anatolia*, 35–6.

[24] For further insights cf. several essays in Moxnes, *Families:* esp. Barclay, "Family," 66–80.

[25] See Gerstenberger, *Religion*, 262–6.

lie down and when you rise."[26] The social, economic, theological and educational tasks that were originally taken care of within the context of the family were later on at least partly taken on by synagogue communities.

Over the last few years there has been a growing scholarly interest in the ancient family. However, our understanding of ancient Jewish families is still quite limited.[27] A deeper understanding of this important social setting would very likely lead us to more insights of how elements of originally domestic religious life finally made their way into institutionalized synagogues.

To sum up, we would like to suggest looking for a multifaceted development of the synagogue. Earliest epigraphic evidence points in the geographic direction of Ptolemaic Egypt. A forerunner especially for the more communal functions was the ancient city-gate while more religious and educational functions had their original place within the family.

Terminology

Whenever something new comes into being it will be given a name. As it took a very long time for Jewish religious gatherings to become what many finally agreed to call a synagogue, it is not surprising to find a number of other terms that were used in this context.[28] Jewish meeting places were referred to as ἀμφιθέατρον, διδασκαλεῖον, εὐχεῖον, τὸ ἱερόν, ἱερὸς περίβολος, μέγιστον οἴκημα, οἰκοδομή and οἶκος, προσευκτήριον, σαββατεῖον, σεμνεῖον, ὁ ἅγιος τόπος or ὁ ἱερὸς τόπος, *templum*, or even τὸ πᾶν ἔργον τῆς Ἑβραϊκῆς.

Jewish gatherings or communities were called: οἱ Ἰουδαῖοι, ἔθνος, κατοικία, λαός, πολίτευμα, συμφοίτησις, συναγώγιον, σύνοδος, *universitas*, and *conventiculum*.

---

[26] Cf. Deut 4:10; 6:4–7; 32:46f.; Ps 78:5.
[27] Kraemer, *Family*; Cohen, *Family*; Perdue et al., *Families*; Blenkinsopp, "Family," 48–103; Collins, "Marriage," 104–62; Meyers, "Family," 1–47; Perdue, "Family," 163–222; idem, "Household," 223–57; Osiek and Balch, *Families*; Jeffers, "Families," 128–50; Claussen, *Versammlung*, 160–4.
[28] Helpful discussions regarding the terminology can be found in Oster, "Supposed Anachronism," 186; Binder, *Temple*, 91–154; Claussen, *Versammlung*, 113–50.

However, focusing especially on the first and second century C.E., we find two terms that are by far the ones most universally used: προσευχή and συναγωγή.

(a) Προσευχή appears already in the earliest inscriptions from the third century B.C.E. Ptolemaic Egypt as we mentioned above.[29] Originally only referring to "prayer" as in the LXX,[30] it then became the common word for a Jewish "place of prayer" in the Diaspora. In the papyri it always means a Jewish place of prayer and gathering.[31] In Josephus it can mean "prayer"[32] or "place of prayer."[33] Philo uses it only to denote a "place of prayer" in the sense of a synagogue in Alexandria and Rome.[34] In the NT it is normally used for "prayer," but in Acts 16:13, 16 προσευχή refers to a Jewish gathering place in Philippi.

(b) Συναγωγή can be found more than 200 times in the LXX. It refers to all sorts of gatherings. Only in Num 16:24 and Sus 28 does it refer to a building. In Josephus it can denote either a synagogue building or a meeting.[35] Philo uses it for a Jewish community—however, only when quoting scripture[36]—as well as for a synagogue building of the Essenes in Palestine. In the NT it is often very difficult to decide whether συναγωγή refers to a building, a community or a meeting of people. There are only two instances where we can be sure that what is meant is a building, i.e. the building in Capernaum that was donated

---

[29] *JIGRE* 22.117 (246–221 B.C.E.); *JIGRE* 24.25.125 (140–116 B.C.E.); *JIGRE* 13.27.28 (2nd or 1st century B.C.E.); *JIGRE* 126 (1st or 2nd century C.E.); *JIGRE* 9 (2nd century B.C.E.?); *JIGRE* 105 (restored; mid-2nd century B.C.E.–early 2nd century C.E..); *CPJ* I 129 (218 B.C.E.); *CPJ* I 134 (late 2nd century B.C.E.); *CPJ* I 138 (second half of 1st century B.C.E.?); *CPJ* II 432 (113 C.E.).

[30] The text of 3 Macc 7:20 is corrupt. It may, however, be the earliest literary reference to a προσευχή in Egypt.

[31] Cf. Philo, *Flacc.* 53

[32] Josephus, *B.J.* 5.388.

[33] Josephus, *C. Ap.* 2,10; both is possible in Josephus, *A.J.* 14.258, however, "prayer" more likely. See Claussen, *Versammlung*, 115f.

[34] Philo, *Flacc.* 41, 45, 47–9, 53, 122; *Legat.* 132, 134, 137f., 148, 152, 156f., 165, 191, 346, 371. Cf. προσευκτήριον in *Mos.* 2.216.

[35] Josephus, *A.J.* 19.300, 305, *B.J.* 2.289, 7.44. For a detailed discussion of the evidence cf. Claussen, *Versammlung*, 124–6. It is worth noticing that Josephus nearly always uses συναγωγή when he refers to synagogues in Israel. The only exception is the προσευχή in Tiberias (Josephus, *Vita* 277, 280, 293), where Josephus uses this word to characterize a probably very large synagogue building, maybe in deliberate contrast to the Temple. Cf. Claussen, *Versammlung*, 117.

[36] Num 27:16–17.

by the Roman centurion (Luke 7:5) and the synagogue in Corinth (Acts 18:7). The papyri from Egypt use συναγωγή only for the Jewish community.[37] Συναγωγή is also very frequent in Greek inscriptions.[38] Here it refers to both buildings and communities.

If we consider the period up to 200 C.E., we notice some transition regarding the use of the word συναγωγή. It is still very much in the process of a change in meaning from the original "meeting" or "community" to the more specific designation of a Jewish synagogue building. If we take this into account, then there is no reason to assume a clear distinction between private and public places for Jewish religious and communal meetings. There were already special buildings designated for more institutionalized types of Jewish communities, but these were very likely in the minority.

The Functions of the Ancient Synagogue

There is a growing consensus among scholars that the Theodotos inscription is pre 70 C.E.[39] Although the synagogue it refers to was placed in Jerusalem it is a useful illustration of a "Diaspora" synagogue providing for the needs of those who came from different parts of the Roman Empire, either as pilgrims or to stay for a longer period of time. It shows that a synagogue was far more than a place for public worship.[40] We know of Diaspora synagogues, which provided opportunities for a treasury, refuge, manumission of slaves and various other needs of the Jewish communities, as well as the more religious functions of ritual bathing, reading and expounding scripture, and saying prayers.

Ancient synagogues are therefore best to be understood as Jewish community centers, which *also* provide a place for Jewish worship. That this religious dimension was, however, by no means marginal can already be seen by the usual designation as προσευχή.

---

[37] *CPJ* 3.473, lines 7 and 9 (291 C.E.).
[38] *CIJ* 718, 720, 722, 781, 861, 1404. *CJZC* 72. See Claussen, *Versammlung*, 122–4.
[39] Kloppenborg Verbin, "Theodotos," 243–80.
[40] For a study of the different functions cf. Binder, *Temple*, 389–450; Levine, *Synagogue*, 124–59; Runesson, *Origins*, 189–232; Claussen, *Versammlung*, 209–23.

The Legal Situation of the Jews in the Diaspora

In the Greco-Roman world one can notice a broad variety of different kinds of voluntary associations (*corpora, collegia, societates*). Already during the first century B.C.E. the Roman authorities viewed Jewish synagogue communities as voluntary associations. For a documentation of the legal status of Diaspora Judaism under Roman Rule we have to rely mainly on some thirty official documents published by Josephus, mostly in books 14, 16, and 19 of his *Antiquitates judaicae* and to some degree on Philo's works *Legatio ad Gaium* and *In Flaccum*. The accounts of both of these authors may be viewed as apologetic in tendency but nevertheless providing illuminating insights into the interactions between the Roman State, municipal authorities and Diaspora Judaism.

Considering the legal status of Jewish communities in the Diaspora one should keep in mind as we look at the Roman decrees and edicts that the local situation may have been quite different from what it should have been according to the law.[41]

(a) What was the official situation like? Josephus hands down documentary material on Jewish rights and privileges from the time of Julius Caesar to that of Claudius. These texts relate to the following eight areas:

1. The permission to decide their own affairs
   (*A.J.* 14.235, 260);
2. The permission to assemble and/or to have a place of assembly
   (*A.J.* 14.214–16, 227, 235, 257f., 260f.);
3. The permission to observe the Sabbath
   (*A.J.* 14.226, 242, 245, 258, 263f.);
4. The permission to observe Jewish festivals
   (*A.J.* 14.213–16, 257);
5. The permission to observe dietary laws
   (*A.J.* 14.226, 245, 261);
6. The permission to contribute money and send the Temple tax
   (*A.J.* 14.214, 227);

---

[41] For more recent treatments of this topic see among others Smallwood, *Jews*; Ameling, "Gemeinden," 34–7; Noethlichs, *Judentum*, 76–90; Pucci Ben Zeev, *Rights*; Sanders, "Judaism," 2f.; Tellbe, *Paul*, 26–63; Claussen, *Versammlung*, 224–55.

7. The exemption from military service
   (*A.J.* 14.223–40);
8. The exemption from the obligation to participate in the imperial cult
   (*A.J.* 19.280–5).

Among these eight areas we shall focus mainly on the second one: the permission to assemble and to have a place to do so. However, the most important is certainly the permission to decide their own affairs. In fact, without this, the right to have a place of assembly would make no sense at all.

The situation in Sardis provides special insight into the legal conditions. Josephus offers two documents: The first is a letter written by Lucius Antonius who was *proquaestor* and *propraetor* in Asia from 49 B.C.E. onwards for at least two years.[42]

> Lucius Antonius, son of Marcus, proquaestor and propraetor, to the magistrates, council and people of Sardis, greeting. Jewish citizens of ours have come to me and pointed out that from the earliest times they have had an association of their own in accordance with their native laws and *a place of their own*, in which they decide their affairs and controversies with one another; and upon their request that it be permitted them to do these things, I decided that they might be maintained, and permitted them to do so.[43]

From this document we can conclude that the Jews of Sardis had turned to the Roman governor. They had requested confirmation of the permission that had been handed down to them from maybe as early as Persian times.[44] The legal situation mentioned here was not invented by the Romans but rather confirmed.

Later on in Josephus' narrative we find another document dealing with the legal conditions of the Jews in Sardis on a local level.

---

[42] Pucci Ben Zeev, *Rights*, 177.
[43] Josephus, *A.J.* 14.235. Transl. by R. Marcus (LCL).
[44] Cf. Pucci Ben Zeev, *Rights*, 409–11.

Decree of the people of Sardis. The following decree was passed by the council and people on the motion of the magistrates. Whereas the Jewish citizens living in our city have continually received many great privileges from the people and have now come before the council and the people and have pleaded that as their laws and freedom have been restored to them by the Roman senate and people, they may, in accordance with their accepted customs, *come together* and have *a communal life* and adjudicate suits among themselves, and that *a place may be given to them in which they gather together with their wives and children and offer their ancestral prayers and sacrifices to God*, it has therefore been decreed by the council and people that permission shall be given them *to come together on stated days to do those things which are in accordance with their laws, and also that a place shall be set apart by the magistrates for them to build and inhabit, such as they may consider suitable for this purpose*, and that the market-officials of the city shall be charged with the duty of having suitable food for them brought in.[45]

Beside other things the Jews of Sardis asked for formal recognition of their permission to "come together and have a communal life" (14.260).

Although content and chronological considerations make it unlikely to link the above two documents directly[46] it is, however, noteworthy to recognize that the Jews of Sardis had to claim their rights, not only on the imperial level but also locally. Both levels of authority had to be asked to confirm and back up—"public backing with muscle behind,"[47] as T. Rajak puts it quite nicely—what had already been decreed long time ago. The same happened with the privileges issued by Julius Caesar,[48] confirmed in a *senatus consultum* in October 47 B.C.E. and then regularly renewed for over a century.[49] However, it would be rather misleading to regard the relevant material in Josephus as "sources ju-

---

[45] Josephus, *A.J.* 14.259–61. Transl. by R. Marcus (LCL) (Italics mine).
[46] Cf. Pucci Ben Zeev, *Rights*, 180f.
[47] Rajak, "Charter", 302.
[48] Josephus, *A.J.* 14.190–5.
[49] Josephus, *A.J.* 14.186.

ridiques"[50] or even as the "Jewish Magna Charta."[51] This would imply a homogeneous overall definition of Jewish religious rights, which clearly did not exist.

(b) As we have seen above, Josephus is able to claim a rather favorable legal *status quo* for the Jews in the Roman Empire. However, this is certainly only one side of the picture. Before we turn again to the above documents referring to the situation in Sardis we should note: The above-mentioned documents, which Josephus includes in his *Antiquitates judaicae* relate to situations where Jewish identity was contested.[52] Antonius' letter is addressed to the local authorities, the magistrates, council and people of Sardis. This implies that the Sardians had questioned the Jewish rights and that the Jews felt unjustly treated.[53] The authorization to have their own "community (σύνοδος) and "place" (τόπος), "in which they decide their affairs and controversies with one another" (*A.J.* 14.235) had to be secured. If one looks a bit closer at the decree of the people of Sardis one can hardly hold back the suspicion that the Sardian Jews did not receive all they were asking for. They got the right to assemble but only "on stated days." The petition to "adjudicate suits among themselves" is not mirrored in the decree. We are also not quite sure whether "a place to be set apart . . . for them to build and inhabit" answers the Jewish request for their own places of prayer. It seems quite likely that Hellenistic cities even under pressure "from above" were only prepared to grant as little as possible.

Jews in other places experienced similar difficulties.[54] We may therefore conclude that, although the legal position of the Jewish communities in the Diaspora seems overall strong, it was threatened at quite a few places. Of course we have not as much information on areas where Jews and non-Jews lived in peace and harmony or where Jewish Diaspora communities where small and insignificant. However, the overall

---

[50] Juster, *Juifs* 1:132–58; 213ff. For a further critique of this view see Rajak, "Charter," 301–33.
[51] Juster, *Juifs* 1: 217.
[52] Cf. for another Diaspora voice on the relationship between Jews and their neighbors: Philo, *Flacc.* 47: "And it was to be feared that people everywhere might take their cue from Alexandria, and outrage their Jewish fellow-citizens by rioting against their synagogues and ancestral customs."
[53] Pucci Ben Zeev, *Rights*, 179; Tellbe, *Paul*, 39.
[54] See Josephus, *A.J.* 14.213–16 (Delos); 14.241–3 (Laodicea); 14.244–6 (Miletus); 14.256–8 (Halicarnassus); 14.262–4 (Ephesus); 16.45 (Ionia); 19.278–85 (Alexandria).

picture that evolves is one in which it is by no means natural or self-evident that Diaspora Jews were able to have synagogues without experiencing any difficulties. The atmosphere seemed to be rather hostile in quite a number of Hellenistic cities. Therefore, we may assume that there must have been many Jewish communities who were just too small or not strong enough to have a local synagogue building where they might live their communal and ritual life. For them meetings in private buildings must have been the obvious type of gathering.

Archaeological Findings of Ancient Synagogues

Although it is now more than twenty years ago since A. T. Kraabel published his seminal essay on "The Diaspora Synagogue: Archaeological and Epigraphic Evidence since Sukenik"[55] we are by and large still dealing with the same archaeological evidence.[56] The findings of Sardis, Priene, Dura, Delos, Ostia, and Stobi are still our most reliable sources when it comes to ancient synagogue buildings in the Diaspora. If we limit ourselves to a period up to 200 C.E. we are only left with Delos (second cent. B.C.E.), Ostia (first cent. C.E.), Stobi (second or third cent. C.E.)[57] and Dura (end of second cent. C.E.). As has been pointed out before[58] the findings in Delos, Stobi and Dura witness to buildings that had originally been private homes that were only later transformed into synagogue buildings. I am not convinced that this is also the case in Ostia.[59] The best-documented example of such a transformation is an inscription found in Stobi, which reads:

---

[55] Kraabel, "Diaspora Synagogue," 477–510.
[56] See for Diapora Synagogues also Binder, *Temple*, 227–341; Levine, *Synagogue*, 232–87; Runesson, *Origins*, 185–9; Claussen, *Versammlung*, 191–208.
[57] Cf. Levine, *Synagogue*, 254–5. The construction of Polycharmos' house may, however, be as early as the first or second century C.E. See Poehlman, "Polycharmos Inscription," 235–46. Poehlman dates the remodeling and donation of the house as a synagogue to the second century C.E. This view is also confirmed by the second century C.E. pottery (242). For historical reasons Hengel dates the donation to the third century C.E. See Hengel, "Synagogeninschrift," 145–83, esp. 150–9, 181–3.
[58] White, *Origins:* 1 and 2.
[59] For the view that the building at Ostia was a synagogue from the time of its construction in the first century C.E. see Runesson, *Origins*, 187f.; idem, "Synagogue" (2001), 29–99; idem, "Synagogue" (2002), 171–220; contra White, "Synagogue," 23–58.

The year 311 (?).[60] Claudius Tiberius Polycharmos, also called Achyrios, father of the synagogue at Stobi, having lived my whole life according to Judaism, have, in fulfillment of a vow, (given) the buildings to the holy place, and the *triclinium*, together with the *tetrastoon*, with my own means, without in the least touching the sacred (funds). But the ownership and disposition of all the upper chambers shall be retained by me, Claudius Tiberius Polycharmos, and my heirs for life. Whoever seeks in any way to alter any of these dispositions of mine shall pay the Patriarch 250.000 denarii. For thus have I resolved. But the repair of the roof tiles of the upper chambers shall be carried out by me and my heirs.[61]

The historical value of this inscription can hardly be overestimated. The building is referred to as a holy place. This clearly indicates the high religious profile. The building history is best to be understood as a gradual move from Jewish religious meetings in private rooms—something one may call a *house synagogue*[62]—towards a specially designated holy place. Thus one may assume that beside highly developed community centers and institutionalized Jewish communities there were also religious Jewish meetings in private houses, as we know them from other contemporary cults and from early Christianity as well.

---

[60] Dates are either 163 C.E. or 279 C.E., with the latter now generally preferred. However, the reconstruction of the first line of the inscription remains very uncertain. Cf. Hengel, "Synagogeninschrift," 146, n. 3; White, *Origins:* 2, 352, n. 120.

[61] Translation generally follows Levine, *Synagogue*, 252.

[62] Talmudic literature knows different terms for the private synagogue (בית הכנסת של יחיד) and the synagogue of a community (בית הכנסת של רבים). Cf. *y. Meg.* 3, 1 73d. See Hengel, "Synagogeninschrift," 162; Krauss, *Altertümer*, 306: "The private synagogue is one, which a single person built for himself and then made it available for public use or which he at once gave as a present, dedicated or donated to the community" (transl. mine). My definition of a house synagogue is closer to the first part of Krauss' definition. Cf. Claussen, *Versammlung*, 37–9, for a history of research on house synagogues. This is, of course, a very likely model for the formation of early Christian house churches. Cf. Krauss, *Altertümer*, 302f.; Stuhlmacher, *Philemon*, 74f.; Klauck, *Hausgemeinde*, 99.

The Organization of the Ancient Synagogue

The large number of publications of inscriptions[63] over the past few decades has led to a growing interest in the leadership of the ancient synagogue.[64] However, as far as epigraphic evidence is concerned, we are usually left with no indication whatsoever of the meaning or function behind a title. The range of titles that appears is often most confusing. The most important designations seem to be those of ἀρχισυνάγωγος and πρεσβύτερος. Beside them one finds ἄρχων, γερουσιάρχης, γραμματεύς. They are still quite common. Still common but less frequent are ἐξάρχων, φροντιστής, and προστάτης. Even less numerous are ἱερεύς, μαθητὴς σοφῶν, διδάσκαλος, νομομαθής, μήτηρ or πατὴρ συναγωγῆς and ψαλμῳδός. Finally some titles seem to denote some kind of servants: νεωκόρος, ὑπηρέτης, ἀρχιυπηρέτης, εἰσαγγελεύς and θυραωρός.

We shall have to focus mainly on the titles of (a) ἀρχισυνάγωγος and (b) πρεσβύτερος and from there try to provide an overview of early synagogue leadership.

(a) So far we know of 38 inscriptions from ancient times mentioning an ἀρχισυνάγωγος.[65] From these, 30 inscriptions are of Jewish origin but not more than two (!) are more or less with certainty to be dated as early as the first century C.E.[66] The earliest inscription naming an ἀρχισυνάγωγος is, of course, that of Theodotos (*CIJ* 2.1404). It refers to—what I would like to call—a pre-70 C.E. Diaspora synagogue inside Jerusalem.

In addition to this, the title is mentioned nine times in the NT, i.e. four times in Mark (5:22, 35, 36, 38), twice in Luke (8:49; 13:14) and three times in Acts (13:15; 18:8; 18:17; cf. 14:2 *v.l.*). It never appears in Philo, Josephus or in a papyrus, and what makes our evidence even smaller and less helpful is that compared with Mark's gospel Matthew always (cf. Matt 9:18–19, 23–26) changes this title to ἄρχων and Luke

---

[63] For an overview cf. van der Horst, *Epitaphs*; Feldman, "Diaspora Synagogues," 577–602; Williams, "Contribution," 75–93. Claussen, *Versammlung*, 51–5
[64] See Williams, "Structure," 129–41.
[65] See Rajak and Noy, "*Archisynagogoi*," 393–429; Horsley, "*Archisynagogos*," 213–20.
[66] *CIJ* 1404 = Lifshitz no. 79; *CIJ* 766 = Lifshitz no. 33; cf. *CIJ* 336, 322 and *JIWE* I 14 where a dating in the first century C.E. may be possible but a second or third century C.E. date may be more likely. Cf. Rajak and Noy, "*Archisynagogoi*," 421–9, esp. 424, no. 18; 427, no. 28.

leaves it out twice (Lk 8:50–51), changes it to ἄρχων τῆς συναγωγῆς in Luke 8:41 and only keeps Mark's text once in Luke 8:49.

Taking into account this very small body of evidence, it is no surprise that scholars come to very different conclusions on what an ἀρχισυνάγωγος may or may not have been.[67] Sources with primary religious concerns emphasize the religious dimension of this title. Dedicatory inscriptions portray them as benefactors or patrons of some honorific standing. However, there is no evidence that they were strong figures of a powerful authority structure.[68] On the other side it must be noted that an ἀρχισυνάγωγος was looked upon and honored by Jews and also by non-Jews as a leader representing his community.[69]

(b) Turning to the elders, the πρεσβύτεροι, we now come to the question of a supposed presbyterial organization of Jewish synagogues ("*jüdische Presbyterialverfassung*"). This has often been used—and I believe abused—trying to explain the origins of early church order in the Pastoral Epistles. Since the times of Hugo Grotius (1583–1645) and Campegius Vitringa (1659–1722) many scholars have believed that the elders formed a ruling council of the synagogue, a model that was then taken over by the early churches.[70]

However, if we take a closer look, we get the impression that the elders were not the governing officers of ancient synagogues.[71] Among the Jewish titles, that of πρεσβύτερος seems to be relatively rare.[72] Jewish elders must rather be viewed as people who were held in high esteem. Sometimes they also held more specific offices. However, most times their influence was not due to an office but rather to the honor they enjoyed as members of traditionally powerful families or high social rank.

Thus we end up with a situation that does not yield many examples of highly developed synagogue organization prior to 200 C.E. The bulk

---

[67] See Rajak and Noy, "*Archisynagogoi*," 404–10.
[68] Rightly so Rajak and Noy, "*Archisynagogoi*," 419.
[69] Cf. Levine, *Synagogue*, 401.
[70] For a recent proponent of this view see Burtchaell, *Synagogue*, esp. 228–33; 292–9.
[71] For a detailed discussion see Campbell, *Elders*, 44–54.
[72] *JIWE* I 59, 62, 71, 75, 163, 148, 149, 157, 163, 176(?), 181; *JIWE* II 24(?), 176(?); *CIJ* (in addition to *JIWE* I and II): 731c. 391, 735, 739, 790, 792, 800, 801, 803, 829, 931, 1137, 1277, 1404; Lifshitz, (in addition to the ones mentioned above: nos. 32, 37, 84(?).

of evidence is from the fourth and fifth century C.E. Therefore, I claim that we have to think of early Diaspora synagogues as little institutionalized social entities, often, if not mostly, meeting in the context of private homes and larger families.

Women in the Ancient Synagogue

The more one claims a highly developed synagogue organization in what is without doubt to be described as a patriarchal society, the less one may believe that there were women officers in ancient synagogues.[73] However, since I believe that *house synagogues* were far more common than one might have expected, there is no question that women played a vital role in ancient synagogue life. There is also no reason to doubt the records of Acts 14:13, 16 where women gather at a place of prayer outside Philippi, or the account of Josephus, who reports that the local authorities in Sardis granted the Jewish population "that a place be given them in which they may gather together with their wives and children."[74] And even regarding the more institutionalized synagogues one should not doubt that as women are identified by a number of office titles they also had some part in the leadership. However, the more institutionalized Jewish communities became, the more the men took over authority and offices.

As we now come to an end what might we say was the focal point of synagogue life in the Diaspora? Let us turn again to Philo, the primary source for Diaspora Judaism. For him the one thing that unites all Jews whatever they call their fatherland is that "they hold the Holy City where stands the sacred Temple of the most high God to be their mother city."[75] This remained the focal point for their synagogues and ancestral customs in the Diaspora. However, after 70 C.E. when Jerusalem and the Temple had been destroyed the shared belief in Monotheism, dietary laws, the Sabbath, special festivals, circumcision of males

---

[73] Brooten, "Evidence," 1–17 and *Women Leaders,* argues strongly in favor of women as officers in ancient synagogues. For a more cautious view cf. Levine, *Synagogue,* 471–90; Binder, *Temple,* 372–9; Claussen, *Versammlung,* 256–93 passim.
[74] Josephus, *A.J.* 14.260.
[75] Philo *Flacc.* 46.

and the study and general observance of the Law of Moses remained among the most important means of achieving cohesion for Judaism in the Diaspora—whatever synagogues would eventually be like in the centuries to come.

Bibliography

Ameling, W., "Die jüdischen Gemeinden im antiken Kleinasien," Pages 29–55 in *Jüdische Gemeinden und Organisationsformen von der Antike bis zur Gegenwart*. Edited by R. Jütte and A. P. Kustermann. Vienna: Böhlau, 1996.

Barclay, J. M. G., *Jews in the Mediterranean Diaspora: From Alexander to Trajan (323 BCE – 117 CE)*. Edinburgh: T&T Clark, 1996.

—, "The Family as the Bearer of Religion in Judaism and Early Christianity." Pages 66–80 in *Constructing Early Christian Families: Family as Social Reality and Metaphor*. Edited by H. Moxnes. London: Routledge, 1997.

Binder, D. D., *Into the Temple Courts: The Place of the Synagogues in the Second Temple Period*. Atlanta: Society of Biblical Literature, 1999.

Blenkinsopp, J., "The Family in First Temple Israel." Pages 48–103 in *Families in Ancient Israel*. Edited by L. G. Perdue, et al., Louisville: Westminster John Knox, 1997.

Brooten, B. J., "Inscriptional Evidence for Women as Leaders in the Ancient Synagogue." Pages 1–17 in *SBL Seminar Papers*, 1981. Society of Biblical Literature Seminar Papers 20. Chico: Scholars Press, 1981.

—, *Women Leaders in the Ancient Synagogue: Inscriptional Evidence and Background Issues*. Chico: Scholars Press, 1982.

Burtchaell, J. T., *From Synagogue to Church: Public Services and Offices in the Earliest Christian Communities*. Cambridge: Cambridge University Press, 1992.

Campbell, R. A., *The Elders: Seniority within Earliest Christianity*. Edinburgh: T&T Clark, 1994.

Charlesworth, J. H., *The Millenium Guide for Pilgrims to the Holy Land*. North Richland Hills: Bibal Press, 2000.

Claussen, C., *Versammlung, Gemeinde, Synagoge: Das hellenistisch-jüdische Umfeld der frühchristlichen Gemeinden.* Göttingen: Vandenhoeck & Ruprecht, 2002.

Cohen, S. J. D., ed., *The Jewish Family in Antiquity.* Alanta: Scholars Press, 1993.

Collins, J. J., "Marriage, Divorce, and Family in Second Temple Judaism." Pages 104–62 in *Families in Ancient Israel.* Edited by L. G. Perdue, et al., Louisville: Westminster John Knox, 1997.

Feldman, L. H., "Diaspora Synagogues: New Light from Inscriptions and Papyri." Pages 577–602 in *Studies in Hellenistic Judaism.* Edited by L. H. Feldman. Leiden: Brill, 1996.

Gerstenberger, E. H., "The Religion and Institutions of Ancient Israel: Toward a Contextual Theology of the Scriptures." Pages 261-276 in *Old Testament Interpretation: Past, Present, and Future. Essays in Honor of Gene M. Tucker.* Edited by J. L. Mays, D. L. Petersen, and K. H. Richards. Nashville: Abingdon, 1995.

Griffiths, J. G., "Egypt and the Rise of the Synagogue." Pages 3–16 in *Ancient Synagogues: Historical Analysis and Archaeological Discovery. I.* Edited by D. Urman and P. V. M. Flesher. Leiden: Brill, 1995.

Hachlili, R., *Ancient Jewish Art and Archaeology in the Diaspora.* Leiden: Brill, 1998.

Hengel, M., "Die Synagogeninschrift von Stobi." *ZNW* 57 (1966): 145–83.

—, "Proseuche und Synagoge. Jüdische Gemeinde, Gotteshaus und Gottesdienst in der Diaspora und in Palästina." Pages 157–84 in *Tradition und Glaube. Das frühe Christentum in seiner Umwelt.* Edited by G. Jeremias, H.-W. Kuhn, and H. Stegemann. Göttingen: Vandenhoeck & Ruprecht, 1971.

Hoenig, S. B., "The Ancient City-Square. The Forunner of the Synagogue." Pages 448–76 in *ANRW* 19.1. Edited by H. Temporini and W. Haase. Berlin: Berlin: de Gruyter, 1979.

Horsley, G. H. R., "An *archisynagogos* of Corinth?" *NDIEC* 4 (1987): 213–20.

Horst, P. W. van der, *Ancient Jewish Epitaphs. An Introductory Survey of a Millenium of Jewish Funerary Epigraphy (300 B.C.E.–700 CE)*. Kampen: Pharos 1991.

Hüttenmeister, F. G., "'Synagoge' and 'Proseuche' bei Josephus und in anderen antiken Quellen." Pages 162-81 in *Begegnungen zwischen Christentum und Judentum in Antike und Mittelalter*. Edited by D.-A. Koch and H. Lichtenberger. Göttingen: Vandenhoeck & Ruprecht, 1993.

Hüttenmeister, F. G., and G. Reeg, *Die antiken Synagogen in Israel :Die jüdischen Synagogen, Lehrhäuser und Gerichtshöfe*. Wiesbaden: Reichert, 1977.

Hüttenmeister F. G., and M. Hengel, "Synagoge." Pages 327–32 in *Biblisches Reallexikon*. 2nd ed. Edited by K. Galling. Tübingen 1977.

Jeffers, J. S., "Jewish and Christian Families in First-Century Rome." Pages 128–50 in *Judaism and Christianity in First-Century Rome*. Edited by K. P. Donfried and P. Richardson, Grand Rapids: Eerdmans, 1998.

Juster, J., *Les Juifs dans l'Empire romain: Leur condition juridique, économique et sociale, I*. Paris: P. Geuthner, 1914.

Klauck, H.-J., *Hausgemeinde und Hauskirche im frühen Christentum*. Stuttgart: Verlag Katholisches Bibelwerk, 1981.

Kloppenborg Verbin, J. S., "Dating Theodotos (CIJ II 1404)." *JJS* 51 (2000): 243–80.

Kraabel, A. Th., "The Diaspora Synagogue: Archaeological and Epigraphic Evidence since Sukenik." Pages 477–510 in *ANRW* 19.1. Edited by H. Temporini and W Haase. Berlin: Berlin: de Gruyter, 1979.

Kraemer, D., ed., *The Jewish Family: Metaphor and Memory*. New York: Oxford University Press, 1989.

Krauss, S., *Synagogale Altertümer*. Berlin: Benjamin Harz Verlag, 1922 (repr., Hildesheim: Olms, 1966).

Levine, L. I., *The Ancient Synagogue: The First Thousand Years*. New Haven: Yale University Press, 2000.

Lifshitz, B., *Donateurs et fondateurs dans les synagogues juives. Répertoire des dédicaces grecques relatives à la construction et à la réfection des synagogues*. Paris: J. Gabalda et Cie, 1967.

Meyers, C., "The Family in Early Israel." Pages 1–47 in *Families in Ancient Israel*. Edited by L. G. Perdue, et al., Louisville: Westminster John Knox, 1997.

Mitchell, S., *Anatolia : Land, Men, and Gods in Asia Minor. II: The Rise of the Church*. Oxford: Clarendon Press, 1993.

Moxnes, H., ed., *Constructing Early Christian Families: Family as Social Reality and Metaphor*. London: Routledge, 1997.

Neusner, J., *The Talmud of the Land of Israel: A Complete Outline of the Second, Third, and Fourth Divisions. I: The Division of Appointed Times. Vol. D: Taanit, Megillah, Rosh Hashannah, Hagigah and Moed Qatan*. Atlanta: Scholars Press, 1996.

Noethlichs, K. L., *Das Judentum und der römische Staat: Minderheitenpolitik im antiken Rom*. Darmstadt: Wissenschaftliche Buchgesellschaft, 1996.

Osiek, C., and D. Balch, *Families in the New Testament World. Households and Housechurches*. Louisville: Westminster John Knox, 1997.

Oster, R., "Supposed Anachronism in Luke-Acts' Use of ΣΥΝΑΓΩΓΗ." *NTS* 39 (1993): 178-208.

Perdue, L. G., "The Household, Old Testament Theology, and Contemporary Hermeneutics." Pages 223–57 in *Families in Ancient Israel*. Edited by L. G. Perdue, et al., Louisville: Westminster John Knox, 1997.

—, "The Israelite and Early Jewish Family. Summary and Conclusions." Pages 163–222 in *Families in Ancient Israel*. Edited by L. G. Perdue, et al., Louisville: Westminster John Knox, 1997.

Perdue, L. G., et al., eds. *Families in Ancient Israel*. Louisville: Westminster John Knox, 1997.

Poehlman, W., "The Polycharmos Inscription and Synagogue I at Stobi." Pages 235-246 in *Studies in the Antiquities of Stobi. III*. Edited by B. Aleksova and J. Wiseman. Titov Veles: Macedonian Review Editions, 1981.

Pucci Ben Zeev, M., *Jewish Rights in the Roman World: The Greek and Roman Documents Quoted by Josephus Flavius*. Tübingen: Mohr Siebeck, 1998.

Rajak, T., "Was There a Roman Charter for the Jews?" Pages 301–33 in *The Jewish Dialogue with Greece and Rome: Studies in Cultural and Social Interaction.* Edited by T. Rajak. Leiden: Brill, 2001 =(*JRS* 74 [1984]: 107–23).

Rajak, T., and D. Noy, "*Archisynagogoi:* Office, Title and Social Status in the Greco-Jewish Synagogue." Pages 393–429 in *The Jewish Dialogue with Greece and Rome: Studies in Cultural and Social Interaction.* Edited by T. Rajak. Leiden: Brill, 2001 (=*JRS* 83 [1993]: 75–93).

Runesson, A., *The Origins of the Synagogue: A Socio-Historical Study.* Stockholm: Almqvist & Wiksell, 2001.

—, "The Synagogue at Ancient Ostia: The Building and Its History from the First to the Fifth Century." Pages 29–99 in *The Synagogue of Ancient Ostia and the Jews of Rome: Interdisciplinary Studies.* Edited by B. Olsson, D. Mitternacht and O. Brandt. Stockholm: Paul Åströms Förlag, 2001.

—, "A Monumental Synagogue from the First Century: The Case of Ostia." *JSJ* 33 (2002): 171–220.

Sanders, E. P., "Common Judaism and the Synagogue in the First Century." Pages 1–17 in *Jews, Christians and Polytheists in the Ancient Synagogue: Cultural Interaction During the Greco-Roman Period.* Edited by S. Fine. London: Routledge, 1999.

Smallwood, E. M., *The Jews under Roman Rule from Pompey to Diocletian: A Study in Political Relations.* 2nd ed. Leiden: Brill, 1981.

Stuhlmacher, P., *Der Brief an Philemon.* 3rd ed. Neukirchen-Vluyn: Neukirchener Verlag 1989.

Tellbe, M., *Paul between Synagogue and State: Christians, Jews, and Civic Authorities in 1 Thessalonians, Romans, and Philippians.* Stockholm: Almqvist & Wiksell, 2001.

Urman, D., "The House of Assembly and the House of Study: Are they One and the Same?" Pages 232–55 in *Ancient Synagogues: Historical Analysis and Archaeological Discovery. I.* Edited by D. Urman and P. V. M. Flesher. Leiden: Brill, 1995.

White, L. M., *The Social Origins of Christian Architecture, vol. 1: Building God's House in the Roman World. Architectural Adaptions among Pagans, Jews and Christians.* Valley Forge: Trinity Press, 1990 (= idem: *Building God's House in the*

Roman World. Architectural Adaptation among Pagans, Jews, and Christians, Baltimore: Johns Hopkins University Press, 1990).

—, "Synagogue and Society in Imperial Ostia: Archaeological and Epigraphic Evidence." *HTR* 90 (1997): 23–58.

—, *The Social Origins of Christian Architecture, vol. 2: Texts and Monuments for the Christian Domus Ecclesiae in Its Environment*. Valley Forge: Trinity Press, 1997.

Williams, M. H., "The Structure of Roman Jewry Reconsidered—Were the Synagogues of Ancient Rome Entirely Homogeneous?" *ZPE* 104 (1994): 129–41.

—, "The Contribution of Jewish Inscriptions to the Study of Judaism." Pages 75–93 in *The Cambridge History of Judaism. Vol 3: The Early Roman Period*. Edited by W. Horbury, W. D. Davies and J. Sturdy. Cambridge: Cambridge University Press, 1999.

10
A Covenant for Gentiles? Covenantal Nomism and the Incident at Antioch

Magnus Zetterholm

IN THE LETTER TO THE GALATIANS Paul gives an account of a schism between himself and Peter that seems to be related to the question of the proper degree of social intercourse between Jewish and Gentile adherents to the Jesus movement. This text is, of course, of great importance being one source of our understanding of the relations between Jews and Gentiles in the early Jesus movement.

In the introduction to the specific account of the clash between the two apostles, we are told that Paul and the representatives of the Jesus movement in Jerusalem had reached an agreement about how missionary activities should be carried out. One easily gets the impression that an agreement was reached also on the issue of the status of Gentiles within the movement. However, after the meeting where this agreement was made, Peter arrived in Antioch. Paul writes in Gal 2:11–14:

> But when Cephas came to Antioch, I opposed him to his face, because he stood self-condemned; for until certain people came from James, he used to eat with the Gentiles. But after they came, he drew back and kept himself separate for fear of the circumcision faction. And the other Jews joined him in this hypocrisy, so that even Barnabas was led astray by their hypocrisy. But when I saw that they were not acting consistently with the truth of the gospel, I said to Cephas before them all, "If you, though a Jew, live like a

Gentile and not like a Jew, how can you compel the Gentiles to live like Jews?"[1]

While these few verses have been subject to an extensive scholarly debate, it would be wrong to claim that there exists any consensus on what the incident was really about.[2]

The reason for this is rather obvious. The answer to the question of what the clash at Antioch was about, is not to be found at the semantic/syntactic level of the text, but rather on a pragmatic, referential level. To understand the incident at Antioch, we are forced not only to deal with the general problems connected with the interpretation of ancient texts, but we are also compelled to reconstruct the specific symbolic universe to which the text refers, in order to fill in the gaps in the text. In the following I will suggest a new reading of the text about the incident at Antioch which, accordingly, does not focus on the semantic/syntactic level of the text, but on the contextual.[3]

But why deal with this text in the context of ancient synagogues? According to the prevalent view, the Christian movement separated from the synagogues and formed separate communities consisting of Gentiles and Jews, who as a result of Paul's theology had become liberated from the burden of Torah obedience. These two ethnic categories, Jews and Gentiles, are usually assumed to have fused together into a new group, with a common "Christian" identity.[4]

There are several reasons to question this view. One problem that is of certain relevance for understanding the incident at Antioch concerns the organizational aspects of the early Jesus movement.

The Organization of the Early Jesus Movement

How are we to perceive the early Christian communities? W. Meeks has investigated four models from the environment: (1) the household, (2) the voluntary association, (3) the synagogue, and (4) the philosophic or

---

[1] Scripture quotations are from the NRSV.
[2] For overviews of the general scholarly discussion, see Wechsler, *Geschichtsbild*, or Kieffer, *Foi*, 80–132.
[3] For a more thorough treatment of the incident at Antioch, see Zetterholm, *Formation*, 129–64.
[4] See e.g. Holmberg, "Christian Identity."

rhetorical school.[5] While Meeks found several similarities between early churches and the assumed model, he finally refuted them all. Instead, he tried to show how "the Pauline Christians developed a 'unique culture.'"[6] Others are more inclined to accept the statement that Pauline churches can be fitted into the spectrum of the Greek and Roman voluntary associations. Thus, M. Tellbe has recently suggested that the Thessalonian church was organized as a *collegium domesticum*.[7]

In my opinion there are two main problems with these kinds of suggestions. My first objection is related to the underlying assumption that "Christians" constituted a group that rather early became separated from the general Jewish communities and developed a common religious identity and a common way of expressing religion. To some extent it is our terminology that leads us astray. Terms like "churches" and "Christians" imply already at a pre-analytical stage that the separation between Jews and Christians had already taken place. If this is assumed to have happened, it is only natural that we find a fitting non-Jewish organization for this new group. This goes hand in hand with the common picture of Paul as the one who establishes the Torah-free gospel for both Jews and Gentiles.

Such assumptions are, however, by no means self-evident. The fact that Christianity originally was a completely Jewish faction should make us more inclined to consider the relations between Jews and Gentiles within the early Jesus movement when looking for its organization. A first step would be to refrain from using sweeping terminology. Instead of the scarcely clarifying designation "Christian," we must take into account that Jews and Gentiles became "Christians" from rather different points of departure.

A Jewish person who came to believe that Jesus was the Messiah did so from within a Jewish symbolic universe that already included a concept of God's Messiah. Such a belief may not have affected his or her religious identity in any profound way. For a Gentile, on the other hand, who became associated with the Jesus movement, the social and cognitive consequences may have been far more serious because of the socio-political system in the Greco-Roman cities. We can thus no longer speak of "Christians" as if they constituted a homogeneous

---

[5] Meeks, *First Urban*, 75–84.
[6] Ibid., 85.
[7] Tellbe, *Paul*, 93. See also Kloppenborg, "Edwin Hatch," 237–8.

group when dealing with the first century situation. Instead, I suggest the following terminology: Jesus-believing Jews together with Jesus-believing Gentiles made up the Jesus movement that eventually turned into the non-Jewish Gentile religion: Christianity.

My second objection, which more directly concerns the organizational aspect of the early Jesus movement, is to some extent a result of an analytical differentiation between Jewish and Gentile adherents to the movement. It could be argued that the Jewish community in the Diaspora was considered one of many *collegia*,[8] although with privileges going far beyond those of other *collegia*.[9] Within the religious/political system of the Greco-Roman cities, cultic and political activities were strictly regulated.[10] Foreign cults were organized as *collegia*, and the introduction of new cults required the approval of the authorities.[11] *Collegia* were, however, not unequivocally supported by Rome, since they sometimes masked revolutionary activities, and there is evidence that suggests that imperial supervision extended well beyond the city of Rome.[12] The Jewish communities were normally exempted from participation in the official cult,[13] which usually meant paying respect to the gods of the city and participating in the frequent festivals and sacrifices. It also meant acknowledging the Roman emperors as deities.

It should thus be clear that Gentiles and Jews related to the religious/political system in rather different ways. Gentiles were expected to participate in the official cult. To fail in duties related to the official *polis* religion, even for an adherent of a foreign cult, was

---

[8] Meeks, *First Urban*, 32; Rajak, "Synagogue," 164–66; Richardson, "Augustan-Era," 18, 19; "Early Synagogues"; "Architectural Case"; Seland, "Philo." Cf. however Levine, "First-Century," 27–8, who also points to the differences between the synagogues and the *collegia*, e.g. the synagogue's wider range of activities and more far-reaching privileges. See also Binder, *Temple Courts*, 229–32, 338–9 and Fitzpatrick-McKinley, "Synagogue Communities," 63–70. Cf. Gruen, *Diaspora*, 24–6, 121–2.
[9] For an overview on Jewish privileges see, Tellbe, *Paul*, 37–51.
[10] See Beard, North, and Price, *Religions of Rome*, 228–36, for examples of Roman judicial measures taken against religious activities labeled as improper.
[11] Cicero, *Leg.* 2.8.19. See also Cotter, "Collegia," 79.
[12] Ibid., 76, 79; Kloppenborg, "Collegia," 16; Price, *Religions*, 155–6.
[13] Josephus, *A.J.* 19.280–5, 19. 305–5. Tellbe, *Paul*, 46–51.

considered *impiety* and could result in exile or even death.[14] Jews, on the other hand, as the only group in the Roman Empire, were permitted to refrain from the cultic activities of the *polis*.

An important question is how these socio-political circumstances affected the relations between the Jewish communities and those Gentiles we know had an interest in Judaism and who interacted with Jews in the synagogues of antiquity.[15] Despite efforts to question the whole idea of a group of Gentiles, usually referred to as "god-fearers,"[16] interacting with Jews in the synagogues, there can be no doubt that such group existed.[17] The most reasonable assumption is that participation in synagogue activities probably did not affect the cultic obligations of the Gentile god-fearer.[18] As pointed out by M. Goodman, the prevalent Jewish attitude to Gentile worship of their ancestral deities was tolerance. As long as Gentile worship was kept outside the Land of Israel, Jews in general would have had little to object to.[19] It may even be the case that the Jewish communities *urged* the Gentile god-fearers not to neglect their commitment to the official cult, since accusations of having lead Gentiles astray could easily affect the Jewish privileges. *Collegia* existed on the condition that they did not violate public law.[20] Thus, god-fearers could continue to maintain their obligation towards the *polis* and the empire and their relation to the Jewish community probably did not affect their identity in any profound way.

There is evidence that supports this view. In one listing of the so-called Aphrodisias inscription (from the third century C.E.) there are nine names of people who are called god-fearers but at the same time are identified *as members of the city council*.[21] These Gentile god-fearers

---

[14] See Price, *Religions*, 82–8 on responses to religious threats in Classical Athens. See also Tcherikover, *Hellenistic Civilizations*, 28; Walker-Ramisch, "Voluntary Associations," 133–4; Tellbe, *Paul*, 34; Bruit-Zaidman and Schmitt-Pantell, *Religion*, 13–15.
[15] On different levels of Gentile involvement in the Jewish communities of antiquity, see Cohen, *Beginnings*, 140–74.
[16] Kraabel, "Disappearance": Kraabel and MacLennan, "God-Fearers." Cf. The critique of Kraabel and MacLennan in Overmann, "God-Fearers."
[17] See Feldman, *Jew*, 244–358; Omnipresence."
[18] Beard, North, and Price, *Religions of Rome*, 309.
[19] Goodman, *Mission*, 49–59.
[20] Walker-Ramisch, "Voluntary Associations," 133.
[21] Καὶ ὅσοι θεοσεβῖς *stop* Ζήνων Βουλ(ευτής) Τέρτυλλος Βουλ(ευτής), see Face *b* lines 34–5 in Reynolds and Tannenbaum, *Jews and Godfearers*, 6–7. City councillors as

seem to have managed to combine their relation to the Jewish community with having an official position in the city council that certainly involved cultic activities, such as public sacrifices at the openings of all council meetings.[22] This makes sense only if one assumes that the Jewish community did not oppose Gentile involvement in the official cult as long as they remained Gentiles.

In this respect, the Jesus movement differed from other Jewish communities that welcomed Gentiles into their midst. A Gentile who associated him- or herself with the Jesus movement could no longer worship other deities. This implies that suggestions of how Gentile adherents to a Jewish faction that did not allow Gentile participation in Gentile cultic activities must take into consideration which organizational options that were available. It must, for instance, be questioned if it was at all possible for Gentile adherents to the Jesus movement to be organized as separate *collegia,* since the only *collegium* that was exempted from participation in the official cult was the Jewish community. So, if Jesus-believing Gentiles were forbidden to participate in Gentile religion, and if the religious/political system only allowed for non-Jewish *collegia* that were loyal to *polis* religion, how are we to imagine the way they were organized?

Let us take a look at how the Jesus movement was introduced in Antioch. In Acts 11:19 we are told that "those who were scattered because of the persecution that took place over Stephen traveled as far as Phoenicia, Cyprus, and Antioch, and they spoke the word to no one except Jews." The most reasonable assumption is that we have here a description of how Jesus-believing Jews influenced other Jews in the context of an ordinary synagogue. Soon, however, Gentiles also became influenced by the message about Jesus. In 11:20 we are informed that "some men of Cyprus and Cyrene who, on coming to Antioch, spoke to the Hellenists also, proclaiming the Lord Jesus." Who were these

---

patrons are known also from Sardis, see Levine, *Ancient Synagogue,* 350. It is possible, but by no means certain, that the inscription *CIJ* 766, where Julia Severa is said to have built a synagogue, indicates the same. From another source (*MAMA* 6.263) she is known to have been a high priestess in a local cult. Feldman (*Jew,* 310) believes that she "sympathized with Judaism." Rajak, ("Synagogue," 168) on the other hand, finds it unlikely that she was "in the process of any sort of conversion" and Levine (*Ancient Synagogue,* 350) states that she "remained fully pagan."
[22] Reynolds and Tannenbaum, *Jews and Godfearers,* 58.

"Hellenists"? The most natural answer is that they were among those god-fearers that had previously related to this synagogue, before the arrival of the representatives of the Jesus movement.

Given the regulations about the *collegia* in the Roman Empire, it is highly unlikely that the earliest Jesus movement in Antioch was organized in any other way than as a synagogue. While the Jewish communities enjoyed protection as long as law and order were maintained, a new cult did not especially if it embraced an ideology of not participating in the official religion. Such a conclusion has far-reaching consequences for how we are to imagine the position of the Jesus-believing Gentiles in the predominantly Jewish Jesus movement. It is likely that the Jesus-believing Gentiles had to hide their existence by pretending to be Jews in relation to the civic authorities. Gentile god-fearers had presumably already adopted a Jewish life style since their motive for associating with Jews in the first place was a profound interest in Judaism, and as S. J. D. Cohen has shown, anyone associating with Jews and with a Jewish behavior may very well have passed as a Jew.[23]

This way of looking at the organization of the early Jesus movement is also in accordance with M. D. Nanos' interpretation of the situation in Rome. Nanos suggests in an admittedly highly controversial interpretation of Rom 13:1–7, that Paul argues that the Jesus-believing Gentiles should subordinate themselves, not to the authorities of Rome, as is usually assumed, but to the *synagogue authorities*.[24] If we, however, assume the existence of a synagogue mainly consisting of Jesus-believing Jews, considering themselves fully rooted within Judaism, with a relation to god-fearing Gentiles who were no longer able to maintain their cultic obligation to the *polis*, this makes perfect sense.

With this in mind, we may now turn our attention to the specific incident at Antioch.

The Incident at Antioch

The conclusion that the incident in Antioch took place within the institution of the synagogue is important. The general existence of god-

---

[23] Cohen, *Beginnings*, 58–62, 66–8.
[24] Nanos, *Mystery*, 289–336.

fearers in a Jewish context implies that the issue of social intercourse with Gentiles was not unique for the Jesus movement. It is, for instance, a fair guess that the four prohibitions known as the apostolic decree in Acts 15:20, 28–9 reflect a prevalent halakha operative among several Jewish groups in Antioch.[25] At least some, presumably Hellenized Jews were accustomed to socializing with Gentiles and it is hard to imagine that this had no halakhic consequences.

At the same time, it is important to note the new situation created by the fact that the Gentiles within the Jesus movement were not allowed to worship other deities. It is likely that this socio-political situation resulted in a closer relationship between Jesus-believing Jews and Jesus-believing Gentiles. Therefore, we may not be surprised by the fact that the clash in Antioch seems to have been related to commensality. Before the arrival of certain people from James, table-fellowship between Jews and Gentiles within the Jesus movement seems to have caused no problems, but the presence of James' representatives changed all that.[26] What was it that attracted James's wrath? Had the whole community realized that Torah obedience was outdated and violated the food laws?[27] That is not likely. If the majority of Jesus-believing Gentiles were recruited among former god-fearers, as suggested above, they had certainly already adopted a Jewish lifestyle. God-fearers did not want to separate from Judaism. Quite the contrary, *one of Paul's major problems seems to have been to prevent Gentiles from observing the Torah or even from becoming Jews.* As for the Jesus-believing Jews, nothing indicates

---

[25] Zetterholm, *Formation*, 143–9.
[26] It has generally been assumed that James was behind the delegation from Jerusalem which is to be identified with the "circumcision faction" (Gal 2:12) and this is also my assumption. This is, admittedly, not the only way to interpret the text. Nanos suggests that the reference to the people from James should be taken as a temporal determinator and that the "circumcision faction" constituted another group within the larger Jewish community in Antioch, see "Peter's Eating," 291–2, 316. While this suggestion cannot be ruled out, I find it more likely that Paul actually meant to imply a casual relationship between the arrival of the people from James and Peter's reaction, which is indicated by the contrast between the very accentuated πρὸ τοῦ γὰρ ἐλθεῖν τινας ἀπὸ Ἰακώβου in the beginning of the phrase and ὅτε δὲ ἦλθον in the second clause. Cf. the discussions in Betz, *Galatians*, 107–8; Bockmuehl, "Antioch," 69; Dunn, *Galatians*, 117–24; Taylor, *Paul*, 128, Witherington, *Grace*, 152–6.
[27] Barrett, "Paul," 54, Betz, *Galatians*, 112; Burton, *Galatians*, 106; Ligthfoot, *Galatians*, 112–14.

that they had done anything that was considered a violation of the Torah.[28]

It appears from Gal 2:11–13 that the Hellenized Jews in Antioch thought it possible to eat together with Gentiles. Despite efforts to make probable that table-fellowship between Jews and Gentiles almost never happened,[29] it is highly unlikely to assume that, for instance, god-fearers never participated in Jewish meals. It is clear that some Jews would never eat with Gentiles and that those Jews found such behavior highly inappropriate. That Hellenized Jews, in spite of this, may have invited god-fearers is almost self-evident.[30] So what was the real problem? To get a hint of what triggered James' reaction we have to turn to the context of the letter to the Galatians.

As a result of a rhetorical reading of Galatians, P. F. Esler has suggested that there is a connection between what is stated in the section in which the Antioch incident appears and issues dealt with in the main part of the letter.[31] One of Paul's main concerns in the letter to the Galatians was to discourage Gentile adherents to the movement from submitting to circumcision (Gal 5:2–2; 6:12–13). Thus, the problem Paul faced in Galatia seems to have been related to the issue of the status of the Gentiles within the Jesus movement: are Gentiles to be circumcised or not?

Circumcision certainly plays an important part also in the Antioch incident. Peter refrained from table-fellowship with the Jesus-believing Gentiles from fear of the "circumcision faction." We may thus assume that since the problem in Galatians was connected to the status of the Gentiles within the Jesus movement as well as the justification of the Gentiles apart from the Torah,[32] this was also the problem in Antioch.

It is important to note the eschatological aspect involved in this. In Gal 1:4 Paul states that Christ has sacrificed himself "to set us free from the present evil age," and in Acts 15:1 it is reported that "certain individuals" questioned whether Gentiles could be saved unless they

---

[28] Nanos, "Peter's Eating," 300–1, Tomson, *Jewish Law*, 228.
[29] This view has most vigorously been advocated by Esler, see e.g. *Community*, 73–86. Cf. Bockmuehl, "Antioch," 167, Sanders, "Jewish Associations," 176–80; Holmberg, "Christian Identity," 402.
[30] See Zetterholm, *Formation*, 149–55 for arguments supporting the view that some Jews certainly could socialize with Gentiles.
[31] Esler, *First Christians*, 61–2.
[32] See e.g., Gal 3:1–18; 5:1–12.

were circumcised. In Acts 15:5 it is explicitly stated that "some believers who belonged to the sect of the Pharisees" made the same remark. We may thus conclude that the incident at Antioch occurred *in a context where the eschatological status of the Gentile adherents to the Jesus movement was at stake*. One way of addressing the problem of what the conflict actually was about could be to relate the narration of the incident to concepts of the eschatological status of the Gentiles within the Judaism of the period.

The Eschatological Status of Gentiles

It seems clear that the Judaism of the first century C.E. did not have *one* view of the eschatological destiny of the Gentiles and certainly not a predominantly negative one. In biblical, pre-rabbinic and Tannaitic literature, we find different ideas of what will happen to the Gentiles. The material can, in fact, be clustered around two poles of extremes, ranging from destruction to salvation.[33] E. P. Sanders has found six discernible predictions about Gentiles in biblical and post-biblical literature: (1) the wealth of the Gentiles will flow into Jerusalem, (2) Gentile nations will serve Israel, (3) Israel will be a light to the nations, (4) the Gentiles will be destroyed or, (5) defeated, (6) Gentiles will survive but will not dwell with Israel.[34]

The fact that there existed *both* positive and negative traditions about Gentiles has an important bearing on the Antioch incident. The early Jesus movement was certainly influenced by traditions with a positive attitude towards Gentiles. While Jesus predominantly, if not completely, directed his mission to the people of Israel, there can be no doubt that the first adherents to the Jesus movement found missionary activities directed towards Gentiles a vital part of the movement's ideology.

Nothing indicates that Jesus ever formulated a specific theological program for the salvation of the Gentiles, but if we assume that he at least confirmed that Gentiles were to be embraced by the final salvation, it is not strange that the early Jesus movement developed different concepts of how this salvation would be realized. As time went by, the question of how the Gentiles would be saved became more and more intense. The awareness of living in a period when the final intervention

---

[33] Fredriksen, "Judaism," 220–1.
[34] Sanders, *Jesus and Judaism*, 124.

was about to take place, triggered specific traditions from a common religious heritage that concerned the future destiny of the Gentile nations. The process of giving this ideology a halakhic form was, of course, dependent on existing concepts of the salvation of Gentiles. Therefore we must give attention to some aspects of salvation in first century Judaism.

Covenant and Salvation

At the center of the relation between Israel and God was the covenant. According to E. P. Sanders, the common pattern in all surveyed literature can be described in terms of *covenantal nomism*. In this system, God certainly rewards obedience and punishes transgressions, but since the Torah provides means of atonement, the covenantal relationship can be maintained or re-established. But even more important, *everyone living within the boundaries of the covenant remaining in the covenant through obedience and atonement will be saved by the mercy of God.*[35] This was probably true for the Tannaitic rabbis, the Qumran community and presumably every other kind of Judaism of the period. It was, however, a soteriological system for Jews only. Exactly how the Gentiles would be saved is less clear. Could it be argued that the Gentiles were to be included into the *covenantal community of Israel*?

There are several factors that speak against this being the general Jewish view. The strong connection between male circumcision and covenantal theology makes it highly unlikely that mainstream Judaism considered this to be a possibility.[36] Not even a Jew who was not circumcised due to some hemorrhagic disease,[37] was allowed to take part in the Passover meal which, of course, is permeated with covenantal theology. In *Jub.* 15:26 the author explicitly states that circumcision on the eighth day is a prerequisite for being included in the covenant.

There are also several texts that deal with Jews who had "removed the marks of circumcision." It seems clear that already during antiquity it was possible to perform operations in order to reconstruct the foreskin. This surgical procedure, first described by the Roman surgeon Celsus,[38]

---

[35] Sanders, *Palestinian Judaism*, 422.
[36] Schäfer, *Judeophobia*, 93.
[37] *b. Yebam.* 64b.
[38] *Med.* 7.25. See also Rubin, "Decircumsion"; Hall, "Epispasm."

is hinted at in several Jewish texts. Paul, for instance admonishes the Jesus-believing Jews in 1 Cor 7:18 not to have this operation performed, and the author of 1 Macc considered this to be the ultimate apostasy, as is clear from the passage 1:14–15.

> So they built a gymnasium in Jerusalem, according to Gentile custom, and removed the marks of circumcision, and abandoned the holy covenant. They joined with the Gentiles and sold themselves to do evil.

Moreover, in *b. Sanh.* 38b, Adam is said to have pulled his foreskin as an expression of having broken the covenant and there are several similar text.[39] We may conclude that if Gentiles were considered to be embraced by the eschatological salvation, this was not thought of in covenantal terms.

It is evident that while there certainly existed traditions that were positive to the eschatological salvation of the Gentiles, the question of *how* this would be obtained had not been reflected upon. Quite naturally, Jewish theologians had been occupied with creating a concrete soteriological system for the present. This is the ideological context in which the incident of Antioch took place. Thus, when the early Jesus movement was about to construct a pragmatic solution to the issue of how to relate to the Gentiles, it was from this symbolic world it had to derive the building blocks.

A Covenantal Theology of Salvation

Is seems as if the early Jesus movement was trapped in a dilemma. On the one hand, Gentiles were to be embraced by the salvation but the only institution that could provide this, namely the covenant, was reserved only for Jews. Could the conflict at Antioch have emanated from the ambition within the Jesus-believing Jewish community to solve this dilemma? In order to find a solution to the problem, Paul may have emphasized the soteriological aspects of covenantal nomism by arguing *that since the covenant provides salvation, Gentiles must be included in the covenant.* There are certainly indications of this: by connecting the inclusion of the Gentiles with the promise given to Abraham in Gal 3:7–29, Paul interprets the salvation of the Gentiles in

---

[39] See Zetterholm, *Formation*, 72–3.

covenantal terms, since the promise given to Abraham is a *covenantal promise* as stated in Gen 15:18: "[o]n that day the Lord made a covenant with Abram."[40]

At the same time, it is clear that Paul emphasized that Gentiles should remain Gentiles. We noted above that this is a main theme in the letter to the Galatians. Paul's message is very explicit—the Galatians are under no circumstances to submit to circumcision. If they do, the result is that they cut themselves off from Christ (Gal 5:4). Even if this is a rhetorical overstatement,[41] it shows how important it was for Paul that Gentile and Jewish identities should be maintained.

It is hard to imagine that Paul was not able to anticipate the reactions against such a solution. However, if he had solved the problem with uncircumcised Gentiles in the covenant by suggesting that they should all convert to Judaism, he may have faced an even more serious problem. The reason why Paul so emphatically discourage Gentiles from becoming Jews may be connected to his belief in the one God. He writes in Rom 3:28–31:

> For we hold that a person is justified by faith apart from works prescribed by the law. Or is God the God of Jews only? Is he not the God of Gentiles also? Yes, of Gentiles also, since God is one; and he will justify the circumcised on the ground of faith and the uncircumcised through that same faith. Do we then overthrow the law by this faith? By no means! On the contrary, we uphold the law.

Nanos is probably right in stating that in Paul's mind the God of Israel would not be the God of all nations if Gentiles were to become Jews in order to be embraced by the final salvation.[42] The conclusion we may draw is that it was of eschatological significance for Paul that Jews and Gentiles maintained their original identities, and above all, that

---

[40] It is generally accepted that Paul's arguing implies an inclusion into a covenantal fellowship with the God of Israel, while the implications of this usually follow the traditional view of Paul as dealing with the salvation of both Jews and Gentiles, see e.g. Martyn, *Galatians*, 341; Boers, *Justification*, 63–4; Dunn, *Galatians*, 173; Wright, *Climax*, 137–56.

[41] Mitternacht, "Korsfäst med Kristus," 33.

[42] Nanos, *Mystery*, 183.

Gentiles were included into the covenant that provided salvation, without becoming Jews.

It is worth mentioning that Paul here uses elements deeply embedded in his own religious tradition. Belief in the One God, the salvation of Gentiles as Gentiles, and covenantal nomism in combination with a firm conviction of living in the messianic age, resulted in an innovative model for the soteriological inclusion of the Gentiles.

It is rather obvious that this ideology may have affected the degree of social intercourse. We have already noted that the problem in Antioch arose from table-fellowship between Jesus-believing Jews and Jesus-believing Gentiles. Peter used to eat with the Gentiles, but stopped at the arrival of the people from James. This custom of eating with Gentiles may have had nothing to do with a specific Pauline ideology, but may have been part of a local halakha prevalent among several Jewish groups in Antioch. However, the fact that Jesus-believing Gentiles were considered to be *covenantal partners* presumably affected the level of social intercourse. As mentioned above, the socio-political situation had presumably forced the Jesus-believing Gentiles to cloak themselves as Jews, which may have resulted in a closer relationship between Jesus-believing Jews and Jesus-believing Gentiles. However, since the Jesus-believing Jews were precisely Jews, we must assume that they obeyed the Torah, and since the Jesus-believing Gentiles presumably were former god-fearers, they had adopted a Jewish life style since their motive for associating themselves with Jews was a profound interest in Judaism. From the point of view of the Jesus-believing Jews, it is unlikely that the Torah was ever violated. So what was the problem?

In one respect commensality may have reached an unusually intimate level: partly as a result of the covenantal theology of Paul, the Jesus-believing Jews in the community in Antioch may, for instance, have felt free to accept dinner invitations from Gentiles and to use food prepared and brought by Gentiles in common meals.[43] This change in the pattern of social interaction between Jew and Gentile was thus motivated by the ideological convictions of Paul that Jews and Gentiles within the Jesus movement had equal status before God, since they were part of the same covenant, let it be from different points of

---

[43] Cf. Nanos, "Peter's Eating," 316.

departure. The Diaspora situation was, however, a contributing factor. Only in a context where we can allow for a rather high degree of social intercourse between Jews and Gentiles in general could such a theological reorientation be tolerated at all. Due to historical circumstances the leadership of the Jerusalem community would not share that tolerance.

When James heard how the Antiochean community realized the agreement from Jerusalem, he evidently reacted by sending a delegation to Antioch. For James this unrestricted table-fellowship implied *covenantal fellowship*. On this point James had got Paul perfectly right! But in the same way as the messianic status of Jesus gave rise to certain associations and expectations, so did the idea of the inclusion of the Gentiles into the covenant. In Jerusalem where a Torah-obedient ideology had been prevailing since the Maccabean uprising, intimate associations with Gentiles may very well have been regarded as a threat to Judaism itself, especially *if Gentiles were said to be part of the covenant of circumcision without circumcision*. Non-circumcision in a covenantal context, we recall, implied a clear break with the covenant and consequently with Judaism. The narration in 1 Macc 1:11–15 which deals with the events during the reign of Antiochus IV Epiphanes connects the fact that the Hellenized Jews made a *covenant* with the Gentiles *and* removed the marks of *circumcision*. Thus, to make a covenant with Gentiles implies apostasy.

From James' point of view, there was no need for a new way of relating to Gentiles, since there already existed an established and halakhic defined way of social intercourse: Gentiles could remain god-fearers and as such be embraced by the final salvation. Exactly how he pictured the relation between Israel and the Gentiles is impossible to say, but it is likely that he, in accordance with prevalent ideas of how Jews and Gentiles should associate, considered the Jesus-believing Gentiles to be connected to the Jewish community as *god-fearers*, while still regarding them to be included in the final salvation. However, if they were to claim part in the *covenant* they had to be circumcised and were to keep the whole of the Torah. The reason why James succeeded in convincing the other Jews about his model was that from a Jewish point of view his solution must be considered the most natural. Thus, the weight of tradition and the authority of *the brother of Jesus*, make it perfectly clear why Paul suffered an ideological defeat. What James consequently demanded was that the unrestricted table-fellowship had to cease and that the Jesus-believing Gentiles should form a separate commensality group.

In practice, the explicit demand for a separation of the community would soon function as an implicit demand on the Jesus-believing Gentiles to become Jews. This would however result in a new dilemma, since according to Pauline teaching, the Jesus-believing Gentiles would risk to cutting themselves off from Christ if they submitted to circumcision. As B. Holmberg has noted, the Jesus-believing Gentiles must have perceived this action as possibly excluding them from the people of God.[44]

Summary and Conclusion

The conflict at Antioch was a conflict in a synagogue between different covenantal models of how the Gentile nations would be embraced by the eschatological salvation. Paul's model meant the inclusion of the Gentiles into the covenant as Gentiles. This model stood in sharp contrast to James', according to which Gentiles had to become Jews to be considered covenantal partners. James probably thought that the Gentile adherents to the Jesus movement should relate to the Jewish community as god-fearers in some sense, certainly not as equals, and certainly not as covenantal partners. Paul, on the other hand, stressed that "in Christ" all distinctions between men become, on one level, superfluous, which at the same time is a paradox: this unity is arrived at *only when the distinction between Jew and Gentile is maintained.* It is as "Jew" and "Gentile" mankind becomes "one in Christ," since the God of Israel is the God, not only of the Jews, but of all humanity.

In the conflict at Antioch we find the earliest evidence of how ideological and social mechanisms working together brought about a social division between Jesus-believing Jews and Jesus-believing Gentiles. In an Antiochean context I believe that this division eventually gave rise to a Gentile movement within the Jesus-believing community to separate from Judaism, that is, Jesus-believing Judaism.[45] It is possible that we find evidence of this process in the writings of Ignatius, the

---

[44] Holmberg, "Christian Identity," 411.
[45] See Zetterholm, *Formation*, 178–230.

bishop in Antioch, in the beginning of the second century, for instance when he states in *Magn.* 10:3:

> It is monstrous to talk of Jesus Christ and to practise Judaism. For Christianity did not base its faith on Judaism, but Judaism on Christianity.[46]

From this and from other comments it is rather clear that Ignatius understood Judaism to be *something profoundly different from Christianity*. Ignatius assumed that Judaism and Christianity were two incompatible religious systems.

We may thus conclude that in the aftermath of the incident at Antioch we find at least three rather different interpretations of the relations between Jews and Gentiles within the Jesus movement. In the Pauline version, Gentiles included into the covenant should remain Gentiles to become "one in Christ" together with Jews who remained Jews and observed the Torah. In James' view, Jews should remain Torah-obedient Jews, while Gentiles should relate to the Jewish community as Jesus-believing god-fearers and be saved according to a theology of righteous Gentiles. In Ignatius' version, Jewishness had become incompatible with being "Christian" and Jewish identity had to cease for a common Gentile identity. It is in this process we can see how Christianity in the form we know it today is born, ironically as a complete contradiction of its own beginning.

Bibliography

Barrett, C. K., "Paul: Councils and Controversies." Pages 42–74 in *Conflicts and Challenges in Early Christianity*. Edited by D. A. Hagner. Harrisburg: Trinity Press, 1999.

Beard, M., North, J., and Price, S., *Religions of Rome: Volume 1: A History*. Cambridge: Cambridge University Press, 2002 [1998].

Betz, H. D., *Galatians: A Commentary on Paul's Letter to the Churches in Galatia*. Philadelphia: Fortress Press, 1979.

---

[46] Translation by K. Lake (LCL).

Bockmuehl, M., "Antioch and James the Just." Pages 155–98 in *James the Just and Christian Origins*. Edited by B. Chilton, and C. A. Evans. Leiden: Brill, 1999.

Boers, H., *The Justification of the Gentiles: Paul's Letter to the Galatians and Romans*. Peabody: Hendrickson, 1994.

Bruit-Zaidman, L., and P. Schmitt-Pantel, *Religion in the Ancient Greek City*. Cambridge: Cambridge University Press, 1992 [1989 in French].

Burton, E. A., *A Critical and Exegetical Commentary on the Epistle to the Galatians*. Edinburgh: T & T Clark, 1921.

Cohen, S. J. D., *The Beginnings of Jewishness: Boundaries, Varieties, Uncertainties*. Berkeley: University of California Press, 1999.

Cotter, W., "The Collegia and Roman Law: State Restrictions on Voluntary Associations 64 BCE–200 CE." Pages 74–89 in *Voluntary Associations in the Graeco-Roman World*. Edited by J. S. Kloppenborg and S. G. Wilson. London: Routledge, 1996.

Dunn, J. D. G., *A Commentary on the Epistle to the Galatians*. London: A & C Black, 1993.

Esler, P. F., *Community and Gospel in Luke-Acts: The Social and Political Motivations of Lucan Theology*. Cambridge: Cambridge University Press, 1996 [1987].

—, *The First Christians in their Social Worlds: Social-Scientific Approaches to New Testament Interpretation*. London: Routledge, 1994.

Feldman, L. H., "The Omnipresence of the God-Fearers." *BAR* 12 no. 5 (1986): 58–63.

—, *Jew and Gentile in the Ancient World: Attitudes and Interactions from Alexander to Justinian*. Princeton: Princeton University Press, 1996 [1993].

Fitzpatrick-McKinley, A., "Synagogue Communities in the Graeco-Roman Cities." Pages 55–87 in *Jews in the Hellenistic and Roman Cities*. Edited by J. R. Bartlett. London, Routledge, 2002.

Fredriksen, P., "Judaism, the Circumcision of Gentiles, and Apocalyptic Hope: Another Look at Galatians 1 and 2." Pages 209–44 in *Recruitment, Conquest, and Conflict: Strategies in Judaism, Early Christianity, and the Greco-Roman World*.

Edited by P. Borgen, V. K. Robbins and D. B. Gowler. Atlanta: Scholars Press, 1998.

Goodman, M., *Mission and Conversion: Proselytizing in the Religious History of the Roman Empire.* London: Clarendon Press, 1994.

Gruen, E. S., *Diaspora: Jews Amidst Greeks and Romans.* Cambridge: Harvard University Press, 2002.

Hall, R. G., "Epispasm and the Dating of Ancient Jewish Writings." *JSP* 2 (1988): 71–86.

Holmberg, B., "Jewish *Versus* Christian Identity in the Early Church." *RB* 105 (1998): 397–425.

Kieffer, R., *Foi et justification à Antioche: Interpretation d'un conflit (Ga 2, 14-21).* Paris: Cerf, 1982.

Kloppenborg, J. S., "Edwin Hatch, Churches and Collegia." Pages 212–38 in *Origins and Method: Towards a New Understanding of Judaism and Christianity: Essays in Honour of John C. Hurd.* Edited by B. H. McLean and J. C. Hurd. Sheffield: JSOT Press, 1993.

Kraabel, A. T., "The Disappearance of the 'God-Fearers'." Pages 119–30 in *Diaspora Jews and Judaism: Essays in Honor of, and in Dialogue with, A. Thomas Kraabel.* Edited by J. A. Overman and R. S. MacLennan. Atlanta: Scholars Press, 1992.

Kraabel, A. T., and R. S. MacLennan, "The God-Fearers—A Literary and Theological Invention." Pages 131–43 in *Diaspora Jews and Judaism: Essays in Honor of, and in Dialogue with, A. Thomas Kraabel.* Edited by J. A. Overman and R. S. MacLennan. Atlanta: Scholars Press, 1992.

Lightfoot, J. B., *The Epistle of St. Paul to the Galatians.* Grands Rapids: Zondervan, 1957.

Martyn, J. L., *Galatians: A New Translation with Introduction and Commentary.* New York: Doubleday, 1997.

Meeks, W. A., *The First Urban Christians: The Social World of the Apostle Paul.* New Haven: Yale University Press, 1983.

Mitternacht, D., "Korsfäst med Kristus och utfryst i Galatien." *STK* 79 (2003): 31–41.

Nanos, M. D., *The Mystery of Romans: The Jewish Context of Paul's Letter.* Minneapolis: Fortress Press, 1996.

—, "What Was at Stake in Peter's "Eating with Gentiles" at Antioch?" Pages 282–318 in *The Galatians Debate: Contemporary Issues in Rhetorical and Historical Interpretation*. Edited by M. D. Nanos. Peabody: Hendrickson, 2002.

Overman, J. A., "The God-Fearers: Some Neglected Features." Pages 145–52 in *Diaspora Jews and Judaism: Essays in Honor of, and in Dialogue with, A. Thomas Kraabel*. Edited by J. A. Overman and R. S. MacLennan. Atlanta: Scholars Press, 1992.

Price, S., *Religions of the Ancient Greeks*. Cambridge: Cambridge University Press, 2000 [1999].

Rajak, T., "The Synagogue Within the Greco-Roman City." Pages 161–73 in *Jews, Christians and Polytheists in the Ancient Synagogue: Cultural Interaction during the Greco-Roman Period*. Edited by S. Fine. London: Routledge, 1999.

Reynolds, J., and R. Tannenbaum, *Jews and Godfearers at Aphrodisias: Greek Inscriptions with Commentary*. Cambridge: Cambridge Philological Society, 1987.

Richardson, P., "An Architectural Case for Synagogues as Associations." In this volume.

—, "Augustan-Era Synagogues in Rome." Pages 19–29 in *Judaism and Christianity in First-Century Rome*. Edited by K. P. Donfried and P. Richardson. Grand Rapids: Eerdmans, 1998.

—, "Early Synagogues as Collegia in the Diaspora and Palestine." Pages 90–109 in *Voluntary Associations in the Graeco-Roman World*. Edited by J. S. Kloppenborg and S. G. Wilson. London: Routledge, 1996.

Rubin, J. P., "Celsus' Decircumcision Operation: Medical and Historical Implications." *Urology* 16 (1980): 121–4.

Sanders, E. P., *Paul and Palestinian Judaism: A Comparison of Patterns of Religion*. Minneapolis: Fortress Press, 1977.

—, *Jesus and Judaism*. Philadelphia: Fortress Press, 1985.

—, "Jewish Associations with Gentiles and Galatians 2:11-14." Pages 170–88 in *The Conversation Continues: Studies in Paul and John In Honour of J. Louis Martyn*. Edited by R. T. Fortna, and B. R. Gaventa. Nashville: Abingdon Press, 1990.

Seland, T., "Philo and the Associations of Alexandria." Pages 110–27 in *Voluntary Associations in the Graeco-Roman World*. Edited by J.

S. Kloppenborg and S. G. Wilson. London: Routledge, 1996.

Schäfer, P., *Judeophobia: Attitudes toward the Jews in the Ancient World.* Cambridge: Harvard University Press, 1997.

Taylor, N. H., *Paul, Antioch and Jerusalem: A Study in Relationships and Authority in Earliest Christianity.* Sheffield: Sheffield Academic Press, 1992.

Tomson, P. J., *Paul and the Jewish Law: Halakha in the Letters of the Apostle to the Gentiles.* Assen/Maastricht: van Gorcum, 1990.

Tcherikover, V., *Hellenistic Civilisations and the Jews.* Peabody: Hendrickson, 1999 [1959].

Tellbe, M., *Paul between Synagogue and State: Christians, Jews, and Civic Authorities in 1 Thessalonians, Romans, and Philippians.* Stockholm: Almqvist & Wiksell, 2001.

Walker-Ramisch, S., "Graeco-Roman Voluntary Associations and the Damascus Document: A Sociological Analysis." Pages 128–45 in *Voluntary Associations in the Graeco-Roman World.* Edited by J. S. Kloppenborg, and S. G. Wilson. London: Routledge, 1996.

Wechsler, A., *Geschichtsbild und Apostelstreit: Eine forschungsgeschichtliche und exegetische Studie über den antiochenischen Zwischenfall (Gal 2,11-14).* Berlin: de Gruyter, 1991.

Witherington, B., *Grace in Galatia: A Commentary on St Paul's Letter to the Galatians.* Edinburgh: T & T Clark, 1998.

Wright, N. T., *The Climax of the Covenant: Christ and the Law in Pauline Theology.* Minneapolis: Fortress Press, 1992.

Zetterholm, M., *The Formation of Christianity in Antioch: A Social-Scientific Approach to the Separation between Judaism and Christianity.* London: Routledge, 2003.

11
The Synagogue and the Separation of the Christians

Judith Lieu

My title is unexceptional; yet it reflects a set of presuppositions and an agenda which, I shall suggest, create more problems than they solve. The metaphoric and visual symbolism of "the synagogue" carries powerful associations from a Christian perspective, yet how do we negotiate between symbol, or what I have called elsewhere "Image," and "Reality"?[1] In this paper we shall explore the way that within the Christian tradition, or within scholarship from that background, the definition of "synagogue" has invariably been determined by a prior understanding of "the church," for which it functions as a reverse mirror-image. This means that "synagogue" comes to signify a shadowy parallel of everything that "church" signifies, and, consequently, generates a similar set of debates to those familiar from contemporary historical and theological discussions of the church: for example, what is the relationship between building and community—when and where is the term, ἐκκλησία/συναγωγή, used with reference to either and which comes first? what is the relationship between worshipping community and more extensive social network? what is the relationship between the practice (or non-observance) by individuals and their stated or felt allegiance? what was the status of individual house-communities, and what degree of mutual recognition was there between them? can there be authentic religious experience apart from the church/synagogue? Each of these questions has been provoked initially by debates about the nature of "the church," and, even when apparently "historical," often reflects powerful theological undercurrents. Transferred to the synagogue, as

---

[1] Lieu, *Image*.

they frequently are, they may indeed prove to be appropriate, but that needs to be established not presupposed; that these should be the primary questions is even less of a given.

Yet we shall also discover that this "reverse image" is already inherent in early Christian references to "the synagogue," which renders the latter highly problematic for any historical investigation, and that it has been taken over unquestioningly by more contemporary scholarship.

To question the, often implicit, assumed equivalence of church and synagogue carries serious implications. Moreover, a possible objection from the other end would be, where did the church come from if not from the synagogue?[2] That, though a serious question, is not our concern here, which is whether we can move from Christian representation to "the real synagogue."

In what follows certain fundamental images that cluster around the contemporary concern for "synagogue and church" will provide a means for exploring this further: they are not mutually exclusive —there is considerable overlap between them—but the categorization offers a framework for further debate. Such debate could extend to the wider issues signaled by both the title and by the texts to be explored, but the focus in what follows is deliberately restricted to "the synagogue."

"Synagogue" *versus* "Church"

The iconography of the blindfolded slave woman, *synagoga*, over against the triumphant, bride-queen, *ecclesia*, is familiar. Belonging to the middle-ages, its roots and its fruits are extensive.[3] It can represent the fundamental image, underlying much of what will follow. Here "the synagogue" serves as the representative of "Judaism," set in opposition to the ἐκκλησία (both singular) as the representative of Christianity.

Justin Martyr is the earliest clear witness to this model; exegeting the two wives of Jacob, he says ἀλλὰ Λεία μὲν ὁ λαὸς ὑμῶν καὶ ἡ συναγωγή,

---

[2] For a sustained argument in this direction see Burtchaell, *Synagogue*.

[3] See Weber, *Geistliches Schauspiel*; Kühnel, "Personification"; Schreckenberg, *Jews*, 16–18, 31–74; Weber notes that there is no simple continuity with earlier artistic depictions of the relationship between the two Testaments, and, like subsequent studies, emphasises the importance of Ps. Augustine, *Altercatio*.

Ῥαχὴλ δὲ ἡ ἐκκλησία ἡμῶν (*Dial.* 134.3). Similarly, he interprets the "donkey and foal of an ass" of Zech 9:9 as "those who were to believe in him from your synagogue (ἀπὸ τῆς συναγωγῆς ὑμῶν) and from the gentiles," then replacing "your synagogue" with "your people" (ἀπὸ τοῦ ὑμετέρου λαοῦ) (*Dial.* 53.4); Origen develops this exegesis to note that "the synagogue at that time was bound in sins" (*Comm. Matt.* XVI.15).

The opposition becomes common in later writers, as they find in every contrasting pair in the scriptures an anticipation of "the church" and its replacement of "the synagogue": so, Prov 30:21–23, "Under three things the earth trembles . . . a maid when she succeeds her mistress," becomes the church replacing the synagogue (Hippolytus, *Fr. Prov.* 26; 54). More commonly the maidservant is the synagogue, following Paul's exegesis of Sarah and Hagar in Gal 4:22–27: here early Christian writers do what Paul does not, adding "synagogue" and "church" to their interpretation: "these are two Testaments . . . one from Mount Sinai referring to the synagogue of the Jews according to the Law . . . the other . . . which is our mother . . . the holy church."[4] Similarly, Isaiah 54:1's contrast between the desolate and the married woman becomes that between the church and the synagogue, although through various means the language of desolation is more readily transferred to the synagogue.[5] For Origen Jairus's daughter is "the synagogue of the Jews" and the woman with the haemorrhage "the church from the gentiles"; the latter, sick for the 12 years while the former was well, is healed as she dies; but the daughter/ synagogue will be raised at the end [Rom 11:25] (*Fr. Luc.* 125).The frequency of female imagery is striking; although casting "the synagogue" as the married woman acknowledges her initial covenantal relationship with God, the concern for the appropriate application of bridal imagery with its NT roots suggests that priority lies with the personification of the church.[6] This concern, particularly within a strict understanding of

---

[4] Tertullian, *Marc.* V.4, *haec sunt duo testamenta . . . unum a monte Sina in synagogam Iudaeorum secundum legem . . . aliud . . . quae est mater nostra . . . in quam repromisimus sanctam ecclesiam.* It is unclear whether Tertullian is quoting Marcion here.

[5] E.g. Origen, *Hom. Jer.* 9.3, ἔχουσα δὲ ἄνδρα τὸν νόμον ἐκείνη ἡ συναγωγὴ λέλεκται; *Hom. Luc.* 21; also *Fr. Lam.* 18 on Lam 1:6 where he interprets "the daughter of Zion" as "the synagogue in her."

[6] In Origen, *Fr. Luc.* 171 Martha represents "the synagogue of the circumcision"—not a reference to Jewish Christians who are described in an alternative exegesis as "the faithful from the circumcision"—and Mary "the church

monogamy and of the prohibition of divorce, rebounds on to the characterization of "the synagogue": thus exegesis of Matt 19 leads to descriptions of "the synagogue" as the adulterous first wife (Origen, *Comm. Matt.* 12.4; 14.17, 19).[7]

Given space it would be interesting to trace further the treatment of "the synagogue" in early Christian exegesis. That is not our task here; what is evident is that by the middle of the second, and more securely by the early third century, Christian writers can speak of, and often personify, ἡ συναγωγή, transliterated into Latin as *synagoga*,[8] as the antithetical equivalent of ἡ ἐκκλησία.

The only possible example of this model earlier than Justin would be the two references in Revelation to "the [a] synagogue of satan," qualifying "those who claim to be Jews but are not" (Rev 2:9; 3:9). Some have concluded from the latter denial that the author would have claimed for "his side" the epithet "Jews": he does not do so explicitly, but he does claim the imagery of the scriptural people of God. However, that he would have envisaged or claimed to be a/the "synagogue of God" seems improbable since he uses the term ἐκκλησία for the individual churches (1:4, 20; 2:1 etc.). Is "the synagogue" here "of Satan" by definition? Does "synagogue" already not simply belong to but represent the Jews?

Jewish parallels for such language are difficult to find; that it is derivative from the LXX's use of συναγωγή for the MT's עדה and קהל, especially of "the congregation of Israel," is possible but there is little to show this—and this would strain any reference to a local institution.[9]

---

from the gentiles." Cf. also the exegesis of Jesus" question, "Who is my mother?" as a reference to the synagogue: Tertullian, *Carn. Chr.* 7.82–7, *figura est synagogae in matre abiuncta et Iudaeorum in fratribus incredulis*.

[7] Tertullian, seeking to accommodate the patriarchs who had concubines as well as wives, suggests, *sed licet figura tum in synagogam et ecclesiam intercesserit* (*Ux.* I.2.8).

[8] First by Tertullian: Lewis and Short, s.v. *synagoga*; Juvenal, *Sat.* III.296 uses *proseucha*.

[9] Lampe, *Patristic Lexicon* s.v. C.1.c sees the use of συναγωγή for the "congregation of Israel" as equivalent to the LXX's translation for קהל, but the "Jewish" examples given, *T. Levi* 11.5; *Pss.Sol.* 10.8, do not explain the Christian use. Perhaps more interesting is 2 Chron 5:6 LXX πᾶσα συναγωγὴ Ισραηλ καὶ οἱ φοβούμενοι καὶ οἱ ἐπισυνηγμένοι (see Reynolds and Tannenbaum, *Jews*, 65 who note the addition of οἱ φοβούμενοι to the MT). Only later do Jewish communities use קהל of themselves, recalling the Biblical congregation of Israel: see Schwartz, *Imperialism*, 275. See below and also n. 19.

Certainly, as is widely recognized, συναγωγή is very rare for "Christian" communities—the few exceptions largely prove the rule;[10] ἐκκλησία, not a Jewish "technical term," becomes the norm, a development yet to be adequately explained.[11] Particularly perplexing for both terms is the relationship between the "universal" and the local.

Perhaps significantly, it is Justin again who first illustrates the exegetical "pay-off" this application supplies; it enables him to cite Ps 22:16, συναγωγὴ πονηρευομένων περιέσχεν με, as a prophecy of Jesus" death: "[Ps. 22.16–19] was a prediction of the manner of death to which the synagogue of the evil doers (ἡ συναγωγὴ τῶν πονηρευομένων) were to condemn him, those whom he also calls dogs" (*Dial.* 98.4; 104.1).[12]

The LXX's use of συναγωγή for the MT's עדה and קהל offers Christian writers further exegetical possibilities: Origen, distinguishing between the "Passover of the Jews" and "the Passover of the Lord," quotes Moses' words to the συναγωγὴ (υἱῶν) Ισραηλ in Exod 12:3, while for Tertullian that same command to kill the Passover lamb anticipates the death of Jesus at the hands of "the whole synagogue of the sons of Israel."[13] Both Origen and Tertullian use the phrase "the synagogue of the Jews," which marks a significant step in the development of the terminology.

This oppositional personification of "the synagogue" is also widely found in contemporary scholarship; while J. Parkes's *The Conflict of Church and Synagogue* shows that it need not be negative, an essay title like "The Saints and the Synagogue," could come straight from the

---

[10] *T. Benj.* 11.2–3 συναγωγὴ τῶν ἐθνῶν; Ignatius, *Pol.* 4.2 πυκνότερον συναγωγαὶ γινέσθωσαν. Justin describes believers as μιᾷ ψυχῇ καὶ μιᾷ συναγωγῇ καὶ μιᾷ ἐκκλησίᾳ (*Dial.* 63.5), and later writers continue to use συναγωγή in a general sense of the Christian assembly (cf. Lampe, *Patristic Lexicon* s.v. C. 2). The Elder cited by Irenaeus, *Haer.* IV.31.1 interprets the two daughters of Lot as αἱ δύο συναγωγαί, although whether this refers to Jews and Christians or to Jewish-Christians and Gentile-Christians is not clear; see Lieu, *Image*, 249–50.

[11] The question whether ἐκκλησία is also drawn from the LXX or from Greek civic practice cannot be explored here.

[12] A christological exegesis of Ps 22:16 occurs earlier in *Barn.* 6.6, but it is Justin who exploits its full potential; yet he can refer Ps 81:1 to believers without stumbling over συναγωγή (*Dial.* 124.1–2).

[13] Origen, *Comm. Jo.* X.13.70: on Origen's reading κυρίου rather than κυρίῳ see Buchinger, "Ex. 12,11.27.48 LXX"; Tertullian, *Adv. Jud.* VIII.142–6, *omnis synagoga filiorum Israel eum interfecit*, followed by Matt 27:25; John 19:12.

pages of the Church fathers.[14] Yet this common hypostatization of "the synagogue" raises a number of problems:

a) It is derivative from the Christian theological language of "the church" as a collective concept and as identical with the body of "the saved"—*extra ecclesiam nulla salus* implicitly generates *intra synagogam nulla salus*. Structures, if not buildings, are seen as the central, indeed the exclusive, locus of identity for Jews as for Christians.

b) It is monolithic: again, in the case of the Christian church a theological rationale of this monolithism is possible, with some justification already in the Pauline and post-Pauline language of "the church" (1 Cor 12:28; Eph 1:22 etc.). Thus it presupposes a single conceptual identity for "the synagogue," something without clear parallel in Jewish sources.[15]

c) Consequently it takes for granted the equivalence of synagogue and community, both local and universal, assuming the centrality of "synagogue" for religious identity.

d) Fundamental to all this is that it assumes that "church" and "synagogue" are analogous.

I have illustrated this model from early Christian writings, and the process by which they adopted the term συναγωγή invites discussion. Yet, conversely, the silence of the same sources is equally telling: the term is rare in much of the NT outside the Gospels and Acts, in the Apostolic Fathers, and in the Apologists.[16] These sources do not use "the synagogue" to talk about Jews and Judaism. Even in the third century, Ps.Cyprian, *de Montibus Sina et Sion* can develop the contrast with "the church" without using the term "synagogue." Moreover, with the partial exception of Justin Martyr, early Christian writers up to 200 C.E. do not explicitly understand Jews or Judaism within a synagogal or even

---

[14] Parkes, *Conflict*; Morris, "Saints," 52: "For the synagogue the law was the central thing and everything followed from that.... But for [Christians] it was of the first importance that when they met, Christ was in their very midst. They gloried in the gospel and Christianity was from the very first a religion of the gospel rather than a religion of the law."

[15] But see above n. 9. However, if the origins of the usage are in the LXX it can not be projected onto local social relations.

[16] Matt: 9; Mark: 8; Luke: 13; John: 2; Acts: 19; Jas: 1; Rev: 2; *Barn.* 5.13; 6.6; Hermas, *Mand.* 11.9,13,14; Ignatius, *Pol.* 4.2; *1 Clem.* 20.6; Justin: *Dial.* 16.4; 47.4; 53.4; 63.5; 72.3; 96.2; 98.4; 104.1; 124.1, 2; 134.3.

a structural framework.[17] The opposition between "church" and "synagogue" is not a primary one in our sources—even less, in fact, than that between "Sabbath" and "Sunday."

Christians as Excluded from "the Synagogue"

In John 9:22 "the Jews" are agreed that any who confessed Jesus to be the Christ or Messiah were to be made ἀποσυνάγωγος, a term apparently coined by the Gospel (cf. 12:42; 16:2). This is the *locus classicus* for the model whereby the synagogue becomes the place from which Christians are excluded, an exclusion that is then seen as constituting "the separation" between Jews and Christians or between Judaism and Christianity. To this interpretation have become attached discussions of the *birkat-hamminim*, the 12th benediction, which is itself understood as effecting exclusion from the synagogue (and hence "the separation"), and is sometimes compared with other forms of exclusion or even "excommunication"—a term laden with ecclesiastical overtones.[18] Even before proceeding further we should note that, in contrast to the Synoptics, the Fourth Gospel has little interest in the synagogue (John 6:59; 18:20 only), which sits oddly with the widespread assumption that the local synagogue and exclusion from it lay at the heart of Johannine self-identity.[19]

"Corroborative" evidence for this interpretation and reconstruction of exclusion has been found in Justin Martyr's references to the cursing of Christians "in the synagogues" (*Dial.* 96.2; 47.4; 16.4), and specifically to the reviling of the king of Israel "after the prayer as instructed by your rulers of the synagogue" (137.2); Justin does not, we should note, interpret this as exclusion but as evidence of hostility from an already separate body.[20] The problems provoked by these references

---

[17] Lieu, *Image*, 284.
[18] The classic account is Martyn, *History*, 59 who uses the term "excommunication." However Meeks, "Breaking," 102 already recognised the *birkat-hamminim* as a "red herring."
[19] See Lieu, "Temple." Schwartz, *Imperialism*, 223, n. 24 accepts that ἀποσυνάγωγος means "from the congregation of Israel."
[20] See also Origen, *Hom. Jer.* 19.12.30 "go into the synagogues of the Jews and see Jesus scourged by them with the language of blasphemy"; *Hom. Ps.* 37.II.8, *Christus usque in hodiernum diem a Iudaeis anathema fiat, cum spiritus sanctus in prophetis*

are well known: on the one hand, there is their surprising and unparalleled specificity; on the other, they stand in tension with objections by Origen, and later by Chrysostom, to "Christians" attending synagogue, apparently unobstructed.[21] Moreover, they are not dispassionate, "objective" accounts: Jewish cursing of Christians plays an important role in Justin's construction of blessing and curse, and the curse of Jesus' death on the cross.[22] The further problems of when, where, how, and for whom, the *birkat-hamminim* functioned would take us too far from our concern here, which is the emblematic role played by "the synagogue."

Another form of this model of "the synagogue" as the locus of "Christian" separation is that which speaks of "the synagogue across the street." Here the classic text is the Gospel of Matthew, which can be seen as at once the most Jewish of the Gospels—a description for which it vies with the Fourth Gospel—and as the most hostile to "the Jews" and their structural representatives. Matthew redacts his Markan model in order to emphasise the synagogue as *their* synagogue (ἡ συναγωγή αὐτῶν: Matt 4:23 [= Mark 1:39]; 9:35; 10:17;12:9; 13:54; 23:34), and as the place of opposition to Jesus as well as of eventual opposition to his followers: "they will hand you over to councils (συνέδρια) and in their synagogues they will scourge you" (10:17; cf. 23:34).[23] These Matthean characteristics have provoked a debate as to whether the conflict reflected in that Gospel is *intra* or *extra muros*, that is, as to whether the communities have split or should be conceptualized as part of the same whole.[24] The problem here, evidently, is "conceptualized by whom?" The model, with its physical metaphor of walls, assumes a structural and unitary Judaism, easily figured as "the synagogue." Matthew's introduction of the term ἐκκλησία (16:18; 18:17), alone in the Gospels, aids this, but it is notable that he does not set the two terms in explicit opposition to each other.

This model has been consciously influenced by contemporary sociological models of sectarianism, which in turn were shaped by the

---

locutus est ab haereticis odio habeatur. For opposing views of the question see Horbury, "Benediction"; Kimelman, "Birkat Ha Minim."

[21] See below.
[22] See Lieu, *Image*, 130–5.
[23] Matthew only: the parallels in Luke 12:11; 20:49 do not refer to synagogues; see Lieu, "Temple," 58.
[24] See Saldarini, "Boundaries"; Stanton, *Gospel*.

experience of sectarianism within the Christian (Protestant) tradition of the post-Enlightenment world. Such studies have been useful as a heuristic tool for analyzing the mind-set of break-away groups, and for tracing connections between world-view, structures, and change; they have not, however, proved able to decide whether sectarianism is to be defined as separation.[25] More important for our purposes, the transference of the sectarian model to Judaism and to the first century C.E. is less straightforward than often recognized: again it presupposes a structural definition of "the synagogue"/"Judaism" analogous to the Christian church in the pre-modern and modern world, and it too easily elides community and place, as well as the local and the connectional ("Judaism"), in a manner adopted from Christian theology if not from the practice of the church.[26] When transferred to the local situation, such as that of John or of Matthew, it both envisages "the synagogue" as the sole locus of Jewish belonging and implies that there was effectively only one "synagogue" in a place, contrary both to our general evidence for Judaism and to the models of variety adopted for "the Christians."

Synagogue as Bridge

In the Acts of the Apostles Paul starts his preaching ministry in each new town that he visits within the synagogue (Acts 13:5, 43; 14:1; 17:1, 10, 17; 18:4, 7, 19, 26; 19:8); encountering opposition from the Jews, he then turns to the Gentiles, frequently, however, having won the support of "those who feared God" (οἱ σεβομένοι φοβούμενοι) (13:43, 50 etc.). This pattern produces a model whereby the synagogue provided the early followers of Jesus with a bridge into the Gentile world. Here we meet another much debated *crux*, the so-called "God-fearers": according to the popular reconstruction these were Gentiles "on the margins of the synagogue," attracted by the "virtues" of Judaism—its monotheism, its high moral tone, its scriptures—and yet

---

[25] For their application to Matthew see Stanton, *Gospel*, 85–107; Saldarini, *Matthew's Community*, 84–123; on John, Freyne, "Vilifying."

[26] Clement of Alexandria, *Strom.* VII.9.53 says Paul did not force Hebrew believers "to separate from the synagogue," (ἀπορρῆξαι τῆς συναγωγῆς) but here "synagogue" functions as "Judaism" for him; cf. also *Strom.* I.19.96. So also Tertullian, *Marc.* III.22 takes Isa 52:11 as a prophetic exhortation "to depart from the synagogue."

unwilling to convert, perhaps because of the physical danger and social stigma of male adult circumcision; however, their acknowledgement of the one God and familiarity with the scriptures would make them easily attracted by and attractive to the preachers of the circumcision-free Gospel.[27]

Clearly the pattern we have noted in Acts is an important one for Luke, established at the beginning of Jesus' public ministry when he reads and interprets Isaiah 61:1ff. in the synagogue at Nazareth (Luke 4:16–30). This is a programmatic incident, signaling Jesus' concern for the oppressed, and provoking a rejection and warning of going to "others" that anticipates the story of Acts; that it is profoundly theological is certain, although scholars continue to debate whether for Luke it presages the final abandonment of the Jews in the ending of Acts or anticipates a recurring pattern of rejection and renewed call. Nonetheless, Luke's picture has proved historically seductive: New Testament scholars have treated the Luke 4 pericope as representative of the nature of the first century synagogue, and have also assigned the presence of God-fearers in the synagogue a pivotal role in the spread of "Christianity."

Two issues need to be distinguished: first, whether the Lukan picture reflects the end rather than the beginning of the first century, that is, the time of writing rather than of the events it purports to describe;[28] secondly, whether this picture of movement from synagogue to beyond, via those already on the margins, is historically verifiable. As often noted, it is not explicitly supported by Paul's own letters, most of which imply a predominantly Gentile readership from a "pagan" background, and which nowhere use the term "synagogue." Elsewhere I have argued that the model of the God-fearers as a bridge is itself more of a scholarly construction, building on the again seductive picture of Acts, and is not otherwise supported by the sources.[29] Moreover, Jewish inscriptions using the term θεοσεβής—not Luke's term—have to be interpreted individually and in their own context, not in that of Acts or of pictures of the early Christian mission.[30] The assumption, or conclusion, that synagogues would have been congenial places for Christian preaching,

---

[27] See Lieu, "Godfearers."
[28] This is a central to the argument of Kee, "Transformation."
[29] See n. 27; also Lieu "Race."
[30] Thus it is not self-evident that the epithet has to be interpreted at Sardis in the same terms as at Aphrodisias.

however that be understood—leading to a definition of them primarily in terms of reading and interpreting the scriptures—and that there would be a ready audience of sympathetic Gentiles—suggesting that they should be defined as geared towards the needs of such—cannot be established on these grounds alone. To do so is to give a stylized model the status of "hard data."

Dependency: Synagogue and Scriptures (LXX)

For Justin it is crucial that his arguments with Trypho about scripture can be substantiated from the synagogue itself. So, arguing from Jer 11:19b, he claims, "This pericope, which comes from the sayings of Jeremiah, is still inscribed in some copies of the Jews in synagogues (ἐν τισιν ἀντιγράφοις τῶν ἐν συναγωγαῖς Ἰουδαίων)—for a little while ago they were excised" (*Dial.* 72.3).[31] Justin is, again, our most explicit witness to a real dilemma for the early "Christians" for whom appeal to the scriptures, soon exclusively in their Greek translation, was central: how did small, scattered, and often impoverished, communities gain access to copies of the scriptures? In debate with Jews this dilemma was underscored when it appeared that Christian versions of the scriptures or collections of "messianic" testimonies diverged from the text of their Jewish interlocutors. Justin introduced the long-lived accusation of Jewish mutilation of their own scriptures, but he also found himself compelled to argue from their text, and so presumably to consult it. He was not the last to do so: according to Eusebius, *Hist. eccl.* VI.16, Origen was still able to seek Jewish manuscripts in the third century.

Tertullian too articulates the problem in an apologetic context. He appeals to the scriptures as prophetic, and cites the story of their translation as evidence of their universal accessibility: not only are they still to be found in Ptolemy's library in the Temple of Serapis, but through the "liberty of tax" there is general access on every sabbath (*vectigalis libertas; vulgo aditur sabbatis omnibus*) (*Apol.* 18.8); in this book, he claims, *thesaurus collocatus totius Iudaici sacramenti et inde iam*

---

[31] On Justin's arguments for Jewish "mutilation" of the scriptures see Lieu, *Image*, 126–9.

nostri (19.2).[32] Similarly, Pseudo-Justin, *Cohort.* 13.5 acknowledges that there are those who dispute Christian use of the scriptures because "they are preserved even now in their synagogues," although he nonetheless affirms that their teaching pertains to the Christian religion.[33] Many have argued that the Christian "take-over" of the LXX was an extended process, and that the overlap between Jewish and Christian use of the LXX was longer than often assumed.[34]

This argument of dependency could be expanded to include other evidence of continuing Jewish—Christian co-development: for example, echoes of synagogue prayers especially as reflected in the *Apostolic Constitutions* 7, of the Passover haggadah, perhaps as reflected in Melito's *Peri Pascha*, or of exegetical traditions as already reflected in Justin but continuing much later. In a number of cases such echoes are not explicable by the origins of Christianity within first century Judaism; instead we can trace a continuing *two-way* interaction as, for example, in the interpretation of the Binding of Isaac.[35]

D. Boyarin has tried to extend such reciprocal development probably as far as is possible, showing the tendency for the categories of "Judaism" and "Christianity" to collapse in the process.[36] Neither "church" nor "synagogue" feature in his, admittedly rudimentary, index. Yet given that it seems appropriate to speak of borrowing, interaction, and even dependency, how far are these to be understood as taking place in relation to or in terms of "the synagogue"? Justin's and Pseudo-Justin's explicit references to "the synagogues" suggest that they should be, although we have already noted the conscious polemical strain in Justin; echoes of synagogue prayers surely also indicate an affirmative answer, but haggadic and exegetical traditions are more

---

[32] On Tertullian's evidence for the synagogue see Horbury, "Early Christians," although in most of his examples the "synagogue" has to be implied. Hippolytus, *Haer.* IX.7 describes his opponent Callistus as creating a disturbance among the Jews of Rome in their synagogue on the Sabbath, where they appeal to their right to read publicly their laws: this is not improbable but their appeal to the rights given them by the Romans recalls Josephus who was known by Hippolytus.

[33] Cf. also Origen, *Cels.* VI.23, "the Jewish books which are read in their synagogues." The problem of Jewish "ownership" of the scriptures is still acknowledged by Augustine, *Tract. Ev. Jo.* 35.7.

[34] See Treu, "Bedeutung," 138–44. On Origen, de Lange, *Origen.*

[35] On the Apostolic Constitutions see Fiensy, *Prayers*; on Melito, Justin, and the traditions about the Binding of Isaac, see Lieu, *Image*, 77–9, 128–9, 220–8.

[36] Boyarin, *Dying.*

ambiguous. Would the synagogue have been the primary, the probable, and/or the only place for such interaction? Where else and how else might such meeting have taken place? These are important questions both in our definition of the terms used, and in our picture of the activities of Jews and Christians within the context of the ancient city.[37]

Synagogue as Refuge/Attraction

As we have already seen, both Origen and Chrysostom harangue those who found the synagogue attractive and attended its services (Origen, *Sel. Exod.* 12; Chrysostom, *Adv. Jud.* IV.7.4, 7). Pionius, bishop of Smyrna, according to the account of his martyrdom, also condemned those who found refuge in the synagogue (*Mart. Pionius* 13). These are later than our period and raise the question whether the phenomenon they reflect is continuous with what some would call the "Judaizing" that was already a problem for Paul (Gal), and perhaps for Ignatius and his rejection of "sabbathizing" (*Magn.* 9:1). Here too the synagogue is to some extent modelled on the image of the church: for Origen that the Passover is to be eaten in one house becomes a warning against eating both ἐν ἐκκλησίᾳ and ἐν Ἰουδαίων συναγωγῇ, although that he can go on to warn of the "synagogue of the heretics" shows how much the term has become the label of "the other" (*Sel. Exod.* 12).[38] Origen vividly distinguishes "synagogal" (συναγωγική) style of prayer from that which his readers should perform "in church," but his purpose is to justify Christian prayer despite Jesus' teaching in Matt 6:5–6 (*Or.* 19–21): "But the saint is not like this: he does not like (φιλεῖν) but loves (ἀγαπᾶν) to pray, and not in synagogues but in churches, and not in corners of streets but in the straightness of the narrow and oppressed way, and not openly but before God" (20.1).[39] Yet such passages are clearly rhetorical and should not on their own lead us to define the synagogue in terms of prayer and meals. Chrysostom condemns the theatricality of the synagogue and denounces the practices associated

---

[37] See Schwartz, *Imperialism* for an attempt to minimise the local religious community as the locus of definition for Jews in our period.
[38] So also Clement of Alexandria, *Strom.* I.19.96 in an anti-heretical context, citing Prov 9:18a (LXX), "Do not stay in her place" says "place signifies the synagogue not church."
[39] Cf. 21.1 βατταλογεῖν rather than θεολογεῖν is to pray in "synagogal style."

with it; but he is intent on its demonization, and demonization is needed where competition is feared, regardless of whether its success is grounded in similarity or dissimilarity.[40] Here "synagogue" is modeled primarily in terms of its "worship experience," but this serves a Christian agenda of contrast. As in the model of dependency, we should also ask whether "attendance at the synagogue," however that be constructed, would (necessarily) have been a (necessary) expression of attraction to "Judaism."

Synagogue as Threat

The final model is both a consequence of the last and returns us back to the beginning. Although Tertullian describes "the synagogues of the Jews" as the *fontes persecutionum*, the evidence for Jewish persecution of Christians is limited, and that any opposition was "synagogal" even more so.[41] Yet, it is often argued, "the synagogue" might also pose a threat because it was more successful and more attractive than "the church." So, in the scholarly literature we sometimes find the model of the powerful synagogue, integrated in the city, in contrast to the small and ostracised struggling Christian "church." When the magnificent synagogue at Sardis was first uncovered and reconstructed, this image played a significant role in understanding and perhaps justifying the virulent polemic of Melito of Sardis's *Peri Pascha*.[42] Here, again, the physical structure identified as a synagogue but also identified with the local community as a social and political entity,[43] becomes a symbol of "Judaism." The site at Capernaum has had a more convoluted history; in the 1960's the grandeur of the synagogue ruins towered over the ground- and below-ground-level remains of the Church of St. Peter. The dramatic Fransiscan construction over those remains now offers the

---

[40] On Chrysostom's unparalleled descriptions see Cohen, "Pagan," 164, 167–8; however, Origen, *Or.* 20.2 already compares the synagogue to the theatre, following the Matthaean Jesus' use of "hypocrites"/"actors."
[41] Tertullian, *Scorp.* 10: although much cited this may be shaped by a reading of Acts since he continues *apud quas apostoli flagella perpessi sunt*; see Lieu, "Accusations"; in *Scorp.* 9 Tertullian cites Matt 10:16 but acknowledges that Christians will not be beaten in synagogues.
[42] See Kraabel, "Melito"; Lieu, *Image*, 203–9, 228; Taylor, *Anti-Judaism*, 55–8.
[43] But ctr. Goodman, "Jews."

visitor a different vision—the ruined synagogue no longer poses a threat to the church and to the self-identity of the pilgrims who visit it. The contiguity of the buildings continues to inspire scholarly imagination in a contemporary rhetoric of "church and synagogue" seeking to mediate between the historical experience of the past and the possibilities of dialogue between the religious communities of the present: it has been hailed as evidence for good relations between the two communities, for the presence of "Jewish-Christians," for actual freedom of action by the Jews of Palestine in the fourth and fifth centuries, or, supposing that the synagogue was built by Christians as a place of pilgrimage, for Christian dominance.[44] Once again, "synagogue" becomes "Judaism," "church" Christianity.

Conclusion

What this last example emphasizes is that these are models or representations. In each case we need to ask what is being represented, and in whose interests? This is equally true whether we are listening to our ancient authors or to contemporary reconstruction. Our early Christian sources are not interested in providing "cold data"; these are models, typologies, often shaped by Biblical exegesis or ecclesiastical need. That they knew synagogues seems certain; that their comments can be easily mined for information less so.[45] What social or historical reality does lie behind, or is claimed to lie behind, the representation?

The same question can be asked of modern accounts of "the ancient synagogue," not only in discussion of the origins of "Christianity": does "synagogue" in each case mean "synagogue" in any useful sense? In modern debate, at one end of the spectrum "synagogue" may simply be

---

[44] For proximity as a sign of good relations see Charlesworth, "Christians," 321; for competition, Taylor, *Christians*, 290–3.

[45] So Tertullian, exegeting Jer 2:10f., interprets the *lacos contritos* of synagogues, which, he says, began in dispersion (understood as a sign of scattering and punishment), and contrasts them with the temple and hence with Christ as the true temple of God (*Adv. Jud.* XIII.14–15). On the other hand, Justin's description of the "house" built by the prophets around Elisha as "where they could read the law and commands of God" (*Dial.* 86.6) is suggestive of his understanding of the synagogue. On the problem of mediating between affirming knowledge of contemporary Judaism and the prism of theological need through which that knowledge is conveyed see Lieu, "History."

a shorthand either for the "Jewish community," whether local or more extensive, or for "Judaism," understood by the interpreter as a unitary phenomenon, whether or not what makes it unitary is open to analysis or description. At the other end, the term is deemed useful only when it means a specific institution, centered on particular physical and organizational structures, and open to a definition which distinguishes it from other Jewish institutions, such as the *beth-hammidrash*, the rabbinic community, those who defined themselves as Jewish (religiously, socially, ethnically) . . . etc. To see these as opposite ends of a spectrum is, of course, to ask whether "the synagogue," as specific institution so defined, did lie at the indispensable center of Jewish life—and, if so, where and when. That is a question our sources cannot answer.

This essay is not about early Christians in the life of the synagogue, nor about the synagogue in the life of the early Christians, although the texts and models it has surveyed have been used to address both topics. Neither does it mean that Christian sources are of no value in any consideration of the synagogue. We should not ignore the rarity of references to the synagogue before the fourth century, a near silence that S. Cohen has pushed as far as it will go, drawing conclusions both about the failure of synagogues to attain "institutional prominence" until that later period, and about the "complexity of the ancient synagogue."[46] Neither, however, should we ignore the more plentiful evidence of Christian acquaintance with practices and ideas that we would associate with "the synagogue," even if they do not always use that term, evidence that W. Horbury has probably pushed as far as it will go.[47] Among our findings have been a degree of openness, prayer, imprecation, and the scriptures; with reference to the title of this paper, "the separation of the Christians," the interest of these is that they point in opposite directions: cursing implies separation, access to the scriptural texts held there implies association, while the effectiveness of either remains unknown. Yet the more fundamental point must be the danger in any exercise of this kind of "reading" the synagogue in the light of the church, or of constructing "the synagogue" as witness to the church.[48]

---

[46] Cohen, "Pagan," 161, 175.
[47] Horbury, "Early Christians."
[48] And so, of course, of repeating the Christian "construction" of the Jews only as witnesses.

Bibliography

Boyarin, D., *Dying for God. Martyrdom and the Making of Christianity and Judaism.* Stanford : Stanford University Press, 1999.

Buchinger, H., "Ex. 12,11.27.48 LXX bei Origenes. Textkritik und Antijudaismus." Pages 285–93 in *Studia Patristica 34.* Edited by M. Wiles and E. Yarnold. Leuven: Peeters, 2001.

Burtchaell, J. T., *From Synagogue to Church: Public Services and Offices in the Earliest Christian Communities.* Cambridge: Cambridge University Press, 1992.

Charlesworth, J., "Christians and Jews in the First Six Centuries." Pages 305–25 in *Christianity and Rabbinic Judaism: A Parallel History of their Origins and Early Development.* Edited by H. Shanks. London: SPCK, 1993.

Cohen, S., "Pagan and Christian Evidence on the Ancient Synagogue." Pages 159–181 in *The Synagogue in Late Antiquity.* Edited by L. I. Levine. Philadelphia: ASOR, 1987.

de Lange, N., *Origen and the Jews: Studies in Jewish Christian Relations in Third Century Palestine.* Cambridge: Cambridge University Press, 1976.

Fiensy, D., *Prayers Alleged to be Jewish.* Chico: Scholars Press, 1985.

Freyne, S., "Vilifying the Other and Defining the Self." Pages 117–44 in *"To See Ourselves as Others See Us": Christians, Jews "Others" in Late Antiquity.* Edited by J. Neusner and E. S. Frerichs. Chico: Scholars Press, 1985.

Goodman, M., "Jews and Judaism in the Mediterranean Diaspora in the Late-Roman Period: The Limitation of Evidence," *Journal of Mediterranean Studies* 4 (1994): 208–24.

Horbury, W., "The Benediction of the Minim and Early Jewish-Christian Controversy," *JTS* 33 (1982): 19–61.

—, "Early Christians on Synagogue Prayer and Imprecation." Pages 296–317 in *Tolerance and Intolerance in Early Judaism and Christianity.* Edited by G. N. Stanton and G. G. Stroumsa. Cambridge: Cambridge University Press, 1998.

—, *Jews and Christians in Contact and Controversy.* Edinburgh: T&T Clark, 1998.

Kee, H. C., "The Transformation of the Synagogue after 70 CE: Its Import for early Christianity." *NTS* 36 (1990): 1–24

Kimelman, R., "Birkat Ha Minim and the Lack of Evidence for an Anti-Christian Jewish Prayer in Late Antiquity." Pages 226–44 in *Jewish and Christian Self-definition II: Aspects of Judaism in the Graeco-Roman Period.* Edited by E. P. Sanders, A. L. Baumgarten, and A. Mendelson. London: SCM Press, 1981.

Kraabel, A., "Melito the Bishop and the Synagogue at Sardis: Text and Context." Pages 77–85 in *Studies presented to George M. A. Hanfmann.* Edited by D. G. Mitten, J. G. Pedley and J. A. Scott. Mainz, 1971.

Kühnel, B., "The Personification of Church and Synagogue in Byzantine Art: Towards a History of the Motif," *Jewish Art* 19/20 (1993/94): 112–23.

Lampe, G., *A Patristic Lexicon.* Oxford: Clarendon Press, 1961.

Lieu, J. M., "History and Theology in Christian Views of Judaism." Pages 79–96 in *The Jews among Pagans and Christians.* Edited by J. Lieu, J. North and T. Rajak. London: Routledge, 1992.

—, "Do Godfearers Make Good Christians?" Pages 329–345 in *Crossing the Boundaries. Essays in Biblical Interpretation in Honour of Michael D. Goulder.* Edited by S. E. Porter, P. Joyce and D. E. Orton. Leiden: Brill, 1994.

—, "The Race of the Godfearers." *JTS* 46 (1995): 483–501.

—, *Image and Reality: The Jews in the World of the Christians in the Second Century.* Edinburgh: T&T Clark, 1996.

—, "Accusations of Jewish Persecution in Early Christian Sources with Particular Reference to Justin Martyr and the *Martyrdom Of Polycarp.*" Pages 279–295 in *Tolerance and Intolerance in Early Judaism and Christianity.* Edited by G. N. Stanton and G. G. Stroumsa. Cambridge: Cambridge University Press, 1998

—, "Temple and Synagogue in John." *NTS* 45 (1999): 51–69.

Martyn, J. L., *History and Theology in the Fourth Gospel.* Nashville: Abingdon, 1979 [1968].

Meeks, W., "Breaking Away: Three New Testament Pictures of Christianity's Separation from the Jewish Communities." Pages 93–116 in *"To See Ourselves as Others See Us": Christians, Jews "Others" in Late Antiquity.* Edited by J. Neusner and E. S. Frerichs. Chico: Scholars Press, 1985

Morris, L., "The Saints and the Synagogue." Pages 39–52 in *Worship, Theology and Ministry in the Early Church. Essays in Honor of Ralph P. Martin.* Edited by M. J. Wilkins and T. Paige. Sheffield: Sheffield Academic Press, 1992.

Neusner, J., and E. S. Frerichs, eds. *"To See Ourselves as Others See Us": Christians, Jews "Others" in Late Antiquity.* Chico: Scholars Press, 1985.

Parkes, J., *The Conflict of Church and Synagogue.* London: Soncino, 1934.

Ps. Augustine, *Altercatio Ecclesiae et Synagogae.* Edited by J. Hillgarth. Turnhout: Brepols, 1999.

Reynolds, J., and R. Tannenbaum, *Jews and Godfearers at Aphrodisias: Greek Inscriptions with Commentary.* Cambridge: Cambridge Philological Society 1987.

Saldarini, A. J., *Matthew's Christian-Jewish Community.* Chicago: University of Chicago, 1994.

—, "Boundaries and Polemics in the Gospel of Matthew." *BibInt* 3 (1995): 239–65.

Schreckenberg, H., *The Jews in Christian Art: An Illustrated History.* London: SCM, 1996.

Schwartz, S., *Imperialism and Jewish Society, 200 B.C.E. to 640 C.E.* Princeton: Princeton University Press, 2001.

Stanton, G. N., and G. G. Stroumsa, eds. *Tolerance and Intolerance in Early Judaism and Christianity.* Cambridge: Cambridge University Press, 1998.

Stanton, G. N., *A Gospel for a New People. Studies in Matthew.* Edinburgh: T&T Clark: 1992.

Taylor, J., *Christians and the Holy Places: The Myth of Jewish-Christian Origins.* Oxford: Clarendon, 1993.

Taylor, M., *Anti-Judaism and Early Christian Identity: A Critique of the Scholarly Consensus.* Leiden: Brill, 1995.

Treu, K., "Die Bedeutung des Griechischen für die Juden im Römischen Reich," *Kairos* 15 (1973): 123–44.

Weber, P., *Geistliches Schauspiel und kirchliche Kunst.* Stuttgart: Ebner and Seubert, 1894.

12
Life in the Diaspora Synagogues: An Evaluation

Mark D. Nanos

THE PAPERS TO WHICH I HAVE the honor of responding analyze a wide range of information. Carsten Claussen undertakes an examination of the origins of the synagogue with a focus on the various forms of congregational meetings, offering a summary of many of the categories that apply. Judith Lieu enumerates the kind of problems that arise when employing Christian sources to define the category of synagogue. And Magnus Zetterholm examines the details and implications of a specific Pauline text and the intra-communal incident it describes in Antioch. In the following I will confine my comments to particular areas of interest that arise among and between each of them, hoping that the presenters will forgive the neglect of the emphases he or she may have wished stressed if their paper was evaluated primarily on its own terms.

A primary goal of each of these papers and the seminar is, it seems to me, to further refine the way the investigation of the ancient synagogue is conceptualized and approached, for example, bringing to bear new sources along with new ways to look at those often discussed. In that light I suggest that these papers might be understood to discuss the theme of church and synagogue. Oversimplified, I might title the propositions exemplified in each of the papers along this line: Carsten Claussen's as "Church, *thus* Synagogue," then Judith Lieu's as "Church, *not* Synagogue," and finally Magnus Zetterholm's as "Church *in* Synagogue."

Private Houses as Synagogues

Carsten Claussen's paper, "Meeting, Community, Synagogue—Different Frameworks of Ancient Jewish Congregations in the Diaspora," offers a careful investigation of a range of issues important to defining, describing, and advancing the discussion of ancient Jewish communal life. He delineates the framework of his survey of the earliest evidence for what was later called the synagogue thus: "What we are looking for is a place of religious meetings and deliberations, as well as one, which provides for other communal needs of a Jewish community up to the time of 200 C.E."[1] There is no need to recite the details of his useful survey; rather, I would like to comment upon a particular line of emphasis that arises in his research. Namely, the probable place of private houses as early places of Jewish communal life, that is, as synagogues.

Claussen notes, for example, 2 Kings 25:9 and Jer 52:13, wherein homes are destroyed, yet at least one rabbinic reference interprets this to indicate the destruction of synagogues, in spite of the fact that, in general, the rabbis retain "a very sharp distinction between private dwellings and sacred places" (*y. Meg.* 3.1 [73d.27–34]).[2] In his search for possible "forerunners" of the synagogues Claussen notes especially that in Asia Minor the evidence suggests most Jews were farmers or craftsmen. He thus suggests that, unlike Judean urban settings, or the special case of Alexandria, "there must have been types of religious or communal gatherings, which were far less institutionalized than the synagogues that may have existed in the provincial capitals," and this brings up the topic of the family setting for social life, that is, the home.[3] It is here that he suggests the need for more research, since it is here that religious and educational functions originated. Even the early usages of προσευχή and συναγωγή do not permit "a clear distinction between private and public places."[4] The logical inference drawn from Josephus's description of the request of the Jews of Sardis for legal permission to have a place built to "gather together with their wives and children and offer their ancestral prayers and sacrifices to God," which is based on the claim to have gathered as an association from ancient times (*A.J.*

---

[1] Claussen, "Meeting," 145.
[2] Ibid., 146.
[3] Ibid., 149.
[4] Ibid., 152.

14.235, 259–61), suggests "meetings in private buildings," all the more so for smaller communities.[5] The inscription from Stobi detailing the donation of a private home to the Jewish community underscores "a gradual move from Jewish religious meetings in private rooms—something one may call a *house synagogue*—towards a specially designated holy place."[6] This evidence blends nicely with the observation that contemporary cults and early Christ-believers met in private houses. Finally, the lack of evidence for titled positions prior to 200 C.E. and the indications of vital roles for women lead Claussen to conclude that house synagogues were far more common than has been recognized to date: "we have to think of early Diaspora synagogues as little institutionalized social entities, often, if not mostly, meeting in the context of private homes and larger families."[7]

I find little to criticize about Carsten's paper. The evidence as he defines it justifies his disposition to find the forerunner of synagogues in family space, in home synagogues, if you will. Surely he is right that Jewish families and neighbors gathered in homes and other private buildings initially and for many years depending upon available resources or the right to own a public building for conducting communal and religious affairs. It is interesting to consider what material or literary evidence yet undiscovered would substantiate the thesis. Would the list A. Runesson offered with respect to his analysis of the Ostia synagogue need to be revised to ascertain the earlier existence of a synagogue house upon which a later public synagogue building stood?[8] Would the discovery of a Torah scroll or menorah or even a niche in an appropriately oriented wall suffice? These and other such items could of course have come to rest in a room for any number of reasons apart from former usage as a location of synagogue meetings, perhaps even indicating a genizah. It is difficult to prove the role of houses, but Claussen argues the case well.

---

[5] Ibid., 157.
[6] Ibid., 158–9.
[7] Ibid., 161.
[8] Runesson, "Synagogue," 82–3.

The Separation and Mirror-Images

Judith Lieu's paper, "The Synagogue and the Separation of the Christians," focuses primarily on different and later data than Claussen analyzed, and to a different end. Lieu challenges both the definitions and dispositions of interpreters who seek to define synagogue life through the lens of the later Christian tradition. In particular, she traces and critiques the way that a prior and largely theological understanding of "the church" has often led to a reverse mirror-image portrayal of "the synagogue," with the result "that 'synagogue' comes to signify a shadowy parallel of everything that "church" signifies, and, consequently, generates a similar set of debates to those familiar from contemporary historical and theological discussions of the church."[9] The two social systems should not be assumed to exemplify the same characteristics or interests, and thus the same questions should not be assumed to pertain to the one as to the other. She notes that the problem is not a new one, it is already present in the references to synagogue that emerge in the early Christian literature itself.

In this paper, Lieu is concerned to reassess the implications not so much for Christians but for defining Jewish communal life, which should be explored on its own terms, instead of merely as a foil for the issues of concern for Christian communal or even personal life. To this end, Lieu explores the shortcomings of six ways that the evidence—especially from the 2nd century and later—has often been modeled to date. First, there is the fundamental image of synagogue (Judaism) versus church (Christianity), with the triumph of the later eventually represented iconographically at the entrance of some middle-age churches, where the blindfolded slave woman is juxtaposed with the bride-queen. Lieu demonstrates that the polemical contrast can be traced to early Christian writers, yet at the same time church/synagogue is not a primary opposition drawn in sources prior to 200 C.E. Analogous institutions should not be assumed. In the second area discussed, Christians as excluded from "the synagogue," one of the several points made is that the modern studies of Christian institutional sectarianism have often been supposed to be analogous to ancient synagogue developments; however, this may not reflect the relationship of community and place in the same way, including even for Clement of Alexandria, for whom reference to synagogue indicates communal life (Judaism)

---

[9] Lieu, "Synagogue," 189.

rather than meeting place per se (*Strom.* VII.9.53).[10] Further points discussed include synagogue as bridge, that is, to supposed "God-fearers";[11] dependency on synagogue and Scriptures (LXX), where the boundaries were perhaps less sharply drawn than often assumed; synagogue as refuge/attraction, which has been taken to suggest a place of worship since that is how, for instance, Chrysostom approaches the matter in his polemical rhetoric, but it is questionable whether this reflects anything more than his own interests and rhetoric; and Synagogue as threat, whether in terms of persecuting Christians or as more successful and thus more attractive than the Church, sometimes portrayed as a "small and ostracised struggling Christian 'church,'"[12] but again, it is arguable whether this reflects anything about the reality of the synagogues' sociopolitical circumstances.

Enlisting early "Christian" literature to frame the discussion of the historical social reality of Jewish life, including the place of reference to synagogues as communities, institutions, or places is, as Lieu argues quite convincingly, a problematic enterprise. Both the methods employed and the kinds of questions posed require refining. Perhaps as we take the route she suggests we will find more available to advance our knowledge of the ancient synagogue than has been realized to date. The next logical step seems to me to be to re-read the earliest evidence of Paul, for example, as intra- and inter-Jewish rather than Christian, and see what it might offer.[13] It is in just this direction that the next paper will lead, nicely framed by the concerns raised by the first two panelists.

---

[10] Ibid., 197.

[11] See ibid., 197–9. One questionable element of Lieu's discussion here is the appeal to sectarian identity for those supposed to be preaching in synagogues to these non-Jews about Christ as though representing "Christianity." She has rightfully questioned defining the social world of synagogue life in this way, so it is striking to see the criticism posed in a way that seems to accept the terms of those she challenges for imagining "Christian preaching" in a context of "Christian mission" within "synagogue . . . places." Should not the criticism be posed in terms of the preaching of a particular Jewish coalition, and thus within the structures of Jewish communal life, apart from supposing a developed level of Christian sectarianism or an emphasis on location per se? In other words, this may be useful information for discussion of Jewish synagogue life in the ways that Judith would approve, if the preaching of Christ within synagogues is defined on its own terms as a Jewish development.

[12] Ibid., 202.

[13] Lieu states that "cursing implies separation, access to the scriptural texts held there implies association," see p. 204. Yet cursing may also indicate concerned interaction continues instead of a complete break, after which there is less need to engage in

Separation and Covenant

Magnus Zetterholm's paper, "A Covenant for Gentiles? Covenantal Nomism and the Incident at Antioch," exhibits a disposition to revisit a Pauline text to redefine the context as intra-Jewish, and thus relevant to a discussion of synagogue life. Zetterholm challenges the prevailing ways to define the groups and situations in sectarian Christian terms, or as separate *collegia*, that is, as non-Jewish voluntary associations, thus obliged to demonstrate piety towards *polis* and Empire. He instead seeks to understand the social dynamics that emerge for Jesus-believing Jews in Antioch organized in the normal Jewish communal way, that is, as synagogues—and thus privileged to refrain from the usual participation of *collegia* in the cultic expressions of *polis* religion—when they maintain that the Gentiles who join them as Jesus-believers are also to discontinue their participation in official cult. That was a unique proposition for a Jewish group, for while other Jewish groups may have incorporated Gentiles in some way as guests, this probably did not alter the expectation of their continued expression of ancestral and official cult. Having redefined the likely categories, Zetterholm turns to a close investigation of the text of Gal 2:11–14.

Zetterholm notes, rightly, I believe, that it should not be assumed that the Jewish people in Antioch were eating in a way that violated Torah when they ate with Gentiles, or that these Gentiles were disposed to separate from Judaism; on the contrary, "*one of Paul's major problems seems to have been to prevent Gentiles from observing the Torah or even from becoming Jews.*"[14] I also think he is right to define the issue at the heart of the conflict as one having to do with the status of Gentiles from various Jewish perspectives of the period; in particular, with conflicting assessments of the eschatological status of the Gentile adherents of the

---

such strategies to define the boundaries of difference and acceptability. In the case of Paul, e.g., his continued persecution by synagogue authorities implies continued interaction within their sphere by one they understand to be a Jewish deviant, and his continued subordination to their discipline (cf. 2 Cor 11:24; Gal 5:11); otherwise it is difficult to understand their willingness to take such matters into their own hands. In the Roman period, Diaspora Jewish communal authority did not extend to discipline of non-members.

[14] Zetterholm, "Covenant," 175 (emphasis his). I have also argued that the issue is not about violating food laws, but to a different conclusion than Zetterholm. I suggest that at issue is the way that the Gentiles at this coalition's table-fellowship were being identified; i.e., as social equals apart from becoming proselytes (Nanos, *Mystery*, 337–71; "Peter's Eating," 300–18).

Jesus groups. Zetterholm brings to bear also the issue of covenant. These Gentiles were understood to be covenant partners, yet at the same time Paul believed that it was important that they remain Gentiles; otherwise his confession of God as the One God of both Israel and the Nations would be compromised. But Zetterholm also argues that they are included in the covenant with Israel.[15] That argument I find confusing, for they would then not remain Gentiles—that is, representatives of the Nations—but become Israelites. Nevertheless, Zetterholm moves the discussion to a very useful area.

Zetterholm understands Paul's accusation that Peter was "living like a Gentile" to indicate that these Jesus-believing Jews were choosing to "accept dinner invitations from Gentiles and to use food prepared and brought by Gentiles in common meals."[16] Although Zetterholm has declared the issue to revolve around unusual identity claims toward Gentiles in this group instead of the compromise of food laws, this move seems to surrender the impact of that point. In other words, he finds the contextual focus to be upon a "high degree of social intercourse between Jews and Gentiles"[17] within Jewish communal space—in synagogues. James is understood to object on normative Jewish grounds to a degree of association with Gentiles that he, like other Judeans shaped by the concerns prevailing since the Maccabean uprising, regarded as collapsing the covenant boundaries signified by circumcision and Torah-observance. These Gentiles may be fearers of God, but they are not to be counted among the circumcised: "What James consequently demanded was that the unrestricted table-fellowship had to cease and that the Jesus-believing Gentiles should form a separate commensality group."[18] Since these Gentiles could not become circumcised according to Paul's teaching they must have perceived this demand to signify that "they had been excluded from the people of God." Thus the conflict at Antioch is understood to bear witness to different covenant models for the inclusion of Gentiles among Jewish groups of believers in Jesus.

Zetterholm advances the discussion not only by his methodological approach to defining the groups in Jewish communal terms, but also by his willingness to listen to this text without first limiting what it might

---

[15] Zetterholm, "Covenant," 179–80.
[16] Ibid., 181.
[17] Ibid., 182.
[18] Ibid., 182–3.

say by what he believes other texts (of Paul's) might be interpreted to say, that is, he is willing to engage in historical-critical exegesis. That is not always the case when we come to texts so central to the convictions of the confessional tradition. Even if I do not share some of his conclusions, with this methodological decision to first seek to listen to this text on its own terms I must agree, for we cannot presume to know what the players in Antioch or audience in Galatia must know about the context of Paul's language before we exegete; namely, whether the issues of identity and concomitant behavior might have arisen within Jewish—that is, pre-"Christian"—social space. We are left to wonder. Apart from new hypotheses in search of answering new questions, or at least questions differently posed, we cannot advance our knowledge, in this case, of what we might learn about Jewish synagogue life from the letters of Paul.

I wish to engage one of the many issues that Zetterholm's paper raises about this incident that is particularly important for this conference. Although he sets out to define the conflict as "between" (inter) and "among" (intra) Jewish groups, I think that his understanding of the players and situation, especially the role of James and those Paul refers to as "the ones who came from" him, leads to a situation that is largely confined to players and issues between and among Jesus-believing Jews. This tendency is heightened by the way Zetterholm understands the incident described to correspond with that found elsewhere (in Acts 15)—although it is questionable whether these two texts describe the same event—as well as his working assumption that the vaguely described "certain ones who came from James" represent the views of James, and that these views are contrary to those of Paul, or in this case, Peter. I question these decisions and instead suggest that there are indications in the text—at least ambiguities that should be explored—that may lead to a deeper investigation of the players and issues in broader terms, that is, as inclusive of non-Jesus-believing Jewish people and groups, as well as their various ways of dealing with the constraints of minority group standing in Roman and local cultic and political terms. I realize that this can be a dangerous move if allowed to be understood in the traditional Christianity against Judaism mode, but that should not result from moving the discussion toward recognition of a conflict among and between Jewish groups and subgroups that predates the institutional separation of some of them as Christianity.

It is not clear that the specific ones to whom Paul refers as coming from James actually represent a challenge to the behavior of Peter in eating with Gentiles in Antioch. The ones whom Peter is said by Paul "to fear" and thus to withdraw "because of" are identified by him differently; they are labeled "the ones for circumcision."[19] It is possible that these advocates of proselyte conversion represent local Antiochene non-Jesus-believing Jewish people and groups which have, because of or simply coincidental to the arrival of certain Judeans in some way linked to James, finally had their fill of the "deviant" behavior that they now learn to be characteristic of Judean as well as Antiochene groups of Jesus-believers. Perhaps certain Antiochene Jewish interest groups raised sufficient objection to what they fear to be taking place within the meetings of the Jesus-believing Jewish groups to gain Peter's compliance. Or in a different direction, perhaps the ones from James were not in any way representing James but interest groups in Judea which were also bringing pressure to bear upon his groups for indiscriminate table-fellowship with gentiles in a manner similar to that being expressed in Antioch (cf. 2:4–5). If something along these kinds of intra- and inter-group lines was taking place, then we have another way to mine this text for first-century synagogue evidence that reaches beyond the confines of the Jesus-movement. At the very least, combined with the many insights offered by these several papers, a new investigation of the early "Christian" literature, especially an effort to read Paul's letters as Jewish communal correspondence, may yield much that is useful for those in search of learning all that we can about ancient synagogue life.

What Claussen is disposed to find, Lieu is suspicious of finding in later Christian sources, but Zetterholm suggests may be found by re-reading Paul, for example, the Antioch Incident. The traditional readings approach Paul's rhetoric as evidence of a sectarian Christian already working outside of Jewish communal space with a primary focus on establishing the boundaries of a Christian identity that is post-Jewish/Judean—that is, in "churches," not "synagogues."[20] To the degree that Zetterholm challenges the consensus assumptions, the textual relevance for investigation of synagogue life is enhanced.

---

[19] See Nanos, *Irony*, 147–54; "Peter's Eating," 286–90, 303–6.
[20] This limitation is perpetuated to the degree that Paul (as well as his disciples) is (are) approached as one(s) who "visited" synagogues rather than "peopled" them.

Conclusion

Like the other papers offered in this conference, each of these arguments exemplifies two aspects of the historical enterprise that ineluctably influence the results; namely, the interplay of definition and disposition.

The order and relative importance placed on both of these aspects is not without significance. The definitions adopted effect the disposition of the investigator (and respondent); at the same time, the disposition of the one doing the research effects the definitions with which he or she begins, in which ways they are likely to be modified, and ultimately, what he or she will probably conclude. We are unlikely to find what we are neither disposed nor equipped to seek. By way of analogy—which of course should not be pushed too far—what minors bring up from a mine is determined before they descend, not least by those who financed and did the research to find the resources, and those who built the mine so as to facilitate a certain kind of result. The final results will reflect their disposition to resources as well as the tools at hand. But they may overlook and thus obscure or even destroy other resources that could prove to be equally or even more valuable to those in search of other ends. From such limitations none of us can ever fully escape, but the kind of critical research undertaken in the Lund project and exemplified in these papers can help all of us expand the sources of information and possible interpretations, and thus enhance our knowledge about ancient synagogue life.

Bibliography

Claussen, C., "Meeting, Community, Synagogue—Different Frameworks of Ancient Jewish Congregations in the Diaspora." In this volume.

Lieu, J., "The Synagogue and the Separation of the Christians." In this volume.

Nanos, M. D., *The Mystery of Romans: The Jewish Context of Paul's Letter*. Minneapolis: Fortress Press, 1996.

—, *The Irony of Galatians: Paul's Letter in First-Century Context*. Minneapolis: Fortress Press, 2002.

—, "What Was at Stake in Peter's 'Eating with Gentiles' at Antioch?" Pages 282–318 in *The Galatians Debate: Contemporary Issues in Rhetorical and Historical Interpretation*. Edited by M. D. Nanos. Peabody: Hendrickson, 2002.

Runesson, A., "The Synagogue at Ancient Ostia: The Building and Its History from the First to the Fifth Century." Pages 29–99 in *The Synagogue of Ancient Ostia and the Jews of Rome: Interdisciplinary Studies*. Edited by B. Olsson, D. Mitternacht and O. Brandt. Stockholm: Paul Åströms Förlag, 2001.

Zetterholm, M., "A Covenant for Gentiles? Covenantal Nomism and the Incident at Antioch." In this volume.

13
The Life in the Diaspora Synagogues: An Evaluation

Bengt Holmberg

THERE IS NO DOUBT that Diaspora Jews living in the same place associated with each other, as did other ethnic groups in the ethnically mixed societies in the Roman empire. The Jews in one place needed one another for mutual support, especially in their religious practices, which distinguished them from other people due to requirements of separateness and restricted association. As any minority within a majority culture wanting to keep its cultural and religious tradition intact from the erosive changes of acculturation and assimilation, they simply had to put in a collective effort to meet together frequently and thus assert their identity. This is what sociologists in the Berger-Luckmann tradition would call "plausibility maintenance." In order to uphold one's personal identity and group identity in the face of a daily barrage of alien religious and cultural influence one has to find frequent support from others who think and act like oneself. The need of remaining Jewish in the Diaspora necessitated an institution like the synagogue, a Jewish assembly.

The need of a Jewish assembly does not, however, necessarily entail the existence of a specific synagogue building. Claussen's paper adds to the realization that an historical study of the synagogue institution in Jewish Diaspora communities should not focus overmuch on the physical manifestation of this institution, i.e. a specific building, in which the local Jews met regularly and specific office-holders performed well-defined functions of communal interest. It is important to remember that to date we have only four or five excavated ancient Diaspora synagogue buildings from the period focused on in the project and conference which preceded this volume (that is, up to 200 C.E.).[1]

The evidence we have points to the synagogue institution as having been primarily embedded in Jewish communal life as a whole, only gradually emerging as a more distinct entity with an articulated tradition and a life of its own. Claussen notes a number of times that the early stages of the synagogue institution are to be sought in Jewish homes, especially those large enough to accommodate gatherings *(synagogai)* of people from outside the family itself. He points out that the home-based type of gathering for educational and religious purposes probably was the only type of "synagogue" possible for many smaller Jewish communities in the Diaspora, which could muster neither the amount of social and political clout needed to assert the legal rights of Jews to assemble in the face of local opposition, nor the money needed to build a house for the assembly.[2] The low degree of institutionalization of offices and leadership roles up into the third century C.E. also points to the prevalence of a more small-scale, domestic setting for Jewish gatherings in the two first centuries of our era.

Realizing this does not mean an unquestioning acceptance of the hypothesis (from L. M. White) that most synagogue buildings began as private houses, whose function as locations for assemblies *(synagogai)* eventually took over their original family-related functions and made them into "synagogues" *(synagogai)* in the later sense: Jewish community buildings for specific religious and educational purposes.[3] The idea that there probably existed a physical house-synagogue beneath more or

---

[1] They are: Delos, Ostia, Priene, Stobi, perhaps also Dura Europos. The magnificent Sardis edifice became a synagogue only after 200 C.E. Cf. the influential presentation and discussion of Kraabel twenty years ago in his "Diaspora Synagogue" together with his "Social Systems." Levine's recent presentation of archaeological remains of diaspora synagogues can only use the same few examples of excavated diaspora synagogues from before 200 C.E.; *Ancient Synagogue,* 97–105 and 232–63.

[2] Claussen, "Meeting, Community, Synagogue," 159–60: "The overall picture that evolves is one in which it is by no means natural or self-evident that Diaspora Jews were able to have synagogues without experiencing any difficulties. The atmosphere seemed to be rather hostile in quite a number of Hellenistic cities. Therefore, we may assume that there must have been many Jewish communities who were just too small or not strong enough to have a local synagogue building where they might live their communal and ritual life. For them meetings in private buildings must have been the obvious type of gathering."

[3] White, "Synagogue and Society," 23–58.

The Life in the Diaspora Synagogues: An Evaluation

less every synagogue edifice in the Diaspora has now been controverted by a more careful look at the synagogues in Ostia and on Delos, which both began their life as public buildings for Jewish communities.[4] As the only certain case for a Diaspora synagogue developing from family dwelling to public building is the synagogue in Stobi, the burden of proof seems to lie with anyone who would hypothesize this as the standard procedure.

One could cautiously suggest a picture where there existed a large number of Jewish assemblies in the Diaspora, in many cases home-based. In some places (for example, larger cities) where the local Jewish community was large and wealthy enough and had achieved a level of cooperation and acceptance from the non-Jewish majority, one could also find specific buildings that functioned as community centers for Jews. Probably they were multi-purpose institutions with several different functions—communal meetings, education, common meals, religious worship.

To this picture one could add the realization that, in even fewer places, there probably existed houses that had been designed for Jewish community worship only, right from their beginning. In his dissertation, A. Runesson has presented previously unnoticed evidence that there existed Jewish temples, *proseuchai*, in the Diaspora (especially in Egypt) up to the first century C.E. It is likely that animal sacrifices had originally been performed in these institutions of worship, and later been replaced by sacrifices of flour, oil and incense. Finally even the non-bloody sacrifices in these places had become overshadowed and substituted by the "synagogue-type" rituals of reading and expounding the Torah.[5]

This intriguing perspective of temples turned into synagogues reminds us of the fact that the institutional manifestations of Jewish Diaspora communities could be highly varied from place to place and from time to time. It would be an anachronism to imagine that there always existed a net of Jewish synagogue buildings, with the same functions inside, all over the Diaspora, similar to the net of parish churches

---

[4] Runesson, *Origins*, 186–8, referring to the work of Mazur, Binder and himself. The large and prominent synagogue in Sardis also began its life as a (non-Jewish) public building. In his "Meeting, Community, Synagogue," 157, Claussen makes an exception for the Ostia synagogue because of Runesson's work, but should have included the Delos synagogue as well.
[5] Runesson, *Origins*, 402–76.

dotting the landscape in some European countries from the Middle Ages. Undoubtedly there existed numerous such buildings—each with its own particular history. Some few were Jewish temples gradually transformed into what we recognize as "synagogues," others were custom-built for communal "synagogal" activities from the beginning (as in Ostia), still others had originated as private homes and were later taken over by and rebuilt for the communal purposes of Jewish assemblies (as in Stobi). And then of course, many Jewish *synagogai* (assemblies) never developed *synagogai* (buildings) at all.

Terminology and Historical Reality

Where Claussen focuses on the development of the Diaspora synagogues, Judith Lieu addresses the difficult question of the relations between the early Christian movement and Judaism as such, usually referred to as the relation between "synagogue" and "church." Her contention is that this usage tends to make ancient Judaism appear as some kind of analogical counterpart to a subject more well-known to Christian scholars, the ancient church. But once articulated, the idea that these two entities somehow must have been mirror images or equivalents of each other, or even similar to each other is revealed as an unwarranted simplification. Judaism was not a kind of "church," nor was the church another Judaism. The real character of the relation between Christian and Jewish communities over time must be more painstakingly investigated in different locations and periods, which will reveal the varying patterns of association and conflict that actually existed.

Lieu does an excellent job of demolishing or at least undermining scholarly clichés and conventional scenarios used to explain historical texts. And that kind of demolition is important for accurate historical work, because "using the wrong words wears ruts of fallacy deep into our unconscious."[6] She criticizes the idea that Christians were excluded from "the synagogue" (especially by the *birkat haminim*), questions the model of "the synagogue across the street" because it again presupposes that "the synagogue" is a place from which a person can be excluded, and she also criticizes the application of the "church-sect" model from contemporary sociology of religion to the relation between ancient Ju-

---

[6] In the felicitous formulation of Akenson, *Saint Saul*, 55.

daism and Christianity. Concerning the church-sect model, I would add to her arguments against using it here, the general criticism that the distinction is a fuzzy one even when used by sociologists of religion, and that its use for describing early Christianity entails a certain amount of circular reasoning.[7]

This terminological cleansing is both needed and very well done here, and it is certainly a task enough for a conference paper. Lieu makes the reader aware of the pervasive influence of rhetoric in any writing of history, both by the ancient actors themselves and by present-day scholars.[8] But a full historical reconstruction must go on to other tasks as well, especially grappling with the data and trying to elicit possible information about what happened in the flesh-and-blood reality of human beings. The historical question underlying Lieu's discussion is of course still there, and it is not answered by a good clearing of the ground as regards (in)appropriate terminology. So, when finishing the paper the reader is still wondering if no Christ-believers were actually excluded from Jewish communities. Are the Johannine term *aposynagogos* and other first-century notations of harsh measures from Jewish authorities against believers in Jesus Christ not related to any historical reality? That Judaism in the first century was not monolithic and that the synagogue institution alone does not define Judaism does not mean that there was no such thing as being excluded from a social and religious Jewish context of which one was formerly a part. Definitional difficulties and deficiencies in the handling of data caused thereby should not tempt us to let the historical question on which the whole discussion is based evaporate together with the unsatisfactory terminology often used to grasp it.

The Role of God-Fearers

I sense the risk of a similar loss of contact with historical reality behind the terminology in Lieu's discussion of the *theosebeis*, "the godfearers." She criticizes the common image of them as a bridge for the early (Jew-

---

[7] For a fuller argument, see my *Sociology*, 86–114.
[8] An earlier, full-scale example of this is Judith Lieu's impressive work on Christian rhetoric about (and against) Jews in the post-New Testament period, *Image and Reality*.

ish) followers of Jesus into the Gentile world. The "godfearers" were a group of non-Jews attracted to the Jewish communities for religious reasons and forming a kind of (half)believing fringe of Gentiles that could very well share Jewish faith and a measure of Jewish observance, but could not bring themselves to full conversion. The reason for this reluctance was mainly the demand for male circumcision, and when a Jewish proselytizing group appeared in some Diaspora synagogues and promised all the benefits of belonging to the covenant without the pain of undergoing circumcision, this group quickly secured a following from among the *theosebeis*.

Lieu's main arguments for disbelieving this hypothesis are (a) that Luke's "seductive" picture of "the godfearers" in Acts is "profoundly theological," and (b) it is not explicitly supported by Paul's own letters, in which he seems to address Gentiles only.[9] Lieu has presented this perspective and her criticism of it more fully in an earlier article, "Do God-Fearers Make Good Christians?"[10] In this 1994 article, which she refers to in the present paper, she provided reasons for thinking that the "god-fearers" probably were attracted to Jewish groups for reasons other than religious interest, such as "social allegiance and status" or even the Jews' reputation for effective magic and exorcism.[11] There is, however, "little trace that these God-fearers were to be found in groups hanging around the doors of the synagogue listening to the debates or preaching going on within."[12]

Lieu does not deny the marginal possibility of religious attraction, eventually leading to full conversion into Judaism by Gentiles, and almost admits that Josephus' dictum about the Jews of Antioch, who "were constantly attracting to their religious ceremonies a multitude of Greeks, and these they had in some measure incorporated with themselves" (*B.J.* 7.45) could refer to converts, *proselutoi*. One could go on, then, and ask if this "multitude" of Greeks made contact with Jewish faith and life only in private contexts and not in Jewish *synagogai* (and if so, why not sitting inside?) Even if there is little trace (in the extant sources) of that kind of contact, there seems to be good reason to believe that it existed. Josephus is quoted and believed when he tells about a large number of women in Damascus "who had gone over to the

---

[9] Lieu," Synagogue and the Separation of the Christians," 197–9.
[10] Lieu, "God-Fearers," 329–45.
[11] Ibid., 337, 341.
[12] Ibid., 343.

Jewish religion, *threskeia*" (*B.J.* 2.560), so why not believe Luke when he tells much the same story about women (Jews and Gentiles of various closeness to Judaism) who converted to the Christian version of that faith in Acts 16:1, 13–15, 33, 17:1–4, 12, 34, etc.? Is the tendentious Luke inherently more unbelievable than the propagandistic Josephus? Surely both can be used in historical work?

The same general observation concerning an over-reluctance to accept some amount of historical fact behind biased sources applies to the weight given by Lieu to the fact that Paul never explicitly mentions synagogues. This fact cannot serve as evidence that Paul did not frequent Jewish assemblies, sometimes probably meeting in Jewish communal buildings. If he had not done so, how did he happen to earn and—five times endure—the maximum physical penalty administered by the intra-Jewish judicial authority of the synagogue (2 Cor 11:24)? And is there any reason to doubt that the Crispus that Paul admits having (converted and) baptized in 1 Cor 1:14 is the former *archisynagogos* from Corinth (Acts 18:8), or is that identification "the again seductive picture of Acts"?

A well-chosen adjective can do wonders as a hidden argument. "Seductive" of a statement implies that it is untrue, only looking like correct historical information, and the same seems to apply to "profoundly theological" statements, which for some reason are devoid of historical truth. It is not clear why a piece of information cannot be historically correct even if Luke attached theological importance to it. Of course it reduces its reliability (as any other kind of bias), but it does not automatically annihilate it. Historians have to work with biased sources most of the time, and can still produce well-founded and testable judgments on historical probability.

Gentile men and women did visit Jewish assemblies (synagogues), and some of them were religiously attracted to Judaism. Paul and other Christ-believers also visited synagogues and made converts to their special brand of Jewish faith. Some of these *Christianoi* were Jews, others were non-Jews. If the preceding three sentences are plausible, the proposition that some of the Gentile Christians were former "godfearers" seems to be an admissible hypothesis that does not flee in the face of historical probability. While Lieu is of course right in pointing to Lukan bias in reporting, I am afraid that she errs on the side of caution when letting the hermeneutics of suspicion disqualify Lukan material altogether from being used for historical reconstruction.

A difficult but highly interesting question is whether the early (Pauline) Christian groups in the Diaspora consisted mainly of Gentiles or of Jews. Lieu leans toward the former alternative, but there are voices for the other alternative too.[13] Of course a conference paper cannot engage all possible questions connected to its theme, and I mention this only to point to another historical issue of great importance for understanding the relations between Jews and Christians in the period focused on here.

"Christians" in a First-Century Context?

Magnus Zetterholm puts forward a number of fresh perspectives and hypotheses in his paper "A Covenant for Gentiles?" in which he suggests a new interpretation of the Antioch Incident (Gal 2:11–21). Especially novel and interesting is his use of sociological perspectives in understanding why the Christians in Antioch eventually separated from the Jewish communities of which they had originally been a part.

The first part of his paper, however, is devoted to attacking the conventional idea that the Christians were already in Paul's time a separate entity, clearly distinct from their Jewish origin. Somewhat like Lieu, he criticizes the use of sweeping terms like "church" and "Christian(s)," which are said to "imply already at a pre-analytical stage that the separation between Jews and Christians has already taken place."[14] In the interest of not separating Christianity from Judaism too early, Zetterholm disallows the term "Christian" altogether as a designation for persons, beliefs, and groups in the first century. He wants to replace "Christian" with "Jesus-believing Jews together with Jesus-believing Gentiles."[15]

I consider this unwieldy term to be a misnomer. These first-century believers did not simply "believe in Jesus," but believed something much more specific, notable, and provocative in the eyes of their con-

---

[13] Stark, *Rise of Christianity*, ch. 3.
[14] Zetterholm, "Covenant," 170.
[15] This is akin to the proposal of Akenson to substitute "Yeshua-faith, Yeshua-followers" for "first-century Christianity," Akenson, *Saint Saul*, 55–67, and n. 9 on pp. 288–90 against the term "Jewish-Christian."

temporaries: that this Galilean was the promised Messiah of Israel, Son of God and Lord—and risen from the dead to prove it.[16]

Further, a case can be made for "Christian" as a proper term for first-century phenomena. The prominence of this Christ-belief in believer groups (cf. the constant reference to "Christ" so characteristic of Paul's letters) made them distinct enough for outsiders to pin the (perhaps somewhat dismissive) label "Christ-ers," *Christianoi,* on them, as evidenced by Acts 11:26, 26:28. Luke testifies that the appellation *Christianoi* started in Antioch in the forties, and later we find it used as a self-designation of believers in Syria in *Did.* 12:4 (Codex Hierosolymitanus 54) and in the letters of Ignatius. Tacitus, who writes around 110 C.E. about the Roman situation in the sixties, mentions that people called the group that Nero blamed the fire of Rome upon *Chrestianoi,* and Suetonius records a more garbled echo of the same naming in the time of Claudius. Josephus' report (*A.J.* 18.63f) where he mentions "the tribe of the Christians" was published in the nineties in Rome, but tells about something that happened in pre-70 Palestine. First Peter is probably written from Rome but addresses the situation in northern Asia Minor, where the believers "bear that name" (4:12) as a slander from outsiders but are encouraged to accept it as an honor.

So, the designation *Christianos* was used for Christ-believers in both Syria, Asia Minor and Rome in the second half of the first century, first by Greek, Roman, and other non-believers (hardly by Jews, though), then by the believers themselves. It does not indicate whether the bearers of the name were originally Jewish or not, and even less that they were no longer Jews. It simply evidences the fact that their belief in Jesus the crucified and risen Christ is so important to them that this name sticks. What began as a handy term, even a nickname, used by outsiders

---

[16] This kind of belief is not as harmless and socially insignificant as overly realist historians think. Drury ("Christ our Passover," 222) puts it forcefully: "Symbolic structures make things happen. Things and people are vulnerable by them. They push people about, killing them, maiming them, making them behave in previously alien ways and altering their material social arrangements. Crucially, when we notice this we are not observing other historical events than those which witnessed to the power of actual events over imaginary symbols. We are watching the same events. Thus Jesus was crucified because he understood the world differently from people with more political power than himself. His symbolic utterances and deeds violated theirs." One could add that later christological utterances and deeds among his followers seem to have had the same (negative) social effectiveness, i.e. caused anger, reprisals, persecution, and eventually separation.

with a keen eye for what was characteristic and important for this new religious movement was gradually accepted by the so-named insiders as simply appropriate for what really defined them: belonging to Christ.

Now, if "Christian" is a term used about a specific group of people and their specific faith and ethos by others and themselves *already in the first century*, it is hard to understand why modern anxieties about how the term might be misunderstood should prevent its use in historical investigation of this very phenomenon. A Jewish *Christianos* in a Pauline community is not separated from Judaism, neither as a religious nor ethnic-social reality, even if he is not an ordinary Jew in all respects. And the term *Christianoi* need not signify a group outside Judaism any more than the term *Pharisaioi* does. On the other hand, both these terms denote groups that are distinct and permanent enough to be given names by others.

Even if designations like "Jewish" and "Christian" cover a wide variety of phenomena through the centuries, they are still adequate terms in describing them from their early stages. The use of such general terms does not necessitate the importing of, say, fourth-century Judaism or Christianity into the term when used about first-century phenomena. Words are not receptacles that *have* to contain every meaning that anybody ever put into them, and to restrict the term "Christian/ity" to the fully (?) separate and developed movement of Christ-believers after, say, 100 or 150 C.E. is simply arbitrary from an historical point of view.

Of course it is important to avoid "fallacy-inducing vocabulary" (Akenson), but this is mainly done by being clear about how one uses important terms. It is just as important for scholars to abstain from developing their own, allegedly neutral and un-misunderstandable terminology and substitute this for terms used by the community of scholars. All too often this new terminology is bound up with a very special interpretation of the historical data under discussion.

Sociology and Theology

Zetterholm goes on to point out an important difference between what is usually termed Jewish and Gentile Christians, that concerns their relation to the surrounding society, specifically their civic religious duties. Only Jews were exempt from participating in civic and imperial cults,

The Life in the Diaspora Synagogues: An Evaluation

which means that the ordinary Gentile God-fearer simply had to fulfill his pagan religious obligations until he became a proselyte, fully converted (and therefore circumcised) to the Jewish religion and people. "It may even be the case that the Jewish communities *urged* the Gentile god-fearers not to neglect their commitment to the official cult"[17] in order not to harm Jewish privileges—a statement one would like to see corroborated from ancient sources.

The Jesus movement differed considerably from normal Jewish Diaspora practice regarding Gentiles by forbidding *any* believer to participate in pagan cults, which meant that even "Gentile Jesus-believers" had to appear as Jews before the authorities. This was easy enough as long as they communed within a synagogue of "Jesus-believing Jews." But, according to Zetterholm, these two groups of Jesus-believers had little in common to begin with. The former group observed the Law and belonged to the Sinai covenant, while the latter did neither. This communion of Jewish and Gentile Christ-believers soon broke apart, which meant that the Gentiles could not hide under the cloak of a Jewish synagogue for long. They simply had to find another way to relate to the local and imperial authorities, namely the way of becoming a recognized (religious) *collegium* of their own. Thus, within the period from Paul to Ignatius, the two groups separated more and more from each other and went on to become two different religions.[18]

The Antiochene synagogue of "Jesus-believing Jews and Gentiles" broke apart because of troubles connected with their original commensality. Zetterholm reads the much-discussed "Antioch Incident" (Gal 2:11-21) in the following way: At first, eating together with Gentiles was not a problem in the synagogues of Antioch, because each party had adapted its own behavior towards the other's: Hellenized Jews lived a bit *ethnikos* in eating with non-Jews (unthinkable in Jerusalem), and the Gentiles who wanted to associate themselves with Jews gladly adapted to live *ioudaikos* in a manner conforming to the four prohibitions of the Apostolic Decree (Acts 15:20, 28–99). The commensality practiced by the *Christianoi* thus was the same as in any Antiochene synagogue, and for the Christians it was strengthened by Pauline theologizing about the one meal symbolizing and manifesting the one Body of Christ.

---

[17] Zetterholm, "Covenant," 172 (emphasis his).

[18] This is only hinted at in Zetterholm's paper, but described more fully in his *Formation*, 136–64.

This changed with the arrival from Jerusalem of "some from James," who made Peter and every other Jewish *Christianos* to change his practice to the Jerusalem custom of not eating with non-Jews. Why Antiochene Jews following the local halakhah, undergirded with local theology, should suddenly swing as one person from their habit of eating with Gentiles to consider this as wrong and the Jerusalem habit as "from a Jewish point of view . . . the most natural"[19] is not explained.

I find several things problematic in this reconstruction. One is the transferal of behavior known to us only among the *Christianoi* to Antiochene Jews and Gentile god-fearers generally, such as eating with non-Jews or practicing the prohibitions from the Apostolic Decree. Another problem of a more methodological character is the theologizing of a conflict that I consider to be better explained with the help of social-scientific perspectives.[20] The conflict between two differing commensality codes in Antioch and Jerusalem is here consistently understood as a conflict between the personal theological opinions of two individuals, Paul and James (who is present by proxy only and whose opinions are not found in any text).

Paul and James are said to agree that if Jews eat together with Gentiles this means that the Gentiles are accepted as belonging to the Mosaic covenant—a far-reaching legal-theological interpretation, alien to Antiochene Jewry (*pace* Zetterholm), possibly also to many Diaspora Jews. And one misses a distinction here: "eating with Gentiles" is not simply one kind of meal. There is a difference, psychological and halakhic, between a meal prepared and offered in a Jewish home by Jews to Gentiles, and a certainly non-kosher one, cooked and served by Gentiles to Jews in a pagan setting. The former may have been acceptable to a Jew who could not stomach the latter.

Paul and James are also said to agree on the fact that Gentiles will be saved together with Jews, but then disagree on a definitional quibble: are they saved (A) inside or (B) outside the Mosaic covenant? Outside, says James, who demands that saved Gentiles should not appear to be saved in the same way as Jews. Why not? Simply because it is not theologically correct to equate salvation B and salvation A (and James was a stickler for correct theology . . . ?).

---

[19] Zetterholm, "Covenant," 182.
[20] Holmberg, "Sociologiska perspektiv," 71–92, and "Jewish *Versus* Christian Identity," 397–425.

Here the author piles hypothesis upon hypothesis about unknowables—James' theology, his interpretation of Gentiles eating with Jews, his knowledge about customs in Antioch and his willingness to intervene there, and generally what took place in individual minds at a great distance from us. Zetterholm, who is clearly adept at using social-scientific perspectives in historical explanation (*vide* his dissertation), seems here to allow himself a visit in another genre of historical explanation, where theological ideas, motives and aims are the controlling factors of an historical event. Theological convictions certainly have social power (see the Drury quotation above), but only *via* their embodiment in a group of humans, enmeshed in behavior patterns and group relations over time. I believe this is the case also when explaining the actions and decisions of the Christian community in Antioch.

Bibliography

Akenson, D. H., *Saint Saul: A Skeleton Key to the Historical Jesus.* New York: Oxford University Press, 2002.

Claussen, C., "Meeting, Community, Synagogue—Different Frameworks of Ancient Jewish Congregations in the Diaspora." In this volume.

Drury, J., " 'Christ our Passover'," Pages 221–33 in *Crossing the Boundaries: Essays in Biblical Interpretation in Honour of Michael D. Goulder.* Edited by S. E. Porter, P. Joyce and D. E. Orton. Leiden: Brill, 1994.

Holmberg, B., "Sociologiska perspektiv på Gal 2:11—14(21)." *SEÅ* 55 (1990): 71–92.

—, *Sociology and the New Testament: An Appraisal.* Minneapolis: Fortress Press, 1990.

—, "Jewish *Versus* Christian Identity in the Early Church." *RB* 105 (1998): 397–425.

Kraabel, A. T., "The Diaspora Synagogue: Archaeological and Epigraphic Evidence since Sukenik." Pages 477–510 in *ANRW* II.19.1. Edited by H. Temporini and W. Haase. Berlin: de Gruyter, 1979.

—, "Social Systems of Six Diaspora Synagogues." Pages 79–91 in *Ancient Synagogues: The State of Research*. Edited by J. Gutmann. Chico: Scholars Press, 1981

Levine, L. I., *The Ancient Synagogue: The First Thousand Years*. New Haven: Yale University Press, 2000.

Lieu, J., "Do God-Fearers Make Good Christians?," Pages 329–45 in *Crossing the Boundaries: Essays in Biblical Interpretation in Honour of Michael D. Goulder*. Edited by S. E. Porter, P. Joyce and D. E. Orton. Leiden: Brill, 1994.

—, *Image and Reality: The Jews in the World of the Christians in the Second Century*. Edinburgh: T&T Clark, 1996.

—, "The Synagogue and the Separation of the Christians." In this volume.

Runesson, A., *The Origins of the Synagogue: A Socio–Historical Study*. Stockholm: Almqvist & Wiksell, 2001.

Stark, R., *The Rise of Christianity: How the Obscure, Marginal Jesus Movement Became the Dominant Religious Force in the Western World in a Few Centuries*. San Francisco: HarperCollins, 1997.

White, L. M., "Synagogue and Society in Imperial Ostia: Archaeological and Epigraphic Evidence." *HTR* 90 (1997): 23–58.

Zetterholm, M., "A Covenant for Gentiles? Covenantal Nomism and the Incident at Antioch." In this volume.

—, *The Formation of Christianity in Antioch: A Social-Scientific Approach to the Separation between Judaism and Christianity*. London: Routledge, 2003.

Part III

The Languages of the Synagogue

14
The Languages of the Synagogue: An Introduction

Jerker Blomqvist

THE STUDIES OF THE LANGUAGE situation in the ancient synagogue that have been carried out within the framework of the Synagogue Project have mainly had the Greek language as their object. The most tangible result of those studies so far is the doctoral dissertation by Georg Walser, *The Greek of the Ancient Synagogue*; the author presents his own conclusions in this volume. In an early phase of the project, Walser also wrote an article on "The Greek of the Jews in Ancient Rome," for the collective volume *The Synagogue of Ancient Ostia and the Jews of Rome* that appeared in print recently. In that volume, another member of the project staff, Per Å. Bengtsson, offers a meticulous edition of all Hebrew and Aramaic inscriptions found in Rome (and some with unknown provenance) and briefly discusses the use of the Semitic languages among the Jews of Rome.

The prominence given to Greek in the linguistic domain of the project was motivated primarily by the availability of expertise necessary for conducting and carrying out the investigation. The different varieties of Greek current in the Hellenistic and Roman periods have been the object of several studies by classicists of Lund, so the Hellenists of the Classics Department were in that sense well prepared for a research project concerning ancient synagogue Greek. But knowledge of Greek, however expert, is not enough in this context. Although one of our basic assumptions was that "synagogal" (or "biblical," or "septuagintal," or "Jewish," or "New Testament") Greek, if it could be proved to exist as a distinct variety of the language, must be equated with, and primarily compared to, other varieties of Greek contemporary with it ("profane," "extra-biblical," etc.), it was also evident that competence in Semitic languages was necessary for defining the distinctive features of the linguistic variety that Walser ultimately chose to designate as Pentateuchal Greek. Such competence, except by Walser himself, was made available by the fact that the project was a joint venture involving Biblical, Classical, Semitic and Jewish studies.

The all but exclusive focussing on one of the languages used in the ancient synagogue does not mean that the Synagogue Project ignored the fact that a number of other languages were used in the synagogue and the geographical environments in which synagogues existed. The heading of this section of the conference volume speaks of *languages of the synagogue* in the plural, and the two scholars who, with Walser, have submitted contributions on that theme do not limit themselves to one language only, but contribute rather to an overview of the whole linguistic situation in the synagogue or in ancient Palestine. Even the first, sketchy plan of our project makes it clear that the ancient synagogue was a multilingual milieu and existed in multilingual environments. The decision to concentrate on Greek was motivated by practical considerations in that plan: the textual evidence available in Greek was richer and more varied than in the other relevant languages, and it was also more accessible for analysis, since databases and electronic retrieval devices could be used.

Thus, Greek is only one of the languages, of which the function in the context of the synagogue could—and should—be investigated. It might be hoped that the study of synagogal Greek carried out by this project will inspire future work on other languages and their interaction with each other and with Greek. The contributions by Emmanuel Tov and Jonathan Watt that follow in this volume provide further inspiration for such projects.

15
The Text of the Hebrew/Aramaic and Greek Bible Used in the Ancient Synagogues

Emanuel Tov

THE TOPIC OF OUR INVESTIGATION is an analysis of the biblical texts used in the ancient synagogues in their original languages and in Greek translation. In this investigation, we are faced with enigmas at all levels because of our fragmentary information regarding the ancient synagogues[1]—their social, religious, and physical structure—let alone the text of the Bible used in these institutions. Since the data regarding the institutions is insufficient, it would appear that inadequate evidence is available for an analysis of the topic under investigation, and that we must learn from inference only, especially from rabbinic and other sources with regard to readings from the Hebrew/Aramaic and Greek Bibles. However, this is one of those fortuitous situations in which archeology comes to our aid, since two biblical scrolls were found at the site of a synagogue, namely under the floor of the Masada synagogue.[2] We are even more fortunate, since it appears

---

[1] See especially the questions raised in the most recent summary by Levine, "First-Century Synagogue." Several queries have also been raised in that scholar's *magnum opus, Ancient Synagogue.*
[2] The definition of the early synagogue is *not* expanded to include houses of prayer in general, so that the buildings of the Qumran community are excluded from the analysis. While it is unknown where in Qumran communal prayers took place, such prayers were held in Qumran and Scripture was read on such occasions. However, we have no way of knowing which of the Scripture texts found in Qumran was read on which occasions. See further below. On the other hand, the detailed analysis of Binder suggests that Qumran may be considered a synagogue, mainly because the holy places of the Essenes (not necessarily that of the Qumran commu-

that the evidence unearthed at Masada corroborates other archeological and literary evidence regarding the use of biblical texts. We first turn to the evidence from Masada, and afterwards to some general observations about the use of Scripture in their original languages.

The Evidence from Masada

Two scrolls were found under the floor of the Zealot synagogue (room 1043): MasDeut (1043/1–4) [Mas 1c] and MasEzek (1043–2220) [Mas 1d].

The archeological evidence is described by Y. Yadin, who noted that the scrolls were found in two pits carefully dug under the floor of the synagogue. The scrolls were deposited at the bottom of the pits which afterwards were filled with earth and stones.[3] A more detailed description is provided by E. Netzer.[4] The scrolls were buried under the ground, and hence most scholars presume this burial to be sound evidence for the practice of a *genizah*. However, C. P. Thiede suggested that at an earlier stage the scrolls were located in a room behind the *ʾaron ha-qodesh*,[5] and that "when the Romans approached, the scrolls were hastily buried under the floor, and when the Romans arrived and found the synagogue, they burnt furniture and other objects and threw them into that room." Although the details in this description may be hypothetical, it is not impossible that the burial does not indicate a *genizah*, and that the scrolls were indeed buried for safekeeping against destruction by the Romans. In any event, the assumption that this was a *genizah* is not crucial to our analysis of the texts, and it is more important to stress that the building was a synagogue.

Beyond these considerations, the only solid piece of evidence concerning the Masada fragments is that two scrolls of Deuteronomy and Ezekiel were buried under the floor of the synagogue. Why these specific scrolls, and not others, were buried there remains unknown since only fragments of the scrolls have been preserved. Possibly these scrolls, or segments of them, were damaged at an earlier stage or were otherwise deemed unfit for public reading, rendering their religious storage in a

---

nity!) were called *synagogai* by Philo, *Prob.* 80–3 and because he identified certain *loci* as rooms for communal prayers. See Binder, *Temple Courts,* 453–68.
[3] Yadin, *Masada,* 187.
[4] Netzer, *Masada III,* 407 ff.
[5] Thiede, *Dead Sea Scrolls,* 74.

special burial place (*genizah*) mandatory. These scrolls were probably buried by the Zealots during their sojourn at Masada (thus providing us with a *terminus ante quem* for their copying and storage, namely 73 C.E.). The burial in separate pits probably shows that the scrolls were discarded at different times. Note that the scrolls probably represented two individual books, and were not segments of larger scrolls. That is, the Deuteronomy scroll probably was not part of a larger Torah scroll, and the Ezekiel scroll did not contain all of the Later Prophets. If the scrolls had been larger, it is probable that some additional fragments would have been preserved.[6] The Deuteronomy scroll contains the very end of the book (Deut 32:46–7; 33:17–24; 34:2–6), as well as an attached uninscribed handle sheet, and it is not impossible that the last sheet(s) was/were damaged due to excessive use (cf. the re-inking of the last column of 1QIsa^a), and hence was/were placed in storage without the remainder of the book.

The two scrolls found in an ancient synagogue provide some information about texts used in that institution. It would be unusual to assume that these scrolls were not used in the synagogue itself, and had only been brought there in order to be buried. Such an assumption could be made about a larger community such as a city, but would not be likely for Masada. The following details are known about the contents and other features of the scrolls found under the synagogue at Masada:

1. The text of the two scrolls is identical to that of the medieval Masoretic Text (MT), and actually much closer to the medieval text than the proto-Masoretic Qumran scrolls.[7] This feature pertains also to the other five biblical scrolls found elsewhere at three different locations at Masada. The scrolls differ from the medieval manuscripts no more than the latter differ among themselves.

2. With regard to their physical features, the two Masada scrolls were probably luxury scrolls. Among the texts from the Judean Desert, I recognized such a category mainly in biblical scrolls,

---

[6] Several *haftarot* are *read* from Ezekiel, but the burying of an Ezekiel scroll under the floor in the Masada synagogue is probably not connected to the reading cycle.
[7] For a detailed analysis of the Masada texts, see Talmon *Masada, VI,* 1–149; Tov, "Qumran Origin," 73, especially the Appendix.

especially among those found at sites other than Qumran.⁸ The main distinguishing features of luxury scrolls are their large top and bottom margins, always more than 3.0 cm, and sometimes extending to 5.0, 6.0, or 7.0 cm. Thus the top margin of the Ezekiel scroll measures 3.0 cm, while that of the Deuteronomy scroll is 3.4 cm. Also the only other Masada scroll for which these data are known, MasPsª, has a top margin of 2.4 cm and a bottom margin of 3.0 cm. Luxury scrolls also usually have a large number of lines, 42 in the cases of MasDeut and MasEzek, and 29 in the case of MasPsª.

3. As a rule, *de luxe* scrolls are characterized by a small degree of scribal intervention, as may be expected from scrolls which were usually carefully written. The fewer the mistakes made, the fewer the corrections needed. However, scribal intervention pertains not only to the correction of mistakes, but also to the insertion of scribal changes. We measure this scribal intervention by referring to the average number of lines in a scroll between two instancesal signs. The lower the number of scribal activities (supralinear corrections, deletions, erasures, reshaping of letters, linear and supralinear scribal signs), the lower the number, the higher the rate of scribal intervention. This number gives a mere impression of the degree of scribal intervention since partially surviving lines are counted as complete ones. One correction per 20 or more lines should probably be considered a low degree of scribal correction, but most scrolls included among the luxury scrolls have (far) fewer corrections. The number of scribal interventions in MasEzek is one per 18 lines, in MasDeut one per 17 lines, and in MasPsª one per 85 lines.⁹

In all three criteria, the characteristics of the luxury biblical scrolls have been prescribed in rabbinic literature for the copying of Scripture scrolls, with regard to the size of the top and bottom margins,¹⁰ the paucity of scribal intervention,¹¹ and precision in the copying.¹²

---

⁸ See Tov, "Biblical Texts."
⁹ For an analysis of the scribal intervention of additional texts, see ibid.
¹⁰ See *b. Menaḥ.* 30a (cf. Massekhet, *Sefer Torah* 2.4) שיעור גליון מלמטה טפח מלמעלה ג' אצבעות ובין דף לדף כמלא ריח רוחב שתי אצבעות ובחומשין מלמטה שלש אצבעות מלמעלה שתי אצבעות ובין דף לדף כמלא ריח רוחב גודל. "The width of the bottom mar-

At the beginning of this study, attention was drawn to the physical evidence for specific biblical scrolls found in a synagogue environment. We now turn to the other archeological and literary evidence for the use of specific biblical texts in the synagogue. We will not dwell on the more general question of evidence for reading from Scripture in the original languages, Hebrew and Aramaic, at religious gatherings. It seems to us that this question has been sufficiently addressed, especially in a recent study by L. Schiffman,[13] and previously also by C. Perrot,[14] L. I. Levine,[15] and S. Safrai, the latter with regard to rabbinic sources.[16] Passages in Philo, Josephus,[17] and the NT (Luke 4:16–21; Acts 15:21; 17:1) refer to the regular reading of Scripture in synagogues in the original languages as well as in translation. The reading from the Torah in a religious gathering is mentioned also in the writings of the Qumran community. It is unclear how this reading took place, but 4QD (4QDamascus Document) clearly refers to the public reading from Scripture[18] and 4QHalakha A (4Q251) 1 ₅ mentions such reading on

---

gin shall be one handbreadth (7.62 cm), of the top margin three finger-breadths (4.56 cm), and of the intercolumnar margin two fingerbreadths (3.04 cm) in all the books of the Bible. In the books of the Torah the bottom margin shall be three fingerbreadths (4.56 cm), the top margin two fingerbreadths (3.04 cm), and the intercolumnar margin a thumb-breadth (2.0 cm)." The calculations are quoted from Yadin, *Temple Scroll,* 1.16. Likewise *y. Meg.* 1.71d and *Sop.* 2.5 prescribe two fingerbreadths (3.04 cm) above the text and three below (4.56 cm) for all the books of the Bible, except for the Torah.

[11] The opinions quoted in *b. Menaḥ.* 29b and *y. Meg.* 1.71c allow for two or three (but not four) corrections per column, while the differing opinions in *Sop.* 3.10 allow for one to three corrections. Scrolls containing a greater number of corrections in a single column could not be used by the public according to those opinions, but according to *b. Menaḥ.* 29b there is a certain leniency with regard to the erasure of superfluous letters.

[12] The precision in the copying is stressed often in the Talmud; see inter alia, below.

[13] Schiffman, "Early History," 44–56.

[14] Perrot, "Reading of the Bible," 137–59; "Luc 4:16–30," 170–86.

[15] Levine, "Development," 123–44; *Ancient Synagogue,* 135–43.

[16] Safrai, "Jewish People," 908–44, 945–70. For the cycles of reading, see especially Mann and Sonne, *Bible as Read and Preached.*

[17] For both authors, see the analysis by Schiffman, "Early History," 46–8.

[18] The combination of several fragments of parallel manuscripts, as reconstructed by Baumgarten *(Qumran Cave 4),* provides the full picture. See 4QD[a] (4Q266) 5 ii 1–3, 4QD[b] (4Q267) 5 ii 3–5, 4QpapD[h] (4Q273) 2 1 and the analysis of Schiffman, "Early History," 45–6.

the Sabbath, while 1QS VI 6-8 is less specific.[19] That scrolls were stored in the synagogue, first in an adjacent room and later in a special niche or in a ʾaron ha-qodesh, is established by an early source such as Luke 4:16–21. According to these verses, Jesus entered the synagogue in Nazareth, a scroll of Isaiah was handed to him, he unrolled it, read the text, and rolled the scroll back after use.[20] Storage of such scrolls in the synagogue is also mentioned in rabbinic literature[21] and is established for several synagogues starting with the synagogue of Dura Europos in the mid-second century C.E. and that of Khirbet Shema in the mid-third century.[22]

Indirect Evidence about Texts Used in the Synagogue

The two scrolls found under the floor of the synagogue at Masada were identical to the medieval MT, and hence were forerunners of that text. The external features of these scrolls are those of luxury editions. When assessing now the other manuscript finds from the Judean Desert together with some literary evidence, we will reach similar conclusions allowing us to understand in much greater detail the textual situation in Israel around the turn of the era.

The only location at which ancient Hebrew and Aramaic scrolls have been found in Israel is the Judean Desert. This is a small region, but we believe that the corpora found there include texts deriving from other places within Israel, thus presenting us with a clear picture of the texts used in the whole country, even though a judgment on the origin of each individual scroll remains hypothetical. Some of the Qumran scrolls were close to the medieval Masoretic texts, although almost never as close as the scrolls from the other sites in the Judean Desert. These scrolls, the largest group at Qumran, must have been based on the texts that were identical to the medieval text such as found at Masada and

---

[19] For an analysis, see Fishbane, "Use, Authority and Interpretation," *Mikra* (see n. 14) 339–77.

[20] From several ancient sources it is also evident that synagogues contained a collection of Scripture scrolls in a special place (ʾaron ha-qodesh), while the name "library" would probably be a little exaggerated for such a collection. Likewise, the implication of Acts 17:10–11 is that Scripture scrolls were stored in the synagogue. *y. Meg.* 3:73d specifically mentions the keeping of separate scrolls of the Torah, Prophets, and Hagiographa in synagogues.

[21] See Safrai, *Jewish People*, especially pp. 927–33, 940.

[22] For the evidence and an analysis, see Meyers, "Torah Shrine," 201–23.

other sites. Of the other texts found at Qumran, some had close connections to the Hebrew source of the LXX, while others were of the vulgar type, often written in a very free orthography and often freely editing the biblical text. As far as we know, none of these groups of texts had a close connection to the texts used in the synagogue. Nor did the Hebrew *Vorlage* of the LXX derive from temple circles, even though the *Let. Aris.* 176 stated that the Torah scroll was sent by Eleazar the High Priest himself to Egypt for the purpose of translation. Had Eleazar indeed sent a copy of the Torah to Egypt, he would probably have chosen the forerunner of MT, which existed at the time of the translation, just as the text of other books existed at that time in Qumran.

The texts that are relevant to the present analysis are those that are close to the medieval Masoretic Text. It is strange that a discussion of ancient texts resorts to medieval sources, but those copies can be characterized sociologically, thus aiding us in the characterization of the ancient texts. Focusing on the consonantal framework of the medieval text, MT, and disregarding the medieval elements of that text (vowels, accents, Masorah), we note that MT was the only one used in earlier centuries in rabbinic circles. This is the only text which is quoted in rabbinic literature, and is used for the various Targumim. Also, the extra-textual details of MT discussed in rabbinic literature, such as the open and closed sections, scribal notations, versification, as well as reading from Scripture, refer exactly to this text. It is therefore assumed that the text which was carefully transmitted through the centuries was previously embraced by rabbinic circles. We would even go so far as to assume that these texts were based on the scroll found in the temple court, but more on this below. First we will focus on the evidence from the Judean Desert.

The texts published in the past, especially those from sites other than Qumran published in the 1990s together with the texts from Murabbaʿat published in *DJD* 2,[23] show beyond doubt that we should posit

---

[23] The biblical texts are available in the following publications: *DJD* 1 (Qumran cave 1), 2 (Murabbaʿat), 3 (minor caves of Qumran), 4 (11QPs^a), 9, 12, 14–17 (all: Qumran cave 4), 23 (Qumran cave 11), 37 (sites other than Qumran). The Masada biblical texts were published by Talmon (see n. 7). These volumes are joined by the following editions: Sukenik, *ʾwṣr* [1QIsa^b]; Parry and Qimron, *Great Isaiah Scroll*; Freedman and Mathew, *Paleo-Hebrew Leviticus Scroll*. A few small fragments were published elsewhere: 4QGen^n (*DJD* 25); XJudges (*DJD* 28); 4Qpap cryptA Lev^h? (*DJD* 36); Mur$^{(a)}$ (Puech, "Fragment," 163–6).

two types of Masoretic scrolls, an inner circle of proto-rabbinic scrolls which agree precisely with codex L and a second circle of scrolls which are very similar to it (Codex L [Leningrad codex B19A] is chosen as the best complete representative of the medieval text.) Most scrolls found at Qumran belong to this second circle, with only a few texts belonging to the first group.[24] On the other hand, *all* the scrolls found at sites in the Judean Desert other than Qumran belong to the inner circle of proto-rabbinic scrolls. Thus, the 23 texts which were found in these sites agree with L to such an extent that they are actually identical with that manuscript. The only differences between the proto-Masoretic scrolls from various sites in the Judean Desert and L pertain to a few details in orthography, minute details in content, paragraphing, and the layout of some individual Psalms. At the same time, these texts always agree with L against the LXX.

This inner circle of 23 proto-rabbinic scrolls includes the following sites and texts: Masada (Genesis, Leviticus [2], Deuteronomy, Ezekiel, and Psalms [2]),[25] Wadi Sdeir (Genesis), Naḥal Seʿelim (Numbers), Naḥal Ḥever (Numbers [2], Deuteronomy, Psalms), Murabbaʿat (Genesis, Exodus, Numbers, Deuteronomy, Isaiah, Minor Prophets),[26] as well as texts from three unknown sites: XJosh, XJudg, and XBiblical Text.[27]

The differences between these scrolls and L are negligible, and in fact their nature resembles the internal differences between the medieval manuscripts themselves. Accordingly, the small degree of divergence between L and texts from the Judean Desert, mainly the texts outside Qumran, allows us to regard these texts as belonging to the same group, or in our terminology, the inner circle of proto-rabbinic texts.[28] This

---

[24] All scrolls are fragmentary, rendering the analysis often inconclusive, but it seems that two Qumran texts belong to the first circle as well: 4QGen^b (one orthographic variant in twelve lines), 4QProv^b (3 differences in 36 lines).

[25] For the publication and an analysis, see Talmon as quoted in n. 7. For my own analysis, see "Qumran Origin," 57–73.

[26] For the first three sites, see Flint, Morgenstern, and Murphy in *DJD* 38. For the last site, see Milik in *DJD* 2.

[27] The texts were published in Gropp, *Wadi Daliyeh II*.

[28] Some medieval manuscripts are almost identical to one another in their consonantal text, such as L and the Aleppo Codex. However, other codices from Leningrad and elsewhere are more widely divergent from these two choice manuscripts. Thus the degree of divergence between the Tiberian and Babylonian codices resembles that between the Judean Desert scrolls and any medieval source.

inner circle contained the consonantal framework of MT one thousand years or more before the time of the Masorah codices. This applies also to the second circle of Masoretic texts.

The texts of the inner circle of proto-rabbinic texts are usually written in *de luxe* editions, and they display very little or no scribal intervention. In both parameters, these texts follow the instructions given in rabbinic literature.

The second circle of ancient scrolls is that of most of the proto-Masoretic texts found at Qumran. These scrolls deviate more from L than the scrolls of the first circle, they are less precise, reflect more scribal intervention, and are usually not written in *de luxe* editions.

We now turn to some thoughts concerning the background of the two groups of scrolls, trying to connect them to data known from rabbinic sources.

The text which is traditionally known as the medieval MT, and earlier representations of which were found in the Judean Desert, were embraced by the spiritual leadership of Jerusalem. They are therefore often called the "proto-rabbinic" or "proto-Masoretic" Text.[29]

All the copies of the proto-rabbinic group of texts such as those found at all sites in the Judean Desert excluding Qumran were to all intents and purposes identical, or at least an attempt was made to make them so as shown by the precision in copying.[30]

In retrospect, it was probably to be expected that the people who left the Hebrew scrolls behind in the Judean Desert possessed biblical scrolls that closely reflected the instructions of the Jerusalem spiritual center for the writing of Scripture scrolls. This characterization which applies to the rebels of Masada and the freedom fighters of Bar Kochba was stressed in 1956 by M. Greenberg for the texts from Murabbaʿat on the basis of the scanty evidence then available: "since the spiritual leaders of this Second Revolt against Rome (132–5) were some of the most emi-

---

[29] See Cross, "Some Notes," 1–14, especially p. 9.
[30] The agreements of these ancient scrolls with L pertain to the smallest details. Thus the agreement between MasLev[b] and the medieval text pertains even to the intricacies of orthography, including details in which the orthography *ad loc.* goes against the conventions elsewhere in the book such as the defective תמימם in Lev 9:2, 3 (col. I, 11, 13) and the defective *hiphil* form ויקרבו in Lev 9:9 (col. I, 21). This has been pointed out in detail by Talmon in his edition of these texts (see n. 7).

nent Rabbis, there is no question as to the orthodoxy of this group."[31] Some scholars even stress the priestly influence on the leadership of the revolt.[32]

We now turn to the question of how such textual identity was achieved, among the scrolls from the Judean Desert internally, between these scrolls and the temple copies, and these scrolls and the medieval manuscripts. The logic prevailing today could not have been different from that of ancient times. It seems to us that identity between two or more texts could have been achieved only *if all of them were copied from a single scroll in this case (a) master copy (copies)* located in a central place until 70 C.E., probably in the temple, and subsequently in another central place (Jamnia?). Identity has to start somewhere, certainly in the pre-printing era and the assumption of a master copy is therefore necessary.[33] Furthermore, that master copy must have been located in a central place, namely the temple.

The data from the Judean Desert allow us to combine the information regarding these manuscripts with the little that is known about the early textual realia from rabbinic sources.

Rabbinic sources provide descriptions of the textual realia which suit the theoretical framework described above. The specific quotations from rabbinic literature to be adduced below have been provided by several scholars, but their connection to the scrolls from the Judean Desert has not been recognized.

Rabbinic sources from a later period provide descriptions of earlier textual procedures, which were also their own. In these descriptions we read of a master copy, namely the scroll of the temple court, and of scrolls copied from or revised according to that master copy. The term *sefer ha-ʿazarah* (ספר העזרה, with a variant ספר עזרא, the book of Ezra)[34]

---

[31] Greenberg, "Stabilization," 157–67, especially p. 165.
[32] See Goodblatt, "Title," 113–32.
[33] This suggestion was already voiced by Krauss, *Talmudische Archäologie,* and Lieberman, *Hellenism in Jewish Palestine,* 22.
[34] The best-known locus is *the baraita* in *y. Taʿan.* 4.68a (cf. *Sop.* 6.4 and *ʾAbot R. Nat.* B ch. 4) concerning the *three* copies found in the temple court and the procedures followed when these copies differed. The scroll of the temple court is mentioned in several additional places in rabbinic literature, e.g., *m. Kelim* 15.6; *m. Moeʾd Qaṭ.* 3.4; *b. b. Bat.* 14b; *b. Yoma* 69a–b; *y. San.* 2.20c.

probably referred only to the Torah,[35] but it stands to reason that the other Scripture books were also found in the temple.[36] Little is known about these master scrolls, and they cannot be dated.[37] Nevertheless, the little that is known about the texts in the temple is consonant with the data from the Judean Desert from sites other than Qumran. This group of scrolls, which must have been copied from or revised according to a master copy, are probably referred to in rabbinic literature.

We suggest that a connection be made between the carefully copied identical biblical texts found in the Judean Desert and the so-called "corrected scrolls" mentioned in rabbinic literature in the singular, *sefer muggah*.[38] The temple employed professional *maggihim*, "correctors" or "revisers," whose task it was to safeguard precision in the copying of the text: "*Maggihim* of books in Jerusalem received their fees from the temple funds" (*b. Ketub.* 106a),[39] which implies that the correcting procedure was financed by the temple resources and must have been based on the master copy in the temple. The temple authorities thus not only gave their *imprimatur* to the corrected scrolls, revised according to the scroll in the temple court, but also financed this activity, which was the only way to safeguard the proper distribution of corrected scrolls. These

---

[35] This is evident from the discussion in *b. B. Bat.* 14b and from the description of the three scrolls found in the temple court which were given names according to passages in the Torah, see *y. Taʿan.* 4.68a (cf. *Sop.* 6.4 and *Abot R. Nat.* B ch. 4).

[36] Note, for example, *m. Yoma* 1.5 according to which the elders of the court read to the High Priest on the day before the Day of Atonement from Job, Ezra, Chronicles, and Daniel. These books, together with the master copy of the Torah were probably part of a temple library. The founding of such a library by Nehemiah was mentioned in 2 Macc 2:13–15 ("books concerning kings, prophets, David, and royal letters"). Josephus mentions the temple library on various occasions (e.g., *A.J.* 3.38; 4.303; 5.61), once also with regard to the copy of the Jewish Law which was taken by Titus (*B.J.* 7.150, 162). For further references to such a library and an analysis, see Klijn, "Library of Scriptures," 265–72.

[37] Gordis, *The Biblical Text*, xl, on the other hand, assumes that "anonymous scholars" chose a precise manuscript and deposited it in the temple "between the accession of Simon the Maccabean (142 B.C.E.) and the destruction of the Temple (70 C.E.)."

[38] For an initial analysis of the *sefer muggah*, see Blau, *Studien zum althebräischen Buchwesen*, 97–111; Krauss, *Talmudische Archäologie*, 3.170–1.

[39] *y. Šeqal.* 4.48a has an interesting מגיהי ספרים בירושלים היו נוטלין שכרן מתרומת הלשכה. variant to this text, viz. מגיהי ספר העזרה היו נוטלין שכרן מתרומת הלשכה, which should probably be translated as "The revisers of Bible scrolls according to the scroll of the temple court" (similarly Gordis, *Biblical Text*, xxvii).

scrolls must have been used everywhere in Israel,[40] especially in synagogues, but also for instruction, as referred to in *b. Pesaḥ.* 112a where R. Akiba urged his student R. Simeon: "and when you teach your son, teach him from a corrected scroll." Another such copy was the scroll of the king, which was not found in the temple but accompanied the king everywhere, and *Sifre* Deuteronomy 160[41] tells us that it was corrected according to the temple copy (*magihim lo misefer ʿazarah*) in the presence of the Levitical priests.[42] Elsewhere, one finds the term *sefer še-ʾêno muggah*, "a book that is not corrected" (*b. Ketub.* 19b) which one could have in his house no longer than thirty days.[43] It is suggested here *that the precise proto-Masoretic texts found in the Judean Desert must have been these "corrected scrolls,"* that is, texts corrected according to the scroll found in the temple court.

The connection made here is no more than an assumption, but a stable one in our mind because of theoretical considerations and the references in rabbinic literature to the writing of Scripture scrolls. Identity can only be achieved by copying from a master copy, and such a scroll was actually mentioned in the Talmud (incidentally, the tradition of the three copies found in the temple[44] is unclear regarding the actual number of copies; the main tradition in rabbinic literature speaks of a single scroll in the temple court [see the references in n. 34]). Elsewhere in the Talmud, *de luxe* editions with large margins were prescribed for the writing of Scripture scrolls. Furthermore, a number of more than three corrections per column was not acceptable in rabbinic literature (see n. 11). Thus the three parameters of the proto-rabbinic texts from

---

[40] This is also the understanding of Safrai, *Jewish People*, 905: "Problems related to the transmission of the text and authenticity of various books of the Bible were examined in the Temple; copyists and correctors sat in the Temple and worked to supply books to *those who needed them in the land of Israel and in the Diaspora* [my italics]. There was a bible in the Temple called 'the book of the court' on the basis of which books were corrected."

[41] Ed. Finkelstein, p. 211. The complicated description of the correcting procedure in *t. San.* 4.7 probably derived from the wording in *y. San.*

[42] In another context we read in *y. Ket.* 2.26b: "a corrected scroll like those which are designated as the books of Assi." Lieberman, *Hellenism*, 25 adds: "From the context it is obvious that these corrected books were written by Assi himself whose handwriting was well known."

[43] Interestingly enough, Rashi explains this book as not only containing the Torah, but any part of Scripture.

[44] For a thorough analysis of this tradition in *y. Taʿan.* 4.68a (cf. *Sop.* 6.4 and *ʾAbot R. Nat.* B ch. 4), see Talmon, "Three Scrolls," 14–27.

the Judean Desert from sites other than Qumran reflect the rabbinic instructions for the writing of Scripture scrolls.

The various pieces of the description fit together well when we realize that these "corrected copies," included in *de luxe* editions, were found at various places in the Judean Desert, but not at Qumran. The Qumranites were not bound by the copying rules practiced in temple circles, as is clear from the unusual orthography used in the copies penned down at Qumran.[45] Therefore, they did not have such "corrected scrolls" in their midst. They must have imported proto-rabbinic texts (of a slightly lower level of precision), which were probably based on these "corrected scrolls," but this assumption cannot be proven in detail. It involves the hypothesis that a scroll such as 4QJer^a or 4QJer^c was copied from a "corrected scroll" of Jeremiah without adhering to the precision which was inherent with the "corrected scrolls." The proto-Masoretic texts from Qumran, one stage removed from the corrected scrolls, were therefore described above as the second circle of proto-Masoretic scrolls.

The relation of the Qumranites to the diversity of texts found in the caves is unknown. That is, they probably did not pay attention to the textual variety found in their midst.[46] One could surmise that Qumran texts of the best quality were used in their religious gatherings, while all other texts were used for different purposes, but this assumption cannot be supported by evidence.

The aforementioned analysis pertains only to copies of the proto-rabbinic text. It did not refer to all other texts that were current in Israel and about which information can be gathered from the Qumran corpus. These texts, such as the scrolls written in the "Qumran scribal practise" and the proto-Samaritan texts were used in Israel alongside the proto-rabbinic texts.

Returning now to the question as to which texts were used in the synagogue, the evidence brought to bear on this question from rabbinic sources is very relevant. But let us first pay attention to the abstract model devised by Lieberman.[47] This scholar distinguished between "inferior" (φαυλότερα) texts which were used by the people, texts used for purposes of instruction and learning (κοινότερα or *vulgata* "widely circulated"), and "exact scrolls" (ἠκριβωμένα) fostered by the temple cir-

---

[45] See Tov, "Further Evidence," 199–216.
[46] See Tov, "Biblischen Handschriften," 1–34.
[47] Lieberman, *Hellenism*, 22–7.

cles. A tripartite division of the texts used in Israel sounds appealing, but from the point of view of the temple circles the evidence should probably be divided into two groups ("exact scrolls" written according to the instructions of the temple circles and all other scrolls) and it can also be divided into three different groups. One problematic aspect of S. Lieberman's abstract model is that it is not based on any known texts (except for the quotations in rabbinic literature from the so-called Severus scroll or "book of R. Meir" which Lieberman considers to be representative of the *vulgata*). Thus, in this model there is no room for precise, early texts different from MT, like 4QJer^{b,d}, in this case close to the LXX. In a way these are also "exact scrolls," but from the point of view of the temple circles which adhered only to the proto-rabbinic texts, these scrolls were not acceptable any more. In short, the known evidence cannot be fitted easily into Lieberman's model. But more crucial for the present analysis is the fact that according to Lieberman's description his "exact scrolls" were found only in the temple, and this model cannot be defended since the evidence reveals that they were also found in the Judean Desert. Furthermore, Lieberman's theory disregards the so-called "corrected scrolls" which he quotes himself from rabbinic sources, and which must have been found in various localities outside the temple (cf. especially *b. Pesaḥ.* 112a and the scroll of the king). It stands to reason that these scrolls were also used in synagogues, and indeed two such luxury scrolls reflecting the proto-rabbinic tradition were found under the floor of the Masada synagogue. Note further that according to Lieberman, the *vulgata* texts were used in synagogues and schools,[48] a view which from the outset is very unlikely because in these places one would expect the most precise scrolls, as corroborated by the scrolls found under the Masada synagogue.

In short, in our view, a combination of the literary evidence and that of the excavations at Masada shows that we may identify the texts used in the synagogue as the "corrected scrolls" mentioned in rabbinic literature. These scrolls contain the proto-rabbinic text. This situation probably prevailed in all of Israel, and many details known about these scrolls are in agreement with the instructions for the writing of Scripture scrolls written down at a later stage in rabbinic literature.

This argument possibly ties in with the assumption of D. D. Binder with regard to a close connection between the temple and the syna-

---

[48] Ibid., 22.

gogues.[49] Without entering into this discussion, it stands to reason that the temple authorities would have been interested in maintaining the copy in the temple as the base for Scripture scrolls used everywhere in Israel, including synagogues.

The analysis referred only to scrolls copied and distributed in Israel, and not to those in the Diaspora. The scrolls sent or brought to Alexandria for the translation of Greek Scripture did not derive from temple sources,[50] and, in our view, it is also unlikely that the vulgar text of R. Meir's Torah, used in Rome in the third century C.E., derived from the temple.[51]

Greek Texts Used in the Ancient Synagogues

Unlike the evidence for the Masada synagogue, there is no direct archeological data for the use of specific copies of *Greek* Scripture in synagogues in Israel or in the Diaspora. It is likely that the Greek translation of the Torah was used in the third and second centuries B.C.E., but this assumption cannot be proven.[52] At the same time, there is ample literary evidence for the notion that Scripture was read in Greek in religious gatherings of Greek-speaking communities in the Diaspora from the first century B.C.E. onwards.[53] Among other things,[54] Philo refers to this

---

[49] Binder, *Temple Courts*, 343–50, 479–500; Levine, "First-Century Synagogue," 26–7 does not accept this view.
[50] See the remarks above, p. 245 and Tov, "Nature."
[51] Rabbinic literature preserves references to a Torah scroll taken by Titus to Rome as booty after the destruction of the temple. In a later period, this scroll was given as a present by Severus (reigned 222–235 C.E.) to a synagogue that was being built with his permission. This scroll, also known as the Severus scroll, was of a vulgar type. From the scant information known about the contents of the Severus Scroll, it appears that its characteristic features are the weakening of the gutturals, the writing of non-final letters in final position, and the interchange of similar letters. For details, see Siegel, *Severus Scroll*. Also Josephus, *B.J.* 7.150, 16 mentions that a copy of the Jewish Law was taken by Titus from the temple. However, it is unlikely that this was the main temple copy analyzed above. The vulgar character of the Severus scroll would not have befitted scrolls found in the temple, and the information given by Josephus is very vague.
[52] Thus also Dorival, *Bible greque,* 120.
[53] Early papyri of the Pentateuch from Egypt (P.Ryl. Gk. 458 [first half of the second century B.C.E.] and P. Fouad [first century B.C.E.]) show that the Greek trans-

custom in Alexandria.[55] 4 Macc 18:10–18, possibly written in Egypt in the first century C.E., expressly mentions the reading of the Law accompanied by reflections taken from the Prophets, Psalms, and Hagiographa. A liturgical use is indicated probably also in the last sentence in the Greek Addition F to Esther which names the book of Esther as a whole "the Epistle of Phrurai [= Purim]" (ἐπιστολὴν τῶν Φρουραι), regarded as an Epistle from Mordecai to the Jewish people concerning the feast of Purim.

For the use of Greek Scripture in Israel, probably the clearest reference is contained in the so-called Theodotos inscription from Jerusalem, usually ascribed to the first century C.E. This inscription[56] states that "Theodotus, son of Vettenos a priest and *archisynagogos*, son of an *archisynagogos* and grandson of an *archisynagogos*, built this synagogue *for the reading of the Law* (εἰς ἀν[άγν]ωσ[ιν] νόμου) and the study of the commandments." The inscription is in Greek, and it may therefore be assumed that the synagogue was used by a Greek-speaking community. M. Hengel cautiously suggests that this synagogue was connected to the Greek-speaking synagogue of Roman freedmen mentioned in Acts 6:9 (Λιβερτῖνοι).[57] Another such synagogue, a "synagogue of the Alexandrians in Jerusalem" is mentioned in *y. Meg.* 73d and *t. Meg.* 2:17.[58] On the other hand, the fact that several scrolls of Greek Scripture were found at Qumran does not indicate that these scrolls were read or used either privately or in religious gatherings. The nature of the Greek text finds in the Judean Desert is such that at all sites in that area there are indications of the active use of Greek as a living language in documentary papyri of different types, including in Naḥal Ḥever where the Greek Minor Prophets Scroll was found together with documentary

---

lation was known in various parts of the country, but they do not necessarily prove use in religious gatherings.

[54] For an early analysis of the evidence, see Frankel, *Vorstudien zu der Septuaginta*, 48–61.

[55] Philo, *Prob.* 81–2: "They use these laws [those of the Torah] to learn from at all times, but especially each seventh day, since the seventh day is regarded as sacred. On that day they abstain from other work and betake themselves to the sacred places which are called synagogues. . . . Then one of them takes the books and reads." See further Philo, *Hypoth.* 7:13; *Mos.* 2:215. The existence of Greek Torah scrolls is also referred to in *m. Meg.* 1.8; 2.1 and *t. Meg.* 4.13.

[56] See *CIJ* 2.232f, no. 1404; Lifschitz, *Donateurs et fondateurs*, 70–1.

[57] Hengel, *The 'Hellenization' of Judaea*, 13.

[58] For a discussion, see Schürer, *History*, 2.76.

Greek papyri. Only at Qumran is this not the case, since, with the exception of a documentary text 4QAccount gr (4Q350), no documentary Greek papyri were found there; the literary Greek texts found at Qumran (mainly Scripture texts) were probably brought there because they happened to be among the possessions of some of the Qumranites.

When turning to the question of which specific text(s) of Greek Scripture was/were used in Greek-speaking communities, we are groping in the dark. Was it the text which we reconstruct as the Old Greek translation such as was reproduced in the critical editions of Rahlfs or the Göttingen Septuagint, or was it a different form, earlier or later? As for the possibility of earlier texts, several Qumran Torah scrolls (especially 4QLXXLev[a] and 4QpapLXXLev[b]) provide glimpses of a text earlier than the Göttingen model which is slightly more distant from MT than the main tradition of the LXX and uses a less fixed vocabulary of Hebrew-Greek equivalents than the main LXX tradition.

When we come closer to the synagogue environment, we find texts that were corrected according to the proto-rabbinic Hebrew text used in rabbinic circles, both B.C.E. and C.E. A major source for this assumption is the Greek Minor Prophets scroll from Naḥal Ḥever dated paleographically to the end of the first century B.C.E. This Greek scroll was revised according to the proto-rabbinic Hebrew text, together with other parts of the Greek Bible, and all of these together are named the *kaige* revision. This development implies that there were central forces in the Jewish world assuring that the text which had been made central in its original, Hebrew/Aramaic shape would be central also in its Greek shape. The fact that the Greek Minor Prophets scroll was found among the remains of the followers of Bar Kochba, linked to the Jerusalem religious circles, is not without importance. It probably implies that this Greek text had the *imprimatur* of the rabbinic circles. In this regard, it should also be mentioned that this scroll, together with other early revisional manuscripts of the LXX, represented the name of God not with κύριος but with paleo-Hebrew characters.[59]

The find of the Minor Prophets scroll in Naḥal Ḥever probably implies that some of the followers of Bar Kochba read the Greek Scrip-

---

[59] Scribes A and B of 8ḤevXIIgr (end of 1 B.C.E); P.Oxy. 50.3522 of Job 42 (1 C.E.); P.Oxy. 7.1007 (leather) of Genesis 2–3 (3 C.E.); P.Vindob. Gr 39777 of Psalms 68, 80 in the version of Symmachus (3–4 C.E.); and the Aquila fragments of Kings and Psalms (5–6 C.E.).

tures in this revised version, and this may also have applied to other Greek-speaking communities in Israel.

By the same token, adherence to the similar revision of Aquila, one-and-a-half centuries later than that of *kaige*, is visible in rabbinic literature, as most quotations in the Talmud from Greek Scripture reflect that translation (see the evidence collected by J. Reider[60] and G. Veltri[61]) and *y. Meg.* 1:71c says about him יפיפית מבני אדם. This acceptance of the Jewish revision of Aquila by the rabbis[62] goes together with the rejection of the main tradition of Greek Scripture, the LXX. Such a rejection is reflected in several places in rabbinic literature, such as *Sop.* 1.7 "It happened once that five elders wrote the Torah for King Ptolemy in Greek, and that day was as ominous for Israel as the day on which the golden calf was made, since the Torah could not be accurately translated." However, according to Veltri, if these traditions are properly analyzed, they do not prove the rejection of the LXX by the rabbinic sources.[63] Since Veltri's analysis is limited to a number of passages in the Talmud, and disregards the manuscript finds of early Greek Scripture texts from Israel and Egypt, it should nevertheless be concluded that the LXX *was* rejected at least from a certain period onwards, described by G. Dorival as being from 100 C.E.[64]

Thus, the manuscript evidence shows a group of Jewish revisions of the LXX[65] in accordance with an ever-changing proto-rabbinic Hebrew text.[66] These revisions reflected the need to use a Jewish-Greek text based on the content of the Hebrew Bible, often different from that of the Greek Bible. Several of these revisions antedated Christianity (*kaige*-Theodotion [reflected among other things in 8HevXIIgr], P.Oxy.

---

[60] Reider, "Prolegomena," 151–5.
[61] Veltri, *Eine Tora*, 186–90.
[62] The Aquila fragments from the Cairo Genizah and the Fayoum probably show a wide distribution of use. Justinian in his *Nov.*, 146 from the 6th century (*PL* 69) 1051–4 settles an argument within the synagogue by allowing the use of Aquila's version alongside that of the LXX: *damus illis licentiam ut etiam interpretatione Aquilae utantur*.
[63] Veltri, *Eine Tora*.
[64] Dorival, *Bible grecque*, 120–2.
[65] A similar development is visible in the Old Testament quotations in the New Testament, which in the Gospels are often closer to MT than the main LXX text, and can often be linked with the *kaige* tradition. For a summary and examples, see Harl in *Bible grecque*, 276–7.
[66] See Tov, "Biblical Texts."

7.1007, and P.Ryl.Gk. 458). Whether or not the circles which moved away from the LXX were identical to those which are commonly named rabbinic is not known, but they were closely related. Note, for example, that *kaige*-Th is rightly described in the subtitle of Barthélemy's *Devanciers* as "sous l'influence du rabbinat palestinien."

The analysis of the Hebrew and Greek texts in ancient Israel points to the influence of the Jerusalem religious circles on the shape of the biblical text in the original languages and in Greek, as well as in Aramaic. Together with this trend, altogether different copies were scorned, so that the Samaritans were accused of falsifying the Torah[67] and the Greek translators were said to have inserted changes in the translation.[68] Had the LXX and the SP not been preserved and the Qumran scrolls not been found, we would have known little about non-rabbinic copies of Hebrew Scripture. At the same time, the rabbinic copies found in the Judean Desert, also used in the synagogues, have been preserved up to the Middle Ages with extreme precision.

Bibliography

Baumgarten, J. M., ed. *Qumran Cave 4.XIII: The Damascus Document (4Q266–273).* Volume 18 of *DJD*. Oxford: Clarendon Press, 1996.

Binder, D. D., *Into the Temple Courts: The Place of the Synagogues in the Second Temple Period.* Atlanta: Scholars Press, 1999.

Blau, L., *Studien zum althebräischen Buchwesen und zur biblischen Literatur- und Textgeschichte.* Strasbourg: Trübner, 1902.

Cotton, H. M., Pages 93–100, 215–28 in *Miscellaneous Texts from the Judaean Desert.* Volume 38 of *DJD*. Oxford: Clarendon Press, 2000.

Cross, F. M., "Some Notes on a Generation of Qumran Studies." Pages 1–14 in *The Madrid Qumran Congress. Proceedings of the International Congress on the Dead Sea Scrolls, Madrid 18-21 March, 1991.* Edited by J. Trebolle Barrera and L. Vegas Montaner. Volume 11 of *STDJ*. Leiden: Brill, 1992.

---

[67] See *y. Sot.* 7.23c, *b. Sot.* 33b (זייפתם תורתכם) with regard to the addition in SP of מול שכם in Deut 11:30.
[68] See Tov, "Rabbinic Tradition," 1–20.

Dorival, G., et. al., *La Bible grecque des Septante: Du judaïsme hellénistique au christianisme ancien.* Paris: Cerf, 1988.

Fishbane, M., "Use, Authority and Interpretation of Mikra at Qumran." Pages 339–77 in *Mikra: Text, Translation, Reading and Interpretation of the Hebrew Bible in Ancient Judaism and Early Christianity.* Edited by M. J. Mulder. Assen–Maastricht/Philadelphia: van Gorcum/Fortress Press, 1988.

Flint, P. W., M. Morgenstern, and C. Murphy, Pages 117–24, 133–66, 207–14 in *Miscellaneous Texts from the Judaean Desert.* Volume 38 of *DJD.* Oxford: Clarendon Press, 2000.

Frankel, Z., *Vorstudien zu der Septuaginta.* Leipzig: Vogel, 1841.

Freedman D. N., and K. A. Mathews, *The Paleo-Hebrew Leviticus Scroll (11QpaleoLev).* Winona Lake: Eisenbrauns, 1985.

Frey, J. B., ed. *Corpus inscriptionum judaicarum: Recueil des inscriptions juives qui vont du III siècle avant Jésus-Christ au VII siècle de notre ère.* Rome: Pontificio istituto di archeologia Cristiana, 1952.

Goodblatt, D., "The Title *Nasi* and the Ideological Background of the Second Revolt." Pages 113–32 in *The Bar Kokhva Revolt—A New Approach.* Edited by A. Oppenheimer and U. Rappaport. Jerusalem: Yad Izhak Ben Zvi, 1984.

Gordis, R., *The Biblical Text in the Making: A Study of the Kethib–Qere.* Philadelphia: The Dropsie College for Hebrew and Cognate Learning 1937. Repr. Ktav: New York, 1971.

Greenberg, M., "The Stabilization of the Text of the Hebrew Bible." *JAOS* 76 (1956): 157–67.

Gropp, D. M., Pages 1–115 in *Wadi Daliyeh II and Qumran Cave 4: The Samaria Papyri from Wadi Daliyeh/Miscellanea, Part 2.* Volume 28 of *DJD.* Oxford: Clarendon Press, 2000.

Harl, M., et al., *La Bible grecque des Septante: Du judaïsme hellénistique au christianisme ancien.* Paris: Cerf, 1988.

Hengel, M., *The 'Hellenization' of Judaea in the First Century after Christ.* London/Philadelphia: SCM Press/Trinity Press, 1989

Klijn, A. F. J., "A Library of Scriptures in Jerusalem?" *TU* 124 (1977): 265–72.

Krauss, S., *Talmudische Archäologie*. Vol. 3. Leipzig: Gustav Fock, 1912. Repr. Hildesheim: Olms, 1966.

Levine, L. I., "The Development of Synagogue Liturgy in Late Antiquity." Pages 123–44 in *Galilee through the Centuries: Confluence of Cultures*. Edited by E. M. Meyers. Winona Lake: Eisenbrauns, 1999.

—, "The First-Century Synagogue, New Perspectives," *STK* 77 (2001): 22–30.

—, *The Ancient Synagogue, The First Thousand Years*. New Haven: Yale University Press, 2000.

Lieberman, S., *Hellenism in Jewish Palestine*. 2nd ed. New York: Jewish Theological Seminary of America, 1962.

Lifschitz, B., *Donateurs et fondateurs dans les synagogues juives, répertoire des dédicaces grecques relatives à la construction et à la réfection des synagogues*. Paris: Gabalda, 1967.

Mann J., and I. Sonne, *The Bible as Read and Preached in the Old Synagogue: A Study in the Cycles of the Readings from Torah and Prophets*. Vols. 1–2. Cincinnati: Mann-Sonne Publ. Committee, 1940–1966.

Meyers, E. M., "The Torah Shrine in the Ancient Synagogue." Pages 201–23 in *Jews, Christians, and Polytheists in the Ancient Synagogue: Cultural Interaction during the Greco-Roman Period*. Edited by S. Fine. London: Routledge, 1999.

Milik, J. T., *Les grottes de Murrabba'at*. Volume 2 of *DJD*. Clarendon Press, 1961.

Netzer, E., *Masada III, The Yigael Yadin Excavations 1963–1965, Final Reports, The Buildings—Stratigraphy and Architecture*. Jerusalem: IES, 1991.

Parry, D. W., and E. Qimron, *The Great Isaiah Scroll (1QIsa^a)—A New Edition:* Leiden: Brill, 1999.

Perrot, C., "Luc 4:16–30 et la lecture biblique dans l'ancienne synagogue." Pages 170–86 in *Exégèse biblique et Judaisme*. Edited by J. E. Ménard. Strasbourg: Université des sciences humaines de Strasbourg, 1973.

Perrot, C., "The Reading of the Bible in the Ancient Synagogue." Pages 137–59 in *Mikra: Text, Translation, Reading and Interpretation of the Hebrew Bible in Ancient Judaism and Early Christianity*. Edited by M. J. Mulder. Assen–Maastricht/Philadelphia: van Gorcum/Fortress Press, 1988.

Puech, E., "Fragment d'un rouleau de la Genèse provenant du Désert de Juda," *RevQ* 10 (1979–81): 163–6.

Reider J., "Prolegomena to a Greek-Hebrew & Hebrew-Greek Index to Aquila." PhD diss. Dropsie College for Hebrew and Cognate Learning, Philadelphia, 1916.

Safrai, S., *The Jewish People in the First Century: Historical Geography, Political History, Social, Cultural and Religious Life and Institutions*. Edited by S. Safrai and M. Stern. Assen – Maastricht/Philadelphia: van Gorcum/Fortress Press, 1976.

Schiffman, L., "The Early History of Public Reading of the Torah." Pages 44–56 in *Jews, Christians, and Polytheists in the Ancient Synagogue: Cultural Interaction during the Greco-Roman Period*. Edited by S. Fine. London: Routledge, 1999.

Schürer, E., *The History of the Jewish People in the Age of Jesus Christ (175 B.C.–A.D. 135)*. Vol 2. Edited by G. Vermes et al. Edinburgh: T & T Clark, 1979.

Siegel, J. P., *The Severus Scroll and 1QIs^a*. Missoula: Scholars Press, 1975.

Sukenik, E. L., *'wṣr hmgylwt hgnwzwt šbydy h'wnybrsyṭh h'bryt*. Jerusalem 1954.

Talmon, S., "The Three Scrolls of the Law That Were Found in the Temple Court." *Textus* 2 (1962): 14–27.

Talmon, S., and Y. Yadin, *Masada VI, The Yigael Yadin Excavations 1963–1965, Final Reports, Hebrew Fragments from Masada*. Jerusalem: IES, 1999.

Thiede, C. P., *The Dead Sea Scrolls and the Jewish Origins of Christianity*. Oxford: Lion Publications, 2000.

Tov, E., "The Rabbinic Tradition Concerning the 'Alterations' Inserted into the Greek Translation of the Torah and Their Relation to the Original Text of the Septuagint" Pages 1–20 in idem *The Greek and Hebrew Bible: Collected Essays on the Septuagint*. Leiden: Brill, 1999.

—, "A Qumran Origin for the Masada Non-biblical Texts?" *DSD* 7 (2000): 57–73.

—, "Further Evidence for the Existence of a Qumran Scribal School." Pages 199–216 in *The Dead Sea Scrolls: Fifty Years After Their Discovery: Proceedings of the Jerusalem Congress, July 20–25, 1997.* Edited by L. H. Schiffman *et al.* Jerusalem: Israel Exploration Society and The Shrine of the Book, Israel Museum, 2000.

—, "The Biblical Texts from the Judaean Desert: An Overview and Analysis of the Published Texts." Pages 139–66 in *The Bible as Book: The Hebrew Bible and the Judaean Desert Discoveries.* Edited by E. D. Herbert and E. Tov. London. British Library, 2002.

—, "The Greek Biblical Texts from the Judean Desert." Pages 97–122 in *The Bible as Book: The Transmission of the Greek Text.* Edited by S. McKendrick and O. A. O'Sullivan. London: British Library and Oak Knoll Press, 2003.

—, "The Nature of the Large-Scale Differences between the LXX and MT S T V, Compared with Similar Evidence from Qumran and the SP and with Reference to the Original Shape of the Bible." Pages 151–81 in *The Earliest Text History of the Hebrew Bible: The Relation between the Masoretic Text and the Hebrew Base of the Septuagint Reconsidered.* Edited by A. Schenker. Atlanta: Scholars Press, forthcoming.

Veltri, G., *Eine Tora für den König Talmai—Untersuchungen zum Übersetzungsverständnis in der jüdisch-hellenistischen und rabbinischen Literatur.* Tübingen: Mohr Siebeck, 1994.

Yadin, Y., *Masada, Herod's Fortress and the Zealots' Last Stand.* London: Weidenfeld and Nickolson, 1966.

—, *The Temple Scroll.* 3 vols. Jerusalem: IES and the Shrine of the Book, 1983.

16
The Greek of the Ancient Synagogue

Georg Walser

THIS PAPER WILL FOCUS on only one of the possible languages of the ancient synagogue, namely Greek. And I will start by quoting a short question which I try to answer at the end of my dissertation:[1] "Was there ever such a thing as a distinct Jewish variety of Greek, or is the language of, for example, the Gospels only an example of a natural phase of the development of the Hellenistic language?" The answer I give to this question is "yes." Yes, there was a distinct Jewish variety of Greek, namely, what I call the Pentateuchal variety of Greek, and, yes, that variety was a quite natural element in the polyglossic spectrum that characterized the ancient Greek language situation. Before I come back to this question I will give a short description of the main outcome of my investigation.

The aim of my investigation has been to test the hypothesis that there existed a peculiar variety of Greek, which was used for certain purposes by Jewish and Christian writers in the context of the synagogue. Synagogue—and, consequently, "the Greek of the ancient synagogue"—should be taken in a very wide sense here. "Synagogue" may be said to denote the environment in which texts with religious content were produced by the Jews and the early Christians in the period about 200 B.C.E. to about 200 C.E. The origin of this peculiar variety used in the synagogue was the translation Greek of the Pentateuch, and the background for the hypothesis is the polyglossic nature of the Greek language, that is, several varieties were used for different genres or situations of speech.

---

[1] Walser, *Greek*, 184.

To test this hypothesis I have investigated some participles, some conjunctions and some particles in the Pentateuch. These features were chosen since it was supposed that, when the Pentateuch was translated into Greek, these features were *not* left unaffected by the Hebrew *Vorlage*. I will come back to the question about which features to choose below. The results from the Pentateuch have then been compared to what was found when two other groups of texts were investigated: one group with texts having an origin within the context of the synagogue and one group with texts having no reference to the synagogue.[2] The comparison led to the conclusion that there is a significant difference between the Pentateuch and all the texts with no reference to the synagogue. Further, it was concluded that some of the texts with an origin within the context of the synagogue differ significantly from the texts with no reference to the synagogue, while the other texts show no difference. It was also noticed that the texts, which differ from the texts with no reference to the synagogue differ in the same way as the Pentateuch, and that some of them show close affinity with the Pentateuch.

To show in some detail, how I have been working and how I have come to these results I will give one example from my investigation, namely the investigation of the conjunctions. However, I will first make a few comments on translation technique, and especially word order.

Since the starting-point of my investigation has been to find differences between the Greek of the Pentateuch and the Greek of texts originally composed in Greek, it was necessary first to find out which level of the language should to be the most likely to reveal such differences. Even if the influence of the Hebrew original of the Old Testament on the Greek translation can hardly be overestimated, it is of great importance to be aware of the fact that not all levels of the language are equally influenced. Further, observations made on one level of the language cannot automatically be regarded as valid for other levels of the language as well. If, for instance, it is observed that the vocabulary of the Pentateuch has very much in common with the vocabulary of the Egypt papyri, this does not mean that the syntax is the same. Or if the syntax of the cases is the same in the Pentateuch as in original Greek texts, this does not mean that the word order is the same as well. Therefore, it is very important to take a close look at the translation technique of the

---

[2] The different texts can be found in the tables below. For more details on the texts see ibid., 8–17.

translators of the Pentateuch to find out which levels of the language that were most effected when the Hebrew original was translated into Greek.

It seems as if there is agreement among scholars that the translators used some kind of everyday Greek when the Hebrew original was translated. Most probably the translators were native Greek speakers. In any case, the translators were very well acquainted with the Greek language. It is also clear that the translators were eager to find good Greek equivalents for the expressions found in the original text. No wonder then if we find the same words and expressions in the papyri and in, for example, Epictetus. However, it is also obvious that the translators translated the Hebrew text without changing the syntax and word order of the original more than necessary. Therefore, it seems probable that it is in the syntax and especially in the word order that we can find Hebrew influence on the Greek translation.

When we concentrate on syntax and word order we can see that there are two factors which are of decisive importance for the Hebrew *Vorlage* to leave traces in the Greek translation: first, often one Greek expression is the translation of one and the same Hebrew expression; and second, the translators were inclined to reproduce the word order of their Hebrew *Vorlage*.

One good example of this is the predicative aorist participle in the nominative case. In most Greek texts these participles are used in most kinds of clauses and in numerous ways. In the Pentateuch, on the other hand, 90 per cent of these participles are translations of one and the same Hebrew expression, namely the Hebrew consecutive forms. Since the Hebrew clauses in which we find the consecutive forms have a very stereotyped word order and since the translators were inclined to reproduce the word order of their Hebrew *Vorlage*, the use of the predicative participles in the translated text is also very stereotyped.[3] Another example is the conjunctions, which I will discuss in some detail below.

Further, since Greek is an inflected or fusional language, many parts of a sentence can be placed in different positions without seriously affecting the overall meaning of the sentence. This fact is the most important condition to make it possible to translate a foreign language into Greek without changing the word order of the translated language. This is what happened when the Pentateuch was translated into Greek.

---

[3] Ibid., 18–79.

As far as possible the translators maintained the word order of the Hebrew original.

Accordingly, the word order in the Pentateuch is greatly influenced by the Hebrew *Vorlage*. This influence of the *Vorlage* is mostly *not* recognizable in any single example, since the Greek word-order rules are seldom violated. However, in larger samples of texts we can see that the word order in the Pentateuch as a whole is not the same as in texts with no reference to the synagogue.

The word order in the Pentateuch is as a whole more stereotyped than in texts with no reference to the synagogue. In some cases a word order, which in texts with no reference to the synagogue is rather rare, can be the common word order in the Pentateuch. In some cases the word order in the Pentateuch is even bound by syntactical rules, quite contrary to what seems to be the case in any other ancient Greek texts where the word order appears to be pragmatically fixed, i.e., the word order is not bound by any syntactical rules, but is decided by pragmatic features such as context and stress.

When choosing features, I have tried to find such expressions in the Greek text, which have no exact equivalent in the Hebrew language, but nevertheless are frequent in the Greek translation. I have also tried to find such features in which the Hebrew sentence structure is likely to deviate from the structure commonly found in Greek texts.

One such feature, which I have chosen as an example for this paper, is the use of conjunctions. Since several of the Greek conjunctions are *not* translations from Hebrew conjunctions, we can suppose that the clause structure in the translated Greek, which follows the Hebrew original, is not the same as in Greek with no reference to the synagogue. Further, these conjunctions are frequent enough to allow detailed investigations.

The conjunctions included in my investigation can be found at the top of Table 16.1 below. What I have investigated is the position of the principal verb in relation to the conjunction. When I studied the conjunctions in the Pentateuch I noticed that the principal verb is very often placed immediately after the conjunction. The origin of this word order can, of course, be found in the Hebrew *Vorlage*. One common Hebrew feature translated into Greek conjunctions is the infinitive construct preceded by a preposition. An example of this can be found in *Gen.* 1:15: להאיר על־ארץ/ὥστε φαίνειν ἐπὶ τῆς γῆς

As we can see the Hebrew text has לְהֵאִיר, i.e., the infinitive construct הָאִיר is immediately preceded by the preposition לְ. When this expression is translated into Greek we get: ὥστε φαίνειν ἐπὶ τῆς γῆς, that is, the Hebrew preposition לְ is translated into the Greek conjunction ὥστε, and the Hebrew infinitive construct is translated into the Greek infinitive φαίνειν. What should be noticed is that the word order of the Hebrew text is preserved in the Greek translation. As can be seen, the Hebrew construction has a fixed word order, that is, there can be no words inserted between the preposition and the infinitive construct. Consequently, since the translation preserves the word order of the original, the Greek translation also gets a fixed word order, that is, in most Greek clauses introduced by these conjunctions the principal verb follows immediately after the conjunction.

The statistics for the texts included in the investigation can be found in Tables 16.1 and 16.2 below. In Table 16.1 we find the absolute figures, that is, the number of each conjunction in every text.[4] Within brackets is given the number of examples in which there are *no* other words than negatives and particles between the conjunction and the principal verb. In Table 16.2 we have the relative frequencies of clauses in which the principal verb follows immediately after the conjunctions. In Table 16.3 the same frequencies are arranged in a falling scale.[5]

---

[4] Only those clauses with more words following the conjunction than the principal verb are taken into account.

[5] For more details on the investigation of the conjunctions see Walser *Greek*, 111–22 and 159–61.

The Greek of the Ancient Synagogue

	ἕως		ἡνίκα		ἵνα		μήποτε		ὅπως		ὅτε		ὥστε		total	
Pentateuch	61	(57)	50	(49)	118	(94)	25	(23)	35	(32)	75	(71)	59	(55)	423	(381)
Josh.	14	(13)	4	(4)	12	(9)	1		3	(3)	9	(9)	8	(7)	51	(45)
Judith	10	(10)	3	(2)	7	(5)	1	(1)	1		2	(2)	—		24	(20)
Tob. I	6	(6)	—		8	(4)	—		2		19	(19)	—		35	(29)
Tob. II	3	(3)	—		9	(8)	4	(3)	10	(9)	34	(34)	—		60	(57)
1 Macc.	7	(6)	—		6	(6)	5	(3)	29	(26)	6	(6)	7	(5)	60	(52)
Dan.-LXX	8	(5)	1	(1)	13	(8)	—		5	(3)	9	(6)	2	(1)	38	(24)
Dan.-Thd.	16	(10)	1	(1)	5	(1)	1	(1)	8	(3)	2	(2)	—		33	(18)
Apc. Dan.-LXX	1		—		4	(4)	—		—		—		—		5	(4)
Apc. Dan.-Thd.	—		2	(2)	1	(1)	—		2	(2)	1		—		6	(5)
ApkMos.	5	(3)	1	(1)	7	(5)	3	(3)	8	(8)	10	(9)	—		34	(29)
JosAs.	3	(3)	—		1	(1)	6	(4)	1	(1)	4	(3)	—		15	(12)
TestAbr. rec. 1	1	(1)	2	(2)	11	(8)	—		7	(5)	4	(4)	4	(1)	29	(21)
TestAbr. rec. 2	2	(2)	1	(1)	13	(8)	—		3	(3)	6	(5)	1	(1)	26	(20)
TestAbr. rec. 3	4	(3)	—		11	(10)	—		9	(9)	6	(6)	2	(2)	32	(30)
TestJob	6	(2)	1	(1)	24	(20)	—		5	(3)	7	(5)	3	(3)	46	(34)
Test12Patr.	13	(8)	—		54	(39)	2		10	(8)	35	(30)	5	(3)	119	(88)
Matt.	19	(14)	—		36	(24)	8	(5)	17	(13)	31	(27)	15	(10)	126	(93)
Mark	4	(3)	—		54	(16)	1	(1)	1		32	(22)	13	(5)	105	(47)
Luke	11	(7)	—		43	(25)	7	(3)	7	(3)	41	(33)	4	(4)	113	(75)
John	3	(2)	—		136	(67)	1		1	(1)	38	(30)	1		180	(100)
Acts	6	(6)	—		10	(2)	2	(1)	12	(7)	12	(9)	8	(4)	50	(29)
Paul	1	(1)	2	(2)	230	(80)	1	(1)	9	(7)	42	(32)	39	(6)	324	(129)
Rev.	1	(1)	—		33	(21)	—		—		22	(22)	—		56	(44)
Arist. Judaeus	1		—		28	(6)	2		16	(2)	9	(2)	12	(2)	68	(12)
Philo Judaeus	4	(1)	5		32	(6)	1		7	(3)	47	(9)	11	(1)	107	(20)
Josephus	2		1		13	(2)	—		6		8	(2)	5	(3)	35	(7)
Yadin Papyri	—		—		2	(1)	—		—		4	(1)	3	(1)	9	(3)
Herodotus	—		—		9	(3)	—		17	(3)	9	(2)	17	(1)	52	(9)
Xenophon	6	(3)	9	(3)	17	(3)	—		31	(10)	18	(4)	49	(9)	130	(32)
Polybius	10	(4)	—		5		—		—		15	(3)	33	(3)	63	(10)
Diodorus Sic.	—		—		5		1	(1)	7		9	(2)	26	(1)	48	(4)
Dion. Hal.	3	(1)	6	(2)	15	(2)	—		5	(1)	12	(2)	11	(2)	52	(10)
Dio Chrys.	4	(3)	—		9	(1)	2	(1)	25	(15)	20	(5)	17	(2)	77	(27)
Plutarch	3	(2)	—		5		—		9	(6)	6	(1)	25	(5)	48	(14)
Epictetus	—		—		63	(17)	—		7	(2)	101	(36)	27	(6)	198	(61)
Selected Papyri	8	(3)	—		66	(20)	—		34	(12)	12	(5)	5	(4)	125	(44)
total	246	(183)	89	(71)	1115	(527)	74	(51)	349	(200)	717	(460)	412	(147)	3002	(1639)

Table 16.1 Position of the principal verb in relation to the conjunctions in the whole corpus.

	ἕως	ἡνίκα	ἵνα	μήποτε	ὅπως	ὅτε	ὥστε	of total
Pentateuch	93	98	80	92	91	95	93	90
Josh.	93	100	75	0	100	100	88	88
Judith	100	67	71	100	0	100	—	83
Tob. I	100	—	50	—	0	100	—	83
Tob. II	100	—	89	75	90	100	—	95
1 Macc.	86	—	100	60	90	100	71	87
Dan.-LXX	62	100	62	—	60	67	50	63
Dan.-Thd.	62	100	20	100	38	100	—	55
Apc. Dan.-LXX	0	—	100	—	—	—	—	(80)
Apc. Dan.-Thd.	—	100	100	—	100	0	—	(83)
ApkMos.	60	100	71	100	100	90	—	85
JosAs.	100	—	100	67	100	75	—	80
TestAbr. rec. 1	100	100	73	—	71	100	25	72
TestAbr. rec. 2	100	100	62	—	100	83	100	77
TestAbr. rec. 3	75	—	91	—	100	100	100	94
TestJob	33	100	83	—	60	71	100	74
Test12Patr.	62	—	72	0	80	86	60	74
Matt.	74	—	67	62	76	87	67	74
Mark	75	—	30	100	0	69	38	45
Luke	64	—	58	43	43	80	100	66
John	67	—	49	0	100	79	0	56
Acts	100	—	20	50	58	75	50	58
Paul	100	100	35	100	78	76	15	40
Rev.	100	—	64	—	—	100	—	79
Aristeas Judaeus	0	—	21	0	12	22	17	18
Philo Judaeus	25	0	19	0	43	19	9	19
Josephus	0	0	15	—	0	25	60	20
Yadin Papyri	—	—	50	—	—	25	33	(33)
Herodotus	—	—	33	—	18	22	6	17
Xenophon	50	33	18	—	32	22	18	25
Polybius	40	—	0	—	—	20	9	16
Diodorus Siculus	—	—	0	100	0	22	4	8
Dion. Hal.	33	33	13	—	20	17	18	19
Dio Chrys.	75	—	11	50	60	25	12	35
Plutarch	67	—	0	—	67	17	20	29
Epictetus	—	—	27	—	29	36	22	31
Selected Papyri	38	—	30	—	35	42	80	35
of total	74	80	47	69	57	64	36	55

Table 16.2 Relative frequency (%) of examples with no words between the conjunction and the principal verb in the whole corpus.

		%	LXX-index
1	Tob. II	95	108
2	TestAbr. rec. 3	94	106
3	Pentateuch	90	100
4	Josh.	88	97
5	1 Macc.	87	95
6	ApkMos.	85	92
7	Judith	83	89
8	Tob. I	83	89
9	Apc. Dan.-Thd.	(83)	(89)
10	Apc. Dan.-LXX	(80)	(85)
11	JosAs.	80	85
12	Rev.	79	83
13	TestAbr. rec. 2	77	80
14	TestJob	74	76
15	Test12Patr.	74	76
16	Matt.	74	76
17	TestAbr. rec. 1	72	73
18	Luke	66	64
19	Dan.-LXX	63	59
20	Acts	58	52
21	John	56	49
22	Dan.-Thd.	55	47
23	Mark	45	32
24	Paul	40	24
25	Dio Chrys.	35	17
26	Selected Papyri	35	17
27	Yadin Papyri	(33)	(14)
28	Epictetus	31	11
29	Plutarch	29	8
30	Xenophon	25	0
31	Josephus	20	-6
32	Philo Judaeus	19	-7
33	Dion. Hal.	19	-7
34	Aristeas Judaeus	18	-9
35	Herodotus	17	-10
36	Polybius	16	-12
37	Diodorus Siculus	8	-24

Table 16.3 Relative frequency of examples with no words between the conjunction and the principal verb in the whole corpus; arranged in a falling scale.

In the first column of Table 16.3 we have the relative frequency of examples in which there are no other words than negatives and particles between the conjunction and the principal verb. In the second column is the LXX-index.[6]

As can be seen the texts with no reference to the synagogue can all be found at the lower part of the table. These texts have the numbers 25, 26, 28–30, 33, 35–37. In these texts only 8–35 per cent of the clauses introduced by the investigated conjunctions have the principal verb immediately after the conjunction. Obviously, in texts with no reference to the synagogue it is more likely that there are words between the conjunction and the principal verb than that the principal verb is placed immediately after the conjunction. We can also see that some of the texts with an origin within the context of the synagogue show close affinity with the texts with no reference to the synagogue. These texts are, for example, Paul, Josephus, Philo Judaeus and Aristeas Judaeus. In the Pentateuch, on the other hand, the principal verb is placed immediately after the conjunction in as much as 90 per cent of the clauses. Further, it is obvious that there are several texts which show close affinity with the Pentateuch. These texts are, for example, Joshua, 1 Maccabees, Judith and Tobit.

It is not possible to go into any details about all features studied in my investigation, but when a mean is calculated upon all features we get the result found in Table 16.4 below.

---

[6] LXX-index = $100 \times (n - X) / (P - X)$ where n = the relative frequency for each text, X = the mean for the texts with no reference to the synagogue and P is the relative frequency for the Pentateuch. This means that the Pentateuch will always get the LXX-index 100, while the mean for the texts with no reference to the synagogue gets the LXX-index 0. Consequently, figures close to 100 indicate agreement with the Pentateuch, while figures close to 0 indicate agreement with the texts with no reference to the synagogue, and figures higher than 50 indicate closer agreement to the Pentateuch than to the mean for the texts with no reference to the synagogue.

The Greek of the Ancient Synagogue

		mean of LXX-index
1	TestAbr. rec. 1	110
2	Pentateuch	100
3	Matt.	99
4	Josh.	98
5	Apc. Dan.-LXX	98
6	ApkMos.	91
7	Tob. II	90
8	Mark	88
9	1 Macc.	86
10	Luke	86
11	Tob. I	80
12	JosAs.	79
13	Judith	76
14	Dan.-Thd.	75
15	TestAbr. rec. 2	73
16	Apc. Dan.-Thd.	72
17	TestJob	71
18	TestAbr. rec. 3	70
19	Test12Patr.	66
20	Dan.-LXX	65
21	Rev.	64
22	John	61
23	Acts	60
24	Epictetus	19
25	Yadin Papyri	16
26	Plutarch	11
27	Xenophon	8
28	Polybius	7
29	Selected Papyri	7
30	Aristeas Judaeus	6
31	Paul	4
32	Josephus	4
33	Diodorus Siculus	-3
34	Philo Judaeus	-7
35	Herodotus	-9
36	Dion. Hal.	-17
37	Dio Chrys.	-22

Table 16.4 Mean of LXX-indexes; arranged in a falling scale.

The LXX-index used here always gives the figure 100 to the Pentateuch and the figure zero to the mean of the texts with no reference to the synagogue. Therefore, a figure higher than 50 shows closer affinity with the Pentateuch and a figure closer to zero shows a closer affinity with the mean of the texts with no reference to the synagogue. As can be seen there is a gap between text number 23 *Acts* and text number 24 Epictetus. Above the gap we find only texts with an origin within the context of the synagogue and all these texts have a LXX-index higher than 50. Consequently, all texts above the gap show closer affinity with the Pentateuch than with the mean of the texts with no reference to the synagogue. Below the gap we find all texts with no reference to the synagogue and some texts with an origin within the context of synagogue. As can be seen, all texts below the gap show closer affinity with the mean of the texts with no reference to the synagogue than to the Pentateuch.

We can also see that the texts with no reference to the synagogue form a rather homogeneous group of texts, that is, none of the texts differs very much from the mean of the same texts. This shows that there seems to be some kind of normal or common Greek usage, at least, as far as the features studied in the present investigation are concerned. We can also see that several of the texts with an origin within the context of the synagogue use this same variety of Greek. These texts are Yadin Papyri, Paul, Josephus, Philo Judaeus and Aristeas Judaeus.

Further, as far as the features investigated are concerned, there is obviously a peculiar variety of Greek which seems to be restricted to texts with an origin within the context of the synagogue. Some of these texts show very close affinity with the Pentateuch, for instance the synoptic Gospels, Joshua and 1 Maccabees.

Consequently, there seems to be good reason to answer the question "if there ever was such a thing as a distinct Jewish variety of Greek" with "yes," even if we might prefer to call this variety of Greek synagogal or Pentateuchal rather than Jewish.

The question is then, why some texts show close affinity with the Pentateuch and why some do not. Therefore, I will try to give a characterization of the Greek of the Pentateuch, especially pointing out what the Pentateuch has in common with the texts showing close affinity with the Pentateuch, but also touching upon the differences between the Pentateuch and other texts with an origin within the context of the synagogue.

First, the Pentateuch is to a great extent a narrative text with small sections of direct speech. When we turn to the texts studied in my investigation, which seem to be closest to the Pentateuch, we can see that they all belong to the same genre as the Pentateuch. In fact, several texts deal with subjects from the Pentateuch. The fact that the Pentateuch and the texts with close affinity to the Pentateuch are all narrative texts clearly distinguishes these texts from, for example, Paul and *Yadin Papyri*, which are found below the gap in Table 16.4.

Secondly, the supposed readers of the translated Pentateuch were most probably those in the context of the synagogue. The same can be said for most texts with an origin within the context of the synagogue with the exception of Josephus, who obviously intended his works to be read outside the context of the synagogue. Therefore, Josephus most probably had the intention of using the proper variety for his purpose, that is, the variety usually used outside the context of the synagogue. Consequently, Josephus is found below the gap.

Thirdly, the subject-matter of the Pentateuch is obviously religious. This is, of course, the case for most of the texts with an origin within the context of the synagogue. However, while the texts with close affinity to the Pentateuch have, or are intended to have, a religious value of their own, Aristeas Judaeus, Philo Judaeus and Josephus are commenting on such texts or subjects.

Although the present investigation only covers a limited number of features, and while the investigation of the language of the Pentateuch is far from complete, let alone the investigation of the language of the other texts, I suggest the possibility that the Greek of the Pentateuch served as a model for subsequent texts composed in the same genre, intended for a similar audience and dealing with the same subject-matter.

The second half of the question which I mentioned above was: "is the language of, for example, the Gospels only an example of a natural phase of the development of the Hellenistic language?" My answer to this question was: "yes, that variety was a quite natural element in the polyglossic spectrum that characterized the ancient Greek language situation."

How is it possible that the translation Greek of the Pentateuch is a natural element of the ancient Greek language? Before I try to answer that question I have to point out that one basic assumption of my investigation has been that Greek texts produced in the context of the synagogue should be viewed against the background of the sociolinguistic situation manifesting itself in other Greek texts of the period.

It is common knowledge that ancient Greek was not a homogeneous language; there existed several varieties of Greek bound to different literary genres or to situations of speech. This diglossic, or rather polyglossic, situation seems to have existed already during the classical period, and the same seems to be true for the Hellenistic period as well. Some of the earlier varieties were even taken into use again during the Hellenistic period, "and resulted, for example, in Hellenistic epic in the language of Homer and Hellenistic epigrams in the language of early Ionian poetry."[7]

Moreover, besides these recognized varieties, other varieties were created when new genres came into existence, for instance, the Doric dialect of the Bucolic poetry and the *senatus consulta* originally written in Latin, but which the Roman senate had translated into Greek. The translations of the *senatus consulta* contain several Latinisms and this seems to be the case during the whole period covered by the texts, even though there can hardly have been a lack of competence in Greek.

As a whole, we could describe the language-situation as polyglossic, and it was in this polyglossic environment during the Hellenistic period that the Hebrew Pentateuch was translated into Greek.

Therefore, when the Pentateuch was translated into Greek a new variety of Greek was created for the genre found in the Pentateuch, just as there was a new variety in the translated *senatus consulta*. This new variety of Greek was just another variety of the polyglossic language-situation mentioned above, that is, only an example of a natural phase in the development of the Hellenistic language. Moreover, this new variety of Greek could later be used when composing other texts. When someone was composing a text in the same genre as the Pentateuch, for example, the *Testament of Abraham*, he could choose either to use one of the varieties used in the texts with no reference to the synagogue, or he could use the variety of the Pentateuch. No surprise then, if he used the latter.

Another question that has to be asked is if those who composed texts after the Pentateuch had been translated into Greek, in any way recognized the Greek of the Pentateuch as a peculiar variety of Greek on a par with other varieties in use at the same time. Of course, we cannot go back and ask those authors. What we can do, is to investigate modern languages in which several varieties of the same language are used for different genres or for different purposes. The results from these investigations can then be applied to the sociolingusitic situation of the ancient synagogue to find out if it seems reasonable to believe that the same could be true for this situation as well.

---

[7] Horrocks, *Greek*, 50.

One such investigation is the famous investigation called "Diglossia" by C. Ferguson.[8] Ferguson studied diglossic situations in Arabic, modern Greek, Swiss German and Haitian Creole. When the results of Ferguson were studied it turned out that several of the factors described by Ferguson seem to be applicable to the sociolinguistic situation of the ancient synagogue as well.

In the situation described by Ferguson there are two varieties of the same language; one mainly spoken and one mainly written. The latter is usually called the prestige-variety. In my investigation, on the other hand, there are only written varieties of the same language. Nevertheless, the same seems to be true about the written varieties in the ancient synagogue as about those written and spoken in Ferguson's examples. The first factor pointed out by Ferguson is that the varieties are used for highly specialized functions. According to Ferguson "The importance of using the right variety in the right situation can hardly be overestimated."[9]

One good example is Josephus. When Josephus retells the story of the Pentateuch, he does not use the same variety of Greek as he found in the Pentateuch. Instead he uses the variety appropriate for his purpose, namely, to make the history of the Jews known to the Greeks.

The exact purpose of the translation of the Pentateuch is not known to us, but we know that the *function* of the translation in later times was chiefly religious. The same *function* is most probably also intended for most, if not all, of the texts written in the same variety as the Pentateuch.

The next factor, which, according to Ferguson, is expected for a prestige-variety of the language, is a strong literary heritage.[10] Not much has to be said about the literary heritage of the Pentateuchal Greek, since it is probably hard to find a literary product, which is held in higher esteem than the Pentateuch. Whether or not the subsequent literary production composed in the same variety of Greek was considered to be part of the existing literature we cannot tell. However, it seems most probable that the reason for composing literature in the same variety of Greek as the Pentateuch was to show that the new texts made an addition to, or somehow had an affinity with, the existing literature.

---

[8] Ferguson, "Diglossia."
[9] Ibid., 329.
[10] Ibid., 330.

Another factor, which is of great importance for the present question, is that according to Ferguson the prestige code had a more highly developed *grammatical* structure.[11] Unfortunately it is not possible to tell if this holds true for the Pentateuchal Greek variety, since we do not know the non-prestige-variety, that is, the spoken variety. The question about which variety is most developed is also very hard to answer. What we do know is that the Pentateuchal Greek variety differs in some respect from other prestige-varieties. Besides the features studied in the present investigation, we know, for example, that the optative mood is not as frequent in the Pentateuchal variety as in other prestige-varieties.

More interesting for the present investigation is the fact that differences between the Pentateuchal variety and other prestige-varieties exist on the level of grammatical structure (and not in a lexicon! I will come back to the question about lexicon below). This means that, if two varieties differ *only* in respect of grammatical structure, this is enough for the two varieties to be recognized as two different varieties. Further, if a new variety is to be "created" it *has* to differ in respect of grammatical structure. This is precisely what happened when the Hebrew text of the Pentateuch was translated into Greek without changing the structure and word order of the original very much. Therefore, it is also very likely that a variety of Greek with a peculiar grammatical structure and word order would be recognized as a *new* and *peculiar* variety.

The last factor described by Ferguson, which I will discuss here, is that both varieties shared most of the *lexicon*, but the prestige variety was broader. According to Ferguson the bulk of the vocabulary of both varieties is shared, of course with variations in form and with differences of use and meaning.[12]

The observation made by Ferguson that both varieties share most of the *lexicon* seems to have some very interesting implications. First, *if* the lexicon was the same for the different varieties of Greek at the time of the ancient synagogue, and *if* there ever was a peculiar Pentateuchal variety at the same time, then it seems highly improbable that this Pentateuchal variety could be recognised by studying the *lexicon*. I.e., when the *lexicon* of the alleged vernacular papyri of the Egypt desert was studied in the beginning of the 20th century, and it was noticed that it has very much in common with the *lexicon* of the New Testament, this

---

[11] Ibid., 333.
[12] Ibid., 334.

is just what we would have expected. Therefore, it is impossible to draw the conclusion from this observation alone that the Egypt papyri and the New Testament are written in the same variety.

The question of whether or not those who composed texts after the Pentateuch had been translated into Greek, in any way recognized the Greek of the Pentateuch as a peculiar variety of Greek on a par with other varieties in use at the same time is, of course, very hard to answer. The comparison of the sociolinguistic situation of the ancient synagogue with similar modern sociolinguistic situations can only give us a hint of how the question could be answered.

When we sum up the four factors, which I mentioned above we can see that there seems to be good reason to believe that the Greek of the Pentateuch was recognized as a particular variety by those who composed texts after the Pentateuch had been translated into Greek. As far as the features studied in my investigation are concerned, there can be no doubt that there is a clear difference on the level of grammatical structure between the Pentateuch on one hand, and texts with no reference to the synagogue on the other. Whether or not this difference is distinct enough to establish a new variety, is hard to tell but several observations in my investigation seem to point in that direction. This difference on the level of grammatical structure taken together with the relatively specialized function of the Pentateuch and the very strong literary heritage seem to give a very good opportunity for establishing a new peculiar variety. Therefore, I think there is good reason to believe that this is just what happened. The fact that several texts, composed after the Pentateuch was translated into Greek and had become a frequently used text, show very close affinity with the Pentateuch, seems to point in the same direction.

Therefore, it seems reasonable as well, to answer the question asked at the beginning of my paper by "yes"; yes, there was a distinct Jewish variety of Greek, namely, what I call the Pentateuchal variety of Greek, and, yes, that variety was a quite natural element in the polyglossic spectrum that characterized the ancient Greek language situation.

Bibliography

Ferguson, C. A., "Diglossia." *Word* 15 (1959): 325–40.

Horrocks, G. C., *Greek: A History of the Language and its Speakers.* London: Longman, 1997.

Walser, G., *The Greek of the Ancient Synagogue: An Investigation on the Greek of the Septuagint, Pseudepigrapha and the New Testament.* Stockholm: Almqvist & Wiksell, 2001.

17
Language Pragmatism in a Multilingual Religious Community

Jonathan M. Watt

Worship may engage the soul only when the language of worship makes it possible. That language which enables one to meditate on things transcendent, involving both heart and mind, will be the medium deemed appropriate for worship. For multilingual communities experiencing ethnic diversity, decisions regarding the language—or languages—of worship can be rather involved, with various criteria coming to bear upon the choices. Sociolinguistic analysis stands at the nexus of language use and social context, and studies those choices. The field may be construed broadly, as R. A. Hudson did when he defined it as "the study of language in relation to society."[1] It may take a decidedly anthropological bent, as with P. Trudgill's contention that it is "concerned with language as a social and cultural phenomenon."[2] It may keep one eye each on community and personal relationships, as J. A. Fishman implied when he called it "the varied linguistic realizations of socio-cultural interactions."[3] But whatever the intent, all would agree that it investigates "socially conditioned linguistic phenomena . . . the social nature of language."[4]

The social environment of a community, perceived objectively and subjectively, conditions language choices. Hence, decisions about which language, dialect or style would be the medium for a synagogue of the late Second Temple Period were *not* mere functions of language

---

[1] Hudson, *Sociolinguistics*, 1.
[2] Trudgill, *Sociolinguistics*, 32.
[3] Fishman, *Language Ethnicity*, 4.
[4] Giglioli, *Language*, 78.

competence within a Jewish community. Factors such as status, literary tradition, ethnic implications, outreach potential and the like all feed into the determination of the code(s) of worship. Whereas monolingual communities are notorious for holding to one language/one ethnicity assumptions and for their imaginations of "purity" and "superiority" of dialect,[5] multilingual communities must balance principle with pragmatism, developing an "ideology of language," the study of which investigates "(n)otions of how communication works as a social process, and to what purpose [these notions] are culturally variable and need to be discovered rather than simply assumed."[6]

While keeping within the conference-assigned period of study (concluding at the end of the second century), I will engage in a sociolinguistic investigation of the hypothetical use of Greek in the early synagogue while adding my own geographic parameter—Palestine —into the equation. I say "hypothetical" because there are virtually no direct data on this subject, so a substantial portion of the work must be accomplished by inference. Though Aramaic would have been the best candidate for use in early Palestinian synagogues because of its native language status and genetic proximity to Hebrew, the fact remains that, within a few centuries of the given time period, Greek was displacing it. Why did Jews in Roman Palestine go for what seems like a counter-intuitive option? To what degree might this have affected synagogues? Why would "a pariah people" (as Max Weber once put it), whose historic identity had established their uniqueness and separation, be willing to use in their community and worship settings the language of a culture of ostensibly mutual abhorrence? I shall attempt to offer some explanations.

Repertoire and Functional Distribution

At the outset, we shall consider some basics. Studies relevant to the language of the ancient synagogue deal largely with linguistic repertoire. The general consensus, of course, is that four language possibilities came into play in some way or another in Jewish Palestine: Aramaic, Hebrew,

---

[5] Woolard and Schieffelin, "Language Ideology," 61.
[6] Ibid., 55.

Greek and Latin.[7] But possibilities are not probabilities, as M. Wise correctly perceived, for after noting the presence of a small minority of Greek scrolls even amongst the sectarian Dead Sea collection, it is said:

> Their discovery has vouchsafed us a further glimpse into the linguistic complexity of first-century Jewish society. Hebrew, Aramaic, Greek: each was being used in particular situations of speech and writing. We are only just beginning to discover some of the rules for those uses, to bring to bear the more sophisticated perspectives of sociolinguistics. Since . . . the Dead Sea Scrolls have but recently become known to a wide range of scholars, we are presently at an early stage of linguistic understanding.[8]

If this paper can identify pertinent terminology and concepts, and effectively illustrate them with some living counterparts, then I trust it can identify "some of the rules" that may have governed those ancient Jewish communities.

The term *repertoire* denotes the collection of languages, dialects, registers and styles that speakers can use competently. But should this concept be applied at the individual or the corporate level? The repertoire of an individual speaker may differ, perhaps dramatically, from that of his community. J. T. Platt differentiates *speech repertoire* ("the functional codes utilized by . . . [the] community") from *verbal repertoire* (that of the individual speaker).[9] It is easier to establish the repertoire of an ancient community because of the collectivity of evidence than it is to verify that of an individual (apart from self-report) or a sub-community. A person's verbal repertoire might have been broader, or narrower, than the speech repertoire that surrounded him. A. Millard reflects this when he states that the highly-literate readers of the Dead Sea Scrolls "could move between Hebrew and Aramaic and some Greek" and then turns his attention to the "more mundane signs of bilingualism in the speech of everyday life."[10]

---

[7] Spolsky, *Triglossia*; Spolsky, *Diglossia*; Rabin, "Hebrew and Aramaic"; Millard, *Reading and Writing*.
[8] Wise, *Dead Sea Scrolls*, 10.
[9] Platt, "Aspects of Polyglossia."
[10] Millard, *Reading and Writing*, 132.

This brings us to the next concept, *functional distribution.* Language repertoire presents more than a simple directory of codes; it ranks their suitability for different occasions or situations. However, conflicting factors may emerge, with language prestige, the age and status of the speaker, the presence of outsiders, the topic of conversation, the medium, or whatever, making conflicting code demands. Unfortunately, many of the sociolinguistic factors we would like to know about ancient synagogues are simply unrecoverable. Even when a language represents an invader or colonizer, and would seem to present an ideological barrier, the functional value of a second language (L2) may prove more powerful than the ostensible traditional or solidarity offerings of a local code (NL or L1). This is where a consideration of language ideology may be helpful.

Ideology of Language

Competency judgments are a function of cognitive processes and NL proficiency, but suitability judgments relate to circumstances outside of the person. K. A. Woolard and B. B. Schieffelin put it this way: "ideologies envision and enact links of language to group and personal identity, to aesthetics, to morality, and to epistemology. Through such linkages, they often underpin fundamental social institution. . . . [S]ocial institutions . . . hinge on the ideologization of language use."[11] Ideology, in turn, may be influenced by ethnicity, "an aspect of a collectivity's self-recognition as well as an aspect of its recognition by outsiders."[12] Ethnicity sometimes equates with nationalism, though the latter may transcend or even unite ethnic differences that are ensconced within it. Nationalism is a function of place, kinship, race, and general commonality of experience—features which have the potential to cut across language barriers.[13] Language can serve nationalistic purposes, providing a unifying role that may overcome barriers raised during the history of the nation. Commonality of language may facilitate ethnicity and nationalism, but it cannot equate with them. Local languages or dialects offer centripetal power to a community to offset centrifugal

---

[11] Woolard and Schieffelin, "Language Ideology," 55.
[12] Fishman, *Language Ethnicity*, 24.
[13] Ibid., 23.

ethnic forces, though they may appear provincial or backward. Languages of wider communication may also function that way, but may not be seen as addressing a community's heart. Which impulse prevailed in ancient Palestinian synagogues—local Aramaic or international Greek—is a vital issue for this paper.

Were ancient rabbis subject to conflicting standards over the language most suitable for instruction? Even if Greek opened doors to learning, would it have been necessary for them to stay with Aramaic for the sake of their students? H. A. Fischel's comment on the difficulties of ascertaining the language use of early rabbis—"[t]he problem is compounded by fluid historical situations prevailing in late antiquity"—seems pertinent, here.[14] Listeners are keenly attuned even to the finest points of grammar and pronunciation. The New Testament depicts this in certain accounts. The apostles Peter and John were recognized by Jewish authorities as *agrammatoi* "unlettered men" (Acts 4:13). Peter is also recognized as being Galilean (Luke 23:59; Matt 27:73) based on "the way you talk"—a sensitivity to regional dialect still evident centuries later in the negative comments about Galilean speech reported in the Babylonian Talmud.[15] Literate communities prize certain varieties of speech while regarding other forms as inadequate, if not defective. Speakers rationalize their preferences by explaining that certain kinds of speech involve "bad grammar," but really it is the ideology of the person, not some inherent structural or aesthetic superiority of a language or dialect, that prompts an individual or a community to use it.

Language Ideology in Jewish Palestine

A sociolinguistic study of a moribund language situation is fraught with the variables of human individuality and sub-communities. Add to this a dearth of explicit sources, and one treads on thin ice. L. I. Levine observes that the "considerable methodological challenges" of studying the Second Temple synagogue are evident in the fact that: "[a]ll told, references to the synagogue in the New Testament, Josephus, Philo,

---

[14] Fischel, "Greek and Latin," 884.
[15] See discussions in Spolsky, "Diglossia," 90; Watt, "Current Landscape," 114–16.

and elsewhere number but several score – for the entire world."[16] And the researcher's situation gets even more precarious: even the concept of "Jewish Palestine" which I have chosen as the additional parameter for this paper is problematic because regional boundaries do not equate either with religious affiliation nor with linguistic isoglosses, as C. B. Paulston notes:

> The notion of Palestine itself is easily misleading. It was neither a country nor an empire but a geographic area, consisting of petty kingdoms and city-states, variously independent, colonized, or occupied with in-between states like client kingdoms; with steadily shifting borders due to conquests and re-conquests, much like eastern Europe. Most of our models for multilingualism refer to ethnic groups within a modern nation-state. We do not really know to what degree such generalization will hold for an area like Palestine, and we need to specify whether we are talking about multilingualism in Judaea, Galilee, Caesarea, Scythopolis or Elephantine as the situations all differed with regard to languages and language use.[17]

An elusive task invites creativity! If ancient synagogues were "first and foremost communal institutions where the gamut of activities of any Jewish community found expression"[18] and where the leadership was "in theory, at least—open and democratic,"[19] then any language used in connection with them must have facilitated involvement of the commoner. Aramaic would be the logical choice, yet a plethora of Greek evidence suggests a more complex picture. Speakers in formal public settings will use a code they considered equal to, or greater than, the status of their NL, but will tend to avoid one considered beneath the dignity of the occasion. An outsider language might normally be considered unsuitable; it is the "marked" (i.e. most unusual) option. But this would *not* be the first time in Jewish history that the not-so-obvious occurred.

---

[16] Levine, "First-Century Synagogue," 22.
[17] Paulston, "Language Repertoire," 82.
[18] Levine, *Ancient Synagogue*, 27.
[19] Ibid., 2.

Consider language shifts in previous centuries. Weitzman commented that "[t]he Jews called Hebrew their 'sacred language', or *leshon ha-qodesh*, almost before it was called Hebrew,"[20] and W. Chomsky elaborates:

> Hebrew has been the sacred language of the Jewish people—the language of its religion, culture and civilization. It has been, in sum, the language of Judaism and intimately identified with the national and religious experiences of the Jewish people throughout the generations.[21]

Yet this did not prevent a switch to Aramaic subsequent to the Babylonian captivity. So, it should not seem remarkable if another shift was occurring beneath the shadow of a Greco-Roman cultural presence in Palestine. The alleged linkage of culture with language is a double-edged sword. A vote for one language could be a statement against another, even a practically useful language of wider communication (LWC). Indeed, there is evidence of nationalistic sentiment amongst early Palestinian Jewry that resisted the use of Greek, but the evidence is slim.[22] Jerusalem would be ideologically and geographically well positioned to resist Egypt-based trends *if* it were of a mind to do so. Otherwise, what need would there have been to "spell . . . out the sanctity of the Torah, in this case in its Greek translation."[23] In fact, a disputed ruling against Greek dating to c. 65 B.C.E. in connection with Roman military actions against Jerusalem is mentioned in the Talmud.[24] Whether or not the reported ruling truly dates to that time, it gives evidence of *someone's* resistance to Greek—but whose, and when?

Another line of evidence regarding shudders of resistance to outsider language (i.e. Greek) can be drawn from Y. Yadin's discussion[25] of the Bar-Kochba Letters – though I prefer R. A. Horsely's interpretation[26] of the matter. And then there appear some mentions of rabbinic

---

[20] Referred to in Sawyer, *Sacred Languages*, 4.
[21] Chomsky, *Hebrew*, 3, 8; also cited in Koffi, *Language and Society*, 128.
[22] Jobes and Silva, *Invitation*, 82; also, Mueller, *First Bible*, 46f.
[23] Levine, *Ancient Synagogue*, 135.
[24] Fischel, "Greek and Latin," 885.
[25] Yadin, *Bar-Kokhba*, 124–39.
[26] Horsely, *Archaeology, History and Society*, 162.

injunctions prohibiting the use of Greek that appear in the Talmud, reportedly issued near the outset of both the First and Second Jewish Revolts[27] (with Fischel noting the irony that one of these injunctions used the Greek loanword *polemos* 'war'). However, S. Liebermann contested this interpretation.[28] Again, *someone* in the line of history was resisting Greek because of its cultural connection, but the sentiments may have been read back into the history by later Jews. Indeed, Moore comments on the "Novel of Justinian" that mentions a Jewish sect which believed public prayers were suitable only in Hebrew, but the source dates to the sixth century.[29] Perhaps even the Hellenistic widow situation of Acts 6:1–6 is suggestive here as well, as were the coins of subsequent generations when, during the First and Second Revolts, Jewish coinage featured paleo-Hebraic script.[30] Reactionary trends of various stripes are mentioned by M. Mueller and others.[31]

But reactionary, anti-language sentiments crescendo at times of armed conflict; otherwise, life continues in whatever code works best and seems suitable. With major Greek populations in the coastal towns of Caesarea and Dor or inland around the Decapolis, the long-term pressure to use Greek in many situations weighed heavily on Palestinian Jews. But to what degree, and how effective, were these pressures?

Factors that Favored Greek

To assess factors that apparently enhanced the use of Greek by Palestinian Jews, I will arrange data under various sociolinguistic headings. It will be suggested that if Greek was considered valuable in various situations outside the synagogue, it may have seemed commensurate with synagogue activities as well. The language that weaves together day-to-day community life would fit with community fellowship.

---

[27] Fischel, "Greek and Latin," 884.
[28] Liebermann, *Hellenism*, 100–14.
[29] Moore, *Judaism*, 111.
[30] Yadin, *Bar-Kokhba*, 86.
[31] Mueller, *First Bible*, 112.

a) The Nationalism-Ethnicity-Language Link

Bursts of ideologically-motivated language resistance are temporary, and such urges certainly have not typified Jewish populations throughout history. Multilingualism is not the archenemy of faith, otherwise, neither the Septuagint nor the second century Greek translations of the Jewish scriptures would ever have been possible. And even in times of warfare, ideological resistance to the "enemy's" code is not foolproof, as the discovery of twenty Greek ostraca at Masada at the time of the First Revolt has shown.[32] Nationalism is a relatively modern phenomenon. Ancient Judaism was never solely Palestinian any more than modern Judaism is solely Israeli. Ethnicity may work for, or against, nationalistic spirit. "Ethnicity tends to stress roots and a shared biological past and the common ancestors (factual or fictional). The basis of personal identification is cultural (including religion), and ethnicity is a matter of self-ascription."[33] With Jewish ethnicity crossing so many cultures and nations, no injunction of any authority could effectively define a community of faith, or its worship, as necessarily holding to one particular language.

The alleged Judaism vs. Hellenism polarity is too simplistic, as Horsley notes when he calls the use of Greek language a "useless barometer" of Hellenism.[34] After all, based on analysis of modern societies, Woolard and Schieffelin observe that:

> Communities not only evaluate but may appropriate some part of the linguistic resources of groups with whom they are in contact and in tension, refiguring and incorporating linguistic structures in ways that reveal . . . [their] ideologies. . . . Linguistic ideology is not a predictable, automatic reflex of the social experience of multilingualism.[35]

b) Language Spread

E. Koffi discusses the concept of language "spread": *horizontal spread* relates to how widely it is being used in a society while *vertical spread*

---

[32] Millard, *Reading and Writing*, 116.
[33] Paulston, *Linguistic Minorities*, 31.
[34] Horsley, *Archaeology*, 154–5.
[35] Woolard and Schieffelin, "Language Ideology," 62.

pertains to its use by the cultural elite.[36] The vertical aspect is evidenced, for example, by Josephus translating his *Antiquitates judaicae* into Greek, something consistent with his predominantly gentile target readership. The same held true for various Jewish histories.[37] That Philo worked in Greek also makes sense: he was part of an expatriate community in Egypt, as was the author of The Wisdom of Solomon in the late first century B.C.E. Evidence of this vertical spread also comes directly from Jewish Palestine of the period in question, with writers using Greek even when they apparently could have employed Aramaic. Some of the deutero-canonical Additions to the Book of Esther, which may have been added by the Alexandrian Lysimachus while residing in Jerusalem c. 114 B.C.E., were prepared in Greek.[38] Ecclesiasticus was translated from Hebrew into Greek by Ben Sira's grandson sometimes between the late 130s and 116 B.C.E. even though the work had a Jerusalem provenance. Second Maccabees, written in the first century B.C.E. and being a summary of Jason of Cyrene's five volume history of Antiochus Epiphanes' anti-Jewish activities, was likely an original Greek product with a Jerusalem provenance. Liturgical Greek from an early period seems to be indicated in the Jerusalem Talmud (*y. Soṭah* 7:1, 21b), something underscored by the discovery of a Greek Minor Prophets scroll at Nahal Hever.[39] However, this kind of evidence is formal, and needs to be supported by evidence of popular, "living" kinds of language of the daily, more informal varieties, in order to be compelling. Such evidence is forthcoming momentarily.

c) Intensity and Duration of Language Contact

The longer communities remain in contact, the more opportunity there is for features to be shared between the languages in the form of lexical or morphophonemic borrowings, calques, and semantic shifts. The more direct the contact, the more likely it is that the community which speaks a regional or ethnic code will shift to the prestige code, i.e. the one spoken by the dominant community. Greek presence in Egypt may be dated as far back as the seventh century B.C.E. under Psammetichus I, who used Greek mercenaries that were later settled in the delta

---

[36] Koffi, *Language and Society*, 12.
[37] See survey in Hurwitz, "Hellenism," 304.
[38] Metzger, *Apocrypha*, 96.
[39] Mueller, *First Bible*, 112.

region, and some time after that (though long before the Ptolemies) it was reaching into the Levant. But usage by immigrants residing in language islands, or for official purposes, is nothing more than an initial step, and falls short of causing language shift. The use of Greek in "impeccable form" on c. 200 B.C.E. inscriptions in Gaza and Sidon helps to establish duration of contact.[40] However, with it being another formalized instance of language, it could not have contributed to the acceptance of Greek by Palestinian Jews any more than Latin on Protestant college seals would prompt North American universities to return to the formal language of the medieval papacy.

By the time the Tobiads were employing a Greek secretary c. 275 B.C.E.,[41] Greek had been established in the Levant for centuries. The precedent was continued later by the Herods and Rome, and of course within the Greek cities of Syro-Palestine. Languages in contact inevitably share features, and shifts by populations do indeed occur.[42] This situation was no exception. Multilingual documents are helpful for showing this. The appearance of Greek back-to-back with Aramaic implies multilingualism, at least of the community as a whole; hence, the Babatha archive from the first to second century, to take one example, is quite suggestive.[43] But we still need more evidence of the daily use of language by Palestinian Jews: did they use Greek in daily interactions?

d) Formal vs. Informal Usage

Investigation into the languages of ancient communities usually is forced to follow along formal lines, for texts inscribed on stone, clay, animal skins, papyrus, wood or metal requires some forethought. But we can look for relative degrees of informality; the less formal data will more closely approximate the language of daily interaction. Religious literature of early Palestinian Jewry would be expected in Aramaic or Hebrew, making those written in Greek all the more noteworthy. We shall not be disappointed.

That Ecclesiasticus was translated from Hebrew into Greek by Ben Sira's grandson, as noted already, is a good place to begin, and there

---

[40] Hengel, *Judaism and Hellenism*, 117.
[41] Ibid. See also Chomsky, *Hebrew*, 175.
[42] Thomason and Kaufman, *Language Contact*.
[43] Lewis, *Documents from the Bar-Kokhba Period*.

were more translations to follow. For example, some of the deutero-canonical Additions to the Book of Esther, perhaps composed by the Alexandrian Lysimachus while residing in Jerusalem c.114 B.C.E., were prepared in Greek.[44] The Epistle of Jeremiah, parts of the book of Enoch and also of the Minor Prophets, at least were circulating in Greek form by the first century B.C.E. Second Maccabees, once again, is illustrative, having a Jerusalem provenance, as are Eupolemus' (2nd century B.C.E.) renderings of biblical narratives. But receptiveness to Greek appears in other contexts as well. Low-denomination coinage that would have had its primary circulation within Jewish Palestine sometimes bore Greek inscriptions.[45] This had been the case with Ptolemaic coinage, and it held true from the late second century B.C.E. until the time of the Herods. A recent, but informal report[46] refers to the discovery of a Hasmonean-period synagogue in Modi'in that may date to the early first century B.C.E. but was destroyed during the Second Revolt. Its architecture is commensurate with contemporary structures in the Herodion, Gamla and Masada, and it included a Greek mosaic inscription of undisclosed contents. However, as noted already, inscriptional evidence must be approached with caution for these purposes because it tends to be official and formal.

If we move further toward informality, the evidence will become more insightful. What were Palestinian laborers – the ones with at least some literacy skills – using at this time? Millard identifies various examples of informal Greek in the Hasmonean and Herodian periods, including erotic graffiti in Marisa (in Judaea), a curse scribbled in Greek on a wall in Gezer, and ostraca from Khirbet el-Kom (near Hebron) that are either Greek or bilingual – some from the early third century B.C.E.[47] Admittedly, we can only surmise that the writers were Jews, as we must in the case of commercial weights from the middle of the first century found in Jerusalem and Masada.[48] Personal identifications scratched on ossuaries were often in Greek as well, even if the individual carried a Semitic name.[49] N. Avigad showed that Jerusalem stone

---

[44] Metzger, *Apocrypha*, 96.
[45] Millard, *Reading and Writing*, 107.
[46] *Artifax*, p. 6, citing the *Jerusalem Post*, June 28, 2001. Cf. Levine, *Ancient Synagogue*, 45.
[47] Millard, *Reading and Writing*, 104f.
[48] Ibid.
[49] Ibid., 113–14.

masons relied on the numerical equivalents of Greek letters for specifying construction sequences.[50] It is these kinds of writings, which come closer to quick human instinct, that point to language competence and a willingness to use Greek in "real life." They come as close as we can to asking ancients the question: "what language do you dream in?" Millard depicts an ostracon originating from the Jewish garrison at Masada that involved a food order.[51] Like etchings on other kitchen ware found around Jerusalem,[52] it was done in Greek.

These samples, rather than literary works or formulaic fragments, provide a clearer window on *why* Greek could have found its way into Jewish synagogues: it had been in use just about everywhere else for a long time. Whether Greek was their second or first language, many Jews seem to have known this language in early Roman Palestine and to have used it in day-to-day settings, from courthouse to kitchen. Such a capacity accords with the use of early liturgical Greek indicated in the Jerusalem Talmud (*y. Soṭah* 7:1, 21b). Feldman appropriately notes that the poor quality of Greek used to scratch identifications into first-century ossuaries argues against Greek being restricted to upper classes.[53] The same could be said for base metal Hasmonean coins with Greek inscriptions discovered at Bethsaida, for their usefulness would presumably have been local.[54] From religions documents to passionate scribbles, Greek was working overtime in Jewish Palestine.

e) Language Prestige

It is an axiom of linguistics that prestige languages and dialects attract speakers. Was Greek really seen as the enemy of Jews? To the contrary, there is evidence that it was perceived as quite serviceable, and sometimes even prestigious. Favorable comments about Greek language appear in early Jewish commentaries (*Esth. Rab.* 4:12; *Gen. Rab.* 16:4, 36:8). Rabbi Simeon b. Gamaliel II is reported to have instructed hundreds of students in this language (*b. Soṭah* 49b) despite his close proximity to the revolt, and he even went so far as to claim that Greek was utterly suitable for the scriptures (*m. Meg.* 1:8). The prevalence of Greek synagogue inscriptions would be most fitting if the prestige of

---

[50] Avigad, *Discovering Jerusalem*, 165.
[51] Millard, *Reading and Writing*, 16.
[52] Avigad, *Discovering Jerusalem*, passim.
[53] Feldman, "Palestinian and Diaspora Judaism," 21.
[54] Strickert, *Bethsaida*, 87.

the language had already been established.[55] Rabbi Judah the Prince himself studied Greek and, at the conclusion of the second century, was encouraging its value over Aramaic in domestic discourse.

Naming of one's children and the renaming of adults are symptomatic of language prestige, and given or taken Greek names of Jewish individuals in Palestine were common. Sawyer mentions Jason for Jeshua in Josephus, and notes as well that half of Jesus' disciples mentioned in the gospels (incl. Peter, Andrew and Philip) had Greek names.[56] Various leaders in the Jewish-Christian church at Jerusalem (c. C.E. 30) mentioned in Acts 6:5 were Greek (Stephen, Philip, Prochorus, Nicanor, Timon, Parmenas and Nicolas), along with Ariston, Berenice, Thenas, Alexander and a growing list of additional names collected from Jewish ossuaries from various sites, including Jerusalem.[57] By the fourth century, seventy-five percent of the epitaphs in the rabbinic cemetery at Beth Shearim involved some Greek.[58] The contrasting situation is also mentioned in Hengel, who proposes that "the increase in Jewish names [of mercenaries in third century B.C.E. Egypt] is also a sign that Jewish national self-awareness had also increased as a result of their stronger political position" there.[59] In and out of Palestine, names pointed to Greek language and implied its cultural acceptance, if not outright prestige.

f) Metaphoric Code-Switching

Code-switching involves alternation between two languages or dialects within the same speech act. A dated yet seminal article by J. -P. Blom and J. Gumperz differentiated between *situational* and *metaphoric* code-switching.[60] The situational type is prompted by circumstances that make simultaneous suggestions or demands upon the communicator. Hispanics in North America have provided the data for many studies of Spanish-English code-switching, much of it situational. Metaphoric code-switching, on the other hand, is done for effect. The speaker uses (or imitates) another code in order to enhance his communication, providing a touch of poetry, humor or artistic realism. Walser has been

---

[55] Roth-Gerson, *Greek Inscriptions*.
[56] Sawyer, *Sacred Languages*, 19.
[57] Millard, *Reading and Writing*, 113.
[58] Sawyer, Sacred Languages, 19; Hengel, *Jews, Greeks and Barbarians*, 115.
[59] Ibid., 86.
[60] Blom and Gumperz, "Social Meaning," 4–34.

able to demonstrate that "there is code-switching not between *two* but between *several* varieties" of Greek in documents connected with ancient Judaism, concluding that "there existed several varieties of Greek side by side. Each variety seems to correlate in one way or another to the genre found in the text."[61] My own research has suggested likewise.[62]

g) The Language Trajectory

Language usage can be functional or emblematic, conveying information or affiliation, respectively. The use of both Semitic and Hellenistic codes over the centuries in Palestine suggests that functionally Hellenized speakers still connected with the languages of their scriptures and their past. For example, the Byzantine-era Bet Shean B synagogue, described by Levine as "probably the most hellenized" of that region's synagogues,[63] has an Aramaic inscription in the prayer room containing a number of linguistic mistakes. E. Y. Kutscher attributes the non-traditional features (including what would be classified as phonemic merger, the co-called "weakening" of previously distinguished gutturals such as aleph and ayin) to influence arising from long-standing language contact with Greek speakers.[64] Why would "a highly acculturated stratum of Palestinian Jewry" put an inscription into Aramaic, and not well-formed at that? Perhaps for the same reason that the sixth century synagogue at Naʿaran used Hebrew in one of its inscriptions—it was not merely the content of the words but their mode of expression that carried this implicit message: affirming the tradition by means of an archaic code. The institution under consideration at this conference has long been identified predominantly by Greek words, συναγωγή and προσευχή, not the Semitic counterparts עדה and קהל. This is a function of the linguistic trajectory. The longstanding acceptance of these words, along with the hundreds of other Greek loanwords in use in common Aramaic by the fifth century, are evidence of the trajectory of increasing Greek usage in a formerly Aramaic-speaking region.[65]

---

[61] Walser, *Greek*, 182–3.
[62] Watt, *Code-Switching in Luke and Acts*.
[63] Levine, *Ancient Synagogue*, 202–4.
[64] Kutscher, *Language*, 59–62.
[65] Sawyer, *Sacred Languages*, 18–19; Kutscher, *History*, 138–41.

That Greek was used in high places, including formal public inscriptions, is not in itself compelling with regard to the synagogue. Verticality of language use can be misleading because trained scholars are notorious ideologues. Horizontal spread is more telling: Greek appears in wide relief, from religious documents to construction sites, from personal letters to legal documents, from family names to public inscriptions. At the least, it was functional, facilitating a network of business and literary connections. But one begins to wonder if its usage wasn't just plain trendy. D. S. Russell suggests:

> In a number of cities the local dialect or language would still be spoken by some, but just as it was fashionable to 'dress with the times' and keep up with cultural trends, so it was essential for all educated men, and indeed for any who had even a modicum of interest in culture, to speak the Greek tongue.[66]

As Millard concluded: "[b]y the end of the second century BC . . . when the Jews had their own state based on Jerusalem, Greek was firmly entrenched."[67]

The trajectory is confirmed by mosaic floors with Greek words in the Byzantine-era synagogues at Tiberias and Sepphoris, by the hundreds of Greek loanwords and morpho-syntactic influence in Talmudic Hebrew, and by the congregation of the fifth-century synagogue at Caesarea that was reciting the *Shema'* in Hellenized syllables.[68] Pragmatism is not a dirty word for, as Koffi asserts, "acquiring a foreign language and retaining one's national or ethnic identity are not mutually exclusive."[69] To the contrary: "[k]nowledge of Greek was the expression of a higher social standing, better education and stronger contacts with the world outside Jewish Palestine."[70]

---

[66] Russell, *Jews*, 86.
[67] Millard, *Reading and Writing*, 107.
[68] Levine, *Ancient Synagogue*, 447.
[69] Koffi, *Language and Society*, 226.
[70] Hengel, *Judaism*, 105.

Conclusion

Half a century ago, Liebermann stated—or rather, understated—that "the general Hellenization of the Mediterranean world did not bypass the Jews . . . [who were] affected by it in not a small degree."[71] More recently, Levine has claimed similarly that: "[t]he synagogue, more than any other Jewish institution of antiquity, demonstrates a fascinating synthesis of Jewish and non-Jewish elements within a single framework."[72] Language usage paralleled this collision of cultures. Whereas in Hasmonean times, coins had been minted in Greek and Hebrew, under the Herods they appear simply in Greek. By the Second Revolt, the reactionary streak that called for paleo-Hebraic script was most revealing about what was *not* present in most people's linguistic venue. By Byzantine times, ten out of eleven dedicatory inscriptions discovered to date at Tiberias were Greek. The pro-Greek trajectory is clear.

The language that served Jews in many settings would not, it seems, have been deemed out of place for community fellowship and worship, assuming of course that it was known to the participants of a particular community. One suspects that in less educated settings, Aramaic-only synagogue activities were the norm.[73] But for those competent in Greek, it could provide commonality, especially when it came to Jews of the Diaspora, including those times when they met on Levantine soil, for as Hengel says:

> There was no stopping the penetration of the Greek language even in Jewish Palestine, and the young Jew who wanted to rise a stage above the mass of the simple people had to learn it. This process was strengthened by contacts with the Diaspora in Egypt, Asia Minor and the Aegean, above all after the temple in Jerusalem attracted more and more festival pilgrims from there. The significance of Jerusalem grew with the growth of the western Diaspora, though it continued to

---

[71] Liebermann, *Hellenism*, 20.
[72] Levine, *Ancient Synagogue*, 4.
[73] Ibid., 145, suggesting that "the educational bent of Galilean villagers" would make it unlikely that they spent Sabbath days engrossed in textual discussions.

remain the centre of world Judaism, now predominantly Greek-speaking.[74]

Three decades later, additional archaeological discoveries and the expanding application of linguistic theory to biblical studies now underscore what earlier writers could only begin to document. Greek apparently was known even to many illiterate Palestinian Jews. The language which on many occasions was engaging their minds and hearts surely would have seemed quite appropriate as well in their synagogues.

Bibliography

Artifax. 2001. "Synagogue Found at Modi'in." Summer, p. 6.

Avigad, N., *Discovering Jerusalem.* Nashville: Nelson, 1988.

Blom, J.-P., and J. Gumperz., "Social Meaning in Linguistic Structure: Code-Switching in Norway." Pages 4–34 in *Directions in Sociolinguistics: The Ethnography of Communication.* Edited by J. Gumperz and D. Hymes. New York: Holt, Rinehart & Winston, 1972.

Chomsky, W., *Hebrew: The Eternal Language.* Philadelphia: Jewish Publications Society, 1957.

Feldman, L., "Palestinian and Diaspora Judaism in the First Century." Pages 1–39 in *Christianity and Rabbinic Judaism.* Edited by H. Shanks. Washington: Biblical Archaeological Society, 1992.

Fischel, H. A., "Greek and Latin Languages, Rabbinical Knowledge of." Pages 884–7 in *Encyclopædia Judaica.* Vol. 7. Edited by C. Roth and G. Wigoder. Jerusalem: Keter 1971.

Fishman, Joshua A. *Language Ethnicity in Minority Sociolinguistic Perspective.* Clevedon: Multilingual Matters, 1989.

Giglioli, P. P., ed. *Language and Social Context.* Harmondsworth: Penguin, 1982.

Hengel, Martin. *Judaiasm and Hellenism: Studies in their Encounter in Palestine During the Early Hellenistic Period.* Vol. 1. Philadelphia: Fortress Press, 1974.

—, *Jews, Greeks and Barbarians.* Philadelphia: Fortress Press, 1980.

---

[74] Hengel, *Judaism*, 60.

Horsley, R. A., *Archaeology, History and Society in Galilee*. Valley Forge: Trinity Press, 1996.

Hudson, R. A. *Sociolinguistics*. Cambridge: Cambridge University Press, 1980.

Jobes, K. H. and M. Silva., *Invitation to the Septuagint*. Grand Rapids: Baker Academic, 2000.

Koffi, E., *Language and Society in Biblical Times*. International Scholars Publications, 1996.

Kutscher, E. Y., *The Language and Linguistic Background of the Isaiah Scroll (IQIsaᵃ)*. Leiden: Brill, 1974.

—, *A History of the Hebrew Language*. Leiden: Brill, 1982.

Levine, Lee I. The *Ancient Synagogue: The First Thousand Years*. New Haven: Yale University Press, 2000.

—, "The First-Century Synagogue: New Perspectives." *STK* 77 (2001):22–30.

Lewis, N. et al., eds. *The Documents from the Bar-Kokhba Period in the Cave of Letters*. Jerusalem: Israel Exploration Society, 1989.

Lieberman, S., *Hellenism in Jewish Palestine: Studies in the Literary Transmission, Beliefs and Manners of Palestine in the I Century B.C.E.-IV Century C.E.* 2nd ed. New York: The Jewish Theological Seminary of America, 1962.

Metzger, B. M., ed. *The Apocrypha of the Old Testament (Revised Standard Version)*. Oxford University Press, 1965.

Millard, Alan. *Reading and Writing in the Time of Jesus*. Sheffield: Sheffield Academic Press, 2000.

Moore, G. F., *Judaism in the First Centuries of the Christian Era: The Age of the Tannaim*. Vol. 1. Cambridge: Harvard University Press, 1927.

Mueller, M., *The First Bible of the Church: A Plea for the Septuagint*. Sheffield: Sheffield Academic Press, 1996.

Paulston, C. B., *Linguistic Minorities in Multilingual Settings: Implications for Language Policies*. Amsterdam: Benjamins, 1994.

—, "Language Repertoire and Diglossia in First-Century Palestine: Some Comments." Pages 79–89 in *Diglossia and Other Topics in New Testament Linguistics*. Edited by S. E. Porter. Sheffield: Sheffield Academic Press, 2000.

Platt, J. T., "Aspects of Polyglossia and Multilingualism in Malaysia and Singapore" (paper presented to the 12th International Congress of Linguistics, Vienna, 1977). Also in *Language and Society* 6 (1977): 361–78.)

Rabin, C., "Hebrew and Aramaic in the First Century." Pages 1007–39 in *The Jewish People in the First Century: Historical Geography, Political History, Social, Cultural and Religious Life and Institutions*. Edited by S. Safrai and M. Stern. Assen: van Gorcum, 1976.

Roth-Gerson, L., *The Greek Inscriptions from the Synagogues in Eretz-Israel and the Diaspora*. Jerusalem: Yad Izhak Ben Zvi, 1987 (in Hebrew).

Russell, D. S. *The Jews from Alexander to Herod*. Oxford: Oxford University Press, 1982.

Sawyer, J. F. A., *Sacred Languages and Sacred Texts*. London: Routledge, 1999.

Spolsky, B., "Triglossia and Literacy in Jewish Palestine of the First Century." *International Journal of the Sociology of Language* 42 (1983):95–109.

—, "Diglossia in Hebrew in the Late Second Temple Period." *Southwest Journal of Linguistics* 10 (1991):85–104.

Strickert, F., *Bethsaida*. Collegeville: Liturgical Press, 1998.

Thomason, S. G., and T. Kaufman., *Language Contact, Creolization, and Genetic Linguistics*. Berkeley: University of California Press, 1991.

Trudgill, P. *Sociolinguistics: An Introduction to Language and Society*. Harmondsworth: Penguin, 1974.

Walser, Georg. *The Greek of the Ancient Synagogue*. Stockholm: Almquist & Wiksell, 2001.

Watt, Jonathan M. *Code-Switching in Luke and Acts*. New York: Peter Lang, 1997.

—, "The Current Landscape of Diglossia Studies." Pages 18–36 in *Diglossia and Other Topics in New Testament Linguistics*. Edited by S. E. Porter. Sheffield: Sheffield Academic Press, 2000.

Wise, M., M. Abegg and E. Cook. *The Dead Sea Scrolls: A New Translation*. San Francisco: Harper San Francisco, 1999.

Woolard, K. A. and B. B. Schieffelin. "Language Ideology." *Annual Review of Anthropology* 23 (1994):55–82.

Yadin, Y., *Bar-Kokhba*. London: Weidenfeld and Nicolson, 1971.

18
The Languages of the Synagogue: An Evaluation

Staffan Wahlgren

BEING A GREEK SCHOLAR I accepted the invitation to comment on the language papers at this conference with some trepidation. As it turned out, however, all papers deal with matters fairly easily understood by anyone with my background and training. There is a sufficient amount of common ground between the classicist and those of you whose speciality is language—which, in a way, is a pity, since it testifies to the fact that many questions of the linguistic world of the ancient synagogue have not been dealt with here.

We have listened to three papers in the language section. First, Emanuel Tov read a paper on *The Text of the Hebrew/Aramaic and Greek Bible used in the Ancient Synagogues*. Tov remarks that here archaeology comes to the rescue of tradition, and he complements the scrutiny of, especially, rabbinic sources with material found at places such as Masada and Qumran. His approach is not theoretical, one could call it philological, and its strong point is his intimate knowledge of the material. But by means of this approach he manages to paint a very convincing picture. I do not intend to go into many of his points. Among other things he discusses the fate of the Greek versions of the Scripture, concluding, which is important, that there is evidence to suggest that the Septuagint was rejected by Jews before the problem caused by its use by Christians had emerged.

He also discusses the *maggihim*, that is, the correctors who ensured that textual identity, literally speaking, could be preserved over time. For a Classical scholar it is interesting and fascinating to learn that we have such a reliable insight into the mechanisms of book production and copying in a pre-printing society. No similar care is taken in the act

The Languages of the Synagogues: An Evaluation

of duplication and dissemination of the Greek Bible, or of any other Greek text—ever. It attests to the special status of the Hebrew text, which is retained under all circumstances.

After Tov followed Georg Walser's paper on *The Greek of the Ancient Synagogue*, basically a summary of his dissertation which was part of the Lund project leading up to this conference. Walser has investigated the use of certain Greek constructions in the (Septuagintal) Pentateuch and other Jewish and early Christian literature, and he has compared it with a corpus of no such provenance. The constructions have been selected according to the principle that they should be normal in Greek and unknown, or at least uncommon, in Hebrew, but that the use of them in Greek translated from Hebrew should be influenced by some peculiarity of the Hebrew *Vorlage*. The example Walser used in his paper to illustrate this principle was the translation into Greek conjunctional clauses of the Hebrew preposition with infinitive construct, where the keeping together of preposition and infinitive in Hebrew influences the Greek word order. This method should, on the one hand, give a satisfactory corpus of instances in a Greek text, since the Greek construction investigated is normal; on the other, the word order should reveal a Hebrew background to this Greek.

The investigation points to a common, unique usage in the majority of the texts written within the synagogue, a usage which is supposed to be a consequence of the use of the Pentateuch as a model. As noted in the discussion, there is not much to be said about the material and the statistics presented by Walser as such. But there are some points of over all interpretation which are not totally convincing.

There are things not shown by statistics. They cannot tell us whether the use of the concept of synagogue is justifiable or not. In this forum it has been natural to us to use the synagogue as the model for explanation. But it should be noted that some concepts spring to mind which are eloquently missing from Walser's treatment, but which may provide an alternative framework. Primarily I am thinking of diachrony and synchrony, and competence.

What would happen if we arranged the synagogal texts according to their time of composition? I admit that this is difficult, in many cases impossible, since we do not know when the texts were written, and that it also may invite circular reasoning. But I do think that we have to try. There are some cases—I am, inter alia, thinking of particles—where it is tempting to believe that chronology is an important factor.

The other thing is competence. Let me argue along two lines. First, the pagan philosopher slave Epictetus and pagan papyri sometimes agree with the synagogal texts. Why not mention, at least as a distant possibility, that part of the explanation of the concordance of Epictetus with synagogal texts lies in a common level of competence? Compare this to Philo, on the other end of the scale, who in most cases does not agree with the synagogal pattern: why not explain this as an uncommon competence in pagan Greek?

This is my first line of argumentation. My second has to do with texts not included in the dissertation. Walser contends that Jewish and early Christian texts usually follow the Pentateuchal pattern if there is not a particularly good reason for them not to do so, as there is in, e. g. Josephus, where the form, which is not synagogal, can be explained as a consequence of the fact that he is writing for a readership of Romans.

In cases like this, one should take great pains hunting for texts which might weaken one's own theory. Let us therefore take a look at the New Testament texts included in the investigation. The whole of the supposedly genuine Pauline corpus of 13 letters is investigated. But not the letter to the Hebrews, and that text is different in language and tone. Here we have a text which fulfills the external criteria of synagogal texts, but which, probably, is not synagogal, or Pentateuchal, in language, and where the possibilities to explain away a pagan form might be less readily available than in the case of Philo or Josephus. So, why not test the theory on that text? Is it not possible that the author of the letter to the Hebrews is writing the kind of Greek which Paul would have used if he had been able to?

These are the points I wanted to raise here. But let me at least touch upon one more subject of some importance, chiefly, perhaps, for Greek scholars but indirectly to the question of whether the tools of our discipline could be of use in a wider humanistic and theological context. Walser has proved the existence of some common linguistic features in a group of texts, texts which in most cases can be associated with the synagogue. He wants to compare this phenomenon—and here he is using a thought originating with J. Blomqvist—with the well-known literary, functionally complementary, Greek dialects, that is, he suggests that here we have something comparable to a Greek dialect. This is an interesting thought, but it should be made clear that the commonly recognised Greek dialects differ from each other, notably in phonology, in ways which are easily recognised, and that that kind of phenomena does not set synagogal Greek apart from ordinary Koine. To cut the argument short, I think that what we have here is, at the very least, a problem of expression. Walser is not clear enough, not specific enough, and I still do not understand what precisely he means when talking about dialect.

However, it should be stressed that Walser has made an important contribution to Greek studies as well as to the agenda of this conference. His investigation will promote scholarship even on those points where the chief effect will be to trigger off further discussion.

Jonathan M. Watt presented a paper with the title *Language Pragmatism in a Multilingual Religious Community*. He views our theme from a sociolinguistic perspective and asks general questions about the ways in which languages compete and interact. His starting-point seems to have been: "How could Hebrew of all languages be marginalized?"

Watt is the pure theorist in this group of three, and it is not easy to know where his suggestions might lead when put into practice. Still, his suggestions are important, and we should consider them carefully.

Watt's paper was followed by a particularly lively discussion, to which many contributed. This discussion widened the theoretical perspective even more and suggested additional questions, such as the significance of geographical factors. Concrete examples, such as inscriptions, were also discussed. And there was a discreet reminder that the author's perspective might depend on a Lutheran standpoint, a fact which he was not unaware of. To this we may add the fact that the multilingual society depicted tends to be rather difficult for us modern Westerners to appreciate fully, and that a general Western bias stands in our way.

Analogy is an important concept in Watt's paper, even more so in the written version than in the actual presentation. And with reference to this I would like to build a bridge between Watt and Walser. This cannot now be done in a very sophisticated way; it is more of a vague feeling of mine. Walser makes reference to the general linguistic situation prevailing in Greece during antiquity, in an effort to understand synagogal Greek, and in an attempt to see the Jewish Greek experience as one of many Greek experiences. Watt suggests that we might understand the sociolinguistic situation of Palestine by looking for analogies in modern societies.

I feel tempted to stress the uniqueness of the case we are studying. I do not think that we can understand the Jews profoundly with the help of analogy.

Finally, a word of desperation. We still do not know what happened to the Hebrew language, and we do not understand the role that the Septuagint played.

19
The Languages of the Synagogue: An Evaluation

Jerker Blomqvist

THE PURPOSE OF THE FOLLOWING remarks is to point out some features which characterize the Greek language and its development, and which are relevant for assessing the functions that Greek had both in the context of the synagogue and elsewhere.[1] Those features may be observable not only in Greek but in certain other languages as well. However, since they seem to be, on the whole, alien to the modern languages of Western Europe, students of ancient languages with their own linguistic background in Scandinavian, German-speaking or Anglophone regions tend to disregard them, thus incurring the risk of transferring ideas of how a language works from their own vernaculars to the object of their studies. The investigation of the Greek language in the context of the ancient synagogue that has been carried out within the Synagogue Project has been designed to avoid that risk.

To make the existence of such features clear, I shall start by pointing out a few facts concerning the development of the Greek language in antiquity. They are uncontroversial, even trivial, as I see them, but obviously relevant and in my view often not given as much attention as they deserve.

First, a definitely uncontroversial point: languages change over time. This fact should be obvious to any observant user of a language; even within the life-time of a single individual, the effects of language change are observable. Changes over a longer period of time in your own language become obvious, for instance, if you put two translations of the

---

[1] What follows here is an adapted version of my contribution to a seminar on Hellenistic Greek arranged by the Danish research project on Hellenism; cf. Blomqvist, "Diglossifenomen."

same ancient text beside each other. Thus, to take an example close at hand, the Swedish New Testament translation of 1526 differs considerably from the one of 1981, and the changes that have occurred during the 455 years that separate them have influenced all levels of the language: phonetics, morphology, syntax, lexicon.

Greek is no exception. The phenomenon of linguistic change is not alien to Greek. We must suppose that, like any natural language, Greek tends to change over time.

I stress this point—that change is a natural effect of the lapse of time on languages—because precisely in Greek there are phenomena that seem to contradict the doctrine of the inevitability of linguistic change over time. The existence of such apparent or real counter-instances is the first of two peculiar features of Greek that I wish to point out. It is not difficult to find pairs of Greek texts that, like the two Swedish Bible translations, are separated by 400–500 years but exhibit only negligible divergences from each other. Take, for example, a section from a speech by the Athenian orator Lysias (Lysias 12.8–13) and put it beside a passage of approximately the same length from Acts (27:19–32).[2] Lysias delivered his speech in 403 B.C.E., Acts is at least 470 years younger, so the time-span between these two Greek texts is about the same as the one separating the two Swedish Bible translations.

In the Lysias passage there is only one word that did not come natural to Luke, viz., ἀνοίγνυμι, for verbs in -νυμι had become rare in Hellenistic Greek,[3] and Luke would have said ἀνοίγω.[4] In the Acts passage we find -σσ- for -ττ- in three words, Luke writes δεκαπέντε instead of πέντε καὶ δέκα, and there is one non-Attic grammatical form, πρῴρης for πρῴρας.[5] That is all. Luke was not an Atticist, who consciously tried to

---

[2] The two texts were not chosen at random (e.g., to make a comparison meaningful, both texts had to be narrative). Two texts prove nothing by themselves, but the examples could easily be multiplied.

[3] BDR §§ 92, 101:54.

[4] Cf. Acts 8:32 ἀνοίγει, 18:14 ἀνοίγειν.

[5] BDR §§ 34:1, 63:2, 43:1. I discuss only grammatical phenomena here, not phonetics or vocabulary. Luke's everyday pronunciation of diphthongs and certain vowels probably differed from Lysias', but the changes in pronunciation had started already in Lysias' own days, so he would probably have understood Luke's speech with only little difficulty, and in the rhetorical schools of the first century C.E. the classical pronunciation is likely to have been taught to the students; cf. Teodorsson, *Ptolemaic Koine*, 253–5, *Phonology of Attic*, 111–12, "Grekiska," 288. Luke's vocabulary is different, of course, mainly due to extra-linguistic factors. On the limited

avoid innovations that had crept into the language after the classical period. Yet, judging from this passage, his Greek could hardly be characterized as non-Attic.[6] Admittedly, there are a few divergences, but the comparison of the two Swedish texts that are also separated by c. 450 years reveals incomparably more differences.

Obviously, certain Greek texts, although separated by a time-span of several hundred years, show no essential signs of change. That reveals itself as an anomaly, when Greek is compared to other languages known by us, and, being an anomaly, it calls for an explanation.

The second peculiar feature I want to point out becomes apparent if we put the same Lysias passage beside a narrative section of comparable length from one of Euripides' tragedies, *Bacchae* 1105–1143. Euripides wrote that tragedy late in his life, and it was staged in Athens for the first time only after his death, in 406, so it is almost contemporary with the Lysias speech. Yet there are many more disagreements between the Euripidean verses and Lysias' speech than between the speech and Acts, although Acts was written more than 450 years later and in a different part of the world. It is probably impossible to find one single Euripidean passage of this length that is less different from Lysias than the passage from Acts is.

One very obvious divergence is that Euripides normally does not use the definite article, which has an important structuralizing function in Lysias' Greek. On the syntactical level we notice that Euripides has fewer prepositions than Lysias and prefers solitary case forms. Morphological divergences are frequent: χέρα, with a different declension stem, for χεῖρα, the dual form χεροῖν, datives in -αισι and -οισι instead of -αις/-οις, the pronouns σέθεν (functionally equivalent to σοῦ) and νιν. ἀπό and ὡς may be placed after the word to which they belong. Phonetic features are the apocope in ἀμβάτην and the -σσ- of

---

value of the lexicon for defining the properties of a linguistic variety, cf. Walser, *Ancient Synagogue*, 145–7.

[6] On the basically Attic character of the so-called koine, see Ebbesen, "Hellenistisk Græsk," 8–9, Horrocks, *Greek*, 33–7. Many scholars, both classicists and theologians, have exaggerated the divergence of koine from classical Attic. The truth is that the linguistic norm established in fourth-century Athens was, with few exceptions, normative for all Greek prose writing throughout antiquity and for many centuries after antiquity. Already Jannaris was aware of this fact, as the programmatic title of his history of Greek indicates: *An Historical Greek Grammar Chiefly of the Attic Dialect as Written and Spoken from Classical Antiquity Down to the Present Time.*

ἐλίσσουσα. Vocabulary is not that important in this context, but it is interesting to notice that the Euripidean passage contains about 70 words[7] that do not appear at all in any speech by Lysias, whereas there are only seventeen words[8] in Lysias 12.8–13 that are absent from the New Testament, and 29[9] in Acts 27:19–32 that never occur in the *Corpus Lysiacum*.[10]

The conclusion is inevitable: Lysias' Greek is much more similar to Luke's than to that of his contemporary Euripides. Thus, Greek texts of the same date may deviate considerably from each other. That is another anomaly that calls for explanation. There are obviously other mechanisms than linguistic change over time that cause these texts to deviate from each other.

Not only two contemporary writers but even the same writer could use more than one variety of Greek. Certain sections of Luke's gospel are obviously written in a variety of Greek different from the one exhibited by Acts 27:19–32. As an example we may use Luke 8:26–39, where even a superficial perusal will reveal the following features that would be alien to a classical writer like Lysias:

1. ἥτις with a definite referent (26).
2. The improper preposition ἀντιπέρα (26).
3. Datives (instead of accusatives) denoting duration: χρόνῳ ἱκανῷ (27), πολλοῖς χρόνοις (29).
4. ἀπό for "out of" (= ἐκ) with ἐξελθεῖν etc. (29, 33, 35, 38).

---

[7] αἱματόω, ἄκρος, ἀλαλάζω, ἀμβάτης, ἀντιβαίνω, ἀποσπαράττω, ἀρβύλη, ἀφρός, βαθύξυλος, βακχέω, βοή, γνωρίζω, γυμνόω, διάστροφος, διασφαιρίζω, δόμος, δυσδαίμων, ἐλάτη, ἑλίσσω, ἐμπνέω, ἐξανασπάω, ἐξανύω, ἐξεργάζομαι, ἔξειμι, ἐπέχω, εὐμάρεια, ζήτημα, θάσσω, θήρ, θύρσος, ἱερέα, ἴχνος, κατακτείνω, κράς, κρυφαῖος, κύκλος, λέων, μαινάς, μέσος, μίτρα, μόχθος, νιν, οἴμωγμα, ὀρέστερος, οὖδας, ὄχλος, παρηίς, πέτρα, πήγνυμι, πλευρά, προσπίτνω, πτόρθος, ῥήγνυμι, σάρξ, σέθεν, σθένος, σπαραγμός, στενάζω, στύφλος, σῶμα, τέρμα, τλήμων, ὑψόθεν, ὑψοῦ, φόβη, χαμαιριφής, χθών, ψαύω, ὠλένη, ὦμος.

[8] ἀνδράποδον, δαρεικός, αὐτόθι, βαδίζω, δωμάτιον, ἐξελαύνω, ἐξώλεια, ἐπαράω, ἐργαστήριον, ἑστιάω, ἐφόδιον, θαρρέω, κυζικηνός, οἴχομαι, ὅποι, παρακελεύομαι, σκέπτομαι.

[9] ἄγγελος, ἄγκυρα, ἀποβολή, ἀποκόπτω, ἀσιτία, ἄστρον, αὐτόχειρ, βολίζω, δεκαπέντε, ἑκατοντάρχης, ἐκτείνω, ἐπίκειμαι, ἐπιφαίνω, εὐθυμέω, ἰδού, λαλέω, λατρεύω, λοιπόν, μέσος, ναύτης, ὀργυιά, πειθαρχέω, πρύμνα, πρῷρα, σκάφη, σχοινίον, τεσσαρεσκαιδέκατος, τραχύς, χαλάω.

[10] For Lysias' vocabulary, cf. Holmes, *Index*; for NT, BDAG.

5. Pluperfect συνηρπάκει (29) as past narrative tense (possibly also ἐξεληλύθει 38).
6. The Latin loan-word λεγιών (30).
7. τὰ δαιμόνια as subject with the verb in plural: παρεκάλουν (31), παρεκάλεσαν (32), εἰσῆλθον (33).
8. Verbs of volition with ἵνα-clauses instead of infinitives: παρεκάλουν (31), παρεκάλεσαν (32), possibly δέομαι (28).
9. Final infinitive: ἰδεῖν (35).
10. αὐτός in the nominative as a (non-emphatic?) personal pronoun (36).
11. ποιεῖν with dative of the person affected (39 (twice)).
12. καί dominates as connective particle.[11]

The two co-existing varieties of Greek exemplified by the Lysias and Euripides passages could be explained as manifestations of a sociolinguistic situation characterised by diglossia or polyglossia. If we use the term diglossia to describe the relation of the Euripidean and Lysiac varieties of Greek to each other, it means that we define the concept of diglossia differently from Ferguson, the author of the "classic" definition.[12] Ferguson deals primarily with situations in which a spoken, "low" variety of a language stands in opposition to a literary, more formalised, "high" variety, but in the case of the Euripides–Lysias relation the two varieties involved are literary. In classical Athens there existed, in fact, even more literary varieties than those two, for epic poetry used a peculiar linguistic form, choral lyric another one, etc., and the spoken vernacular, we may suppose, differed from everyone of these literary varieties.

The concept of diglossia was introduced into the discussion on the post-classical development of Greek in 1974 by the Finnish scholar J. Frösén.[13] Later on scholars have mostly used the term to describe a

---

[11] On these phenomena in NT Greek, cf. BDR §§ 293:1, 203, 201, 209, 5:1, 133, 388:2, 390, 277:3, 151:1, and 442. Some of the phenomena used by Walser, *Ancient Synagogue*, for defining Pentateuchal Greek also recur in Luke 8:26–39. Cf. Walser's analysis of *T. Ab.* 13.1–5 and Matt 2:19–23 (*Ancient Synagogue*, 171–2).

[12] Ferguson, "Diglossia." A slightly different definition, involving bilingualism and therefore more adequate to the multilingual environments in which the ancient synagogues functioned, is given by Watt, "Current Landscape," 18. Cf. Walser, *Ancient Synagogue*, 176–7.

[13] Frösén, *Prolegomena*, 229–30. Frösén describes the situation as polyglossia rather than diglossia.

situation that is supposed to have arisen after Atticism had had its impact on literary Greek in the first centuries C.E. In 1997, for example, Horrocks wrote:

> [T]he eventual triumph of Atticism can ultimately be attributed to the fact that it found its natural milieu in the context of the antiquarianism of the Second Sophistic . . . While the written Koine could be accepted as the language of business, the expression of the highest forms of Greek culture demanded better, and only Attic, the embodiment of the 'purest' language, could serve as its vehicle . . . . The resulting dichotomy between an unchanging Attic ideal and the Koine in all its heterogeneity quickly established a formal state of diglossia that became steadily more problematical with the passage of time, and which was not to be finally abandoned until the late twentieth century.[14]

However, the linguistic norm adhered to by the Atticists was essentially the same as the one that had been followed by prose writers of the Hellenistic period as well. The language of those writers, whether we call it *koine* or not, can only be described as Attic, and Luke, for one, could write the same sort of Greek as Lysias; the divergences that we observe are few. Atticism did not create Greek diglossia; it only made it more manifest and turned it into an ideological issue. The Attic linguistic norm had been established in the fourth century B.C.E. That norm was valid for written prose. We must assume, from what we know about the inevitability of linguistic change over time, that spoken Greek had not remained unchanged in the period between, say, Lysias and Luke. Phonetic data indicate that spoken, everyday Greek differed noticeably from the literary variety in the fourth century B.C.E., perhaps already in the late fifth century. At that time several literary varieties were long since established. Greek polyglossia is much older than Atticism.

Thus, the sociolinguistic situation in classical Athens was characterised by polyglossia; the everyday vernacular stood in opposition not to one but to several literary varieties, and these, in their turn, were opposed to each other. The main cause of this multiplicity is that every

---

[14] Horrocks, *Greek*, 81. Similar views have been expressed by Bubeník and Niehoff-Panagiotidis.

literary genre tended to use a linguistic variety of its own. The number of those genre-bound varieties—"literary dialects," as they are sometimes styled—was not constant, but a new genre could create its own linguistic norm, as happened when bucolic poetry developed in the third century B.C.E.[15] As Walser has argued, it is possible to regard what he calls Pentateuchal Greek as a variety of that sort, created as a linguistic norm at a certain point of time and then utilised in the context of the ancient synagogue and for particular purposes in that milieu.

Diglossia also has an effect that proves particularly relevant to one of the points raised above: diglossia situations are stable and often remain with few changes throughout centuries.[16] As a consequence, at least one of the varieties of the language involved in the situation will be preserved unchanged or with very few changes over long periods. Classical Arabic has, in principle, remained unchanged throughout its history, and the variety of Greek used by Lysias and his colleagues in the late fifth and fourth centuries B.C.E remained the primary linguistic norm for prose writers throughout antiquity and the Byzantine period; for certain purposes it is still in use today.[17] In a language as pervaded by diglossia or polyglossia as Greek is, it is no wonder that the same variety of the language may have been used both around 400 B.C.E. and 75 C.E.

The advantage of introducing the concept of diglossia in the discussion on the nature of the Greek used in the religious writings of ancient Jews and early Christians is that it transforms the rather peculiar variety of Greek used in those texts from an abnormality, as seen from the viewpoint of classical linguistic norms, into a normal variety of the language, tied to a certain literary genre or a certain functional domain. Just as the variety of Greek used by Euripides is the normal language of Greek tragedy, in the same way Pentateuchal Greek becomes the normal way for a speaker of Greek to express himself when writing on subjects and to an audience in the context that we somewhat vaguely define as the ancient synagogue. This way of regarding the "Penta-

---

[15] Horrocks, *Greek*, 50, Walser, *Ancient Synagogue*, 175.
[16] This is an empirical fact, resulting from Ferguson's survey of diglossia situations known to him and confirmed by later investigations. Cf. Walser, *Ancient Synagogue*, 180–1.
[17] Documents in Classical Greek are still produced by orthodox church authorities, e.g., the documents authorising the Modern Greek translation of the *New Testament* in 1986–7 (*Η Καινή Διαθήκη*, δ΄-η΄); cf. Blomqvist, "Ett språk," 74–5.

teuchal," "synagogal" or "Jewish-Christian" variety of the language takes into account those two peculiar features of Greek that have been pointed out above.

Bibliography

BDAG = *A Greek-English Lexicon of the New Testament and other Early Christian Literature.* Third edition (BDAG), revised and edited by F. W. Danker, based on Walter Bauer's *Griechisch-deutsches Wörterbuch zu den Schriften des Neuen Testaments und der frühchristlichen Literatur,* sixth edition, ed. K. Aland and B. Aland, with V. Reichmann and on previous editions by W. F. Arndt, F. W. Gingrich, and F. W. Danker. Chicago: Chicago University Press, 2000.

BDR = Blass, F., and Debrunner, A., *Grammatik des neutestamentlichen Griechisch.* Bearbeitet von F. Rehkopf. 14. Aufl. Göttingen: Vandenhoeck & Rupprecht, 1975.

Blomqvist, J., "Diglossifenomen i den hellenistiska grekiskan." Pages 25–38 in *Sproget i Hellenismen.* Edited by Engberg-Pedersen *et al.* Århus: Aarhus Universitetsforlag, 1995.

—, "Ett språk som motstått tiden – grekiskan genom 3000 år." Pages 73–82 in *Språket och tiden.* Edited by J. Blomqvist and G. Bruce. Lund: Studentlitteratur, 1998.

English translation by C. Parada: "3,000 Years of Greek: The Language that Withstood Time," http://homepage.mac.com/cparada/GML/003Signed/JBGreek.html, January 2002.

Bubeník, V., *Hellenistic and Roman Greece as a Sociolinguistic Area.* Amsterdam: J. Benjamins, 1989.

Ebbesen, S., "Hellenistisk Græsk – Koiné." Pages 7–24 in *Sproget i Hellenismen.* Edited by T. Engberg-Pedersen *et al.* Århus: Aarhus Universitetsforlag 1995

Ferguson, C. A., "Diglossia." *Word* 15 (1959): 325–40.

Frösén, J., *Prolegomena to a Study of the Greek Language in the First Centuries A.D. The Problem of Koiné and Atticism.* Helsinki: 1974.

Η Καινή Διαθήκη. Το πρωτότυπο κείμενο με μετάφραση στη δημοτική. Αθήνα. Ελληνική Βιβλική Εταιρία/ *The New Testament in Today's Greek Version.* United Bible Societies, 1995.

Holmes, D. H., *Index Lysiacus.* Amsterdam: Servio, 1962.

Jannaris, A. N., *An Historical Greek Grammar Chiefly of the Attic Dialect as Written and Spoken from Classical Antiquity Down to the Present Time.* Hildesheim: Olms, 1987 [1897].

Niehoff-Panagiotidis, J., *Koine und Diglossie.* Wiesbaden: Harrassowitz, 1994.

Teodorsson, S.-T., *The Phonology of Ptolemaic Koine.* Göteborg: Acta Universitatis Gothoburgensis, 1977.

—, *The Phonology of Attic in the Hellenistic Period.* Göteborg: Acta Universitatis Gothoburgensis, 1978.

—, "Grekiska språket, språkhistoriskt studieobjekt par excellence." Pages 282–90 in *Språkets speglingar. Festskrift till Birger Bergh.* Edited by A. Jönsson and A. Piltz. Lund: Skåneförlaget, 2000.

Walser, G., *The Greek of the Ancient Synagogue. An Investigation on the Greek of the Septuagint, Pseudepigrapha and the New Testament.* Stockholm: Almqvist & Wiksell, 2001.

Watt, J. M., "The Current Landscape of Diglossia Studies: The Diglossic Continuum in First-Century Palestine." Pages 18–36 in *Diglossia and Other Topics in New Testament Linguistics.* Edited by S. E. Porter. Sheffield: Sheffield Academic Press, 2000.

Part IV

The Worship of the Synagogue

20
The Worship of the Synagogue: An Introduction

Sten Hidal

For all who studied New Testament Exegesis at Lund University 1933–1964 the liturgy of the synagogue was a familiar phenomenon. This was especially true from 1943, when Professor Hugo Odeberg (1898-1973) founded his famous society Ereuna with the purpose of "an immanent, unbiased and scholarly study of the New Testament."[1] Generations of students—and some colleagues of professor Odeberg—gathered each Saturday morning during semesters in order to recite "the morning prayer from the Ancient Church" and to listen to a short paper on a biblical subject. Also in his academic teaching Odeberg continually dwelt upon the liturgy of the synagogue. This, no doubt, has had a vast influence on many students of theology in Sweden and has created a tradition of Judaic studies in Lund, in which this conference partly stands.

Hugo Odeberg started as a thorough expert on Jewish mysticism. His edition in 1928 of *3 Enoch, or, The Hebrew book of Enoch* (*editio princeps* with introduction, translation and commentary, re-edited in 1973) betrays an impressive knowledge of a Jewish tradition, until then not much studied. This interest in Jewish mysticism was combined in Odeberg with a keen appreciation of the Hellenistic influence on Judaism. In this respect he was close to Rudolf Bultmann. Greek, but also Samaritan och Mandaic sources are repeatedly consulted in all his early writings, including a famous commentary on parts of the Fourth Gospel (1929). Gradually Odeberg ceased to publish in English and German; all his later writings are in Swedish.

---

[1] For an introduction to Odeberg's life and work, see Gerhardsson, "Hugo Odeberg."

According to Odeberg, the ancient Jewish liturgy gives a clear picture of a Judaism standing, as it were, above the various parties and traditions in the contemporary Jewish community. This was important: Pharisaism represented according to him, a distortion of central features in "authentic" Judaism. The liturgy of the synagogue was primarily a creation of Jewish mysticism, and the Pharisees and rabbinic Judaism had contributed very little. This was the reason why early Christianity could so easily accept the liturgy of the synagogue, which they did with a few adaptations. "The morning prayer from the Ancient Church" as said in the Ereuna was simply an abbreviation of the morning prayer of the synagogue with a few additions from the New Testament, mainly from christological and trinitarian formulas in the epistles. It should be noted that Ereuna gathered on Saturday morning, not Sunday. The keeping of the Sabbath was regarded as a divine commandment.

It was continously stressed—also in the academic teaching—that according to the Gospels, Jesus took part in the liturgy of the synagogue each sabbat "as was his custom" (Luke 4:16; cf Acts 17:2). Attending this liturgical service was, admittedly, nothing unusual to him, but this observance carried a much greater significance according to Odeberg. The synagogal worship was instituted by God as a gift to his people and was not to be replaced by something else. It was nothing less than part of the divine revelation, and thus normative for all times—also for the Christian Church.

The liturgy of the synagogue—and therefore also of the Ancient Church—was characterized by *joy*. This word was central to Odeberg and as a proof of its importance, Is 56:7 was often quoted: "I will bring them to my holy mountain, and make them joyful in my house of prayer." A house of prayer—this was what the synagogue was intended to be and a binding heritage was taken over by the Church. The prayers were the central part of the liturgy, some of them perhaps going back to the temple. The reading of the Torah was not an important part of the liturgy, although the homily was central. A collection was always taken up and said to be a part of the liturgy itself, not to be omitted.

No doubt Odeberg's view of the synagogue was a rather bold combination of the scarce references in the New Testament, later traditions of the synagogue and the immense literature of Jewish mysticism. The historical correctness of such a combination of very diverse sources may indeed be questioned, and problems of dating texts or critically analysing them never interested Odeberg. He saw Jewish mysticism as a very old, coherent phenomenon and so it had had all the opportunities of influencing the liturgy from the very beginning. No doubt the unknown origin of the synagogue was a fascination to him, as also the small and intimate milieu of the synagogue in comparison to the temple (and later Christian churches). Odeberg always felt himself close to "those who are quiet in the land" (Ps 35:20). The synagogue was in his view never taken over by the priests or the rabbis from an ideological point of view. It was a creation by laymen for laymen, but above all it was a divine gift to Israel. It was a place where the Psalms were recited, and where the divine light permeating all creation was perceived by the faithful in great joy and gratitude.

When it came to investigations of the development of the Jewish liturgy, Odeberg confidently left this task to his disciples. He himself preferred reading Jewish texts in his higher seminar, but more often Samaritan than rabbinic ones. Most of his writings in later years were in Swedish and not primarily intended for learned readers. 1951 David Hedegård published his doctoral dissertation *Seder R. Amram Gaon, Part I* containing the Hebrew text with critical apparatus, translation with notes and introduction. In the introduction section X, temple and synagogue, he gives a short summary of the views on the Jewish liturgy as prevalent in Odeberg's seminar. It is pointed out that the synagogue and its service emerged as a substitute for the temple. "All these facts indicate that prayer in the synagogue service is regarded as a ceremonial rite, which at least in some respects is analogous to the ceremonies of the temple service."[2] But also in Hedegård there is no real interest in the *development* of the Jewish liturgy. To edit and comment upon one of the oldest liturgies extant is seen as a relevant task, but genetic questions and still more questions of the further development are not taken up in the agenda.

Hedegård's dissertation covered only the first part of R. Amram Gaon's prayer book. The task of editing the second part containing the prayer order for sabbaths and festivals fell upon another of Odeberg's disciples, Tryggve Kronholm (1939–1999), and the title of the book is *Seder R. Amram Gaon Part II, The Order of the Sabbath Prayer: Text Edition with an Annotated English Translation and Introduction* (1974). This is a scholarly work of meticulous accuracy. The overall view of synagogal liturgy is very close to Odeberg and Hedegård, but the author

---

[2] Hedegård, *Seder Aram*, xxxviii.

is more interested in philology. Kronholm was not a theologian; he became in due time professor in Semitic languages at Uppsala University.

Neither Hedegård nor Kronholm make any attempts at describing the impact of Jewish mysticism on the liturgy of the synagogue, nor do they say anything about the origin of the synagogue or its relation to the temple—except in a very vague wording. In Lund the tradition originating from Hugo Odeberg was very much orientated towards texts and it was seen as the scholar's first duty to be able to grasp a totality, not to analyse. The aim was synthesis, not analysis (except from a philological aspect). After Kronholm's dissertation no work has been done on the liturgy of the synagogue and the tradition from Odeberg seems to have become extinct. However, Jewish liturgy in a wider sense has not been neglected. Håkan Ulfgard published in 1998 *The Story of Sukkot. The Setting, Shaping and Sequel of the Biblical Feast of Tabernacles,* where this feast is analyzed in regard to biblical and post-biblical history and theology. Irene von Görtz-Wriesberg offers in her contribution in this volume, *No Second Temple—No Shavuot?* a picture of her doctoral dissertation to come. Work on Jewish liturgy continues in Lund, and has been stimulated by this conference.

Bibliography

Gerhardsson, B., "Hugo Odeberg and his vision 'Christ and Scripture.'" Pages 112–25 in *Evangelium Schriftauslegung Kirche Festschrift für Peter Stuhlmacher zum 65. Geburtstag.* Edited by J. Ådna et al. Göttingen: Vanderhoeck & Ruprecht, 1997.

Hedegård, D., *Seder R. Amram Gaon. Part I. Hebrew Text with Critical Apparatus Translation with Notes and Introduction.* Lund: Ph. Lindstedts universitetsbokhandel, 1951.

Kronholm, T., *Seder R. Amram Gaon, Part II. The Order of the Sabbath Prayer: Text Edition with an Annotated English Translation and Introduction.* Lund: Gleerup, 1974.

Odeberg, H., *3 Enoch or the Hebrew Book of Enoch: Edited and Translated for the First Time with Introduction, Commentary & Critical Notes*. Cambridge: Cambridge University Press, 1928 (new edition New York, 1973).

—, *The Fourth Gospel: Intrpreted in Its Relation to Contemporaneous Religious Currents in Palestine and the Hellenistic-Oriental World. Part I.* Uppsala: Almqvist & Wiksell, 1929 (reprinted Amsterdam 1968).

Ulfgard, H., *The Story of Sukkot: The Setting, Shaping, and Sequel of the Biblical Feast of Tabernacles*. Tübingen: Mohr Siebeck, 1998.

21
Again Blessing Formulae and Divine Sovereignty in Rabbinic Liturgy[1]

Reuven Kimelman

THE FOCUS ON DIVINE sovereignty distinguishes the liturgy of rabbinic Judaism from earlier Jewish liturgies. Examples of this focus are the Shema liturgy, the Rosh Hashannah liturgy, and blessing formulae. The how, when, and why of this phenomenon is the subject of this study. I shall begin with a discussion of the presence of מלכות (kingship) in the *baruk* (blessing) formula that succeeds the Shema verse (Deut 6:4) in the liturgy, ברוך שם כבוד מלכותו לעולם ועד (Blessed be the name of His glorious kingship for ever and ever), hereafter referred to by the acronym BŠKML"W. I then focus on the almost total absence of this sovereignty motif in pre-rabbinic blessing formulae and the total absence of *baruk* formulae containing references to both מלכות and שם (name). This leads into a discussion of the interpolation of the sovereignty motif to create BŠKML"W, which in turn leads into an investigation of the introduction of said motif into the official rabbinic blessing formulary. After clarifying the "when and why" of the insertion of the sovereignty motif in the blessing, I offer an explanation for the development of the sovereignty motif in rabbinic liturgy as a whole.

---

[1] An earlier version of this study is slated to appear in *Liturgy in the Life of the Synagogue: Studies in the History of Jewish Prayer*, eds., Steven Fine and Ruth Langer.

BŠKML"W

The rabbinic claim that the Second Temple liturgy included BŠKML"W presents the primary objection to our thesis that divine sovereignty became central to the liturgy only in the rabbinic period. However, the claim of temple origins for BŠKML"W is problematic on several fronts.

There is no consensus in rabbinic literature on either the function or the origin of the BŠKML"W. According to most of Tannaitic literature, it functioned in the temple as a response to the enunciation of the Tetragrammaton by the High Priest on the Day of Atonement,[2] or as the "amen" after a blessing.[3] The Tannaitic *Sifre* and Amoraic literature agree that it served as the response to the recitation of the Shema verse by Israel, but disagree on whether it was the angels,[4] Jacob[5] or Moses[6] who were responding. BŠKML"W also appears without the Shema in the story of Moses hearing it from the angels upon arriving on high.[7] In addition, its recitation served to make amends for reciting an

---

[2] *m. Yoma* 3:8, 4:1–2, 6:2, *t. Kippurim* 2:1, ed. Lieberman, 2:229, line 9; *Sifra, Aḥare Mot*, ch. 1, *paršah* 2, and ch. 4, *paršah* 4, ed. Weiss, pp. 80d, 82a; *Qoh Rab.* 3, 11, 3 (end).

[3] See *Mek., Pisḥa* 16, ed. Lauterbach, 1:138, line 137; *Sifre Deut*, 306, ed. Finkelstein, p. 342, line 10; *t. Taʿan.* 1:11–13, ed. Lieberman, p. 326–7; *t. Ber.* 6:22, ed. Lieberman, p. 39, lines 101–2; *y. Taʿan.* 2:11, 65d; *y. Ber.* 9:8, 14c; *b. Ber.* 63a; *b. Taʿan.* 16b; *b. Sota* 40b. *Sifre Deut*, ibid., should be corrected according to the *Mek.*, ibid. For the use of "amen" as a response, see Schürer, *History*, 2:450, n. 108.

[4] *Gen Rab.* 65, 21, ed. Theodor-Albeck, p. 739 with notes; *Deut Rab.*, ed. Lieberman, p. 68; and *Cant Zutta*, 1, 1, ed. Buber, p. 7.

[5] *Sifre Deut* 31, ed. Finkelstein, p. 53; *Gen Rab.* 96, and 98, 3, ed. Theodor-Albeck, pp. 1202, 1252; *b. Pesaḥ.* 56a; *Deut Rab.* 2, 35; *Midr. Sekel Tob*, Gen 49:1, ed. Buber, p. 311; *Leqaḥ Tob*, Gen 49:1, ed. Buber, p. 231; Ginzberg, *Genizah Studies*, 1:44, 122; *Bet Ha-Midrasch.* ed. Jellinek, 2:74; *Midr. Ha-Gadol, Gen*, ed. Margulies, p. 835. lines. 17–18; *Yal.* I:257, *Gen*, ed. Heyman-Shiloni, p. 832, line 6, p. 834, line 26 and possibly ibid., 1:836, Deut, p. 109, line 3; and the Targumim cited below (pp. 334ff.).

[6] *Deut Rab.* 2, 31.

[7] This idea appears in relatively late sources; see *Deut Rab.* 2, 35; ibid., ed. Lieberman, pp. 68–99 with p. 69, n. 2; Ginzberg, *Genizah Studies*, 1:123 with n. 35; and *Yal.* 1:836, *Deut*, ed. Heyman-Shiloni, p. 108, and n. 6 with Lerner, "New Light," 139–43.

unnecessary blessing.[8] BŠKML"W also shows up frequently in Hekalot literature. There it serves three functions: as part of angelic liturgies in response to the *Qedušah*, as a response to the enunciation of divine names, and as a finale.[9] The most common function of BŠKML"W—whether it be the temple of Tannaitic literature,[10] or the Shema and/or angels of Amoraic and Hekalot literature—is that of a response.

Nonetheless, if BŠKML"W with its motif of divine sovereignty was not part of the temple liturgy, then its function as a response may have resulted from its later perceived role in the Shema. The difficulty in assuming that Second Temple liturgy employed this *baruk* formula is that its reference to God's name (שם) and its mention of kingship (מלכות) are not combined in any other extant Second Temple *baruk* formula.

So how did BŠKML"W come about? According to Amoraic literature it is based on Neh 9:5:

קומו ברכו את ה' אלהיכם מן העולם ועד העולם
ויברכו שם כבודך ומרומם על כל ברכה ותהילה

Rise, Bless the Lord your God from eternity to eternity.

---

[8] See *y. Ber.* 6:1, 10a with Lieberman, *Hilkot Ha-Yerušalmi*, pp. 38–9, n. ד; and Lamm, *Halakot Ve-Halikot*, 39–40.
[9] See Schäfer, *Konkordanz*, 2:416c–417a.
[10] The exception is the attribution to Jacob in the Tannaitic *Sifre Deut* 31, ed. Finkelstein, p. 53. This, however, is unlikely of Tannaitic provenance as its Aggadic and anonymous character suggest an Amoraic one. Moreover, when BŠKML"W appears elsewhere in the *Sifre* (306, ed. Finkelstein, p. 342) it serves as a liturgical response to the name of God. There is no mention of Jacob. Such a response fits its standard Tannaitic use. Also when the *Sifre* (323, ed. Finkelstein, p. 372) describes Jacob urging his sons to accept divine sovereignty there is no mention of BŠKML"W. The lateness of the BŠKML"W episode in *Sifre Deut* 31 is also evidenced by the fact that it is disconnected from what precedes or succeeds it. It was apparently interpolated when the Amoraic rendition of the story of Jacob became widely known. In the *Babylonian Talmud*, the tradition is attributed to the late third century Amora, R. Simeon b. Pazzi; see Rabbinovicz, *Diqduqei Sofrim, Pesaḥim*, 165, n. ד.

And they blessed your glorious name exalted above every blessing and praise.[11]

This verse contains all the elements of our blessing formula except for the mention of kingship. MaHaRSHA (R. Shmuel Eliezer Edels, 16th century) tried to resolve this discrepancy by suggesting that מלכותו (His kingship) of BŠKML"W derives from מרומם (exalted). He interprets Nehemiah's שם כבודך ומרומם (Your glorious name and exalted) to be the source of the blessing formula's שם כבוד מלכותו (name of His glorious kingship).[12] The difficulty with this suggestion is the unsupported contention that מלכות and מרומם are equivalent terms.[13] A similar tactic had been made long before by the *Mekilta*:

ומה הם עונין אחריו המברך ברוך ה׳ המבורך לעולם ועד.

וכשהוא קורא בשמו יהיו עונין אחריו ואומרין:

ברוך שם כבוד מלכותו לעולם ועד.

וכן דוד אומר: גדלו לה׳ אתי ונרוממה שמו יחדו

And what do they respond after the one who recites the benediction,
"Blessed be YHVH [hereafter: the Lord] who is to be blessed for ever and ever"?
And whenever he mentions His name, they shall respond by saying:
"BŠKML"W,"
For so David also says: "O magnify the Lord with me and let us exalt His name together" (Ps 34:4).[14]

---

[11] The Tannaitic sources (see n. 3) do not explicitly associate BŠKML"W with Neh 9:5 whereas Amoraic sources do; see *y. Taʿan.* 2:11, 65d; *y. Ber.* 9:8, 14c; and b. *Taʿan.* 16b. In any event, it is unclear whether the alleged response was BŠKML"W or 1 Chr 16:36; see the notes of Malter, *Treatise*, 60b.

[12] At *b. Soṭah* 40b, s.v., ומנין; see Lieberman, *Tosefta*, 1:124, line 102.

[13] The closest they come to equivalency is their juxtaposition in Ps 145:1 and Dan 4:34. The other examples for the association of the two cited by Eleazar b. Judah of Worms, *Perušei Siddur Ha-Tefillah La-Roqeaḥ*, 1:257, lack מלך.

[14] *Mek., Pisḥa* 16, ed. Lauterbach, 1:138

In both cases the justification for reciting BŠKML"W is a verse which mentions exalting His name, but no mention of מלכות. In actuality, there is no biblical evidence for a response mentioning kingship nor is there a biblical warrant for one. Based on Neh 9:5, the temple response should have been first ברוך ה' אלהינו מן העולם ועד העולם or[15] ברוך שם כבודך ומרומם and then[16] ברוך ה' אלהי ישראל מן העולם ועד העולם על כל ברכה ותהילה.

Since liturgical responses often reformulate just the initial strophe, or at most add the motif of divine eternity, it is strange to find our response adding the motif of divine sovereignty to a strophe that makes no mention of it.[17] Indeed, in Anan's Karaite liturgy, which hews to biblical precedent, the response consists only of ברוך ה' אלהי ישראל (Blessed be the Lord God of Israel) and ברוך שם כבדו (Blessed be His glorious name) among other *baruk* verses.[18]

Sovereignty in Pre-Rabbinic Blessing Formulae

Were BŠKML"W pre-rabbinic it would be unique among pre-rabbinic *baruk* formulae in its inclusion of both שם (name) and מלכות (kingship). In biblical *baruk* formulae that mention שם the common staples are ברוך and עולם (forever). None mention מלכות. Such is the case in the aforecited Neh 9:5 as well as Dan 2:20 which reads: להוא שמה די-אלהא מברך מן עלמא ועד עלמא (May the name of God be blessed for ever and ever). Even Ps 145, the only biblical psalm with the expression "my God the king" (Ps 145:1), mentions these three elements without mentioning kingship in the actual blessing of God's name.[19] After the strophe, ארוממך אלהי המלך (I will extol You, my God, the king), it continues with only ואברכה שמך לעולם ועד. בכל יום אברכך ואהללה שמך לעולם ועד (and bless Your name for ever and ever.

---

[15] As in Ps 41:14, 106:48; 1 Chr 16:36, or ברוך אתה ה' אלהי ישראל מעולם ועד עולם a là 1 Chr 29:10; see Wiliamson, "Structure and Historiography," 117–18, n. 3 and *Ezra and Nehemiah*, 303–4.

[16] As noted by RaLBaG (R. Levi b. Gerson) to Neh 9:5 (*Miqra'ot Gedolot*, p. 218).

[17] See Büchler, *Types of Jewish-Palestinian Piety*, 224–7.

[18] Such as Pss 41:14a; 72:18a, 19a; 89:53; and 106:48, namely, the *baruk* formulae that conclude the first four book of Psalms; see Mann, *'Anan's Liturgy*, 352.

[19] Even though its central theme is divine sovereignty; see Kimelman, "Psalm 145," 37–58.

Again Blessing Formulae and Divine Sovereignty in Rabbinic Literature

Every day I bless You and praise Your name for ever and ever [vv. 1–2]). The Psalm also ends, ויברך כל בשר שם קדשו לעולם ועד (and all flesh shall bless His holy name for ever and ever [v. 21]), without mention of מלכות.

Similarly, Ps 113:2 states: יהי שם ה' מברך מעתה ועד עולם (Let the name of the Lord be blessed now and forever). The two cases in the Psalter of actual blessing formulae that contain שם simply state: ברוך שם כבודו לעולם (Blessed be His glorious name forever [72:19]) and ברוך ה' [שם =] אלהי ישראל מן העולם ועד העולם (Blessed be the Lord, the God of Israel, from now and forevermore [106:48]). Ps 10:16 does mention מלכות and עולם but lacks a blessing context and any mention of שם.

The blessing formulae of extra-biblical literature in the Second Temple period follow the same pattern of mentioning the three elements of ברוך, שם, and עולם (the sources appear in the original Hebrew or in Hebrew translation to facilitate comparison). Tob 3:11–15 begins: ברוך אתה אל רחמן וברוך שמך לעולמים (Blessed are You, merciful God, and blessed is Your name forever); 8:5–7 begins: ברוך אתה ה' אלהי אבותנו וברוך שמך לכל דורות העולם (Blessed are You, O Lord God of our ancestors, and blessed is Your name in all generations forever). The Aramaic 4Q196:7 reads: [וברי]ך שמך קדישא [וי]קריא לכל ע[למין] (and blessed be Your holy and honored name forever). Tob 11:14 begins: ברוך האלהים וברוך שמו הגדול (Blessed be God and blessed be His great name); and 13:17 ends: ברוך אלהי ישראל וברוכים יברכו את שמו הקדוש לעולם ועד (Blessed be the God of Israel and the blessed will bless His holy name for ever and ever). *The Prayer of Azariah* also begins: ברוך אתה ה' אלהי אבותנו ומהולל ומפואר שמך לעולמים (Blessed are You, O Lord, God of our ancestors and worthy of praise and glorious is Your name forever [1:3]). *The Song of the Three Jews*, which is appended to *The Prayer of Azariah*, repeats the aforecited verse (1:3) and then adds: ברוך שם כבודך הקדוש ומפואר מאד ומרומם לעולמים (And blessed is your glorious, holy name, and to be highly praised and highly exalted forever [1:30]). Similarly, *1 Enoch* says: ברוך אתה וברוך שם אלוהי הרוחות לעולם ועד (Blessed are You, and blessed is the name of the Lord of the spirits for ever and ever [39:14]), and ברוך הוא וברוך שם אלוהי הרוחות לעולם ועד (Blessed is He, and blessed is the name of the Lord of the spirits for ever and ever [61:11]). *The Wisdom of Ben Sira* 51 concludes with: ברוך ה' לעולם ומשובח שמו לדר ודר (Blessed is the Lord forever and praised is His name from generation to generation) and יהי שם ה' מבורך מעתה ועד עולם (May the name of the Lord be blessed from now and forever).

At Qumran there are two examples of the coalescing of the three elements both of which are followed by a double amen: לבר]ך את שם [עו]ל[מים] אמן אמן כבודך בכל קיצי (To bless Your glorious name in all the ends of the worlds amen amen [4QBer^a 7:7]); and ברוך שמכה לעולמי עד. אמן אמן (Blessed is Your name forever amen amen [4Q510–11, frg. 63, 4:2]).[20] Blessing formulae with just "name" also abound at Qumran.[21]

This three-fold combination was so standard that even Hekalot literature with all its preference for kingship language contains a blessing with the three elements without an expression for kingship. One, which begins and ends with the formula ברוך אתה ה׳ (Blessed are You, Lord), has a strophe combining the three elements שם, ברכה and עולם, with קדוש (holy) either as in ואברך קדושת שמך לעולם (and I will bless the holiness of Your name forever), or ואברך שמך הקדוש לעולם (I will bless Your holy name forever).[22] Another simply states ברוך שבח שמך . . . לעולם (Blessed is the praise of your name . . . forever).[23] Indeed, there is even an occurrence[24] of BŠKML"W without מלכות namely ברוך שם כבוד לעולם ועד. The three elements of עולם, שם, ברכה also constitute known liturgical responses. In the Qumran version of Ps 145, the refrain after each verse is ברוך הוא וברוך שמו לעולם ועד (Blessed is He and blessed is His name for ever and ever).[25] In what became the response of the *Kaddish*, the three elements appear as יהא שמיה רבא מברך לעלם ולעלמי עלמיא (May His great name be blessed for ever and ever and ever).[26] Assuming the

---

[20] On the liturgical significance of the double amen, see Charlesworth, *Dead Sea Scrolls*, 49.

[21] See Schuller, "Observations on Blessing of God," 137, 140; the chart of closing formulae from 4Q503 in Falk, *Festival Prayers*, 37; 4QBerakhot (4Q286–90) ויברכו את שם קודשכה (And they blessed the name of Your holiness) or וברכו את שם כבוד אלוהותכה (And they blessed the glorious name of your God) with Nitzan, "Textual, Literary and Religious Character," 642, 651.

[22] Schäfer, *Synopse*, 569, pp. 218–19, lines 24–5.

[23] Ibid. 676, p. 248, lines 26–7.

[24] Ibid. 376, p. 158, line 36. The parallel (ibid., 702, p. 258, lines 10–11) which does contain מלכות may represent an interpolation to what became the standard form. On the whole topic, see Schlüter, "Untersuchungen," 83–148.

[25] 11Q Ps^a; see Kimelman, "Psalm 145," 56–7.

[26] *ʾAbot. R. Nat.* A 31, ed. Schechter, p. 91 cites in the name of the Tanna R. Yosi Ha-Galilee this strophe in Hebrew: יהא שמו הגדול מבורך לעולם ולעולמי עולמים (May His great name be blessed for ever and ever and ever). *Sifre Deut* 306, ed. Finkelstein, p. 342, line 11, also cites the Hebrew, albeit as a responsorial. The first voice is יהא שמו הגדול מבורך and the response is לעולם ולעולמי עולמים. In post-Tannaitic literature, it appears both in Hebrew and Aramic, see Lehnardt, "Once

Tetragrammaton (abbreviated in Hebrew as 'ה) functioned as the equivalent of שם, the Tannaitic congregational response ברוך ה' המבורך לעולם ועד (Blessed is the Lord who is to be blessed for ever and ever)[27] would also count as an example of combining the three (ברכה, שם, עולם) in a liturgical response.

Similarly, the Second Temple blessing formulae that contain references to divine kingship lack שם. Tob 13:1 reads: ברוך אלהים חי עולמים וברוכה מלכותו [או: מלכותו לעולם ועד] (Blessed be God, who lives forever, and blessed is His kingship [or: for His kingship lasts for ever and ever]).[28] *First Enoch* 22:14 reads: ברוך ה' אדני-הצדק המושל עד [או: על ה] עולם (Blessed be my Lord, the lord of righteousness who rules forever/over the world) [4QEn^d 1:11 reads], בריך דין קושט[א] ולהוה בריך מרא רבותא וקושטא דמריא לעלמא] (Blessed be the judgement of righteousness and blessed be the Lord of Majesty and of righteousness who is ruler of eternity)[29] and 84:2 reads: ברוך אתה ה' המלך הגדול וגבור . . . מלך המלכים ואלהי עולם (Blessed are You, O great and powerful king . . . king of kings and God of the world/eternity).[30] *Psalms of Solomon* 5:19 may read: ברוך כבוד ה' כי הוא מלכנו (Blessed be the glory of God, for He is our king).[31] *The Song of the Three Jews* reads: ברוך

Again," 23, nn. 36–7. There is also an expanded form in Hebrew that inserts in the middle "and be sanctified" יהא שמו הגדול מבורך לעולם ולעולמי עולמים (*Midreshei Ge'ullah*, p. 341, lines 271–2). For the spelling of שמיה, see Sperber, *Minhagei Yisrael*, 1:71–7.

[27] m. Ber. 7:3; *Sifre Deut* 306. For an earlier partial treatment of the three elements, see De Sola Pool, *Kaddish*, 46–51.

[28] The Qumran 4QTob (4Q200), frg. 7, reads: ברוך אלוהים חי אשר לכל העולמים היה מלכותו (Blessed is the living God whose sovereignty has been forever). Tob 13:6 also states: וברכו את אלוהי הצדקה ורוממו את מלך העולמים (Bless the Lord of righteousness and exalt the king of the ages) [Aramaic 4Q196 17 2:2–3 reads: וברכו למרה[ן] קושטא ורו[ממו לה] (bless the Lord of righteousness and extol Him) and 13:10/11 states: וברכי מלך עולמים (Bless the king of the ages). God is also addressed as βασιλεῦ τῶν αἰώνων (king of the ages) in *1 Clem.* 61:2 and 1 Tim1:17. Although the authenticity of chs. 13 and 14 of Tob have been questioned, there is no reason to deny their Second Temple provenance; see Weitzman, "Allusion," 50–1, nn. 4–6.

[29] For the translation and variant, see Charlesworth, *Old Testament Pseudepigrapha*, 1:25, n. 2. *1 En.* 25:7, 27:3 and 81:3 speak about blessing the Lord of Glory, the eternal king (or king of ages) but provide no blessing.

[30] Chs. 83–4 are not represented among the Qumran Aramaic manuscripts.

[31] The other references to God as eternal king there (17:1, 46) do not comprise blessing formulae.

אתה על כסא כבוד מלכותך ומהולל ומרומם לעולמים (Blessed are You on the throne of Your kingdom and exalted forever [1:33]). At Qumran, a line from *4QSongs of the Sage* reads ברוך אתה אלי מלך הכבו[ד] (Blessed are You, my God, king of glory);[32] while *4QSongs of the Sabbath Sacrifice* records a possible human response to the angelic heavenly liturgy,[33] which may read: ברוך [הא]דון מלך] הכל (Blessed is the Lord, king of all),[34] and a line from 4Q405, frg. 14 + 15, 1:3, that reads קול ברך למלך מרוממים (the sound of blessing to the king from above/of exalters/of exalted ones),[35] which lacks otherwise any blessing formula.

Other references to divine kingship in Second Temple prayer lack a blessing context. The LXX contains a prayer wherein God is addressed βασιλεῦ πάντων κρατῶν (King ruling over all) and βασιλεῦ τῶν θεῶν (King of gods).[36] A prayer in *The Testament of Moses* states: "Lord of all, king of the lofty throne, You who rules the world" (4:2).[37] Judith prayed: "God . . . Lord of heaven and earth, Creator of the waters, King (βασιλεῦ) of all your creation" (Jdt 9:12). The high priest Simon prayed: "Lord, Lord, King (βασιλεῦ) of heaven, ruler (δέσποτα) of all creation, holy among the holy ones, sovereign (μόναρχε), ruler of all (παντοκράτωρ) (3 Macc 2:2). And the priest Eleazar prayed: "King (βασιλεῦ), great in power, most high, ruler of all, God, who governs the whole creation with mercy" (3 Macc 6:2).

Qumran literature also has few references to divine kingship. They are concentrated in the *Songs of the Sabbath Sacrifice*, and the *War Scroll* (chapter 12) where the term מלכות is frequently combined with כבוד (glory). In the *Songs of the Sabbath Sacrifice*, the theme of sovereignty appears primarily in scenes of the heavenly angels or of the temple and on the Sabbath.[38] The references to kingship in a blessing context are limited to the few just mentioned above. The absence of kingship references is underscored by the fact that the *Daily Prayers* (4Q503),

---

[32] 4Q511, frgs. 52–9, 3:4.
[33] 4Q403 1:28; see Schuller, "Observations on Blessing of God," 138; and Falk, *Festival Prayers*, 146–7.
[34] 4Q403, frg. 1, 1:28; see Newsom, *Songs of the Sabbath Sacrifice*, 206.
[35] For the text and its translation see Davila, *Liturgical Works*, 137.
[36] Add. Esth. 13:9; 16:18, 21.
[37] A translation of the Latin. The original Greek, which may have been based on a Hebrew or Aramaic original, is lost.
[38] See Newsom, *Songs of the Sabbath Sacrifice*, 424–7; Carmignac, "Roi, royauté et royaume,"177–86; Schwemer, "Gott als König," 49–76, 117; Preuss, *Theologie des Alten Testaments*, 1:123–74; and *ABD*, 4:52.

which alone contain twenty nine blessing formulae, make no mention of kingship.[39] The virtual absence of kingship in the blessing formulae of Qumran, the liturgy which has the greatest affinity to post-temple rabbinic liturgy, is telling.[40]

The infrequency of the sovereignty motif in Second Temple liturgy is not surprising in view of its rarity in the Hebrew Bible itself. The closest biblical expression to the rabbinic acceptance of divine sovereignty—קבלת עול מלכות שמים—is Jer 5:5 which uses עול (yoke) as a metaphor of commitment and loyalty to God.[41] The expression מלכות שמים (kingship of "Heaven," i.e., God) is not biblical at all. The closest expressions are מלכות ה׳ (1 Chr 28:5) and ממלכת ה׳ (1 Chr 13:8).[42] The Pentateuch contains at most three references to divine kingship, all of which appear in poetic selections.[43] There are other references scattered throughout,[44] most prominently in Psalms, especially in those odes that

---

[39] Falk, *Festival Prayers*, 37. 4QBerᵃ 7i does juxtapose מלכות to ברכות but not as part a *baruk* formula; see Nitzan, "Textual, Literary and Religious Character," 653, with n. 57.

[40] For the otherwise considerable commonality between rabbinic and Qumran liturgical expressions, see Schiffman, "From Temple to Torah," 10; Talmon, "Emergence," 200–43; Chazon, "Prayers from Qumran," 265–84; and Sarason, "Intersections," 169–81.

[41] See Rashi and Abarbanel, *ad loc*. Targum, Rashi, and Radak understand it as the yoke of Torah. Dr David Bernat of Welseley College informs me (private communication, Nov. 1999) that the Akkadian equivalent is *niru* (its Aramaic cognate *nir* is used to translate עול [e.g., Gen 27:40]) in both political and theological contexts. An example of the latter is the epigram, "he who bears the yoke of his god (*nir ili*) never lacks food, however sparse," about which Bernat says, "in this instance *nir ili* is paired poetically with *tem ili* the will of the god" (*Theodicy*, 239–40, as cited in Lambert, *Babylonian Wisdom Literature*, 85). This is especially pertinent since elsewhere, as Bernat comments, "Akkadian political language and forms have taken on theological garb in the Bible, particularly to denote the covenantal relationship of Israel and God"; see McCarthy, *Treaty and Covenant*; Moran, "Ancient Near Eastern Background," 77–87; Tadmor, "Treaty and Oath," 127–52; Weinfeld, "Covenant Terminology," 190–9; and idem, *Deuteronomy 1-11*, 351–2. He also notes that "Numerous studies have pointed to concepts and locutions common to Akkadian and Rabbinic literature that are unattested in the Bible"; see, *inter alia*, Muffs, *Studies in the Aramaic Legal Papyri*.

[42] About which, see Hurvitz, *Transition Period*, 83–4, n. 36.

[43] Exod 15:18; Num 23:21. On Deut 33:5; see Tigay, *Deuteronomy*, 407, n. 41. For the rest of the Bible, see Brettler, *God is King*, 30–3; and *ABD*, 4:43.

[44] Such as 1 Sam 12:12; Jer 10:10; Isa 33:22; Mic 4:7; Obad 21.

celebrate God's sovereignty.⁴⁵ The various images of God as sovereign in Psalms depict Him as ruler over all gods, over all the world, and over all the nations, that is, over the divine, the natural, and the human realm.

Early rabbinic prayer also lacks references to divine kingship. It is missing from the aforementioned response,⁴⁶ יהא שמיה רבא מבורך לעלם ולעלמי עלמיא. It is also absent from the blessing perorations, which are the oldest parts, of the standard Babylonian-based ᶜAmidah except for some versions of blessing 11 with its petition for divine justice.⁴⁷ Indeed its mention in the body of blessings 1, 2, 3 and 5 of current versions is frequently absent in Medieval versions.⁴⁸ It is absent as well from the Palestinian-based Genizah versions,⁴⁹ from the *Habinnenu* abridgement of the daily ᶜAmidah,⁵⁰ and from the *Magen ʾabot* abridgement of the

---

⁴⁵ Such as Pss 93, 95–9; see also 3 5:3; 10:16; 22:29; 24:7–10; 29:10; 44:5; 47:3, 7–9; 48:3; 68:25; 74:12; 84:4; 145:1, 11–13; 149:2 along with Kimelman, "Psalm 145," 45, 55, n. 95.

⁴⁶ On the dating of the sovereignty motif in the *Qaddiš*; see Goldschmidt, *Maḥzor Le-Yamim Ha-Noraʾ im*, 1:25.

⁴⁷ For its absence in blessing 11, see Luger, *Weekday Amidah*, 131; Goldschmidt, *On Jewish Liturgy*, 199, line 20; Abraham b. Nathan of Lunel, *Sefer Ha-Manhig*, 1:305, n. 66; Judah b. Yaqar, *Peruš Ha-Tefillot Ve-Ha-Berakhot*, 1:48; and Abudarham, *Abudarham Ha-Šalem*, 100. Not only is God not called מלך in blessing 11, but the strophe that asks God: מלוך עלינו (reign over us), is absent from a Genizah MS (see Luger, ibid., 120) and from the version of *Siddur Rabbenu Šelomoh b. R. Natan*, 15.

⁴⁸ See Jacobson, *Netiv Binah*, 1:272–8. In blessing 8, מלך is absent in *Seder Rav Amram Gaon*, p. 25, but does appear by the early thirteenth century in Judah b. Yaqar, *Peruš Ha-Tefillot Ve-Ha-Berakoth*, 1:47 and in Eleazar b. Judah of Worms, *Perušei Siddur Ha-Tefillah La-Roqeah*, 1:337.

⁴⁹ See Luger, *Weekday Amidah*, 42, 55, 65, 82, 87, 120; Assaf, "Me-Seder Ha-Tefillah Be-ʾEretz Yisrael," 116–31; Schechter, "Genizah Specimens," 656–7; Mann, "Genizah Fragments," 296, 309–10 and Schechter, *Studies in Jewish Liturgy*, 97. An exception is the אבינו מלכנו of the *Modim* blessing cited only in Mann, ibid., 310. A comparison of it with the text cited by Schechter ("Genizah Specimens") shows that it is interpolated along with, and is related to, the expressions for prostration of the Mann text. For an additional insertion, see Luger, ibid, 190.

⁵⁰ See *y. Ber.* 4:3, 8a = *Taᶜan* 2:2, 65c; and *b. Ber.* 29a. For these three forms of the ᶜAmidah in English, see Petuchowski, "Jewish Prayer Texts," 27–36; for the Palestinian versions of the ᶜAmidah with the Babylonian and Palestinian versions of the *Habinnenu* in Hebrew and in English, see Evans, *Jesus and His Contemporaries*, 277–80. Kingship is also absent from the other versions of the abridgement (see Schechter, *Studies in Jewish Liturgy*, 97; Hadani, "Habinenu," 302, 313–16; and Fleischer, "Occasional," 14 with the literature cited in n. 15) as well as from the

Sabbath ᶜAmidah.⁵¹ Indeed, the absence of kingship as opposed to the mention of the divine name (שם שמים) was deemed the distinguishing mark of the blessing formulae of the ᶜAmidah.⁵² The Palestinian version of the ᶜAmidah even resisted the Babylonian practice of changing the peroration of the third blessing from "the holy God" to "the holy King" to mark the High Holidays.⁵³ The absence of any mention of sovereignty in the original ᶜAmidah may explain the need for the interpolation of the *Qedušah* with its ceremony for emulating the angelic acceptance of divine sovereignty.⁵⁴ Through the interpolation of

---

short alternatives to the ᶜAmidah (see *t. Ber.* 3:3, ed. Lieberman, p. 13 and parallels).

⁵¹ See *Seder Rav Amram Gaon*, 64. That both abridgements lack מלך was noted by Abraham b. Nathan of Lunel, *Sefer Ha-Manhig*, 1:140.

⁵² *Midr. Ps* 16, 8, ed. Buber, p. 123; and *b. Ber.* 21a ("The ᶜAmidah is different, it lacks mention of divine kingship;") see Rashi and Tosafot ad loc.; and Eleazar b. Judah of Worms, *Ha-Roqeaḥ Ha-Gadol*, p. 253. Accordingly, מלך is absent from Saᶜadyah Gaon's paraphrase of the ᶜAmidah; see Zulay, *Liturgical Poetry*, 248–57, as well as from all the divine appelatives added to blessing 1; see *b. Ber.* 33b, *y. Ber.* 9:1, 12d; *Midr. Ps* 19, 2, ed. Buber, p. 163; *Midr. Ha-Gadol Deut*, ed. Fish, p. 191; and Schäfer, *Synopse*, #419, p. 178, lines 25–6. Since God was not originally addressed as king in the ᶜAmidah the metaphors for the posture and choreography of the worshipper lack royal images such as a servant before a king; see Ehrlich, *Non-Verbal Language Prayer*, 33–63, 116–27. The rabbinic material focuses on the models of a slave taking leave of his master, of a disciple taking leave of his teacher, and of a worshiper taking leave of the divine presence as opposed to models of royal entrance and exit etiquette such as that used for the Holy of Holies (see ʾ*Abot R. Nat.* A 15 and B 29, ed. Schechter, p. 61). Although the royal metaphor for the ᶜAmidah is implicit in the Talmud (*b. Ber* 33a, ᶜ*Erub.* 64a. The case in *b. Ber.* 34b with R. Yohanan b. Zakkai does not deal with the ᶜAmidah), it does not become explicit until the medival period; see *Siddur R. Saᶜadyah Gaon*, p. 20; Maimonides, "Laws of Prayer," 5:11; Rashi, *b. Ber* 25b, s.v., ʾ*aval le-tefillah; Tosafot Rabbenu Yehudah Sirleons*, p. 358, s. v., beʾ*avot*; *Maḥzor Vitry*, p. 15; *Siddur of R. Solomon ben Samson of Garmaise*, pp. 102–4; Abudarham, *Tehillah Le-David*, p. 213, Abraham b. Nathan of Lunel, *Sefer Ha-Manhig* 1:87; and "Rashi" to *Gen Rab.* 39, 12, Vilna edition, p. 81a. The bowing at blessing seventeen in particular came to be understood as bowing to a king; see Abudarham, *Tehillah Le-David*, p. 217, nn. 97–8.

⁵³ See *b. Ber.* 12b; Fleischer, "Seridim Nosafim," 8; Jacobs, "Kingship and Holiness," 68–9; and Luger, *Weekday Amidah*, 71–7, with literature cited in notes.

⁵⁴ For the lateness of the *Qedušah* in the ᶜAmidah, see Fleischer, "Qedushah," 301–50. Note that the sole Tannaitic reference to the *Qedušah* (*t. Ber.* 1:9, ed. Lieberman, 1:3–4,) has only "Holy, holy, holy . . . (Isa 6:3) followed by a *baruk* verse (which could be Ezek 3:12 as MS Erfurt reads or some other *baruk* verse such

the *Qedušah* the ʿAmidah was updated to the rabbinic understanding of communal liturgy as the occasion for declaring divine sovereignty.

The absence of any reference to divine kingship in the earliest formulations of the ʿAmidah correlates with its near absence in the contemporaneous writings of Josephus. Such an absence is most telling in the intellectual portrait of the Pharisees in his *Antiquitates judaicae*,[55] which was issued in the early nineties of the first century C.E., the very decade that the ʿAmidah was being formulated under the auspices of Rabban Gamaliel.[56] Despite the golden opportunities for contrasting the sovereignty of God with that of Emperor Vespasian, neither Josephus' report of the Zealot Eleazar ben Jair at Masada, which contains the statement "We determined to serve neither the Romans nor anyone else but only God,"[57] nor his description of the Sicarii, who "honor God alone as their Lord and Master,"[58] make any mention of divine sovereignty.[59] The closest Josephus comes to the idea of the sovereignty of God is his neologism "theocracy" which he defines as "placing all rule and authority in the hands of God."[60] The end of the

---

as those in *1 En.* 39:14 or 61:12 or Schäfer, *Synopse*, #555, p. 210, lines 10–11, 20–1, 25–6. For the liturgical phenomenon of alternating *baruk* verses, see Ginzberg, *Genizah Studies* 1:256). At this stage the *Qedušah* still lacks a kingship verse. Kingship verses such as Ps 146:10 or Exod 15:18 could not figure in the *Qedušah* since the *Qedušah* itself was not yet understood as a ceremony for proclaiming divine sovereignty. Thus the mid-third century Amora Rav refers to Isa 6:3 only as the song of the angels (*b. Ḥul.* 91b), whereas the late third century Amora R. Abin (or R. Abbahu) who promoted the understanding of the angelic "Holy, holy, holy" as an acclamation of divine sovereignty, said: "Every day the angels crown God . . . saying: 'Holy, Holy, Holy'" (*Lev Rab.* 24:8, ed. Margulies, p. 564); see Kimelman, "Shema Liturgy," 61–2. According to *3 En.* (40:2; see Charlesworth, *Old Testament Pseudepigrapha*, 1:291), the angels receive a crown for saying holy. On the phenomenon of the crowning of the crowner, see Kimelman, *Mystical Meaning*, 8, n. 48.

[55] *A.J.* 13.171–2; 18.12–15; see *B.J.* 2.162.
[56] See Kimelman, "Literary Structure," 175; and Levine, *Ancient Synagogue*, 510–16.
[57] *B.J.* 7.323.
[58] *B.J.* 7.410; see also *A.J.* 18.23, where God is called ἡγεμόνα καὶ δεσπότην.
[59] Indeed, there is no explicit mention of God at all in Josephus' general description of the Jewish three schools of Jewish thought in *A.J.* 13.171–3, albeit in *A.J.* 18.11–25, but not as king.
[60] *C. Ap.* 2.165.

first century thus provides us with a *terminus a quo* for the interpolation of the sovereignty motif into the rabbinic liturgy.[61]

In sum, except for the rabbinic claim of BŠKML"W as a Second Temple response,[62] no other blessing formula containing both name and kingship has shown up in Second Temple literature.[63] Had the

---

[61] This late dating is supported by the rarity of the motif in other first century C.E. Jewish Hellenistic literature. The author of Wis, ca. 40 C.E., mentions only once the expression "kingdom of God" (βασιλείαν θεοῦ) (10:10). His contemporary, Philo, does not even cite the Shema verse (Deut 6:4) (see Wolfson, *Philo*, 2:95; and Leonhardt, *Jewish Worship*, 140), though he does use βασιλεῦ τῶν θεῶν (king of gods) in Conf. 173 as well as τοῦ θεοῦ βασιλείαν (the kingship of God) in *Spec.* 4.164 (see also 1.207) as does *Pss. Sol.* 17:3 (ἡ βασιλεία τοῦ θεοῦ). So far the expression has not cropped up in the Dead Sea Scrolls, though some have tried to read 1QSb 3:5 and 4Q525 5:3 to say so. The absence of the expression is quite telling "given the frequency of the word 'kingdom,' especially in the texts found in cave 4" (Evans, *Jesus and His Contemporaries*, 304, n. 21). Of course, "the kingdom of God" (ἡ βασιλεία τοῦ θεοῦ) does appear in the sayings of Jesus, but they are notoriously difficult to date and even more difficult to establish their meaning. For a full discussion, see Meier, *Marginal Jew*, 2:237–42, 289–506. In any case, Jesus does not address God as king.

[62] As noted the Qumran *Songs of the Sabbath Sacrifice* come closest especially with the expression כבוד מלכותו (4Q403 1:32) which also occurs in 4Q510 1:4. כבוד מלכותך appears in 1QM 12:7. All of these lack reference to שם (cf. Schwemer, "Gott als König," 115–18). The alleged Christian parallels are all post-70 C.E. (see Werner, "Doxology," 288–9) as are those of Hekalot literature (see, e.g., Schäfer, *Synopse*, #553, p. 209, lines 33–4; 555, p. 210; and 571, p. 218, lines 47–8).

[63] Flusser mistakenly holds that the blessing of *The Song of the Three Jews* is the antecedent of the mention of kingship in our blessing formula. In "Psalms, Hymns, and Prayer," 554, he writes: " 'Blessed is the holy name of your glory . . . forever . . . blessed are you in the temple of your sacred glory . . . forever . . . blessed are you on the throne of the glory of your kingship.' This is an expansion of the doxology recited in the Temple of Jerusalem: 'Blessed be the name of the glory of his kingship forever,' and the apocryphal prayer can serve as a kind of explanation of this famous doxology." In presenting the material this way, Flusser creates the impression that the three "blessed" statements form a unit, whereas in actuality they are the second, third, and fifth of six distinct blessings (1:28–34). Since they are not linked in any way (cf. Urbach, *Sages*, 705, n. to p. 348 [ET: p. 858, n. 3a]) there is no reason to extract them from the whole just to establish an antecedent for our formula. Indeed, the fact that none of the six blessings combine שם and מלכות supports the contention that there was no norm for combining both of them in a single blessing formula. Accordingly, Tob 13 which begins: "Blessed be God, who lives forever, for His kingdom lasts throughout all ages" and ends: "Blessed be the God of Israel and the blessed will bless the holy name forever and ever," mentions "kingship" and "name" in two distinct blessing formulae, but not together. A

temple response included שם and מלכות their absence elsewhere would be conspicuous as no blessing formula would be better known or more imitated than that of the temple. Since no single element of BŠKML"W is unique, nor is any element of it specifically linked to the temple, there is no reason to assume that in combination it was limited to the temple.

The History of BŠKML"W

Whence the formulation BŠKML"W? In the absence of any corroborating evidence for the full BŠKML"W in the Second Temple period, it is possible that the temple response was only ברוך שם כבודו לעולם ועד (Blessed is His glorious name for ever and ever) without מלכותו. Such a formulation appears in Ps 72:19 and is alluded to in Neh 9:5. It is also the appropriate response to hearing the name of God alone.[64] Scholars have speculated that the insertion of מלכות was aimed at countering the claims of kingship of the Hasmonaeans, specifically Alexander Jannai, or of the Sadducees,[65] or of Herod.[66] But the absence of such a formula in any other text makes its unlikely that its introduction was in opposition to any pre-70 C.E. political figure.[67] It would be peculiar for a polemic of this nature to lack multiple attestations. A more likely scenario is that an expression that lacked mention of kingship in Second Temple times was expanded to include it.

The phenomenon of adding the kingship motif to an extant tradition seems to have transpired also with regard to the related episode of Jacob. According to the aforenoted rabbinic sources,[68] Jacob on his deathbed called his twelve sons and addressed them saying:

---

similar division of labor obtains at Qumran's 4Q403 where one strophe (1:28) says: מברכים ומצדיקין בשם כבודו while the next states: ברוך האדון מלך הכל.

[64] As noted by Wiesenberg, "Liturgical Term," 26–7, and confirmed by the Syriac *Peshitta* to Neh 9:5.

[65] See Aptowitzer, "Geschichte," 101–10.

[66] See *Sifre Deut*, ed. Friedmann, pp. 72b–73a, n. 17.

[67] See Urbach, Sages, 349, n. 8 (ET, p. 859, n. 8). For the cult of the emperor, see below (pp. 348 ff).

[68] See n. 5.

Is it possible that you harbor reservations about the Holy One, blessed be He? They said to him, "Hear O Israel" (Deut 6:4), our father, just as you harbor no reservations about God, so we harbor no reservations about God, rather "the Lord is our God, the Lord is one" (ibid.). He too whispered BŠKML"W.

The targumic tradition here lacks mention of מלכות. Instead of BŠKML"W, *Tg. Ps.-J.* Deut 6:4 substitutes: ברוך שום יקריה לעלמי עלמין (Blessed is His glorious name for ever and ever), which is virtually the Targum to Ps 72:19—ברוך שום יקריה לעלמא (Blessed is the name of His glory forever). Other Targumim[69] substitute for BŠKML"W: יהא שמיה רבא מברך לעלם לעלמי עלמיא (May His great name be blessed for ever and ever and ever), an expression that is almost identical to Dan 2:20 and in Hebrew to that of Ps 113:2 and Job 1:21.

Apparently, the targumic tradition reflects an early stage of the story before BŠKML"W, with its mention of kingship, was incorporated into the recitation of the Shema. Then it was still adequate to just praise the divine name upon hearing it. The later ascription of BŠKML"W to Jacob is an attempt to explain and ground the peculiar practice of whispering a response. It thus assumes two developments, namely, the association of BŠKML"W with the Shema and the practice of whispering it (see below). The attribution of the explanation to late third century rabbis likely points to the time of its origin.[70]

---

[69] *Tg. Yer.* Gen 49:1–2, Deut 6:4; *Tg. Neof.* Deut 6:4; see Heinemann, *Prayer*, 86, n. 38; and Kasher, *Sefer Šemaʿ*, 19. Similarly, the response of Tgs. *P.-J.* and *Neof.* to Exod 15:3 to the name of God is יהי שמיה מברך לעלמי עלמין. In other places (Exod 20:2; Num. 15:2; 21:34) some Targumim leave out the term for forever. Those that include it follow the liturgical principle that the congregation should exceed the precentor's praise so that when the precentor says, "Bless the Lord who is to be blessed," the congregation responds with "Blessed be the Lord who is to be blessed for ever and ever" (*Sifre Deut* 306, ed. Finkelstein, p. 342); see Shinan, *Embroidered Targum*, 118, n. 73. The survival of ברוך שם כבוד לעולם ועד in Hekalot literature (see above, n. 24) may be added to the many indications of linkage between Hekalot and the temple adduced by Elior, "From Earthly Temple," 341–80. Another Hekalot text, *Masseket Hekalot* (not in Schäfer, *Synopse*) associates ברוך הוא וברוך שמו with Neh 9:5 (*Bet Ha-Midrasch*, ed. Jellenik, 2:47).

[70] According to one tradition, the author is R. Simon b. Pazzi, see above n. 10. According to another tradition, the author is Eleazar b. Aḥmi/ Aḥvi (see *Deut Rab.*,

The Shema verse itself does not make, or demand, mention of kingship. Indeed, there is no necessary connection between declaring the singularity of God and the motif of sovereignty in the Bible. Thus Nehemiah juxtaposes its blessing formula (9:5), with its employment of the term שם כבודך (the name of Your glory), with a statement that in substance parallels the Shema verse, namely, "You are the Lord, You alone" (Neh 9:6),[71] without any mention of divine kingship. When the recitation of the Shema verse became understood as an act of acceptance or realization[72] of divine sovereignty, the כבודו (His glory) of Ps 72:19 was expanded to כבוד מלכותו (His glorious kingship)[73] resulting in its infelicitous syntax. This infelicity is best demonstrated by the exception to the targumic tradition, *Tg. Neof.* Gen 49:2, which reads: ברוך שמיה כבודיה דמלכותיה לעלמי עלמין (Blessed is His glorious name of His kingdom for ever and ever).[74] Instead of the common Aramaic יקריה this text retains the Hebrew with an Aramaic suffix כבודיה, a term which otherwise is unattested in *Targum Neofiti*,[75] and which suggests editing according to a Hebrew original. This text also had obvious difficulties in rendering the syntax of BŠKML"W into Aramaic. In order to translate the two consecutive construct forms found in שם כבוד מלכותו, it had to insert the genitive ד (of) before the third word. Similarly, R. Saʿadya Gaon, aware of the peculiarity of a statement that constitutes, what he calls, "praises applied to the attribute of the attribute of an attribute" renders the formula into Arabic as if it read: "Blessed be the name of the

---

ed. Lieberman, p. 67, n. 3), a name that also appears in Tannaitic literature (see *Sifra*, end of ch. 2, ed. Weiss, p. 4b).

[71] The concluding words of the Shema verse ה' אחד can mean "the Lord is one" as well as "the Lord alone"; see Tigay, *Deuteronomy*, 65, 438–9; and Kimelman, "Shema Liturgy," 80, n. 255.

[72] An understanding which may have been triggered by Zech 14:9 ("And the Lord will become king over all the earth; on that day the Lord will be one and His name one"); see *Midr. Ha-Gadol, Deut*, ed. Fisch, p. 127, line 25. In late midrashic literature, Israel actually realizes divine kingship, see *Exod Rab.* 23, 1; *Midr. Ps* 25, 9; *Pirqe R. El.* 11, ed. Luria, p. 28a; and Heschel, *Theology of Ancient Judaism*, 1:65–82.

[73] See Finkelstein, "Meaning," 36–8. The expression itself is found only in late biblical, Second Temple Hebrew; see Hurvitz, *Transition Period*, 82–3. Its Akkadian equivalent may be *melam šarrūti*; see Weinfeld, *Deuteronomy 1–11*, 352.

[74] Courtesy of Professor Avigdor Shinan of the Hebrew University.

[75] Nor in *Tgs J.* and *Onq.*, according to their concordances.

glory of His kingdom."⁷⁶ Such difficulties in translating BŠKML"W into the cognate languages Arabic and Aramaic underscore the roughness of the Hebrew, a telltale indicator of an interpolation.

The reason that מלכות was interpolated to create BŠKML"W was to guarantee that the recitation of the Shema verse would be grasped as an act of the acceptance of divine sovereignty.⁷⁷ This, however, created a new problem, namely, the insertion of a non-biblical element into the recitation of the biblical Shema. In order to legitimate the new formulation it was stamped with sacred or heavenly authority by retrojecting it back to the temple and/or projecting it onto the celestial choir or by placing it in the mouth of Jacob.

There were two modes of reciting the Shema verse to make the point that its recitation was an act of acceptance of divine sovereignty. One was the communal ceremony of dividing the Shema verse of (*porsin et šemaᶜ*).⁷⁸ The other was the addition of BŠKML"W after it. The duplication of function is underscored by the onetime Palestinian practice of reciting both aloud.⁷⁹ It is precisely due to the overlap of

---

⁷⁶ Saᶜadyah Gaon, *Book of Beliefs*, 2:13, p. 136. This point is reflected in the Hebrew translation of Yosef Kapaḥ (p. 115) but not in that of Yehudah ibn Tibbon (p. 104). I am indebted to Professor Haggai ben Shammai of the Hebrew University for this clarification.
⁷⁷ As noted by Bahya to Deut 5:4, ed. Chavel, 3:277, lines 6–7; and Ibn Šuᶜeib, *Sefer Derašot Ibn Šuᶜeib*, p. 19b; see *Sifre Deut* 31, ed. Friedmann, 72b, n. 17; and Urbach, *Sages*, 350 at n. 15 (ET, p. 402).
⁷⁸ That is, the precentor says: "Hear O Israel," and the congregation responds: "The Lord our God the Lord is one"; see Kimelman, "Shema Liturgy," 94–5. This division of the Shema verse follows contemporaneous acclamation rites; see ibid., 63–8.
⁷⁹ For the Shema, see Kimelman, "Shema Liturgy," 92–3 For BŠKML"W, see *b. Pesaḥ.* 56a; and *Deut Rab.*, ed. Lieberman, p. 69, n. 2. According to the commentary of R. Ḥannanel and to two Yemenite MSS of *b. Pesaḥ.* 56a, the recitation of BŠKML"W aloud was instituted at Usha; see Urbach, *Sages*, 349, n. 9 (ET, p. 859. n. 9). The reference to Usha supports the assumption that the Shema became the liturgical acclamation of divine sovereignty (*m. Ber.* 2:2) in the mid-second century during the Ushan period. R. Abbahu's explanation (*b. Pesaḥ.* 56a) that BŠKML"W was instituted to squelch heretical allegations reflects the milieu of his own fourth century Caesarea, not that of second century Usha; see Levine, *Caesarea Under Roman Rule*, 73, 76–7. The heresy of fourth century Caesarea may have simply consisted of the denial that the Shema affirms divine kingship, or the corollary that the God of Israel is Lord of all, as noted by the fourth century Emperor Julian (see below, n. 190). Thus the need to proclaim BŠKML"W aloud

function between responding with "the Lord our God, the Lord is one" and BŠKML"W that the various Midrashim assigned the role of BŠKML"W to a third party, be it Jacob or Moses, rather than having the same respondents say "the Lord our God, the Lord is one" and BŠKML"W. Another way of avoiding the appearance of duplication of function was to whisper the BŠKML"W,[80] producing the anomaly of a whispered response in public worship.[81] Apparently, BŠKML"W was originally reserved for the individual recitation as the dividing of the Shema was reserved for the communal recitation, which accordingly required a quorum.[82] Alluding to the time when one sufficed, R. Judah surmised that the people of Jericho divided the Shema verse but did not say BŠKML"W.[83]

---

with its emphasis on מלכותו לעולם which may have been understood also as affirming His kingship over the world.

[80] In contrast, Albeck, who holds that BŠKML"W was the response—based on the temple model—writes: "Once they ceased splitting the Shema, and the precentor and congregation recited the Shema together, there was no place for the congregation to respond with BŠKML"W, but since they did not want to abolish the practice totally, they instituted the saying of BŠKML"W in a whisper" (Albeck, Šišah Sidrei Mišnah, 1:328). Albeck does not explain why there was no place for the congregation to respond. If they could respond with BŠKML"W when the Shema was split why could they not respond so when it was not, unless, as I hold, the splitting of the Shema and the saying of BŠKML"W were originally two distinct practices for indicating the theme of divine sovereignty.

[81] See Aptowitzer, "Geschichte," 110. The various Aggadic explanations (above, n. 5) for the whispering are struggling with the incongruity of whispering something that should be proclaimed aloud. For example, according to *b. Pesaḥ.* 56a (followed by the later midrashic tradition, cited in n. 5) BŠKML"W is whispered to mediate between Jacob having said it and Moses having not said (or written [following Abraham b. Isaac of Narbonne, *Sefer Ha-Eškol*, p. 15, and Eleazar b. Judah of Worms, *Perušei Siddur Ha-Tefillah La-Roqeaḥ*, 1:283.]) it, that is, it is not biblical.

[82] See *m. Meg.* 4:3; and *Sop.* 10:6, ed. Higger, pp. 212–14, with n. 26. R. Nehemiah (*t. Soṭah* 6:3, ed. Lieberman, pp. 183–4, lines 31–2) specifically refers to the division of the Shema as a synagogue practice.

[83] See *t. Pisḥa* 3:19, ed. Lieberman, 2:157, lines 77–8 with Lieberman, *Tosefta*, 4:541–2. Urbach, accepting the temple origin of BŠKML"W, gives the following scenario: "[BŠKML"W] originated in the reading of the Shema in the temple, only the usage spread beyond its precincts. However, when the recital of the Shema became an individual obligation, some Sages abolished completely the saying of BŠKML"W, because they were concerned not to make an unnecessary breach between two verses of the Torah; but the majority continued to pronounce the response in a low voice" (*Sages*, 349, ET, p. 401). There is, however, no evidence

A third way of underscoring the sovereignty theme of the Shema verse consisted of introducing it with a blessing that states that God "commanded us with regard to the recitation of the Shema to make Him king over us."[84] Since this blessing is only attested in a Genizah text, it is likely a later development intended to underscore the function of the Shema verse when the other two indicators of divine sovereignty—the division of the Shema verse and the recitation of the BŠKML"W aloud—were no longer practiced.[85]

In sum, the theme of divine sovereignty in the Shema verse was indicated by splitting it, or by preceding or succeeding it with a blessing formula that spells out the theme of divine sovereignty. The splitting of the verse enacted the theme, whereas the blessing stated it. Confusion set in when the significance of the splitting was no longer understood necessitating the insertion of BŠKML"W to include explicitly the theme of sovereignty.

Sovereignty in the Rabbinic Blessing Formulary

The absence of "kingship" in early blessing formulae is consistent with its late appearance in the rabbinic blessing formulary, ברוך אתה ה' אלהינו מלך העולם (Blessed are You, Lord our God, king of the world). The earliest recorded discussion of the mandatory elements of the formulary appears in Amoraic literature, attributed to teachers of the mid-third century, Rav and R. Yoḥanan.[86] It was also in the mid-third

---

that BŠKML"W was part of the temple recital of the Shema, nor that the Shema only later became an individual obligation (indeed, its individual status preceded its communal status), nor that the issue consisted in making an unnecessary break between two verses of the Torah.

[84] See Flesicher, Qetaʿim," 112; Mann, "Genizah Fragments," 286; and the shorter version in Ginzberg, *Geonica*, 1:136. In the same vein, since the Sabbath is the day of divine sovereignty its psalm, Psalm 92—which makes no mention of sovereignty—was coupled with Psalm 93 which begins with it—"The Lord has reigned"; see Kimelman, *Mystical Meaning*, 9, n. 58.

[85] See Urbach, *Sages*, 350, n. 15 (ET, p. 860, n. 15).

[86] *y. Ber.* 9:1, 12d; *b. Ber.* 40b; *Midr. Ps* 16, 8, pp. 122–3 with nn. 32–3. According to Wiesenberg, there is no unambiguous attestation of the whole blessing formulary even in this period; see Wiesenberg, "Liturgical Term," 38-46, 53; and idem, "Gleanings," 57–8. The innovative aspect of the kingship requirement is underscored by the fact that the Talmud (*b. Ber.* 40b) can find Tannaitic support

century that a blessing formula addressing God as "king of the world" (ברוך א מלך העולם) appeared at Dura Europos.[87] Not long after there appeared synagogue inscriptions at Jericho and Ḥamat Gader in which God is designated "king of the world" (מלכיה דעלמא or מלך עלמה).[88] Also the thirteenth *Sibylline Oracle*, which has been attributed to a Jew and dated to 265 C.E., concludes with a reference to God as "King of the world" (13:172).[89] Heretofore, the most common blessing formula started with ברוך followed by a reference to the Deity, without the "you" of direct address. This formulation characterizes much of the Bible,[90] the Qumran *Daily Prayers*,[91] the blessing formulae of the Christian Scriptures,[92] and the beginnings of Tannaitic blessing formulae.[93] The opening formula ברוך אתה (blessed are You), followed by a reference to the Deity, also became increasingly common. In the Bible it only appears twice, both times in late biblical literature.[94] Its presence

---

(see *Sifre Deut* 303, ed. Finkelstein, p. 322) for mentioning the divine name, but not for mentioning kingship.

[87] The א or X may stand for אדוני, אתה or אלהינו; see Sukenik, *Synagogue of Dura-Europos*, 158; Finkelstein, "Prayer of King David, 110a, n. 1; and Wiesenberg, "Liturgical Term," 46–7. A similar example, of Syrian provenance like Dura Europos, is the *Constitutiones Apostolorum* with its blessing εὐλογητὸς εἶ, κύριε βασιλεῦ τῶν αἰώνων (Blessed are You, O Lord, king of the ages) which in the original Hebrew may have been ברוך אתה ה' מלך עולם\עולמים. Besides the Jewish liturgical material, this work is based upon the *Did.*, finally redacted in the mid-second century Syria, and the *Didascalia* from the first half of the third century Syria. The Jewish liturgical material has been dated to the mid-third century; see Fiensy, *Prayers*, 19–21, 210–27. Such a dating corresponds to that of the Dura Europos synagogue and of the Amoraim Rav and R. Yohanan thereby creating three independent mid-third century attestations of the blessing formula.

[88] See Foerster, "Synagogue Inscriptions," 25, 33; and Naveh, *On Stone and Mosaic*, nos. 32–4, 69, and 82. In contrast, a first century inscription (see Levine, *Ancient Synagogue*, 114) which reads θεῶι ὑψίστωι παντοκράτορι εὐλογητῶι (the most high God, almighty, and blessed) contains three epithets for God without mention of kingship.

[89] Charlesworth, *Old Testament Pseudepigrapha*, 1:453.

[90] See Heinemann, *Prayer*, 55, n. 9.

[91] Falk lists fifteen cases of opening formulae with ברוך אל (blessed is God), generally followed by ישראל, see *Festival Prayers*, 37.

[92] Luke 1:68; 2 Cor 1:3; Eph 1:3; 1 Pet 1:3.

[93] See *Sifre Deut*, p. 324, line 7 (as opposed to later versions [see Lieberman, *Tosefta*, 4:801] which incorporate "you") 306, p. 342; *t. Ḥag.* 2:11, *Taʿan.* 1:11–14, *ʾAbot R. Nat.* 3, ed. Schechter, p. 9a (R. Akiba); *y. Meg.* 4:2, 74a (R. Judah); with Finkelstein, "Prayer of King David," 111b.

[94] Ps 119:11; 1 Chr 29:10.

increases in Second Temple blessings, as noted above, indeed at Qumran it becomes almost the norm.[95] It also appears in conclusions of Tannaitic blessings[96] and Hekalot blessings.[97]

Why was kingship added to the blessing formulary? The Talmud justifies mandating the inclusion of God's kingship in the blessing formulary by citing Ps 145:1—"I extol You, my God, the king, and bless Your name for ever and ever."[98] In fact, this verse (and only this biblical verse) contains all four requirements of the statutory rabbinic blessing formulary: ברכה (blessing—"bless"), שם (the divine name—"my God"),[99] הזכרת מלכות (mention of kingship—"the king") and עולם (world/eternity—"forever"). Even אתה ("you") is indicated through the second person ארוממך ("I extol You").[100] Although this verse can serve as a biblical warrant for the Amoraic requirements of a blessing, not being a blessing it cannot serve as its source.

It is simpler to claim that the blessing formulary is a combination of the blessing formulae of Chronicles and the kingship motif as shown in the following chart:

	C	B	A
1 Chr 29:10	מעולם ועד עולם	אלהי ישראל אבינו	ברוך אתה
blessing:	מלך העולם	ה' אלהינו	ברוך אתה

In Chronicles and in the blessing formulary the A units are identical. Assuming that "our God" of the blessing is equivalent to "God of Israel our father" of 1 Chr 29:10 makes the B units equivalents.[101] However,

---

[95] For instances of ברוך אתה at Qumran, see Schuller, "Observations," 134–42, who notes that "the second person formula ברוך אתה אל ישראל (blessed are You, God of Israel), is surprisingly standard" (p. 141, see ibid., n. 44, for examples). See also Strugnell and Schuller, "Further Hodayot Manuscripts," 70. The Hodayot and 4Q408 1:6 also contain the formula ברוך אתה אדוני (Blessed are You, Lord); see Falk, *Festival Prayers*, 96–7.
[96] Such as *m. Pesaḥ*.10:6; *Taʿan*. 2:4.
[97] See Schlüter, "Untersuchungen," 83–148.
[98] *y. Ber.* 9:1, 12d; *Midr. Ps* 16, 8, ed. Buber, p. 122.
[99] I.e., אדני not שם.
[100] See *y. Ber.* 9:1, 12d; *b. Ber.* 40b; and *Midr. Ps* 16, 8, ed. Buber, pp. 122–3 with nn. 32–3.
[101] The blessing formula of 1 Chr 16:36 reads: ברוך אדני אלהי ישראל מן העולם ועד העולם (Blessed is the Lord, the God of Israel, from everlasting to everlasting). Its use

by calling God מלך העולם (king of the world), the C unit of the rabbinic blessing underscores the innovation of the kingship motif. If, as most assume, עולם here is spatial and translates as "world," it strikes a new note. In the Bible the same word, lacking the definite article, has a temporal sense. Thus when God is designated מלך עולם in Jer 10:10 and Ps 10:16, it indicates eternal king.[102] In any case, the meaning of עולם is not as consequential as its presence since consistency of terminology in liturgy is more important than consistency of meaning.

The question of the origin of the mention of kingship in the blessing formulary remains. It is possible that the kingship element was derived from other Second Temple blessings such as those found in Tobit and *1 Enoch*.[103]

> Blessed be God, who lives forever, for His kingdom lasts forever (Tob 13:1);
>
> Blessed be my Lord, the Lord of righteousness who rules forever/over the world (*1 En.* 22:14); and
>
> Blessed are You, O great king . . . king of kings and God of the whole world (*1 En.* 84:2)

If all these texts hark back to the Second Temple period, then in the aggregate all the elements of the rabbinic formulary, namely, ברכה (blessing), הזכרת השם (name of God), מלכות (kingship), אתה (You), and עולם/ם (forever/world) were then extant among the various blessing formulae.

Nonetheless, because the rabbinic formulary appears only in Amoraic sources, it is unlikely that it is the product of a linear development from Second Temple blessings. Were it so, its absence in Tannaitic blessings would be inexplicable. Moreover, the reference to God as "our God" or "the God of Israel" appears in the blessing formulary and the blessing

---

of אלהי ישראל instead of אלהי ישראל אבינו of 1Chr 19:10 suggests that אלהינו is yet another equivalent.

[102] Weisenberg, "Liturgical Term," 8–9, argues that even with the definite article העולם retains its temporal meaning. This may, as he argues, apply also to the equivalent Greek expression τοῦ κόσμου βασιλεύς (2 Macc 7:9) whose spatial reference is anomalous; see Goldstein, *II Maccabees*, 305.

[103] For the relationship and common liturgical vocabulary of *1 En.* and Tob, see Nickelsburg, "Tobit and Enoch," 65–6.

formulae of Chronicles respectively, but not in Second Temple blessings that mention kingship. Second Temple blessing formulae stressed that God is king over all, or God of Israel, but not both,[104] apparently recognizing the incongruity of affirming both together.[105]

Why then did the blessing formulary insist on affirming that God is God of Israel and King of the world in precisely six words? The answer may lie in the content and lengths of the other two litugical affirmations of divine sovereignty, namely, the Shema verse and the BŠKML"W, both of which contain six words.[106] The Shema verse has additional correspondences with the blessing formulary. Both six-word formulae can be shown to contain the following tripartite structure:[107]

	C	B	A
Shema	ה' אחד	ה' אלהינו	שמע ישראל
blessing:	מלך העולם	ה' אלהינו	ברוך אתה

Whereas the B units are identical, the A units consist of a direct address—of God in the blessing, and of Israel in the Shema—the C units consist of functional equivalents as both phrases are understood

---

[104] See above, nn. 28–35. Judith mentions both elements in a prayer (9:12), but not in a blessing.

[105] A similar charge can be leveled against "the Lord is our God the Lord is one" of the Shema verse. If "the Lord is one" why also say "the Lord is our God?" The Midrash resolves the apparent redundancy saying : " 'the Lord our God' applies to us; 'the Lord is one' applies to all humanity" (*Sifre Deut* 31, ed. Finkelstein, p. 54, lines 5–6). The Midrash elsewhere (see ibid., 53, and parallels in nn. 11, 12, 14; *Ruth Rab.*, "Introduction," 1, *Exod Rab.* 29, 4; and *Midr. Ha-Gadol, Exod*, ed. Margulies, p. 399) is acutely aware of the incongruity of affirming that God is the God of Israel in a context of affirming that God is the God of all humanity. Its answer is that the God of all is particularly related to Israel (indeed known as the God of Israel). A similar answer is attributed to Alexander, who said: "God was the common father of us all, but more particularly of the best of us" (Plutarch, *Alex.*, end of 27). This incongruity of the Shema verse is paralleled by the similar syntax of the blessing formulary about which could be be asked similarly, as does the *Sifre* (ibid., p. 53, line 11), namely, why does the blessing say "the Lord our God" if it also says "king of the world." The answer is that indeed God is "king of the world," but most particularly "the Lord our God."

[106] A commonality underscored by medieval sources (see *Midraš Sekel Tob, Gen* 49:1, ed. Buber, p. 311; *Leqah Tob, Gen* 49:1, ed. Buber, p. 23; R. Eleazar of Worms as cited in Wolfson, *Along the Path*, 30, 151, n. 205; and the *Zohar* 1:12a, 18b, 2:139b).

[107] A parsing supported by the traditional cantillation of the Shema verse.

rabbincally as expressions of divine sovereignty.[108] Thus *Sifre Deut* 31, glosses, "the Lord is one," with "for all humanity," understanding "one" to imply one for all, ergo sole sovereign.[109] Both of these texts also move through the three stages of second person singular[110] to first person plural to third person singular.[111] Since this tripartite shift is otherwise without parallel in biblical or post-biblical prayer,[112] it is possible that the structure of the Shema, at least subconsciously, informed the structure of the blessing formulary. Since the blessing formulary incorporated the motif of kingship only after the Shema verse was understood as the acceptance of divine kingship this possibility increases. It thus seems that the blessing formulary, containing the elements mandated by the Talmud, took its cue from the blessing formulae of Chronicles while adhering to the syntax of the six-word Shema whose rabbinic meaning was made explicit by the six-word BŠKML"W.

The result of adding "king" to the blessing formulary is that the function of the Shema verse, the expansion of BŠKML"W, and the construction of the blessing formulary all reflect the same liturgical goal of highlighting God as sovereign. Originally, neither the Shema verse, the antecedent of BŠKML"W, or early blessing formulae were associated with divine sovereignty. When the Shema verse became the verse for the acceptance of divine sovereignty, it was linked to an expanded form of Ps 72:19 which now included מלכותו. It is unclear whether originally ברוך שם כבוד מלכותו לעולם ועד was said as a response to the Tetragrammaton of the Shema verse, following temple usage, and that מלכותו was added when the Shema assumed its function of declaring divine sovereignty, or whether BŠKML"W only became attached to the Shema when the Shema became the verse for the acceptance of divine sovereignty. In any case, the adding of kingship to Ps 72:14 to produce BŠKML"W parallels the adding of kingship to the blessing formulae of 1 Chr 16:36 and 29:10 to produce the rabbinic blessing formulary.

---

[108] See *m. Ber.* 2:2; *Sifre Num*, 115, ed. Horovitz, p. 126, line 7.
[109] For a discussion of God as אדון, see Urbach, *Sages*, 16, n. 7 (ET, p. 696, n. 7)
[110] Albeit one imperative and the other a passive participle.
[111] Assuming that the verb to be is implied in both, about which see below.
[112] A conclusion based on the software *Accordance*, courtesy of my colleague Marc Brettler. See also material cited above and Nitzan, *Qumran Prayer*, 72–8.

Divine Sovereignty in Rabbinic Liturgy

The positing of a parallel evolution of BŠKML"W and the blessing formulary makes it possible to speculate, however tentatively, about the trajectory of the theme of divine sovereignty in rabbinic liturgy. The theme first appears in non-liturgical contexts attributed to rabbis of the late first century. R Eleazar b. Azariah relates it to desisting from sin.[113] An anonymous Tannaitic statement equates living in Israel with the acceptance of divine sovereignty[114] while another contrasts the rejection of the yoke of heaven with the acceptance of the yoke of man.[115]

With regard to the liturgy, the first stage in the incorporation of the theme of divine sovereignty was the introduction of a separate *malkuyot* blessing into the Rosh Hashannah liturgy,[116] probably in R. Akiba's time[117] in the early part of the second century.

---

[113] *Sifra, Qedošim,* end of *pereq* 11, ed. Weiss, 93d.
[114] *Sifra, Behar,* end of *parša* 5, ed. Weiss, 109c.
[115] *t. Sota* 14:4 and *t. B. Qam.* 7:5. Only in the Amoraic parallel (*y. Qidd.* 1:2, 59d), attributed to R. Yohanan b. Zakkai, does עול מלכות שמים appear.
[116] The arguments for the innovative nature of *malkuyot* were advanced by Liebriech and Finkelstein (see Heinemann, *Studies in Jewish Liturgy,* 44–6; Spiegel, *Last Trial,* 96–7, nn. 77–8; and now Mack, *Source,* 205–18). Liebriech notes that whereas the liturgy of Rosh Hashannah mentions three themes, *malkuyot, zikronot* and *šofarot,* only the latter two have traces in the Bible ("Aspects of the New Year Liturgy," 138). Finkelstein cites the position of Ginzberg that *malkuyot* were inserted at the time of R. Akiba. He then cites the order of the prayers recorded in *m. Roš. Haš.* 4:5 and concludes: "It will be seen that omitting the reference to *Malkuyot,* the statement of R. Akiba and R. Johanan b. Nuri are identical. This shows that they had before them an old Mishnah in which no mention was made of *Malkuyot.* The fact that the *Malkuyot* is very young would in any case follow from its not having an independent benediction like *Zikhronot* and *Shofarot.* Finally, it will be noted that in the Fast Day ritual (*m. Taᶜan.* 2:3) *Zikhronot* and *Shofarot* are included but not *Malkuyot* . . . The identification of Rosh ha-Shannah as the festival of the Divine Kingdom was a result of the inclusion of the Malkuyot, and not the cause" (Finkelstein, "Development," 108, n. 43). Finkelstein reinforces his association of the kingship motif with R. Akiba by noting that Akiba is accredited with the prayer "Our Father, Our King, we have no king but You (*b. Taᶜan.* 25b), in which the Kingship of God receives the same emphasis as His Fatherhood" (ibid., 107). It should be noted that these two epithets for God do not appear together in the Bible or at Qumran. For example, Isaiah refers to God as "our King" (33:22), "King" (43:15, 52:7) and "our Father" (63:16, 64:7) but not both together. R. Akiba's contemporary, however, the sophist Dio Chrysostom (40–120), refers to the deity as "Father and King" as did Philo (see below, n. 172). Akiba is also credited with providing an explanation for the choice of the daily

The second stage was the explanation of R. Akiba's student, R. Simeon b. Yoḥai, for the structure of the Decalogue. According to Simeon, the sequence of the first two sayings of the Decalogue adheres to the theory that the acceptance of God's sovereignty precedes the acceptance of His commandments.[118] He understood the words "I am the Lord your God," (of the Decalogue as well as of Lev 18:2) to mean, "Am I not He whose sovereignty you have accepted at Sinai?" When the Israelites replied, "Yes," (God continued): "As you accepted My sovereignty accept My decrees: 'You shall have no other gods besides Me.' "[119]

---

psalm for Monday and Friday in terms of divine sovereignty (*b. Roš. Haš.* 31a; see *m. Tamid* 4:8; and *ʾAbot R. Nat.* A, 3, ed. Schechter, p. 5). Heinemann rejected Liebriech's and Finkelstein's contentions and argued instead for the antiquity of the kingship motif by asserting that the temple liturgy was replete with references to divine sovereignty (*Studies in Jewish Liturgy*, 46, n. 8. In a previous study, ibid., 55, n. 6, he had accepted their positions). For evidence, Heinemann referred to his book *Prayer*, 85ff., 173ff. The references there to divine kingship, however, turn out to be only the aforecited blessing formulae and the ʿ*Aleynu* prayer. With regard to the ʿ*Aleynu*, Bar-Ilan, ("Source," 22, n. 85) has shown that the terms that convinced Heinemann (ibid., 174) of its temple provenance can equally point to a Hekalot provenance. With regard to the blessing formulae, the only one that mentions kingship and has an alleged temple setting is the BŠKML"W. Having discounted that evidence, as we have done, Heinemann's objections are neutralized and the arguments for the innovation of a *malkuyot* blessing, based on Liebriech's observation that *malkuyot* lacks a biblical correlate and on Finkelstein's (see also idem, *Akiba*, 312) that it lacks a separate blessing, retain all their cogency.

[117] See *t. Roš. Haš.* 2, 13, ed. Lieberman, 2:318, lines 71–3 with parallels there. It may be significant that the Hekalot blessing (above, n. 24) that includes עולם, שם, ברכה, but no מלכות is transmitted in the name of a Tanna of the generation preceding R. Akiba, R. Neḥunyah b. Ha-Qaneh (on the text, see the discussion of *Maʿaseh Merkavah* in Gruenwald, *Merkavah Mysticism*, 181–6). Note that the expression מלכו של עולם (king of the world) which appears in Hekalot literature more than a dozen times (Schäfer, *Konkordanz*, 2:414a-b), frequently in prayers, is, when not anonymous, consistently associated with R. Neḥunyah ben Ha-Qaneh and/or his disciple R. Ishmael (see *b. Šebu.* 26a); see Altmann, "Širat Qedušah," 22, n. 12.

[118] *Mek., Ba-Ḥodesh* 6, ed. Lauterbach, 2:238.

[119] For this reading of the *Mekilta* see Nachmanides to Deut 22:6, ed. Chavel, 2:451, which reads: "The Holy One, blessed be He, said: 'You accepted my sovereignty—I am the Lord your God, accept My decrees—You shall no other Gods besides Me.' " This reading may have also been that of R. Eleazar Ha-Qallir, for he integrated the two by saying: "When my servants accepted the yoke of my kingdom, I commanded: You shall have no other Gods besides Me" (cited by

The third stage was the application of this two-part sequence to the first two biblical sections of the Shema by his younger contemporary, R. Joshua b. Qorḥa. According to Joshua, the first section of the Shema (Deut 6:4–9), because it constitutes "the authority of God's kingship," logically precedes the second (Deut 11:13–21), which constitutes "the authority of the commandments."[120] Accordingly, the first section of the Shema functions as an equivalent to the first statement of the Decalogue, both constituting "the authority of God's kingship;" whereas the second section functions as the second statement (and probably the rest) of the Decalogue, both constituting "the authority of the commandments." In stages three and four, the acceptance of divine sovereignty has replaced the biblical terminology of covenant. In the Torah,[121] the Decalogue constitutes the covenant; whereas here, it and its equivalent constitute the acceptance of divine sovereignty

The fourth stage was the insertion of BŠKML"W after the Shema verse. This likely took place at this time since its recitation out loud, as noted, was associated with Usha which was the rabbinic center of the mid-second century. This late development helps accounts for its absence in the traditions of the prior death of R. Akiba, all of which deal with the Shema.[122] The fifth stage was the insertion of the kingship motif into the ʾEmet ve-yaṣiv in the next generation by R. Judah Hanasi (ca. 200 C.E.)[123] and subsequently into the first and third blessing of the

---

Mirsky, Haʾ Piyut, 25). Another reading has "in Egypt" for "at Sinai"; see *Sifra, Aḥarei Mot, Pereq* 13:3, ed. Weiss, p. 85d; and Büchler, *Studies in Sin and Atonement*, 39–40. For the biblical roots of God as king at Sinai, see Weinfeld, *Justice and Righteousness*, 109–12, 139–41.

[120] *m. Ber.* 2:2. Since this understanding of the Shema is new, the other reference to the Shema as מלכות שמים by R. Gamaliel (*m. Ber.* 1:8) must be attributed to the early third century R. Gamaliel, the son of R. Judah Hanasi; see *m. ʾAbot* 2:2. As here, so elsewhere (*b. Ḥul.* 106a), this R. Gamaliel was known for his scrupulous observance.

[121] Exod 34:28, Deut 4:13, 5:19, 9:11.

[122] See *y. Ber.* 9:7, 14b = *Sota* 5:7, 20c, *Tanḥ, Tabo* 4, ed. Buber, p. 47; *Midr. Mišlei* 9, ed. Visotzky, p. 67, lines 19–20; and *b. Ber.* 61b; along with the discussion in Lieberman, *Studies*, 357–61, and in Boyarin, *Dying for God*, 105–8, 120–3.

[123] *t. Ber.* 2:1, *y. Ber.* 1:9, 3d. The other positions, all anonymous, cited there advocate inserting an element of the Exodus story. When cited in *Exod Rab.* 22, 3, R. Judah Hanasi's position is not mentioned, as if it were not yet known when the cited material was formulated. This conforms to those Genizah texts of ʾEmet ve-yaṣiv that lack מלכות ; see Goldschmidt, *Maḥzor Le-Yamim Ha-Noraʾim*, 1:23–4.

Shema liturgy.[124] The sixth stage was the addition of the kingship motif to the blessing formulary in the next generation by Judah's students, Rav or R. Yoḥanan,[125] as noted above. The requirement of mentioning kingship in the third and eleventh blessing of the ʿAmidah during the High Holiday period is attributed to the same Rav.[126] Thus from the early second century C.E. to the mid-third century, the rabbinic liturgy became centered around the idea of acknowledging God as sovereign. This drive toward the "sovereignization of the liturgy" helps account for the later interpolation of the *Qedušah* into the Palestinian ʿAmidah[127] and the many interpolations of "king" in the Babylonian ʿAmidah.[128]

Why Was There a Sovereignization of the Liturgy?

Some explain the sovereignization of the liturgy as a response to the claims of the ruling authorities. Those who date the response to the Second Temple period prefer a Jewish ruler. Those who date it later prefer a Roman one.[129] The infrequency of the sovereignty motif in Second Temple blessings, however, argues against a polemical thesis being applicable then.

---

[124] See Kimelman, "Shema Liturgy," 58–63; and Lehnardt, "Der Gott der Welt," 295–307.
[125] See above, n. 86.
[126] *b. Ber.* 12b.
[127] See above, n. 54.
[128] Above, nn. 47–8. It even accounts for the "sovereignization" of the Bavli's presentation of R. Akiba's death. All the sources that mention R. Akiba's death (above, n. 117) record that it was the time for the recitation of the Shema and that the issue was the fulfillment of the requirement to love God "with all your soul" (Deut 6:5). Only the Bavli (*b. Ber.* 61b, see *Diqduqei Sofrim, Ber.*, p. 356, n. 8) adds that Akiba was involved in the act of acceptance of divine sovereignty, an addition that conforms to its general updating and theological embellishment of Palestinian sources. On the whole incident, see Goldberg, "Martyriuim," 1–82.
[129] See above, nn. 65–7; Heinemann, "Formula," 177–9; and Finkelstein, "Impact," 39–45. Büchler suggests "The stress on God's Kingship" was to counter "Caligula's claim to be god and his demand of actual worship" (*Studies in Sin and Atonement*, 45). Weiss, "Formula *melekh haʿolam*," 169–71, suggests a gnostic background, but cites no gnostic documents. This lack of documentation is not atypical for claims that rabbinic comments are responding to gnostic positions. Indeed the possibility itself should be reconsidered in the light of Williams, *Rethinking "Gnosticism."*

The thesis that the sovereignty motif was introduced to counter the cult of the emperor is also difficult to maintain. As the former thesis, it relies on the questionable assumption that political events spur liturgical innovation and that political claims can be countered by liturgical ones.[130] Moreover, it suffers from a lack of correlation between the dating of the Roman, rabbinic, and Christian data. The various cults of the emperor would have been as threatening to Christianity as they were to Judaism, yet Christian liturgy was not characterized by the sovereignty motif. In fact, Christian literature of the time rarely mentions the imperial cult at all.[131] On the contrary, there is a slew of both Patristic and rabbinic sources that expatiate on the positive value of the Roman Empire and of having a single emperor.[132] Indeed, Christians prayed for its welfare,[133] as may have rabbis.[134] Of course,

---

[130] See Kimelman, "Liturgical Studies," 65.

[131] As noted by Bowersock, "Imperial Cult," 175. According to Millar: "Although Christian apologists are found defending the Christian refusal to worship the Emperor . . . we do not find refusal of Emperor-worship, as such, as an initial charge forming the basis of any accusations of Christians. What we do find is that various forms of recognition of Imperial divinity, along with acts of worship of others gods, were used as a test of apostasy, after which Christians were almost always allowed to go free . . . undoubtedly the issues of the worship of the pagan gods in general, of the recognition of the Emperor as divine and of loyalism in a broader sense are closely intermingled. But the primary issue was not the Imperial cult as such" ("Review of W. H. C. Frend," 235). For the Patristic material on the imperial cult, see Beaujeu, "Les apologètes," 101–42.

[132] For the Patristic sources, see Origen, *Cels.* 2:30, ed. Chadwick, p. 92 with n. 2; and Momigliano, *Pagans*, 135–6, 151–2. For the rabbinic sources, see Feldman, *Jew and Gentile*, 102–6. For such first century Christian material and Second Temple Jewish material, see Légasse, "La prière," 236–53.

[133] Even Tertulllian (c. 160–c. 220), a Christian with an avowed hostility to *religio Romanorum*, conceded that all men owed the emperor "their piety and religious devotion and loyalty" (*Apol.* 36.2). In fact, he argued that Christians preserve the Empire by constant prayer to the one God, "always for all the emperors, long life to them, secure rule, a safe house, strong armies, a faithful Senate, an honest people, a peaceful world" (ibid., 30.4; see ibid. 30–2; Matt 22:21; and 1 Tim 2:2 along with Tertullian, *Idol.* 15; and Ando, *Imperial Ideology*, 393). Similarly, a generation later in the 250's, Dionysius of Alexandria when asked to worship "the gods that preserve the empire," answered: "We worship and venerate the one God, creator of all, who has entrusted the empire to the Augusti Valerian and Gallienus, whom he loves greatly, and to him we pray continuously on behalf of their empire, that it should remain unshaken" (Eusebius, *Hist. eccl.*, 7.11.7–8). For additional sources, see Alföldy, "Crisis," 94, n. 15; and Gabbo, "Holy Spirit," 56–7.

[134] m. ʾAvot 3:2.

anti-Roman invective is also noted in rabbinic literature. What is rare, however, is material contrasting the kingdom of Rome with the kingdom of God[135] as opposed to just contrasting the King of the king of kings with a king of flesh and blood. Were rabbinic liturgy about the kingship of God aimed primarily at the imperial cult, material contrasting the heavenly king and His authority with that of the earthly king would abound.[136] What does abound in both Patristic and rabbinic literature is anti-iconic material, which, *inter alia*, includes the image of the emperor, but without special focus on the imperial cult as such.[137]

Attempts at explaining the kingship motif in the liturgy with the anti-emperor thesis also ignore how emperors, desiring to maintain the façade of the republican tradition, were circumspect in appropriating

---

[135] Such as: "The time for the kingdom of wickedness to be uprooted from the world has arrived, the time for the kingdom of God has arrived" (*Pesiq Rab Kah.* 5:9, ed. Mandelbaum, p. 97 and parallels) as opposed to complimentary material such as: "Rabbi Simeon ben Laqish said, 'Behold it was very good' [Gen 1:30], this is the kingdom of heaven, 'And behold it was very good,' this is the kingdom of the Romans" (*Gen. Rab.* 9.13), or Sheshet's comment: "Earthly kingship is like heavenly kingship" (*b. Ber.* 58a). On the literary, as opposed to the political, significance of the many kingship parables, see Stern, *Parables in Midrash*, 19–21.

[136] As for example in 2 Macc 15:4–5. The political significance of the story of the death of R. Akiba, which is frequently used to contrast loyalty to God with loyalty to the emperor, is diminished upon realizing that the part about the Shema verse as the expression of the acceptance of divine sovereignty appears only in the *Bavli* (see above, n. 122). A graver challenge to the thesis that the Shema, as an expression of divine sovereignty, functioned as an anti-Roman protest is its absence in the episodes of the rest of the ten martyrs; see Lieberman, *Studies*, 362; and idem, "Martyrs of Caesarea," 425–7.

[137] For the Patristic material, see chapter seven of Price, *Rituals and Power*, 170–206. For the rabbinic, see Urbach, "Rabbinical Laws, 149–65, 229–45; Blidstein, "Nullification, 1–44; Hadas-Lebel, "Le paganisme," pp. 397–485; and Veltri, *Römische Religion*, 81–138. For the rare polemical material against emperor worship in rabbinic literature, see *m. ʿAbod. Zar.* 3:1 with *t. ʿAbod. Zar.* 5:1, *b. ʿAbod. Zar* 41a, and *y. ʿAbod. Zar.* 3:1, 42b, along with Lieberman, *Tosefta*, 3:281–2, and Hadas-Lebel, ibid., 422–3. Were the reference to worshiping even human beings (*b. ʿAbod. Zar.* 55a; Mek. *Ba-Ḥodeš* 6, ed. Lauterbach, 2:246) or wood (*Tanḥ. Terumah* 3) a reference to emperor worship, it would have mentioned the worship of a king of flesh and blood. Indeed, midrashic literature records the fear that Adam (*Pirke R. El.* 20, ed. Luria, p. 48a) Jacob (see *Gen Rab.* 96, 5, ed. Theodor-Albeck, p. 1196 with parallels and notes), Aaron (see *Bet Ha-Midrasch* 1:95), and Moses (see *Midr. Leqaḥ Tov, Deut*, p. 68a; and *Sefer Pitron Torah*, ed. Urbach, p. 237) might become objects of worship.

the title "king" (βασιλεύς/ rex).[138] In the context of the imperial cults, emperors were more likely to be dubbed θεός (god), in accordance with their function as visual gods.[139] There are rabbinic traditions that protest and satirize the deification of kings/emperors,[140] even one that specifies Emperor Hadrian.[141] In such a context, however, instead of proclaiming God as מלך העולם (King of the world), the rabbis should have acclaimed God as אלהי האלהים (God of gods) à la the Bible,[142] or מלך אלים and אל אלים (King of gods) à la Qumran[143] or Philo (βασιλεῦ θεῶν).[144] Such is the tactic of *1 Enoch* who states that God is "the God of

---

[138] As was pointed out to me by Professor Louis Feldman. According to the rabbis, "Caesar, Augustus, Basileus" referred to the same thing (*y. Ber.* 9:1, 9d at end). Calling a king any of them was a capital offense (*Tanḥ*, ed. Buber, *Va'era* 7, pp. 22–3, with n. 61).

[139] According to Price "Some part [of the ritual system] treated the emperor like a god. The ceremonial of the imperial cult was closely modelled on divine ceremonial. Imperial temples and their images were called by the same names . . . as those of the traditional gods. They also looked identical . . . The image of the emperor, despite being partially controlled by Rome, was largely comprehensible within divine categories. Sacrifices were sometimes offered to the emperor as to a god. So too the emperor was called *theos* (god) and the main aim of the cult was to display piety *(eusebeia)* towards him" (*Rituals and Power*, 231–2). On the use of the term *theos* for the emperor, see idem, "Gods and Emperors," 93–5. The thesis that emperors were actual objects of worship in the Eastern Empire, as opposed to Rome itself, is supported by Harland, "Honours and Worship," 322–3.; and Friesen, *Twice Neokoros*, 150. Still, Emperor Domitian (81–96 C.E.) claimed the title "*dominus et deus noster*" (our lord and god) (Suetonius, *Dom.* 27) and R. Samuel b. Naḥman (late third century) noted that "There [in Rome?] kings are called gods" (*Lev Rab.* 33, 6, ed. Margulies, p. 769).

[140] See *Mek., Shirta,* ed. Lauterbach, 2:61 with Goldin, *Song at the Sea*, 193; *Gen Rab.* 9, 5, ed. Theodor-Albeck, p. 70; *Tanḥ. Bereišit* 7; Urbach, *Sages*, 76, and 378, n. 26 (ET, pp. 91, and 877, n. 27); and Ginzberg, *Legends of the Jews*, 5:427, n. 175; 6:423, n. 99. Such humor was not limited to the rabbis; see Scott, "Humor," 317–28.

[141] *Tanḥ. Bereišit* 7, *Šofṭim* 12, see Herr, "Persecutions," 116, n. 113.

[142] Deut 10:17; Dan 2:47. This title is also preferred by their contemporary Christian compatriot, Origen; see *Cels.* 7:4, ed. Chadwick, p. 455. This usage by gentiles is noted by the Talmud (*b. Menaḥ.* 110a, commenting on Mal 1:11).

[143] 4Q403 1:34 may have both in one strophe: אל אלים ומלך מלכים; see Newsom, *Songs of the Sabbath Sacrifice*, 217. The Qumran *Canticles of the Instructor* has ברוך אתה אלהי האלהים (Blessed be you God of gods) (*DJD*, VII, p. 229).

[144] *Flacc.* 170. Philo uses βασιλεῦ τῶν θεῶν "king of gods" (*Conf.* 173), as does the LXX (Add Esth 4 [14:12]), as well as τοῦ θεοῦ βασιλείαν "the kingship of God" (*Spec.* 4.164, see ibid., 1, 207) as do Pss. Sol. 17:3 and Wis 10:10.

gods, the Lord of lords and King of kings" (9:4).[145] Alternatively, they could have stressed that God was the savior of the world since "In the mythology of imperial propaganda the Roman emperor is a universal saviour. As coins of Trajan proclaim, he is *Salus Generis Humani* (saviour of the human race) or, in the words of various inscriptions, he is saviour and benefactor of the entire world."[146]

Rabbinic attacks on the imperial cult, independent of the general attack on idolatry, may have been blunted by the fact that Jews had a privileged status in the Roman Empire from the time of Emperor Augustus that generally exempted them from participation in the imperial cult.[147] In the early third century, Emperors Severus and Caracalla even affirmed their right to civic honors while exempting them from any attendant religiously offensive obligations.[148]

Near the end of the second century there seems to have been a shift in imperial claims towards what has been dubbed an oriental theory both of divinity and of its associated monarchy. In any event, Emperor Commodus, who reigned from 180–192, made *invictu* (= invincible) a component of the imperial title and had the sun god portrayed on his coins.[149] Emperor Caracalla (d. 218) came to be regarded as world-ruler (*cosmocrator*) through whom shone the divinity of *Sol Invictus* (The Invincible Sun).[150] And Emperor Aurelian in 274 sought to found a

---

[145] See Nickelsburg, *I Enoch*, 202 with discussion of the titles on pp. 211–12.
[146] Fears, "Rome," 103.
[147] See Schürer, *History*, 1:378–81.
[148] *Digest* 27.1.15.6 and 50.2.3.3; see Linder, "Roman Imperial Legislation," 103–10; and Cohen, "Judaism to the Mishnah," 202–5.
[149] See Brent, *Imperial Cult*, 265–8.
[150] The sun served as a symbol of the supreme god to Christian and pagan alike; see Liebeschuetz, *Continuity and Change*, 281, 285-289. Indeed, so pervasive was this in Christian circles that it accounts for the earlier rumor, cited by Tertullian (*Apol.* 16.9ff.), in the last years of the second century that the sun was the god of the Christians; see the sources and literature cited in *Octavius of Marcus Minucius Felix*, p. 345, n. 541. This worship which bordered on solar monotheism may have been sufficiently compatible with Jewish monotheism to allow for synagogue mosaics with Helios holding a globe in his left arm; see Leicht, "*Qedushah*," 156. In any case, the "Prayer of Jacob" (ibid., 161) describes the Creator in terms of solar theology. *Sefer Ha-Razim*, ed. Margoliot, p. 12, also contains a prayer to Helios that uses the titles *polokrator* and *tyrranos*. Note that the role we are ascribing to the blessing formulary matches the role that Ness ascribes to the zodiac which, he opines, "reminded the worshiper that God of Israel ruled all things " ("Astrology and Judaism," 131). For the debate on the role of the sun in ancient Judaism, see

state cult of *Sol Invictus* at Rome in order to enhance the cult of the emperor by associating it along with that of the sun.[151]

This development may have contributed to the expansion of the motif of divine sovereignty in the liturgy. R. Judah Hanasi, who lived under Emperor Caracalla, introduced the motif into the ʾ*Emet ve-yaṣiv* and incorporated into the Mishnah the position of R. Joshua b. Qorḥa that the first two paragraphs of the Shema reflect respectively the acceptance of the authority of divine sovereignty and the acceptance of the authority of the commandments. The authors of the requirement of kingship in the blessing were also students of R. Judah Hanasi.

In its Roman context, the thrust of the blessing is "Blessed are You the Lord our God (who is [the real]) king of the world." The emphasis on the God of Israel as the king of the world also appears in a passage of

---

Leicht, ibid., 171, n. 104; Levine, *Ancient Synagogue*, 572–9; and Weiss, "Zodiac." The difficulty may have been resolved as did Plutarch who was able to reconcile the worship of the sun and yet believe that God (Apollo) who is "one and one alone" (*Mor.* 393 C—LCL V: 247) was not to be identified with the sun, for "as the body is to soul, vision to intellect, and light to truth, so is the power of the sun to the nature of Apollo" (*Mor.*, 433E—LCL V, p. 475). Thus it is not improper "to pay honor also to this imagery of him in the sun and to revere the creative power associated with it, in so far as it is possible by what is perceived through the senses to gain an image of what is conceived in the mind" (*Mor.* 393E—LCL, V:249). Of the stories told about Antoninus and Rabbi Judah Hanasi, one (*b. San.* 91b) has Antoninus ask him why the sun which rises in the east specifically sets in the west? To which he responded, "in order to pay respects to its master/creator (שלום לקונה כדי ליתן) as it says, 'The host of heaven bow down to you' (Neh 9:6)." By setting in the west, the sun pays obeisance to God whose presence dwells in the west. If Antoninus represents Emperor Caracalla (see Avi-Yonah, *Days of Rome*, 50–1, 89–90), then the answer may be directed against Caracalla's elevation of the sun as the supreme god, for here the sun is to God as a client is to his Roman patron to whom he must pay his daily respects. For this ceremony called *Salutatio* in Latin and שואלים בשלום in Hebrew; see Kimelman, "Conflict," 135–7. The accomodationism with sun symbolism, which emerges in the fourth century, parallels in time and thrust the accomodationism with images on mosaics; see Levine, *Ancient Synagogue*, 455–6. One source (*Tg. Ps.-J.*, Lev 26:1) even permits figured images on synagogue floors as long as they are not bowed down to; see Hachili, "Synagogues," 113–14.

[151] See Smith, *Julian's Gods*, 163–6. The head of the Sun was placed on the obverse of bronze Roman coins, described as "Master of the Roman Empire" (*SOL DOMINVS IMPERI ROMANI*). For the differences of the cult of *Sol invictus* under Emperor Elagabal (218–22) and Emperor Aurelian (270–75), see Halsberghe, *Cult of Sol Invictus*, 69–88, 135–62.

the Rosh Hashannah ʿAmidah which awaits the day when all humanity will proclaim: ה׳ אלהי ישראל מלך מלכותו בכל משלה (The Lord, God of Israel is king and His kingship rules over everything).[152] This point that what makes God truly king is that He rules over all is made explicit in the following talmudic statement cited in the name of the late third century Amora, R. Eleazar:

> What is the relationship between (the first part of Psalm 146:5) "Happy is he that has the God of Jacob for his help" (and the second part) "who made heaven and earth?" It is like this: a king of flesh and blood having a patron (above him) rules in one province but not another province. And even if you say he is a cosmocrator and rules the earth, does he rule the sea? But the Holy One, blessed be He, is not so. He rules the sea and the land.[153]

In this statement, the extent of divine rule is contrasted with rule of the greatest of human rulers the so-called *cosmocrator*. The irony is clear. Whereas a human king, such as an emperor, can be called a *cosmocrator*, only the God of Jacob is actually so. Similarly, the blessing formulary affirms that the God of Israel is the real *cosmocrator* of the world. It is worth noting thus that the attestations of the term *cosmocrator* for God as well as for the emperor in rabbinic literature are, as the statements regarding the content of the blessing formulary, post-Caracalla Amoraic statements.[154]

It would be most helpful to correlate the sovereignty motif in rabbinic liturgy with that of the Church Fathers. Lamentably, each instantiation has difficulties. For example, R. Akiba's contemporary, Clement of Rome, around the turn of the first century, addresses God as δέσποτα ἐπουράνιε, βασιλεῦ τῶν αἰώνων (heavenly master, king of the ages) (*1 Clem.* 61:2), but this is just standard Scriptural parlance.[155] It is

---

[152] *Seder Rav Amram Gaon*, p. 136, lines 30–1. This liturgical statement is an adaptation of Ps. 103:19: ה׳ בשמים הכין כסאו ומלכותו בכל משלה. The second to fourth word, בשמים הכין כסאו have been replaced by אלהי ישראל מלך which serves to emphasize that the God of Israel is king. The second strophe states, as does the blessing formulary, that God's kingdom extends over everything.

[153] *y. Ber.* 9:1, 13b = ʿ*Abod. Zar.* 3:1, 42c.

[154] See Krauss, *Griechische and Lateinische Lehnwörter*, 2:502.

[155] See above nn. 28–9. The epithets Clement normally uses for God are δεσπότης (twenty four times) μόνος (four times) and κύριε (three times); see Bowe, "Prayer,"

claimed that the self-defined Samaritan,[156] Justin Martyr—of the mid-second century, when R. Akiba's students flourished—wrote a work on the monarchy of God, but the only evidence for it comes more than a century later.[157] A generation or so later, during the time of R. Joshua b. Qorḥa, Theophilus (ca. 180 C.E.), Bishop of Antioch, comments upon the names of God, saying: "He is called God because He founded all things ... but He is Lord because He rules the universe."[158] He further argued that the unique sovereignty (μοναρχία θεοῦ) of God cannot be demonstrated were the world uncreated.[159] Theophilus' use of the monarchy of God, however, is atypical. Moreover, he is hardly representative of Christianity vis-a-vis Judaism in view of his affinity with the Judaism or Jewish Christianity of his day.[160] At the end of the third century, Arnobius may have referred to God as *rex mundi* ("king of universe"), but the reading might just as well be *rerum dominus* ("Lord of things").[161] Apparently, God's sovereignty was not a significant motif of Roman Christianity.[162] That imperial developments left so few traces on formulations of second and third century

---

85–97. This survey of Christian use of King in addressing God excludes the *Constitutiones Apostolorum* as it is based on a Jewish text. Still, note that God is referred to as παντοκράτωρ throughout and as king in three ways: as ὁ βασιλεὺς τῶν θεῶν (the King of the gods [7.33.2]); as βασιλεῦ τῶν αἰώνων (King of the ages [7.34.1]), and as βασιλέα δὲ καὶ κύριον (King and Lord [8.12.7, see 8:37.1]), all of which are common Jewish usages.

[156] Justin, *Dial.* 120.6

[157] See Eusebius, *Hist. eccl.* 4.18.4. The extant work on the subject collates references from Classical writers on the sole rulership of God.

[158] Theophilus, *Autol.* 1:4; see Barn. 21:5.

[159] *Autol.* 2:4–8; see Brent, *Imperial Cult,* 308.

[160] See Grant, *Greek Apologists,* 165–8. On the problem of crossovers from Christianity to Judaism, see Kimelman, "Identifying Jews and Christians," 301–31. Interestingly, Theophilus, the first Christian theologian to argue explicitly for *creatio ex nihilo* (cf. Justin, *1 Apol.* 10 and 59), makes the argument in the context of a polemic with Greek thought just as does Rabban Gamaliel (*Gen Rab.* 1, 1, ed. Theodor-Albeck, p. 8).

[161] See Arnobius, *The Case Against the Pagans,* 2:39, ed. McCracken, pp. 151, and 328, n. 246.

[162] See Ferguson, "Kingdom of God," 191–208. The discussion of Meeks, *Origins,* 166–9 of "God as Monarch" in early Christianity lacks documentation. The theme of divine sovereignty does, of course, emerge with Emperor Constantine. Eusebius, in his panegyric, highlights the significance of divine sovereignty in order to underscore the significance of that of Constantine; see Eusebius, *Laud. Const.,* 3:5–7 (336 C.E.), cited in Stevenson, *A New Eusebius,* p. 392.

Christianity challenges any assumption that it left more traces on rabbinic formulations.[163]

In sum, the correlation among Jewish, Christian, and Roman data for the imperial cult is weak. None of the data is concentrated in any generation. A century or two is too long a period to explain a politically motivated liturgical innovation. If any specific cult of the emperor, and there were many earlier,[164] had triggered rabbinic counter claims, there should be a concentration of such claims during the reign of a single emperor. Since the sovereignization of the liturgy was a process lasting over a century, not associated with any single individual or generation, it is unlikely that it was caused by a single political factor.

Apparently, the centrality of divine sovereignty in rabbinic liturgy is more the fruit of internal theological developments than the result of external political events. As noted, the image of God as sovereign becomes increasingly prominent in the Second Temple period where about a half a dozen Second Temple blessing formulae address God as king. Although the references to divine kingship do not confirm the existence of BŠKML"W or the blessing formulary, they do point to a growing tendency of the liturgy to image God as king. This tendency flourishes in later rabbinic,[165] targumic,[166] and Hekalot literature.[167]

Under rabbinic auspices biblical covenant imagery was transformed into monarchical imagery. I have argued elsewhere that the original covenantal ceremony of the Shema liturgy consisted of the three biblical sections that constitute the Shema lectionary and the Decalogue, preceded by a blessing on Torah and succeeded by the ʾEmet ve-yaṣiv. Under rabbinic auspices, ʾEmet ve-yaṣiv absorbed the kingship motif, the Decalogue was removed, and the remaining part was flanked by two

---

[163] Similarly, Philo's confrontation with the imperial cult failed to elicit a liturgical response on divine sovereignty; see above, n. 59; Goodenough, *Introduction to Philo*, pp. 69–74; and Leonhardt, *Jewish Worship*, 346, Index, ruler cult.

[164] See Price, *Rituals and Power*; Friesen, *Twice Neokoros*; and Schowalter, *Emperor*.

[165] See above; Wiesenberg, "Liturgical Term," 1–56; and idem, "Gleanings," 47–72.

[166] See *ABD*, 4:53b–54a

[167] See Schwemer, "Himmlischer König," 310–11, n. 1. According to Alexander, "It [the celestial court of the Hekalot texts] correlates best with the situation that emerged with the reforms of Diocletian in the late third century CE" ("Family of Caesar," 288). Such parallels, however, can be found among the emperors of the Byzantine period or later; see, e.g., Kantorowicz, *Laudes Regiae*, 137–79.

blessings which incorporate the events of creation and redemption along with their heavenly and historical coronation ceremonies. The result was the transformation of an ancient pact form into a comprehensive rite for the realization of divine sovereignty. Accordingly, the biblical understanding of covenant was updated terminologically and conceptually to the rabbinic understanding of the acceptance of divine sovereignty.[168] This shift from a focus on covenant to one on sovereignty is reflected in the terminological distinction between Qumran and rabbinic Judaism. The Qumran *The Rule of the Community* alludes to the Shema by saying: "With the coming of the day and night I shall enter the covenant of God" (1QS 10:10), whereas the rabbinic Mishnah designates the recitation of the Shema as an acceptance of divine sovereignty.[169] Thus an expression for a convert entering the covenant is השלים עצמו להקב״ה, וקיבל עליו מלכות שמים (he dedicated himself to the Holy One, blessed-be-He, and (or: that is) he accepted divine sovereignty).[170]

Understanding the Shema as an expression of divine sovereignty paved the way for the incorporation of the kingship motif into the blessing formulary. Such a development was undoubtedly enhanced by living in an empire that sought the convergence of political and theological imagery and terminology. But that is quite different from saying "the formula *melekh ha'olam* . . . is indeed a protest . . . against Roman Emperor-worship."[171]

It is more precise to say that by the late third century, paganism, Christianity, and Judaism were claiming that their god was the world ruler. Centuries earlier, the *Epistle of Aristeas* (15–16) quotes a Hellenistic Egyptian who states that

---

[168] Kimelman, "Shema Liturgy," 82–91.
[169] See Talmon, "Dead Sea Scrolls," 137; and Bernstein, "Hymn," 36, n. 10; 37, n. 16. On the annual covenantal ceremony of Qumran, see Nitzan, "Benedictions," 263–71. On the idea of covenant, see idem, "Concept of the Covenant," 85–104. In rabbinic literature, the meaning of the term *brit* shifted from the general meaning of covenant to specific commandments; see Urbach, "Ten Commandments," 134; and Sanders, *Jesus and Judaism*, 141.
[170] *Tanḥ. Lekh Lekha* 6, ed. Buber, p. 63. Note that this is attributed to a mid-third century Palestinaian Amora, Resh Laqish, for the acceptance of divine kingship is not mentioned with regard to conversion in Tannaitic or Second Temple literature; see Cohen, *Beginnings*, 129–238.
[171] Heinemann, "Formula," 177, who cites Baumstark, *Comparative Liturgy*, 68.

They [the Jews] worship the same God—The Lord and Creator of all the universe, as all other men, as we ourselves, O King, though we call him by different names, such as Zeus or Dis. This name was very appropriately bestowed upon Him by our first ancestors, in order to signify that He through whom all things are endowed with life and come to into being is necessarily the ruler and lord of all.

At the end of the first century C.E., this statement is cited by Josephus (*A.J.* 12.22). Josephus in his own voice cited the idea that "the wisest of the Greeks learnt to adopt these conceptions of God from principles with which Moses supplied them" (*C. Ap.* 2.168). Not much later, the pagan Dio Chrysostom designated Zeus as the "God who governs the universe" and who is "the common father and savior and guardian of mankind." According to him, Zeus "alone of the gods is entitled 'Father' [πατήρ] and 'King' [Βασιλεύς] . . . He is addressed as King because of his dominion and power; as Father . . . on account of his solicitude for us and his kindness."[172] The famous statement of Plato—"All things center in the King of all, and are for his sake, and he is the cause of all that is good"[173]—was cited approvingly by Christian and pagan alike in the latter half of the second century.[174] In the same period, the philosopher Numenius of Apamea writes that "the first god abstains from every work and is the king."[175] Maximus of Tyre writes about 180 of a universally accepted truth by Greeks and barbarians alike, namely, "There is only one God, King and Father of all."[176] Such a religious reality also stands behind Tertullian's question, posed at the

---

[172] Chrysostom, *Dei Cogn.* (Or. 12), 2:61, 77. For similar sentiments see his contemporary, Plutarch, *Mor.*, 601B. A century earlier, Philo often referred to God as Father or King. In *Opif.* alone, he calls God "Father of the universe" (τὸν πατέρα τῶν ὅλων [72, see 74]), "Father and Ruler of all" (πατρὸς καὶ ἡγεμόνος τῶν πάντων [135]), "Maker and Father" (ποιητοῦ καὶ πατρός [7, see also 10, 21, 77]) (à la Plato, *Tim.* 28c), and "Father and King" (πατρὸς καὶ βασιλέως [144]).

[173] Plato, *Ep.* 312E.

[174] By Clement of Alexandria, *Protr.* 6 (60), *Strom.* 5.103.1; by Celsus (Origen, *Cels.* 6.18) and by Numenius (Eusebius, *Praep. ev.* 11.18.3).

[175] Fragment 12. Numenius, *Fragments*, p. 54. On Numenius and Judaism, see Stern, *Greek and Latin*, 2:206–7.

[176] Ed. Hobein, 17:5; see 39:5. He also refers to "the God who is the father and creator of all" (cited from Grant, *Hellenistic Religions*, 168). See the similar view of his contemporary Celsus as cited in Origen, *Cels.* 8.68.

end of the second century: "Do you not grant, from general acceptance, that there is some being higher and more powerful, like an emperor of the world, of infinite power and majesty?"[177] Jews were quite aware of the philosophical proclivity to expatiate about God in terms of divine sovereignty. Trypho, a reputed Jewish refugee from the Bar-Kokhba war in Palestine and student of philosophy, when asked by Justin whether he expects to derive the kind of enlightenment from philosophy one gets from Moses and the prophets, answered, "Do not the philosophers talk all the time about God and do not their enquiries always concern divine monarchy (μοναρχίας) and providence."[178]

In the early third century, a Christian philosopher, Marcus Minucius Felix, concedes that "Those who would have Jupiter to be sovereign are misled in name but are in agreement about his unique power."[179] After summarizing various philosophical conceptions of God, he concludes: "These opinions are pretty well identical with ours: we recognize God, and we also call Him Father of all." About a quarter of a century later, the pagan philosopher, Porphyry describes the god of the Jews as "one truly God, the creator and the king prior to all things" (*in deum vero generatorem et in regem ante omnia*).[180] In a third century funerary inscription from Thessaly the deity is designated "the King, the greatest *pantokratora* god, creator of everything."[181] In the same century the *Orphic Hymns* refer to God as "begetter of all and great King," (βασιλέα μέγιστον) or as "the greatest King of eternal earth" (βασιλεύτατε πάντων).[182] There is even a hymn which, as the rabbinic blessing formulary, addresses the Deity as both ruler of one group and King of all: "O blessed ruler of Phrygia and supreme king of all."[183]

---

[177] Tertullian, *Apol.* 24.3.

[178] Justin, *Dial.* 1.

[179] *Octavius of Marcus Minucius Felix*, 18, 11, p. 82. Zeus is also called "βασιλεύς of all the gods" (Musurillo, *The Acts of the Christian Martyrs*, p. 163) as Jupiter is called *regem omnium deorum* (Varro, *apud*, Augustinus, *Civ.* 4.31).

[180] *Philos. orac.*, cited by Augustine, *Civ.* 19.23.

[181] IG, IX, 2, 1201, as cited by Henrichs, "Despoina Kybele," 277, n. 64. This source is cited by Pleket, "Religious History," 173 who also lists other references wherein the deity is referred to as *Basilius* and even as βασιλεὺς ὁ θεός (ibid., 174, n. 100).

[182] Athanassakis, *Orphic Hymns*, #20, line 5, p. 33,; #39, line 1, p. 55.

[183] Ibid., #48, l. 5, p. 65.

In the next century, Emperor Julian also notes that "the creator is the common Father and King (βασιλεύς) of all things."[184] He also says, "These Jews ... revere a God who is truly most powerful and most good and governs this world of sense, and, as I well know, is worshipped by us also under other names."[185] He himself, however, in *The Hymn to King Helios*, calls Helios τὸν πάντων βασιλέα (king of the whole world),[186] a title that harks back to the βασιλεῦ πάντων κρατῶν (king ruling over all [or almighty]) that the LXX (Esth 4) calls God.[187]

The affirmation of God as king of the world in the blessing formulary corresponds to this growing consensual monarchial theology of the Late Antique Roman Empire.[188] The point of the blessing that "it is our God who is king of the world."[189] also counters the contention that "the God of the Hebrews was not the begetter of the whole universe with Lordship over the whole but rather ... that he is confined within limits."[190] In any case, the blessing highlighted divine sovereignty in a period in which the chief deity was presented more and more in terms of rulership of the world.[191]

In this theological universe, the particularistic covenantal theology of the Bible and Qumran yielded to the universalistic coronation theology

---

[184] *Against the Galilaeans* 115D (*The Works of the Emperor Julian*, 3:345).

[185] *Letter to the High-Priest Theodorus*, 20, 454a, (*The Works of the Emperor Julian*, 3:61).

[186] 132C (*The Works of the Emperor Julian*, 1:358).

[187] See above, n. 36.

[188] On the empire as an increasingly monotheistic-minded society, see MacMullen, *Paganism*, 83–94; idem, *Changes*, 323, n. 18; and *Octavius of Marcus Minucius Felix*, p. 263, n. 229. For parallels between rabbinic Judaism and developments in the Roman Empire, see Levine, *Judaism and Hellenism*, 134–8.

[189] The Shema verse was also understood as "It is our God who is God of the world/humanity," (see above, nn. 105, 109) as Exod 15:10 was understood as "It is the Lord who will reign for ever and ever;" see Goldin, *Song at the Sea*, p. 47, n. 58.

[190] *Against the Galilaeans*, 100C, see 148C (*The Works of the Emperor Julian*, 3:345, 359). In contrast, the Midrash says: "God said: 'The owner of a ship is not called *nauklerus* (ship owner) unless he has a ship, so I am not called God unless I created for myself a world" (*Seridei Tanḥuma Yelamdenu*, ed. Urbach, *Koveṣ Al Yad* 6 (16) 1, 1966, p. 12).

[191] There is also a corresponding use of the Greek καλός to praise or acclaim the deity in pagan, Christian, and Jewish prayers, a practice borrowed from the acclamations of the Emperors "καλός ὁ βασιλεύς"; see Lieberman, *Studies*, 434–5.

of the rabbis.[192] What covenant was to biblical theology, the acceptance of divine sovereignty became for rabbinic theology.[193] The focus on the sovereignty of God became so significant for the rabbis that it became the distinguishing mark of their liturgy.

Bibliography

Abraham b. Isaac of Narbonne, *Sefer Ha-Eškol.* Edited by S. Abeck Jerusalem: Wagsel, 1984.

Abraham b. Nathan of Lunel, *Sefer Ha-Manhig.* Edited by Y. Raphael. 2 vols. Jerusalem: Mossad Harav Kook, 1978.

Abudarham, D., *Abudarham Ha-Šalem,* Jerusalem: Usha, 1963.

—, *Tehillah Le-David.* Edited by M. Baron. Jerusalem: Or Ha-Sefer, 2001.

Albeck, H., *Šišah Sidrei Mišnah,* 6 vols. Jerusalem: Dvir, 1968.

Alexander, P. S., "The Family of Caesar and the Family of God: The Image of the Emperor in the Heikhalot Literature." Pages 226–97 in *Images of Empire.* Edited by L. Alexander. Sheffield. Sheffield Academic Press, 1991.

Alföldy, G., "The Crisis of the Third Century as Seen by Contemporaries." *GRBS* 15 (1974): 89–111.

---

[192] For the increased use of king-parables in rabbinic literature of the period, see Stern, *Parables in Midrash,* 97, and 292, n. 35.

[193] On the biblical understanding of covenant, see Tigay, *Deuteronomy,* xiv–xv. Note the model of "royal covenants in which a citizenry accepted someone as its king," (ibid., 63). In rabbinic parlance, however, *brit,* unless a verse is being cited, was reserved for the covenant of Abraham, i. e., circumcision (see above, n. 169), Note that Josephus also avoids using covenantal language. Instead of recasting it in terms of divine sovereignty, however, he employs a patron-client relationship (see Spilsbury, "God and Israel," 172–91), a relationship that has biblical precedent (see Tigay, ibid., 59, and 372, n. 43). The parallels are obvious. The fact that Josephus uses the patron-client model may indicate that the rabbinic sovereignty model had not yet been formulated. Indeed, there is no evidence for such a model until the next century. The development from the language of covenant to that of kingship explains the absence of the term in the Mishna which, however, does virtually open with mention of God's kingship (*m. Ber.* 2:2). Thus the contentions (see material cited in Schwartz, *Imperialism,* 65, n. 41) that the covenant is unimportant for the mishnaic system or that the system takes covenant legal theory for granted are misleading.

Altmann, A., "Širat Qedušah Be-Sifrut Ha-Hekhalot Ha-Qedumah." *Melilah* 2 (1946): 2–23.

Anchor Bible Dictionary, The, 6 vols., New York: Doubleday, 1992.

Ando, C., *Imperial Ideology and Provincial Loyalty in the Roman Empire.* Berkeley: University of California Press, 2000.

Aptowitzer, A., "בשכמל״ו Geschichte einer liturgischen Formel." *MGWJ* 73 (1929): 93–118.

Assaf, S., "Me-Seder Ha-Tefillah Be-Ereṣ Yisrael." Pages 116–31 in *Sefer Dinaburg.* Edited by I. Baer. Jerusalem, 1949.

Athanassakis, A., *The Orphic Hymns: Text Translation and Notes.* Missoula Montanta: Scholars Press, 1977.

Avi-Yonah, M., *In the Days of Rome and Byzantium.* Jerusalem: Bialik Institute, 1970 (in Hebrew).

Bar-Ilan, M., "The Source of the Prayer 'Aleynu Leshabeaḥ' [Hebrew]." *Daat* 43 (1999): 5–24 (in Hebrew).

Baumstark, A., *Comparative Liturgy.* London: Mowbray, 1958.

Beaujeu, J., "Les apologètes et le culte du souverain." Pages 101–42 in *Le culte des souverains dans l'Empire romain: sept exposés suivis de discussions par Elias Bickerman.* Genève: Fondation Hardt 1973.

Bernstein, M. J., "Hymn on Occasions for Prayer (1QS 10:8b–17)." Pages 33–7 in *Prayer from Alexander to Constantine: A Critical Anthology.* Edited by M. Kiley. London: Routledge, 1997.

Blidstein, G., "Nullification of Idolatry in Rabbinic Law." *PAAJR* 41 (1974):1–44.

Bowe, B., "Prayer Rendered for Caesar? I Clement 59.3–61.3." Pages 85–99 in *The Lord's Prayer and Other Prayer Texts from the Greco-Roman Era.* Edited by J. H. Charlesworth *et al.* Valley Forge: Trinity Press, 1994.

Bowersock, G. W., "The Imperial Cult: Perceptions and Persistence." Pages 171–82, 238–41 in *Jewish and Christian Self-Definition.* Vol. 3. Edited by B. Meyer and E. P. Sanders. Philadelphia: Fortress Press, 1982.

Boyarin, D., *Dying for God: Martyrdom and the Making of Christianity and Judaism.* Stanford: Stanford University Press, 1999.

Brent, A., *The Imperial Cult and the Development of Church Order: Concepts and Images of Authority in Paganism and Early Christianity before the Age of Cyprian.* Leiden: Brill, 1999.

Brettler, M., *God is King: Understanding an Israelite Metaphor.* Sheffield: Sheffield Academic Press, 1989.

Büchler, A., *Studies in Sin and Atonement in the Rabbinic Literature of the First Century.* New York: Ktav, 1967.

—, *Types of Jewish-Palestinian Piety from 70 B.C.E. to 70 C.E.: The Ancient Pious Men.* New York: Ktav, 1968.

Carmignac, J., "Roi, royauté et royaume dans la liturgie angélique." *RQ* 12 (1985): 177–86.

Charlesworth, J. H., ed. *The Dead Sea Scrolls: Pseudepigraphic amd Non-Masoretic Psalms and Prayers.* Vol. 4A. Louisville: Westminster John Knox Press, 1997.

—, ed. *The Old Testament Pseudepigrapha.* 2 vols. Garden City: Doubleday, 1983–1985.

Chazon, E., "Prayers from Qumran and Their Historical Implications." *DSD* 1 (1994): 265–84.

Chrysostom, Dio, *Discourses.* 1961. Translated by J. W. Cohoon. 5 vols. LCL. Cambridge: Harvard University Press.

Cohen, S. J. D., "Judaism to the Mishnah: 135–220 C. E." Pages 195–223 in *Christianity and Rabbinic Judaism: A Parallel History of Their Origins and Early Development.* Edited by H. Shanks. Washington: Biblical Archeology Society, 1992.

—, *The Beginnings of Jewishness: Boundaries, Varieties, Uncertainties.* Berkeley: University of California Press, 1999.

Davila, J. R., *Liturgical Works.* Grand Rapids: Eerdmans, 2000.

De Sola Pool, D., *The Kaddish.* Leipzig: Rudolf Haupt, 1909.

Discoveries in the Judean Desert. Vol 7. Edited by M. Baillet, Oxford: Clarendon Press, 1982.

Ehrlich, U. *The Non-Verbal Language of Jewish Prayer.* Jerusalem: Magnes Press, 1999 (in Hebrew).

Eleazar b. Judah of Worms, *Ha-Roqeaḥ Ha-Gadol.* Edited by B. Schneerson. Jerusalem: Oṣar Haposqim, 1967.

—, *Perušei Siddur Ha-Tefillah La-Roqeaḥ.* 2 vols. Edited by M. and Y. Hershler. 2 vols., Jerusalem: Machon Harav Hershler, 1992.

Elior, R., "From Earthly Temple to Heavenly Shrines: Prayer and Sacred Liturgy in the Hekhalot Literature and Its Relation to Temple Traditions." *Tarbiz* 64 (1995): 341–80 (in Hebrew).

Evans, C. A., *Jesus and His Contemporaries: Comparative Studies*. Boston: Brill, 2001.

Falk, D. K., *Daily, Sabbath, and Festival Prayers in the Dead Sea Scrolls*. Leiden: Brill, 1998.

Fears, J. R., "Rome: The Ideology of Imperial Power." *Thought* 55 (1980): 98–109.

Feldman, L. H., *Jew and Gentile in the Ancient World*. Princeton: Princeton University Press, 1993.

Ferguson E., "The Kingdom of God in Early Patristic Literature." Pages 191–208 in *The Kingdom of God in 20th-Century Interpretation*, Peabody: Hendrickson, 1987.

Fiensy, D., *Prayers Alleged to be Jewish: An Examination of the Constitutiones Apostolorum*. Chico: Scholars Press, 1985.

Finkelstein, L., *Akiba: Scholar, Saint and Martyr*. New York: Atheneum, 1970.

—, "The Meaning of the Word פרס in the Expressions, בפרוס הפסח, בפרוס העצרת, פורס על שמע and בפרוס החג." *JQR* 32 (1941/1942): 387–406; *JQR* 33 (1942/1943): 29–48.

—, "The Development of the Amidah." Pages 91–177 in *Contributions to the Scientific Study of Jewish Liturgy*. Edited by J. Petuchowski. New York: Ktav, 1970.

—, "The Prayer of King David according to Chronicles." *Eretz Israel* 13 (1978): 110–16 (in Hebrew).

—, "The Impact of the Roman Emperors on the Synagogue Liturgy." Pages 39–45 in *Threescore and Ten: Essays in Honor of Rabbi Seymour J. Cohen on the Occasion of His Seventieth Birthday*. Edited by ed. A. Karp, et al. Hoboken: Ktav, 1991.

Fleischer, E., "Between Occasional and Standardized in Public Prayer in Early Eretz-Yisrael." Pages 7–33 in *Studies in Memory of the Rishon Le-Zion R. Yitzhak Nissim*. Vol 5. Jerusalem: Yad Harav Nissim, 1985 (in Hebrew).

—, "Qetaʻim Me-Qovṣei Tefillah Ereṣ-yisraeliim Min Ha-Genizah." *Koveṣ Al Yad* 13 (23) Jerusalem: Mekize Nirdamim, (1996): 92–198.

—, "The *Qedušah* of the *Amidah* (and other *Qedušot*): Historical, Liturgical and Ideological Aspects." *Tarbiz* 67 (1998): 301–50 (in Hebrew).

—, "Seridim Nosafim Me-Qovṣei Tefillah 'Ereṣ-yisraeliim Min Ha-Genizah." *Koveṣ Al Yad* 15 (25) (2001): 3–37.

Flusser, D., "Psalms, Hymns, and Prayer." Pages 551–77 in *Jewish Writings of the Second Temple Period.* Edited by M. Stone Philadelphia: Fortress Press, 1984.

Foerster, G., "Synagogue Inscriptions and Their Relation to Liturgical Versions." *Cathedra* 19 (1981): 12–40 (in Hebrew).

Friesen, S. J., *Twice Neokoros: Ephesus, Asia and the Cult of the Flavian Imperial Family.* Leiden: Brill, 1993.

Gabbo, E., "The Holy Spirit, the Roman Senate, and Bousset." *JANES* 16–17 (1984–1985): 55–65.

Ginzberg, L., *A Commentary on the Palestinian Talmud.* 4 vols. New York: The Jewish Theological Seminary of America, 1941–1961 (in Hebrew).

—, *Geonica,* 2 vols. New York: Hermon Press, 1968.

—, *Legends of the Jews.* 7 vols., Philadelphia: The Jewish Publication Society, 1968.

—, *Genizah Studies.* 2 vols. New York: Hermon Press, 1969 (in Hebrew).

Goldberg, A., "Das Martyriuim des Rabbi Aqiva zur Komposition einer Märtyrererzählung." *Frankfurter Judaistische Beiträge* 12 (1984): 1–82.

Goldin, J., *The Song at the Sea.* New Haven: Yale University Press, 1971.

Goldschmidt, E. D., *Maḥzor Le-Yamim Ha-Nora'im.* 2 vols. Jerusalem: Koren, 1970.

—, *On Jewish Liturgy.* Jerusalem: Magnes Press, 1980 (in Hebrew).

Goldstein J., *II Maccabees.* Garden City: Doubleday, 1983.

Goodenough, E. R., *An Introduction to Philo Judaeus.* Oxford: Blackwell, 1962.

Grant, F., *Hellenistic Religions: The Age of Syncretism.* Indianapolis: Bobbs-Merrill, 1963.

Grant, R. M., *Greek Apologists of the Second Century.* Philadelphia: Westminister Press, 1988.

Gruenwald, I., *Apocalyptic and Meravah Mysticism.* Leiden: Brill, 1980.

Hachli, R., "Synagogues in the Land of Israel: The Art and Architecture of the Late Antique Synagogues." Pages 96–129 in *Sacred Realm: The Emergence of the Synagogue in the Ancient World.* Edited by S. Fine. New York: Oxford University Press, 1996.

—, "The Zodiac in Ancient Jewish Synagogal Art: A Review." *JSQ* 9 (2002): 219–58.

Hadani, J., "Habinenu: Tefillah Qeṣarah Me'en Šemoneh Esreh." *Sinai* 100 (1987): 299–324.

Hadas-Lebel M., "Le paganisme á travers les sources rabbiniques des IIe et IIIe siècles." Pages 397-485 in *ANRW* II.19.2. Edited by H. Temporini and W. Haase. Berlin: de Gruyter, 1979.

Halsberghe, G. H., *The Cult of Sol Invictus.* Leiden: Brill, 1972.

Harland, P. A., "Honours and Worship: Emperors, Imperial Cults and Associations at Ephesus (First to Third Centuries C.E.)." *SR* 25 (1966): 319–34.

Heinemann, J., "The Formula *melekh ha-'olam.*" *JJS* 9 (1960): 177–9.

—, *Prayer in the Period of the Tanna'im and Amora'im* Jerusalem: Magnes Press, 1964 (in Hebrew).

—, *Studies in Jewish Liturgy.* Jerusalem: Magnes Press, 1981 (in Hebrew).

Henrichs, A. "Despoina Kybele: Ein Beitrag zur relgiösen Namenkunde." *HSCP* 80 (1976): 253–86.

Herr, M., "Persecutions and Martydom in Hadrians's Days." *ScrHier* 23 (1972): 85–125.

Heschel, A. J., *Theology of Ancient Judaism.* 3 vols. Vols 1–2, London: Soncino Press, 1962-65; vol. 3, New York: Jewish Theological Seminary of America, 1995 (in Hebrew).

Hurvitz, A., *The Transition Period in Biblical Hebrew: A Study in Post-Exilic Hebrew and its Implications for the Dating of Psalms.* Jerusalem: Bialik Institute, 1972 (in Hebrew).

Ibn Shu'eib, J., *Sefer Derašot Ibn Šu'eib.* Edited by S. Abramson. Jerusalem: Maqor, 1969.

Jacobs, I., "Kingship and Holiness in the Third Benediction of the Amidah and in the Yoẓer." *JJS* 41 (1990): 62–74

Jacobson, I., *Netiv Binah*. 5 vols., Tel Aviv: Sinai, 1964–1978.

Judah b. Yaqar, *Peruš Ha-Tefillot Ve-Ha-Berakhot*. 2 vols. Jerusalem: Meorei Yisrael, 1968,

Julian. *The Works of the Emperor Julian*. 1923. Translated by W. Wright. 3 vols. LCL. Cambridge: Harvard University Press.

Kantorowicz, E. H., *Laudes Regiae: A Study in Liturgical Acclamations and Mediaeval Ruler Worship*. Berkeley: University of California Press, 1958,

Kasher, M., *Sefer Šema' Yisrael*, Jerusalem: Beth Torah Shelemah, 1980.

Kimelman, R., "The Conflict Between the Priestly Oligarchy and the Sages in the Talmudic Period (An Explication of *J. Shabbat* 12:3, 13c = *Horayot* 3, 48c." *Zion* 48 (1983): 135–47 (in Hebrew).

—, "Psalm 145: Theme, Structure, and Impact." *JBL* 113 (1994): 37–58.

—, "Liturgical Studies in the 90's." *Jewish Book Annual* 52 (1994–1995/5755): 59–72.

—, "The Literary Structure of the Amidah and the Rhetoric of Redemption." Pages 171–218 in *Echoes of Many Texts: Essays Honoring Lou H. Silberman on His Eightieth Birthday*. Edited by W. G. Dever and E. J. Wright. Atlanta: Scholars Press, 1997.

—, "Identifying Jews and Christians in Roman Syria-Palestine." Pages 301–31 in *Galilee through the Centuries: Confluence of Cultures*. Edited by E. M. Meyers. Winona Lake: Eisenbrauns, 1999.

—, "The Shema' Liturgy: From Covenant Ceremony to Coronation." *Kenishta: A Journal of Synagogue Life* 1 (2001): 9–105.

—, *The Mystical Meaning of Lekhah Dodi and Kabbalat Shabbat*. Jerusalem: Magnes Press, 2003 (in Hebrew).

Krauss, S., *Griechische und lateinische Lehnwörter im Talmud, Midrasch und Targum*. 2 vols. Hildesheim: Olms, 1964.

Ladouceur, D. J., "Josephus and Masada." Pages 95–113 in *Josephus, Judaism, and Christianity*. Edited by L. Feldman, and G. Hata. Detroit: Wayne State University Press, 1987.

Lambert, W., *Babylonian Wisdom Literature*. Oxford: Clarendon Press, 1960.

Lamm, N., *Halakot Ve-Halikot*. Jerusalem: Mosad Harav Kook, 1990

Légasse, S., "La prière pour les chefs d'état: antécédents judaïques et témoins chrétiens du premier siècle," *NT* 29 (1987): 236–53.

Lehnardt, A., "Once Again: 'Oseq be-Ma'ase Merkava' and Qaddish in bBerakhot 21b." *Frankfurter Judaistische Beiträge* 27 (2000): 23–7.

Lehnardt, T., "Der Gott der Welt ist unser König: Zur Vorstellung von der Königsherrschaft Gottes im Shema und seinen Benediktionen." Pages 285–307 in *Königsherrschaft Gottes und himmlischer Kult in Judentum, Urchristentum und in der hellenistischer Welt*. Edited by M. Hengel and A. Schwemer. Tübingen: Mohr, 1991.

Leicht, Reimund, "*Qedushah* and Prayer to Helios: A New Hebrew Version of an Apocryphal Prayer of Jacob." *JSQ* 6 (1999): 140–76.

Leonhardt J., *Jewish Worship in Philo of Alexandria*. Tübingen: Mohr Siebeck, 2001.

Lerner, M. B., "New Light on the Spanish Recension of Deuteronomy Rabba [1] The Evolution of Ed. Lieberman." *Te'udah* 11 (1996): 107–145, xiv–xvi.

Levine, L. I., *Caesarea Under Roman Rule*. Leiden: Brill, 1975.

—, *Judaism and Hellenism in Antiquity: Conflict or Confluence?* Seattle: University of Washington Press, 1998.

—, *The Ancient Synagogue: The First Thousand Years*. New Haven: Yale University Press, 2000.

Lieberman, S., "The Martyrs of Caesarea." Pages 395–445 in *Annuaire de l'institue de philologie et d'historie orientales et slaves* 7 (1939–1944).

—, *Hilkot Ha-Yerušalmi*. New York: The Jewish Theological Seminary of America, 1947.

—, *Tosefta Ki-fšutah*. 10 vols. New York: The Jewish Theological Seminary of America, 1955–1988.

—, *Studies in Palestinian Talmudic Literature*. Edited by D. Rosenthal, Jerusalem: Magnes Press, 1991 (in Hebrew).

Liebeschuetz, J. H. W. G. *Continuity and Change in Roman Religion*, Oxford: Clarendon Press, 1986.

Liebreich, L. J., "Aspects of the New Year Liturgy." *HUCA* 34 (1963): 125–76.

Linder, A., *The Jews in Roman Imperial Legislation*. Detroit: Wayne State University Press, 1987.

Luger, Y., *The Weekday Amidah in the Cairo Genizah*. Jerusalem: Orhot Press, 2001 (in Hebrew).

Mack, H., "The Source of *Malkhuyyot* Benediction." *JSQ* 9 (2002): 205–18.

MacMullen, R., *Paganism in the Roman Empire*. New Haven: Yale University Press, 1981.

—, *Changes in the Roman Empire: Essays in the Ordinary*. Princeton: Princeton University Press 1990.

Maḥzor Vitry, R. Simḥah ben Samuel. Edited by S. Horowitz. Mekize Nirdamim, 1923. Reprint, Jerusalem: Alef, 1963.

Malter, H., ed., *The Treatise Ta'anit of the Babylonian Talmud*. New York: The American Academy for Jewish Research, 1930 (in Hebrew).

Mann, J., " 'Anan's Liturgy and His Half-Yearly Cycle of the Reading of the Law." *Journal of Jewish Lore and Philosophy* 1 (1919): 329–53.

—, "Genizah Fragments of the Palestinian Order of Service." *HUCA* 2 (1925): 269–338.

Margulies, M., *The Differences Between Babylonian and Palestinian Jews*. Jerusalem: Rubin Mass, 1938 (in Hebrew).

McCarthy, D., *Treaty and Covenant*. Rome: Pontifical Biblical Institute, 1963.

Meeks, W. A., *The Origins of Christian Morality: The First Two Centuries*. New Haven: Yale University Press, 1993.

Meier, J. P., *A Marginal Jew: Rethinking the Historical Jesus*. 3 vols. New York: Doubleday, 1991–2001.

Midrešei Ge'ullah. Edited by Y. Even-Shemuel. Jerusalem: Bialik Institute, 1954.

Millar, F., "Review of W. H. C. Frend, Martyrdom and Persecution in the Early Church," *JRS* 56 (1966): 234–5.

Miqra'ot Gedolot. New York: M. P. Press, 1974.

Mirsky, A., *Ha'Piyut: The Development of Post Biblical Poetry in Eretz Israel and the Diaspora*. Jerusalem: Magnes Press, 1990 (in Hebrew).

Momigliano, A., *On Pagans, Jews, and Christians*. Hanover: Wesleyan University Press, 1987.

Moran, W., "The Ancient Near Eastern Background of the Love of God in Deuteronomy." *CBQ* 25 (1963): 77–87.

Muffs, Y., *Studies in the Aramaic Legal Papyri from Elephantine*. Leiden: Brill, 1969.

Musurillo, H., *The Acts of the Christian Martyrs*. Oxford: Clarendon Press, 1972.

Naveh, J., ed., *On Stone and Mosaic: The Aramaic and Hebrew Inscriptions from Ancient Synagogues*. Jerusalem: Israel Exploration Society & Carta, 1978 (in Hebrew).

Ness, L. J., "Astrology and Judaism in Late Antiquity." Pages 126–33 in *The Ancient World: Mystery Cults in Late Antiquity*. Vol. 26:2 Chicago: Ares, 1995

Newsom, C., *Songs of the Sabbath Sacrifice: A Critical Edition*. Atlanta: Scholars Press, 1985.

Nickelsburg, G., "Tobit and Enoch: Distant Cousins with a Recognizable Resemblance." *SBL Seminar Papers, 1988*. (SBLSP 27; Atlanta: Scholars Press, 1988), 54–68.

—, *I Enoch*. Minneapolis: Fortress Press, 2001.

Nitzan, B., *Qumran Prayer and Religious Poetry*. Leiden: Brill, 1994.

—, "The Textual, Literary and Religious Character of 4QBerakhot (4Q286-290)." Pages 636–56 in *The Provo International Conference on the Dead Sea Scrolls: Technological Innovations, New Texts, and Reformulated Issues*. Edited by D. Parry and E. Ulrich. Leiden: Brill, 1999.

—, "The Benedictions from Qumran for the Annual Covenantal Ceremony." Pages 263–71 in *The Dead Sea Scrolls Fifty Years After Their Discovery*. Edited by L. Schiffman, E. Tov, and J. VanderKam. Jerusalem: Israel Exploration Society, 2000.

—, "The Concept of the Covenant in Qumran Literature." Pages 85–104 in *Historical Perspectives: From the Hasmoneans to Bar Kokhba in Light of the Dead Sea Scrolls.* Edited by D. Goodblatt, A. Pinnick and D. Schwartz. Leiden: Brill, 2001.

Numenius, A., *Fragments.* Edited by E. des Places. Paris, 1973.

Octavius of Marcus Minucius Felix. Edited by G. W. Clarke. *ACW.* New York: Newman Press, 1974.

Petuchowski, J., "Jewish Prayer Texts of the Rabbinic Period." Pages 21–44 in *The Lord's Prayer and Jewish Liturgy.* Edited by J. Petuchowski, and M. Brocke. New York: Seabury Press, 1978.

Pleket, H. W., "Religious History as the History of Mentality: The 'Believer' as Servant of the Deity in the Greek World." Pages 152–92 in *Faith Hope and Worship: Aspects of Religious Mentality in the Ancient World.* Edited by H. S. Versnel. Leiden: Brill, 1981.

Preuss, H. D., *Theologie des Alten Testaments.* Stuttgart, 1991.

Price, S. R. F., "Gods and Emperors: The Greek Language of the Roman Imperial Cult." *JHS* 104 (1984): 93–5.

—, *Rituals and Power: The Roman Imperial Cult in Asia Minor.* Cambridge: Cambridge University Press, 1984.

Rabbinovicz, R., *Diqduqei Sofrim (Variae Lectiones in Mischnam et in Talmud Babylonicum).* 14 vols. Jerusalem: 1960.

Saadia Gaon, *The Book of Beliefs and Opinions.* Edited by S. Rosenblatt, New Haven: Yale University Press, 1967.

Sanders, E. P., *Jesus and Judaism.* Philadelphia: Fortress Press, 1986.

Sarason, R. S., "The 'Interesections' of Qumran and Rabbinic Judaism: The Case of Prayer Texts and Liturgies." *DSD* 8 (2001): 169–81.

Schäfer, P., *Synopse zur Hekhalot-Literature.* Tübingen: Mohr, 1981.

—, *Hekhalot Studien.* Tübingen: Mohr, 1988.

—, *Konkordanz zur Hekhalot-Literatur.* Tübingen: Mohr, 1988.

Schechter, A. I., *Studies in Jewish Liturgy.* Philadelphia: Jewish Publication Society, 1930.

Schechter, S., "Genizah Specimens." *JQR* 10 (1898): 654–9.

Schiffman, L., "From Temple to Torah: Rabbinic Judaism in Light of the Dead Sea Scrolls." *Shofar* 10 (1992): 2–15.

Schlüter, M., "Untersuchungen zur Form und Funktion der Berakha in der Hekhalot-Literatur." *Frankfurter Judaistische Beiträge* 13 (1985): 83–148.

Schowalter, D. N., *The Emperor and The Gods: Images from the Time of Trajan*. Minneapolis: Fortress Press, 1993.

Schuller, E., "Some Observations on Blessing of God in Texts from Qumran." Pages 133–42 in *Of Scribes and Scrolls: Studies in the Hebrew Bible, Intertestamental Judaism and Christian Origins Presented to John Strugnell on the Occasion of His Sixtieth Birthday*. Edited by H. Attridge. J. Collins and T. Tobin. Lanham: University Press of America, 1990.

Schürer, E., *The History of the Jewish People in the Age of Jesus Christ (175 B.C.–A.D. 135)*. 3 vols. Edited by G. Vermes, *et al*. Edinburgh: T & T Clark, 1973–1987.

Schwartz, S., *Imperialism and Jewish Society: 200 B. C. E. to 649 C. E.* Princeton: Princeton University Press, 2001.

Schwemer, A., "Gott als König und seine Königsherrschaft in der Sabbatlieder aus Qumran." Pages 45–118 in *Königsherrschaft Gottes und himmlischer Kult in Judentum, Urchristentum und in der hellenistischer Welt*. Edited by M. Hengel and A. Schwemer. Tübingen: Mohr, 1991.

—, "Irdischer and himmlischer König: Beobachtungen zur sogenannten David-Apokalypse in Hekhalot Rabbati §§ 122–126." Pages 310–59 in *Königsherrschaft Gottes und himmlischer Kult in Judentum, Urchristentum und in der hellenistischer Welt*. Edited by M. Hengel and A. Schwemer. Tübingen: Mohr, 1991.

Scott, K., "Humor at the Expense of the Ruler Cult." *CP* 27 (1932): 317–28.

Seder Rav Amram Gaon. Edited by D. Goldschmidt. Jerusalem: Mossad Harav Kook, 1971

Seridei Tanḥuma Yelamdenu. Edited by E. Urbach. *Koveṣ Al Yad* 6 (16) (1966): 3–75 (in Hebrew).

Shinan, A., *The Embroidered Targum: The Aggadah in Targum Pseudo-Jonathan of the Pentateuch*. Jerusalem: Magnes Press, 1992 (in Hebrew).

Siddur of R. Solomon ben Samson of Garmaise including the Siddur of the Haside Ashkenas. Edited by M. Hershler. Jerusalem: Hemed, 1971 (in Hebrew).

Smith, R., *Julian's Gods: Religion and Philosophy in the Thought and Action of Julian the Apostate.* London: Routledge, 1995.

Sperber, D., *Minhagei Yisrael: Meqorot Ve-Toledot.* 6 vols. Jerusalem: Mossad Harav Kook, 1989–1998.

Spiegel, S,. *The Last Trial.* New York: Schocken, 1969.

Spilsbury, P., "God and Israel in Josephus: A Patron-Client Relationship." Pages 172–91 in *Understanding Josephus: Seven Perspectives.* Edited by S. Mason. Sheffield: Sheffield Academic Press, 1998.

Stern, D., *Parables in Midrash: Narratives and Exegesis in Rabbinic Literature.* Cambridge: Harvard University Press, 1991.

Stern, M., *Greek and Latin Authors on Jews and Judaism.* 3 vols. Jerusalem: The Israel Academy of Sciences and Humanities, 1974–1984.

Stevenson, J., ed., *A New Eusebius: Documents Illustrative of the History of the Church to A.D. 337.* London: SPCK, 1968.

Strugnell, J., and E. Schuller, "Further *Hodayot* Manuscripts from Qumran?" Pages 51–72 in *Antikes Judentum und frühes Christentum Festschrift für Hartmut Stegemann zum 65. Geburtstag.* Edited by B. Kollmann, W. Reinbold, and A. Steudel. Berlin: de Gruyter, 1999.

Sukenik, E. L., *The Synagogue of Dura-Europos and Its Frescos.* Jerusalem: Bialik Institute, 1947 (in Hebrew).

Tadmor, H., "Treaty and Oath in the Ancient Near East: A Historian's Approach." Pages 127–52 in *Humanizing America's Iconic Book.* Edited by G. Tucker, and D. Knight. Chico: Scholars Press, 1982.

Talmon, S., "The Emergence of Institutionalized Prayer in Israel in Light of Qumran Literature." Pages 200–43 in *The World of Qumran from Within: Collected Studies,* Jerusalem-Leiden: Magnes Press-Brill, 1989.

—, "The 'Dead Sea Scrolls' or 'The Community of the Renewed Covenant?'" Pages 115–45 in *Echoes of Many Texts: Essays Honoring Lou H. Silberman on His Eightieth Birthday*. Edited by W. G. Dever, and E. J. Wright. Atlanta: Scholars Press, 1997.

Tigay, J., *Deuteronomy, The JPS Torah Commentary*. Philadelphia: The Jewish Publication Society, 1996.

Tosafot Rabbenu Yehudah Sirleons. Edited by N. Sachs. Jerusalem, 1969.

Urbach, E., "The Rabbinical Laws of Idolatry in the Second and Third Centuries in the Light of Archaeological and Historical Facts." *IEJ* 9 (1959): 149–65, 229–45.

—, *The Sages: Their Concepts and Beliefs*. Jerusalem: Magnes Press, 1969 (in Hebrew).

—, "The Place of the Ten Commandments in Ritual and Prayer." Pages 127–45 in *The Ten Commandments as Reflected in Tradition and Literature Throughout the Ages*. Edited by B. Z. Segal. Jerusalem: Magnes, 1985 (in Hebrew).

Weinfeld, M., "Covenant Terminology in the Ancient Near East and Its Influence on the West." *JAOS* 93 (1973): 190–9.

—, *Justice and Righteousness in Israel and the Nations: Equality and Freedom in Ancient Israel in Light of Social Justice in The Ancient Near East*. Jerusalem: Magnes Press, 1985 (in Hebrew).

—, *Deuteronomy 1–11*. New York: Doubleday, 1991.

Weiss, J. G., "On the formula *melekh ha'olam* as anti-Gnostic protest." *JJS* 10 (1959): 169–71.

Weiss, Z., "The Zodiac in Ancient Synagogue Art: Cyclical Order and Divine Power." *La Maique gréco-romaine* IX (forthcoming).

Weitzman, S., "Allusion, Artifice and Exile in the Hymn of Tobit." *JBL* 115 (1996): 49–61.

Veltri G., "Römische Religion an der Peripherie des Reiches: Ein Kapitel rabbinischer Rhetorik." Pages 81–138 in *The Talmud Yerushalmi and Graeco-Roman Culture*. Vol. 2. Edited by P. Schäfer, and C. Hezser, Tübingen: Mohr Siebeck, 2000.

Werner, E., "The Doxology in Synagogue and Church: A Liturgico-Musical Study." *HUCA* 19 (1945/46): 275–351.

Wiesenberg, E. J., "The Liturgical Term *melekh ha-'olam*." *JJS* 15 (1964): 1–56.

—, "Gleanings of the Liturgical Term *Melekh Ha-'Olam*." *JJS* 17 (1966): 47–72.

Wiliamson, H. G. M., *Ezra and Nehemiah*. Waco: Word Books, 1985.

—, "Structure and Historiography in Nehemiah." Pages 117–31 in *Proceedings of the Ninth World Congress of Jewish Studies: Panel Sessions, Bible Studies*. Jerusalem, 1988.

Williams, M. A., *Rethinking "Gnosticism": An Argument for Dismantling a Dubious Category*. Princeton: Princeton University Press, 1966.

Winston, D., *The Wisdom of Solomon*. Garden City: Doubleday, 1979.

Wolfson, E. R., *Along the Path: Studies in Kabbalistic Myth, Symbolism, and Hermeneutics*. Albany: SUNY, 1995.

Wolfson, H. A., *Philo: Foundations of Religious Philosophy in Judaism, Christianity, and Islam*. 2 vols. Cambridge: Harvard University Press, 1968.

Zulay, M., *The Liturgical Poetry of Sa'adya Gaon and His School*. Jerusalem: Schocken, 1964 (in Hebrew).

22
No Second Temple—No Shavuot?
The Book of Jubilees as a Case Study

Irene von Görtz-Wrisberg

MANY YEARS AGO I read a poem by the famous Polish author Adam Mickiewicz. This poem "Pies i wilk" or in English, "The Dog and the Wolf," made a great impression on me. And then, later was I ever surprised when during a high school class in Latin, I found a similar poem, "Lupus ad Canem," a poem about a wolf and a dog. This poem was written by the Latin fabulist Phaedrus of first century C.E.

At first I thought that Mickiewicz had been inspired by Phaedrus. Instead it turned out that he had borrowed the poem or parts of the poem from the fabulous French writings of Jean de La Fontaine. La Fontaine was so to speak, the bridge between Mickiewicz and Phaedrus. For some reason I decided to study Phaedrus a bit closer, and realized that he in his turn owed a lot to Aesop. If I would have continued this line of investigation I might have discovered that also Aesop should be grateful to somebody.

But indeed one can ask how this introduction relates to the present paper. The purpose of this introductory part was to serve as an example of how sources can be re-used, in being re-read, re-written and re-interpreted, by future generations. My point here is that each author not only copies but also alters the text of a former writer, either by expanding, condensing or changing it. Further, in what respect a former text is transformed, may depend upon the contemporaneous situation. In the case of the Polish author Mickiewicz the theme of the poem, being free or fettered, was even more striking since the poem could also be read as an allegory about the severe Polish situation of that time.

No Second Temple—No Shavuot?

This corresponds well with how one can understand the shaping of *The Book of Jubilees*.[1] Firstly, with regard to its relation to, or its dependence on different sources, above all various biblical sources. Secondly, when a text is re-used it is perhaps because it primarily wants to transmit a certain message to a contemporary reader or listener. Just like Mickiewicz had a further purpose in reusing La Fontaine's poem, than only presenting a fable.

After having done a survey of research on the festival of Shavuot, I wanted to label it a forgotten festival, since I noticed that both the primary sources as well as the secondary literature that treat the festival were astonishingly scarce. There is, however, one exception when it comes to the primary sources on Shavuot, namely *Jubilees*. This is one reason why I have chosen to discuss Shavuot in relation to this source in the present paper. Even if other festivals are also found in *Jubilees*, Shavuot is understood as the main festival,[2] which gives a further reason for analyzing this festival in particular.

In the secondary literature the commentary parts on *Jubilees* are mainly paraphrases or quotations of the text.[3] And this is not of much help. Furthermore, many of these works tend to concentrate on the calendrical issues when discussing the festival, and thereby neglect the features of the festival. The purpose of the present paper is therefore to analyse *Jubilees* with the aim of grasping the meanings of the festival and gaining a deeper understanding of it.

The problem—or actually problems—examined in this paper are threefold, based on three underlying questions. Firstly, a descriptive

---

[1] In the prologue of *Jub.* the full title can be found: "These are the words regarding the divisions of the times of the law and of the testimony, of the events of the years, of the weeks of their jubilees throughout all the years of eternity" (*Jub.* Prol.). "The (Book) of Jubilees" or "The Little Genesis" are brief titles stemming from the Greek, Syriac, Latin and later Hebrew texts, see Wintermute, "Jubilees," 41. The quotations in this paper are taken from VanderKam's critical edition of *Jubilees*.

[2] Davenport, *Eschatology*, 12, n. 7; Endres, *Biblical Interpretation*, 202; van Goudoever, *Biblical Calendars*, 63, 65; Kraus, *Gottesdienst*, 77; Le Déaut, "Pingsten," 152; Noack, "Pentecost," 82, 86–7, *Pinsedagen*, 98, 100–1; Potin, *Pentecôte*, 122.

[3] There are nevertheless two monographs that can be described as detailed commentaries on *Jub.* Endres, *Biblical Interpretation*, however, only dealing with the Jacob cycle in *Jub.* (19–45), and van Ruiten, *Primaeval History*, who solely concentrates on Gen 1–11 in relation to *Jub.* VanderKam's recent guide, *Book of Jubilees*, also deserves to be mentioned in this context. Even if it is not a verse by verse commentary it is still a valuable introduction to *Jub.*

one: how is the festival described in *Jubilees*? The intention here is to look closer at the term or terms designating the festival as well as at the understanding of the festival. This means that rites[4] connected with the festival, will also be scrutinized. Secondly, an interpretative approach: why is there a reference to the festival in *Jubilees*? The purpose is to find a reason for the mentioning of the festival. Thirdly, on a more synthetic level: what kind of mechanisms can be discerned through the references to the festival? The aim is to study whether there might be any theological or ideological considerations behind the understanding of the festival. Questions number one and two will be in focus within the textual analyses, whereas question number three will be discussed in connection with the conclusions.

A famous problem for everyone working especially with ancient sources is that you can always ask different questions, but finding any answers within the sources, is another matter. Instead what often happens, is that you end up with a bunch of new questions and answers to totally different issues. This means that I am well aware of the difficulties connected with my project.

Briefly, something about the title "Shavuot." I have chosen to use "Shavuot," "Weeks," as a general term when speaking about this festival, and this is also why I have it in the title of this paper. The reason for this is that "Shavuot" does not automatically point to the agrarian side of the festival, as would have been the case with for instance the other names connected with the festival. However, when analysing a specific source, e.g. *Jubilees*, I adopt the term or terms used by the actual source.

Finally, a couple of words about the title of the present paper: "No Second Temple—No Shavuot? *The Book of Jubilees* as a Case Study." Since *Jubilees* is mainly occupied with some of the events of the books of Genesis and Exodus, the mentioning of a Second Temple is anachronistic and one could further correctly object, that not even the First Temple of Jerusalem existed so early. I admit that these objections are legitimate, but the purpose of the title is really to put the focus on *Jubilees*' own time, sometime in the second century B.C.E. A time when the Second Temple surely existed, and my purpose is not to deny this fact, instead my question is a bit provocative with the intention to suggest

---

[4] There is a vast discussion on how to define "rite." For this paper I apply a broad definition of the term and hereby understand "rite" to be a form of procedure in connection with the festival under scrutiny.

that some groups, in this case the authorship or producers of *Jubilees*, may for some reasons have neglected the Second Temple. I do not want to anticipate the results, but promise to return to the title and my suggestion later in the final part.

What I now intend to present is a short introduction to *Jubilees*. Thereafter I will continue with textual analyses and sum up my results in a concluding synthesis.

The Book of Jubilees and Textual Analyses

The Book of Jubilees

Jubilees is a retelling or rewriting[5] of mainly Gen 1 to Exod 20. The narrative starts off in Sinai, where Moses is summoned to the mountain by God to receive the two stone tablets. He is furthermore told to write down the revelation given to him during the forty days' and nights' stay (*Jub.* Prol.; 1:1–5, 7), that is *Jubilees*. Thereby *Jubilees* wants to be understood as a fully authorised revelation and text.[6] After the prologue where God is directly addressing Moses, the retelling is taken over by the angel of presence (*Jub.* 1:26–7; 2:1),[7] and at times the narrative of Genesis and Exodus gets interrupted by direct exhortations to Moses with the purpose of transmitting them to the Israelites.

---

[5] A discussion on rewriting the Bible, that is to rewrite it with an aim, and especially focusing on the rewriting of *Jubilees*, is found in Endres, *Biblical Interpretation*, 15–17, and in van Ruiten, *Primaeval History*, 3–5. See also VanderKam, "Biblical Interpretation," 97–8, 117–25.

[6] VanderKam, *Book of Jubilees*, 12, 23–4.

[7] See *Jubilees* (VanderKam), and the text-critical apparatus to *Jub.* 1:26–7. Here VanderKam discusses the ambiguity in the Mss with regard to the authorship, that is the angel of presence or Moses. I agree with the translation of VanderKam, who understands the angel to be dictating the text for "the secretary" Moses, see also VanderKam, *Book of Jubilees*, 17–18. The real author of *Jub.* is God, whereas the angel just serves as a mouthpiece (*Jub.* 1:4–5, 7, 26–7; 2:1). Thus instead of using the term "authorship" in relation to Moses, I prefer the term "secretaryship," since this term better reflects the task of Moses. VanderKam denies that the ambivalence would indicate different editions, see "Putative Author," 209–17.

Jubilees is not a simple transcript, because sometimes the biblical story is expanded[8] or condensed, and occasionally changed, possibly because of its aim. As for the form, it has been suggested that it is reminiscent of a narrative midrash.[9] Even if *Jubilees* is a retelling to Moses and in extension also to the Israelites, one may however assume that one particular group of Israelites is specifically in focus, namely the generation contemporary to *Jubilees* sometime around mid-second century B.C.E.[10]

Where is the authorship to be sought? An important indication may be revealed through the eminent position of Jacob's son Levi. According to *Jubilees* Levi and his descendants are to become priests and Levi is even appointed priest in *Jubilees* (30:18; 32:1, 3). Levi and Judah get the blessing of Isaac (*Jub.* 31:9–20); Levi is, however, the first to be blessed. Apart from this, other practices connected with priests, such as regulations about sacrifices and calendrical issues, are also frequent. This points to an authorship among priestly circles.[11] Furthermore, the provenance is with a high degree of probability to be found among a group that rejected interchange, that is assimilation with the Hellenistic ideas, and apparently tried to keep up with old traditions such as the 364-day solar calendar,[12] which probably also had ancient priestly roots.[13]

Through the findings at Qumran it was finally concluded what only up to then had been assumed, *Jubilees* was initially indeed written in

---

[8] Halpern-Amaru, *Empowerment*, 133–8, discussing the exegesis of *Jub.*, rightly states that one has to be careful not to over-emphasize the notion of the expansions.
[9] In Wintermute, "Jubilees," 40, the following definition can be found: "the narrative Midrash scarcely distinguishes between text and comment, but interweaves them to form a continuous narrative." The same genre for *Jub.* is also suggested in Berger, *Jubiläen*, 285.
[10] VanderKam, *Textual*, 282–4. Recent discussions on the dating may be found in Ulfgard, *Sukkot*, 156–7, and VanderKam, *Book of Jubilees*, 18–21.
[11] Jaubert, *Notion d'alliance*, 91–2; Potin, *Pentecôte*, 129; VanderKam, "Origins and Purposes," 19. The special concern for Levi should perhaps also be put in relation to Moses, being himself a descendant of Levi (Exod 2:1–2).
[12] Nickelsburg, *Jewish Literature*, 74; VanderKam, "Origins and Purposes," 17–18. Cf. also *Jub.* 6:30–8, where the calendar is described as being given to Moses to command to the Israelites. It is the same calendrical tradition as in *1 En*, see García Martínez, "Heavenly Tablets," 251–2, who also directs attention to *Jub.* 2:9 where only the sun is mentioned—leaving out the moon—and "as a great sign."
[13] García Martínez, "Heavenly Tablets," 252; VanderKam, "Origin," 390–411.

Hebrew. Today we only have Hebrew fragments[14] and the complete *Jubilees* is only to be found in Ethiopic. Despite the fragments at Qumran, *Jubilees* is usually interpreted as a pre-sectarian document, since no split with the larger community can be noticed out of the source.[15] It is, however, a document that in a later phase became connected with Qumran.[16]

Textual Analyses

Two important notes before I start analyzing. Firstly, during the analyses I will at times make comparisons with what I call the "biblical sources." By "biblical sources" I mean the biblical sources today accessible to us, for example the Masoretic text and the Septuagint. The version of Genesis and Exodus available to the author of *Jubilees* is lost to us, but it apparently bears witness to a Palestinian text. At times *Jubilees* is very close to the Masoretic text, but where it differs, many of the varieties can also be noted in the Septuagint and the Samaritan Pentateuch.[17] Thus when in the following I state something like "not found in the biblical sources," this means it cannot be found in the sources known to us, and most likely stems from the textual tradition of *Jubilees*. Secondly, it may seem anachronistic in the following to refer to Exodus, Leviticus, Numbers and Deuteronomy when discussing the patriarchal stories, but *Jubilees* has not only retrojected the festival, but also its rites.

In connection with this, I would like to quote G. Boccaccini: "If in Jubilees the ancient patriarchs are said to keep some of the laws later revealed to Moses, it is not because the Mosaic torah was preexistent, as it would be in later Rabbinic Judaism, . . . but because the patriarchs had direct access to the heavenly archetype,"[18] that is to the heavenly tablets, which "are the only and all-inclusive repository of God's revelation."[19] Therefore, I also allow myself to compare the patriarchal festival

---

[14] The earliest Hebrew fragments probably stem from late second century B.C.E., see further VanderKam, *Book of Jubilees*, 18, and Wintermute, "Jubilees," 43.
[15] Berger, *Jubiläen*, 282; Boccaccini, *Beyond*, 86–7, 97; Eiss, "Wochenfest," 171–2 with n. 40 on p. 172; Potin, *Pentecôte*, 129; Wintermute, "Jubilees," 44, 48.
[16] VanderKam, "Origins and Purposes," 3.
[17] VanderKam, *From Revelation*, 460–1; *Textual*, 103–205.
[18] Boccaccini, *Beyond*, 90.
[19] Ibid. For further comments on the term "heavenly tablets," see n. 34.

practices attested in *Jubilees* with the Pentateuch.[20] In this paper I have limited my analysis to four texts. The reason for this "special selection" is that these texts serve as good examples of the festival. The starting point as well as the fundamental text will be *Jub*. 6, which is located within the Noah cycle. I will thereafter continue with the three other texts, chosen because each text is mainly connected to each one of the patriarchs.[21]

In this part, I will concentrate on two questions. First, I will examine how the festival is described in each text and secondly, scrutinize why there is a reference to this festival in the different texts.

Jub. 6:1–22: The Formation of the Festival

In my opinion Chapter 6 is crucial to the understanding of the festival in *Jubilees* and therefore I will give a closer rendering of this chapter.[22] Our text begins at the ending of the story of the flood. After the waters have dried up, Noah disembarks the ark to construct an altar on Lubar, a mountain in the chain of Ararat (*Jub*. 5:28; 6:1).

There are close parallels between this text and the biblical one. As is typical for *Jubilees*, we find a precise date for the event, namely "the first of the third month" (*Jub*. 6:1).[23] Furthermore, *Jubilees*' interest in sacrifices is notable also in this story. The primary sacrifice offered by Noah after his disembarkation is obviously a sacrifice of atonement, because the blood of a kid is shed for the expiation of "the sins of the earth" (*Jub*. 6:2). Noah performed further offerings and God apparently accepted them, since he established a covenant with Noah and promised that floods would neither ruin the earth, neither would the seasons end (*Jub*. 6:3–4).[24]

---

[20] Cf. also Noack, "Pentecost," 84, who states "that Jubilees wishes to be in accord with the Old Testament regulations regarding the Feast of Weeks," and van Ruiten, *Primaeval History*, 248, who mentions that the biblical festival calendars on Shavuot are indirectly applied by the author of *Jub*.

[21] Explicit references to the festival can be found in the following texts: *Jub*. 6:17–22; 14:20; 15:1; 16:13; 22:1; 44:4. Furthermore, in *Jub*. 29:5, 7–8 a feast is held and Jacob and Laban swear an oath on precisely the fifteenth of the third month. The festival is, however, not mentioned. For comments on the date, see nn. 55 and 56. Further remarks on the passage in *Jub*. 29 can be found in n. 57.

[22] The text in this paragraph corresponds to Gen 8:18–9:17 in the Hebrew Bible.

[23] This date is also given in some LXX Mss to Gen 8:19.

[24] The important covenant making by God is often neglected when discussing the covenants in *Jub*. Instead the starting point is Noah's covenant and acceptance (*Jub*.

Then follows the exhortations to reproduce and instructions for not consuming the blood of animals or spilling human blood (*Jub.* 6:5–9). As already mentioned, there are several parallels between this rendering and the biblical story, but this is about to change, because of a major expansion in *Jubilees* (6:10), which is of particular interest to us:

> Noah and his sons swore an oath not to consume any blood that was in any animate being. During this month he made a covenant before the Lord God forever throughout all the history of the earth.

At least three things are to be observed in this agreement to God's demands. Firstly, the swearing of an oath[25] not consuming blood. In other words, this is a positive answer to the commandment of God and the prohibition concerning blood. Secondly, we find a reference to a date, "this month," which most probably refers to the third month (cf. *Jub.* 6:1), since no other month has been mentioned in this chapter. A month, which in *Jubilees* appears to be—as we shall soon see—intimately connected with Shavuot. But in this text the exact day is left open. And thirdly, just as God made a covenant earlier with Noah (*Jub.* 6:4), Noah now makes a covenant with God. It appears to be an *imitatio Dei*, and it is a full acceptance of the instructions of God.[26]

After the covenant of Noah, the expansion continues and a sudden shift of addressee occurs in the text. It is almost possible to note a change of volume as well; from *piano* to *forte*. Now the story-telling angel cuts off the story of Noah, and addresses Moses, and instantly we are, so to speak, taken from Mount Lubar to Mount Sinai (*Jub.* 6:11).

> For this reason he [the Lord] told you, too, to make a covenant—accompanied by an oath—with the Israelites during this month on the mountain and to sprinkle blood on them because of all the words of the covenant which the Lord was making with them for all times.

6:10). There is, however, at least one exception, van Ruiten, *Primaeval History*, 216–22, 238–9 with n. 72 on p. 239.

[25] For the oath as the basis of a covenant, see Mettinger, *King*, 302.

[26] The covenants between God and Noah can be understood in terms of a "contractual relation." On "contractual relation," see Mettinger, *King*, 302.

Hereby Moses is reminded of the covenant-making in Sinai, which resembles that of Noah. Not only the setting is similar, a mountain, but also the date, "this month," and the swearing of an oath in connection with the establishing of a covenant. The reason for the oath also seems to be a parallel to Noah's oath, namely not to consume any blood, and this becomes even clearer through the passages that follow (*Jub.* 6:12–13). The sprinkling of blood gives an allusion to Noah's use of blood as atonement during his primary sacrifice after his disembarkation (*Jub.* 6:2). In this case the blood is sprinkled on the Israelites and appears to be a sign of confirmation of the covenant. Furthermore, the sprinkling of blood may perhaps also be understood here in terms of atonement, that is the atonement of the people.[27] Why the blood should not be consumed is because the "spirit" or "vital force" is in the blood (*Jub.* 6:7).[28] The blood is allowed to be used in connection with offerings (*Jub.* 6:14). Based on this one may perhaps conclude that the blood, that is the life, is seen as something that adheres to God. Thus just as Noah imitated God when establishing a covenant, Moses apparently imitated Noah. What may further underline the parallel is the small word "too"[29] in the beginning of the last quoted passage where it says: "you, too, . . . make a covenant" (*Jub.* 6:11).

One can ask if the sudden change of focus, to Moses and his time, in reality should be understood as a double addressing, that is to even later generations and then perhaps to the generation in the time of *Jubilees*. What makes this probable is the way the commandments are said to be kept "for all times," "for all time" and "forever," which are expressions frequently found in this context (*Jub.* 6:11–14). And this gets further stressed by a "halakhic"[30] utterance indicated by a formulaic phrase, which reads as follows: "Now you command the Israelites,"[31] and it

---

[27] See also the following passage, *Jub.* 6:14, where there seems to be a link between the use of blood and forgiveness.

[28] Eiss, "Wochenfest," 171–2, has argued that not consuming blood due to the covenant could perhaps be understood as a sign of separation just like circumcision (*Jub.* 15:26, 28).

[29] "Jubilees" (Wintermute) has "also," whereas in *Jubiläen* (Berger), nothing similar can be found. In *Jubilees* (VanderKam), there is no comment to this word in the text-critical apparatus.

[30] The purpose in using this term is only to stress the fact that in this passage a commandment is given, that is an instruction or "law," see furthermore *Jub.* 6:14.

[31] For further examples of this formulaic expression—with some minor differences—probably indicating halakhah, see e.g. *Jub.* 2:26; 6:20, 32; 15:28; 30:11;

continues: "not to eat any blood so that their name and their descendants may continue to exist before the Lord our God for all time" (*Jub.* 6:13). These kinds of phrases are found on several occasions throughout *Jubilees* in connection with more instructional or legalistic passages, and seemingly extend the group of addressees.

Thereafter we are for a short moment brought back to the Noah story by the mentioning of the symbol of the everlasting covenant. The bow in the sky[32] shall serve as a symbol of no more floods ruining the earth (*Jub.* 6:15–16). One can rightly ask why I present this lengthy discussion about the covenants of God, Noah and Moses. How does this relate to Shavuot? These are good and appropriate questions, and the answer as well as the link to Shavuot can be found precisely in the passage following the one with the bow. The browsing through the different covenants serves as a background to this passage, namely to the crescendo (*Jub.* 6:17):

> For this reason it has been ordained and written on the heavenly tablets that they should celebrate the festival of weeks during this month—once a year—to renew the covenant each and every year.

Here we find the first mentioning of the festival of weeks in *Jubilees* and also a general explanation of it. Apart from this, a reference is again found to "this month," presumably the third month, since no other month has occurred in this chapter. This is the same month as for the covenants just mentioned (*Jub.* 6:1, 4, 10–11). The most interesting thing is that this passage reveals the cause for the celebration, namely as a festival for the purpose of *renewing* the covenant annually. And this is a unique statement, since it seems to be the earliest explicit reference in the ancient sources to an interpretation of this festival in terms of a

---

33:13; 41:26; 49:15, 22. Also the reference to "heavenly tablets" at times apparently does indicate halakhah, see García Martínez, "Heavenly Tablets," 255–8, and Nickelsburg, *Jewish Literature*, 74–5, both rendering examples. On "heavenly tablets", cf. further n. 34.

[32] van Ruiten, *Primaeval History*, 247, 250, states that the festival can be seen as a sign of the covenant, despite the bow in the sky (*Jub.* 6:15–16). I would, however, modify this interpretation and suggest the following: whereas the bow in the sky is the sign of God's covenant, the festival is the covenantal sign of God's counterpart (*Jub.* 6:17).

covenant renewal.[33] This general explanation is further given heavenly authorization by the reference to the heavenly tablets.[34] The festival is even given the oldest possible roots, since *Jubilees* states that this festival had already been observed "in heaven from the time of creation" (*Jub.* 6:18). And thereby the apparently new meaning of the festival is turned into an old one.[35] Thereafter we learn—and this I take as crucial passages for the present paper—that Noah and his sons celebrated it. After the death of Noah it was perverted by his sons, since they consumed blood (*Jub.* 6:18). Abraham and his sons were the next to observe it. Then it was no longer remembered, but finally a renewal took place on Mount Sinai (*Jub.* 6:19).

Again we find Moses confronted with a halakhic part, introduced by the formulaic phrase: "Now you command the Israelites" (*Jub.* 6:20). What then follows seems to be the answer to several underlying questions and one almost gets an association to something like a Haggadah for Shavuot. Firstly, the response to the assumed question "when" shall we celebrate it? The answer is: annually during one day in this month, that is the third month (*Jub.* 6:20, 22; see *Jub.* 6:1 for the date), however no exact day is mentioned.[36]

Secondly, we get an answer to "why" shall we observe it? The obvious responses are, because it is a commandment (*Jub.* 6:20–2) and furthermore: "because it is the festival of weeks and it is the festival of

---

[33] de Vaux, *Ancient Israel*, 494.
[34] The term "heavenly tablets" derives from the Enochic literature (*1 En.* 81:1–10), see further Boccaccini, *Beyond*, 88–90. Davenport, *Eschatology*, 10 with n. 5, detected two different traditions within the heavenly tablets. This is in line with Davenport's view maintaining different redactions within *Jub.*, see pp. 10–18, in the above mentioned volume. The redaction theories suggested for *Jub.* have mainly been rejected. García Martínez, "Heavenly Tablets," 243–60, states that the term "heavenly tablets" may be systematized into five different groups. The relevant references for the present purpose are found within the fourth group, categorized as "The Calendar and Feasts," 251–5, which contains regulations about feasts and calendars not found in the biblical texts. For VanderKam's classification, see *Book of Jubilees*, 90. VanderKam, *Book of Jubilees*, 90–3, further puts attention to the fact that the meaning of the terms "heavenly tablets" and "testimony" at times seem to coincide. Ulfgard, *Sukkot*, 162.
[35] See further Noack, "Pentecost," 84, *Pinsedagen*, 100.
[36] Regarding a specific weekday for the festival Eiss, "Wochenfest," 168, is certain that *Jub.* 6 vv. 20 and 22, refer to a Sunday. Cf. however the text-critical apparatus to *Jub.* 6:22 in *Jubilees* (VanderKam), where it is stated that according to the Ethiopic text the reference to a Sunday is not plausible.

firstfruits," a twofold festival (*Jub.* 6:21). Here something gets added, apart from being a festival of the covenant, it is apparently also understood as a festival of the firstfruits. The combination of the festival of weeks and firstfruits can also be found in the biblical sources (cf. Exod 34:22a; Num 28:26a).[37] There is no specification in this passage about the kind of firstfruits, but perhaps one may assume some type of firstfruits that were ripe during the third month.

As for the title, festival of weeks, something further may be noted. The Hebrew unpointed form, שבעות, gives rise to at least two associations, namely to שָׁבֻעוֹת ("weeks") and שְׁבֻעוֹת ("oaths").[38] Since nothing is said specifically about the counting of the seven weeks, which is the case in the biblical sources (Lev 23:15–16; Deut 16:9–10), the Hebrew unpointed word hereby becomes open to different interpretations, which may also be the purpose. One only has to think of the oaths, which were included when the covenants by Noah and Moses were established.[39] No oaths are, however, mentioned in the last quoted passage (*Jub.* 6:21), but they may, so to speak, be included in the association that comes with the unpointed Hebrew form.

A further association or word-play can also be hiding in the above mentioned Hebrew word, namely the figure of "seven," שֶׁבַע.[40] The fig-

---

[37] In the calendrical pericope in Numbers about the day of the firstfruits and the festival of weeks (Num. 28:26–31), a reference is also made to atonement through a goat (v. 30). The reference to atonement is reminiscent of the primary sacrifice of Noah after his disembarkation (*Jub.* 6:2).

[38] "Jubilees" (Wintermute), the text-critical apparatus n. f. to *Jub.* 6:17, prefers—despite the text-critical comment that the Ethiopian word means "weeks"—to "reflect the ambiguity of an unpointed text" by translating: "the feast of Shebuot;" Kraus, *Gottesdienst*, 77, sees it as "Fest der Eide;" Testuz, *Idées*, 146–9, esp. 148, understands it as the festival of oaths ("La Fête des Serments"). VanderKam, "Weeks," 896, comprehends the title to be "*šābuôt*" ("weeks") and not "*šĕbuôt*" ("oaths"), but counts on the possibility of a word-play between Shavuot and Shevuot. I find VanderKam's suggestion plausible. An understanding in terms of a word-play, has been suggested earlier by, e.g. van Goudoever, *Biblical Calendars*, 64, and Jaubert, *Notion d'alliance*, 104.

[39] Eiss, "Wochenfest," 165–6, 171–2.

[40] Otto, "שֶׁבַע," 1020–1, however denies any etymological connections between "seven" and "oath." Still, in *Jub.* seven is a prominent and often used figure (for references in *Jub.*, see n. 41), thus I think that at least on the level of connotations there may possibly be a connection, see also Gen 21:27–32. Note the location for this covenant, Beer-sheba (Gen 21:31–2), a place often referred to in *Jub.* and at times also in connection with this festival. It is rendered in, e.g. *Jub.* 22:1 as "Brun-

ure of seven seems to have an eminent position within this source,[41] and it is a figure expressing fullness.[42] It would not be surprising if the figure of completeness also underlies the understanding of this festival as the festival of festivals, since this is apparently how it was understood by *Jubilees*.[43] A festival that even originates in heaven!

Let us return to the implied questions, and the third one: "how do we know it is legitimate to celebrate the festival?" The answer is given in a passage that reads as follows: "I [that is, the angel of presence communicating with Moses] have written (this) in the book of the first law in which I wrote for you that you should celebrate it" (*Jub.* 6:22).[44] Thus there can be no doubt about the legitimacy of the festival, since God is to be found behind the angel and the first law, which is *Jubilees*' own term for the Pentateuch.[45]

And finally: "how is it to be celebrated?". In other words: is there a hint at any rites or procedures in these passages? Not surprisingly sacrifices are mentioned, but the regulations are apparently to be found in the first law, if the following expression: "I have told you about its sacrifice" (*Jub.* 6:22), should be understood as a reference to it. Furthermore, the oaths connected with the covenant could also be mentioned in this context as a special feature or mark of the festival (cf. *Jub.* 6:10–11).

Before we continue, just a short reflection about *Jubilees*' own time and the assumed addressees, and the understanding of the festival. Not surprisingly, plenty of questions remain, despite the analysis and discussion. Questions to which no answers can be found. For example: where

---

nen des Schwures," *Jubiläen* (Berger), or "the well of the oath," *Jubilees* (VanderKam), and the same translation, "the Well of the Oath," is also found in "Jubilees" (Wintermute).

[41] See, e.g. *Jub.* 3:17; 4:13, 29; 6:18; 7:39; 11:10; 12:16; 17:15; 20:1; 22:26; 24:1; 34:2; 41:21; 42:23; 47:1.

[42] Otto, "שֶׁבַע," 1013–16.

[43] For references on being the main festival, see n. 2.

[44] However, it is not clear out of the context which biblical texts are referenced. Shavuot is described in connection with calendars in the biblical sources, i.e. in Exod 23:16a; 34:22a; Lev 23:15–21; Num 28:26–31, and Deut 16:9–12, 16–17. García Martínez, "Heavenly Tablets," 252, sees in *Jub.* 6:22 "a direct allusion to" Lev 23:15. How the allusion is to be understood, is not further elaborated, and therefore lacks a convincing argumentation.

[45] Davenport, *Eschatology*, 11, n. 7; García Martínez, "Heavenly Tablets," 252; VanderKam, *Book of Jubilees*, 12; Wintermute, "Jubilees," 38.

was the festival to be celebrated among the coming generations? In the case of Noah and Moses, the setting was a mountain. But how about the future? Nothing is said that it should always be celebrated on, or in relation to a mountain, but one cannot help thinking of Zion.

Jubilees sees its own Second Temple period rather darkly. God presents glimpses into the future for Moses and says: "They will forget all my law, all my commandments, and all my verdicts. They will err regarding the beginning of the month, the Sabbath, the festival, the jubilee, and the decree" (*Jub.* 1:14; cf. *Jub.* 6:32–8). But seemingly, after the dark times, a bright future will arise when the people will come back to God and "[t]hey will become a blessing, not a curse" (*Jub.* 1:16). This is most probably an allusion to the curses and blessings mentioned in Deuteronomy (Deut 26:16–19; 27:11–28:69 [27:11–29:1 NRSV] that is, when the obligations connected with the covenant are mentioned. Those who keep the covenant are guaranteed blessings. Furthermore, God reveals to Moses that there will be a new temple (*Jub.* 1:17). In a way this means that the present situation is depraved both with regard to the festivals, as well as to the Second Temple. Still, *Jubilees* is hoping for a prosperous future for the people, if they only separate themselves from the present threat, namely the Hellenistic culture, which apparently has tempted some.[46]

Back to the present text. How about the reason for connecting the festival to this text? The main point of this chapter in *Jubilees* seems to be something else that cannot be found within the biblical sources. It goes without saying that the "invention" concerns the interpretation of the festival,[47] namely the renewal of the covenant.[48] Since both the Noah story, as well as the event in Sinai are associated with the covenant theme, this most likely is the reason or incitement for *Jubilees* to attach this festival to the present chapter. Apparently, it is important to *Jubilees* to state that this is an extremely old festival, which was even

---

[46] Boccaccini, *Beyond*, 92–8.
[47] Noack, "Pentecost," 84, *Pinsedagen*, 100.
[48] In the Hebrew Bible there are two references to a covenant setting and the third month, namely Exod 19–24 and 2 Chr 15:10–15. None of these texts is found within a calendar, and moreover none of the texts refer to a festival. They may, however, have inspired the dates for the festival in *Jub*. Jaubert, *Notion d'alliance*, 105, suggests that an annual rite to renew the covenant may have old roots, but she admits that it is difficult to come to a definite conclusion about this, and even more difficult to obtain a date for such a rite.

celebrated in heaven, further by Noah and the patriarchs,[49] and also a festival in accordance with the word of God. All this effort to stress the ancient background of the festival and to legitimize it, may in fact point to the opposite.[50] It may be something totally new that is being commanded, stemming from the time of *Jubilees*. If so, we are thus witnessing an inauguration of a new meaning being added to the festival, and this despite *Jubilees*' concern for preserving old traditions.

Jub. 14:1–20: Abram and the Festival

The most elaborated descriptions of this festival are found within the Abraham cycle,[51] that is the stories in *Jubilees* associated mainly with Abraham,[52] despite the far greatest part of *Jubilees* being concentrated on the Jacob story.[53]

The first of the episodes, connected to the festival, starts off on the first day in the third month and is found in *Jub.* 14.[54] Abram—since this occurs before the changing of his name—is comforted by God when he asks about offspring. He is promised as many as the stars and he believes (*Jub.* 14:1–6). The introduction of the story is almost a parallel to the account found in the biblical sources, with one main excep-

---

[49] Cf. Lohse, "πεντηκοστή," 48, who points out that *Jub.* gives the festival a higher status through its celebration by the patriarchs and that they should further be seen as examples to future generations to copy their behaviour, i.e. to observe the festival. These antiquarian tendencies in *Jub.* have also been noticed by Endres, *Biblical Interpretation*, 3; VanderKam, "Jubilees, Book," 1032, and Wintermute, "Jubilees," 38.

[50] See further Noack, "Pentecost," 84, who states that "[i]t cannot be decided whether the book is right in claiming that the celebration of the feast as a covenant festival was already an old practice when the book was written, or if it is a completely new one. For our present purpose, however, it may suffice to observe that the book is convinced that, to contemporary Judaism as a whole, this is a new aspect of the feast."

[51] In the Abraham cycle the associations to the festival are found in *Jub.* 14:1–20; 15:1–14; 16:1–4, 10–14 (cf. 15:21); 17:1 (the festival is not explicitly mentioned), and 22:1–6.

[52] For a disposition of *Jubilees*, see e.g. Wintermute, "Jubilees," 35.

[53] See further ibid., 36.

[54] Also *Jub.* 15:1–14 could have been discussed, but for the present purpose only the first text about Abraham and the festival has been chosen. The text dealt with in this paragraph has its counterpart in the Hebrew Bible in Gen 15:1–21.

tion: the date, that is the mentioning of the first day in the third month (*Jub.* 14:1). The reference to this month is a reason to be on the alert.[55]

In the next passage the story continues with God promising Abram the land of the Canaanites, eternally. Additionally God also guarantees he will be the God of Abram and his offspring (*Jub.* 14:7). This guarantee is an extension not found in the biblical story. There are also some expansions associated with favourite themes of *Jubilees*. One of these, again concerns a date, namely a date two weeks later when the story continues. There has been no shift of month, which infers a reference to the middle of the month of main interest (*Jub.* 14:10).[56] The setting here is a covenant making,[57] namely Abram and the covenant, which apparently was established "[o]n that day" (*Jub.* 14:18), a reference not found in the biblical sources. No change has been made with regard to the date, thus it seems safe to suggest that it refers to the same date as recently mentioned. On that day a covenant was made promising the land to the future generations of Abram (*Jub.* 14:18).

This covenant is obviously to be understood as an imitation of the one Noah made (*Jub.* 6:10), since it says: "we concluded a covenant with Abram like the covenant which we concluded during this month with Noah" (*Jub.* 14:20).[58] But how about the festival? So far we have

---

[55] There are both direct and indirect references to the third month, which may be connected with the festival, see *Jub.* 6:1, 10, 11, 17, 20, 22; 14:1, 10, 18, 20; 15:1, 21; 16:13; 17:1; 28:15; 29:5, 7; 44:1, 3, 5, 8.

[56] For references to a date around the middle of the third month and which may be associated with the festival, see *Jub.* 14:10; 15:1, 21; 16:13; 28:15; 29:7; 44:3, 5, 8.

[57] *Jub.* has a preference for connecting covenants with this month, see *Jub.* 1; 6; 14; 15. de Vaux, *Ancient Israel*, 494, states that "the Book of Jubilees . . . puts all the covenants it can discover in the Old Testament (from Noah to Sinai) on the day of the feast of Weeks." Also *Jub.* 29 may be added, despite no mentioning of a covenant. Instead we here find a mutual agreement: "Jacob swore to Laban and Laban to Jacob" (*Jub.* 29:7). In the biblical sources there is an explicit reference to a covenant, ברית, in this context (Gen 31:44), see also VanderKam, *Book of Jubilees*, 65.

[58] In this verse the date is specified to "[d]uring this night," which most likely is a reference to the same occasion as in *Jub.* 14:18. Cf. the text-critical apparatus to *Jub.* 14:20 in *Jubilees* (VanderKam), where "day" apparently has good support also in *Jub.* 14:20. The reason for choosing "night" is, however, articulated as follows: "It [day] may be original, though «night» is preferable because it differs from v 18 where «day» appears." To me this comment makes no sense. Instead "day" also in *Jub.* 14:20 would have suited the context better. Both *Jubiläen* (Berger) and "Jubilees" (Wintermute), retain the same word in *Jub.* 14:18 as well as in *Jub.* 14:20: "Tag" respectively "day."

found no hint of a festival. Still there is a clear link. There is not only a reference to the covenant in the recently quoted passage, but also in the following, an explicit mentioning of Abram renewing the festival: "Abram renewed the festival and the ordinance for himself forever" (*Jub.* 14:20).[59] This is probably an allusion to the commandment in *Jub.* 6. In this ordinance or commandment the following was stated: firstly, to observe the festival, which was specified as the festival of weeks. Secondly, it should be celebrated in the third month, and thirdly the purpose was "to renew the covenant" annually (*Jub.* 6:17).[60]

Thus this concluding passage in the Abraham cycle touches upon several passages in *Jub.* 6. And even if an explicit title for the festival is not found in the present chapter, it seems safe to conclude that the reference is to the same festival as in the referred chapter. Still, a further comment may be added. The mentioning of Abram renewing the festival in this chapter and in fact the whole text about God's covenant with Abram, also serves as a confirmation. A confirmation of the statement in *Jub.* 6:19, where it said that Abraham observed this festival. Furthermore, the renewing of the festival included a covenant renewal (*Jub.* 14:20; cf. *Jub.* 6:17),[61] which did in fact take place in the third month.[62] Thus the above mentioned statements are indeed verified. But how about the reason for adding the festival in this text? This was most probably because of the covenant setting already found within the biblical sources.

Jub. 22:1–6: Isaac and the Festival

As previously noted several times, the passages tend to open by a certain date. Also the current text, in *Jub.* 22, begins similarly by referring to among all others a certain jubilee and year, but a day and a month are not mentioned (cf. *Jub.* 22:1). However, we are again placed in a festive context. The text under scrutiny is an expansion when compared to the biblical sources.

What about the festive context then? Isaac and Ishmael are visiting their father Abraham. The reason for the visit is to observe "the festival

---

[59] Also "Jubilees" (Wintermute), has "renewed," and so does *Jubiläen* (Berger), "erneuerte."

[60] A reference to *Jub.* 6:20–2, would be anachronistic, since it is directed to Moses and the generations to come.

[61] Jaubert, *Notion d'alliance*, 102.

[62] VanderKam, *Book of Jubilees*, 49.

of weeks," here explained as being "the festival of the firstfruits of the harvest" (*Jub.* 22:1). Thereby we get a precision of the firstfruits, namely as being connected with the harvest.[63] Another thing to be noted is that this is the only time in the patriarchal stories when the two titles are rendered together. This also indicates that the titles may be used interchangeably.[64] Furthermore, we get proof of Isaac and also Ishmael celebrating the festival. But it is obvious that Isaac is seen as the main actor, and the one carrying out the festival (*Jub.* 22:3–4).[65]

In this text we find one of the most elaborate descriptions of the festival, and this gives us a unique opportunity to "participate" in the festival. Not surprisingly sacrifices are mentioned. Isaac prepares both a burnt offering as well as a "peace offering,"[66] which were offered on presumably the same altar in Hebron that Abraham used when his covenant was established (*Jub.* 22:3; cf. *Jub.* 14:10–11). It is also stated that Isaac made a "joyful feast" (*Jub.* 22:4).

The one and only time a woman is explicitly referred to as being involved in the festival celebrations is in this very chapter. The woman in question is Rebecca.[67] Both in the Bible[68] as well as in *Jubilees* she is given an eminent position.[69] Also in this text she is no passive incidental character, but plays an active part. She bakes "fresh bread" and thereby

---

[63] Cf. also *Jub.* 15:1: "the festival of the firstfruits of the wheat harvest;" *Jub.* 16:13: "the festival of the firstfruits of the harvest." It is only in *Jub.* 44:4 that the title diverges a bit more: "the harvest festival—the firstfruits of grain." Even if the titles differ slightly, it seems safe, based on the context, to conclude that the references are to the same festival.

[64] This means that each title may be connected to either one or both of the festival aspects, i.e. to the covenantal aspect and/or to the agrarian aspect. See further *Jub.* 15:1–14, where "the festival of the firstfruits of the wheat harvest" is connected with a covenant setting.

[65] For further comments, see n. 72.

[66] According to the translation in *Jubilees* (VanderKam), cf. also here the text-critical apparatus to *Jub.* 22:4, where it says that it literally ought to be translated "a sacrifice for safety;" *Jubiläen* (Berger) has "ein Heilsopfer," and the literal translation to *Jub.* 22:4 is given in n. a) in the text-critical apparatus as "Ein Opfer für Rettung;" "Jubilees" (Wintermute), renders it as "a thank offering."

[67] Halpern-Amaru, *Empowerment*, 137, who asserts that Rebecca is the only matriarch in *Jubilees* who has been portrayed with additional material if compared to the biblical sources.

[68] Meyers, "Her Mother's," 43–4.

[69] Halpern-Amaru, *Empowerment*, 37–40, 55, 84, 90; VanderKam, *Book of Jubilees*, 114.

uses "new wheat"[70] (*Jub.* 22:4). The reference to new wheat may among all others, be an indication of a date, perhaps even to the third month when the wheat may have been ripe.

The question is whether the fresh bread should be regarded as belonging to a rite in connection with the festival. It seems as if the expression in this context to "the firstfruits of the land," which Jacob is instructed by his mother to take to Abraham, may be understood as a reference to the bread (*Jub.* 22:4). It is possible that the bread in relation to the present festival may be an allusion to Lev 23 (vv. 15–21), where the festival is described. Perhaps more precisely an allusion to the description of the elevation offering, which consists of two loaves of bread and is referred to as "לחם הבכורים," "the bread of the firstfruits" (Lev 23:20a). But admittedly, we do not know the amount of bread brought by Jacob. Still, there seems to be some similarity to the text in Leviticus. Then we learn that Abraham is to consume it and "bless the Creator of everything" (quotation from *Jub.* 22:4, see also v. 6). Especially the reference to Abraham and him performing a blessing, may be a hint of a further rite connected with this festival.[71]

Let us now remind ourselves of the statement in *Jub.* 6:19 where it was reported that the patriarchs observed the festival. In the case of Isaac we can note that he indeed celebrated the festival, here rendered with its two different names, which apparently should be understood as equivalents. The date is not given explicitly, but the reference to the festival as well as to the firstfruits, that is, the new wheat, could point to

---

[70] "Wheat" is the term preferred here by *Jubilees* (VanderKam); "Jubilees" (Wintermute), has "grain." It is interesting to note that in *Jubilees* (VanderKam) the terms "wheat" and "grain" are applied contrary to "Jubilees" (Wintermute), see e.g. also the following texts: *Jub.* 15:1 and 44:4. *Jubiläen* (Berger), does not in any single case specify the kind of grain in connection with the festival, cf. *Jub.* 15:1; 22:4; 44:4. In the Hebrew Bible in Exod 34:22a an explicit reference to "wheat" (חטים) is found in connection with the festival: וחג שבעת תעשה לך בכורי קציר חטים, "and you shall keep the festival of weeks, the firstfruits of wheat harvest." There are only two instances in the Hebrew Bible (Lev. 23:16b and Num 28:26a) where the mentioning of "offering of new grain," or literally "new offering" (מנחה חדשה), can be found and this in calendars connected to the festival, see further Jaubert, *Notion d'alliance*, 101. See also *Jub.* 15:2 where "a new sacrifice" is mentioned and further *Jub.* 44:4 where Jacob had to celebrate the festival with "old grain" because of the famine, which is most likely to be understood tacitly that under normal circumstances "new grain" would have been used. See furthermore the comment on *Jub.* 44.

[71] See also Testuz, *Idées*, 147.

the third month. Last but not least, how about the covenant renewal in connection with the festival that was mentioned in *Jub.* 6:17? The answer must be negative, since no reference is made to it. However, what does the use of Abraham's altar imply? This may be a vague connection to a covenant, but nothing is explicitly rendered. Then the question remains why this festival and more precisely the agrarian aspect, that is the firstfruits, is emphasized within this text. My suggestion is that an answer may be found on a symbolic level, namely the fact that Isaac himself was regarded as a firstfruit, even born on this festival (*Jub.* 16:13). Furthermore, he was the one who made it possible for the covenant to continue. This may also be a hint of a covenant, however not of a covenant renewal.[72]

Jub. 44:1–8: Jacob and the Festival

Within the Jacob cycle there are usually three episodes that are connected with the festival.[73] In the third and last one found in *Jub.* 44,[74] we find Jacob in doubt as to whether or not he should go down to

---

[72] But cf. e.g. Endres, *Biblical Interpretation*, 40–5, and VanderKam, *Book of Jubilees*, 56, who interpret *Jub.* 22 against a covenantal setting. They also argue that Abraham and Jacob are in focus in this chapter. According to my opinion one has to divide *Jub.* 22 into at least three major sections to sharpen the picture. The first section, *Jub.* 22:1–6, where the main part of the festival is carried out by Isaac, who here clearly stands out against Ishmael; the second section, *Jub.* 22:7–9, where the blessing of the Creator is being performed by Abraham; and the third section, *Jub.* 22:10–30, where Abraham blesses Jacob. The following question may be a help to retaining the focus of the present paper: which are the rites of the festival according to *Jub.* 22? Obviously the first section of the chapter is substantial, and perhaps also the second part. As for the last portion, the blessing of Jacob, one can ask whether this really is a rite belonging to the festival? The answer must be left open. Endres and VanderKam state that there are connections to the covenant within this blessing, but does this suffice to be understood as a covenant renewal? Still, the crucial issue remains, namely where do we find the actual covenant renewal, since we are here just witnessing a *blessing*? To sum up: covenant aspects may well be reflected through the blessing, but in my opinion there is no covenant renewal actually taking place in *Jub.* 22. Cf. furthermore the covenants and covenant renewals in *Jub.* 6, 14 and 15.

[73] Apart from the episode being analyzed in this paragraph, *Jub.* 44:1–8, the following two episodes are often related to the festival: *Jub.* 28:15 (the naming of Judah) and *Jub.* 29:5, 7–8 (a feast is held for Laban by Jacob). Even if the events in these two episodes take place on the fifteenth of the third month, no reference to the festival can be noted.

[74] The text in this paragraph has its equivalent in the Hebrew Bible in Gen 46:1–6.

Egypt to Joseph (*Jub.* 44:2–3). Also in this case the expansions, if compared to the biblical sources, contain interesting information. Not surprisingly, we find an exact date in this account as well. In the introduction to this chapter we can read how Jacob left Hebron[75] on the first day of the third month and on the seventh day he sacrificed "to the God of his father Isaac" (*Jub.* 44:1). He waits another seven days hoping for a vision, which may inform him what to do. It would then have been the fourteenth of the third month (*Jub.* 44:3).

Now comes the central part with regard to the present study—not found in the biblical sources. We learn that Jacob observed "the harvest festival," explained as "the firstfruits of grain" (*Jub.* 44:4; cf. Exod 23:16a: חג הקציר בכורי מעשיך, "the festival of the harvest, of the firstfruits of your labour"). This title reminds us for example, of *Jub* 22:1, where the festival of the firstfruits of the harvest was mentioned.[76] And truly Jacob has already been mentioned in connection with the festival in that chapter, but in contrast to *Jub.* 22, he is here himself accomplishing the festival. No exact date is given, but in two of the following passages the sixteenth is mentioned (*Jub.* 44:5, 8). This is also the day when Jacob leaves for Egypt after having received comforting words from God (*Jub.* 44:5–6, 8).[77]

Why did Jacob leave on the sixteenth? A possible answer would be, because it was the day after he had celebrated the festival. And therefore a suggestion to the fifteenth as the date for the festival is plausible.[78] Furthermore, this would be in accordance with the main part of the texts in *Jubilees* where the festival is connected with the middle of the

---

[75] Following the suggestion by *Jubilees* (VanderKam) to read "Hebron," see also the text-critical apparatus to *Jub.* 44:1. Cf. *Jubiläen* (Berger), who has "Haran," but see the text-critical apparatus n. a) to *Jub.* 44:1, where a somewhat cryptic comment is given: "Das ist wohl Haran (=Hebron)," and "Jubilees" (Wintermute), who also has "Haran", but in the text-critical apparatus n. a. to *Jub.* 44:1 gives the following remark: "Haran is apparently a corruption."

[76] Cf. also *Jub.* 15:1 "the festival of the firstfruits of the wheat harvest;" *Jub.* 16:13 "the festival of the firstfruits of the harvest." In *Jub.* 22:1 both of the titles are rendered: "the festival of weeks (this is the festival of the firstfruits of the harvest)." See also n. 63.

[77] Cf. *Jub.* 1:1, where the revelation of God to Moses on Mount Sinai also takes place on the sixteenth in the third month, see further Potin, *Pentecôte*, 125.

[78] Eiss, "Wochenfest," 168; van Ruiten, *Primaeval History*, 249; Testuz, *Idées*, 149; VanderKam, *Book of Jubilees*, 80, who mentions that *Jub.* 44 presents a unique opportunity "to determine the exact date for" the festival, "Weeks," 896.

third month.[79] Thus we can conclude that even if it was not celebrated by Jacob on exactly the fifteenth, it was at least celebrated in the middle of the third month.

But how about the celebration of the festival? The name preferred in this context is "the harvest festival," further defined as "the firstfruits of grain" (*Jub.* 44:4).[80] As we have noticed in *Jub.* 22, Rebecca baked bread of new wheat, which was seen as firstfruits (*Jub.* 22:4). So perhaps the grain thought of could be wheat (cf. Exod 34:22a), which may have been ripe by the third month and thus possibly could have served as firstfruits. And also a further thing may be noted. It is explicitly mentioned that Jacob used "old grain" (*Jub.* 44:4). This implies that no *new* grain could be found. Thus we can conclude that new grain, perhaps new wheat, ought to be used when celebrating the festival.

What is the reason then for mentioning the festival? Seemingly, to stress the seriousness of the ongoing famine in the land, which may be illustrated by the following quotation: "because in all the land of Canaan there was not even a handful of seed in the land" (*Jub.* 44:4).[81] Apparently, Jacob could not have celebrated the festival properly, since preferably new grain should have been used. So the mentioning of precisely the harvest festival fits well with the biblical theme of food shortage and the Joseph story. Thereby, the harvest festival becomes a splendid illustration of a critical situation and perhaps further supports the legitimization of going down to Egypt.[82] In addition a note concerning the use of the title: just as Isaac was regarded as a firstborn, so was Jacob. Perhaps this is a further reason here as well, on a symbolic level for why exactly the firstfruits are mentioned; namely because of Jacob, who was a successor and guarantor for the continuation of the covenant.

Let us in conclusion, also in this case, check whether the statements in *Jub.* 6, vv. 17 and 19, hold true for Jacob. Firstly, since we concluded

---

[79] For references to the date, see nn. 55 and 56.
[80] "Grain" is here in accordance with the translation in *Jubilees* (VanderKam), whereas "Jubilees" (Wintermute) has "wheat." For further comments, see n. 70.
[81] See also God's words to Noah in *Jub.* 6:4, where God among all others promised that "seedtime and harvest would not cease." Anyhow, this appears to be exactly what has happened according to *Jub.* 44, since there had been nothing to harvest. But now when this severe situation has come about, there is still a place for Jacob and his family to move to. A new rescue campaign will be conducted on dry land—not on an arch—and it will be a protected journey to Egypt (*Jub.* 44:5–8).
[82] See *Jubiläen* (Berger) and the text-critical apparatus n. a) to *Jub.* 44.

out of the Isaac episode that both of the titles for the festival are interchangeable, we can give a positive response to Jacob indeed celebrating the festival. And this is true even if only the more agrarian features of the festival were mentioned. Secondly, we assumed the date to be in the middle of the third month, perhaps even on the fifteenth. Thirdly, however, no covenant renewal was explicitly reported and thus we reach a negative conclusion as regards this criteria of the festival. Even if there may be a vague link to a covenant through Jacob, the successor of the covenant, this is not sufficient for interpreting the festival as an occasion of covenant renewal.

Conclusions

The purpose of this survey was to answer three questions. Two of them have been dealt with during the analyses and the aim was here to answer how the festival was described in each text and why there was a reference to it. Firstly, the festival was apparently described as both the festival of weeks as well as the festival of firstfruits in the different texts. These titles are to be understood as being interchangeable. Secondly, the reason for the application of the festival in each text.[83] In these chapters there are three reasons to be found, of which some are met more than once in the texts. Firstly, as a result of a covenant setting, secondly, because of a famine, and thirdly due to an interpretation on a symbolic level with regard to firstfruits.

Since I have argued that all of the patriarchs observed the festival, thus the statement in *Jub.* 6:19 seems, but just seems, to be verified. There is however, also a reference to a covenant renewal in *Jub.* 6:17 as a feature or criteria of the festival. A covenant renewal was only recorded in the case of Abraham. *Jubilees* remained silent in the case of the two other patriarchs and a covenant renewal; this despite the mentioning of the festival. Thus the assertion in *Jub.* 6:19 that the patriarchs observed the festival must partly be falsified, since the texts analyzed on the one hand certainly showed the patriarchs observing the festival, but on the other hand no explicit reference to a covenant renewal could be

---

[83] Cf. also *Tg. Ps.-J.* that connects Passover with events in Genesis in Bengtsson, *Passover*. An assumption may be that *Tg. Ps.-J.* is an example of another tradition, where it was important to promote the Passover.

pointed out in the cases of Isaac and Jacob. Still the data obtained is important, as will soon be shown.

What now remains is the third question, that is on a synthetic level to try and grasp what kind of mechanisms can be found behind the understanding of the festival. In other words to discover the theological and ideological considerations which most likely are to be interpreted in light of the contemporary society. Two aspects are central: first, why was it important to state that above all, the patriarchs celebrated the festival and secondly, why was a new meaning added to this festival? What could have been the "trigger"?

In the first chapter of 1 Maccabees there is an interesting text—also noted by others[84]—that deserves to be quoted in this connection: "In those days[85] certain renegades came out from Israel and misled many, saying, 'Let us go and make a covenant with the Gentiles around us, for since we separated from them many disasters have come upon us'." (1 Macc 1:11). In a further verse it is stated that they "abandoned the holy covenant" (1 Macc 1:15a). According to 1 Maccabees there seems to have been some who longed for a "paradise lost," where there had been no separation among people.

In this Hellenistic crisis *Jubilees* holds the contrary opinion. Firstly, there was never such a time when there was no separation. *Jubilees* here gives the perfect examples: Noah and all the patriarchs already observed, for instance the festivals. This was no new practice due to the Mosaic covenant. Secondly, the "paradise" is for those who keep the covenant. Since, the covenant was in danger, this could also have promoted the authorship and the community behind *Jubilees* to claim a covenant renewal annually. A covenant renewal that was made old, that is pre-Mosaic, through the recorded practice by at least Abraham (*Jub.* 14:20). Thus in a way *Jubilees* can be seen as a response to the situation referred to in 1 Maccabees.

The authorship behind *Jubilees* seems further to have been more than aware of the former history of the people; the exile and the reason for this catastrophe. A reason that was promoted in the post-exilic time, namely because of the transgression of the commandments and the

---

[84] Cf. further the documentation brought together by VanderKam, *Book of Jubilees*, 139–41, "Origins and Purposes," 20–2, and to which this conclusive section is partly indebted. See also Davenport, *Eschatology*, 13 with n. 4.

[85] Referring to the time of Antiochus IV Epiphanes (175–164 B.C.E.).

covenant. *Jubilees* may have wanted to prevent a similar catastrophe, therefore the advice to renew the covenant once a year may have served as a good safeguard against such a transgression. Thereby regularly reminding the people of their obligations and also of the blessings that would come out of it (cf. *Jub.* 1:16 and see also the discussion about curses and blessings above).

One last question: why was the Shavuot, the twofold festival, chosen for such a renewal? Since the authorship or producers of *Jubilees* were eager to keep to tradition, it is not surprising that they attached a new meaning to something old, a way of re-using or recycling. The two other pilgrimage festivals, Passover and Sukkot, were already so to speak "occupied" by additional interpretations connected with the Exodus event. In passing: *Jubilees* itself is also marked by the Exodus event, since it starts off in Sinai and the covenant making, but traces this tradition to pre-Mosaic times; the reasons for this have already been presented. A further note may be added to why this festival was chosen as an occasion for covenant renewal. There is good reason to assume that the Hebrew name of the festival שָׁבֻעוֹת, "weeks," and a word-play on the word שְׁבֻעוֹת, "oaths," which are intimately connected with the covenant, played a significant role. And the possible relation to the number "seven," שֶׁבַע, expressing fullness, which emphasized the festival as the foremost one in *Jubilees*. These associations could also have supported the choice of this festival specifically.

The priest-oriented authorship behind *Jubilees* was apparently not interested in mixing in Hellenistic ideas. Their message was to the people as a whole. Still, their concern for the correct calendar and for the correct cult probably forced them to distance themselves both from the corrupt calendar that was in use, and consequently also from the temple cult, which was affected by this calendar.

Thus, I will finally return to what I promised in the beginning, namely to the title of my paper. In this respect the title "No Second Temple—No Shavuot?" makes sense. To *Jubilees* the Second Temple was no temple, but does this also imply no Shavuot? Yes, in a way, since it was perhaps not seen as properly celebrated because of the wrong calendar and maybe the lack of the covenant aspect. If it was not correctly observed in the temple, where may it then have been celebrated? Could it at some stage perhaps, have been in a synagogue?

Bibliography

Bengtsson, P. Å., *Passover in Targum Pseudo-Jonathan Genesis. The Connection of Early Biblical Events with Passover in Targum Pseudo-Jonathan in a Synagogue Setting*. Stockholm: Almqvist & Wiksell, 2001.

Berger, K., ed. *Das Buch der Jubiläen*. JSHRZ 2, Lief. 3. Gütersloh: Mohn, 1981.

Boccaccini, G., *Beyond the Essene Hypothesis. The Parting of the Ways between Qumran and Enochic Judaism*. Grand Rapids: Eerdmans, 1998.

Davenport, G. L., *The Eschatology of the Book of Jubilees*. Leiden: Brill, 1971.

Eiss, W., "Das Wochenfest im Jubiläenbuch und im antiken Judentum." Pages 165–78 in *Studies in the Book of Jubilees*. Edited by M. Albani, *et al*. Tübingen: Mohr Siebeck, 1997.

Endres, J. C., *Biblical Interpretation in the Book of Jubilees*. Washington: Catholic Biblical Association of America, 1987.

García Martínez, F., "The Heavenly Tablets in the Book of Jubilees." Pages 243–60 in *Studies in the Book of Jubilees*. Edited by M. Albani, *et al*. Tübingen: Mohr Siebeck, 1997.

Goudoever, J. van, *Biblical Calendars*. Leiden: Brill, 1959.

Halpern-Amaru, B., *The Empowerment of Women in the Book of Jubilees*. Leiden: Brill, 1999.

Jaubert, A., *La notion d'alliance dans le judaïsme aux abords de l'ère chrétienne*. Paris: Éditions du Seuil, 1963.

Kraus, H.-J., *Gottesdienst in Israel. Grundriß einer Geschichte des alttestamentlichen Gottesdienstes*. 2nd ed. München: Kaiser Verlag, 1962.

Le Déaut, R., "Šāvūʿōt och den kristna pingsten i NT." *SEÅ* 44 (1979): 148–70.

Lohse, E., "πεντηκοστή," Pages 44–53 in *TDNT* 6. Edited by G. Friedrich. Grand Rapids: Eerdmans, 1980 [1968].

Mettinger, T. N. D., *King and Messiah. The Civil and Sacral Legitimation of the Israelite Kings*. Lund: Gleerup, 1976.

Meyers, C., "'To Her Mother's House.' Considering a Counterpart to the Israelite Bêtʾāb." Pages 39–51 in *The Bible and the Politics of Exegesis. Essays in Honor of Norman K. Gottwald on His Sixty-Fifth Birthday*. Edited by D. Jobling, et. al. Cleveland: Pilgrim Press, 1991.

Nickelsburg, G. W. E., *Jewish Literature between the Bible and the Mishnah. A Historical and Literary Introduction*. Philadelphia: Fortress Press, 1987 [1981].

Noack, B., "The Day of Pentecost in Jubilees, Qumran, and Acts." *ASTI* 1 (1962): 73–95.

—, *Pinsedagen. Litterære og historiske problemer i Acta kap. 2 og drøftelsen af dem i de sidste årtier: Festskrift udgivet af Københavns universitet i anledning af Hans Majestæt Kongens fødselsdag 11. marts 1968*. Copenhagen, 1968.

Otto, E., "שֶׁבַע *šæba* שְׁבוּעוֹת *šābûʿôt*." Pages 1000–27 in *ThWAT* 7. Edited by H.-J. Fabry and H. Ringgren. Stuttgart: Kohlhammer, 1993.

Potin, J., *La fête juive de la pentecôte. Étude des textes liturgiques*. Vol. 1. Paris: Cerf, 1971.

Ruiten, J. T. A. G. M. van, *Primaeval History Interpreted: The Rewriting of Genesis 1-11 in the Book of Jubilees*. Leiden: Brill, 2000.

Testuz, M., "Les idées religieuses du Livre des Jubilés." Ph.D. diss., Université de Paris, 1960.

Ulfgard, H. *The Story of Sukkot. The Setting, Shaping, and Sequel of the Biblical Feast of Tabernacles*. Tübingen: Mohr Siebeck, 1998.

VanderKam, J. C., *Textual and Historical Studies in the Book of Jubilees*. Missoula: Scholars Press, 1977.

—, "The Origin, Character, and Early History of the 364-Day Calendar: A Reassessment of Jaubert's Hypotheses." *CBQ* 41 (1979): 390–411.

—, "The Putative Author of the Book of Jubilees." *JSS* 26 (1981): 209–17.

—, *The Book of Jubilees*. Translated by James C. Vanderkam. Leuven: Peeters, 1989.

—, "Jubilees, Book of." Pages 1030–2 in *ABD* 3. Edited by D. N. Freedman, et al. New York: Doubleday, 1992.

—, "Weeks, Festival of." Pages 895–7 in *ABD* 6. Edited by D. N. Freedman, *et al.* New York: Doubleday, 1992.

—, "Biblical Interpretation in *1 Enoch* and *Jubilees*." Pages 96–125 in *The Pseudepigrapha and Early Biblical Interpretation*. Edited by J. H. Charlesworth and C. A. Evans. Sheffield: JSOT Press, 1993.

—, "The Origins and Purposes of the *Book of Jubilees*." Pages 3–24 in *Studies in the Book of Jubilees*. Edited by M. Albani, *et al.* Tübingen: Mohr Siebeck, 1997.

—, *From Revelation to Canon. Studies in the Hebrew Bible and Second Temple Literature*. Leiden: Brill, 2000.

—, *The Book of Jubilees*. Sheffield: Sheffild Academic Press, 2001.

de Vaux, R., *Ancient Israel. Its Life and Institutions*. Grand Rapids: Eerdmans, 1997 [1961].

Wintermute, O. S., "Jubilees: A New Translation and Introduction." Pages 35–142 in *The Old Testament Pseudepigrapha. Volume 2: Expansions of the 'Old Testament' and Legends, Wisdom and Philosophical Literature, Prayers, Psalms, and Odes, Fragments of Lost Judeo-Hellenistic Works*. Edited by J. H. Charlesworth. New York: Doubleday, 1985.

23
Qumran and the Synagogue Liturgy

Daniel K. Falk

THE TWO FOCI THAT DOMINATE the synagogue liturgy as we know it are Scripture and communal prayer.[1] But determining when the synagogue liturgy came to take this shape remains a tantalizing puzzle. By the first century C.E. the reading of Torah is well attested as a dominant function in synagogues, but the evidence for communal prayer is much more difficult.[2] In pre-70 sources about synagogues, there is a puzzling silence about prayer. The strongest evidence for prayer as an important element in synagogues of the Second Temple period is the widespread use of the term *proseuche* ("place of prayer") for Jewish places of assembly in the Diaspora.[3] But this evidence is equivocal at best, and implies nothing about the nature or status of prayer. For Judea there is no evidence at all. Does the virtual silence in pre-70 sources about prayer in synagogues indicate that institutionalized prayer, which became a hallmark of the synagogue was a novel development only after the destruction of the temple?[4] Or is the origin of the synagogue prayers to be sought elsewhere in pre-70 Judaism? How are we to explain the relationship between synagogue prayers and prayer practices developing in the Second Temple period? What is the relationship between synagogue prayer and the temple?

For answering these questions, the Dead Sea Scrolls are probably the most instructive source, because they present a remarkably rich store of evidence for liturgical prayer. Here at least there are collections of prayer texts for various designated occasions and indications of a detailed cycle of liturgical prayer such as is otherwise only clearly attested after the de-

---

[1] See Elbogen, *Jewish Liturgy*, 15–84.
[2] Levine, *Ancient Synagogue*, 135–59.
[3] Ibid., 153–5.
[4] This position is argued most forcefully by Fleischer, "Beginnings."

struction of the second temple. Moreover, these prayers contain numerous similarities to the synagogue prayers in terms of thematic content, phrasing, times and occasions, types of prayer, and formal features.

There are several surveys that treat Qumran prayer broadly.[5] In this paper, I will limit the discussion to daily public prayer, as this is the most debatable feature of synagogue liturgy in the Second Temple period and the Qumran evidence is most useful. The evidence falls into four categories of prayer practice: recital of the *Shema*, blessings, petitions, and songs of praise. For evaluating the import of such practices in relation to the development of the synagogue liturgy, it is necessary to consider the practices holistically rather than merely comparing individual features, and to give weight to parallels without biblical precedence.[6]

Recital of the Shema

There are two pieces of evidence for the daily recital of the *Shema* at Qumran. A calendar of appointed times in the *Rule of the Community* (1QS IX, 26–X, 8) specifies two times of daily prayer: sunrise and sunset. From the following passage with strong allusion to Deut 6:4–9, it appears that this twice daily prayer included at least recital of the *Shema*.

> With the arrival of day and night, I will enter into the covenant of God. And with the departure of evening and morning, I will recite his laws. In their existence I will place my boundary without turning back. I will declare his judgement concerning my sins, and my transgressions are before my eyes as an engraved statute ... as soon as I stretch out my hand or my foot, I will bless his name; as soon as (I) go out or come in, to sit down or rise up, and while I recline on my couch, I will praise him. I will bless him with the lifting up of the utterance of my lips in the assembly of men ... (1QS X, 10–14)

---

[5] Chazon, "Historical Implications," "Hymns," and "Psalms"; Nitzan, *Qumran Prayer*; Schuller, "Prayer"; Falk, *Prayers*; idem, "Prayer."
[6] See Maier, "Zu Kult," 543–7; Falk, *Prayers*, 17–20. Also Fleischer, "Essential Nature"; Zahavy, "New Approach"; Hoffman, *Beyond the Text*, 1–19.

The discovery of numerous *tefillin* at Qumran supports this conclusion.[7] Several other Jewish texts from the Second Temple period regard recitation of the *Shema* and the use of *tefillin* to be a Mosaic ordinance, thus attesting that this was a well-established practice, at least in private prayer (*Let. Aris.* 158–60; Philo, *Spec.* 4.141–2; and Josephus, *A.J.* 4.212–3).

Beyond Deut 6:4–9, however, it is not clear that the biblical passages recited would necessarily have been identical to that assumed already in the earliest rabbinic literature, namely Deut 6:4–9, Deut 11:13–21, and Num 15:37–41 (see *m. Ber.* 2:2).[8] Indeed, several passages preserve recollections that the Decalogue was at one time part of the recitation, and they cite different reasons why this practice was abandoned,[9] indicating that this was probably a live liturgical dispute. This makes it all the more likely that there is at least a kernel of accurate recollection in *m. Tamid* 5:1 when it depicts priests reciting the Decalogue with the *Shema* in a morning service. There is no indication that this was a universal practice, but several pieces of evidence from Egyptian sources probably reflect the Decalogue included with the *Shema*.[10]

In the light of these considerations, it is likely that the phrase "I will recite his laws" in 1QS X, 10 points to a practice of reciting the Decalogue with the *Shema*.[11] That nine of the *tefillin* found at Qumran

---

[7] See Milik, "Tefillin," 34–79; Schiffman, "Phylacteries," 675–77, and references there.

[8] Reif notes that the rabbinic evidence seems to suggest that the third passage (Num 15:37–41) was not adopted until much later than the first passage (Deut 6:4ff.), and apparently "had not yet acheived an equal status in the second century CE" (*Judaism*, 83). See further Kimelman, "Shemaʿ," 12–13, and n. 14.

[9] Reasons include: because "heretics" (*minim*) claimed that only the Decalogue was revealed by God to Moses; so as not to burden the people with prolonged recitation; because "these words" that are subject to daily recitation (Deut 6:6–7) refers specifically to Deut 6:4-9 not the preceding Decalogue in Deut 5 (*b. Ber.* 12a; *y. Ber.* 1:8, 3c [lines 30–33; = *TLI* 1:4, III.F]; *Sipre Deut* 34). Note: for ease of locating passages cited from the Jerusalem Talmud, I provide in addition to the standard reference both line numbers to printed editions and a reference to the English translation in the *Talmud of the Land of Israel* (*TLI*).

[10] Philo's overall argument in *Spec.* 4.137–42 assumes that the Decalogue is included in the *tefillin* and the *Shema*, as also probably in *Let. Aris.* 158–60; a close link between the Decalogue and the *Shema* is also attested by the Nash Papyrus (2nd c. B.C.E.) and the preface to LXX Deut 6:4.

[11] Kimelman disagrees, on the grounds that evening recitation of the Decalogue is otherwise unattested, and furthermore "no reference to the law is made three lines

include the Decalogue among their passages points in the same direction.[12]

Benedictions

There are four sources of evidence for a practice of daily recitation of blessings at Qumran: a scroll consisting of morning and evening blessings (4Q503 *Daily Prayers*); a few fragments of another scroll that mentions morning and evening blessings (4Q408); a passage in the *Rule of the Community* that prescribes nightly corporate blessings (1QS VI, 7–8); and another passage in the *Rule of the Community* that ascribes blessings to appointed times of sunrise and sunset (1QS X, 10–14). It is not at all clear that all or any of these relate to the same phenomenon. In the following discussion I will focus primarily on the one source for which both occasion and content are explicit, 4Q503.

Daily Prayers (4Q503) is a collection of blessings to be recited by the congregation sunset and sunrise each day of a month.[13] The short blessings (4–6 lines each) display a remarkably regular form:

1. Statement of setting/ritual:
   "In the fifteenth of the month in the evening they shall bless"

---

later where it says, 'as soon as (I) go out or come in, to sit down or rise up, and while I recline on my couch, I will cry out to him'" (Kimelman, "Shema‘," 70, n. 211). I do not regard the objections as compelling. If the Decalogue was recited with the *Shema*, there is no rationale for this to be restricted to the morning, even though *m. Tamid* 5:1 only describes a morning service. The logic for its recitation (taken up and refuted in *Sipre Deut* 34) would apply equally to morning and evening. In any case, the evidence of the *tefillin* (see below) indicates that practice at Qumran may have been distinctive. The second objection does not take account of the poetic nature of the passage.

[12] 1Q13, 4Q128, 129, 134, 135, 137, 139, 140, 142. It seems that this was a disputed practice: Tov has observed that the *tefillin* found at Qumran fall generally into two main groups (Tov, "*Tefillin*," 44–54). Those *tefillin* that include passages—such as the Decalogue—not in accordance with rabbinic regulations display a distinctive "Qumran" scribal practice. The remaining *tefillin* form a group lacking these scribal distinctives and more closely corresponding to rabbinic norms concerning content.

[13] Baillet, "Prières quotidiennes," 105–36; Olson, "Daily Prayers," 235–85; Falk, *Prayers*, 21–57; Davila, *Liturgical Works*, 208–38; Chazon, "Function," 217–25.

"And when the sun rises to shine on the earth they shall bless"
2. Speech formula: "they shall recite, saying"
3. Opening benediction: "Blessed be the God of Israel who has done . . ."
4. Body of prayer: short, related to occasion
5. Closing benediction:[14] "Blessed be You, God of Israel, You did . . ."
6. Concluding rubric (response?): Peace be on you, Israel

In these blessings, the community praises God especially for the creation and daily renewal of the lights, consciously united with angelic praise. Other motifs include God's election of Israel from the nations, the covenant, God's gift of knowledge, God's kingship, glory and holiness, God's acts of deliverance, rest and delight, festivals, and priesthood. It appears that the prayers are tailored to both the time of recital (evening, morning) and occasion (Sabbath, festival)—that is, prayers that fall on a Sabbath or a festival include appropriate motifs. Although this collection seems specific to the first month of the year (Nisan), Chazon notes that the essential character of these as daily prayers celebrating the daily renewal of lights suggests that these are somehow part of a regular cycle of daily prayers.[15]

By whom were these prayers to be recited? As Chazon has noted, these are explicitly prayers of the congregation, with no indications of group differentiation.[16] Thus, Maier's argument on the basis of style and content that these were prayers for priests is unlikely.[17] Still, I consider it likely that the concluding rubric "Peace be on you Israel" may represent a responding blessing of peace over the congregation by a priest or

---

[14] Due to the fragmentary nature of the scroll, it is not certain that all of the prayers had a closing benediction as well as an opening benediction, and in several cases this seems unlikely. On the whole, it seems probable that the usual pattern was for a prayer to have both. See Falk, *Prayers*, 36–37 and Nitzan, *Qumran Prayer*, 70.

[15] Chazon, "Function," 220. Contrast Maier, "Zu Kult," 579. On the allusions to Passover, see Falk, *Prayers*, 29–35.

[16] Chazon, "Function," 222; e.g., "they will bless" and "answering they will say" in the introductory formula; "we his holy people exalt . . .," frg. 11 3, cf. 4 9; "[and we] the sons of your covenant, we praise [your name]," frg. 9 3; first-person plural speech throughout.

[17] Maier, "Zu Kult," 579.

group of priests.[18] In any case, whether or not these prayers were composed by priests or with priestly interests, and whether or not they were followed by a responding priestly blessing, for our purposes the most significant datum is that these are prayers of the congregation. The highly formulaic content and limited vocabulary are what one would expect of congregational prayers.[19]

The question of provenance is more difficult. Evidence from content and calendar is ambiguous. Although some scholars believe it was probably not composed by Qumran sectarians because of a lack of distinctive features, I am led on the basis of some formal similarities with other sectarian prayers from Qumran to think it possible that they did originate in or close to the *Yaḥad*.[20] On the basis of paleography, the scroll dates around the early first century B.C.E. (100–75 B.C.E.).[21]

These prayers have evoked comparison above all with the benedictions accompanying recital of the *Shema* in the synagogue liturgy. Before making comparison, let us consider the early evidence for the na-

---

[18] Falk, *Prayers*, 53–4. Chazon ("Function," 222) rejects this proposal, noting that in contrast to the opening instruction for communal prayer, there is no instruction that the final blessing on Israel is a priestly response. She prefers to explain the awkward transition from address of God to address of the congregation as a "standard formulaic conclusion" following the main blessing. This might be possible, but there is no true analogy. Chazon refers to use of the phrase "Peace be on Israel" (שלום על ישראל) in the Psalms of Ascent Ps 125 and 128, some synagogue inscriptions, and synagogue prayers such as the *Kaddish* and final *Amidah* benediction. But in these examples the formula is consistently in the third person. This merely reinforces the oddity of our text in which the key feature is the second person address to Israel following a prayer addressed to God. Moreover, even the third person phrase "peace be on Israel" in the Psalms of Ascent is suspected by some scholars of reflecting a priestly response (e.g., Allen, *Psalms 101–150*, 167, following Mowinckel). Also, the last benediction of the *Amidah* was sometimes referred to as the "priestly blessing" and was originally a repsonse to the blessing by the priests (Elbogen, *Jewish Liturgy*, 27). Moreover, Heinemann has argued that second person address to the congregation in prayer was distinctive of priestly blessings (Heinemann, *Prayer*, 104-11). In addition to my arguments elsewhere, it should also be noted that of the Qumran prayers that have concluding benedictions, most are followed by "Amen, Amen," which is almost certainly a response (*Words of the Luminaries* [4Q504, 506]; *Festival Prayers* [4Q507, 508, 509+505, 1Q34-34bis]; *Songs of the Sage* [4Q511]). In 4Q503, the rubric "Peace be on you, Israel" takes the place of "Amen, Amen" in these other prayers.

[19] See Nitzan, *Qumran Prayer*, 321–55, esp. 346, 348, 353.

[20] See Chazon, "Historical Implication," 271–3, 282, n. 68; Falk, *Prayers*, 22–29.

[21] Baillet, "Prières quotidiennes," 105–36.

ture of these benedictions.[22] The basic ritual is assumed in the Mishnah: blessings recited twice a day with the morning and evening *Shema*, specifically two blessings before the *Shema* and one after, with a fourth added to the evening recital (*m. Ber.* 1:4). The Babylonian Talmud assumes knowledge of the thematic content of these benedictions, formal structure, and at least some specific wording (*b. Ber.* 11a–12a).

1. The first benediction before the morning *Shema* is known as "Creator of Light" (*Yotzer 'Or*) in both Talmuds (*b. Ber.* 11b; *y. Ber.* 1:8, 3c [lines 39–40; = *TLI* 1:4, III.M]), and consists of praise to God as creator and renewer of the luminaries. From *b. Ber.* 11a–12a is known not only this basic thematic content, but also that it had both an opening benediction "who forms light and creates darkness, who makes peace and creates all things" and a concluding benediction ending "who creates the luminaries."[23] This is essentially the same as the short form of the "Creator" blessing in Saadia Gaon's prayerbook.[24]

> Blessed be you, LORD our God, king of the universe
> who forms light and creates darkness
> who makes peace and creates all things
> In his great mercy he gives light to the earth
> and those who dwell on it
> (In) his goodness he renews every day the work of creation.
> Blessed be YHWH creator who forms the luminaries

2. The second benediction was called the "Benediction of the Torah" in the Jerusalem Talmud (*y. Ber.* 1:8, 3c [line 39; = *TLI* 1:4, III.L]).[25]

---

[22] See Ellbogen, *Jewish Liturgy*, 15–24; Hoffman, *Canonization*, 24–49; Kimelman, "Šěma'," 73–86; Kimelman, "Shemaʿ Liturgy," 12–79.
[23] Ellbogen, *Jewish Liturgy*, 17–18.
[24] Davidson, Assaf, and Joel, *Siddur Saadja*, 13.
[25] This occurs in a discussion as to the identity of the one blessing recited before the *Shema* by the priests. I follow the judgment of Elbogen that ברכת תורה here refers to what is the second benediction before the *Shema* in the synagogue service (Elbogen, *Jewish Liturgy*, 19), rather than the benediction over the study of Torah, as is sometimes maintained (e.g., Finkelstein, "Development," 39–40; Zahavy, *Berakhot*, p. 45 [III.L]). In favor of the latter position is the argument that in this passage it is followed by recitation of the Decalogue, which may be the basis of the reasoning. In favor of the former position, this statement in the Jerusalem Talmud is spoken in the authority of R. Samuel, and in *b. Ber.* 11b, R. Samuel's authority is cited in favor of the identification as the "With great love" benediction. Since the content of

This name provides a précis of its essential thematic content: thanksgiving for the gift of Torah/revelation. In the Babylonian Talmud, it is known by two variants of its opening line, "With great love" and "With everlasting love" (*b. Ber.* 11b). In the blessing as it has come down to us (and intimated in the opening line reported in the Babylonian Talmud), the gift of Torah is in the context of God's loving choice of Israel and the covenant ("who has chosen his people Israel in love").

3. The benediction that follows the *Shema* is known in the Mishnah and Tosefta by its opening line, "True and certain" (*m. Tamid* 5:1; *t. Ber.* 2:1), which points to its function as an affirmation of the *Shema*. In the talmuds, it is known as the "Redemption" blessing (*ge'ullah*) after its main content, which praises God as redeemer of Israel (*b. Ber.* 9b; *y. Ber.* 1:1, 2d [line 64; = *TLI* 1:1, XIV.Q]). This content is related to the third passage of the *Shema*, Numbers 15:37–41, which mentions the Exodus. It is assumed in the debate recorded in *t. Ber.* 2:1:

> One who recites the *Shema* must mention the exodus from Egypt in "True and certain." Rabbi says, "in it one must mention [God's] sovereignty." Others say, "in it one must mention the smiting of the firstborn and the splitting of the sea."

In the Jerusalem Talmud is recorded a resolution by R. Joshua b. Levi (3rd c. C.E.) that all of these should be mentioned, concluding with the benediction "the rock of Israel and its redeemer" (*y. Ber.* 1:9, 3d [lines 69–70; = *TLI* 1:5, IV.D]). The concluding benediction in the prayerbook is the Babylonian form approved by Rava (4th c. C.E.): "blessed are you, Lord, the redeemer of Israel."

4. After the evening *Shema* is added a fourth benediction about God as guardian of Israel.

That this liturgy of blessing accompanying the *Shema* is very ancient is beyond question. The critical question is whether it originated in the Second Temple period or only later. All our direct sources, after all, post-date 200 C.E. For this question, it is crucial that we distinguish between the liturgy as we know it (3 benedictions in the morning, 4 in the evening; relatively stable wording), and the essential nature of the

---

this benediction focuses on the gift of Torah, it is likely that the same benediction is intended in both of these citations of R. Samuel's authority.

liturgy. There can be little doubt that the liturgy as we know it is post-70. The number and arrangement of benedictions were established at least by the end of the Tannaitic period, but there is not a shred of evidence for such an enumeration of blessings pre-70, and into the Amoraic period there continued to be debates reflecting development of themes and wording. Especially interesting in this regard are *t. Ber.* 2:1 and *y. Ber.* 1:9, 3d (cited above) which indicate thematic variety within a general parameter ultimately resolved by combining them. If we may take the rabbinic directives as attempts to establish or affirm a practice, we may identify essential elements of a basic liturgy assumed already by the Mishnah:

> type of prayer: blessings
> time: twice daily, morning and evening in relation to sunrise and sunset
> context: accompanying the *Shema*
> content: general themes related to cycle of luminaries (creation, renewal) and the *Shema* (Torah, knowledge, election, redemption)

This is especially supported by the tradition in *m. Tamid* 5:1 about a prayer service by the priests between the offering of daily sacrifices and the incense offering.

> The officer said to them, "recite a blessing," and they recited a blessing. They recited the decalogue, the *Shema* [Deut 6:4ff.], and the "and it will be if you obey" [Deut 11:13ff.], and the "and he spoke" [Num 15:37ff.]. They blessed the people with three blessings: "True and certain," the "*Abodah*," and the Priestly Blessing. On the Sabbath they added a blessing for the departing course of priests.

Here a practice of reciting blessings in connection with the *Shema* is attributed to temple times. Amoraim of the third century tried to identify the unspecified benediction. Both the Jerusalem and Babylonian talmuds cite the authority of R. Samuel that this was the benediction immediately preceding the *Shema* in the synagogue service.[26] They both mention and refute the opinion that the one benediction might instead have been the "Creator," but the logic in the Babylonian Talmud particularly pursues how best to explain that there is only one benediction preceding the *Shema* whereas in the ritual they know there are two. That third century rabbis perceived continuity but struggled to relate this tradition to contemporary practice reinforces the basic authenticity of the Mishnah report. How seriously is one to regard the identifications of the three blessings with the people mentioned in *m. Tamid* 5:1? Almost certainly at play here is an attempt by tannaim to relate this purported practice to the central liturgical cycle known to them in the synagogue consisting of *Shema* with benedictions (where "True and certain" is the benediction following the *Shema*) and the *Amidah* (which contains both an "Abodah" benediction and a "Priestly blessing"), and so we should not think that we have here attested simply the synagogue benedictions of those names. On the other hand, that it is not brought into closer correspondence suggests the authenticity of at least the broad outlines. That is, we may have here a basically authentic Second Temple tradition of blessings with themes broadly comparable to some in the synagogue liturgy, but not similarly differentiated or amenable to identification.

We need to consider one further element. In the "Creator" blessing known today, there is a liturgical recitation of the heavenly praise (Isa 6:3 combined with Ezek 3:12) known as the *Qedushah*. When the liturgical *Qedushah* originated and how early it was a component of the "Creator" blessing continue to be debated, and the evidence is notoriously difficult.[27] Fleischer has argued that the *Qedushah* in the "Creator" blessing was in the ancient Palestinian rite restricted to Sabbath and festivals.[28] Heinemann accepted this conclusion ("it never became part of the daily order of prayer" in Palestine) but retained the conviction that the *Qedushah* of the "Creator" blessing "is of Palestinian origin and is

---

[26] Referred to as the "Torah benediction" in *y. Ber.* 1.8, 3c [lines 27–28, = *TLI* 1:4, III.B], and as the "With great love" benediction in *b. Ber.* 11b; see the preceding note.

[27] For a good summary of older views, see Werner, "Doxology" and Elbogen, *Jewish Liturgy*. More recently, see Fleischer, "Diffusion"; Heinemann, *Prayer*, 230–4; Spinks, *Sanctus*; Lehnardt, "Gott der Welt," 300–6. For a recent discussion of the Qumran evidence, see Chazon, "*Qedushah.*"

[28] Fleischer, "Diffusion."

probably quite ancient."[29] There is, on the other hand, some early evidence associating the angelic song especially with creation and the daily renewal of the luminaries.[30] Even though it seems impossible to establish whether these in any way support a practice of liturgical use of the *Qedushah* in morning prayer, they would provide a natural context for it.

E. Chazon has shown that 4Q503 *Daily Prayers* resembles the rabbinic "Creator" benediction (*b. Ber.* 11a–12a) "in content, language, form and function."[31] Furthermore, although these prayers do not contain the textual elements associated with the *Qedushah* in the rabbinic liturgy (the angelic acclamation "holy, holy, holy" of Isaiah 6:3 combined with the angelic blessing of Ezekiel 3:12), Chazon demonstrates that they do attest what she regards to be the constituent element of this liturgy, namely "the liturgical phenomenon of human praise with the angels."[32] Thus, she argues that

> 4Q503 witnesses joint [human and angelic] praise in the context of a blessing for the daily renewal of the heavenly lights as found later in the *Qedushah* of the *Yoser* liturgy. 4Q503 also displays additional thematic and linguistic parallels with the *Yoser* blessing in which the *Qedushah* is embedded which suggest some continuity between the two liturgies. These include: the verbs להאיר (to shine) and לחדש (to renew), the practice of mentioning darkness during the morning prayer and light during the complementary evening prayer (מעריב ערבים) and the incorporation of the same, traditional

---

[29] Heinemann, *Prayer*, 230–4.
[30] Job 38:7 (see Septuagint and Targum); *Targum Ps.-J.* Gen 32:27; *L.A.B.* 18:6; 11QPs[a] *Hymn to the Creator* XXVI, 11–12; *2 En.* 15; *3 Bar.* 6–10; *T. Adam* 1–2; *Apoc. Mos.* 7:2; 17:1; *3 En.* 40:1–4 (this last passage associates the angels who recite the *Qedushah* with luminaries and daily renewal). See further on the angelic liturgy Philonenko, "Priere," 225–7.
[31] Chazon, "Historical Implications," 282. See also Schiffman, "Dead Sea Scrolls," 37–40; Nitzan, *Qumran Prayer*, 55.
[32] Chazon, "Qedushah," 7, 12–13. Chazon also finds the "liturgical phenomenon" but not the *Qedushah* verses in Ps 103:2–22; 148; Tobit 8:15; *Jub* 2:21 ("Qedushah," 7, n. 1).

Sabbath and festival themes in the expanded blessings for those holy days.[33]

She draws important implications for the history of the *Qedusha*. Whereas the *Qedushah* is often thought to have originated in the context of merkabah mysticism, and in Palestine its use to have been restricted to Sabbath and festivals, 4Q503 is witness to the basic liturgical phenomenon of the *Qedushah* of the "Creator" blessing (angelic/human praise in context of blessing for creation of lights) in daily use in Palestine as early as the second century B.C.E., not associated with merkabah mysticism. It may also suggest that the *Qedushah* of the "Creator" blessing is earlier in origin than that in the *Amidah*, a point that has often been debated.[34]

These conclusions are sound, but I believe that comparison can be expanded and extended more widely to the essential *Shema* liturgy as a whole as I have traced above. The common elements are as follows. (1) These are benedictions praising God. (2) They are recited twice daily, morning and evening in relation to sunrise and sunset. (3) Taken as a whole (and excluding special Sabbath and festival motifs), the themes reflected in 4Q503 correspond remarkably well to the thematic content of the *Shema* benedictions: creation and renewal of the lights, joint angelic and human praise, revelation and knowledge, election and covenant, and redemption.[35] In other words, these are all motifs related to the cycle of luminaries (creation, renewal) and the *Shema* (Torah, knowledge, election, redemption).

(4) In this context, similarities in language are all the more significant. These occur especially with regard to the motif of light.[36] More particularly, Chazon noted that the benediction in 4Q503 24–25 3–4 הגוים] [ה]גוים אש[ר חֹר] בנו מכול is "virtually identical" with R. Hammuna's (3rd c. C.E.) blessing before the study of Torah: אשר בחר בנו מכל העמים ונתן לנו את תורתו (*b. Ber.* 11b). Of course, election is a common motif, and R.

---

[33] Ibid., 12.
[34] Ibid., 14–16.
[35] The motif of God's kingship is possible but uncertain in 4Q503 (see ff. 33–4, 40–1). Elsewhere, the earliest evidence attests it as a sabbath motif; Judah the Prince advocated its mention in the benediction following the *Shema* (*t. Ber.* 2:1). See Lehnardt, "Gott der Welt."
[36] E.g., renewal of lights 3 2, 29–30 9, 33 II + 35 2; illumination of the earth (להאיר על הארץ) 2 12, 10 1, 48–50 7.

Hammuna's benediction belongs to a different setting, but there is no precise biblical precedent for these two election benedictions, whose exact correspondence probably points to a common tradition of blessing language. Because in 4Q503 this benediction occurs in a prayer for Sabbath, Chazon suggests that election should probably be regarded as a special Sabbath motif, as also attested in *Jub.* 2:19.[37] I suggest, however, that the comparison is even more significant if one considers that the second *Shema* benediction in the synagogue also combines the motifs of Torah and election: "you have chosen us from all peoples and tongues" (ובנו בחרת מכל-עם ולשון) and "who has chosen his people Israel in love." The wording is not as close, but for most prayers wording is still fluid into the amoraic period,[38] and R. Hammuna's Torah blessing would work equally for the benediction preceding the *Shema*. Moreover, as Chazon has noted, the prayers for Sabbath and festivals in 4Q503 are in character daily prayers like the rest with merely the addition of special motifs for the occasion.[39] And in 4Q503, election as a motif is also found in the prayer for the morning of the 6th day (frgs. 7–9) which is certainly not a sabbath, and perhaps in fragments 33–34, also probably not a sabbath.[40] I think it preferable, then, to consider the election blessing in 4Q503 24–25 3–4 as reflecting a motif suitable for a daily *Shema* blessing.

(5) 4Q503 exhibits the use of both opening and closing benediction formulas, analogous to the "long form" for blessings determined by the rabbis, although they do not correspond in precise form.[41] This is the

---

[37] Chazon, "Historical Implications,"278; Chazon, "Sabbath Prayer," 9 and n. 26; Baumgarten, "4Q 503," 402.

[38] See Hoffman, *Canonization*, 4, 36.

[39] Chazon, "Function," 224.

[40] In frgs. 33–34 16, Baillet reads ועלמדנו לגורלנו. But this is part of a closing benediction (*vacat* on following line, and new prayer begins in line 18), which addresses God in the second person in these prayers. Furthermore, the closing benediction of the following prayer (in line 20) refers to God "establishing" (אשר העמדת]). Therefore, I read for line 16 ותעלמדנו לגורלנו "and you es]tablished us for [our] l[ot]" or "for [your] l[ot]" (for analogous language of the people as God's lot, see 1QS II, 2; 1QM XIII, 12; XV, 1; XVII, 6–7).

[41] Chazon, "Function," 221. It is possible that not all the prayers had closing benedictions in addition to opening benedictions, as noted by Nitzan, *Qumran Prayer*, 70, but it seems likely that the usual pattern was to have both. For a catalogue of the prayer formulas in 4Q503, see Falk, *Prayers*, 35–41, cf. 19–20. For detailed discussion of blessing formulas in the Dead Sea Scrolls, see Schuller, "Observa-

earliest known example of the use of opening and closing benedictions, and it is thus important to appreciate the significant degree of uniformity throughout the prayers.[42]

Individually, the similarities listed here might not be significant, but together they relate the two practices holistically to a degree that requires explanation. How are we to account for this? I would propose a hypothesis that 4Q503 may represent daily benedictions to accompany recital of the *Shema*. Admittedly, the evidence is circumstantial: there is no explicit indication of such a function in the scroll itself. The argument is based at this point on a comprehensive web of similarities with a practice of blessings alongside the *Shema*, and especially the inclusion in these daily prayers of motifs extraneous to the renewal of luminaries, but integrally relevant to the *Shema*. Considering the indications that the blessings in 4Q503 accommodate the occasion as well as the time by incorporating sabbath and festival motifs on those days, it would not be surprising to find motifs relevant to the *Shema* included if they were used in conjunction with it.

I will consider some further (still circumstantial) evidence in a moment, particularly with regard to the plausibility of such a suggestion, but first it is important to clarify what I am *not* suggesting in this hypothesis. I am *not* implying *any* sort of equation between 4Q503 and the *Shema* liturgy of the synagogue, nor *any* model of linear development, such as a prototype or precursor. The differences must not be underestimated (and the following is not a comprehensive list): (1) 4Q503 provides only one benediction per occasion instead of a series as with the synagogue *Shema*. (2) The blessings in 4Q503 are different morning and evening as well as each day of the month, with recurring general themes. The *Shema* benedictions are the same every morning and every evening. Over the cycle of prayers in 4Q503, the main themes of the daily *Shema* benedictions are covered. (3) In 4Q503, joint angelic and human praise is celebrated in both morning and evening prayers, whereas the *Qedushah* occurs only in the morning "Creator" blessing.[43] (4) The benediction formulas in 4Q503 do not correspond to rabbinic instructions for the liturgical benediction. (5) The

---

tions," 133–43. On the historical development of rabbinic benediction formulas, see Heinemann, *Prayer*, 77–103.

[42] Falk, *Prayers*, 40.

[43] Chazon notes this as a previously unattested practice ("Qedushah," 12).

final rubric "Peace be on you, Israel" in 4Q503 is unparalleled, and could represent a priestly response.

It seems that there must be contact, but not direct contact. In seeking a plausible context for this, the report in *m. Tamid* 5:1 (cited above) warrants serious consideration. Here is attested a practice from the Second Temple that is not to be identified with the synagogue *Shema* but that is *perceived* to bear some continuity. It is placed in a unique context (priests in the temple) but one that allows the possibility of diverse imitation and influence. If this vague report corresponds even partially to an actual practice by priests, and it provided (by imitation, adaptation, indirect influence) the shared essential character of blessings accompanying the *Shema*, several distinctive features would be explained. (1) The report in *m. Tamid* 5:1—especially the one, unspecified blessing—and the attempts to relate it to the synagogue *Shema* suggest undifferentiated blessing without fixed themes or wording. 4Q503 would reflect the use of a single benediction with varying thematic content among a small lexicon of motifs; the synagogue *Shema* would reflect the crystallization of customary motifs in differentiated blessings.[44] (2) 4Q503 combines in prayers of the congregation the "dignified liturgical style" that suggests to Maier the priestly realm with short and simple content that Nitzan finds a hallmark of popular prayer.[45] (3) The consistent formal structure, and especially the use of opening and closing benedictions without biblical precedent, point to deliberate liturgical shaping and a tradition with which the rabbis show general continuity but divergence in particulars. (4) If the final blessing "peace on you, Israel" in 4Q503 is a priestly response, it would correspond to the "priestly blessing" with which the priests concluded their service in *m. Tamid* 5:1.[46]

---

[44] In support of this, the debate concerning the content of the "redemption" benediction in *t. Ber.* 2:1 implies the existence of various suitable expressions of related motifs; *y. Ber.* 1:9, 3d shows the trend toward combination.

[45] Maier, "Zu Kult," 579; Nitzan, *Qumran Prayer*, 351.

[46] It is widely accepted that the priestly blessing does indeed go back to the temple, and that there is reflection of some awkwardness accommodating it to the synagogue liturgy (Reif, *Judaism*, 85; Hoffman, *Canonization*, 53–5: "the Palestinian communities omitted the actual Priestly Benediction if no priests were available to say it. In such cases only a symbolic priestly recitation occured, by which the lay leader recited the instructions from the biblical narrative" (54)). The concluding peace of 4Q503 *Daily Prayers* may reflect attempt to incorporate the priestly blessing. In the context of *Daily Prayers* it may not have been recited by priests but may

How plausible is it that *Daily Prayers* could be a collection of blessings associated with the *Shema*? The practice of joining blessings to the *Shema* is commonly disputed for the Second Temple period, but besides the claim of *m. Tamid* 5:1, there are two probable pieces of evidence from the Second Temple period.[47] First, in the context of describing daily prayer at sunrise and sunset, with allusions to the recital of the *Shema* and Decalogue in 1QS X, 10–14a, is the statement:

> As soon as I stretch out my hand or my foot, I will bless his name;
> As soon as (I) go out or come in, to sit down or rise up,
> And while I recline on my couch, I will praise to him

Although there is a danger of over-interpreting, the language of blessing (ברך) and praise (רנן; cf. 1QS X, 17 where it is parallel הלל) here probably alludes to the recitation of blessings (of praise) along with the *Shema*. If this is correct, it would provide a plausible context for such blessings in the *Yaḥad*.

Second, it is probable that Josephus also refers to blessings with the *Shema* in *A.J.* 4.212 [Thackery, LCL].

> Twice each day, at the dawn thereof and when the hour comes for turning to repose, let all acknowledge before God the bounties which He has bestowed on them through their deliverance from the land of Egypt: thanksgiving is a natural duty, and is rendered alike in gratitude for past mercies and to incline the giver to others yet to come.

It is clear that he has the *Shema* in mind, since he is expounding Deut 6:4–9 as a Mosaic ordinance to pray twice daily, to wear *tefillin* and set up *mezuzot*. But it can hardly be the biblical passages alone that he describes as "thanksgiving." Moreover, although "deliverance from the land of Egypt" might be seen as an allusion to Num 15:41 (end of the third passage of the traditional *Shema*), this passage merely mentions the deliverance; nothing in the traditional *Shema* passages speaks

---

have been used as a standard closing, as Chazon suggests ("Function," 222; see discussion above). Either way, it is probable that its inspiration was the priestly blessing in the temple.

[47] See Falk, *Prayers*, 113–14; cf. Reif, *Judaism*, 83 and references in n. 69.

properly of the bounties as a result of the deliverance.[48] This is, however, precisely the theme of the benediction immediately following the *Shema* in the rabbinic liturgy, and *m. Tamid* 5:1 also claims that the priests in the temple recited this benediction following the *Shema*. The short form of this blessing recorded in the talmud would very well fit Josephus' description: "We give thanks to you, who delivered us from Egypt and redeemed us from the house of slavery to praise your name."[49] Whether or not Josephus had in mind a blessing with fixed wording, his description best suggests a practice of accompanying the *Shema* with blessing. That he could speak of this as a Mosaic ordinance would imply that this would have to be a reasonably well-established practice before the destruction of the temple, at least in the private prayers of some individuals.[50]

Petitions

Another collection of daily prayers found at Qumran consists of communal petitions, and is entitled *Words of the Luminaries* (4Q504, 4Q506).[51] These too seem to have been intended for liturgical recitation in connection with the interchange of luminaries,[52] but this is a completely different type of prayer practice from that attested in *Daily Prayers*. (1) Unlike 4Q503 which gives 2 short and simple benedictions for each day of a month, this collection prescribes a single long and

---

[48] Moreover, it is not clear that the Num 15 paragraph would have been part of the *Shema* at this time. Its status was less secure than the Deut paragraphs even into the amoraic period (see Kimelman, "Shemaʿ Liturgy," 13). It should be noted, however, that the motif of the benefits of the exodus is found in Deut 6:10–12, immediately following on from the first traditional passage Deut 6:4–9.

[49] *Y. Ber.* 1:9, 3d [lines 57–58; = TLI 1:5, II.D]; *b. Ber.* 14b. This is presented as a means of fulfilling the obligation to mention the exodus in the *Shema* even if the Num 15 passage is omitted from the evening recital.

[50] There is no hint that this is public prayer, and apart from the Dead Sea Scrolls and *m. Tamid* 5:1, all the evidence for recital fo the *Shema* seems to assume a private setting, *viz.*, the home. When Josephus performs the "customary service" with prayer in the morning at the Tiberias *proseuche*, it is possible that this attests recital of the *Shema* in a public setting, but both the content and nature of the prayer are uncertain (*Life*, 294–5; see Binder, *Temple Courts*, 410–11).

[51] 4Q505 is not a copy of *Words of the Luminaries*. See Falk, *Prayers*, 59–61, 156.

[52] As Chazon has argued, the self-title probably refers to recitation of these prayers at sunrise and/or sunset ("Liturgical Document," 57).

elaborate petitionary prayer for each weekday, followed by a song of praise for the sabbath. (2) It is based on a weekly cycle, likely to be repeated throughout the year,[53] rather than monthly. (3) The weekday petitions follow a very consistent form that is fundamentally different than *Daily Prayers*:[54]

(a) a superscription indicates the type of recital and the occasion (e.g., תפלה ביו[ם הרביעי, 3 ii 5),

(b) the prayers begin with an invocation summoning God to remember (זכור אדוני) his holiness or his past dealings with Israel, followed by

(c) an extended historical summary that chronicles Israel's relationship with God and

(d) a petition, concluding with

(e) a benediction and

(f) a response "Amen, Amen."

(4) Given their length and complexity, it seems likely that the petitions of *Words of the Luminaries* were recited by a prayer leader to which the congregation responded "Amen, Amen."[55] In contrast, *Daily Prayers* are congregational prayers, perhaps with a responding priestly blessing of peace. (5) The thematic content is very different. Three components are dominant in the weekday prayers: the recounting of God's past acts of mercy, confession of sin and petition for forgiveness, and supplication for both deliverance and strengthening for the fulfillment of Torah. For the sabbath, there is a hymn that praises God in the third person with doxological language. Its themes of joint human and angelic praise and God's holiness are characteristic sabbath themes, and the use of praise instead of petition on sabbath is consistent with some rabbinic concerns.[56]

Since the one copy (4Q504) dates from around the middle of the second century B.C.E. and the other (4Q506) from the middle of the first century C.E., and the composition lacks any reference to the history or self-perception of the *Yaḥad*, it is likely that *Words of the Luminaries*

---

[53] But cf. Maier, "Zu Kult," 579.
[54] The form is almost identical to that in the *Festival Prayers* (4Q507–9).
[55] Note that there are no rubrics indicating congregational recital as in *Daily Prayers*.
[56] Chazon, "Sabbath Prayer," 5–6.

is pre-Qumran in origin but was copied and used there.[57] It is the earliest example of a collection of daily supplications for physical deliverance not connected with situations of distress,[58] and has thus naturally been compared with the daily petitions of the *Amidah* (= *Tefillah* or Eighteen Benedictions).

The *Amidah* as we know it is a series of 19 petitions recited three times a day, but earlier 18 benedictions recited twice daily.[59] The origin and development of this liturgy has long been debated, and it is unnecessary to rehearse that debate here.[60] What does seem secure is that what we now have is the product of a lengthy process of development incorporating material from diverse times and settings. Many regard a version of the prayer found in the Cairo Genizah (9th c. C.E.) to represent a Palestinian form, and the earliest known of the liturgy as a whole.[61]

The Mishnah presupposes daily recital of the *Amidah* morning and afternoon, apparently to correspond to the times of sacrifice, and an evening recital that appears less well established (*m. Ber.* 4:1). The *Amidah* as known to the Tannaim seems to have general themes, but not fixed wording (*m. Ber.* 4–5). The Mishnah assumes it to be a public liturgy recited by a precentor who represents the congregation, and the congregation affirms each benediction with "Amen."[62] R. Gamaliel II in the late first c. C.E. is given credit for significant efforts at institutionalizing this prayer (*m. Ber.* 4:3; *b. Meg.* 17b), which seem to concern promulgating the *Amidah* as a religious obligation on all Jews, arrangement, and thematic content.[63] But this is instructive for us, because on the one hand, even into the Amoraic period there continue to be debates about specific content, themes, and form. And on the other hand, it is assumed that R. Gamaliel II builds on earlier practice of petitionary prayer. How early does it extend, and what may be regarded as an early expression of the same essential practice?

---

[57] Chazon, "Sectarian Prayer."
[58] Chazon, "Liturgical Document," 108.
[59] Morning and afternoon, corresponding to the times of sacrifice. The addition of a third recital in the evening was debated in the Amoraic period, and the basis of a famous feud between R. Gamaliel and R. Joshua (*b. Ber.* 27b).
[60] For a survey of Jewish liturgical research that highlights the major trends, see Sarason, "Method." On the problems, see Elbogen, *Jewish Liturgy*, 24–54; Heinemann, *Prayer*, 218–27; Hoffman, *Canonization*, 50–5.
[61] For a translation, see Heinemann, *Literature*, 33–6.
[62] Elbogen, *Jewish Liturgy*, 25.
[63] Hoffman, *Canonization*, 50.

Scholars have long noticed texts from the Second Temple period which exhibit strong thematic and terminological similarities with the later *Amidah* benedictions.[64] Although one can trace biblical precedents for individual points of contact, this does not explain the numerous collocations of such motifs and language, especially the remarkable correspondences between the Hebrew hymn following Sir 51:12 to seven or eight of the *Amidah* benedictions with regard to phrasing, ordering, and even prayer form.[65] Heinemann's explanation is widely accepted. This state of affairs

> can only be explained by assuming that a great number of "series of benedictions" like these must have existed in a variety of forms and styles. The "Eighteen Benedictions" which we now possess is to be regarded as only one of these many forms (which ultimately crystallized and became normative), and is itself most likely a combination of several previous "series" of benedictions and petitionary prayers.[66]

Nevertheless, only *Words of the Luminaries* represents a holistic analogue to the Amidah definitely from the Second Temple period. Here one finds thematic and terminological parallels to most of the thirteen intermediate petitions of the *Amidah* in a prayer of the same essential

---

[64] See Heinemann, *Prayer,* 219–20. Besides the hymn following Sir 51:12, other proposed parallels (of varying value) include: Sir 36:1–17 (content, not wording); *m. Tamid* 5:1; the eight benedictions recited by the high priest after reading from the Torah on the Day of Atonement; 2 Macc 1:24–9 (see Goldstein, *II Maccabees,* 178, and my own list of parallels, Falk, *Prayers,* 200–1), Psalms of Solomon (see the critique in Elbogen, *Jewish Liturgy,* 394, n. 7), Pap. Egerton 5 (recently edited by van der Horst, "Neglected Greek Evidence," 278–96, cf. Marmorstein, "Oldest Form"); 1QS 10:8–11:16; 1 Clement (Lightfoot, *St. Clement of Rome,* 1:393–6); Apostolic Constitutions Book 7(Fiensy, *Prayers Alleged to be Jewish,* 129–34; cf. Kohler, "Essene version"). Also, Weinfeld ("Prayers for Knowledge") proposed the existence of a triple petition for knowledge, repentance and forgiveness (*Amidah* #4, 5, 6) that he found reflected in a prayer of Levi (4QTLevi^a), two non-canonical psalms found at Qumran (11QPs^a Plea; 11QPs^a 155 [Syriac Ps III], several hymns from the *Hodayot,* and early Christian catechetical prayers (*Ap. Const.* 8.6.5–7; cf. Col 1:9–14; Eph 1:3–14); in *Words of the Luminaries,* see Chazon, "Liturgical Document," 104–5.
[65] See Marmorstein, "Jesus Sirach," 288.
[66] Heinemann, *Prayer,* 220–1.

form and function.[67] (1) It is likely that *Words of the Luminaries* was for twice daily recital at sunrise and sunset (although possibly just once a day). It also seems that the *Amidah* was originally a twice daily recital.[68] (2) *Words of the Luminaries* is the earliest example of petitionary prayers for public, daily liturgical recital. (3) Probably in both cases, the petitions were recited by a prayer leader with the congregation affirming with "Amen." (4) *Words of the Luminaries* exhibits a consistent use of formulas, including a closing benediction that epitomizes the prayer. This is the earliest attestation of an impulse to frame prayers with stereotyped formulas at the beginning and end, although not yet truly an example of opening and closing benedictions.[69] Moreover, although the specific formulas do not correspond to those of rabbinic liturgical prayers, the form of the concluding benediction is virtually identical to the "missing link" that Heinemann hypothesized between the "biblical pattern" of blessings and the rabbinic liturgical blessings.[70]

Of course the differences are substantial. Most significantly, *Words of the Luminaries* does not have a series of benedictions repeated daily, but one benediction per weekday on a weekly cycle. It would not be accurate to say that *Words of the Luminaries* is an early form of the *Amidah* or even a precursor to it.[71] Nevertheless, these weekday petitions represent the same essential type of prayer practice, and the shared language

---

[67] Nitzan (*Qumran Prayer*, 108) discusses parallels to *Amidah* benedictions #4 (knowledge), #5 (repentance), #6 (forgiveness), #7 (redemption), #8 (healing), #10 (gathering of exiles), and #14 (compassion). On the triple petitions for knowledge, repentance and forgiveness (*Amidah* #4, 5, 6), see further Chazon, "Liturgical Document," 104–5. It could be added that "book of life" (see 4Q504 1–2 VI 14) also appears in the Palestinian version (Cairo Genizah) of the curse against apostates (*Amidah* 12, in a quotation from Ps 69:29) and that the focus on Jerusalem and David in the historical summary for Thursday may imply a (lost) petition for the restoration of Jerusalem and the Davidic dynasty (*Amidah* #14). See Maier, "Zu Kult," 560. In the prayer-book, these are two separate benedictions (14 and 15), but the Cairo Genizah shows that in Palestine these were originally a single benediction.

[68] See n. 59.

[69] Falk, *Prayers*, 79–80; cf. Chazon, Liturgical Document," 12 [English abstract], 100–1.

[70] Falk, *Prayers*, 79–84.; see Heinemann, *Prayer*, 77–103.

[71] Nitzan, *Qumran Prayer*, 110, and n. 68.

goes beyond the common biblical heritage.[72] For example, 4Q504 1–2 II 13 is the earliest attestation of the expression "to implant Torah in our heart," which came to have a standard place during the Tannaitic period in the benediction spoken after the Torah reading.[73] In addition, although the phrase "circumcise the foreskin of our heart" is based on biblical passages (Deut 10:16; Jer 4:4), this is the earliest instance of the petition which appears in similar form in the *Habinenu*, an abbreviated *Amidah*. All this points to a common stream of liturgical tradition, although probably not direct relation.

Psalms and Hymns

The remaining evidence for daily prayer at Qumran can all be classified as psalms or hymns. A hymn fragment (4Q408) praises God for creating morning and evening as times of prayer. A few small fragments remain of a liturgical calendar (4Q334) that prescribes the number of "songs" and "words of praise" to be recited on the evening and morning of specified days of a month. Although this may describe angelic praise analogous to *Songs of the Sabbath Sacrifice*, the idea that human praise mirrors heavenly praise is prominent in the Qumran texts and thus this scroll gives at least indirect support for a practice of morning and evening praise.[74] This is further supported by two of the headings in the *Hodayot* which seem to imply that at least some of these were available for use in daily prayer at sunrise and sunset (1QHa XX, 4–11 [XII, 4–11]; V, 12–14 [frgs. 15 1–3 + 31]).[75] 11QPs[a] *David's Compositions* speaks of "songs" (שיר) of David "to sing before the altar over the whole-burnt *tamid* offering every day, for all the days of the year, 364." This last example contrasts with all the other pointers to times of daily prayer in relation to the luminaries.

---

[72] The following examples are pointed out and discussed by Chazon, "Liturgical Document," 104–5, 167. See also Flusser, "He Has Planted It," and Weinfeld, "Prayers for Knowledge."

[73] It also appears in the Christianized Jewish liturgy of the Apostolic Constitutions (7.26.1–3; 8.6.5–7). Weinfeld, "Prayers for Knowledge," 194; Flusser, "He Has Planted It," 151.

[74] See Falk, *Prayers*, 98–9.

[75] See ibid., 100–3.

Liturgical Cycle

Considering the evidence for daily prayer at Qumran, we find that all of it falls into four basic types: recital of the *Shema* (with Decalogue), blessings, petitions, songs of praise. The material is of diverse character and even origin. Were these used completely independently, or could these diverse prayers have been used in a liturgical cycle? First of all, we may notice that each of these types of prayers are for morning and evening—usually specifically sunrise and sunset. Secondly, a description of the *Yaḥad's* cycle of daily prayers (1QS X, 9–14)[76] seems to allude to four types of prayer for sunrise and sunset:

> 1. Songs of praise:
> "I will sing with knowledge, and all my song (will be) for the glory of God, and the strings of my harp (will be) for the measure of his holiness, and the flute of my lips I will raise as the cord of his judgement

> 2. Recital of the *Shema* and Decalogue:
> "With the arrival of day and night, I will enter into the covenant of God. And with the departure of evening and morning I will recite his laws"

> 3. Blessings added to the *Shema*:
> "as soon as I stretch out my hand or my foot, I will bless his name; As soon as I go out or come in, to sit down or rise up, and while I recline on my couch, I will praise him"

> 4. Supplication/confession of sins:
> "I will declare his (God's) judgement concerning my sins, and my transgressions are before my eyes as an engraved statute . . . I will delight in however he judges me"

Moreover, this "inventory" of prayer accounts well for the various daily prayers found at Qumran, making it plausible that these prayers of diverse nature and origin could have been used in the *Yaḥad* as part of a daily liturgical cycle. At any rate, they provide a reasonably reliable picture of the basic types of prayer used in some way in daily liturgy.

---

[76] See the discussion in Falk, "Qumran Prayer Texts," 115–18, 120–1.

Remarkably, this distinctive combination of prayer types is roughly analogous to the elements of daily prayer in the later synagogue:

1. psalms
2. *Shema*[77] with
3. blessings
4. supplications (*Amidah*)

Thus, both at Qumran and in the later synagogue we find a comparable conglomeration of similar types of prayer from diverse origin combined into a daily liturgical cycle.

Conclusion

The similarities between prayers at Qumran and the synagogue liturgy are too substantial to ignore, especially since these pertain to basic elements of form and content of individual prayers as well as broader aspects of performance, time, and liturgical sequence. How is one to explain them? Apart from the "Qumran" context, there is no evidence for a comparable liturgical cycle. Moreover, it is very difficult to imagine a direct line of development from this one community to the rabbinic prayers. And the similarities do not indeed suggest a direct lineage, but rather that both shared similar influences. Where is a context to explain the apparent shared tradition? Evidence is lacking for the synagogue as a context for comparable traditions of daily prayer in the Second Temple period.

I would suggest that there is one possible context. All the basic practices of daily prayer found both in the Qumran "cycle" and the synagogue liturgy are attested or claimed in the pre-70 period in relation to the temple area, and only there.[78] There is only one setting in the Second Temple period for which daily corporate recital of the *Shema* is attested: a service held by priests in the temple (*m. Tamid* 5:1). This same passage also attests the adjoining of blessings to the *Shema*. Although

---

[77] Rabbinic texts attest that the Decalogue was eliminated from the synagogue service at some point (*m. Tamid* 5:1; *b. Ber.* 12a; *y. Ber.* 1.8, 3c).
[78] See Falk, "Jewish Prayer Literature," 269–92.

this source is late and shows confusion and likely harmonization with the synagogue liturgy, its general outlines are plausible. Likewise, the popular prayers and prostrations of the people at the temple prominently mentioned in several sources (Sir 50; Luke 1:10; Acts 3:1; Josephus, *C. Ap.* 2.196–7; *m. Tamid* 5:1; cf. 2 Macc 1:23–30) is the only setting in the Second Temple period for which daily supplications in a public context may be attested. Furthermore, the songs of the temple singers at the daily sacrifices is the only setting for daily public singing of psalms attested in sources for the Second Temple period, apart from the descriptions of sectarians (Essenes and Therapeutae) by Philo and Josephus. Judging from the descriptions by Ben Sira and others, this was a popular liturgical event with the people, who participated by prostrating themselves and saying their own prayers.[79]

I must hasten to add two qualifications. First, these prayer activities do not belong to the official temple cult, but they are various activities that are carried out for the most part loosely and informally around the temple. What is significant is that the temple provides the locus that attracts these activities because of its perceived status as a place especially appropriate for prayer. In contrast to the remarkable silence about prayer in the pre-70 synagogue, there is significant and consistent testimony about the temple as a place where people prayed. Second, it would not be correct to identify these prayer practices around the temple with either prayers found at Qumran or in the later synagogue liturgy. Neither is there any evidence of a linear development among these.

In attempting to explain these data, I would speculate that the temple may have provided the means of dissemination of various prayer traditions. It was a setting where pilgrims from all locales and social contexts met, and it would be natural to bring home traditions of song and prayer that one encountered. This is not to claim that the temple provided the prototype of synagogue prayers. But certain prayer practices had already developed in public settings as customary institutions around the temple. I would suggest that these may have provided the basic practices and lexicon for the liturgies developed both at Qumran and later in the synagogue.

---

[79] Sir 50:16–21; Luke 1:10; Acts 3:1; *m. Tamid* 7:3–4; cf. 1 Macc 12:11; Josephus, *C. Ap.* 2.193–8; Luke 2:36–8; 18:10; Acts 2:46–7; 5:12–14; 22:17.

Bibliography

Allen, L., *Psalms 1–150*. Waco: Word, 1983.

Baillet, M., "Prières quotidiennes." Pages 105–36 in *Qumrân grotte 4, III (4Q482-4Q520)*. Oxford: Clarendon, 1982.

Baumgarten, J., "4Q 503 (Daily Prayers) and the Lunar Calendar." *RevQ* 12 (1986): 399–407.

Bickerman, E., "The Civic Prayer for Jerusalem." *HTR* 55 (1962): 163–85.

Chazon, E., "A Liturgical Document from Qumran and Its Implications: 'Words of the Luminaries' (4QDibHam)." Ph.D. diss., Hebrew University, 1991 (in Hebrew).

—, "4QDibHam: Liturgy or Literature?" *RevQ* 15 (1992): 447–55.

—, "Is Divrei Ha-Me'orot a Sectarian Prayer?" Pages 3–17 in *The Dead Sea Scrolls: Forty Years of Research. Papers Read at a Symposium Sponsored by Yad Izhak Ben-Zvi at the University of Haifa and at Tel Aviv University March 20–24, 1988*. Edited by D. Dimant and U. Rappaport. Leiden: Brill, 1992.

—, "On the Special Character of Sabbath Prayer: New Data from Qumran." *Journal of Jewish Music and Liturgy* 15 (1992/93): 1–21.

—, "Prayers from Qumran and Their Historical Implications." *DSD* 1 (1994): 265–84.

—, "Hymns and Prayers in the Dead Sea Scrolls." Pages 244–70 in *The Dead Sea Scrolls After Fifty Years: A Comprehensive Assessment*. Vol. 1. Edited by P. Flint and J. VanderKam, with assistance of A. Alvarez. Leiden: Brill, 1998.

—, "The Function of the Qumran Prayer Texts: An Analysis of the Daily Prayers (4Q503)." Pages 217–25 in *The Dead Sea Scrolls Fifty Years After Their Discovery. Proceedings of the Jerusalem Congress, July 20–25, 1997*. Edited by L. Schiffman, E. Tov, and J. VanderKam. Jerusalem: Israel Exploration Society, in cooperation with The Shrine of the Book, Israel Museum, 2000.

—, "The Qedushah Liturgy and Its History in Light of the Dead Sea Scrolls." Pages 7–17 in *From Qumran to Cairo: Studies in the History of Prayer*. Edited by J. Tabory. Jerusalem: Orhot, 1999.

—, "Psalms, Hymns, and Prayers." Pages 710–15 in *Encyclopedia of the Dead Sea Scrolls*. Vol. 2. Edited by L. Schiffman and J. VanderKam. Oxford: Oxford University Press, 2000.

Davidson, I., S. Assaf, and B. Joel. *Siddur R. Saadja Gaon*. Jerusalem: Mekize Nirdamim, 1941 (in Hebrew).

Davila, J., *Liturgical Works*. Grand Rapids: Eerdmans, 2000.

Elbogen, I., *Jewish Liturgy: A Comprehensive History*. Translated by Raymond P. Scheindlin. Jerusalem: Jewish Publication Society/Jewish Theological Society, 1993.

Falk, D., "Jewish Prayer Literature and the Jerusalem Church in Acts." Pages 267–301 in *The Book of Acts in Its Palestinian Setting*. Edited by R. Bauckham. Vol. 4 of *The Book of Acts in Its First Century Setting*. Edited by B. W. Winter. Grand Rapids: Eerdmans, 1995.

—, *Daily, Sabbath, and Festival Prayers in the Dead Sea Scrolls*. Leiden: Brill, 1998.

—, "Prayer in the Qumran Texts." Pages 852–76 in *Cambridge History of Judaism*. Vol. 3. Edited by W. Horbury. Cambridge: Cambridge University Press, 1999.

—, "Qumran Prayer Texts and the Temple." Pages 106–26 in *Sapiential, Liturgical and Poetical Texts from Qumran. Proceedings of the Third Meeting of the International Organization for Qumran Studies, Oslo 1998. Published in Memory of Maurice Baillet*. Edited by D. Falk, F. García Martínez, and E. Schuller. Leiden: Brill, 2000.

Fiensy, D. A., *Prayers Alleged to be Jewish: An Examination of the Constitutiones Apostolorum*. Chico, California: Scholars Press, 1985.

Finkelstein, L., "The Development of the Amidah." *JQR* 16 (1925/1926): 1–43, 127–70.

Fleischer, E., "On the Beginnings of Obligatory Jewish Prayer [Hebrew]." *Tarbiz* 59 (1990): 397–441.

—, "Rejoinder to Dr Reif's Remarks [Hebrew]." *Tarbiz* 60 (1991): 683–8.

Flusser, D., "Qumrân and Jewish 'Apotropaic' Prayers." *IEJ* 16 (1966): 194–205.

—, "'He Has Planted It [i.e., the Law] as Eternal Life in Our Midst'." *Tarbiz* 58 (1989): 147–53.

Goldstein, J., *II Maccabees*. Garden City: Doubleday, 1983.

Hammer, R., "What Did They Bless? A Study of Mishnah Tamid 5.1." *JQR* 81 (1991): 305–23.

Heinemann, J., *Prayer in the Talmud: Forms and Patterns*. Berlin: de Gruyter, 1977.

Heinemann, J. and J. Petuchowski, *Literature of the Synagogue*. New York: Behrman, 1975.

Hoffman, L., *The Canonization of the Synagogue Service*. Notre Dame: University of Notre Dame Press, 1979.

—, *Beyond the Text: A Holistic Approach to Liturgy*. Bloomington: Indiana University Press, 1987.

Horst, P. W. van der, "Neglected Greek Evidence for Early Jewish Liturgical Prayer." *JSJ* 29 (1998): 278–96.

Kimelman, R., "The Šĕma' and Its Blessings: The Realization of God's Kingship." Pages 73–86 in *The Synagogue in Late Antiquity*. Edited by L. Levine. Philadelphia: American Schools of Oriental Research, 1987.

—, "The Shemaʻ Liturgy: From Covenant Ceremony to Coronation." Pages 9–105 in *Kenishta: Studies of the Synagogue World*. Edited by J. Tabory. Bar-Ilan University Press, 1999.

Kohler, K., "The Essene Version of the Seven Benedictions as Preserved in the vii Book of the Apostolic Constitutions." *HUCA* 1 (1924): 410–25.

—, "The Origin and Composition of the Eighteen Benedictions with a Translation of the Corresponding Essene Prayers in the Apostolic Constitutions." *HUCA* 1 (1924): 388–425.

Lehnardt, T., "Der Gott der Welt ist unser König: zur Vorstellung von der Königsherrschaft Gottes im Shema und seinen Benediktionen." Pages 285–307 in *Königsherrschaft Gottes und himmlischer Kult in Judentum, Urchristentum und in der hellenistischer Welt*. Edited by M. Hengel and A. M. Schwemer. Tübingen: Mohr, 1991.

Levine, L. I., ed. *The Synagogue in Late Antiquity*. Philadelphia: ASOR, 1987.

—, *The Ancient Synagogue: The First Thousand Years.* New Haven: Yale University Press, 2000.

Lévi, I., *The Hebrew Text of the Book of Ecclesiasticus.* Reprint. 1904. Leiden: Brill, 1951.

Liebreich, L. J., "The Impact of Neh 9:5-37 on the Liturgy of the Synagogue." *HUCA* 32 (1961): 227–37.

Lightfoot, J. B., *The Apostolic Fathers. Part 1. St. Clement of Rome. Vol. 1.* London: Macmillan, 1890.

Maier, J. "Zu Kult und Liturgie der Qumrangemeinde." *RevQ* 14 (1990): 543–86.

Marmorstein, A., "Jesus Sirach 51:12ff." *ZAW* 29 (1909): 287–93.

—, "The Oldest Form of the 18 Benedictions." *JQR* 34 (1943): 137–59.

Milik, J. T., "Tefillin, Mezuzot et Targums (4Q128–4Q157)." Pages 33–91 in *Qumrân Grotte 4, II (Archéologie et 4Q128-4Q157).* Edited by R. de Vaux and J. T. Milik. Oxford: Clarendon, 1977.

Nitzan, B., *Qumran Prayer and Religious Poetry.* Translated by Jonathan Chipman. Leiden: Brill, 1994.

Olson, D. T., "Daily Prayers (4Q503 = 4QPrQuot)." Pages 235–85 in *Pseudepigraphic and Non-Masoretic Psalms and Prayers.* Vol. 4A of *The Dead Sea Scrolls. Hebrew, Aramaic, and Greek Texts with English Translations.* Edited by J. Charlesworth, et al. Tübingen: Mohr; Louisville: Westminster John Knox, 1997.

Petuchowski, J., "The Liturgy of the Synagogue: History, Structure, and Contents." Pages 1–64 in *Studies in Liturgy, Exegesis and Talmudic Narrative.* Vol. 4 of *Approaches to Ancient Judaism.* Edited by W. Green. Chico, California: Scholars Press, 1983.

Philonenko, M., "Prière au soleil et liturgie angélique." Pages 221–8 in *La littérature intertestamentaire: Colloque de Strasbourg (17–19 octobre 1983).* Edited by A. Caquot, *et al.* Paris: Presses Universitaires de France, 1985.

Reif, S., "On the Earliest Development of Jewish Prayer." *Tarbiz* 60 (1991): 677–81 (in Hebrew).

—, *Judaism and Hebrew Prayer: New Perspectives on Jewish Liturgical History.* Cambridge: Cambridge University Press, 1993.

Sarason, R.,"On the Use of Method in the Modern Study of Jewish Liturgy." Pages 97–172 in *Theory and Practice.* Vol. 1 of *Approaches to Ancient Judaism.* Edited by William Scott Green. Missoula: Scholars Press, 1978.

Schiffman, L., "The Dead Sea Scrolls and the Early History of Jewish Liturgy." Pages 33–48 in *The Synagogue in Late Antiquity.* Edited by L. Levine. Philadelphia: The American Schools of Oriental Research, 1987.

—, "Phylacteries and Mezuzot." Pages 675–77 in *Encyclopedia of the Dead Sea Scrolls.* Edited by L. Schiffman and J. VanderKam. Oxford: Oxford University Press, 2000.

Schuller, E., "Some Observations on Blessings of God in Texts from Qumran." Pages 133–43 in *Of Scribes and Scrolls: Studies on the Hebrew Bible, Intertestamental Judaism, and Christian Origins Presented to John Strugnell on the Occasion of His Sixtieth Birthday.* Edited by H. Attridge, J. Collins, and T. Tobin. Lanham: University Press of America, 1990.

Skehan, P., and A. Di Lella. *The Wisdom of Ben Sira.* New York: Doubleday, 1987.

Spinks, B., *The Sanctus in the Eucharistic Prayer.* Cambridge: Cambridge University Press, 1991.

Tov, E., "Tefillin of Different Origin from Qumran?" Pages 44–54 in *A Light for Jacob: Studies in the Bible and the Dead Sea Scrolls in Memory of Jacob Shalom Licht.* Edited by Y. Hoffman and F. Polak. Jerusalem: Bialik Institute, 1997.

Weinfeld, M., "The Prayers for Knowledge, Repentance and Forgiveness in the 'Eighteen Benedictions'—Qumran Parallels, Biblical Antecedents, and Basic Characteristics [Hebrew]." *Tarbiz* 48 (1979): 186–200.

Werner, E.,"The Doxology in Synagogue and Church." *HUCA* 19 (1945/1946).

White, S. A., "4QDt^n: Biblical Manuscript or Excerpted Text?" Pages 13–20 in *Of Scribes and Scrolls: Studies on the Hebrew Bible, Intertestamental Judaism, and Christian Origins Presented to John Strugnell on the Occasion of His Sixtieth Birthday.* Edited by H. Attridge, J. Collins, and T. Tobin. Lanham: University Press of America, 1990.

Zahavy, T., "A New Approach to Early Jewish Prayer." Pages 45–60 in *History of Judaism: The Next Ten Years*. Edited by B. M. Bokser. Chico, California: Scholars Press, 1980.

—, *Berakhot. The Talmud of the Land of Israel 1*. Chicago: University of Chicago Press, 1989.

24
The Worship of the Synagogue: An Evaluation

Håkan Ulfgard

THE TASK OF COMMENTING upon the contributions to this section of the conference is not an easy one. The three papers have little in common, and the content of two of them does not really deal with what one would expect from the title of the section, especially since the common denominator of all sections in this conference is stated as ". . . of the Synagogue". Nevertheless, as discussions about the development of Jewish liturgical practice and of related theological concepts, these studies—each with its own particular profile—are bound together by a common historical interest, resulting in an increased awareness of the various factors that help to explain both the diversity and the unity of ancient Judaism.

The paper apparently most in line with the title chosen by the organizing committee, that of Reuven Kimelman, focuses on how the emphasis on divine sovereignty provides a distinguishing feature in the liturgy of rabbinic Judaism in comparison with earlier Jewish liturgies. Perhaps in order to whet the appetite of the conference participants, the original title of his contribution is cited in the conference programme as "When and Why Did the Acceptance of Divine Sovereignty Become the Distinguishing Mark of Rabbinic Liturgy?" In the print version, however, less disclosure of historical and ideological circumstances is promised: "Again Blessing Formulae and Divine Sovereignty in Rabbinic Liturgy." Nonetheless, the whole argumentation of the paper focuses on precisely these generical questions.

As his argument goes, Kimelman begins by problematizing the rabbinic claim that the mention of God's kingship in various liturgical blessing formulæ—particularly those called by the acronym

BŠKML"W, "Blessed be the name of His glorious kingship for ever and ever"—goes back to the Second Temple period. According to him, there are no indications that the theme of God's divine royal sovereignty was mentioned in pre-rabbinic liturgical contexts, especially in conjunction with a reference to the divine "name," such as in the phrase "the name of His glorious kingship". Instead, one has to reckon with an interpolation of this motif into the liturgical repertoire of rabbinic blessings, and it is the discussion about "when" and "why" this has taken place that constitutes the main contribution of his paper.

In his very detailed study—the footnotes abound with an overwhelming plethora of references to ancient sources and modern scholars—Kimelman has an obvious point in observing that an accentuation of God's divine sovereignty seems to have taken place in Jewish liturgy after the end of the Second Temple period, at least according to the rabbinic tradition. For him, it is the introduction of the phrase "His [God's] kingdom/sovereignty" into the blessing after the recital of the Shema verse that is of the greatest significance. This should be understood as a conscious "act of the acceptance of divine sovereignty"—and by retrojecting or projecting this formula (which, as he correctly observes, creates some syntactical difficulties in the blessing as a whole) into the liturgy of the earthly or celestial temple, the rabbis wanted to ensure maximal legitimization of both the formula and the idea contained in it.

What I have problems with, however, is that the obviously liturgical material from Qumran is not given quite the attention that it deserves. Although Kimelman does acknowledge that the idea of divine kingship is expressed in the *Songs of the Sabbath Sacrifice* (4Q400–7, 11QShirShab and MasShirShab; also in the *War Scroll*, col. xii), for him this is counterbalanced by the absence of expressions proclaiming God's divine rule and sovereignty in other Qumranite liturgical formulae. Here I think that the important study by A. M. Schwemer,[1] merits more attention than just a brief mention in a foot-note. Taking as her starting-point the abundant use of the word group *mlk/mlkwt* in these texts, her article is not only a thorough study of how God's kingship is conceived and articulated within this particular liturgical framework. She also puts the idea of divine rule and sovereignty into its larger context of the development of Jewish worship from the Old Testament

[1] Schwemer, "Gott als König."

Psalms through Qumran to the Hekalot literature, providing the reader with abundant references to ancient sources and scholarly literature on the subject.

To my mind it seems that Kimelman in his search for the antecedents of the BŠKML"W formula is perhaps too narrowly focused on looking for a particular phraseology. Thus, he tends to make too much out of the absence of some precise formulations about God's divine kingship in the early Jewish liturgical material, despite the fact that the idea is present in so many other parts of the biblical and post-biblical tradition (cf. his brief treatment of the New Testament expression ἡ βασιλεία τοῦ θεοῦ, a phrase given full significance in Schwemer's article). For him, there is a problem in finding any logical development from blessings dating to the time of the Second Temple that mention either God's universal kingship or his sovereignty over Israel to the full BŠKML"W formula as it is convincingly attested in the Amoraic period. Technically, his suggestions about how the formula was created and appended to the Shema verse in combination with additions to Ps 72:19 and 1 Chr 16:36 and 29:10 by the Amoraim may be correct, but one gets the impression that his overall concern is to reduce the possible existence of a mention of God's divine kingship in early Jewish liturgy to a minimum (cf. n. 116, where the Hekalot literature is emphasized as the source for liturgical phrases on divine sovereignty—with no discussion about the evidence from the *Songs of the Sabbath Sacrifice*).

The main problem addressed in Kimelman's paper is how to explain the "when" and "why" of the appearance of the BŠKML"W formula—in his own words: the "sovereigntization of the liturgy." Here he takes issue with such scholars as Heinemann, Finkelstein and Büchler, who have proposed that this may have been a protest against Roman emperor worship. This "relies on the questionable assumption that political events spur liturgical innovation and that political claims can be countered by liturgical ones."[2] As a further argument he also claims that emperor worship does not appear to have been a central problem in early Christian literature, quoting instead from Church Fathers who regard the Roman empire and its single emperor as positive factors. In both cases, I do not see that this is a convincing argumentation. Especially, Kimelman does not at all seem to pay any attention to the way in which the NT Book of Revelation is saturated with liturgical language

---

[2] Kimelman, "Blessing Formulae," 349.

proclaiming God's (and the Lamb's) universal kingship and sovereign dominion in sharp reaction to the claims of an earthly (Roman) power, even personified by the mysterious number 666 (Rev 13:18). I also have problems with his contention that—if the addition of the the BŠKML"W formula was a reaction to the imperial cult—the rabbinic response to Roman emperors who dubbed themselves *theos* should rather have been to call their God by the epithet "God of gods" instead of "King of the world" (which is the usual designation). Such an argument seems to ask for more "logic" than one has the right to demand from this kind of texts.[3]

According to the many textual examples provided by Kimelman and the historical development reconstructed by him, his answer concerning the introduction of the BŠKML"W formula in Jewish liturgy would be that this came about gradually, from the end of the second century onwards, as a liturgical innovation aimed at countering the claims of the Roman rule to represent some kind of a divine imperial order, especially in the way this came to expression under emperors as Commodus, Caracalla, and (later) Aurelian. Theologically speaking, this meant a shift from stressing the worshipper's covenantal relationship with God to emphasizing in public worship his subordination under God's supreme and universal sovereignty and monarchic rule. I can agree with his contention that there was a trend among both Jews and Christians of this epoch and afterwards (especially among Christians, with the Christianization of the empire under Constantine and his successors)—paralleled by a henotheistic tendency among "ordinary" Hellenistic-Roman worshippers—to claim universal dominion for precisely their God. Thus, although I have some critical remarks on the way in which Kimelman has focused on the precise wording of the BŠKML"W formula and on technical details of its historical development, there is much to be learnt from this paper about the development of Jewish liturgy and, in the end, about its interaction with its surrounding religious and cultural milieu.

---

[3] I would also question his conclusion: "That imperial developments left so few traces on formulations of second and third century Christianity challenges any assumption that it left more traces on rabbinic formulations" (pp. 355–6). Was not the situation vis-à-vis the Roman authorities during this period quite different among Christians than among Jews? Earlier in his paper, Kimelman himself has conceded that Jews had a privileged position in the Roman Empire—and this was not the case with Christians.

The Worship of the Synagogue: An Evaluation

From the perspective of liturgical development within ancient Judaism, more fundamental historical issues are touched upon by Daniel K. Falk in his paper "Qumran and the Synagogue Liturgy." Here as well as in the case of Kimelman, the initial promise of historical explanation in the title of his conference presentation is reduced: The original title in the conference programme has been emended from "Qumran and the *Origins* of [my italics] Synagogue Liturgy." Although this is a reasonable limitation in view of what his paper actually contains, there is no doubt that a thorough study of Qumranite liturgical traditions can provide some very illuminating comparative material for research on the early forms of Jewish liturgical life outside the temple. When it comes to drawing conclusions concerning the process which resulted in the formation of early synagogal liturgical patterns, however, many other factors have to be considered—especially the question about the scientific perspectives and fundamental presuppositions of the scholars themselves.

Falk's initial questions about the origins of institutionalized prayer in Judaism and about the relationship between synagogue prayer and the temple are precise and concrete.[4] As it turns out, however, the reader will have to look elsewhere for his answers, but what emerges from his paper is a well-informed and well-structured presentation, which provides a strong argument for the opinion that there is much to be learned from the Dead Sea Scrolls in the study of the origins of synagogal communal prayer.[5] Both witness to attempts at approaching God in a cultic context without the traditional sacrifices, and even if there are obvious differences between synagogal Judaism and Judaism as it is expressed in the Qumran writings,[6] both share a common stock of liturgical ideas and features.

Among the various forms of communal prayer practices, Falk limits his discussion to daily public prayer, subdivided into the following four

---

[4] "Does the virtual silence in pre-70 sources about prayer in synagogues indicate that institutionalized prayer, which became a hallmark of the synagogue was a novel development only after the destruction of the temple? Or is the origin of the synagogue prayers to be sought elsewhere in pre-70 Judaism? How are we to explain the relationship between synagogue prayers and prayer practices developing in the Second Temple period? What is the relationship between synagogue prayer and the temple?"

[5] In his bibliography, however, one notes the absence of Talmon, "Emergence."

[6] Cf. the remarks on the absence of any fixed place of prayer in Qumran by Schiffman, *Reclaiming*, 292.

categories: recital of the Shema, blessings, petitions, and songs of praise. For daily (morning and evening) recital of the Shema at Qumran, Falk has a good point in referring to 1QS X,10–14, which can be combined with the archaeological evidence of the tefillin found at Qumran, as well as to other documents of the period. It is also difficult to object to his demonstration that blessings were recited daily in communal prayer (4Q503; 4Q408; 1QS VI,7f; X,10–14), and that these can be compared with later Mishnaic and Talmudic formulations both regarding form, content and location in the context of liturgy (cf. especially *m. Tamid* 5:1). This comparison is relevant, of course, regardless of whether the material from Qumran is considered sectarian or not.

That 4Q503 is a particularly important documentation of liturgical practice in Palestine long before there is any evidence for the synagogue institution is rightly emphasized by Falk (with due credits especially to the studies of E. Chazon).[7] Especially interesting is his reflection about the similarities between the combined angelic and human praise, set into a context of blessing God for the creation of lights, and the Qedushah of the synagogal liturgy. With evidence for this kind of prayer in the second century B.C.E., this observation is important not only in studying the early forms of Jewish liturgy, but also for discussion of the origin and development of later merkavah mysticism. For this discussion, Falk's remark serves as a most stimulating contribution, but otherwise, his main hypothesis concerning this text—that it may be seen as an exponent of a liturgical practice in which daily recitation of the Shema was combined with particular sets of benedictions—is, at least to my mind, less controversial, especially as he is careful not to overemphasize the similarities between 4Q503 and later Shema liturgy, nor the possibility of a more or less direct development between them. But taken together, the references to liturgical activity in *m. Tamid* 5:1, 1QS X,10-14a, and Josephus, *A.J.* 4.212, serve to strengthen his contention that there was a practice of combining recital of the Shema with certain blessings already before the destruction of the Temple.

From the study of 4Q503 in particular, but also from Falk's presentation of petitions, psalms and hymns in other Qumran texts, the picture emerges of a particular "Qumranite" pre-history of later synagogal

---

[7] One would have preferred, however, to get at least some examples of those similarities with generally recognized sectarian prayer from Qumran that make him locate it in this particular spiritual milieu; instead, the reader is referred to his book on the subject.

practices. However, as he is careful to point out, the similarities should not lead to a myopic focusation on Qumran alone as providing the background milieu. It seems a wise conclusion to point instead to public worship in the temple of Jerusalem, especially as evidenced by *m. Tamid* 5:1, as the matrix of liturgical practices (with examples, quoted by Falk, also in 2 Macc 1:23–30, Sir 50, Luke 1:10, Acts 3:1 and Josephus, *C. Ap.* 2.196f). After all, Second Temple Judaism had one focal point where man could meet God—whether in actual daily liturgical practice or in ideal worship—and that was in the context of his Temple. Until there is substantial evidence pointing in that direction, it does not seem necessary to hypothesize on synagogal worship as the formative context of daily communal prayer within Judaism.

The third contribution in the section on the worship of the synagogue, "No Second Temple—No Shavuot? The Book of Jubilees as a Case Study," by Irene von Görtz-Wrisberg, stands apart from the other two papers of the section. Within the larger Lund University research project on the origins of the synagogue institution in ancient Judaism and in its interaction especially with the emerging institutions of early Christianity, von Görtz-Wrisberg is writing her doctoral thesis on the origins and development of the Shavuot festival (Feast of Weeks). Since there is a lack of scholarly studies focusing on the broader aspects of this festival—one of the three main annual festivals in biblical tradition—this should be regarded as a most valuable contribution to the study of the development of ancient Judaism. In this paper she is presenting some observations on how the festival is depicted in one of the oldest—and richest—post-biblical sources on the festival, namely the Book of Jubilees, commonly dated to the second century B.C.E. This is thus a report from work in progress—and work dealing with a text which was composed well before there is any evidence for an established synagogue institution, and hence no particular forms of synagogal worship. With these caveats in mind, the promising character of von Görtz-Wrisberg's paper for the study of the interaction between biblical interpretation, theological and ideological preferences, and liturgical innovation within Second Temple Judaism should, however, be acknowledged.

The many copies of the *Book of Jubilees* found among the Qumran writings, together with the way in which the book itself is most probably referred to in CD 16:3f, indicate its great esteem at least among those Jewish circles that resisted the politically dominant Hasmoneans.

Thus, in recent years it has attracted increased scholarly attention as an important witness to the theological and ideological development within Second Temple Judaism. The paraphrasing and expansion of the biblical narrative from Gen 1 to Exod 12, where each event in the story is carefully dated as to year, month, and day (as well as its insistence on a 364-day calendar, combined with a criticism of the common calendar reckoning; cf. 1:14) make it a most rewarding text to work with for scholars interested in early biblical *Wirkungsgeschichte*, as well as for those who focus on Jewish calendrical matters. In von Görtz-Wrisberg's case all these interests converge. Combining a descriptive, interpretative and synthetic approach, her study on how the Shavuot festival appears and is understood in *Jubilees* sheds some very significant light on the development of this festival, which has so far not attracted as much scholarly attention as the other major Jewish festivals.[8]

Behind the somewhat provocative title "No Second Temple—No Shavuot? The *Book of Jubilees* as a Case Study" lies the suggestion that there was a critical attitude towards the whole institution of the Second Temple among those responsible for producing *Jubilees* If it to my mind—and to most scholars as well—is uncontroversial to claim that the attitude of the author(s) of *Jubilees* is "No Second Temple" (cf. the implicit criticism of the present situation in 1:17), the appended question "No Shavuot?" may seem a bit problematic. "(D)oes this also imply no Shavuot?" von Görtz-Wrisberg asks, and her reply is: "Yes, in a way, since it was perhaps not seen as properly celebrated because of the wrong calendar and maybe the lack of the covenant aspect." Thus, it is not the existence of the festival as such which is questioned (as the title might suggest), but rather the way it was celebrated and understood within the kind of "main-stream" Judaism which *Jubilees* is criticizing.

In her brief introduction to *Jubilees*, von Görtz-Wrisberg correctly points out how its priestly orientation is revealed by the way the roles of Levi and Judah (mainly that of the former) among Jacob's sons are emphasized. She also draws attention to its apparent negative attitude towards Hellenistic influence, an attitude which she connects with its general conservatism and, in particular, with its emphasis on the 364-day calendar. These cultic and calendrical interests merge in the way *Jubilees* depicts how Noah and the three patriarchs Abraham, Isaac, and

---

[8] Cf. the recent studies on the Feast of Tabernacles by Rubenstein, *History of Sukkot*; Vicent, *Fiesta judía* and Ulfgard, *Story of Sukkot*.

Jacob celebrate the Feast of Shavuot. By choosing four texts from *Jubilees* (6:1–22; 14:1–20; 22:1–6; 44:1–8), asking how the feast is depicted in each case, and why this is so, a picture emerges of the ideological and/or theological understanding of the festival, which in itself gives valuable knowledge about *Jubilees*, but which also can be used within the broader investigation of the historical development of Shavuot from the biblical to the rabbinic period.

As a general conclusion from the study of the texts chosen for analysis (the main passages concerned with Shavuot in *Jubilees*, although there are a few more briefly noted by von Görtz-Wrisberg), it is rightly stressed how *Jubilees* wants to emphasize the ancient roots of the correct celebration of the festival, but that this effort of legitimization may in fact point in the opposite direction: In order to be able to introduce a new way of celebrating and interpreting the festival, its authors have taken recourse to the most ancient authorities possible, such as Noah, Abraham, Isaac, and Jacob (and it was even celebrated in heaven "from the day of creation," 6:18). This normative ambition is also implied through the way in which there is a "double addressing" in the book, i.e. a shift from its narrative focus on the patriarchal story to the Moses story which provides the wider setting (meta-narrative) of the whole book. Confronted with such an absolute authority as the "heavenly tablets," the traditional ordinances of the Mosaic law—both the written torah and its oral, pharisaic-rabbinic complement—must give way. But the main thrust of *Jubilees* is not so much a concern for what should be the correct halakah as an attempt at providing, in the guise of a divine revelation, an alternative biblical setting for that particular covenantal theology which is so typical for this book (which, in its turn, gives a legitimation for a different halakah than the generally accepted one: if already Noah, Abraham, Isaac and Jacob, in concluding their covenants with God, were fulfilling his torah in a certain way, then the authority and traditional interpretation of the much later biblical law of Moses is questioned).

Thus, with her analysis of the four Shavuot passages pointing to the main character of Shavuot as that of a festival of covenant or covenant renewal (as well as a festival of "first-fruits"—especially in the way this combination is presented in the roles of Isaac and Jacob as "firstlings"), von Görtz-Wrisberg is contributing not only to the study of the history and development of this particular festival, but—even more important—to the study of the theological and ideological development within Second Temple Judaism in general. What I have problems with in this paper are mainly two things that need to be respectively clarified and supplied.

First, the clarification concerns to what extent *Jubilees* should be regarded as an anti-Hellenistic document. Is it really Hellenistic culture per se which is under attack—or is it not rather a Judaism which, to the mind of the author(s), is too assimilating and too susceptible to Hellenistic influence? It is certainly correct to point to 1 Macc 1 for a reference to contemporary tensions between assimilating and more conservative Jews, but it should be asked if there are not signs within *Jubilees* itself of concepts and ideas that seem to function as some kind of a Jewish counterpart to its corresponding Hellenistic parallels. Are not, e. g., the "heavenly tablets" in some respect a Jewish response to the Greek concept of μοῖρα? But what really matters for the author(s) of *Jubilees* is to find a way of showing how one's general idea of the covenant (and of its halakah) has a better divine authorization than the one which appears to be the dominating one within the Judaism of its time.

Second, the absence within the earliest material from the synagogal liturgy of any real evidence for an annual celebration of the covenant (or for the renewal of the covenant) is problematic. There is no doubt that Shavuot in *Jubilees* is the festival especially associated with the idea of covenant or covenant renewal—the word-play between שָׁבֻעוֹת ("weeks") and שְׁבֻעוֹת ("oaths") is commonly acknowledged—and it seems highly probable that this festival was the occasion for the annual ceremony celebrating the covenant, according to Qumranite practice; cf. 1QS 2:19. What one would like to see from continued studies on Shavuot, bridging the gap until the era of the Tannaim and Amoraim (when, e.g., Exod 19:6ff is declared as the prescribed torah reading for Shavuot), is how the connection between the festival and covenant celebration is maintained and developed further in other forms of Second Temple Judaism. Here, the New Testament depiction (Acts 2) of the events that took place on Shavuot just after the death and resurrection of Jesus—the reaction to Peter's speech and the gift of the Spirit pointing to some kind of a covenant renewal (in Luke's theological paradigm: the starting-point of God's widened covenant)—may be a most significant expression of how the festival was understood in other forms of marginal (or, better: subsequently marginalized) Jewish movements. But with *Jubilees* totally suppressed from the sacred scriptures of ancient synagogal Judaism, I think that the final suggestion of this third paper on the liturgy of the ancient synagogue; that the proper celebration of Shavuot in the way this is envisaged by *Jubilees* could have been meant to take place in a synagogue, would need a divine revelation to be really convincing—or the discovery of a synagogal community of quite another kind than this conference has had in mind.

Bibliography

Kimelman, R., "Again Blessing Formulae and Divine Sovereignty in Rabbinic Liturgy." In this volume.

Rubenstein, J. L., *The History of Sukkot in the Second Temple and Rabbinic Periods*. Atlanta: Scholars Press, 1995.

Schiffman, L., *Reclaiming the Dead Sea Scrolls. The History of Judaism, the Background of Christianity, the Lost Library of Qumran.* Philadelphia: The Jewish Publication Society, 5755/1994.

Schwemer, A. M., "Gott als König und seine Königsherrschaft in den Sabbatliedern aus Qumran." Pages 45–118 in *Königsherrschaft Gottes und himmlischer Kult im Judentum, Urchristentum und in der hellenistischen Welt*. Edited by M. Hengel and A. M. Schwemer. Tübingen: Mohr, 1991.

Talmon, S., "The Emergence of Institutionalized Prayer in Israel in Light of Qumran Literature." Pages 200–43 in *The World of Qumran from Within: Collected Studies*. Jerusalem: Magnes Press, 1989.

Ulfgard, H., *The Story of Sukkot: The Setting, Shaping, and Sequel of the Biblical Feast of Tabernacles*. Tübingen: Mohr Siebeck, 1998.

Vicent, R., *La fiesta judía de las cabañas (Sukkot). Interpretaciones midrásicas en la Biblia y en el judaísmo antiguo*. Estella: Editorial Verbo Divino, 1995.

Part V

The Hermeneutics of the Synagogue

25
The Hermeneutics of the Synagogue: An Introduction

Birger Olsson

THE ANCIENT SYNAGOGUE AND its various activities was of crucial importance for the Jews as a basic and effective means of constructing the meaning of their lives. This applies not the least to the liturgy in a broad sense, including the reading and teaching of the Torah. The public, communal ritualizing says a lot about Jewish identity.[1]

The Bible was the center of this process. The reading and teaching of the Torah is the most unique and most continuous feature of the ancient synagogue. And the prayers are heavily influenced by Biblical rhetoric. Therefore, the fifth and last research area of our project has the title "Hermeneutic and Ideological Analysis". The Bible was read, translated, taught, preached and used in prayers and hymns. This synagogal use of the Bible includes a complicated and fascinating hermeneutic process, which can be studied in the rituals as such, in prayers, in the translations into the people's languages and in the sermons. Unfortunately, most material from this process comes from the time after 200 C. E. We decided in our project to focus on the Targums. I quote from the description of the project:

> An extensive interpretation enterprise, often centering on the translation from one language to another, was a significant characteristic of activity in the synagogue. From a hermeneutic point of view, the Targums occupied a special place in the synagogue and therefore represent a primary source material within this fifth and last area of analysis.

[1] See Hoffman's latest presentation in "Jewish Liturgy."

Conditions for different forms of targumic analysis have never been as good as they are today. A comprehensive wave of research has gained momentum during the last three decades, and within the framework of the present project it is planned a monograph in each of the following two subject areas:

1) A content-oriented comparative analysis in which the specific interpretations of passages in the Hebrew Bible are often linked with similar commentaries in other Jewish literature. The hermeneutic principles will themselves become manifest, so that the development of the interpretation of a given scripture passage or biblical theme can be accounted for, and the theme's contents then be presented. For example, we wish to address such questions as how the Targums view God, the Torah, revelation, prayer, holiness, conversion, redemption, the messiah, and the resurrection of the dead. From a perspective such as this the relations between interpretations of the New Testament and the Targums become particularly significant. This particular approach, which is the most usual, can be expected to have both historical and literary qualities.

2) A more form-oriented, primarily internal analysis of Targum texts with the aim in part of examining the interpretation of sacred writings. This study may focus on certain kinds of texts, such as blessings, or unique characteristics of discourse, such as the use of the rejoinder. This particular research project is still in its infancy. Modern translation studies that proceed from the text as a semiotic whole suggest that a fruitful study would concentrate on semantic discourse markers, e.g., terminal characteristics, transition markers, temporal, spatial or logical relations, various types of references within the text, incorporation of old and new information, or the author's own comments on what he is saying. Different forms of rhetorical analysis will be relevant here as well. In the area of inner textual studies there is still much that remains to be done to describe the

hermeneutic "handiwork" of the synagogue and the religious socialization that took place there.

This is an ambitious program which in itself could be a separate project. Modern targumic studies concentrate on manuscripts, translations, comparisons between different versions and other Jewish literature, philological helps, and the hermeneutic principles and not so much on the ideological aspects or on the relation to the ritualizing in the synagogue and its identity-shaping effect.[2] And I have found very few more synchronic or narrative analyses.[3] In the project we had to limit ourselves to an investigation by Karin Hedner Zetterholm (*Portrait of a Villain. Laban the Aramean in Rabbinic Literature*. Leuven: Peeters, 2002) of a biblical figure, the interpretation of Laban in biblical and post-biblical Jewish literature, using methods from both fields mentioned above, and to an analysis of the references to Passover in the Targums on Genesis by Per Å. Bengtsson (*Passover in Targum Pseudo-Jonathan Genesis. The Connection of Early Biblical Events with Passover in Targum Pseduo-Jonathan in a Synagogue Setting*. Stockholm: Almqvist & Wiksell, 2001).

In this volume we find a presentation of the most important results in Hedner Zetterholm's dissertation, a contribution by Paul Flesher on the relationship between Targums and the ancient synagogue together with an evaluation by Bruce Chilton.

Bibliography

Bengtsson, P. Å., *Passover in Targum Pseudo-Jonathan Genesis. The Connection of Early Biblical Events with Passover in Targum Pseduo-Jonathan in a Synagogue Setting*. Stockholm: Almqvist & Wiksell, 2001.

Grossfeld, G., *A Bibliography to Targum Literature*. Cincinnati: Hebrew Union College, 1972.

---

[2] See the bibliographies by Grossfeld 1972, 1977 and 1990, and also Hayward, "Major Aspects". You do not find "synagogue" in Grossfeld's subject index, only "Liturgy" and "Meturgeman".

[3] See, however, the dissertation by Samely, *Interpretation of Speech*.

—, *A Bibliography to Targum Literature. Volume II.* Cincinnati: Hebrew Union College Press, 1977.

—, *A Bibliography to Targum Literature. Volume III.* New York: Sepher-Hermon Press, 1990.

Hayward, R., "Major Aspects of Targumic Studies 1983–1993. Pages 107–22 in *Currents in Research* 2 (1994).

Hedner Zetterholm, K., *Portrait of a Villain. Laban the Aramean in Rabbinic Literature.* Leuven: Peeters, 2002.

Hoffman, L. A., "Jewish Liturgy and Jewish Scholarship: Method and Cosmology." Pages 732–55 in *The Oxford Handbook of Jewish Studies.* Edited by M. Goodman. Oxford: Oxford University Press, 2002.

Samely, A., *The Interpretation of Speech in the Pentateuchal Targums: A Study of Method and Presentation in Targumic Exegesis.* Tübingen: Mohr Siebeck, 1992.

26
The Attempted Murder by Laban the Aramean: Rabbinic Hermeneutics and the Emergence of an Ideology

Karin Hedner Zetterholm

LABAN THE ARAMEAN IS perhaps not a very well-known biblical figure. He is the father-in-law of Jacob and the father of Leah and Rachel and appears in a few chapters in the book of Genesis where he is a minor character with no great significance. Yet, he is known in Jewish tradition as a major enemy of Jacob and thereby of all of Israel, and his main characteristics are deceit and wickedness. He is even repeatedly said to have attempted to kill Jacob. Since this is hardly the image of Laban that emerges from a reading of the biblical story alone, the question of how and why this portrait came into being arises.

Toward a New Theory of Interpretation

For several years there has been an ongoing debate among scholars as to whether midrash (in its broad sense of biblical interpretation) is to be viewed primarily as scriptural interpretation, i.e. as a legitimate reading practice responding essentially to real exegetical difficulties in the biblical text although ideological concerns are also evidenced in it, or whether it is largely unconcerned with these difficulties and better understood primarily as a vehicle for the expression of rabbinic values and concerns, with the biblical verse merely serving as a pretext. Even though some scholars still emphasize only the ideological aspect of interpretation, assuming that when an ancient interpreter deviated from the biblical narrative in his retelling of it, the reason for that deviation must be sought in factors outside of the text such as his political views or religious agenda,[1] there is a growing consensus that there is no such thing as a sharp distinction between ideology and exegesis. All interpretation is rather seen as the outcome of interaction between the text and the reader in a process where the reader's experiences, and his/her ideological, theological, and/or political concerns affect his/her understanding of the text but where the text also affects the reader and the formation of his/her ideology or theology. It has been pointed out that it is not very useful to attempt to make a distinction between ideology/theology and exegesis, since we do not know how much ideology or theology in rabbinic Judaism originally came into being as a result of exegesis. Even in cases of clearly ideological interpretations, it is hardly possible to determine whether the exegete started out with an idea and then went looking for a verse to attach it to, or whether when faced with an exegetical problem, he found its solution amid the historical baggage of his age, a solution that reflected his own ideology or the issues of his day.[2]

Moreover, scholars have also drawn attention to the fact that whatever other motives and concerns that may be evidenced in the rabbinic narrative expansions they are *presented* as a form of exegesis. These expansions are ultimately based on something which is found in the biblical text, an unusual word or grammatical form or some problem in the plot, and even though such irregularities may have been perceived as difficulties because of an underlying ideology, they are presented as a form of exegesis. One ought therefore to take seriously the rabbis' claim that what they are doing is reading, rather than automatically regarding their interpretations as a result of the extratextual reality of the rabbinic period.[3]

---

[1] Neusner, *Comparative Midrash*, Neusner, *Midrash in Context*, Neusner, *Judaism and Scripture*. For an earlier example of the view of midrash as a communication of rabbinic ideology or theology with hardly any attention paid to its hermeneutical function, see, Urbach, *Sages*.

[2] Boyarin, "Inner Biblical Ambiguity," 5, 43, Boyarin, *Intertextuality*, 11–19, Samely, *Interpretation of Speech*, 81–5, 181, Kugel, *Potiphar's House*, 250, Kugel, *Bible as it was*, 26, Shinan, "מדרשת הפסוק," 203–5.

[3] Kugel, *Bible as it was*, Fraade, "Interpreting Midrash," 186ff, Boyarin, *Intertextuality*, 15.

Thus, there is a growing number of scholars who claim that rather than taking for granted that the political/ideological/theological concerns of each rabbi wholly determined the interpretation of the biblical text, one ought to consider the possibility that his political/ideological/theological views may have been, at least partly, generated by his understanding of the biblical text. Rabbinic biblical interpretation, then, is not a reflection of an already existing ideology but rather the outcome of a process where the interpreter's experiences and his ideological/theological/political concerns naturally affect his understanding of the text, but where the text is also assumed to affect the interpreter and the formation of his ideology or theology.[4] It is this approach to rabbinic biblical interpretation that is the point of departure for the present study of Laban the Aramean.

A Case of Intertextuality

The idea that Laban attempted to destroy Jacob is repeated in every observant Jewish household every Pesah, since it appears in the Passover Haggadah where Laban is even said to be worse than Pharaoh:

> Go and learn what Laban the Aramean attempted to do to our father Jacob! Pharaoh decreed only against the males but Laban attempted to uproot everything, as it is said: *An Aramean destroyed my father* [Deut 26:5]. Then he went down to Egypt . . .

It is nowhere stated in Genesis that Laban attempted to kill Jacob or his family, which evokes the question of how this idea originated. The key appears to be the traditional Jewish rendering of the phrase ארמי אבד אבי in Deut 26:5, which in modern bible translations is translated as, "My father was a fugitive Aramean" (NJPSV), "A wandering Aramean was my ancestor" (NRSV), "My father was a wandering Aramean" (NIV), "An Arammian nomad was my father" (JB), or something very similar. The wandering Aramean is by modern biblical commentators as well as by Jewish medieval ones usually understood to

---

[4] For a more thorough survey of the issues discussed here, see Boyarin, *Intertextuality*.

refer to Jacob, or possibly to all the patriarchs. Israel's ancestors came from a region known as Aram naharaim which could explain the designation "Aramean." Jewish tradition, however, as expressed in the midrashim and targumim has a completely different rendering of the phrase, usually understanding it to mean "An Aramean destroyed my father" and identifying the "Aramean" with Laban. The earliest evidence of this understanding is found in Tannaitic literature and since it also appears in a large number of later rabbinic texts,[5] it was apparently widely accepted. In the following the earliest references are listed in rough chronological order:

Targum Onqelos

לבן ארמאה בעא לאובדא ית אבא ונחת למצרים ...

Laban the Aramean sought to destroy my father, and he went down to Egypt . . .

Sifre

מלמד שלא ירד אבינו יעקב לארם אלא על מנת לאבד ומעלה
על לבן הארמי כאילו איבדו

This teaches that our father Jacob went down to Aram only in order to perish, and Laban the Aramean is regarded as if he destroyed him.

Targum Neofiti

לבן ארמייה סבר למובדה לאבונן יעקב מן שירויה ושיזבת יתיה מן ידיה ונחת
למצרים ...

Laban the Aramean sought to destroy our father Jacob from the beginning, but you saved him from his hand, and he went down to Egypt . . .

---

[5] See, *Tanḥ.* (Buber edition) *Eqev* 5; *ʾAg. Ber.* ch. 53 [54]; *Midr. Psalms* 30.4; *Midrash ha-Gadol* on Gen 31:22–3; *Yalqut Shimoni* vol. 1 *remez* 938; *Leqaḥ Tov* on Deut 26:5.

The Attempted Murder by Laban the Aramean

Targum Pseudo-Jonathan

לארם נהריא נחתת[6] אבונן יעקב מן שירויא ובעא לאובדותיה ושיזבי מימרא דייי מן
ידוי ומבתר כדין נחת למצרים...

> Our father Jacob went down to Aram Naharaim from the beginning and he [Laban] sought to destroy him, but the Memra of the Lord saved him from his hands. Afterwards, he went down to Egypt...

Midrash Tannaim and the comments in the margins of *Neofiti* have the same interpretation. The rendering of the phrase depends on the understanding of the root אבד which can be interpreted in at least two different ways, since the biblical text was not yet vocalized at the time the early midrashim and targumim came into being. אבד can be perceived as אֹבֵד (*qal* participle) in which case the phrase is intransitive and אבי most likely the subject, "My father was a wandering Aramean," but it could also be understood as אִבַּד (*piel* perfect) in which case the phrase becomes transitive and ארמי the subject and אבי the object: "An Aramean destroyed my father." The root אבד in *qal* has the meaning of "perish, die, be destroyed, be lost, stray, wander, disappear," and it is the understanding of אבד as a *qal* participle which is the basis for the translation "my father was a wandering Aramean." The *piel* form of the root means "cause to perish, destroy, kill," and interpreting אבד as a *piel* perfect thus gives the meaning "an Aramean destroyed my father." This is essentially how the phrase was understood in Jewish tradition, the intransitive understanding making its first unambiguous appearance in the 12th century in the commentaries of Ibn Ezra and Rashbam. It is possible that *Sifre* and *Pseudo-Jonathan* contain a combination of both the intransitive and the transitive interpretation, but the transitive is undoubtedly the predominant one.[7]

---

[6] נחת =

[7] There is a third possibility of understanding אבד, which has been used to explain the Masoretic text where אבד is vocalized אֹבֵד although the cantillation marks suggest the transitive reading, and that is the suggestion that the Masoretes understood אבד not as *qal* participle but as the more rare conjugation *poel* perfect. According to Kautzsch and Cowley, *Hebrew Grammar*, § 55, *poel* is the equivalent of *piel* in a limited number of verbs in the Bible.

Thus, both the understanding "My father was a wandering Aramean" and "An Aramean destroyed my father" are grammatically possible, but the first interpretation seems to fit the context better and there is an almost complete scholarly consensus that the phrase originally meant "My father was a wandering Aramean" and that it was at some point reinterpreted to mean "An Aramean destroyed my father," and the "Aramean" being identified with Laban. This reinterpretation has puzzled scholars and the most common attempts to explain it have been to attribute it to historical factors outside of the text, identifying Laban with historical enemies of Israel, such as the Seleuchid rulers of Syria[8], Antiochus Epiphanes,[9] Rome (noting the similarity between ארמי and רמאי)[10], or Herod.[11]

The problem with identifying Laban with a historical enemy of Israel, however, is that such identifications are not stated or even hinted at in rabbinic literature, (as opposed to Esau, who is clearly identified first with Edom and later, with Rome) and in view of the new insights into the workings of midrash I would like to suggest an altogether different approach to the problem.[12]

The fact that Jacob is called "Aramean" in Deut 26:5 probably seemed peculiar to the rabbis who regarded the Bible as a unified whole containing no inconsistencies, since he is nowhere else in the Bible referred to as such. On the contrary, Genesis seems to go out of its way to emphasize that Jacob, in contrast to Laban was *not* an "Aramean" (25:20, 28:5, 31:20, 31:24). Given this sensibility to inconsistencies in the Bible, they would naturally be disturbed by the designation of Jacob as an Aramean in Deuteronomy, a fact that has been pointed out by several scholars.[13] Accordingly, it seems likely that the word "Aramean" would rather evoke associations to Laban, who is commonly referred to as "Laban the Aramean" (לבן הארמי Gen 25:20, 31:20, 31:24). Laban is the best known Aramean in the Bible, and it would be natural for the rabbis to understand the word "Aramean" to refer to him. If the "Aramean" is identified with Laban, the root אבד must be understood as

---

[8] Finkelstein, "Oldest Midrash," 299–300.
[9] Seeligmann, *Septuagint Version*, 85–6.
[10] Aberbach, "Jacob," 9: 1197 and personal communication Nov. 8, 1999.
[11] Yuval, "הפוסחים," 22.
[12] For a more thorough survey of the issues discussed here, see Hedner Zetterholm, *Portrait*.
[13] See e.g., Dreyfus, "L'araméen," 152–3, Steiner, "Aramean," 129.

a *piel* form meaning "destroy," but since that is grammatically possible it probably did not cause great difficulties. This is not to say that the rabbis interpreted ארמי אבד אבי to mean "My father was a wandering Aramean" and then consciously distorted it to mean something else because the original sense seemed strange to them. Rather, I propose that the transitive reading was the way they understood the verse, given their assumptions and presuppositions.

Once ארמי אבד אבי was understood to mean "An Aramean sought to destroy my father" and the Aramean identified with Laban, the question of when Laban attempted to destroy Jacob immediately presents itself. *Aggadat Bereshit*, a tenth century midrash, supplies an answer by reading Deut 26:5 and Gen 31:23–5 in conjunction with each other[14]

ד״א שיר למעלות אשא עיני [אל ההרים] בשעה שברח יעקב מן לבן. והלך
לו ויושב בהר. ושמע לבן והשיגו. שנאמר וישג לבן את יעקב ויעקב
תקע את אהלו בהר (בראשית לא כה) והיה לבן מבקש לילך ולהרוג
ליעקב. שכן משה אומר ארמי אבד אבי וגו׳ (דברים כו ה) ומה הוא כן.
אלא מן לבן הארמי אבד יעקב אבינו. התחיל יעקב אומר אשא עיני וגו׳
והקב״ה הלך כביכול ונגלה לרשע ועשה עצמו שלוחו. בשביל לעשות צרכו
של יעקב. שנאמר ויבא אלהים אל לבן וגו׳ (בראשית לא כד)

Another interpretation: *A song for ascents. I turn my eyes to the mountains;* [Ps. 121:1] When Jacob fled from Laban he went and encamped on a mountain. Laban heard [that Jacob had fled and he pursued after him] and he overtook him, as it is said: *Laban overtook Jacob. Jacob had pitched his tent on the Height* (Gen. 31:25). And Laban attempted to go and kill Jacob, as Moses said: *An Aramean destroyed my father* (Deut. 26:5) What does this mean? [It means that] through Laban the Aramean our father Jacob was destroyed. And Jacob said: *"I turn my eyes."* The Holy One blessed be He went, as if it were possible [to speak in this manner], and revealed himself to the wicked one and made himself his [Jacob's] messenger in order to carry out the needs of Jacob, as it is said, *but God appeared to Laban* etc. (31:24).[15]

---

[14] *Midrash ha-Gadol* on Gen 31:22–3 likewise juxtaposes Deut 26:5 and Gen 31:22–3.
[15] *Aggadat Bereshit* ch. (53) [54].

The phrases, "when Jacob fled from Laban he went and encamped on a mountain. Laban heard and he overtook him" summarize Gen 31:21–3, and it is concluded by the quotation from v. 25. Accordingly, *Aggadat Bereshit* interprets the story in Genesis as follows: Jacob escapes to the hill country of Gilead (v. 21), Laban hears about his flight and pursues him with the intention of killing him (vv. 22–3, 25 and Deut 26:5), God intervenes and as a result Jacob is saved (v. 24).

There are hints of Laban's hostile intentions in Gen 31:23–5, and an intertextual reading of Deut 26:5 and Gen 31:23–5 may well have produced the idea that Laban wished to kill Jacob when the latter fled from Haran.

Gen 31:23–5 reads:

ויקח את אחיו עמו וירדף אחריו דרך שבעת ימים וידבק אתו בהר הגלעד:
ויבא אלהים אל-לבן הארמי בחלם הלילה ויאמר לו השמר לך פן-תדבר
עם-יעקב מטוב עד-רע:וישג לבן את יעקב...

So he took his kinsmen with him and pursued him a distance of seven days, <u>catching up</u> with him in the hill country of Gilead. But God appeared to Laban the Aramean in a dream by night and said to him, "Beware of attempting anything with Jacob, good or bad." Laban <u>overtook</u> Jacob . . .

The root דבק in *hiphil* often has a connotation of hostility in biblical Hebrew and is frequently used in the context of war (Judg 20:42, 2 Sam 1:6, Judg 20:45, 1 Sam 14:22, 1 Sam 31:2).[16] Read in the light of Deut 26:5 which reinforces the notion of hostility, these verses would give good reason to state that Laban pursued Jacob with the intention of killing him.

Such an intertextual reading, where one verse evokes associations to another verse and where these verses read together generate a new meaning that each one of them could not have on their own is a com-

---

[16] In poetic texts the *hiphil* form of the root דבק has the meaning of "cleave to, cling to," (e.g. Jer 13:11, Ezek 29:4, 3:26, Deut 28:21, Ps 22:16) but in all the historical books, with the exception of Judg 18:22, it has a clear connotation of hostility and war. The word וישג in v. 25 also has a hostile connotation (Exod 14:9, 1 Sam 30:8, 2 Sam 15:14, Lam 1:3, 1 Chr 21:12) although it has a wider range of meanings and nuances than וידבק.

mon feature of midrash.[17] Thus, confronted with a biblical phrase that seemed to be saying that Laban destroyed Jacob, the rabbis came to think of Gen 31:23–5, which read together with Deut 26:5 could be understood to mean that Laban intended to kill Jacob when the latter fled from Haran. This is not to say that the rabbis interpreted ארמי אבד אבי to mean that Laban sought to destroy Jacob and then went looking for a verse to prove this idea, but rather that an unintentional association to Gen 31:23–5 made possible this interpretation of Deut 26:5.

These texts which attest to an understanding of Gen 31:22–5 and Deut 26:5 in light of each other are admittedly late (the tenth and thirteenth century respectively), but there are earlier indications of such an understanding even though the verses from Genesis are not explicitly quoted. *Midrash Tanhuma* (Buber edition) *Eqev* 5 describes Jacob's hardships in chronological order from his birth: already in the womb Esau tried to kill him, when he had received the blessings Esau planned to kill him again, he escaped to Laban where he suffered because of the latter's daughter, and after that Laban attempted to kill him. Due to the chronological account and the words "after that," it seems reasonable to conclude that "after that" refers to Jacob's escape and Laban's pursuit of him even if the verses are not quoted.

וברח ללבן ונצטער בבתו. ואחר כך ביקש לבן להרגו. שנאמר ארמי אובד אבי (דברים כו ה)

> And he escaped to Laban and suffered because of his daughter[18] and after that Laban attempted to kill him, as it is said: *An Aramean destroyed my father* (Deut 26:5).

Targum Pseudo-Jonathan and also the marginal glosses of *Targum Neofiti* understand Deut 26:5 in the context of Jacob's stay with Laban. The addition "but the Memra of the Lord saved him from his hands," present also in *Targum Neofiti* to Deut 26:5, is most likely a reference to Gen 31:24 where God intervenes and warns Laban not to hurt Jacob. Even though there is admittedly no text from Tannaitic times that ex-

---

[17] See Boyarin, *Intertextuality*, 22–32.
[18] בבתו could perhaps also be interpreted to mean "in his house," but the parallel version in *Tan Eqev* 3 has בבנותיו של לבן ("because of Laban's daughters"), which indicates that it is probably "his daughter" that is meant here also.

plicitly quotes Deut 26:5 together with Gen 31:23–5, it nevertheless seems reasonable that an understanding of these verses in light of each other gave rise to the idea that Laban attempted to destroy Jacob and that these later texts reflect an understanding that originated in earlier times. It also seems reasonable to assume that the idea that Laban attempted to kill Jacob, which is widely spread in rabbinic literature, played a significant role in forming a negative view of Laban although this is by no means the only negative statement about him.

Laban the Deceiver

Apart from being presented as attempting to destroy Jacob, Laban is generally considered to be a wicked person whose most outstanding characteristic is deceit according to the midrashim and targumim.[19] The epithet "deceiver" can easily be derived from Laban's behavior in the biblical story but most midrashim and targumim emphasize this out of proportion. One reason for this is probably the similarity between the Hebrew words ארמי ("Aramean") and רמאי ("deceiver"), permitting a double reading of ארמי as meaning both "Aramean" and "deceiver." It is repeated a number of times in Genesis that Laban was an Aramean and since in the view of the rabbis the Bible does not contain any repetitions they understood the recurrence of the word "Aramean" to hint at another meaning.[20] Due to the similarity of ארמי and רמאי they accordingly considered the repetition to mean that Laban was both an Aramean and a deceiver. Thus, the characteristic "deceiver" attributed to Laban in rabbinic literature was not arbitrarily chosen out of a wish to provide him with a certain set of negative characteristics, but is rather the outcome of a reading of the biblical text although this reading is naturally conditioned by a certain set of assumptions.

The Significance of Jacob for the Image of Laban

An additional reason for the emphasis on Laban's deceit is most probably the wish on the part of the rabbis to excuse Jacob's behavior and make him appear in a more favorable light. The rabbis saw Jacob as the

---

[19] See e.g., *Gen. Rab.* 63.4, 70.19, 75.5; *Tan Vayishlah* 1; *Gen Rabbati* on Gen 31:23–4, Gen 30:35, 31:8; *Midrash Aggadah* on Gen 29:24, 31:33; *Tg. Ps.-J.* Gen 29:12, Gen 29:19.

[20] For a summary of the most important assumptions underlying rabbinic biblical interpretation, see Kugel, *Bible as it was,* 17–23.

representative and the embodiment of the people of Israel, and given this identification it is scarcely surprising that part of his behavior as described in the biblical story such as making his brother sell him his birthright in return for a bowl of stew, and tricking his father into giving him the blessing intended for the first-born seemed disturbing to them and in need of reinterpretation.[21] By exaggerating Laban's deceit, Jacob's deceitful actions such as his manipulation of the mating of Laban's sheep and his secret departure from Paddan-aram will be seen as necessary measures in order to survive when dealing with such an unreliable person as Laban. All the midrashim and targumim are very careful either to reinterpret Jacob's deception of his father and brother calling it an act of wisdom, or to simply pass over it in silence. By reinterpreting or ignoring Jacob's deception and emphasizing Laban's deceitful behavior toward Jacob, an impression is created of an innocent Jacob who is unjustly ill-treated by a deceitful Laban.

The improvement of Jacob's image is significant for the structure of the whole narrative and the effect that this new structure, or lack of structure, has for the impression the reader gets of Laban. Redefining Jacob's taking of the blessing as an act of wisdom results not only in making Jacob appear in a more favorable light, but also in a different evaluation of the subsequent events.[22] While the biblical narrative implies that Laban has the role of an instrument with which justice is meted out to Jacob giving him what he deserves when he, the younger brother who deceived his father and brother, is deceived by Laban in much the same way by being given the elder daughter in marriage in-

---

[21] Ibid., 199–200. Kugel points out that the rabbinic assumption that the Bible is perfect, containing no inconsistencies or contradictions to some extent also included the conduct of biblical heroes. Thus, Jacob and other meritorious figures ought not to behave improperly, and if at times they appear to do so, the rabbis conclude that something else *must* have been meant. The Bible's perfection ultimately meant that it was in accordance with the interpreters' ideas and standards of conduct (p. 21).

[22] Bar-Efrat, *Narrative Art*, 93 has pointed out that events in a plot receive their meaning from their position and role in the system as a whole. The events are like building blocks, each one contributing to the entire structure, and the removal of one building block may cause the entire structure to collapse, or at least cause severe damage to it. The main relations between the different building blocks are those of cause and effect, parallelism and contrast. Redefining Jacob's taking of the blessing as an act of wisdom must be regarded as the removal of such a building block, resulting in the elimination of the connection between cause and effect, thereby causing severe damage to the whole structure.

stead of the younger, he fulfills no such function in the midrashic and targumic renderings of the story thus making his deceit seem unwarranted and therefore more emphasized. Laban's deception of Jacob is no longer understood to be an expression of measure for measure, and the basis for understanding Laban's deception as a rebuke of Jacob is accordingly eliminated. Thus, altering the structure of the narrative makes Laban automatically look bad, without necessarily attributing any additional negative characteristics to him (as is the case with Esau). The wish to make Jacob appear in a more favorable light accordingly has consequences also for the understanding of passages which are not actively reinterpreted and brings with it an image of Laban that was perhaps at first unintended. It seems likely that the automatic negative portrait of Laban that emerges as a result of the rabbinic reinterpretation of certain elements in the biblical story contributed to the further vilification that the rabbis made him undergo. It becomes a circle where everything works to Laban's disadvantage. He automatically appears more negative as a result of the improvement of Jacob's image, and in addition he is deliberately attributed with negative characteristics (although they are not arbitrarily chosen but derive from a serious albeit biased reading of the biblical text) in order to further improve Jacob's image.[23]

Conclusions

It is argued that that the portrait of Laban as a villain developed as a result of rabbinic hermeneutics, and that the characteristics which are attributed to him in rabbinic literature were not arbitrarily chosen due to some extra-textual issue or an ideologically motivated wish to provide him with a set of negative characteristics, but that it is rather the outcome of a reading of the biblical text, albeit a reading that is naturally biased and conditioned by a certain set of assumptions. The rabbis were involved in a constant interaction with the biblical text in a process where they filled in the gaps that they perceived in the text and ex-

---

[23] The phenomenon of denigrating an opponent, initially not necessarily out of interest in him but for the purpose of presenting oneself in a more favorable light seems to be a common human behavior. It appears to be one reason for Christianity's denigration of Judaism and in this case it had far-reaching consequences. In the case of Laban it does not seem to have had any significant consequences, perhaps precisely because he was not identified with a historical figure.

plained inconsistencies with material provided by the Bible itself and by material taken from their ideological code.

Accordingly, grappling with a text that is full of gaps, inconsistencies and repetitions by interpreters with a set of assumptions of how these features are to be understood, may be sufficient to create an image of an enemy. It is interesting to see that this is all it takes for an ideology to emerge. Of course this is not to say that this is how all images of enemies or ideologies are created, but the fact that it seems to be the case with Laban illustrates the power of hermeneutics. An ideology of a wicked Laban emerges as the outcome of interaction between the biblical text and the rabbis with their specific concerns and assumptions, and this ideology then influences further interpretation creating an image of Laban as a villain. The study further suggests that an image of an enemy can develop primarily as a side-effect of concerns other than an interest in the enemy himself. Accordingly, a portrait of a villain can emerge more or less by chance but once this image or ideology has come into being it acquires a life of its own and influences future interpretations.

Bibliography

Aberbach, M., "Jacob." Pages 1197–201 in *Encyclopaedia Judaica*. Vol 9. Edited by C. Roth and G. Wigoder. Jerusalem: Keter, 1978 [1972].

Bar-Efrat, S., *Narrative Art in the Bible*. Sheffield: Almond Press, 1989 [1979 in Hebrew].

Boyarin, D., "Inner Biblical Ambiguity, Intertextuality and the Dialectic of Midrash: The Waters of Marah." *Prooftexts* 10 (1990): 29–48.

—, *Intertextuality and the Reading of Midrash*. Bloomington: Indiana University Press, 1990.

Dreyfus, F., "'L'araméen voulait tuer mon père': L'actualisation de Dt 26,5 dans la tradition juive et la tradition chrétienne." Pages 147–61 in *De la Tôrah au Messie: Mélanges Henri Cazelles*. Edited by J. Doré, P. Grelot and M. Carrez. Paris: Desclée, 1981.

Finkelstein, L., "The Oldest Midrash: Pre-Rabbinic Ideals and Teachings in the Passover Haggadah." *HTR* 31 (1938):

291–317.

Fraade, S. D., "Interpreting Midrash 1: Midrash and the History of Judaism: Review of Judaism and Scripture: The Evidence of Leviticus Rabbah by J. Neusner." *Prooftexts* 7 (1987): 179–194.

Hedner Zetterholm, K., *Portrait of a Villain: Laban the Aramean in Rabbinic Literature*. Leuven: Peeters, 2002.

Kautzsch, E., and A. E. Cowley, *Gesenius' Hebrew Grammar as Edited and Enlarged by the Late E. Kautzsch: Second English Edition Revised in Accordance with the Twenty-Eighth German Edition (1909) by A. E. Cowley*. Oxford: Clarendon Press, 1985 [1910].

Kugel, J. L., *In Potiphar's House: The Interpretive Life of Biblical Texts*. New York: HarperCollins, 1990.

—, *The Bible as it was*. Cambridge: The Belknap Press of Harvard University Press, 1997.

Neusner, J., *Comparative Midrash: The Plan and Program of Genesis Rabbah and Leviticus Rabbah*. Atlanta: Scholars Press, 1986.

—, *Judaism and Scripture: The Evidence of Leviticus Rabbah*. Chicago: The University of Chicago Press, 1986.

—, *Midrash in Context: Exegesis in Formative Judaism*. Atlanta: Scholars Press, 1988 [1983].

Samely, A., *The Interpretation of Speech in the Pentateuchal Targums: A Study of Method and Presentation in Targumic Exegesis*. Tübingen: Mohr, 1992.

Seeligmann, I. L., *The Septuagint Version of Isaiah: A Discussion of Its Problems*. Leiden: Brill, 1948.

Shinan, A., מדרשת הפסוק אל האגדה החופשית. Pages 203–20 in מחקרי ירושלים בספרות עברית לזכר יוסף אבן. Jerusalem, 1984.

Steiner, R. C., "The 'Aramean' of Deuteronomy 26:5: Peshat and Derash." Pages 127–38 in *Tehilla le-Moshe: Biblical and Judaic Studies in Honor of Moshe Greenberg*. Edited by M. Cogan, B. L. Eichler and J. H. Tigay. Winona Lake: Eisenbrauns, 1997.

Urbach, E. E., *The Sages: Their Concepts and Beliefs*. Jerusalem: Magnes Press, 1987 [1975].

Yuval, I. J., הפוסחים על שתי הסעיפים: ההגדה של פסח והפסחא הנוצרית. תרביץ 65 (1996): 5–28.

27
The Literary Legacy of the Priests? The Pentateuchal Targums of Israel in their Social and Linguistic Context

Paul V. M. Flesher[1]

THE DESTRUCTION OF JERUSALEM and its temple in 70 C.E. should have brought an end to Judaism. Gone was the religious center ordained by God and his Torah. Gone were the sacrifices by which the People Israel atoned for their transgressions. Gone was God's home on earth. But Judaism survived and reshaped itself into a vibrant, living religion that has sustained Jews for nearly 2000 more years. Under whose leadership did Judaism manage to accomplish this in the years and centuries following that destruction? While there is no doubt that the Babylonian rabbis and their Talmud

---

[1] I want to thank Birger Olsson and all the members of the Synagogue Project at Lund University for organizing and hosting The Ancient Synagogue: From the Beginning to about 200 CE: An International Conference at Lund University, during the week of October 14–17, 2001. This opportunity for interaction and collaboration among scholars interested in the ancient synagogues was a delight to all involved. For sharing their sage wisdom, I particularly wish to thank Lee Levine, Philip Alexander, Avigdor Shinan, Emmanuel Tov, Anders Runesson, and Reuven Kimelman. Versions of this paper were also given at the Third Congress of the International Organization for Targum Studies, in Basel Switzerland, August 2001 and at the annual national meeting of the Society for Biblical Literature in Denver, November 2001. Many scholars have made comments and observations that have improved this paper. In particular, I wish to thank Moshe Bernstein, Jodi Magness, Willem Smelik, Robert Hayward, Hayim Lapin, Eric Meyers, Sean Freyne, and Steven Fine. At the University of Wyoming, I wish to thank linguists Pamela Innis and Patricia Hamel.

provided Judaism's foundation from the sixth or seventh century onward, who led during the period immediately following 70?

The classic answer has been that the Palestinian rabbis provided the social foundation and the religious theology that led Judaism out of this disaster into a new era. It was their vision, as found in the early rabbinic texts of the Mishnah, the Tosefta and the halakhic *midrashim*, that gave the demoralized Jews a new direction for their religion. They not only provided the leadership for post-70 Judaism, but in Galilee the rabbinic movement guided the institutions—the synagogues, the schools, and the courts—that gave the new Judaism its distinctive shape and strength.

But over the past few decades, scholars have shown that the rabbis did not "run" or "control" Jewish society in the Galilee. J. Neusner has shown that the earliest rabbinic text, the Mishnah, reveals little interest in the synagogue at all.[2] The archaeological finds of synagogue mosaics indicate that in later centuries Jews did not follow rabbinic prescriptions concerning images. And L. Levine and others have developed a chronological picture charting the lack of a relationship between the rabbis and the common people during the first centuries following the destruction.[3] Furthermore, while Graeco-Roman literature and law of this period recognizes many kinds of Jewish leaders, it never even mentions rabbis.[4] These observations all support the conclusion that the rabbis did not provide religious leadership, or at least not widely recognized leadership, for the Galilean Jewish community at this time. This new scholarly picture leaves a large hole in our understanding of post-70 Galilee. Who provided the leadership if the rabbis did not? Scholars have struggled with this question because nearly all written evidence of this time comes from rabbinic literature which provides a woefully incomplete picture of Galilean society.

In this paper, I argue that the religious leadership of the Jewish community following 70 was provided by the same group as beforehand, namely, the priests—at least in part. The key evidence for this conclusion comes from their own writings, which have until now generally been attributed to the rabbis. These writings are the Pentateuchal

---

[2] See Neusner, "Synagogue in Law," 170–3. For a more indepth discussion of the place of rabbis in the first few centuries of the common era, and related bibliography, see below.
[3] See Cohen, "Place," and Levine, "Sages."
[4] Ibid., 215.

The Literary Legacy of the Priests?

Targums,[5] not only the Palestinian Targums and *Targum Pseudo-Jonathan*, but also the original form of *Targum Onqelos*, whose final form was claimed by the Babylonian rabbis. In fact, it was this original *Onqelos*, now generally called Proto-Onqelos or the Old Palestinian Targum, that provided the basis for the translations and some of the expansions of the Palestinian Targums and *Pseudo-Jonathan*.[6] The links between Proto-Onqelos and the two later Targums show that the prestige of the priests inhered in their earliest Targum, Proto-Onqelos, and was carried forward in the Land of Israel into the two later Targums.

The close ties of Proto-Onqelos with the Palestinian Targum and *Targum Pseudo-Jonathan* indicate that this early version of *Targum Onqelos* remained in Palestine following 70 and was influential there. Thus A. Berliner's conclusion, "To procure recognition and respect for this Targum [i.e. *Onqelos*] in its country of origin [i.e., the Land of Israel] was not possible," is simply incorrect.[7] Like P. Kahle after him, Berliner looked to the "all-powerful rabbis" for evidence, and found it lacking. But as W. Smelik shows, the Palestinian rabbis rejected Aramaic translations of Scripture, and so the lack of mention in Palestinian *rabbinic* literature is not indicative of Proto-Onqelos' place in Palestine.[8] Smelik's study shows that the rabbinic literature is the wrong place to look for corroboration; the Pentateuchal Targums themselves constitute the best evidence, for they come from a social location outside rabbinic circles, namely, the priests.

My argument that the priests were responsible for the Targums and that they thus provided religious leadership in the synagogue is developed in two parts. The first part describes the ties that link the three Targums. These ties are incisive yet problematic, for the Targums are composed in different dialects. This sets up the question, why are the Pentateuchal Targums linked together, even though they are composed in three different dialects? The answer is provided in the second part,

---

[5] Targums for books outside the Pentateuch may also derive from the Priestly caste, but I have not yet explored that possibility.

[6] As I have studied the Targums of Israel, I have become convinced that the Old Palestinian Targum and Proto-Onqelos are one and the same. Although it would be appropriate to use either term in this essay, I will restrict myself to using Proto-Onqelos in order to emphasize its link with *Tg. Onq.* See my discussions in Flesher, "Palestinian Targum?," 35–79 and "Translations," 75–101.

[7] Berliner, *Zeiter Teil*, 108f, cited in Kahle, *Cairo Geniza*, 194. Brackets mine.

[8] See Smelik, "Language," 201–26. For further discussion, see below.

namely, that the Targums were written at three different historical stages, each time under the aegis of the priests. The Targums thus reflect, through their interpretations, the goals of the priestly caste. But even beyond this, they reflect the linguistic and dialectal vicissitudes undergone by the priests over the early centuries of the common era.

The Targums of Israel

Before the dawn of the twentieth century, it might have seemed to the casual observer that the classification of the Pentateuchal Targums was straightforward. On the one hand, there was *Targum Onqelos*, the Babylonian Targum which was promoted by the Babylonian Talmud and claimed by the Babylonian rabbis as "our Targum." On the other hand, there were the two Palestinian Targums, each of which carried the Aramaic designation *ty*, which was short for *Targum yerushalmi* (= "Jerusalem Targum"). Scholars rendered this term into English as "Palestinian Targum." The first of these Targums, *Targum Pseudo-Jonathan*, comprised a complete Targum to the Pentateuch, translating essentially all the Hebrew text, but also adding many expansions, both large and small. The second Palestinian Targum, known as the *Fragmentary Targum*, comprised fragments of, or selections from, a complete Targum to the Pentateuch.

But the casual observer would have been wrong in assuming a clearcut geographical division, for scholars had already recognized that *Targum Onqelos* had elements of both Eastern and Western Aramaic, and that *Targum Pseudo-Jonathan*, despite its extensive additional material, had clear ties to the more literal *Targum Onqelos*. Then, in the middle of the twentieth century, two new types of pentateuchal Targums were unveiled. In 1930, Kahle published fragments from the Cairo Geniza that bore significant links with the Palestinian Targums.[9] This was followed by A. Diez Macho's discovery and publication of another Pales-

---

[9] Kahle, *Masoretens des Westens*. Additional Targum fragments from the Cairo Geniza have since been discovered and all known fragments were published by Michael L. Klein in his *Genizah Manuscripts of Palestinian Targum to the Pentateuch* (1986). A few fragments have been identified since then, and have been noted in the posthumous publication of Klein's writings, forthcoming in the Brill Academic Press series, *Studies in the Aramaic Interpretation of Scripture*.

tinian Targum, *Targum Neofiti* (or MS Neophyti 1) in 1957.[10] These finds enlivened the debate concerning the place of each Targum, a debate from which the dust is only now settling.

In the aftermath of this scholarly discussion, the apparently straightforward targumic classification has been turned on its head. *Targum Onqelos* was apparently written primarily in Palestine, while *Targum Pseudo-Jonathan* has been removed from the classification of Palestinian Targum, despite the *ty* designation on its manuscript, and the new finds have redefined the category of Palestinian Targum. How has this change come about? Let me start the explanation with *Targum Onqelos*.

In 1958, E. Y. Kutscher set forth an apparently enduring solution to *Targum Onqelos*' dialect problem, namely, why *Onqelos* has elements of both Eastern and Western Aramaic dialects.[11] He argued that *Targum Onqelos* was composed in two stages. The first stage, the creation of Proto-Onqelos, took place in Judea, probably in the first century C.E. Kutscher demonstrated this by showing that *Onqelos* was composed in the same dialect as the *Genesis Apocryphon* of Qumran. This dialect is now termed Jewish Literary Aramaic.[12] In the second stage, Proto-Onqelos was taken to Babylonia, where it was later recast into the Targum we now know as *Targum Onqelos*.

While I think that this picture of *Onqelos*' development is correct, one corollary is not; namely, that when Proto-Onqelos left Palestine, no copies remained behind.[13] Hence Proto-Onqelos had no influence on the development of Targums in Palestine until it returned with the westward movement of Babylonian Judaism in the early Middle Ages.[14] By contrast, my research reveals that Proto-Onqelos remained in Pales-

---

[10] Diez Macho, *Neophyti 1*.

[11] See Kutscher, "Language," 9–15. Kutscher follows Dalman and Nöldeke in seeing *Onqelos*' origins in Judea. See also Goshen-Gottstein, "Language of Targum Onqelos," 169–79. For a deeper discussion of the scholarly history, see Cook, "Rewriting the Bible," 10–14. For bibliography, see Beyer, *Aramaic Language*.

[12] See Kaufman, "Languages (Aramaic)" for the terminology, now used by the *Comprehensive Aramaic Lexicon*. Kutscher, "Genesis Apocryphon," 9–10, did not directly address the question of the dating of *Tg. Onq*. Although he discussed Proto-Onqelos in a first century context, his comments also allow a dating up to 135.

[13] Kutscher, "Genesis Apocryphon," 10, esp. n. 44.

[14] As stated by Berliner and Kahle above. I have myself used this formulation to explain how *Tg. Ps.-J.* and *Tg. Onq.* are related. See Flesher, "Targumim in the Context," 614–16.

tine and played a key role in the development of the Palestinian Targums and *Pseudo-Jonathan*.

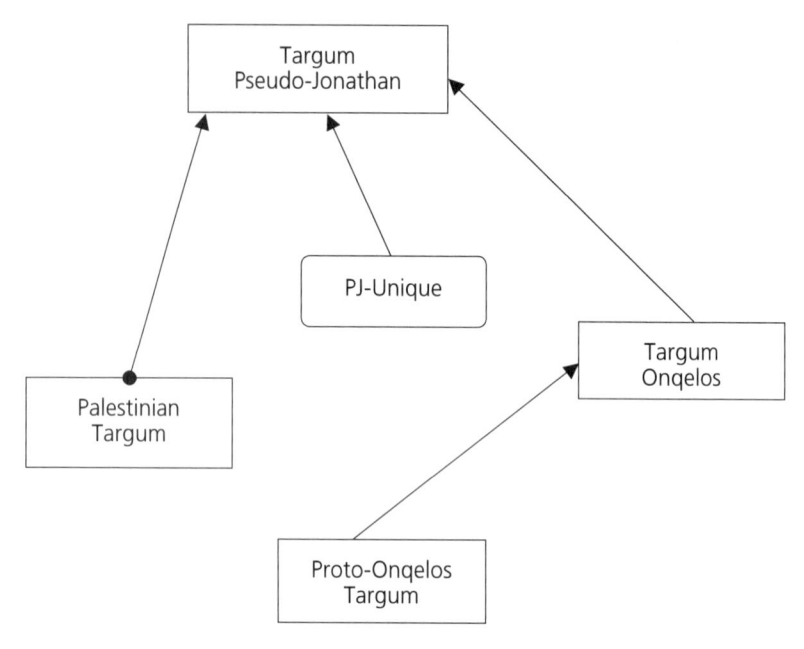

```
                    ┌──────────────┐
                    │   Targum     │
                    │Pseudo-Jonathan│
                    └──────────────┘
                       ▲        ▲
                       │        │
                    ┌──────────────┐
                    │  PJ-Unique   │
                    └──────────────┘
                                              ┌──────────┐
                                              │  Targum  │
                                              │  Onqelos │
    ┌──────────────┐                          └──────────┘
    │  Palestinian │                              ▲
    │    Targum    │                              │
    └──────────────┘                              │
                              ┌──────────────┐
                              │ Proto-Onqelos│
                              │    Targum    │
                              └──────────────┘
```

Figure 27.1 Standard view.

Although the Palestinian Targums can immediately be differentiated from *Targum Onqelos* by their dialect—they were written in Jewish Palestinian Aramaic rather than Proto-Onqelos' Jewish Literary Aramaic[15]—the key difference lies in the many expansions added into the Palestinian Targums' translation while *Onqelos'* translation is comparatively literal. These expansions by and large are shared across the different Palestinian Targums and hence derive from a single source. In my early research, I determined that 539 of the expansions are shared among these Targums, where the Targums are extant.[16] I have designated this collection of expansions the Proto-PT Source. Although I

---

[15] This also indicates a time difference, for Jewish Literary Aramaic belongs to Middle Aramaic, while Jewish Palestinian Aramaic fits into Late Aramaic. See Kaufman, "Languages," 174–5.

[16] See Flesher, "Mapping," 250. Even though *Tg. Ps.-J.* is not a Palestinian Targum, as I shall explain, it contains the Proto-PT source.

have yet to publish a complete presentation of my source analysis, a study of the expansion sources found in Gen 28–50 has appeared.[17]

The expansions provide the first indication that Proto-Onqelos remained in Palestine and influenced the Palestinian Targums. This becomes clear from an analysis of the Proto-PT expansions of the second half of Genesis in which I compared them to the non-translational aspects of *Targum Onqelos,* mostly added words.[18] I found that 35 per cent of the expansions in the Proto-PT Source drew from this additional material found in *Targum Onqelos.* Given *Onqelos'* two-stage development, this can only mean that the Palestinian Targums derived these expansions, at least in part, from Proto-Onqelos.

The second indication of Proto-Onqelos' presence in Palestine derives from comparing its translation with that of the Palestinian Targums. The Palestinian Targums share a common translation, as well as the Proto-PT expansion source. That translation depends in part on Proto-Onqelos' translation. In a recently published essay, I argue this result indicates that the translation shared among the Palestinian Targums comprises a dialectal translation of Proto-Onqelos.[19] In turn, it provides clear evidence that Proto-Onqelos remained in Palestine following the first century, and played an influential role in the creation of the Palestinian Targums.

The notion that Proto-Onqelos remained in Palestine affects the scholarly interpretation of *Targum Pseudo-Jonathan* as well. The later Targum combines the expansions of the Proto-PT source with the translation of *Onqelos,* and seasons it with a large collection of other additional material. In the scholarly picture based on Kutscher's model, *Pseudo-Jonathan's* use of *Onqelos'* translation requires its creation sometime after the final Onqelos returned to Palestine, that is, in the early Middle Ages. However, since Proto-Onqelos remained in Palestine, it

---

[17] This information derives from the source-critical analysis of the Palestinian Targums which I directed in the early 1990s with three of my then doctoral students: B. P. Mortensen, R. M. Campbell, and L. Simon. Mortensen and I are moving our studies towards publication, but some results have already appeared. See Flesher, "Mapping"; "Exploring the Sources"; Campbell, "Fragment-Targum"; Mortensen, "Targum Pseudo-Jonathan"; "Economics"; "Pseudo-Jonathan's Temple."

[18] Flesher, "Is Targum Onkelos a Palestinian Targum," 35–79.

[19] Flesher, "Translations of Proto-Onqelos," 75–101. Le Déaut sees some hint of impact of *Tg. Onq.* on *Tg. Neof.,* but interprets it as coming during the process of transmission rather than creation. He does not provide any evidence to support his observation, see Le Déaut, "Targumim," 579–81.

becomes clear that *Pseudo-Jonathan* drew its Onqelos-like translation from Proto-Onqelos instead. Although *Pseudo-Jonathan* has Onqelos' translation and some of its added words, the further Onqelos gets from a literal translation of the Hebrew text, the less likely that rendering is to show up in *Pseudo-Jonathan* (or in the Palestinian Targums for that matter). Given *Pseudo-Jonathan's* predilection for expansions and additions of all sorts, the best explanation for this missing material is that *Pseudo-Jonathan* used Proto-Onqelos which did not have it.[20]

Despite the similarities between the Palestinian Targums and *Pseudo-Jonathan*, *Pseudo-Jonathan's* character brings us to a rather ironic observation. It turns out that *Pseudo-Jonathan* is not a Palestinian Targum after all, even though it has carried that designation (as Aramaic *ty*, "*Targum yerushalmi*") for centuries.[21] This is because the connections among *Targum Neofiti*, the *Fragmentary Targums*, and the Cairo Geniza Fragments impose a new definition of Palestinian Targum. Not only do these Targums share the Proto-PT expansion source and the same dialect, but they also share a common translation.[22] These common elements thus indicate that these Targums derive from the same Targum, that is, from an original Palestinian Targum, an initial translation of the Pentateuch containing the expansions of the Proto-PT source.[23] The differences among the different representatives of the Palestinian Targum stem from a free approach to reproduction, one which allowed changes in wording (especially within expansions) and the addition of new expansions. This approach differed radically from the Babylonian treatment of *Targum Onqelos*, which consisted of careful copying from

---

[20] Alexander anticipates some of the results of my analysis in his essay, "Jewish Aramaic Translations," 248–9.

[21] Kaufman and others have argued this point, see Kaufman, "Dating" 118–41, and Kaufman and Maori, "Targumim to Exodus 20," 24–5. The observation of the composite nature of *Tg. Ps.-J.* has been made by a number of scholars in the past, see Vermes, "Targumic Versions," 110 and Cook, "Rewriting the Bible," 2–5 whose discussion gives some history of the scholarly views on this matter.

[22] This general observation is apparent to any scholar who has compared the translations of the Palestinian Targums. See also the important study by Kaufman and Maori. For a discussion of Aramaic dialects in general, see Kaufman, "Dating" and Kaufman, "Languages."

[23] The "original Palestinian Targum" should not be confused with the Old Palestinian Targum, which is Proto-Onqelos. This original Palestinian Targum was translated from the Hebrew text into the Jewish Targumic Aramaic dialect with constant close consultation of Proto-Onqelos and the careful incorporation of expansions of the Proto-PT source.

manuscript to manuscript and even the development of a *masorah* to help ensure the accuracy of succeeding copies.

Targum Pseudo-Jonathan has a composite character that differentiates it from the true Palestinian Targums. It contains the expansions of the Proto-PT source in their Palestinian dialect of Jewish Targumic Aramaic. Its translation reproduces that of Proto-Onqelos in dialect and for the most part in wording. It also contains a further collection of expansions, even larger than Proto-PT, which is called the PJ-unique Source.[24] These expansions are composed in yet a third dialect, that of Late Jewish Literary Aramaic—a dialect recently identified by Kaufman and E. Cook.[25] *Pseudo-Jonathan's* features thus indicate that it is not a Palestinian Targum.[26]

Even though it is clear that neither *Pseudo-Jonathan* nor Proto-Onqelos belongs to the classification of Palestinian Targum, they are clearly related to it. These commonalities suggest all these Targums should be classified together, despite their differences. Indeed, if we look at all the Pentateuchal Targums using the criteria of translation, expansions, and dialect, they are closely bound together. They are all Targums of Israel.[27] Here is how they are linked. First, the Proto-PT expansions appear in the Palestinian Targums and *Pseudo-Jonathan*. Second, a significant percentage of the Proto-PT expansions derive from added words in *Targum Onqelos*. Third, the translations likewise link these sets of Targums together, not directly, but through a common source found

---

[24] Mortensen terms this source "Unique Pseudo-Jonathan" in her work (see Mortensen, "Targum Pseudo-Jonathan") or "Pseudo-Jonathan's distinctive material" (Mortensen, "Economics").

[25] See Kaufman, "Dating" and Cook, "Rewriting the Bible." See also Kaufman, "Late Jewish Literary Aramaic," 363–82. In a paper delivered to the Aramaic Studies Section of the Society of Biblical Literature in 2000, I explored the dialectal character of the sources identified by my source-critical analysis of the Palestinian Targums. I found that the dialectal differences in *Tg. Ps.-J.* outlined by Kaufman and Cook largely coincided with the sources of *Tg. Ps.-J.* For further discussion of PJ and its dialects, see below.

[26] Although the literary flexibility to create such a composite Targum is that found in Palestine rather than the *masorah*-obsessed approach of Babylonian Jewry.

[27] This grouping is anticipated by the *Comprehensive Aramaic Lexicon (CAL)* project, where *Tg. Onq.* and *Tg. Ps.-J.* are presented as Palestinian texts. I want to thank Stephen Kaufman and Jerome Lund of CAL for making their expertise and resources available to me and for the assistance they have given me with regard to Aramaic dialectology.

in *Targum Onqelos*.[28] Fourth, dialect links the Palestinian Targums and *Pseudo-Jonathan*, for both present Proto-PT in the dialect of Jewish Targumic Aramaic. Fifth, dialect also links *Pseudo-Jonathan* and *Targum Onqelos*, for both their translations are in Jewish Literary Aramaic. So the classification Targums of Israel brings together all the Pentateuchal Targums, based on their interconnections.

If it makes sense to term these Targums "Targums of Israel," then not only must the similarities be explainable within the context of the Land of Israel, but so must their differences, especially the dialectal differences. Thus we need to know who composed these Targums, who used these different dialects, and why the Targums shifted among the dialects? In particular, as historians, we want to be able to identify the social or religious group responsible at different stages for these developments.

The initial identification of priests as the social group responsible for the Targums comes from two observations. First, my colleague B. Mortensen has demonstrated that the expansions of the PJ-unique source are highly focused on issues of direct priestly concern.[29] It reveals extensive interest in apects of sacrifice, down to small details like in which hand the sacrificial knife should be held. More general matters of temple activities and management also appear. And, where the temple is not involved, priests often are. For instance, when *Pseudo-Jonathan* discusses judges, it depicts them as priests, not as rabbis.[30]

Since priests were involved in the last stage of the Pentateuchal Targums, could they have been involved in earlier stages as well? A second aspect of *Pseudo-Jonathan* suggests the answer is yes, for the additional material distinctive to *Pseudo-Jonathan* was written in the dialect of Late Jewish Literary Aramaic. The social group who developed the expansions used this new dialect, namely, the priests. Although this dialect was heavily influenced by Jewish Palestinian Aramaic and other dialects, its foundation comes from Jewish Literary Aramaic whose heyday was the first century, a time when priests were more prominent. To trace the development of the later dialect, then, we need to return to the first century and see what we can discover about Jewish Literary Aramaic,

---

[28] This is Proto-Onqelos.
[29] See Mortensen, "Economics," Mortensen, "Temple," and Mortensen, "Targum Pseudo-Jonathan," 68–194.
[30] See for example *Tg. Ps.-J.* to Exod 18:26 and 22:27, and Mortensen's discussion in "Targum Pseudo-Jonathan," 96, 122.

Proto-Onqelos (the Targum which used it in its composition), and the priestly class.[31]

The Priestly Impact

The Targumic Evidence

The Targums of Israel consist of three different Targums, which, while they are clearly linked, come from different historical and social circumstances. We can begin to place them into specific periods when we look at the dialects in which the Targums are composed. Each Targum was written in a different dialect, or, in the case of *Pseudo-Jonathan*, three dialects. These dialects can, in varying degrees, provide the initial placement of the Targum in their historical periods and geographical locations.

But the problem of explaining the connections among these different Targums is not answered simply by fixing them in space and time. We need to understand the dynamics—the historic and linguistic changes—that took place between these periods, and how those dynamics shaped the Targums. The Targums of Israel were created during a time that contained not only great historical change but also significant linguistic change. To explain the characters of these three Targums, we must unite the historical and the linguistic into a single explanation. By bringing them together, we construct an argument that is stronger than either aspect alone.

Stage One – The First Century

Proto-Onqelos was composed in the dialect of Jewish Literary Aramaic, which scholars classify as a form of Middle Aramaic. This dialect stands at the end of a trajectory that begins in the Official Aramaic of the Persian Empire and comes through the Biblical Aramaic of Daniel, before it appears in Qumran, Proto-Onqelos and *Targum Jonathan*. The latest

---

[31] This essay will focus exclusively on the use and development of Aramaic, to the exclusion of the other languages in use in Palestine during this time. For scholarly discussion and analysis of the interaction of Aramaic, Hebrew and Greek, as well as Latin, see: Fitzmyer, "Languages of Palestine," 62–91; Horsley, *Archaeology*, 154–75; and Hezser, *Jewish Literacy*, 227–50.

exemplars are the Bar Kokhba Letters, *Megillah Taʿanit*, and older legal formulas preserved in the Taanitic writings. Thus while this dialect falls into the chronological period of Middle Aramaic, which ranges from the start of the second century B.C.E. to the third century C.E., the latest compositions in Jewish Literary Aramaic seem to have been written by about 135.[32]

Jewish Literary Aramaic was a literary standard, a concept which has two important implications. First, a literary dialect requires a support structure, both educational and financial. That is, it needs to be taught so that people can learn to read it and acquire the techniques and skills necessary to write it. Students must have the leisure to study; teachers and schools must have the financial support to teach them. Thus a literary dialect must serve an important function for a moneyed elite, usually a political or religious structure, who would supply that support. This means a literary dialect has a centralizing tendency that focuses it on the location of its support structure. Second, a literary dialect is portable, in a way that a local, spoken dialect is not. That is, a spoken dialect needs speakers—more than one—in order to perform communication acts. Outside a dialect's locality, such speakers are rare. A literary dialect, by contrast, can be moved anywhere that a single reader or writer of that dialect wishes to go. When ascertaining a geographical location for a literary dialect, these two tendencies pull in opposite directions. The centralizing tendency brings people around the center, while the portability provides a possiblity for the dialect to appear anywhere.

When we turn to an attempt to establish a geographical location for Jewish Literary Aramaic, however, only one tendency seems to be in play, that of centralization. Three factors point to the conclusion that Jerusalem provided the home for Jewish Literary Aramaic's educational support structure prior to 70 C.E., and that the dialect was probably known throughout Judea.[33]

The first indication stems from the more than 40 Aramaic inscriptions archaeologists have found dating to the first century C.E. from tombs and ossuaries surrounding Jerusalem.[34] While most of these in-

---

[32] Kaufman, "Languages," 174 puts the end of Middle Aramaic at 250 C.E., while Fitzmyer, "Phases," 61, puts the end at 200 C.E.
[33] The following argument supports the conclusions of Kutscher, even though it is based on different types of evidence.
[34] Beyer, *Aramäischen Texte*, 339–47 and its *Ergänzungsband*, 205–8. There are a few named priests among the inscriptions.

scriptions consist only of names, and thus give no dialectical information, a few contain more linguistically useful material. The small amount of dialectal information in them suggests that these inscriptions are composed in Jewish Literary Aramaic. The clearest indication of this is their use of Jewish Literary Aramaic's masculine plural pronomical suffix -נה (and -ונא) rather than the form found in the later Jewish Palestinian (and Targumic) Aramaic -ן (and -ינן).[35]

The second indication that Jewish Literary Aramaic is a Jerusalem-based dialect of Judea comes from the Qumran Aramaic documents and the Bar Kokhba letters. These writings were found in Judea. While the users of a literary dialect could move around, it seems these stayed near home. The texts were either written or preserved by people with strong Jerusalem connections. Indeed, the Qumran community, according to the Community and the Damascus Rules, formed around a group of priestly exiles from Jerusalem and its temple. They aimed to return to Jerusalem and to restore their ideas of pure and correct worship to the temple. Similarly, Bar Kokhba and his army focused on Jerusalem, with the goal of driving out the Romans and restoring Jewish rule there. So these writings reveal that Jewish Literary Aramaic was used by people who viewed Jerusalem as the focus of their activities.

A third factor bearing on our question is that of language and dialect decay.[36] Jewish Literary Aramaic in Palestine goes from a vibrant, productive dialect in the first century—indeed this is its heyday—to a decaying, marginal language in the second. Its latest compositions seem to have been written by about 135, such as the Bar Kokhba Letters and *Megillah Taʿanit*.[37] After that, the dialect seemed incapable of producing

---

[35] These examples are drawn from Beyer's texts yJE 3, 4, and 5 (Beyer, *Aramäischen Texte*, 1984, 340). These ossuary inscriptions also show a tendency to archaize. For example, they sometimes spell "wife" in a form drawn from Official Aramaic, that is, אנתתה instead of the JLA אתתה. See Beyer, yJE 11, 17 and 29.

[36] Language and dialect decay and decline constitutes part of the larger area of study generally termed "language death." For general studies in this field, see Crystal, *Language Death*, 19–24, 68–90; and Nettle and Romaine, *Vanishing Voices*, 50–6. See also Dressler, "Language Decay," 321–36 and Dorian, *Investigating Obsolescence*.

[37] The Mishnah and other Tannaitic literature occasionally contain older legal formulas written in this dialect. Their exact provenance is unclear. With regard to the standard chronological framework for understanding the history of Aramaic dialects, see Fitzmyer, "Phases." He places the end of Middle Aramaic at 200 C.E.

further literature. Why this sudden decline? Dialects do not just disappear on their own. There must be a reason. W. Dressler sees the central feature of a decaying language as a decline in the number of people who can produce communication, either spoken or written, filling the same sociolinguistic functions for which their elders had used it.[38] This happens when the language or dialect becomes "impoverished in comparison with earlier stages of the language." What would suddenly impoverish this thriving Aramaic dialect? A catastrophic event that removed its educational and financial support structure.[39] The obvious candidate for this event is the destruction of Jerusalem in 70 by the Romans. Jewish Literary Aramaic declined not because of linguistic shift, but because of historical events—events which point to Jerusalem as its center.

Cook has recently posited that *Targum Onqelos'* dialect stems not from Palestine, but from a location—a linguistic and geographic location—between Eastern and Western Aramaic, which he calls "Central Aramaic."[40] Using linguistic evidence, he argues that rather than Middle Aramaic showing a clear distinction between Eastern and Western, Middle Aramaic should be conceived of as a dialectal continuum, with each dialect shading off into those geographically positioned next to it. That would place *Onqelos'* dialect as being used somewhere in the upper Euphrates region. Although Cook provides a possible explanation of the linguistic evidence, it does not fit the historical data. With regard to the points just mentioned, we have shown that the Jerusalem inscriptions locate *Onqelos'* Jewish Literary Aramaic in Judea. Nor do we know of any large, well-educated or influential society of Jews in the region Cook identifies that could have been responsible for writing, distributing, and popularizing *Onqelos*—a society that could have provided its support structure. Finally, Cook closes with the observation that there is no indication that *Onqelos* ever was in Palestine, a point my research has shown to be incorrect.[41] So despite Cook's analysis, Jerusalem remains the only real possibility for the main area for use of Jewish Literary Aramaic.

Kaufman, the editor of the *Comprehensive Aramaic Lexicon*, places it at 250 C.E., see Kaufman, "Languages."

[38] Dressler, "Language Decay," 324.

[39] See Nettle and Romaine, *Vanishing Voices*, 51–3, and Crystal, *Language Death*, 70–6.

[40] See Cook, "New Perspective," 142–56 and "Qumran," 1–21.

[41] Cook, "Language," 155–6

The Literary Legacy of the Priests?

If Jerusalem was the center of the dialect, then who provided its support structure? The educational purpose of that structure would have been accomplished by scribes, but the institutional support and employment would be found among the governing elite, whether political or religious. Given the continuous instability and even absence of the Jewish political elite in Jerusalem, the location must have been within the temple administration under the supervision of the priests.[42] The priests were in no way the only users of the dialect, anyone who learned it could use it. And, from the evidence of the inscriptions, that was certainly true among those who could afford tombs in which to bury their dead. But it was the priests who used and sponsored the means necessary for the continuation of this dialect.

Even though the support structure for Jewish Literary Aramaic was centered in Jerusalem, that does not mean that knowledge of Jewish Literary Aramaic was restricted to the city. On the contrary, we know that Qumran sectarians read and wrote in Jewish Literary Aramaic. This is not surprising, given the group's priestly orientation and Jerusalem connections. Furthermore, the system of *mishmarot* by which 24 families of priests rotated from their homes outside Jerusalem in and out of their temple service at different times of the year would have spread the knowledge and use of Jewish Literary Aramaic throughout Judea.[43] So Jewish Literary Aramaic was geographically centered in Jerusalem, and it was probably used throughout Judea. Its support structure was provided by the temple and its priests.

Turning from linguistic to historical evidence, can we show that the priests' knowledge of Proto-Onqelos' dialect leads to the conclusion that they wrote Proto-Onqelos?[44] Not directly. But we can show that, as a class, the priests had responsibility for the Torah and for teaching it, and had become known as Torah experts. Indeed, from biblical times,

---

[42] Goodman, *Ruling Class*, 36–50, shows that following the deposition and exile of Archelaus in 6 C.E., priests essentially become the only non-foreign, political power in Judea. The issue here is not, as for Goodman, whether the new priesthood commands the respect of Judeans, but whether they manage the temple as an institution and keep its support structure functioning.

[43] For the institution of *maamadot* and *mishmarot*, see 1 Chron 24:7–12, Josephus, *J.A.* 7.366, *m. Taʿan.* 4:2 and *y. Taʿan.* 68a. The best bibliography appears in Schürer, *History*, vol. 2, 245–50. See also Levine, *Ancient Synagogue*, 36; and Runesson, *Origin*, 125–7.

[44] For general analysis of priests in the first century, see: Goodman, *Ruling Class*; Schwartz, *Josephus*; Schürer, *Jewish People*, vol. 2, 237–308; Sanders, *Judaism*.

the priestly duties included the responsibility for instructing the People Israel in the Torah's ethical and legal regulations, and enforcing their practice of them.

Even though we typically associate priests with the temple's sacrificial practices, Scripture has also been under the provenance of the priests from the earliest portrayals in Jewish sacred writings. The Pentateuch relates how after Moses received the Ten Commandments and the rest of the Torah, they were put in the Ark that became the center of the Tabernacle.[45] It thus became the responsibility of Aaron the Priest. This responsibility appears in stories of both the tribal and the monarchical periods, with the priests carrying the ark into battle and Solomon establishing it at the heart of the temple.[46] In terms of teaching, Deut 31: 9–13 depicts Moses giving the Torah to the priests and assigning them the task of publicizing and teaching the commandments to the People Israel every seven years. In 2 Chronicles, priests share their teaching (and judging) duties with the Levites.[47] Similarly, when Israel returned from the exile in Babylonia, it was Ezra the Priest (and scribe) who taught the Torah to the returnees. Neh 8 makes clear that it is not just the teaching that is important, but practicing the commandments that have been taught. Twice in this chapter Ezra reads from the Torah and twice the people go away to practice what was read—the activities of the Feast of Sukkot.

This link between the priests teaching Torah and the People Israel practicing it continues down into the first century. Josephus presents the priests as the class of people to whom God the Lawgiver assigned responsibility for the knowledge and implementation of His Laws. Josephus's admittedly idealized picture shows the priests as responsible for administration of and instruction in the Torah. In *C. Ap.* 2.185–7, he writes:

> Could there be a finer or more equitable polity than one which sets God at the head of the universe, which assigns the administration of its highest affairs to the whole body of priests? . . . But this charge further embraced a strict superintendence of the Law and of the pursuits of everyday

---

[45] Exod 25:10–22.
[46] 1 Sam 4:1–6; 1 Kgs 8:6–11.
[47] See 2 Chron 17:7–9 and 19:8–10, and the discussion in Sanders, *Judaism*, 170–3.

The Literary Legacy of the Priests?

life; for the appointed duties of the priests included general supervision, the trial of cases of litigation, and the punishment of condemned persons.

Thus priests are in charge of administering the Law, up to and including the operation of courts and the punishment of law-breakers. But they are also supposed to superintend the Law and its application to the life of each Jew, the "pursuits of everyday life."

In the late Second-Temple period, the priests do this by teaching Israel in the synagogue. While it has been widely recognized that one of the earliest and most well-documented synagogue activities is that of Scripture reading and interpretation, two points have been less understood.[48] First, Scripture study is for the purpose of practicing Torah. Josephus (*C. Ap.* 2.175–8) makes it clear that Scripture study is not important in-and-of-itself, but so that the People Israel can do God's commandments and Torah.

> For ignorance [God] left no pretext. He appointed the Law to be the most excellent and necessary form of instruction, ordaining, not that it should be heard once for all or twice or on several occasions, but that every week men should desert their other occupations and assemble to listen to the Law and to obtain a thorough and accurate knowledge of it. . . . The result, then, of our thorough grounding in the laws from the first dawn of intelligence is that we have them, as it were, engraven on our souls.

Second, this "study for practice" takes place under priestly auspices, as well as lay. Priests are presented by Philo as the preferred leaders of Scripture reading and instruction in the synagogue. In his *Hypoth.* 7:12–13 we read:

> He [Moses] required them to assemble in the same place on these seventh days, and sitting together in a respectful and orderly manner hear the laws read so that none should be

---

[48] For Scripture reading in synagogues, see, for example, Josephus, *C. Ap.* 2.175; Philo, *Legat.* 156; Acts 13:14–15; and the Theodotus inscription—translation in Kloner, "Ancient Synagogues," 11. For scholarly discussion of this question, see Levine, *Ancient Synagogue*, 135–51.

ignorant of them. And indeed they always assemble and sit together, most of them in silence except when it is the practice to add something to signify approval of what is read. But some priest who is present or one of the elders reads the holy laws to them and expounds them point by point till about the late afternoon, when they depart having gained both expert knowledge of the holy laws and considerable advance in piety.

It is clear here that the priests are ones who should instruct the People Israel in the Torah. But there has been a change from earlier times. They share that task with knowledgeable laymen. In this passage, the elders have that position. In the New Testament, that right is not even limited to elders; even visitors can comment on Scripture. In Luke 4:16-22, Jesus gets into trouble when he dares to interpret the Isaiah passage he has just read as referring to himself.[49]

This association between priests and non-priests can even be found with regard to Scripture translation, albeit into Greek rather than Aramaic. In *The Letter of Aristeas*, King Ptolemy sends to the High Priest in Jerusalem asking him to send translators who can render the Hebrew Bible into Greek. He appoints "men of the most exemplary lives and mature experience, skilled in matters pertaining to their Law, six in number from each tribe."[50]

Finally, on a related matter, leadership roles in the synagogue can be held by the laity or by priests. Most identified synagogue leaders are laymen, but Theodotus the Priest led his Jerusalem synagogue as the *archisynagogos*, as did his father and grandfather. Similarly, a priest was one of the leaders of the synagogue in Berenice, as can be seen from his privileged position on a dedicatory inscription.[51]

---

[49] In their *Excavating Jesus*, 27–8, Crossan and Reed observe that Luke has recast this story beyond its Markan basis. In Mark 6:2–6, Jesus teaches in the synagogue, but there is no link to Scripture reading.

[50] *Let. Aris.* 32.

[51] See Binder, *Temple Courts*, 257–63, 355–60. For bibliography on the extensive recent discussion of the Theodotus inscription, see Riesner, "Synagogues in Jerusalem," 179–212. Kee has been an important participant in these debates, see "Defining," 7–26, as well as the bibliography in Riesner. For my own perspective, see Flesher, "Prolegomenon," 143–7 and "Palestinian Synagogues," 33–4.

The Literary Legacy of the Priests?

So the priests were the guardians of Scripture, its assigned interpreters, and had the duty of ensuring that the people Israel knew the Torah and practiced it, throughout the centuries prior to the temple's destruction in 70. Most importantly, by the first century C.E., Scripture reading and instruction had become part of synagogue practice and thus were available to all Jews.[52] While this enabled people of all classes to take part in Scripture study, it still left the priests as the class of divinely ordained instructors and interpreters, and gave them an active role that involved continual interaction, in a religious context, with the masses of the People Israel.

It is interesting to note that despite the general expertise scholars have assigned to specific Jewish groups, such as scribes, Pharisees and Sadducees, these groups are not depicted by our sources as participating in Scripture interpretation in synagogues, unless they are priests or Levites.[53] But these are religious parties or occupations, not rival social institutions, and so their members functioned as priests or as employees of the temple complex. Sadducees, rather than representing alternative "Scripture experts," apparently dominated the priesthood.[54] The Pharisees, according to Josephus, had fewer members of the priestly caste, but were part of the body of people who served as support personnel for the educational, governing, and diplomatic functions of the temple complex—the latter functions having fallen to the priesthood following the exile of Archelaus in 6 C.E.[55] Furthermore, the Pharisees were not

---

[52] At least to those who lived in places that could afford it. Some small villages may not have been able to afford Torah scrolls. Furthermore, small rural villages may not have had anyone literate enough to read Scripture. For an in-depth discussion of literacy in this period, see Hezser, C., *Jewish Literacy*.

[53] For scribes, see Binder, *Temple Courts*, 363–8. For Pharisees, see Grabbe, "Synagogues in Pre-70 Palestine," 23–4; Levine, *Ancient Synagogue*, 37–8; and Sanders, *Judaism*, 380–452. Neusner's surveys of all the material referring to Pharisees reveal no connection between Pharisees and the synagogue, and little connection between Pharisees and Scripture interpretation. His comprehensive analysis finds only two references to possible Pharisees and Targums: a late comment about Jonathan b. Uzziel and the *Writings Targum* (*b. Meg.* 3a), and an observation about a Job Targum (*t. Šabb.* 13:2). See *Rabbinic Traditions*, vol. 1, 355–6, 369, 371; vol. 3, 192, 211. For the non-rabbinic material, see Neusner, *Politics to Piety*. In the 2nd edition, see also the essays by Smith and Ziesler.

[54] On the Sadducees, see Schürer, *Jewish People*, vol. 2, 404–14; and Sanders, *Judaism*, 332–6.

[55] On the Pharisees, see Neusner, *Politics to Piety*; Schürer, *Jewish People*, vol. 2, 388–403; Sanders, *Judaism*, 380–451; Schwartz, *Josephus*, 172–200.

known for their Scripture interpretation, but for their knowledge of alternative traditions "handed down from former generations."[56] These religious parties thus provide no alternative to the understanding that it was the priests who had responsibility not just to interpret the Holy Books, but to guide the people in the practice of God's Torah.

So we have arrived at the penultimate step in our argument, but we can go no further. We have built a case that indicates the role of priests encompasses Scripture interpretation as much as temple sacrifice. We have also shown that priests and their support structure are most likely the main focus for the teaching and use of Jewish Literary Aramaic. Both are necessary conditions for Proto-Onqelos' composition. However, we lack the direct evidence to take the final step that would demonstrate without question that the priests either wrote or sponsored the writing of Proto-Onqelos. If the priests were responsible for Proto-Onqelos, then I have provided the answer to the mystery of the Targum's prestige in the next stage, for its association with the priests would have given it a high status. After the banishment from Judea, the priests would have carried Proto-Onqelos north to Galilee to become the literary exemplar of their prestige and standing.

Stage 2 – The Second Century

Stage one came to a catastrophic end with the destruction of Jerusalem and its temple in 70 C.E., and then the failure of Bar Kokhba's rebellion in 135. In Galilee, there was comparatively little disruption, except in the few cities where the Roman armies fought at the start of the war (in 67). Galilee's catastrophe did not begin until the mid-second century, when the banishment of all Jews from Judea caused thousands of them to migrate north.[57] Among the migrants were large numbers of priests. While many priests probably moved with only their immediate families to whatever villages would give them welcome, every priestly *mishmarah* had families that moved and settled together. Partial lists of the *mishmarot* in their Galilean locations are known from archaeological finds as

---

[56] Josephus, *J.A.* 13.297.

[57] It is unclear exactly how many Judeans migrated to Galilee following the two revolts against Rome. As Groh, "Clash," 29–38, makes clear, there seems to be little interruption in occupation patterns in Galilee in the first and second centuries, except for those cities like Yodefat which were directly attacked by the Romans.

early as the third century and entire lists appear among sixth and seventh century *piyyutim*.[58]

```
        ┌─────────────┐
        │ Palestinian │
        │   Targum    │
        └─────────────┘
            ↑     ↑
           /       \
          /         \
┌──────────────┐     \
│  Proto-PT    │      \
│  Expansions  │       \
└──────────────┘        \
        ↑                \
         \                \
          ┌──────────────┐
          │ Proto-Onqelos│
          │    Targum    │
          └──────────────┘
```

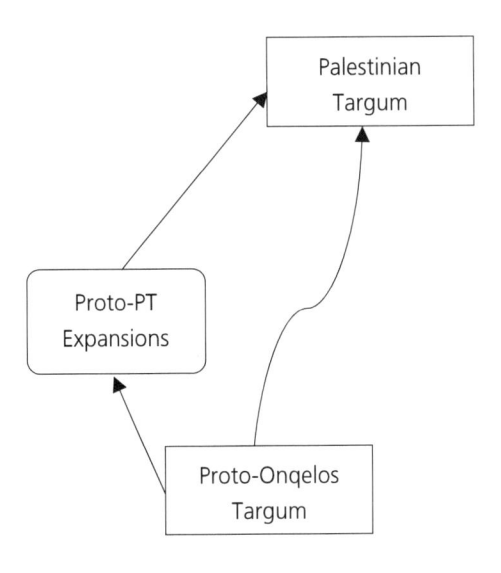

Figure 27.2 Palestine: second century.

Despite the enormous social and economic disruption this large-scale immigration must have had on Galilee, the available evidence suggests that the linguistic situation remained stable. The Aramaic literature and inscriptions closest in time to the second century and third century were all composed in a single dialect, that of Jewish Palestinian Aramaic.[59] Or to be more precise, they were composed in one of the sub-dialects of Jewish Palestinian Aramaic. For *Targum Neofiti* and the other Palestinian Targums were composed in a sub-dialect of Jewish Palestinian Aramaic Kaufman identifies as Jewish Targumic Aramaic.[60] He goes on to

---

[58] See Schürer, *Jewish People*, vol. 2, 245–50; Avi-Yonah, "Caesarea Inscription," 46–57.

[59] Sokoloff's *Dictionary of Jewish Palestinian Aramaic* treats these as a single dialect. Naveh's work also treats the inscriptions as part of the same dialect. See also Yahalom's "Synagogue Inscriptions in Palestine," 47–56, esp. n. 13.

[60] There are a few exceptions to this characterization, such as Exod 20 in the Paris *Frg Tg*. See Kaufman and Maori, "Targumim to Exodus 20," 28.

distinguish the related sub-dialects of the post-first century Jewish Palestinian inscriptions as well as that of Galilean Aramaic.[61]

Kaufman and Fitzmyer class Jewish Palestinian Aramaic as part of Late Aramaic, which begins in the third century.[62] Thus they indicate a clear separation between Jewish Literary Aramaic which is Middle Aramaic and Jewish Palestinian Aramaic which is Late Aramaic. This division appears to be more than chronological;s it is also developmental. Although more attention needs to be devoted to this question, it seems that Jewish Palestinian Aramaic developed along a trajectory that avoided both Jewish Literary Aramaic and Biblical Aramaic.[63]

So where does Jewish Palestinian Aramaic come from? It seems that prior to this period, it was the spoken Aramaic dialect of Jewish Galilee. This is because the Galilean synagogue inscriptions, despite being from the third century and later, seem to represent a version of the dialect that is closer to the spoken tongue.[64] They show indications of phonologic change that develops in a spoken mileau rather than a written one. For example, the inscriptions regularly use הי- instead of the targumic יהי- as the masculine singular pronomial suffix. The loss of the yod indicates a shift in the spoken language.[65] In addition, an inscription from Capernaum has shortened the feminine singular jussive תהי to תי, as a speaker would have done.[66] Similarly, an inscription from Hammat Gader wrote דהב instead of the expected דיהב, again a shortening com-

---

[61] See Kaufman, "Languages."

[62] See ibid., and Fitzmyer, "Phases."

[63] Jewish Palestinian Aramaic not only lacks several features found in Biblical Aramaic and Jewish Literary Aramaic, but it has unrelated, alternative features in their place.

[64] The inscriptions in this dialect date mostly from the fourth to the seventh century, with a few as early as the third. The texts containing Galilean Aramaic are largely fourth century or later. My own position on the dating of the first Palestinian Targum which contained the Proto-PT source is late second century, based on the work of Alexander's "Toponomy." My hypothesis concerning the position of these dialects expects that this spoken language be active in the second century and perhaps a century or two earlier. The problem is of course that there is no direct evidence, known to me, supporting this position—or contradicting it. If this dating of the Palestinian Targum is correct, then it is perhaps the earliest evidence of this dialect. Such dating must be established on a non-linguistic basis.

[65] See Naveh, *Mosaic*, 36 (Kursi), and 107 (Ein Gedi). I want to thank Jerome Lund of the *Comprehensive Aramaic Lexicon* for helping me understand dialectical aspects of these inscriptions.

[66] Ibid., 38–9.

mon to speech.[67] In comparison to the written language of the Palestinian Targums, these forms have changed more rapidly. The Palestinian Targums seem to be a written version of this dialect created for the synagogue, while Galilean Aramaic may be a written sub-dialect created by the more scholarly rabbinic circles.[68]

When Jewish Palestinian Aramaic retained its position as the dominant Aramaic dialect of post-135 Galilee, what happened to Jewish Literary Aramaic? It could have died out. Instead, it seems that a small social group—the priestly caste—struggled to maintain it. This scenario derives from the observations made by Ferguson, who articulated the link between religious groups and language preservation. Ferguson points out that religious groups frequently guard their distinct identity vis-à-vis the surrounding culture by maintaining their linguistic differences.[69] He further argues that if this religious difference is linked to mi-

---

[67] Ibid., 57–60.

[68] If Jewish Targumic Aramaic derives from the spoken dialect of Galilee and the Golan, then it fair to ask where this spoken Galilean dialect comes from. The answer lies in the source of Galilee's population. After much debate and sifting of evidence, archaeologists are coming to the conclusion that an essentially deserted Galilee was repopulated by Judeans during the Hasmonean period. They certainly seem to share a common material culture, including the extensive use of immersion pools and stone vessels. These items are quite rare outside of Judea and Galilee and indicate a concern with cultic purity. Reed, *Archaeology*, 23–51, discusses the evidence for the various positions, along with extensive bibliography, and shows why this is the only workable conclusion. Freyne has also taken this position, see "Town and Country," 53. If this scenario is correct, then the Aramaic of Galilee stems from the spoken dialect of Judea in the second century B.C.E., rather than from Judea's Jewish *Literary* Aramaic. Thus, in a way, Tal's idea (see "Dialects," 447–8), that the Palestinian Targums were written in the spoken dialect of Judea points in the right direction. This would explain why Jewish Palestinian Aramaic appears in inscriptions throughout the Land of Israel during the third through sixth centuries C.E. and not just Galilee, a phenomenon which Tal also comments on (pp. 442–3). The explanation is that the inscriptions come from the geographic areas in which the Judean spoken dialect (=Jewish Palestinian Aramaic) continued in use through these centuries.

[69] See Ferguson, "Religious Factors," 59–68. Ferguson based his analysis on several earlier studies, such as the collection of essays edited by Fishman et al., *Language Loyalty;* Samarin, *Language in Religious Practice*; and the work of Blanc, (*Communal Dialects in Baghdad*) who studied Arabic dialects in early twentieth century Baghdad. Blanc observed that dialect difference was not a matter of geographic location, but of religion. Each of the three religious groups—Muslim, Christian, and Jewish—spoke a different dialect of Arabic. A parallel situation of course appears in Palestine in the period under study with Samaritan Aramaic, Christian Palestinian

gration of the group, then the impetus to maintain the difference of language or dialect is even stronger.[70]

When we bring these observations to second-century Galilee, we find they help explain the continuation of Jewish Literary Aramaic. The caste status of the priests certainly gives them a standing as an independent social group, even within their own religion. The purity regulations, the marital laws, and the continuing priestly privileges erected, at one level, a solid boundary between them and other Jews. While the priests maintained their biblically emphasized holy status, recent events had cost them their dominant position. Most important for our purpose, their literary dialect no longer had widespread acceptance.

So Jewish Literary Aramaic became a distinctive dialect of the priestly caste, and lost the standard character it had in stage one. Although the priests lacked the ability to make their dialect known and accepted among the wider population of Jewish Galilee, they were able to continue knowledge of the dialect among themselves.[71]

Even with a strong support structure, any minority dialect remains constantly under pressure from the dominant dialect, and, over the generations, will be influenced by it. In the terminology of Dressler's concept of language decay, "[once] social change subordinat[es] the respective speech community to another speech community," then the necessary circumstances for a situation of language decay have been met.[72] In other words, once the priestly dialect of Jewish Literary Aramaic became subordinated to the dominant Jewish Palestinian Aramaic,

---

Aramaic and Jewish Palestinian Aramaic. See the more recent observations on this link between religion, immigration and language preservation by Haugen, Huffines, Mougeon and Beniak, and Woolard in Dorian, *Investigating Obsolescence*.

[70] Ferguson, "Religious Factors," 61–4. Let me be clear that I do not think that this was a diglossic situation, at least not a Ferguson defined diglossia. See Ferguson, "Diglossia," 1–26. Thus I agree with Schwartz, "Power and Identity," 3–47, on this point, although I do not think that diglossia is limited to modern, industrial societies, as he argues.

[71] Ferguson is careful to point out that there may be many factors in play in these linguistic situations that we do not yet recognize. However he does claim, "It may still be safe to assume that in voluntary migration for socioeconomic reasons, religious affiliation or commitment will tend to be language-conservative (i.e., maintenance-oriented), to the greatest extent for the language of sacred texts, next greatest for the language of public ritual and explanation of the texts," Ferguson, "Religious Factors," 64.

[72] Dressler, "Language Decay," 325. Brackets mine.

The Literary Legacy of the Priests?

then the weaker dialect continually struggled against corruption by the stronger. As we shall see momentarily, the priestly caste was only partly successful in fighting against this.

Although the priests did not manage to promote their dialect, they were successful in promoting their Targum, Proto-Onqelos. Successful, to the extent at least, that Proto-Onqelos served as the basis for a new Targum, the Palestinian Targum. How were the priests able to achieve this acceptance? The priests were able to retain their position of influence within the synagogue, which they had had in stage one. This influence brought their Targum to the attention of the other Jews. The Targum became a model for how to explain Scripture, but since it was in a dialect not readily understood in Galilee, it needed to be translated.

Several points of this scenario need to explained, the first being control of the synagogues. How do we know that the priests were active and authoritative in the synagogues from the second century onwards? Did not the rabbis run the synagogues? Well, that was the standard scholarly picture up to a couple of decades ago. The earliest rabbinic texts, the Mishnah and the Tosefta, talk about three main institutions: the *bet din*, the courts; the *bet midrash*, the study house; and the *bet kneset*, the synagogue. It was assumed that since the rabbis talked about these institutions, the rabbis ran these all three institutions and made extensive use of them.

In recent decades it has become clear that this is not the case. In the Mishnah, the rabbis draw a picture of society in which they themselves run the courts, as well as the law schools, the *batei midrash*, that train students to work in that court system.[73] But the rabbis do not claim to control the synagogues. In fact, they are not particularly interested in them. As Neusner points out, compared to their attention to the temple and the household farm, the rabbis' interest in the synagogue is almost negligible, focusing only on two topics: sale and disposal of synagogue property, and rules concerning the reading of Scripture.[74]

Neusner is not the only person to notice the lack of connection between the Tannaim and the synagogue. Levine has made the broadest

---

[73] The extent to which the rabbis actually ran the courts seems to vary over time.
[74] See Neusner, "Synagogue in Law." This two-part list leaves out prayer, not because the Mishnah does not discuss it, but because the rabbis imagine it happening in private or in the school house—it only occasionally is depicted as occurring in the synagogue.

and strongest case for the absence of rabbis in the synagogue.[75] He argues that the rabbis saw their main institution as the *bet midrash*. Prior to the mid-third century they had no significant place in the synagogue, while some rabbis began to participate in some activities in some synagogues after that. However up to the end of the fourth century, their interest seems occasional and individual.

Levine goes on to make the observation that the Theodosian Code, from the first half of the fifth century, mentions priests and synagogue officials as leaders of Jewish communities, but never refers to rabbis.[76] The same is true of the writings of Epiphanius, fourth century, and of Jerome in the fourth to fifth century. When we recall that this is the same period, the fourth century through the sixth century, in which synagogues are being built with extensive art work in their floor mosaics—against all rabbinic dicta—we realize that even as the rabbinic literature suggests greater involvement of rabbis in synagogues, they are in no way in a controlling position. In fact, most rabbis would not have allowed themselves to worship in such decorated synagogues. So the idea that we can explain the growth of the synagogue and its centrality in the Jewish community by reference to the rabbis is simply no longer tenable.

So who was running the synagogue? The same people who seem to have been doing it before the destruction: the local people of the community, a mix of "average" Jews and members of the priestly class. Despite the small numbers of priests, percentage-wise at least, their prestige and status would have made them prominent and active participants. Indeed, we should recall the two-part role priests played prior to 70: they were the guardians and interpreters of Scripture as well as as temple sacrificers. They may have lost their temple and their sacrificial role in the destruction, but the synagogues and their association with Scripture continued on. The synagogues following the destruction were highly influenced by synagogue organization prior to the destruction.

The influence of priests within synagogues led to an acceptance of their Targum. Their participation in the synagogue would have brought to everyone's attention the priestly Targum, Proto-Onqelos. The idea of having a version of the Torah in their spoken language seems to have appealed to many Jews. But any desire to use the Proto-Onqelos trans-

---

[75] See Levine, "Sages."
[76] Ibid., 215.

lation of the Hebrew Bible for public reading, however, would have run head on into the problem of the audience not being able to understand it easily.

Proto-Onqelos' problem in a Jewish Palestinian Aramaic environment was actually twofold. First, the Targum's adherence to Jewish Literary Aramaic used words and grammatical and morphological constructions that fell woodenly on the ear of a Jewish Palestinian Aramaic listener. Second, its style of translating the Hebrew Text made it difficult for the listener to follow much of it. For example, Proto-Onqelos follows the Hebrew Text when it makes a verbless clause or attaches suffixes directly to verbs, which it does frequently. This close adherence to Hebrew grammar makes oral comprehension more difficult, requiring a greater precision and exactness of listening.

So someone decided to make a new Targum. Who was responsible for creating this new Targum? Most likely, the priestly/lay coalition of the synagogues. Certainly the rabbis would not have composed it. As Smelik shows in a recent article, the Palestinian rabbis were highly antagonistic to translation into Aramaic; the only translations of which they approved were into Greek. Given their consistent antagonism, it is difficult to argue that they would be responsible for writing them.[77]

The new Targum would be based on the prestigious Proto-Onqelos, but it would overcome its two drawbacks. First, it would be written in a vesion of Jewish Palestinian Aramaic to overcome differences of vocabulary and grammar. Second, it would be written in a style more condusive to listening, one which put less information into small linguistic packages. We can see this decision in *Neofiti's* regular insertion of a copula into verbless clauses and its use of the direct object marker *yath* to separate suffixes from verbs.

But once it was decided to create a new Targum, a third factor came into play, namely, the priestly duty to teach and instruct, and it is here that the Palestinian Targum acquired its distinctive feature. Under-

---

[77] See Smelik, "Language," 201–26. Smelik points out early on, "When we . . . have a closer look at the appreciation of the translations in the Yerushalmi, we find that praise is reserved for Greek translations, whereas Aramaic translations are deemed impossible, rejected, or corrected." See also the study by Aaron, "Judaism's Holy Language," 49–108. In addition, the rabbinic dicta about the dangers of Targum translation essentially prohibit translation in the form contained in the Palestinian Targums. *t. Meg.* 4:41 forbids translating exactly as well as adding to the translation. For discussion, see Alexander, "Targumim," 25–6.

standing became not just a matter of dialect and translation style, but of interpretation, of helping the listeners to understand the meaning of Scripture. This became the impetus for adding the expansions of the Proto-PT Source, which were most likely created as the new Targum was being written.

How do we know that the original Palestinian Targum was a teaching Targum? Because of the expansions' location within the text and their educational purpose. The Pentateuch contains three types of material: narrative, legal/moral, and priestly.[78] Figure 3 below shows how the Proto-PT expansions appear primarily in only two of the Pentateuch's three types of material, narrative and legal/moral, but not priestly.[79] The narrative and legal/moral types have between three and and four-and-a-half expansions per chapter (with Deuteronomy's narrative rising to just over six and a half), while the expansions in the priestly sections average just over one per chapter. Furthermore, the educational character of all these expansions emphasizes the distinction; they focus on Doing Torah. While this is explicit in the opening story of Genesis—that of Adam and Eve—and in Deuteronomy's final chapters, it also takes place in specific details in many additions throughout the narrative and legal/moral sections, and even in the few expansions located in the priestly material.[80] So the Proto-PT Source parallels the emphasis Josephus assigned to the priests in the first century, namely, the importance of doing Torah and practicing the commandments.

---

[78] These classifications of material basically conform to the Documentary Hypothesis. The three classes of material are as follows: Narrative—Gen all; Exod 1–11; 12:19–50; 13:17–22; 14–20; 24; 32:1–34:9; Lev none; Num 1–4; 7; 9:15–14:45; 16–17; 20–27; 31–34; 36; Deut 1–11; 27–34. Legal/Moral—Exod 21–23; Lev 17–27; Deut 12–26. Priestly—Gen none; Exod 12:1–18; 13:1–16; 25–31; 34:10–40:38; Lev 1–16; Num 5–6, 8:1–9:14; 15; 18–19; 28–30; 35; Deut none.

[79] Expansions in narrative sections of the Pentateuch appear at an average rate of about 4.28 per chapter, while expansions in the legal/moral codes of the Pentateuch appear only slightly less frequently at 3.88 expansions per chapter. The interest in recasting priestly passages in the Palestinian Targums falls drastically, to a rate of only 1.09 per chapter.

[80] See Flesher, "Afterlife," 1–48 and "Resurrection," 311–31.

The Literary Legacy of the Priests?

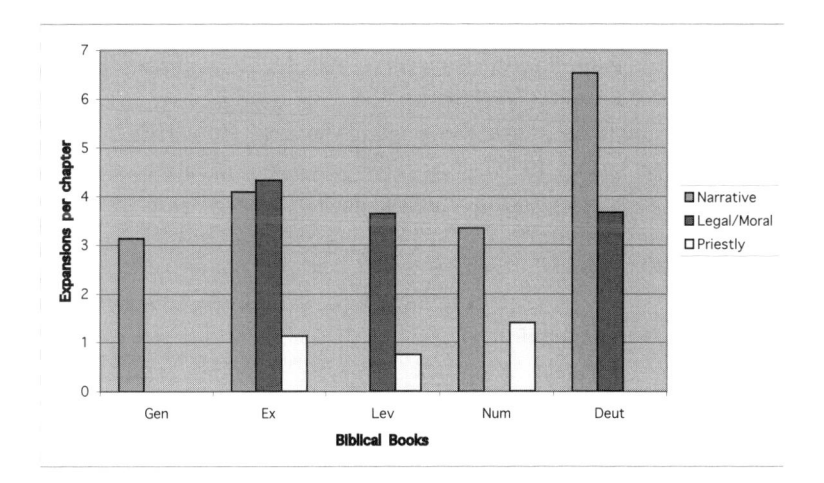

Figure 27.3 Expansion location in Palestinian Targum.

The Palestinian Targum subtly but clearly emphasizes that the priests are responsible for teaching Torah, just as we found in the first-century. In both Deut 17:9–11 and 33:10, the extant Palestinian Targums add material to endorse Scripture's assignment of priests as teachers. Deuteronomy 33:10 says, for instance, that "[the priests] *shall be fit* to teach the judicial ordinances *in the midst of those of the house* of Jacob, and *the decrees of* your law [=Torah] to *the assembly of the tribes of the children of Israel*."[81] Furthermore, the Palestinian Targums depict both Isaac and Rebecca studying with or visiting Shem in his legendary school, and then identify Shem as Melchizedek, God's high priest in Jerusalem.[82] Thus the Palestinian Targum continues to view priests as teachers of Torah.

Why would it make sense for priests to create a Targum that specifically excludes additional material about priestly temple practices? I think there are three answers. First, priestly knowledge was private, perhaps even secret. It would not be the kind of information that priests would have wanted to share with the masses. Second, temple knowledge by and large was irrelevent to the purpose of teaching how to practice the commandments of the Torah. Third, focusing on the tem-

---

[81] This is McNamara's translation of *Tg. Neof.*, see *Deuteronomy,* 166–7. Italics indicate where *Tg. Neof.* adds to a translation of the Hebrew text. Brackets mine.
[82] See *Tg. Neof.* and the *Frg Tg.* to Gen 14:18, 24:62 and 25:22. The Cairo Geniza fragments are not extant at these verses.

ple might actually have been detrimental to Torah practice. This would be because God promised Israel a temple, a promise which seem to have been abrogated after 70. Emphasizing the temple would have led people to question God's promises, and perhaps even to doubt their need to adhere to their side of the Covenant, the practice of Torah. So the Targumists jumped over the Pentateuchal material directly concerned with the temple to focus on the Patriarchs, the Matriarchs and Moses. Here could be found models of behavior and promises from God about his concern for Israel that did not involve awkward and painful reminders of the non-existent temple.[83]

So the Proto-Onqelos Targum became the basis of a new Targum because it had gained prestige from its association with the priests.[84] The Palestinian Targum, which used Proto-Onqelos in its creation, became quite popular and was copied many times. Its teaching character derived from the priests' role of instructing Israel in how to practice the Torah. Once the new Targum was made, however, Proto-Onqelos ceased to be important in the general populace of Jewish Galilee. The accessibility of the new Targum made Proto-Onqelos obsolete there. But Proto-Onqelos was preserved among the priests, and they attempted to maintain its dialect—Jewish Literary Aramaic.

---

[83] Why do the rabbis discuss the temple so much in the Mishnah and the Tosefta, then? I think that it is because they are trying to appropriate it for the purpose of heightening their status. Since the priests, as the only religious group continuing its status from the pre-70 period, set the model for status, the rabbis are trying to immitate them by developing their own temple-based knowledge. The priests, by contrast, aim to keep their true knowledge of the temple secrets and are attempting to carry out their other function, that of teaching Torah to Israel.

[84] Indeed, the Palestinian Targum represents a new type of Scripture interpretation in Israel. Unlike midrash, pesher, and other forms of interpretation, the Targum does not make a clear distinction between Scripture and interpretation. Unlike other forms of the rewritten Bible, the Targum creates a close rendering of the Hebrew Text, rather than paraphrasing it. Thus the Palestinian Targum presents interpretation as if it were Scripture. Who would have the audacity to do this? I think the answer can only be the priests. Certainly not the rabbis who were so careful to identify interpretations with specific individuals. Furthermore, they seem to have no agreed-upon body of interpretation that they could have put into a Targum. In the Tannaitic literature they rarely resolve a dispute or give a definitive ruling. They prefer to let debates hang.

Stage 3 – Beyond 200

This last observation essentially brings the discussion up to the year 200, the closing date of this conference's period of focus. However, to provide further support to this model of the development of the Targums and their dialects, I need to discuss *Targum Pseudo-Jonathan*, which was probably not composed before the mid-fourth century.

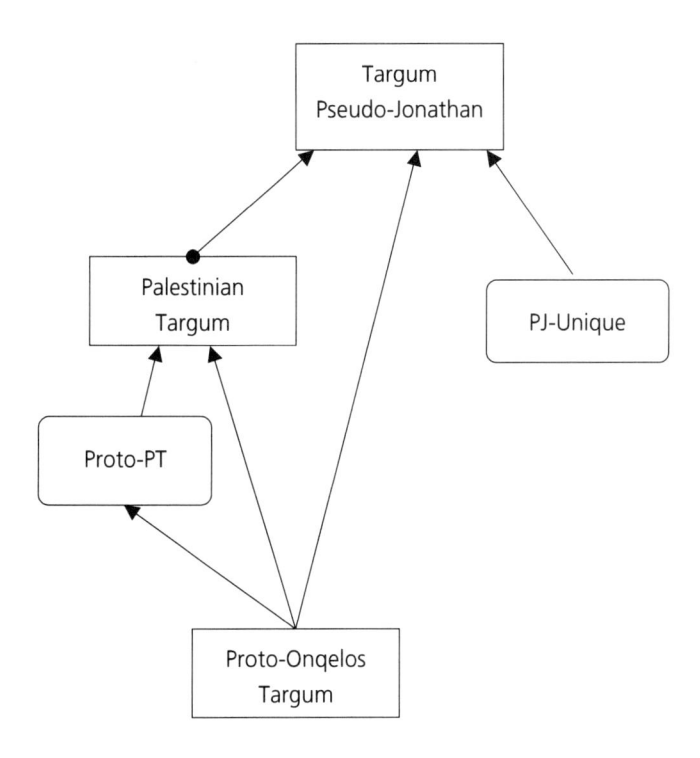

Figure 27.4 Palestine: fourth century or later.

Targum Pseudo-Jonathan is a thoroughly priestly Targum, for it owes all three of the main elements of its mixture to the priests, albeit at different periods of time. As I observed earlier, *Pseudo-Jonathan's* translation is essentially that of Proto-Onqelos and is composed in its dialect of Jewish Literary Aramaic, while the expansions of the Proto-PT Source come from the Palestinian Targum and are usually cast in the

Palestinian Targum dialect of Jewish Palestinian Aramaic.[85] But the additions of the PJ-unique source are written in a new dialect, called Late Jewish Literary Aramaic, and reveal a dominant interest in matters of concern to priests.

It is at this stage that the priests for the first time combine their temple and Scripture interests in targumic form. For the focus of PJ-unique expansion source on priestly concerns indicates an interest in incorporating the priests' knowledge about sacrificial and temple practices into a Targum, a teaching text of Scripture. Beverly Mortensen's work on the PJ-unique source sets forth this point.[86] On the one hand, a large percentage of the PJ-unique expansions appear in the priestly sections of the Torah. Indeed, the highest ratio of expansions per chapter in PJ-unique appears in Leviticus, followed by Exodus and Numbers.[87] That is, the three books that have the greatest amount of priestly material have the greatest number of expansions. On the other hand, Mortensen's work also reveals that the PJ-unique expansions tend to reflect priestly concerns wherever they appear. That is, they focus on matters discussing priests and their activities. These are usually in the temple, but often appear outside as well. For instance, PJ-unique presents priests as judges, a picture decidedly at odds with that presented by the rabbinic material.[88]

So the new material in *Targum Pseudo-Jonathan* is focused on priestly matters: What of its dialect, Late Jewish Literary Aramaic?[89] Recognized independently by Kaufman and Cook, it is, in the words of Kaufman, a "real, albeit literary, dialect with its own grammar and lexicon."[90] It can be described as a combination of grammatical elements from Jewish Literary Aramaic and Jewish Palestinian Aramaic, with the addition of lexical items otherwise known only in Samaritan Aramaic, Christian Palestinian Aramaic, Syriac and Jewish Babylonian Aramaic, combined with a strong liking for Hebraizations, archaisms, and borrowings from Biblical Aramaic

---

[85] Occasionally *Tg. Ps.-J.* recasts these expansions and elements of Late Jewish Literary Aramaic can be found.

[86] Mortensen, "Targum Pseudo-Jonathan."

[87] Ibid., 71. Lev averages 10.4 expansions per chapter, Exod has 8.8, and Num 8.5. Gen actually has the fewest expansions per chapter at 7.5.

[88] Mortensen, "Targum Pseudo-Jonathan," 75.

[89] See Kaufman, "Late Jewish Literary Aramaic"; "Dating," and Cook, "Rewriting."

[90] Kaufman, "Languages," 175.

The Literary Legacy of the Priests?

From a linguistic perspective, how do I argue that it is related to the priests? As I theorized in stage two, the priestly class attempted to preserve Jewish Literary Aramaic while living in a Jewish Palestinian Aramaic environment. Over time, this dialect was corrupted, primarily by the influence of the dominant dialect, namely, Jewish Palestinian Aramaic.

Cook's work demonstrates in part that my hypothesized process actually took place, for he makes it clear that the base of Late Jewish Literary Aramaic was the earlier Jewish Literary Aramaic, while the key changes away from it derived from Jewish Palestinian Aramaic.[91] This is most apparent with regard to one of the earliest signs of decay, namely, "the loss of productive word-formation."[92] To compensate, lexical enrichment must come from outside the dialect. While these lexical items usually come from the dominant dialect, in this case Jewish Palestinian Aramaic, they can also come from any dialect (or language) with which the weaker dialect comes into contact. Thus it is not surprising that Late Jewish Literary Aramaic brings in lexical items from the two Aramaic dialects nearby: Christian Palestinian and Samaritan. Furthermore, it incorporated Hebraisms and archaic Aramaic forms (real and imagined) to make *Pseudo-Jonathan's* added material seem more "biblical" and "authentic." The only surprising aspects are the lexical borrowings from Syriac and Jewish Babylonian Aramaic. These may perhaps be accounted for by trade and travel in the Fertile Crescent region. Thus, the dialect of Late Jewish Literary Aramaic which seems to appear newly formed upon the creation of *Pseudo-Jonathan*, actually shows signs of having been a decaying dialect under pressure from a dominant one for several centuries.[93]

---

[91] See the linguistic analyses in Cook, "Rewriting," 107–280. The overall conclusion that one reaches from Cook's extensive grammatical analysis is that of Jewish Palestinian Aramaic penetration into what was once Jewish Literary Aramaic.
[92] Dressler, "Language Decay," 325.
[93] This characterization of Late Jewish Literary Aramaic can be tested and analyzed in greater detail, for linguists have identified a number of features common to most decaying languages, in addition to the loss of new word formation. These include a decrease in the ability of language producers to form relative clauses, numerous phonological changes, and alignment of grammatical characteristics with the dominant language, and so on. See, for example, the essays by Hill, Campbell and Numtzel, Huffines, Mougeon and Beniak, and Woolard in Dorian, *Investigating Obsolescence*.

Putting together the the topical emphases of the PJ-unique Source and the linguistic situation, the following historical picture appears. When the priests in Galilee decided to create a Targum for themselves, they drew the translation from the Targum they had been preserving over the generations, Proto-Onqelos, written in Jewish Literary Aramaic. Since they no longer had the ability to compose in that dialect, they wrote their priest-oriented additions in the dialect that had developed from it, namely, Late Jewish Literary Aramaic. Finally, they drew the expansions of the Proto-PT Source, which they had created generations earlier, and gave them in the dialect in which they were written. Occasionally, the translation and the Proto-PT expansions were recast, and some linguistic traits of that recasting indicate that they were done by a Targumist who was writing in Late Jewish Literary Aramaic. Thus this last priestly dialect provides the overall linguistic character of *Targum Pseudo-Jonathan*.

The three stages of targumic development—Proto-Onqelos, the Palestinian Targums, and *Targum Pseudo-Jonathan*—were paralleled by three stages in the history of Jewish Literary Aramaic. In our analysis, the dialect began as a wide-spread Judean dialect in the first century, but then became restricted during the second century to the priestly class in northern Palestine. During this period, it lost much of its linguistic vitality and became influenced by the dominant dialect, Jewish Palestinian Aramaic, and others. In the fourth century or later, however, the transformed Jewish Literary Aramaic, now Late Jewish Literary Aramaic, broke from hiding upon the composition of *Targum Pseudo-Jonathan*. Again it functioned as an active dialect, at least at the literary level, becoming the linguistic basis for other Targums, including the Targums of Psalms and Job.

What was the historical impetus that caused *Pseudo-Jonathan* to be written? I think that the historical events surrounding Julian's plan to rebuild the Jerusalem temple in 362 provide this impetus. For this is a Targum written for priests by priests. It teaches about sacrificial and other priestly practices, in a dialect created by and known primarily within priestly circles. It lays out "secret" knowledge about how to be and act like a priest. The rebuilding of the temple is the time at which this information would be useful and practical.[94]

---

[94] In this dating, I follow specifically follow Mortensen, "Economics," 61–4; and in general I follow the dating of Hayward. See, for example, Hayward, "Red Heifer,"

Conclusion

So we have now come full circle, to the point where we can see that the fate of Proto-Onqelos in Palestine and its dialect Jewish Literary Aramaic was intimately linked to the fate of the priestly class. At the earliest stage, prior to the destruction of the temple, Proto-Onqelos was composed under the auspices of the priestly elite in Jerusalem. Following the defeat of Bar Kokhba, the priestly class, along with other Judeans, moved north into Galilee, taking both their dialect and their Targum with them. The priests and their Targum gained respect, but their dialect did not. So, again under priestly auspices, a new Targum—which scholars now call the Palestinian Targum—was written with Proto-Onqelos providing its foundation. The Palestinian Targum became quite popular, being rendered into a number of related versions, of which we now know several. At the same time, some priests kept Proto-Onqelos and worked to preserve knowledge of its dialect. They were only partly successful in this, for the dialect acquired grammatical features from Jewish Palestinian Aramaic and other dialects of Aramaic and Hebrew. So when *Pseudo-Jonathan* was composed, its main dialect was not the widely accepted and used Jewish Palestinian Aramaic, but a development from Jewish Literary Aramaic which had been preserved within the priestly class, now called Late Jewish Literary Aramaic.

Thus, the Pentateuchal Targums can play an important role in helping modern scholars ferret out a more complete picture of developments in Palestine during the first centuries of the common era. To fully understand these centuries, study of these Targums and their dialects must be included alongside other types of analysis.

Bibliography

Aaron, D., "Judaism's Holy Language." Pages 49–108 in *Approaches to Ancient Judaism, New Series.* Vol. 16. Edited by A. Avery-Peck and J. Neusner. Atlanta: Scholars Press, 1999.

Alexander, P. S., "The Toponomy of the Targumim with Special Reference to the Table of Nations and the Boundaries of the Holy Land." Ph.D. diss., Oxford University, 1974.

9–32 as well as the bibliography in Flesher, "Afterlife," 44, n. 117. For opposing views, see the bibliography in Flesher, "Afterlife," 45, n. 118.

—, "The Targumim and the Rabbinic Rules for Delivery of the Targum." *VTS* 36 (1985): 14–28.

—, "Jewish Aramaic Translations of Hebrew Scriptures." Pages 216–53 in *Miqra*. Edited by M. J. Mulder and H. Sysling. Assen: Van Gorcum and Minneapolis: Fortress, 1990.

Avi-Yonah, M. "The Caesarea Inscription of the Twenty-Four Priestly Courses." Pp. 46-57 in *The Teacher's Yoke*. Edited by E. J. Vardaman and J. L. Garrett. Waco: Baylor University Press, 1964.

Beyer, K., *Die aramäischen Texte vom Toten Meer samt den Inschriften aus Palästina, dem Testament Levis aus der Kairoer Genisa, der Fastenrolle und den alten talmudischen Zitaten*. Göttingen: Vandenhoeck & Ruprecht, 1984

—, *The Aramaic Language: Its Distribution and Subdivisions*. Göttingen: Vandenhoeck & Ruprecht, 1986.

—, *Die aramäischen Texte vom Toten Meer samt den Inschriften aus Palästina, dem Testament Levis aus der Kairoer Genisa, der Fastenrolle und den alten talmudischen Zitaten. Ergänzungsband*. Göttingen : Vandenhoeck & Ruprecht, 1994.

Binder, D. D., *Into the Temple Courts: The Place of the Synagogues in the Second Temple Period*. Atlanta: Scholars Press, 1999.

Blanc, H., *Communal Dialects in Baghdad*. Cambridge: Harvard University Press, 1964.

Campbell, R. M., "A Fragment-Targum without a Purpose? The raison d'etre of MS Vatican Ebr. 440." Ph.D. diss., Northwestern University, 1994.

Cohen, S. J. D., "The Place of the Rabbi in Jewish Society of the Second Century." Pages 157-74 in *The Galilee in Late Antiquity*. Edited by L. I. Levine. New York: Jewish Theological Seminary of America, 1992.

Cook, E. M., "Rewriting the Bible: The Text and Language of the Pseudo-Jonathan Targum." Ph.D. diss., University of California Los Angeles, 1986.

—, "Qumran Aramaic and Aramaic Dialectology." Pages 1-21 in *Studies in Qumran Aramaic*. Edited by T. Muraoka. Louvain: Peeters, 1992.

—, "A New Perspective on the Language of Onqelos and Jonathan." Pages 142–56 in *The Aramaic Bible: Targums in their Historical Context*. Edited by D. R. G. Beattie and M. McNamara. Sheffield: Sheffield Academic Press, 1994.

Crossan, J. D., and J. L. Reed, *Excavating Jesus: Beneath the Stones, Behind the Texts*. HarperCollins: New York, 2001.

Crystal, D., *Language Death*. Cambridge: Cambridge University Press, 2000.

Diez Macho, A. *Neophyti 1: Targum Palestinense ms. de la Biblioteca Vaticana*, 6 vols. Madrid-Barcelona: Consejo superior de Investigaciones Científicas, 1968–79.

Dorian, N. C., ed., *Investigating Obsolescence: Studies in Language Contraction and Death*. Cambridge: Cambridge University Press, 1989.

Dressler, W. U. "Acceleration, Retardation, and Reversal in Language Decay?" Pages 321–36 in *Language Spread: Studies in Diffusion and Social Change*. Edited by R. L. Cooper. Bloomington: Indiana University Press, 1982.

Ferguson, C., "Diglossia." Pages 1–26 in *Language Structure and Language Use: Essays by Charles A. Ferguson*. Edited by A. S. Dil. Stanford: Stanford University Press, 1971.

—, "Religious Factors in Language Spread." Pages 59–68 in *Language Spread: Studies in Diffusion and Social Change*. Edited by Robert L. Cooper. Bloomington: Indiana University Press, 1982.

Fishman, J. A., *Language Loyalty in the United States*. The Hague: Mouton, 1966.

Fitzmyer, J. A., "The Phases of the Aramaic Language." Pages 57–84 in *A Wandering Aramean: Collected Aramaic Essays*. Edited by J. A. Fitzmyer. Missoula: Scholars Press, 1979.

Flesher, P. V. M., "Exploring the Sources of the Synoptic Targums to the Pentateuch." Pages 101–34 in *Textual and Contextual Studies in the Pentateuchal Targums*. Vol. 1 of *Targum Studies*. Edited by P. V. M. Flesher. Atlanta: Scholars Press, 1992.

—, "Mapping the Synoptic Palestinian Targums of the Pentateuch." Pages 247–53 in *The Aramaic Bible: Targums in their Historical Context.* Edited by D. R. G. Beattie and M. H. McNamara. Sheffield: Sheffield Academic Press, 1994.

—, "The Targumim in the Context of Rabbinic Literature." Pages 611–29 in *Introduction to Rabbinic Literature.* Edited by J. Neusner. New York: Doubleday, 1994.

—, "Palestinian Synagogues before 70 C.E.: A Review of the Evidence." Pages 27–39 in *Ancient Synagogues: Historical Analysis and Archaeological Discovery.* Vol. 1. Edited by D. Urman and P. V. M. Flesher. Leiden: Brill, 1995.

—, "Is *Targum Onkelos* a Palestinian Targum? The Evidence of Genesis 28–50." *JSP* 19 (1999): 35–79.

—, "The Theology of the Afterlife in the Palestinian Targums to the Pentateuch: A Framework for Analysis." Pages 1–48 in *Approaches to Ancient Judaism: New Series.* Vol. 16. Edited by J. Neusner. Atlanta: Scholars Press, 1999.

—, "The Resurrection of the Dead and the Sources of the Palestinian Targums to the Pentateuch." Pages 311–31 in *Death, Life-After-Death, Resurrection and The World-to-Come in the Judaisms of Antiquity.* Vol. 4 of *Handbuch der Orientalistik. Judaism in Late Antiquity.* Edited by A. J. Avery-Peck and J. Neusner. Leiden: Brill, 2000.

—, "Prolegomenon to a Theory of Early Synagogue Development." Pages 121–54 in *Judaism in Late Antiquity, Part Three, Where We Stand: Issues and Debates in Ancient Judaism, Vol. Four, The Special Problem of the Synagogue.* Edited by A. J. Avery-Peck and J. Neusner. Leiden: Brill, 2001.

—, "The Translations of Proto-Onqelos and the Palestinian Targums." *Journal of the Aramaic Bible,* 3 (2001): 75–101.

Freyne, S., "Town and Country Once More: The Case of Roman Galilee." Pages 49–56 in *Archaeology and The Galilee: Texts and Contexts in the Graeco-Roman and Byzantine Periods.* Edited by D. R. Edwards and C. T. McCollough. Atlanta: Scholars Press, 1997.

Goodman, M., *The Ruling Class of Judea.* Cambridge: Cambridge University Press, 1987.

Goshen-Gottstein, M. H., "The Language of Targum Onqelos and the Model of Literary Diglossia in Aramaic." *JNES* 37 (1978): 169–79.

Grabbe, L. L. "Synagogues in Pre-70 Palestine." Pages 17–26 in *Ancient Synagogues: Historical Analysis and Archaeological Discovery*. Vol. 1. Edited by D. Urman and P. V. M. Flesher. Leiden: Brill, 1995.

Groh, D. E., "The Clash between Literary and Archaeological Models of Provincial Palestine." Pages 29–38 in *Archaeology and The Galilee: Texts and Contexts in the Graeco-Roman and Byzantine Periods*. Edited by D. R. Edwards and C. T. McCollough. Atlanta: Scholars Press, 1997.

Hayward, R., "Red Heifer and Golden Calf: Dating Targum Pseudo-Jonathan." Pages 9–32 *Textual and Contextual Studies in the Pentateuchal Targums*. Vol. 1 of *Targum Studies*. Edited by P. V. M. Flesher. Atlanta: Scholars Press, 1992.

Hezser, C., *Jewish Literacy in Roman Palestine*. Tübingen: Mohr Siebeck, 2001.

Horsley, R. A., *Archaeology, History and Society in Galilee: The Social Context of Jesus and the Rabbis*. Valley Forge: Trinity Press, 1996.

Kahle, P., *Das palästinische Pentateuchtargum, die palästinische Punktation, der Bibeltext des Ben Naftali*. Vol. 2 of *Masoreten des Westens*. Stuttgart: Kohlhammer, 1930.

—, *The Cairo Geniza*, 2nd ed. Oxford: Blackwell, 1959.

Kaufman, S. A., "Dating the Language of the Palestinian Targums and their Use in the Study of First Century CE Texts." Pages 118–41 in *The Aramaic Bible: Targums in their Historical Context*. Edited by D. R. G. Beattie and M. J. McNamara. Sheffield: Sheffield Academic Press, 1994.

Kaufman, S. A., "Languages (Aramaic)." Pages 173–8 in *The Anchor Bible Dictionary*. Vol. 4. Edited by in D. N. Freedman. New York: Doubleday, 1992.

—, "Targum Pseudo-Jonathan and Late Jewish Literary Aramaic." Pages 363–82 in *Moshe Goshen-Gottstein—In Memoriam*. Edited by M. Bar-Asher, et al. Ramat Gan: Bar Ilan University Press, 1993 (in Hebrew).

Kaufman, S. A., and Y. Maori, "The Targumim to Exodus 20: Reconstructing the Palestinian Targum." *Textus* 16 (1991): 13–78

Kee, H. C., "Defining the First-Century C.E. Synagogue," Pages 7–26 in *Evolution of the Synagogue: Problems and Progress*. Edited by H. C. Kee and L. H. Cohick. Harrisburg: Trinity International Press, 2000.

Klein, M. L., *Genizah Manuscripts of Palestinian Targum to the Pentateuch*. Cincinnati: Hebrew Union College Press, 1986.

Kloner, A., "Ancient Synagogues in Israel: An Archaeological Survey." Pages 11–18 in *Ancient Synagogues Revealed*. Edited by L. I. Levine. Jerusalem: Israel Exploration Society, 1982.

Kutscher, E. Y., "The Language of the 'Genesis Aprocryphon': A Preliminary Study." *ScrHier* 4 (1957): 1–35.

Le Déaut, R., "The Targumim." Pages 563–90 in *The Cambridge History of Judaism*, vol. 2. Edited by W. D. Davies and L. Finkelstein. Cambridge: Cambridge University Press, 1989.

Levine, L. I., "The Sages and the Synagogue in Late Antiquity: The Evidence of the Galilee." Pages 201–24 in *The Galilee in Late Antiquity*. Edited by L. I. Levine. New York: Jewish Theological Seminary of America, 1992.

—, *The Ancient Synagogue: The First Thousand Years*. New Haven: Yale University Press, 2000.

McNamara, M., *The Aramaic Bible: The Targums. 5A, Targum Neofiti, 1. Deuteronomy*. Collegeville: Liturgical Press, 1997.

Meyers, E. M., and J. F. Strange, *Archaeology, the Rabbis, and Early Christianity*. Nashville: Abingdon, 1981.

Mortensen, B. P., "Targum Pseudo-Jonathan: A Document for Priests." Ph.D. diss., Northwestern University, 1994.

—, "Pseudo-Jonathan and Economics for Priests." *JSP* 20 (1999): 39–71;

—, "Pseudo-Jonathan's Temple, Symbol of Judaism." Pages 129–140 in *Targum and Scripture: Studies in Aramaic Translation and Interpretation in Memory of Ernest G. Clarke*. Vol. 2 of *Studies in the Aramaic Interpretation of Scripture*. Edited by Paul V.M. Flesher. Leiden: Brill Academic Press, 2002.

Naveh, J., *On Stone and Mosaic*. Jerusalem: Maariv, 1978, (in Hebrew).

Nettle, D. and S. Romaine, *Vanishing Voices: The Extinction of the World's Languages.* Oxford: Oxford University Press, 2000.

Neusner, J., *The Rabbinic Traditions about the Pharisees Before 70.* 3 vols. Leiden: Brill, 1971.

—, *From Politics to Piety: The Emergence of Pharisaic Judaism.* Englewood Cliffs: Prentice-Hall, 1973. 2nd ed. New York: KTAV Publishing House, 1979.

—, "The Synagogue in Law: What the Texts Lead Us to Expect to Find." Pages 151–74 in *Religious Texts and Material Contexts.* Edited by J. Neusner and J. F. Strange. Lanham: University Press of America, 2001.

Reed, J. L., *Archaeology and the Galilean Jesus: A Re-examination of the Evidence.* Harrisburg: Trinity Press International, 2000.

Riesner, R., "Synagogues in Jerusalem." Pages 179–212 in *The Book of Acts in Its Palestinian Setting.* Edited by R. Bauckham. Grand Rapids: Eerdmans, 1995

Runesson, A., *The Origins of the Synagogue: A Socio-Historical Study.* Stockholm: Almqvist & Wiksell, 2001.

Samarin, W. J., ed., *Language in Religious Practice.* Rowley: Newbury House Publishers, 1976.

Sanders, E. P., *Judaism: Practice and Belief, 63 BCE-66 CE.* London: SCM Press, 1992.

Schwartz, S., "Language, Power and Identity in Ancient Palestine." *Past and Present* 148 (1995): 3–47.

—, *Josephus and Judaean Politics.* Leiden: Brill, 1990.

Schürer, E., *The History of the Jewish People in the Age of Jesus Christ.* Revised and edited by G. Vermes et al. Edinburgh: T&T Clark, 1979.

Smelik, W., "Language, Context, and Translation Between the Talmudim." *Journal of the Aramaic Bible* 3 (2001): 201–26.

Sokoloff, M., *A Dictionary of Jewish Palestinian Aramaic of the Byzantine Period.* Ramat Gan: Bar Ilan University Press, 1990.

Tal, A., "The Dialects of Jewish Palestinian Aramaic and the Palestinian Targum of the Pentateuch." *Sefarad* 46 (1986): 441-8.

Vermes, G., "The Targumic Versions of Genesis 4:3-16," Pages 92–126 in *Post-Biblical Jewish Studies.* Edited by G. Vermes. Leiden: Brill, 1975.

Yahalom, J., "Synagogue Inscriptions in Palestine—A Stylistic Classification." *Immanuel* 10 (1980): 47–56.

28
The Hermeneutics of the Synagogue: An Evaluation

Bruce Chilton

TWO TARGUMISTS, THREE OPINIONS. Karin Hedner Zetterholm and Paul V. M. Flesher invite us to join a long-standing debate within Targumic studies, which addresses the relationship of the Targums both to the rabbis and to the synagogue. Zetterholm explicates the relationship between between targumic readings of Deut 26:5 and the rabbinic hermeneutics concerning Laban, construed along the intertextual lines. Flesher, on the other hand, forcefully takes up the case for a priestly origin of the Targums, and in doing so also invokes the category of an ancient "Palestinian Targum."

It is tempting to wade directly into the implicit dispute between two coherent positions, but this volume is better served by reflecting on these divergent points of view through the lens of the synagogue, the topic to which the project is devoted. What does it mean when extant targumic contradict *and* correspond to rabbinic teaching concerning translation in the synagogue? For example, *m. Meg.* 4:9 insists that Lev 18:21 ("You must not give of your seed, to deliver it to Moloch") should not be interpreted in respect of sexual intercourse with Gentiles; the *Targum Pseudo-Jonathan*—a late work, produced long after rabbinic authority had been established—takes just that line. On the other hand, *b. Qidd.* 49a proudly points out that "our Targum" solves the conundrum of rendering Exod 24:10. If one were to translate literally, and have Moses and his companions see God, that would be a lie; if one were to have them see anyone but God, that would be blasphemy. Answer? They saw the "glory" of God.

The relationship between the rabbis and the Targums was ambivalent, and that ambivalence had plenty of opportunity to flourish.

Among the Targums to the Pentateuch, *Targum Onqelos* appears to correspond best to rabbinic ideals of translation. Although paraphrase is evident, especially in order to describe God and his revelation in suitably reverent terms, the high degree of correspondence with the Hebrew of the Masoretic Text (and probably with the Hebrew text current in antiquity) is striking. The dialect of *Onqelos* is commonly called "Middle Aramaic," which would place the Targum between the first century B.C.E. and 200 C.E. A better designation, in my opinion, would be "Transitional Aramaic" (200 B.C.E.–200 C.E.) embracing the various spoken dialects (Hasmonaean, Nabataean, Palmyrene, Arsacid, Essene, as well as targumic) that came to be used during the period, since what followed was a strong regionalization in dialects of Aramaic, which we can logically refer to as Regional Aramaic (200 C.E.–700 C.E.). Precisely because Transitional Aramaic was transitional and because Regional Aramaic as spoken by Jews embraced a variety of dialects, various Targums were produced in Transitional Aramaic *after* its demise as a common language. For that reason, the year 200 C.E. is not a firm date, after which a Targum in Transitional Aramaic cannot have been composed. *Onqelos* should probably be dated towards the end of the third century, in the wake of comparable efforts to produce a literal Greek rendering during the second century, and well after any strict construal of the principle that Targums were to be oral. By contrast with the rabbinic ethos that permitted the creation and preservation of *Onqelos*, one might recall the story of Rabbi Gamaliel, who is said during the first century to have immured a Targum of Job in a wall of the temple (*b. Šabb.* 115a).

The *Targum Neophyti I* was discovered in 1949 by A. Díez Macho in the Library of the Neophytes in Rome. The paraphrases of *Neophyti* are substantially different from those of *Onqelos*. Entire pericopae are added, as when Cain and Abel argue in the field prior to the first case of murder (Gen 4:8); such "renderings" are substantial additions, and it is impossible to predict in literary terms alone when remarkable freedom of this kind is to be indulged. The dialect of *Neophyti* is known as "Palestinian Aramaic," although "Tiberian" (or Galilean) is a more accurate designation. However designated, this example of Regional Aramaic (200 C.E.–700 C.E.) is distinct from the "Babylonian Aramaic" of *Onqelos*.

That distinction between "Tiberian" and "Babylonian" manifests the increased regionalization in the Aramaic language to which I have referred. But *Neophyti* is produced in a frankly Regional Aramaic such as was apparently current among teachers whose center became Tiberias, while *Onqelos* appears in a Transitional Aramaic that is on the way to becoming Regional. Although the language of *Neophyti* appears somewhat later, the chronology of these two Targums is about the same; the differences between them are a function more of program than dating. The Rabbis of Babylonia, who called *Onqelos* "our Targum" exerted greater influence than did their colleagues in the west.

A later representative of the type of expansive rendering found in *Neophyti* is *Targum Pseudo-Jonathan*. Its reference to the names of Mohammed's wife and daughter in Gen 21:21 put its final composition in the seventh century C.E. or later. (This oddly designated Targum is so called in that the name "Jonathan" was attributed to it during the Middle Ages, because its name was abbreviated with a *yod*. But the letter perhaps stood for "Jerusalem," although that designation is also not established critically. The title *"Pseudo-Jonathan"* is therefore an admission of uncertainty.) *Neophyti* and *Pseudo-Jonathan* are conventionally called "Palestinian Targums," to distinguish their dialects and their style of interpretation from those of *Onqelos*. In fact, however, *Pseudo-Jonathan* was produced at the dawn of the period of Academic Aramaic (700 C.E.–1500 C.E.), during which rabbinic usage continued to develop the language in a literary idiom after it had been supplanted by Arabic as a *lingua franca* in the Near East. In addition to being excessively general, the designation "Palestinian" has produced problems in research, because in the past it has been argued that this was the only indigenous and ancient (indeed, pre-Christian) Targum.[1]

Neophyti and *Pseudo-Jonathan* are to be associated with two other Targums, or to be more precise, groups of Targums. The first group, in chronological order, consists of the fragments of the Cairo Geniza. They were originally part of more complete works, dating between the seventh and the eleventh centuries, which were deposited in the Geniza of the Old Synagogue in Cairo. In the type and substance of interpretation, these fragments are comparable to the other Targums of the Tiberian type. The same may be said of the *Fragments Targum*, which was collected as a miscellany of targumic readings during the Middle Ages, representing the continued interest in Aramaic as a theological language. An interesting feature of the Targums of the Tiberian type is that

---

[1] On this topic, see Chilton, "Four Types of Comparison," 163–88.

their relationship might be described as a synoptic one, in several ways comparable to the relationship among the Gospels. All four of the Tiberian Targums, for example, convey the debate between Cain and Abel to which I have referred, and they do so with those variations of order and wording which are well known to students of the Synoptic Gospels.

In a comparison of the synoptic relationship of the Gospels to those of the Targums and other rabbinic documents, I have suggested that the paradigm of strict literary dependence might not always be helpful. In an environment in which meaning is developed both orally and in writing—which was manifestly the case within early Judaism and primitive Christianity—exegeses could evolve by means of interactions that have left to literary trace.[2] Within the limits of the evidence, we might be able to characterize types of exegesis, but that does not necessarily imply direct contact among those who thought along similar lines, and every distinctive interpretation does not imply that an entire document had to be involved.

An example of this sort of evolution might illustrate the point. The Tiberian Targums to the Pentateuch in aggregate present four different versions of what the Hebrew text leaves in silence: the presumed argument between Cain and Abel just prior to the primordial fratricide (Gen 4:8). I have elsewhere analyzed the differences among those versions as an analogy for understanding variations and coincidences among the Synoptic Gospels.[3] Here only two of the targumic versions will concern us, since the interest is in the substantive meaning involved.

Neophyti I presents the dispute clearly. In what follows, I present the text in translation with sigla that will be used to compare it later with the *Fragments Targum*.

> A I Cain answered and said to Abel,
> I know the world is not created with mercies,
> and it is not led in respect of fruits of good deeds,
> and there is accepting of person in judgment:
> for what reason was your offering received with favor
> and my offering was not received from me with favor?

---

[2] Chilton, *Profiles of a Rabbi*.
[3] See Chilton, "Comparative Study," 553–62 and *Targumic Approaches*, 137–49.

A II Abel answered and said to Cain,
I know the world is created with mercies,
and in respect of good deeds it is led:
and because my good deeds surpassed yours
my offering was received from me with favor
while your offering was not received from
you with favor.

B I Cain answered and said to Abel,
there is no judgment and there is no judge,
and there is no other world,
there is no giving good reward to the righteous
and there is no repaying from the wicked.

B II Abel answered and said to Cain,
there is judgment and there is a judge,
and there is another world,
and there is giving good reward to the righteous
and there is repaying from the wicked in
the world to come.

In a single passage, a complete, rational theodicy is enunciated. In this world, God's favor is a matter of justice and mercy, because it hangs on good deeds. In the world to come, all wrongs are to be righted.

In a finely written essay, A. Cohen called attention to the principle of rabbinic Judaism that "the rejection of moral laws implies a denial of God."[4] He cites the example of *t. Šebu.* 3:6, where Rabbi Reuben during a discussion with a philosopher in Tiberias insists that both the failure to keep commandments and the commission of transgression necessarily involve a denial of God, making one into the most hateful person in the world. That is just what Cain becomes here in *Neophyti I*. He denies God in his mercy and his justice, and in so doing implicitly refuses the imperative that because God is "compassionate and gracious, so you be compassionate and gracious; as he is called righteous, you be

---

[4] Cohen, "Ethics of the Rabbis," 69–96, 73.

righteous" (*Sifre* 49).[5] Cain is the anti-model of the virtue for which Abel is the model.

So it comes as little surprise that Cain also, in B I, leaps into the explicitly stated clause of exclusion from resurrection which is specified in *m. Sanh.* 10:1:

> All Israelites have a share in the world to come.... And these are the ones who have no portion in the world to come: He who says, the resurrection is a teaching which does not derive from the Torah, and the Torah does not come from Heaven; and an Epicurean.

As J. Neusner has pointed out, by definition Israel here "is anticipated to be the people of eternity," and the exceptions to that rule are specific.[6] Having said that, however, he goes on to show that *m. Sanh.* 10:2–5 names other excluded persons (all Israelites, but for Balaam) in order to insist upon that initial definition of Israel.

What we find in *Neophyti I*, then, is a rational theodicy consistent with the rabbinic theology of its time (the period of the Mishnah and the Tosefta), stepping from a consideration of this world to that of the world to come. When we turn to the Talmudic treatment of the Mishnaic teaching (*b. Sanh.* 90b–91a), however, what is striking is the disproportionate emphasis upon deriving the resurrection of the dead from the Torah.[7] A conspicuous example is when Gamaliel's daughter is portrayed as contradicting Caesar in his doubt that dust could live again:

> There are two potters in our town, one who works with water, the other who works with clay. Which is the more impressive? He said to her, The one who works with water. She said to him, If he works with water, will he not create even more out of clay?

---

[5] So Cohen paraphrases this passage in the midst of an excellent discussion of the *imitatio Dei* in rabbinic Judaism.

[6] See Neusner, *Theology of the Oral Torah*, 563–6.

[7] Ibid., 567–74.

Poor Caesar will not even have known his argument had been slain, unless he recognized that the water-potter and the clay-potter were one: the timelessly creative God of Genesis.

This is precisely Neusner's point: "that resurrection of the dead is a doctrine set forth by the Written Torah and demonstrable within the framework of the Torah, occupies a principal place in the Oral Torah's exposition of the topic."[8] The increasing focus upon resurrection as a key issue within theodicy helps to explain what I could not account for in my earlier treatment of the dispute between Cain and Abel: the deviant structure of the post-Talmudic *Fragments Targum* in its presentation.

In order to underscore and identify that deviance, I will use the sigla already introduced above:

B I   Cain answered and said to Abel,
there is no judgment and there is no judge,
and there is no other world,
and there is no giving good reward to the righteous
and no repaying from the wicked,

A I   and the world is not created with mercies
and it is not led with mercies
for what reason was
your offering received from you with favor
and from me it was not received with favor?

B II   Abel answered and said to Cain,
there is judgment and there is a judge,
and there is another world,
and there is giving good reward to the righteous
and repaying the wicked;

A II   and the world is created with mercies
and it is led with mercies. It is still led
according to fruits of good deeds:
because the fruits of my deeds surpassed yours
my offering was received from me with favor
and from you it was not received with favor.

[8] Ibid., 566.

In this case, the next world has superseded this world in importance, which explains the comprehensive transformation of the structure of the passage in this later Targum.

But for all that the theodicy within the Tiberian Targums develops an increasingly other-worldly emphasis, what is evident is a metaphysics of divine mercy and judgment in the next world and this, a metaphysics which is grounded in the Torah's reflection of the nature of God. I have chosen this passage, because the sacrificial topic and occasion is of immediately priestly interest, while the interpretative pattern and content of the exegesis is evidently rabbinic. No contradiction is necessitated in seeing such influences at work, although tensions must have featured as differing interpretative strategies deployed in synagogues.[9] The rabbis acknowledged that (*b. Meg.* 3a), because what gathered in a synagogues were not only people, but opinions and meanings, some expert in the estimation of many (rabbis and priests, for example), some embedded in local custom, but all attesting the vital diversity of early Judaism and rabbinic Judaism.

Bibliography

Chilton, B., "A Comparative Study of Synoptic Development: The Dispute Between Cain and Abel in the Palestinian Targums and the Beelzebul Controversy in the Gospels." *JBL* 101 (1982): 553–62.

—, "Four Types of Comparison between the Targumim and the New Testament." *Journal for the Aramaic Bible* 2 (2000):163–88.

—, "Two in One: Renderings of the Book of Isaiah in Targum Jonathan." Pages 547–62 in *Writing and Reading the Scroll of Isaiah. Studies of an Interpretive Tradition 2.* Edited by C. C. Broyles and C. A. Evans. Leiden: Brill, 1997.

—, *Profiles of a Rabbi. Synoptic Opportunities in Reading about Jesus.* Atlanta: Scholars Press, 1989.

---

[9] The best way to investigate these tensions is to trace the exegetical frameworks that lace these skeins of meaning within a Targum; see Chilton, "Two in One," 547–62.

—, *Targumic Approaches to the Gospels. Essays in the Mutual Definition of Judaism and Christianity.* Lanham: University Press of America, 1986.

Cohen, A., "The Ethics of the Rabbis," Pages 69–96 in *Essays in honour of the Very Rev. Dr. J. H. Hertz.* Edited by I. Epstein, E. Levine and C. Roth. London: Edward Goldston, 1942.

Neusner, J., *The Theology of the Oral Torah. Revealing the Justice of God.* Montreal: McGill-Queen's University Press, 1999.

Part VI

The Synagogue of Ancient Ostia and the Jews of Rome

29
Current Views on the Synagogue of Ostia Antica and the Jews of Rome and Ostia

Dieter Mitternacht

During the fall of 1997 a team from Lund University and Olof Brandt, an archeologist from the Swedish Institute in Rome, began to study the synagogue of ancient Ostia and the Jews of Rome in antiquity. The results have been published as *The Synagogue of Ancient Ostia and the Jews of Rome: Interdisciplinary Studies* in Acta Instituti Romani Regni Sueciae, Series in 4°, 57, 2001. The investigations were part of a larger research project, headed by Professor Birger Olsson and concerned with the ancient synagogue from its beginning to around 200 C.E.[1]

Since the contributions were completed in 1999, there have been some crucial developments in related research. Besides subsequent publications on the origin of the synagogue building in Ostia and the Jews in the Diaspora, the DAI 2001 excavation campaign of navalia and temple at the Tiber mouth, and the discovery of the *Villa suburbana* in the south of region IV have brought to light new data with implications for Ostia synagogue research. In this article I will appraise the current situation and contribute some additional insights.

---

[1] The project went under the heading: *The Ancient Synagogue: Birthplace of Two World Religions.* For details, see the preface to this volume.

The Jews of Rome

In an effort to provide a backdrop for the archaeological evidence from Ostia and the understanding of the Jewish community in Ostia, four of the contributions to *The Synagogue of Ancient Ostia and the Jews of Rome: Interdisciplinary Studies* (henceforth *SAOJR*) investigated: (a) the situation and organization of the Jews of Rome, (b) the way the Romans viewed the Jews, (c) the languages of the Jews of Rome, and (d) Jewish inscriptions in Rome.

Situation and Organization

Karin Hedner Zetterholm appraised recent research on Jewish communities of ancient Rome from the first century B.C.E. to the beginning of the fourth century C.E. She excluded the second century B.C.E. since she considers the reference to an expulsion of Jews from Rome in 139 B.C.E. in Valerius Maximus 1.3.3. to be inconclusive as to whether those expelled had settled permanently or were just sojourners.[2] In her opinion the earliest reliable evidence of a Jewish presence in Rome is found in Cicero's speech *Pro Flacco* in 59 B.C.E.

Since then, E. Gruen has argued persuasively that the expulsion in 139 B.C.E. was one in a series of "periodic expulsion decrees" that served the purpose of pointing out "the undiluted character of their ancestral traditions". The expulsion did include Jews but also other peoples. Not a certain group of sojourners was targeted by the Romans, but foreign resident groups. "The government in short was making a statement, not purging itself of alien ethnic groups."[3] Thus, Gruen holds that the Jews expelled in 139 B.C.E. were residents of Rome. He also considers the inference usually drawn from Philo's reference in *Leg.* 155 that Jews first came to Rome as captives of the campaigns of Pompey in 63 B.C.E., Gabinius, 57 B.C.E., and Cassius, 53 B.C.E. to be unwarranted. The inference is uncalled for both because Philo only refers to the Jews of the Trastevere, and also because "no known prisoners arrived from that land [=Judaea] between the time of Cicero and that of Philo."[4] Jews had

---

[2] Relying on Leon, *Jews*, 3.
[3] Gruen, *Diaspora*, 18–19.
[4] Ibid., 23. Barclay concludes from Josephus, *A.J.* 14.70–1, 79, that Aristobulus and his children must have been accompanied by many of humbler status and that therefore "Jews must have featured prominently in the Roman slave markets of that time" (Barclay, *Diaspora*, 289). Josephus specifies only the family of Aristobulos,

come to Rome for many different reasons and for the reasons already mentioned, more likely than not, much earlier than 63 B.C.E.[5]

E. Baltrusch, in a volume also published after *SAOJR*, adds another interesting point to the discussion. He thinks that the boldness of the Jews' activities in 139 B.C.E. may have been due to the fact that they had recently come to Rome and were not yet accustomed to a "Roman kind" of tolerance. Whereas under Persian and Greek rule the autonomy of religion could be used as a claim to considerable liberties; for the Romans, tolerance ended wherever the interest of the state began.[6]

Following H. J. Leon, Hedner Zetterholm asserts that from the few sources pertinent to the period up to the beginning of the Common Era, it may be deduced that the Jews of Rome fared quite well until the times of Augustus. They were granted special rights by Caesar.[7] Augustus even made donations to the temple in Jerusalem and asked that burnt offerings be made there at his expense (Philo, *Leg.* 155–7). But from the times of Tiberius, Gaius Caligula and Claudius (14–54 C.E.) on, the conditions for Jews became less favorable. During that period, Judaism was increasingly perceived to pose a threat to the Roman way of life, which lead to the expulsion from Rome under Tiberius in 19 C.E.[8] of a great number of Jews who lacked Roman citizenship[9] and of a limited number under Claudius in 49 C.E.[10]

Again Gruen offers a somewhat different perspective by pointing out that Jews were not the only sect named in the edict or edicts of the year 19. Tacitus names Egyptians, Suetonius refers to foreign sects in gen-

---

however, and Gruen therefore emphatically rejects any assertions of mass deportations of Jewish slaves to Rome during that time (Gruen, *Diaspora*, 23, n. 48). It seems however likely that rulers were accompanied by some slaves at least.

[5] Gruen, *Diaspora*, 23.
[6] Baltrusch, *Juden*, 118–20.
[7] According to Josephus (*A.J.* 14.155–216) Caesar issued decrees that granted the Jews the rights to hold assemblies, observe the Sabbath and send the temple tax to Jerusalem. They were exempted from military service and their own courts to a certain extent were recognized by Roman authorities.
[8] Barclay, *Diaspora*, 301.
[9] Leon, *Jews*, 19.
[10] For a discussion of whether or not Claudius' actions against the Jews occurred on one or two occasions (41 C.E. and 49 C.E.) see Hedner Zetterholm, "Jewish Communities," 133–4, or e.g. Gruen, *Diaspora*, 36–41.

eral, Seneca broadly to alien rituals, Josephus includes Isis worshippers.[11] Gruen also points to the conspicuous temporal coincidence between the edict(s) and the death of Tiberius' nephew and adopted son Germanicus who perished in the east that same year. Rumors that arts of black magic had hastened Germanicus' demise (Tacitus, *Ann.* 2:69, 82), may well have triggered action against alien religions in Rome. And since Tiberius was suspected of having wished for Germanicus' death secretly, a public show of rage would have been the appropriate response.[12] Even the maniacal Gaius, although he planned to erect a statue for himself in the temple of Jerusalem, left the Jews of Rome alone, for all we know.

Gruen considers it more probable that the Jews of Rome did fare rather well during the time period in question. Yes, together with other foreign cults they were treated badly on occasion, but usually these were times when scapegoating was considered necessary by Roman authorities and special circumstances prompted "the need for a public polishing of the imperial image."[13]

The expulsion under Claudius recorded in Acts 18:2 and Suetonius, *Claud.* 25.4 is another case where Jews in Rome fell under a broad imperial policy to crack down on undesirable assemblages that included a number of other ethnic groups and was designed to advance the image of the ruler. Claudius can hardly be considered to have been a Jewbaiter. His ascent to the throne received vital support by the Jewish ruler Agrippa. The very same year that he is reported to have suppressed the Jews in Rome, he expressly allowed the Jews in Alexandria to keep to their traditional ways unmolested (*CPJ* 2.153, lines 86–7).[14]

The reference to the instigation of *Chrestus* by Suetonius[15] is (hesitantly) taken by Barclay as a reference to "perhaps only or especially Christian Jews".[16] The obstacles are that Chrestus is a widely attested name for freedmen or freed foreigners from the east, yet never attested

---

[11] Gruen, *Diaspora*, 32f. Also Baltrusch observes that modern scholars much too quickly reduce to "Jewish" revolts incidents that clearly involve other people as well (Baltrusch, *Juden*, 120).

[12] Gruen, *Diaspora*, 34.

[13] Ibid., 36.

[14] One must also take into consideration that the Romans ruled more strictly in the centre of the Empire than in Egypt or Palestine (cf. Baltrusch, *Juden*, 116.).

[15] Suetonius, *Claudius* 25.4: "*Iudaeos impulsore Chresto assidue tumultuantis Roma expulit.*"

[16] Barclay, *Diaspora*, 305. The original suggestion goes back to the fifteenth century and has been reiterated numerous times since (see Boterman, *Judenedikt*, 72–85).

of a Jew. Also, the reference implies that Chrestus would have been present in Rome at the time. Thirdly, Suetonius is known to have called the Christians by their proper name at other times (*Nero* 16.2). I tend to side with Gruen that the identification of Chrestus with Christ is "an uphill battle, better given up."[17] But the assertion that there were Christ-believing Jews among those expelled is not affected by this (Acts 18:2). It simply shows that Roman authorities at this time did not differentiate between Christ-believing Jews and Jews in general. A decade or so later, Nero's brutal persecution of Christians subsequent to the great fire in Rome appears not to have affected the Jews as a community.[18] The shift of perception that seems to underlie these measures may indicate that *in Rome* the Christ-believers were no longer considered part of synagogue communities.

Apart from the rigorous enforcement of the *fiscus Iudaicus* and prohibitions for Roman citizens to adopt Jewish practices,[19] Jews do not seem to have been treated especially harshly in the late first century.[20] Even during the reign of Hadrian (117–138), the emperor most hated by Jews because of his erection of a temple for Jupiter in Jerusalem and his prohibition of circumcision, Jews were able, for instance, to maintain a major synagogue building in Ostia.

All in all Roman authorities seem to have cared little for religious preferences and practices and were primarily interested in quelling political unrest. Up to the fourth century Roman law did not have a technical term for religious offenses. Under certain circumstances alien cults were lumped together, worshippers of Isis were treated the same way as Jews. This of course does not indicate that Rome was religiously tolerant, it simply underlines the fact that it was set on maintaining law and order.[21]

From catacomb inscriptions of the Vigna Randanini, Villa Torlonia and the Monteverde in Rome (third and fourth centuries C.E.) it seems evident that Roman Jewish families chose freely among Greek, Latin

---

[17] Gruen, *Diaspora*, 39.
[18] Barclay, *Diaspora*, 306–8, Leon, *Jews*, 36, Levinskaya, *Acts*, 181.
[19] Barclay, *Diaspora*, 311–13.
[20] Leon, *Jews*, 36.
[21] Rutgers, *Jews in Rome*, 93–116. Baltrusch, *Juden*, 118. Emphatically agreed to by Hedner Zetterholm, "Jewish Communities," 135.

and Semitic names and that Jews interacted with non-Jews.[22] Also, the high frequency of single names typical for the *plebs urbana,* as opposed to long sequences of names typical for the upper classes, indicates that the Jews did not belong to Rome's upper class. L. V. Rutgers affirms that no inferences can be drawn from the inscriptions (including the imperial *gentilicia*) with regard to the social composition of the Jewish communities of earlier time periods.[23] Hedner Zetterholm maintains, still, that they were at first partly made up of slaves who had been taken to Rome in the first centuries B.C.E. and C.E.[24] In light of the assertions made by Gruen (cf. above) we may now wish to be more vigilant with regard to this issue.

Since the expulsion of Jews from Rome under Claudius happened not long before the erection of the synagogue building in the Quarter outside the Porta Marina, Hedner Zetterholm ponders the idea that it may have been Jews expelled from Rome that moved to Ostia and soon thereafter built for themselves a house of worship close to the sea.[25] In any case, titles mentioned on inscriptions from Castel Porziano and Porto (*CLJ* 533, 535–51) suggest that the Jews of Ostia were organized similarly to those of Rome,[26] yet they preferred Latin over Greek for Jewish names more than the Jews of Rome.[27]

In the Eyes of the Romans

Sten Hidal sketches the opinions of Roman authors in the first five centuries C.E. about Jews and Jewish religion and compares the evidence to what those same authors have to say about other groups of people in and around the empire. Drawing on sources from Valerius Maximus, Cicero, Suetonius, Horace, Ovid, Seneca, Quintillian, Dio

---

[22] On the issue of distinguishing different factions among the Jews based on names, Hedner Zetterholm sides with Rutgers against Leon that the evidence does not support such distinctions. On the issue of sensitivity with respect to name practices she sides with Rutgers against Frey (Hedner Zetterholm, "Jewish Communities," 135–6). Rutgers suggests that the Jews in Rome switched gradually from Greek to Latin and that the Vigna Randanini came into use as a catacomb at a later date (Rutgers, *Jews in Rome*, 160, 176–81).

[23] Ibid., 166–9, 268. All Jewish funerary inscriptions preserved are from earlier periods.

[24] Hedner Zetterholm, "Jewish Communities," 136.

[25] Ibid., 134.

[26] Floriani Squarciapino, "La sinagoga di Ostia," 332, idem, "Ebrei," 138.

[27] Hedner Zetterholm, "Jewish Communities," 136.

Cassius, Tacitus, Martial, Juvenal, Petronius and Rutilius Namatianus, he observes that whereas the earlier writers refer to the Jews as one of the many oriental cults and do not pay them any special attention, the situation changes with Seneca and Quintillian. From these writings onwards anti-Semitic sentiments are voiced against lower class Jews especially, and Jewish royalty occasionally.[28]

The best-known non-Jewish description of Jewish life comes from the fifth book of Tacitus' *Historiae* where he makes an effort to give an etiological account of Jewish customs. Compared to his superficial treatment of the remote and fairly unknown Germans, it becomes apparent that Tacitus describes the Jews for readers who have a certain familiarity with their customs. Tacitus takes offense at the preposterous and offensive rites of the Jews, he abhors both their ceremonies and their national origin; their way of life is simply incompatible with Roman tradition.

Hidal sees a contemptuous bias among Roman authors against Jews compared to other groups of people, and takes fear of cultural invasion rather than anti-Semitism as the best explanation for the bias. Whereas the Germans were considered an external enemy and their religion an exotic foreign phenomenon, the Jews were perceived to be a threat to Roman culture and everyday life. Thus, Jewish religion is described with overly depreciatory adjectives such as e.g. *absurdus, foedus, pravus, sinister, sordidus*. As we get to Rutilius Namatianus in the fifth century, the last of the classical Latin poets, the bias appears to have become a prejudice (*De reditu suo*, 386–98).[29]

E. Baltrusch has argued since that among the reasons why the Romans at times may have perceived the Jewish way of life as a threat to their state, would be their conception of an antithesis between the τιμή, the splendor of the Roman state, and the ἀρχαία συνήθεια of the Jewish communities.[30]

Gruen's caution against overemphasizing the Romans' interest in the Jews seems justified, however. Even though Jewish customs and habits have generated an unusual number of comments from Roman authors, "on the whole, they show indifference to Jews. The preserved remarks

---

[28] Juvenal (*Sat.* 6.153–60) ridicules Agrippa the Barbarian and his incestuous sister Berenice who came from "that country where kings with bare feet observe the Sabbaths, and where an inherited clemency allows pigs to grow old (vv. 159–60).
[29] Hidal, "Jews," 144.
[30] Baltrusch, *Juden*, 123.

are far more often dismissive than probing. . . . Jews simply had too little importance for Roman intellectuals to undertake any serious research or inquiry about them."[31] Horace's equation of the Sabbath with the thirteenth day, the emperor Augustus' remarks to Tiberius that the Sabbath was a day of fasting,[32] Tacitus' suggestion that the Jews abstain from eating pork because they had suffered a disease through contact with that animal,[33] confirm Gruen's caution. Without bothering too much about precision, the Romans treated the Jews as one of those groups from the east that practiced despicable outlandish customs. In order to grasp what actually caused disdain and irritation we must look for aspects of the Jewish faith that surfaced in Jews' relation to non-Jews.

However wrongly interpreted, the effect of attitudes and behaviors was real for the ones affected. As the Greeks before them,[34] the Romans disdained what they considered to be anti-social behavior. Both Tacitus and Juvenal record with displeasure the Jews' loyalty among themselves and their hatred for everybody else. "They don't eat with other people; they don't sleep with them. There is nothing they won't do with one another—but they won't have intercourse with Gentiles . . . Jews will not even give directions in the street to non-Jews."[35]

Nonetheless, none of these references indicates that the Romans felt threatened by Jewish faith. Not even Jewish monotheism was perceived as a problem. Rather, Romans could simply consider YHWH to be another name for Jupiter.[36] "As one among many immigrant minorities in Rome, Jews were subject to the cultural and social snobbery of the Roman elite". And so "with their hand clean of the wars in Judea and the Diaspora Revolt of 116–117 C.E., the Jewish community in Rome

---

[31] Gruen, *Diaspora*, 48, 52.
[32] Horace, *Sat.* 1.9.60–78, Suetonius, *Aug.* 76.2. See also Strabo, 16.2.40.
[33] Tacitus, *Hist.* 5.4.2. see also Plutarch, *Quaest. Conviv.* 4.5.2–3.
[34] E.g. Hectateus of Abdera, *Diodorus* 40.4 attributes to Moses as having introduced an "unsocial and intolerant code of life." (Stern, *Greek and Latin Authors I*, 28). Manetho, Josephus *C. Ap.* 1.239, emphasizes that Moses framed laws completely opposed to Egyptian custom, demanding among other things "that they should have intercourse with none save those of their own confederacy." (Stern, *Greek and Latin Authors I*, 82). Further references in Gruen, *Diaspora*, 274.
[35] Ibid., 45–6, referring to Tacitus, *Hist.* 5.5.1–2; 5.3.1; Juvenal, 14.103–4.
[36] Ibid., 42–3.

could sustain an unbroken history, which has lasted to the present day."[37]

Language Skills

Georg Walser set out to investigate whether any Judeo-Greek varieties of Greek may be identified in ancient Rome. The primary source material available consists of inscriptions, most of which are funerary inscriptions: 467 Greek, 127 Latin and 8 Semitic[38] inscriptions, all later than 200 C.E.[39] Though impressive in their sheer bulk, funerary inscriptions are of limited value. They are often very short, stereotypical and repetitive, using the same formulas and expressions over and over again, the production process of inscriptions involves several persons with different levels of language competence. Walser concludes that investigations into varieties of *spoken* language are impossible. Whatever conclusions one arrives at, be it that "the Jews formed no linguistic island in ancient Rome,"[40] or that there is no difference in terms of phonology, morphology and syntax from non-Jewish Greek,[41] such statements can refer only to funerary inscriptions. Nothing can be known of other contexts.[42]

However, a comparison of languages shows that Hebrew and Aramaic inscriptions are rather clumsy, presenting more interpretative problems than do the Greek and Latin inscriptions. Also, even scriptural quotations are in Greek (three renderings of Ps 10:7: ‎זכר צדיק לברכה . . . are all reminiscent of either LXX or Aquila's Greek translation). Considering the fact that the Jewish slaves which were brought to Rome already had knowledge of Greek and were reading the LXX in their services, it may be surmised that their competence in Greek surpassed their competence in Hebrew and Aramaic. Hebrew retained a certain function as a sacred language but not enough language competence was preserved to cite from the Hebrew Bible in fu-

---

[37] Barclay, *Diaspora*, 318–19.
[38] Cf. the list of (more or less) Semitic inscriptions below.
[39] In southern Italy the distribution of Jewish funerary inscriptions is quite different: 4 Greek, 12 Latin and 14 Semitic inscriptions. In northern Italy there are a few Greek and Latin but no Semitic inscriptions. Figures from Noy, *Inscriptions Italy*, and idem, *Inscriptions Rome*.
[40] Leon, "Jews," 92.
[41] Rutgers, *Jews in Rome*, 184.
[42] Walser, "Greek," 149.

nerary inscriptions. Judging from the prevalence of Greek over Latin one may further surmise a preference for Greek over Latin.[43] Thus, while the inscriptions do not allow inferences with regard to spoken varieties of Greek they inform us that the Jews used the same Greek as non-Jews when writing funerary inscriptions.

Edition of Jewish Inscriptions in Rome

Per Å. Bengtsson provides an edition of all the Jewish inscriptions in Rome that contain a Semitic element, such as fragments assumed to be Semitic, stereotypical phrases in Hebrew such as שלום or שלום על ישראל or even a picture of the menorah. The following list presents the texts and translations of the inscriptions. For detailed analyses of each inscription, the reader is asked to consult *SAOJR*.[44]

List of the inscriptions that include a Semitic element:
Abbreviations: A = Aramaic; G = Greek; H = Hebrew; *CIJ* = Frey, *Corpus*; Noy = Noy, *Inscriptions Rome*; Kanzler = Kanzler, "Scoperta"; Lang = Language; L = Latin.

Monteverde catacomb, all 3rd–4th C.E.

CIJ 290, Lang: A	אניה חתנה | דבר קלבריה
	Annia (?), son-in-law(?) of Bar-Calabria(?)
CIJ i, 291, Lang: A & G	| [--] ברת אסדורה |
	Isidora, daughter of... (Aramaic)
	΄[--Ισ]ιδώρα θυγά| [τηρ--] ἄρχ(οντος) Εβρέων
	...Isidora, daughter of... an archon of the Hebrews
CIJ i, 292, Lang: H	שלו[ם]
	Peace
CIJ i, 293, Lang: H	שלום על (menorah) שאל
	Peace upon... Israel(?)

---

[43] Ibid., 147.
[44] Bengtsson, "Inscriptions," 154–63.

CIJ i, 294[45], Lang: G   (menorah) Σαβ|άτυς

CIJ i, 295 1.1, Lang: H or A [--]א[--]

CIJ i, 295 II. 2–3, Lang: A   לברכתה | תהי
May it be for a blessing (?)

CIJ i, 296, Lang: G & H   ἔνθα κῖτε Αμμ|ιὰς Ιουδέα
ἀπὸ | Λαδικίας ἥτις | ἔζησεν ἔτη (menorah)|
ב πε´ שלם
Here lies Ammias, a Jewess from Laodicea,
who lived 85 years
In peace

Kanzler 3, Lang: H? & L?   կ ս ժ ի Ր Հ
facsimile (illegible)

CIJ i, 349, Lang: G & H   ἐνθά<δ>ε κῖτεν Ιούδας| νήπιους· ἐν εἰρηνε
κύμυ|σες αὐτοῦ
אל (menorah) ישר
Here lies Judas, child
In peace his sleep
Israel

CIJ i, 397, Lang: G & H   ἐνθάδε {ε} κεῖθεν |Σαββάτις δὶς ἄρχων |
ἔζησεν ἐτῶν (hedera) λε´. | ἐν ἰρήνη κύμυσις
αὐτοῦ |
ישרשל (shofar) (menorah) (lulav with a root?)
שאלום על
Here lies Sabbatius, twice archon. He lived 35 years
In peace his sleep
Peace upon Israel

Trastevere (?)

CIJ i, 497, 5th C.E.   ἐνθάδε κεῖται Τουβίας Βαρζαρω|να καὶ
Lang: G, L & H   Παρηιόριος υἱὸς Τουβία | Βαρζα-αρωνα. (hedera) (hede-
ra) (hedera) [vac.]|
hic est positus Tubias Barzaha| rona (hedera) et
Paregorius filius || Tubiae Barzaharona. (hedera) |

---

[45] First treated by Frey as two inscriptions, nos. 294 and 395.

	[ם]שלום (menorah) שלום (hedera) שלום (menorah) שלום Here lies Tobias Barzaarona and Paregorius son of Tobias Barzaarona Here was placed Tobias Barzaarona and Paregorius son of Tobias Barzaarona Peace Peace Peace Peace
CIJ i, 513, 3rd–4th C.E. (?) Lang: G & H (?)	ἔνθα κεῖται Τι[–]∥μῆνας[–] ∣ (illegible Hebrew) Here lies Ti . . . months . . .
Noy 546, 3rd–4th C.E. (?) Lang: G & H (?)	[–]∥βα ζήσασα [ἔτη] ∣ ε´ θυγάτη[ρ]∥ Βίκτω∣ρος ∣ (illegible Hebrew) . . . va having lived 5 years, daughter of Victor
Via Appia, 3rd C.E.	
CIJ i, 283, Lang: G & H	ἐνθάδε κεῖ∣ται Φαυστῖνα∣ (shofar) (menorah) (lulav) שלום Here lies Faustina. Peace
Via Casilina catacombe	
CIJ i, 73, Lang: H or G (?)	בשא (conj. Marucchi, abbr. for בית שלום אמן) or ΛωΖ (conj. Frey) Bet schalom. Amen
CIJ i, 74, Lang: H(?)	נות שרה (conj. Marucchi) rest(ing-place) of Sarah
Via Portuense, 5th C.E.	
CIJ i, 499, Lang: L & H	hic requ[iescit--]∥ Sigismundu(s) [--]∥ Sarra c[- -]∥ Runtin[--men-]∥ sis VI die,[s--] ∥ dies vite [--]∥ quievi[t in pace (?) --] left: בשלום (lulav) (menorah) (shofar) Here lies . . . Sigismund . . . Sarra . . . 6 months . . . days . . . day of (his/her) life . . . fell asleep in peace (?) . . . In Peace
Villa Torlonia catacombe, 3rd–4th C.E.	
Noy 529, Lang: H	שלום על ישראל∥[---] Peace upon Israel

Provenance unknown

CIJ i, 319, 3rd–4th C.E. (?) Lang: G & H	ἐνθάδε κῖτε Εἰρήνα| παρθενικὴ σύμβιος|Κλωδίου ἀδελφὸς| Κούντου Κλαυδίου| Συνεσίου πατρὸς|συναγω-γῆς Καμπησίων Ῥώμης שלום Here lies Irene, previously unmarried bride of Clodius the brother of [or bride of Clodius, sister of] Quintus Claudius Synesius (the) father of the synagogue of the Campesians of Rome. Peace
CIJ i, 732, 4th C.E.(?) Lang: G & H	ἐνθάδε κεῖνται | Ἀναστασία μήτηρ καὶ | Ασθῆρ θυγάτηρ· ἐν [εἰ]ρήνῃ ἡ κοίμησεις | αὐτῶν ἀμ<ήν> שלום right: (shofar) below: (5-branched menorah) Here lie Anastasia the mother and Asther the daughter In peace their sleep Amen Peace
CIJ 108, 3rd–5th C.E. Lang: G, L & H(?)	(hedera)[46] | Ερμειόνη θυγατρὶ | Πισίννα μήτηρ ἀνέθηκεν |ἢ ἀπέδωκεν μῆν(ας) η´ <κ>αὶ ἡμ(έρας) ζ´· | ἢ<τ>ιν ἐπίκλην Barveoda For her daughter Hermione, Pisinna her mother put up (this). She gave up (her soul aged) 8 months and 7 days, who was by surname Barsheoda

The Synagogue Building at Ostia

Two of the contributions to *SAOJR* deal with the synagogue building at Ostia and the quarter outside the Porta Marina. Olof Brandt presents a survey of the developments of the quarter from the first century B.C.E. to the fourth century C.E. Anders Runesson focuses on questions pertaining to the structure and function of the synagogue building from the first to the fifth century C.E.

To begin with I shall present briefly the most important assertions of the excavator as outlined by Runesson. Then I shall turn to the contri-

---

[46] The "hedera" or ivy leaf is a common symbol in the Monteverde inscriptions.

butions of Runesson in *SAOJR* and the subsequent debate between Runesson and L. M. White. Brandt's presentation of the Quarter will be amended with some new archeological data that have come to light since *SAOJR*, that may alter some of the assertions made by Brandt.

The Initial Discoveries

In 1961 in the far south-east corner of the quarter outside the Porta Marina at Ostia, the remains of a building were discovered. Based on analyses of masonry techniques, building materials and comparative evidence from other sites at Ostia, the excavator M. Floriani Squarciapino, who led the two excavation campaigns in 1961 and 1962, dated the original edifice to the second half of the first century. Her dating was subsequently confirmed by G. Zappa's identification of brick stamps.[47]

As the excavations were completed, Floriani Squarciapino asserted that a first century synagogue had been discovered. With its clear affiliation to Ostian architecture in general the building was recognized for being without comparison to any other known synagogue building. Its monumental character was taken as a testimony to the high level of integration and economical well-being of the Jews of Ostia.

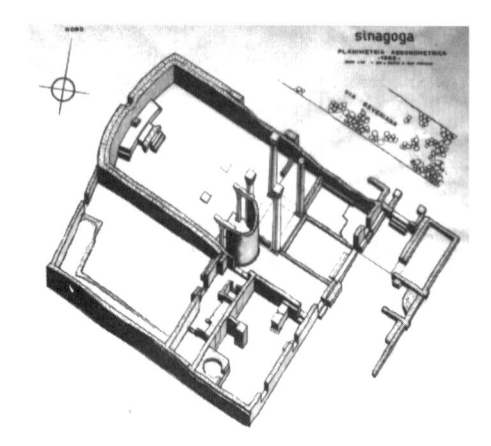

Figure 29.1 Isometric drawing of the Ostia synagogue in its fourth century state. Courtesy of ArchSAO.

---

[47] Floriani Squarciapino, "La sinagoga di Ostia," 327, idem, "Ebrei," 139. Zappa, "Nuovi bolli laterizi di Ostia," 285.

According to the excavator's preliminary excavation report, the earliest building was constructed in *opus reticulatum*. It included a main hall with broad benches along the walls and a podium. Also included in the original construction were four monumental columns with doors on either side leading into the main hall (see figs. 29.1 and 29.3). The different areas of the building have subsequently been labeled with the letters A-K by White (see fig. 29.3).

In the fourth century, a major renovation and enlargement of the building included the addition of some areas (A, F and E, fig. 29.3), the laying out of mosaic floors and the construction of two doors to flank the entrance from A to B. During this renovation phase the doors from area D towards the Via Severiana to the north were blocked, the benches of the main hall removed and additional columns installed in D. From outside and around most of the exterior walls of D, supporting walls were added. Some time later a Torah *aedicula* on a podium was put up in C3, now partly blocking the south entrance to D (cf. figs. 29.1 and 29.3).

Between the construction of the original building and its renovation in the fourth century, Floriani Squarciapino alleged that there may have been an intermediary phase with a few minor changes, like the division of area B by wooden walls and the laying out of some mosaics.[48]

Since no adjacent building or road construction have been identified that might have influenced the original building's geographical orientation, Floriani Squarciapino suggested that the building was designed from the beginning in an east-west direction for religious purposes, i.e. looking towards Jerusalem from the podium in D. For this she also takes the three doors from B to A into account, two of which were added much later, however. Adding to that the evidence from the Mindus Faustus inscription with its reference to an ark for the holy law (τὴν κειβωτὸν ἀνέθηκεν νόμῳ ἁγίῳ) which she considered to belong to the synagogue,[49] and the continuity of plan between the earliest and the latter building, Floriani Squarciapino considered it reasonable to assume that the building was designed from the outset for synagogal purposes.[50]

---

[48] Floriani Squarciapino, "La sinagoga di Ostia," 311–12; idem, "Plotius Fortunatus archisynagogus," 191. Cf. Runesson, "Synagogue," 33.

[49] For a detailed discussion of the many intricate issues with regard to the usefulness of the Mindus Faustus inscription for the building's history see Runesson, "Synagogue," 85–8.

[50] Floriani Squarciapino, "Ebrei," 469.

The Building's History and Functions

In 1990, White challenged Floriani Squarciapino's position. White argued that the original building could not be dated before Trajan (98–117), or even Hadrian (117–138). Also, in his opinion the original edifice must have been a private two-storey building with street front shops in B_1. In addition, and most importantly, according to White all of area D consisted of two stories. During a minor renovation towards the end of the second century, benches and a podium were introduced in D and a dining hall (E) added to the building.[51] Only from then on the building was used as a synagogue. Not before the late third or early fourth century was the building monumentalized by the removal of the first storey floor in D and the addition of columns in C_2.[52]

Thought-provoking as it seemed, White's reassessment of the building's history appears beset with a number of incredible assumptions. Under the influence of Runesson's criticism, he has retracted in several respects. In his later publications he is accepting a date of the original building as early as late Flavian-Trajan, i.e. from the beginning of Domitian's reign in 81 C.E.[53] Also, he now reaffirms the excavator's position that the original foundation structures presuppose four columns in C_2,[54] and acknowledges that "some sort of colonnade was original."[55]

Nonetheless, White retains his two-storey theory for D and claims that, based on the dating of the capitals, the extant large columns cannot be dated earlier than the end of the first century. The original but no longer extant columns could therefore have been of lower height and could have served the purpose of supporting the first floor ceiling of D.[56] Some support for White's replacement theory comes from the fact that the capitals of the columns cannot be dated before the first half of the second century. But since the capitals may have been exchanged or

---

[51] White, *Social Origins I*, 69.
[52] White, "Synagogue and society," 23–58. Already Kraabel had expressed doubts as to whether such a "temple-like" construction could have belonged to a first century synagogue (Kraabel, "Diaspora Synagogue," 499).
[53] White, "Reading," 459. In his earlier work White had dated the original building to Trajan-Hadrianic (White, "Synagogue and Society," 28–9, n. 19.)
[54] This had been pointed out clearly by Floriani Squarciapino, "La sinagoga di Ostia," 314, who had argued that the foundation structure beneath the columns is inseparable from the whole building structure (cf. Runesson, "Synagogue," 71f).
[55] White, "Reading," 443.
[56] Ibid., 443.

added later[57] the assertion of an installment of new and larger column shafts at a later date remains a conjecture. Also, there are no signs of any column foundation enlargements, which one might have expected had such a change in column size been carried out.[58]

Figure 29.2 The restored northern wall of area D (the former window filled in), looking northwest. Photo by Dieter Mitternacht.

Runesson had suggested that White's two-storey theory depended on a misreading of Floriani Squarciapino's article from the second campaign, namely that there were remains of a staircase under the Torah *aedicula*.[59] Admitting his misreading,[60] White asserts however, that a

[57] Zevi, "La sinagoga di Ostia," 140. In Runesson's view they were added in what he calls the first major renovation activity (Runesson, "Synagogue," 72).
[58] Runesson, "Monumental Synagogue," 197, see also ibid., 188, n. 70.
[59] Runesson, "Synagogue," 73–4.

staircase under the Torah aedicula never played an important role in his argument for an original two storey structure. Instead, his two "main" arguments have always been (a) the staircase in K (presuming an original connection between K and D) and (b) the second floor window in room D and the brick band in that wall. In Whites scheme the brick band carried the support structure for the upper floor ("its position *above* a layer of brick in three courses gives the appearance of a second level" [italics mine]).

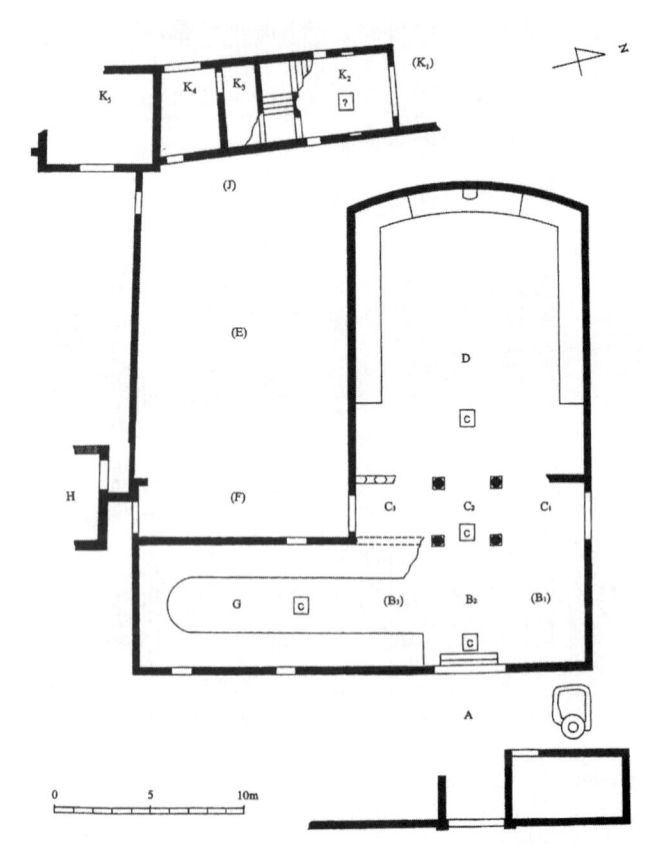

Figure 29.3 The Synagogue at Ostia—first phase, second half of the first century C.E. Courtesy of Anders Runesson.

---

[60] White, "Reading," 441f.

Current Views on Jews and the Synagogue in Rome and Ostia

Again, both of these arguments are problematic: (a) there is no evidence of K ever having been connected with D; (b) the window in question rests directly on the brick band (fig. 29.2) that would have carried the support structure for the second floor. Not only would a floor above the brick band have covered the lower part of the window, the window itself would have been at the bottom of the room.[61]

White recognizes that even with lower support columns in C_2 the thin original walls of D could hardly have carried an upper floor stretching over all of area D, but argues that there would have been piers or partition walls that divided D into a number of smaller spaces.[62] Again, there are no remains of such piers or partition walls.

Figure 29.4 The eastern wall of one of the two *tepidaria* in the *Terme del Foro*. Photo by Dieter Mitternacht.

---

[61] Cf. Runesson, "Monumental Synagogue," 196–7.
[62] White, "Reading," 441.

If instead we accept that the colonnade in C indicates a monumental gestalt of the building from the start,[63] another architectural feature falls into place, namely the slightly curved wall in the main hall, which is reminiscent of walls in other halls in Ostia as for instance in one of the *tepidaria* of the *Terme del Foro* (fig. 29.4).[64]

A third matter of dispute between Runesson and White concerns the *triclinium* benches in areas G/B$_3$. White claims that the benches were put up during renovations in the early second century, assuming an original floor (of which there are no remains) that was removed during the renovation and replaced with a lower floor on which the benches were then installed,[65] implying that the benches could not be original.

Figure 29.5 The rough bedding course on the lower inside of the wall between A and G. Photo by Dieter Mitternacht.

---

[63] Everybody, including White, agrees that the *aedicula* with its podium must be secondary to the south-east column of area C.
[64] The curved inner wall of the guild house of the house builders that has been suggested for comparison by Runesson may be of interest because of the function of the room (Runesson, "Synagogue," 90). It is an interior ledge on which statues may have been displayed, however, rather than a wall.
[65] White, "Reading," 445.

But there are no remains of an original floor and the lowering of floors is extremely uncommon in Roman architecture. Also, the lowest (supposedly subsequent) floor lies directly on the sandy ground and on the same level as the surrounding walls. In addition, there are no compelling reasons why the benches would have blocked any original doors, or windows rather,[66] from A and F to G. Finally, the rough bedding course below the brickband on the lower inside of the walls coincides with the wall space that was covered by the benches (fig. 29.5). On the outside the wall is in smooth reticulate all the way down to ground level (fig. 29.6). This again would seem to indicate that the benches belonged to the original design.

Figure 29.6 Smooth reticulate wall structure on the lower outside of the wall between A and G. Photo by Dieter Mitternacht.

White also rejects Floriani Squarciapino's suggestion that the original geographical orientation of the building was religiously motivated and argues that in its early stages the building was oriented not on an east–west but on a north–south axis facing the Via Severiana with its main entrance.[67] While Runesson rejects this possibility, I am inclined to at-

---

[66] Runesson, "Monumental Synagogue," 191.
[67] White, "Synagogue and Society," 387.

541

tribute more weight to the entrances from the north (see below). Also, Runesson's assertion that "the orientation of the synagogue could have been in any direction the builders liked since they were not constrained by other structures"[68] seems somewhat exaggerated. Even though no remains of an earlier road have been identified yet, the assumption of the existence of such a road seems plausible, especially now that *Villa suburbana* has been discovered close to the synagogue and a considerable amount of traffic in the area can be taken for granted (cf. fig. 29.10:6).[69]

According to Runesson, there are three factors that speak for a synagogal purpose of the building from the start. First, there is a continuity of plan between the first and the later building, which would seem to indicate that the building was considered suitable from the start for synagogal purposes. Second, the inscriptions and the mosaics that appear during the second century indicate early Jewish ownership. Thirdly, the podium in the front is reminiscent of the *bimah* of synagogues.[70]

Some questions remain with regard to these factors. First, the assertion of a continuity of plan does not, to my understanding, take into account appropriately the three original entrances from the north. If, as Runesson claims, the entrance from the north to D was added later,[71] the question remains, since the entrance to C is the most important. Also, the assertion by Floriani Squarciapino that the three entrances from A to B were oriented towards Jerusalem, must consider the fact that only one of these entrances was original. It is true of course that this original (middle) entrance is the largest entrance to the building(s), but the size of the entrance from the north to C_1 is also considerable. With regard to the podium and the benches, all that can be asserted is that this supports the existance of a large room where people were gathering from the beginning.

In conclusion of this section I would like to point out one more issue that still awaits consideration. During a visit to the site I was discussing with Olof Brandt the soft erosion on the surface of the marble slab floor

---

[68] Runesson, "Synagogue," 40. In reaction to White's critique, Runesson has since toned down his position on this issue somewhat (see Runesson, "Monumental Synagogue," 175).
[69] See also Heinzelmann, "Ostia, Regio III," 221–2.
[70] Runesson, "Synagogue," 90.
[71] Ibid., 78.

between the western columns of C (fig. 29.7). We agreed that that the erosion could hardly have come about from a curtain sliding between the columns, since for most of the time the passage between the columns was probably closed by a barrier (indicated by holes in the columns, the distinct groove in the marble slabs and the lack of a second hole on one of the columns that would have been necessary for the lower hinge[72]). A more plausible explanation would seem that over a long period of time water has been dripping down in a straight line between the columns.

Since the centre of the erosion is located towards the western conclusion of the columns, the drippings could have gathered from a roof that ended with the western columns, leaving at least area C_2 roofless. Whether or not C_2 had a marble floor from the beginning is unclear. The floors of the original building were generally covered with cocciopesto and most of the marble was added during subsequent renovations of the building. On the other hand, if marble was used somewhere from the start, an open floor area inside the building structure would have been a plausible choice. Also, as is evident from the column foundations, the floor level in C_2 was not changed during the different renovations of the building.

Figure 29.7 Looking north between the two western columns of C. Note the soft erosion in the marble slab surface that runs between the columns (2) and the parallel groove to the left (1). Photo by Dieter Mitternacht.

[72] Ibid., 51.

One explanation for the opening in area C_2 that caused the erosion may be that the western columns of C were part of a wall construction that delimited area D from C. In that case all of area C could have been roofless and the entrance to C from the north (first to third century) could have led to an open passage between two buildings. Entering the passage, one would either turn to the right and enter the synagogue hall, to the left and enter the triclinium or pass through the passage in order to exit through the door at the south end and into area F. Since the doors from the north were blocked in the fourth century, the passage would then have become an interior open space, or maybe the roof construction would have been extended from D to B. The latter would have to have been the case at least as the Torah aedicula was installed in C_3. In consequence, a division of the building construction in the early period would seem possible. The composed foundation structure of the colonnade however still suggests that the two buildings were designed together, including also a west-east axis for the main hall that may have served religious purposes.

The Quarter Outside the Porta Marina

As we turn to the Quarter outside the Porta Marina, there have been some major developments since *SAOJR*, with regard to the first century. Before I turn to a description of these new insights and discoveries, I will sum up Olof Brandt's detailed and useful description of the developments in the Quarter outside the Porta Marina of Ostia during the first four centuries C.E. (with a few additional comments).[73]

Having started out as a naval base in the fourth century B.C.E., Ostia developed into the leading harbor of Rome from the middle of the second century B.C.E., grew into a city with a population total of between 75 to 100 thousand people, and was gradually turning into a residential environment for traders and merchants who made their living at Portus.[74] During the reign of Hadrian (117–138 C.E.) Ostia experienced a "building boom" and was rebuilt to a great extent. Due to socio-economical changes, impressive mansions in the center of the city were being torn down and replaced by apartment buildings, workshops and guild seats. As Ostia's economic significance began to diminish from

---

[73] Brandt, "Quarter,"19–28.
[74] Eventually Portus outgrew Ostia and was made by Constantine a city in its own right (Civitas Constantiniana).

the second century onwards, its inhabitants retained their status for various reasons.

Brandt notes that the Quarter outside the Porta Marina did not experience the same economical and political decline as the late town of *Ostia antica* from 250 C.E. and especially 420 C.E. onwards. While the town within the walls began to disintegrate, the Quarter continued to expand. Well into the early decades of the fourth century elegant and fashionable building structures were being put up outside the city walls.[75] Even as people began to abandon the town of Ostia from 420 C.E. onwards, the Quarter outside the Porta Marina continued to be used. Under Theodericus (493–526 C.E.) the thermae of the Porta Marina went through a fourth phase of restoration.[76]

From the third century on, there are signs of a Christian presence throughout Ostia. Constantine donated a Christian basilica to Ostia, and at the Council of Rome in 313 C.E. Ostia was represented by its own bishop. From 336 C.E. and onwards the bishop of Ostia even consecrated the new pope. In the immediate vicinity of the synagogue a fourth century *opus sectile* building is decorated with a portrait of Christ.[77]

Hand in hand with the expansion of Christianity went the spread of Mithraism that seemed to have gradually replaced the oriental cults in the third century.[78] At the same time traditional Roman religions retained a degree of influence, evidenced most impressively by the remarkable *Tempio rotondo*. However, none of the thirteen *mithrae* that have been found,[79] was located outside the Porta Marina. Of course, neither was there any indication of Jewish religion in the Quarter before the discoveries made in 1961.

In the end Ostia was abandoned by its inhabitants. C. Pavolini, who suggested a division of late *Ostia antica* into three periods of development, defined the third period (420 C.E. onwards) as one of disintegration and decline. In fact, Ostia's decline was so rapid that Alaric and the Visigoths who sacked Rome in 410 C.E. did not find it necessary to

---

[75] Excavated during the campains of Floriani Squarciapino in 1977 and Pavolini in 1978 and 1979 (Floriani Squarciapino, "Synagogue d' Ostie," Pavolini, "Ostia (Roma): Saggi Lungo la via severiana.").
[76] Brandt, "Quarter," 26.
[77] Ibid., 26.
[78] Meiggs, *Roman Ostia*, 354–77.
[79] Becatti, *Scavi di Ostia II. I mitrei*, fig. 25.

concern themselves with Ostia. And as the Vandals sacked Rome again in 455 C.E., Portus was included in the destruction, but Ostia not even mentioned.

From Naval Base to Suburban Living Environment

The notion that the river mouth of the Tiber was almost abandoned as a doorway to Ostia and Rome as Claudius (41–54 C.E.) initiated the construction of the new harbor further to the north[80] has to be reassessed in light of the construction work at the river mouth that has come to the fore in the DAI/AAR 2001 excavation campaign.[81]

Portus, as the new harbor was simply called, was completed by Nero (54–68 C.E.) and enlarged and secured with an inner hexagon-shaped harbor in the early second century C.E. by Trajan (98–117 C.E.). For obvious nautical reasons, Portus became the main port of Ostia, in fact a world port of Rome. But the old harbor at the Tiber mouth was not abandoned, as has often been assumed. In region III a harbor basin and a navalia complex that consisted of a square platform of 70 x 65 m with an underlying structure of numerous vaulted channels that had been used as boat halls have now been discovered (figs. 29.8 and 29.9).[82]

On top and right in the center of the platform, there is a podium with a formerly 20 m high temple (fig. 29.9). Two construction phases have been identified, one from the early empire and one from the time of Marcus Aurelius (161–180 C.E.).[83] The discovery substantiates several

---

[80] The new harbor included a channel from the Tiber and into the sea, a huge lighthouse and a basin of 850,000 m². Several other large harbors of Rome were built (Antium by Nero, Tarracina and Centumcellae by Tajan) but Portus was the most significant.

[81] I am referring to the Aug 27 to Oct 13, 2001 joint American Academy in Rome (AAR) - German Archaeological Institute (DAI) excavation campaign in regions III and IV, conducted under the leadership of M. Heinzelmann. The following account is based on the preliminary report available on the DAI website and on an excerpt from the Grabungsvorbericht 2001 that was made available to me by Dr. Heinzelmann. I was told that the complete Grabungsvorbericht 2001 is scheduled for publication in Römische Mitteilungen by the end of 2002. The volume has however not been in print as of June of 2003.

[82] Based on aerial photographs and geophysical prospections, the existence of a large harbor basin had been suspected for some time and was first confirmed through soundings during the excavation campaign in 2000.

[83] Cf. *CIL* 14.376.

Current Views on Jews and the Synagogue in Rome and Ostia

written sources mentioning annual processions that were conducted from Rome to a Castor and Pollux temple at the mouth of the Tiber.

It is important for the present purpose to note that the construction of the harbor to the north (Portus) did not lead to the abandonment of the harbor at the Tiber mouth. As Ostia (with Portus) became a world port and experienced a period of great commercial expansion, construction activities that upheld the town itself as a place of commerce and trade also continued.

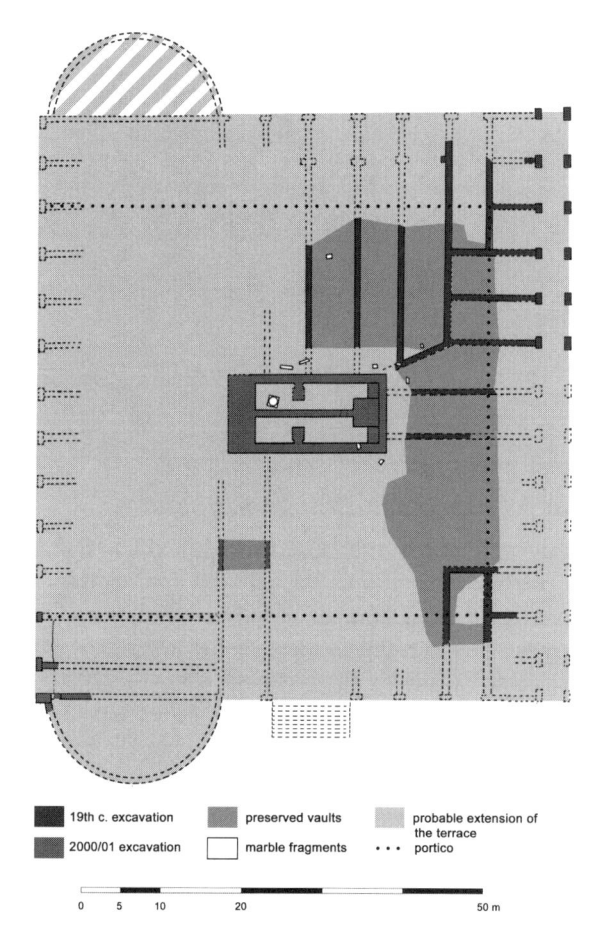

Figure 29.8 Navalia and temple construction at the Tiber mouth. Courtesy of Michael Heinzelmann.

Well into the second century, traders and merchants did not just use Ostia as a residential environment but the town continued to function as a place of commerce. Floriani Squarciapino's suggestion that among the Jews that moved to Ostia during the first centuries C.E. there were merchants who were attracted by the blossoming town of commerce, is further strengthened.

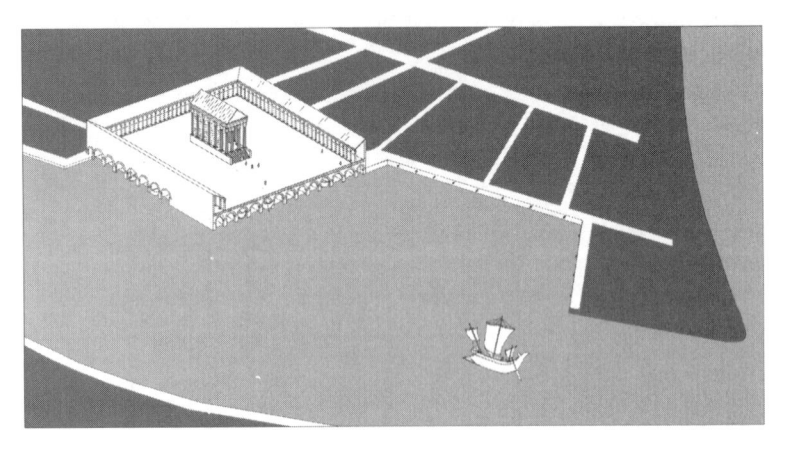

Figure 29.9 Reconstruction of the harbor basin and the Navalia with temple. Courtesy of Michael Heinzelmann.

The *Villa suburbana* and the Synagogue

With regard to the first century C.E., Brandt had stated that, except for the synagogue building, all building activities outside the Porta Marina had been confined to its immediate vicinity: two *mausolea* during the first century B.C.E. and a small sanctuary for Bona Dea, the goddess of the fertility of the fields (built in 30–40 C.E., fig. 29.10:1), and the *Domus fulminata* (built in 65–75 C.E., fig. 29.10:2). The synagogue building (fig. 29.10:3) appeared to have been put up far away from any other building, and the choice of location so far to the east of the Porta Marina and close to the ancient shoreline seemed unexpected.

The notion of remoteness was further strengthened by the supposition that it took half a century before any other building or road constructions appeared anywhere close to the synagogue building. In the second century some insulae were set up to the north and north-west of the synagogue and towards the end of that century (198–209 C.E.) the ground level of the Quarter was raised so that the shoreline retreated. Also, the Via Severiana was laid out between the insulae and the synagogue building.

In the meantime, new information has come to the fore that sheds new light on the positioning and the surroundings of the synagogue. Already in 1985, based on an aerial photograph, indications of a large villa complex between the late republic city wall and the Via Severiana had been reported. In response, part of the DAI/AAR 2001 excavation campaign in regio IV was dedicated to sounding some of that terrain. The four soundings (34–37) performed in the area confirm the existence of a sizable Villa complex (fig. 29.10) that consisted from north to south of a large living area, including an almost square peristyle (fig. 29.10:4). Towards the south it culminated in a 125 m long garden stadium that ran from west to east almost parallel to the seashore and concluded in the east with a pavilion-like *Kopfbau* (fig. 29.10:5). The ground level underneath the garden stadium and the Kopfbau was about 1 m higher than that of the rest of the villa. The Kopfbau was paved with mosaics and frescos and must have had a second floor that was richly decorated with *opus sectile*. The second floor was most likely to have provided a grand view both over the stadium and towards the sea.

Sounding 37 was conducted in a large room in the north east section of the Villa's living area, most probably a *triclinium*. Opus mixtum walls and older substructures underneath indicate a second building phase. A *terminus post quem* is provided by a brick stamp (type *CIL* 15.708a) from 138 C.E.

The fact that the garden stadium appears to have been designed with an open view of the sea in mind may indicate that it was built earlier than the insulae which were to block its view of the sea.[84]

---

[84] The excavation report states that "im Verlauf des 2. Jhs. südlich dieses Komplexes entlang der Via Severiana mehrere Insulabauten entstanden, welche die Villa vom Meer abschnitten." This statement is somewhat misleading, since the Via Severiana was built between 198 and 209 C.E. and the insulae under discussion were built already in the beginning of the second century (cf. Brandt, "Quarter," 23–4). There are even some remains of walls underneath some of the insulae that date to the end of the first century C.E. (see fig. 29.10:7, cf. Heinzelmann, "Ostia, Regio III," 221). Also, the foundation level of these early insulae is 0.9 m below the Via Severiana. The assumption of an earlier road no later than towards the end of the first century C.E., resembling the direction of the Via Severiana no later than towards the begin-

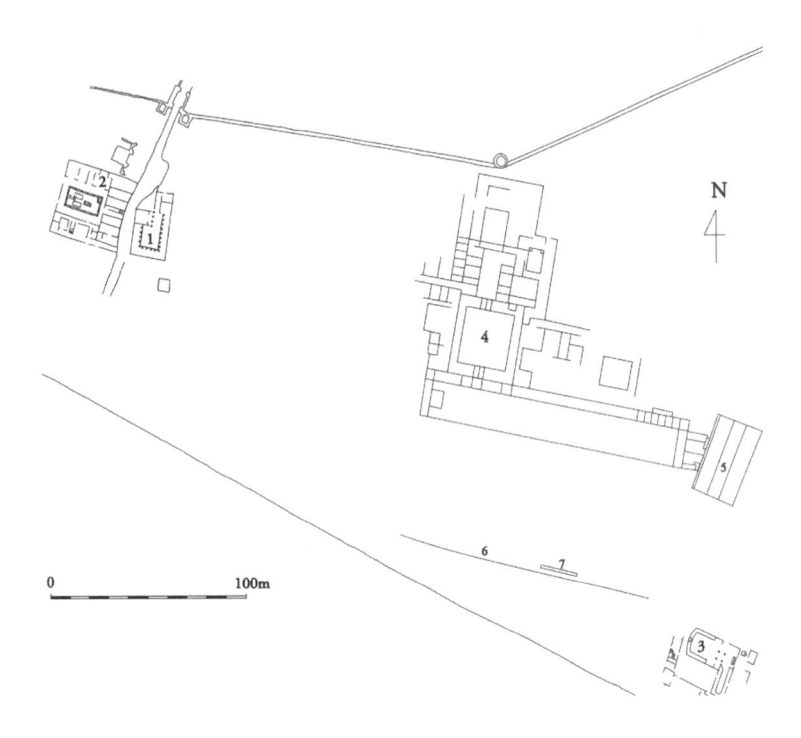

Figure 29.10 Map of the Quarter outside the Porta Marina in the second half of the first century C.E. Some parts of the villa structure belong to the second century. The villa plan was included with courtesy of Michael Heinzelmann. (1) Sanctuary for *Bona Dea*, (2) *Domus fulminata*, (3) synagogue building, (4) peristyle of *Villa suburbana*, (5) pavillion of *Villa suburbana*, (6) presumed road that preceded the *Via Severiana*, (7) *insulae* remains from the first century (*saggio b*).

In addition, sounding 34 on the Kopfbau showed "auffallend groben *opus reticulatum*." These indications together with ceramic finds from the foundations of the Garden stadium and the Kopfbau make it now possible to date the basic structure of the building to 60–80 C.E.

Based on these soundings the building history of the Villa complex can be divided into two phases: the original construction of the villa in 60–80 C.E.; reconstructions and new decorations during the second

---

ning of the second century C.E., seems reasonable, however (Heinzelmann, "Ostia, Regio III," 221–2).

century Hadrianic period. Towards the end of the third century the whole complex was completely destroyed, possibly by an earthquake.[85] Three subsequent construction phases in the fourth and fifth century do not seem to take any notice of the structures of the earlier complex.

It must be noted further that the existence of a Villa complex outside the city walls at such an early date confirms what the excavation campaigns in 1999 and 2000 in regions III, IV and V had brought to light, namely that the periphery of the town was beginning to be filled by rich and large private houses as early as the second half of the first century. During the DAI Rome excavation campaign 1999 a huge, almost square, private *domus* (60 x 65 m) which had been identified by an areal photograph, could now be dated by the excavators to the second half of the first century C.E., probably Flavian.[86] The building was richly decorated with *opus sectile* floors and paintings. Somewhat east of the formerly unknown gate of the *Via degli Aurighi* in regio III, a large *domus* with several wings was found sitting right on the city wall. Its earliest building phase has been dated to the late first or early second centuries C.E. During another sounding not far from "the villa on the wall" two smaller villas that lean against the city wall from the outside appeared. The older of the two was built in the second half of the first century.[87]

These villas seem to be just the beginning of what may be a series of discoveries that will require reconsiderations of the development of the periphery of the city of Ostia during the first century. Later on during the second century "construction boom" the *Villa suburbana* was integrated into an unbroken chain of seashore villas, stretching several kilometers southwards. Given the special interest in the synagoguge, one is especially curious as to what soundings of the buldings northwest of the synagogue may bring to the fore.

---

[85] Until RM 109, 2002 becomes available, see the report at the DAI home site (http://www.dainst.org). Also the domus discovered in regio III collapsed because of an earthquake. None of the ancient earthquakes listed in Guidoboni, *Catalogue*, fits the time frame. Two that are listed come close, but none of them seems to have affected Ostia. No. 131 is based on an unclear reference in the *Historia Augusta* (*Tac.* 17.4-5) and occurred, if at all, during the reign of Tacitus (275–276 C.E.). It was limited, however, to the city of Rome. No. 127 is based on a reference in *Historia Augusta* (*Gall.* 5.2) which says that a number of great disasters occurred during the consulship of Gallienus (262 C.E.), and adds: "Rome, too, was shaken."

[86] Bauer, Heinzelmann, and Martin, "Ostia. Ein urbanistisches Forschungsprojekt," 397.

[87] Heinzelmann, "Ostia, Regio III," 321–2.

From what can be known at this point, the circumstances of the Quarter outside the Porta Marina during the first century C.E. will have to be reconsidered in some respects. Brandt's map in *SAOJR*[88] has been redrawn accordingly (fig. 29.10).

Implications For the Dating of the Synagogue Building

What implications emerge for the earliest dating of the synagogue building? As the excavator stated, the construction of the Garden stadium presupposes a view of the sea. A look at fig. 29.10 indicates that the synagogue building did not infringe on that view.

One is tempted therefore to speculate, whether the positioning of the synagogue so far to the south could have been due to requirements for the stadium's shore view? Also, towards the end of the first century C.E. (wall 22 in *saggio b,* fig. 29.10:7) and continuing into the second, third and fourth centuries, *insulae* were erected that in fact did block the shore view of the garden stadium. In other words, from the turn of the century and onwards, the requirement of a shore view for the villa's garden stadium where not implemented.

If these speculations are allowed to carry some weight, they would imply that there has been an interdependence between the positioning of the synagogue and the demand for a shore view for the villa's garden stadium, and the notion of a temporal proximity between the erection of the *Villa suburbana* and the synagogue building around the years 60–80 C.E. is strengthened.

In conclusion, I want to point out two aspects that may enrich the discussion of the building's history in the future.

First, in her latest contribution to the discussion Floriani Squarciapino, where she asserts her overall agreement with Runesson versus White,[89] presents an earlier unpublished detail of a Trajanic coin that was found,[90] in the cement of the mosaic in B_1. The coin constitutes a terminus post quem for the dating of the reconstructions during the Hadrianic period. One is left to wonder, of course, how many more such important details are known only to the excavator.

---

[88] Brandt, "Quarter," 22.
[89] ". . . avec lequel je suis d'accord à peu de points près," Floriani Squarciapino, "Synagogue d' Ostie," 277.
[90] Ibid., 276. I thank A. Runesson for pointing this out to me.

Second, the assertion that the *Villa suburbana* may have been destroyed by an earthquake could have major implications for the history of the synagogue building. Since the earthquake seems to have brought about the collapse of the whole villa complex and even affected a *domus* in regio III[91] one may surmise that the synagogue building with its thin walls would have been affected somehow as well. One could therefore deduce that the reason behind the reinforcement of the walls of D from outside and the addition of supporting piers indicates an alerted awareness on account of the effect of the earthquake on the earlier building. In that case, the idea that the reinforcements were added in order to be able to change the two-storey structure of area D into a hall structure would be further weakened. The supporting walls would have been added in order to retain the main hall structure and guard it against further damage from earthquakes.

An additional socio-religious explanation as to why the synagogue was "embellished" with Jewish symbols during the major rebuilding phase has been suggested by M. Zetterholm in his contribution to *SAOJR* (see below). The two explanations would seem to complement each other.

A number of unanswered questions are still pending. From the point of view of the synagogue building, the most important issues concern (1) the area west of the synagogue building, where signs of building structures have been identified but still await excavation and dating; (2) the structures north of the synagogue along the Via Severiana, that to my knowledge have not been investigated at their lowest levels (c.f. *saggio b*, fig. 11:7). In both of theses instances, the assertions that have been made with regard to the synagogue building's location and geographical direction could be either confirmed or shown to be in need of further revision.

The Jews of Ostia

Three contributions to *SAOJR* are marked by an exploratory approach to the data available on Ostian Jewry. Taking peculiarities such as the unexpected location of the synagogue and coincidences of building activities together with knowledge of historical developments and worship

---

[91] See above n. 85.

habits of the time in general, as well as with theories from the sociology of knowledge, they manage each it its own right, to illustrate possible, sometimes even probable, causes, effects and practices.

From Meeting Facility to Holy Place

In his second contribution to *SAOJR* Anders Runesson concerns himself with possible religious motives for the location of the synagogue outside the city walls and near the seashore. In order to substantiate his case, he argues as follows:[92] There are no Jewish regulations regarding the location of synagogues except for *t. Meg.* 4.23 where it is said that synagogues are built on the highest place in town. Yet in Halicarnassus' decree it is said that Jews were permitted to "build προσευχάς near the sea, in accordance with their customs" (Josephus, *A.J.* 14.258) and according to Acts 16:13 the place of prayer in Philippi was expected to be outside the city gates by the river. In addition, there is archaeological evidence that at least four Diaspora synagogues were built near water (Delos, Aegina, Hammam-Lif and Ostia). In the land of Israel on the other hand none of the synagogues that are known were built near water (with the exception of Capernaum I, but that location may be coincidental to the fact that the whole town lies by a lake).

Two factors seem to account for the apparent preference to situate Diaspora synagogues outside the city and close to water. First, Jews avoided worshipping within city walls that contained pagan sanctuaries (unless whole quarters were Jewish, as in Alexandria).[93] Second, in *m. Miqw.* 5.4 the rabbis state that all seas are valid as *miqwaoth*, especially the "Great Sea," i.e. the Mediterranean. In addition *Mek. Pisha* 1:4–6 states that God did not reveal himself outside the land of Israel except at a pure spot (במקום טהרה) near water. In Philo, *Flacc.* 120–3, we are told that the Jews of Alexandria met for prayer at a pure spot at the beach because their προσευχάς had been taken from them. By implication the destroyed house of prayer is identified as the pure spot for which the location at the beach was chosen as a substitute.[94]

Not only was water essential for the identification of pure locations for worship in the Diaspora, in many Diaspora synagogues (Ostia,

---

[92] Runesson, "Water and Worship," 115–29.
[93] Elbogen, *Jewish Liturgy*, 340.
[94] For an emphasis on pure places Runesson refers to Josephus, *A.J.* 3.241, 4.79–81, Philo, *Mos.* 1.25–37)

Sardis, Priene, Dura Europos, Gerasa, Side, Lydian Philadelphia) we find water facilities such as basins, fountains and cisterns. Contrary to the *miqwaoth* of the land of Israel, however, these water facilities were located in the entrance areas and they were not designed for immersion.[95] Rather they seem to have corresponded to the vessels for ritual washings, sprinklings or just the dipping of a hand outside non-Jewish temples.[96]

In addition to the purity of places there was a concern for the purity of people. Rabbinic literature is ambivalent with regard to whether one should wash before or after the handling of sacred texts, prayer, or meals.[97] But the importance of ablutions one way or another is never questioned. The Essenes immersed themselves before meals[98] and made ablutions prior to prayer.[99] There are passages from the Hasmonean period (Jdt 12:7–8), the New Testament (1 Tim 2:8; Jas 4:8) and later Christian authors (*1 Clem.* 29:1; Hippolytus, *Trad. ap.* 41; Tertullian, *Or.* 13ff) that testify to the praxis of ritual hand washing before prayer both among Jews and Christians. Of the Jews of the Diaspora it is said that they used ritual ablutions in order to attain ritual purity.[100] A great number of texts interconnect requirements of ritual cleanness with prayer, the handling of sacred scripture and communal meals.[101]

During the fourth century renovation of the Ostia synagogue both the basin in area B_1 and the cistern in A were covered and room K_5 rebuilt into a *nymphaeum*. At the same time, baths were being constructed on the other side of the Via Severiana. Maybe, Runesson

---

[95] With the possible exception of Delos, where a bather may have been able to descend into the water on steps.

[96] Even more to the point, in a Cairo Geniza text Lev 19.30: "You shall revere my sanctuary" is followed by the statement: "Therefore the men of old set up in the courtyards of synagogues whole sinks to sanctify the hands and the feet." Cf. Margaliot, *Laws from the Geniza*, 132.

[97] Some made distinctions between regular and sacred meals, see Sanders, *Judaism*, 437–8, Sanders, *Jewish Law*, 261.

[98] Josephus, *B.J.* 2.129, 132.

[99] Wright, "Jewish Ritual Baths," 210.

[100] Cf. e.g. Philo, *Spec.* 1.261ff., 3.63, Justin, *Dial.* 14.1, Clement of Alexandria, *Strom.* 4.22.142

[101] Ritual washings were performed (1) before prayer (*Sib. Or.* 3.591–3, Philo, *Virt.* 57, Josephus, *B.J.* 5.380, Clement of Alexandria, *Strom* 4.22.142; (2) before the handling of sacred scriptures *Let. Aris.* 305–6, Josephus, *A.J.* 12.106); (3) before eating, Philo, *Contempl.* 64–90.

speculates, the Jews of Ostia had come under the influence of "rabbinic Judaism on the rise" and had accepted the demand for immersion bathing, including a clearer dissociation from Hellenistic customs. So they began to use the public baths across the road. Maybe also a growing sense of marginalization in light of the "success" of Christianity boosted homeland affinities. So it may have been decided to remove the washing facilities from the entrance area and to implement immersion practices instead.[102]

In sum then, the sources seem to suggest that synagogue worship required ritual ablutions for various reasons. At first the purpose of the ablutions was to prepare the worshipper for prayer, scripture reading and communal meals. With time, the places where ablutions were performed, i.e., the synagogue buildings, were perceived as holy places.[103]

The synagogue at ancient Ostia may indeed be an example, where a location on the shore was chosen because of religious convictions and rituals. Suggestions that the choice of place would indicate Jewish ghettoization tendencies were never quite compatible with other indices that showed the Jews' adjustment to and fairly good status in Roman society. Based on the insights now available into construction activities in the quarter outside the Porta Marina (see above), such notions can be ruled out all together. Even the fact that the building is placed farther to the south than necessary at first sight, may appear reasonable in light of the shore view requirement for which the garden stadium of the *Villa suburbana* was designed. But as has been pointed out, these assertions will have to be revised, if future excavations west of the synagogue bring to light building structures that predate the synagogue.

Competition as Identity Boost

Magnus Zetterholm takes the *temporal coincidence* of the fourth century synagogue renovations with Constantine's erection of a basilica as his point of departure for an investigation into the relations between Jews and Christians in Ostia. He emphasizes that, even though there were other religious systems present at the time in Ostia, only Judaism and Christianity participated in the architectural monumentalization typical for parts of Ostia during the decades around 300 C.E.

---

[102] Runesson, "Synagogue," 125, 127.
[103] Ibid., 127.

That the renovation of the synagogue after 306 C.E. involved a stronger emphasis on religious symbols than did the earlier building, is evident especially from the erection of the Torah *aedicula*. The addition of two new doors flanking the entrance on either side may have been an attempt to emphasize consistency with Palestinian synagogues and even the temple.[104]

Regarding the correlation of synagogue and church construction Zetterholm adds the few bits and pieces known about Ostian Jewry and Christianity and fits them into a puzzle of fundamental reasons for the development of Judaism and Christianity throughout the empire. Committed to using the two building activities as mirror images of socio-religious circumstance, he ventures to investigate whether it is "possible to understand the *action* of the Jewish community as a *reaction* to the threat of the rising Christianity."[105]

In order to compensate for the scarcity of historical data Zetterholm interrelates the data with social scientific theories that treat germane phenomena such as the impact of *high social ethics* on group credibility, the motivating and persuasive effect of *martyrdom* on in-group identities, *resource mobilization* within a social and religious movement, and procedures of *reality maintenance*.[106]

Based on the assumption of similarities of development throughout the Roman Empire, which saw growth from a few thousand in the first century to millions of Christians in the third, Zetterholm is convinced that "there was a vigorous Christian community in Ostia around the year 300 C.E.."[107] Similarly he asserts that the Jewish community conceived of the massive rise of Christian presence as an ideological threat. The assertion finds support from the fact that Jews converted to Christianity.[108]

Considering thus the *temporal coincidence* of the fourth century synagogue monumentalization and Constantine's erection of a basilica, Zetterholm thinks that the renovation of the synagogue was an example of ideological resource mobilization in light of the threat posed by

---

[104] Zetterholm, "Struggle," 110, 112.
[105] Ibid., 101.
[106] On "*marginalization elements*" inherent in Diaspora Judaism and the effect of *the two epidemics* that swept throughout the empire, he relies especially on Stark, *Rise of Christianity*, Berger and Luckman, *Social Construction of Reality*,.
[107] Zetterholm, "Struggle," 107.
[108] Ibid., 109.

Christianity. Starting as a defensive action, the resource mobilization proved to have an immensely positive effect on Jewish identity and may be an example of the mechanisms by which Judaism survived.

One might wish to add that from the first to the third century C.E. threats and opportunities based on confessions of faith in Christ must have shifted in various ways. In the early years when such confessions were practiced within Judaism the question was whether Gentile Christ-believers would be allowed by the Jewish community control agents to profit from the established Jewish religious liberties.[109] As we get to the end of the first century and into the second, Christ-believers begin to define their religious identity as non-Jewish and the relationship between Jews and Christ-believers shifts dramatically. Jewish converts to Christianity are required to leave their former religious identity.[110] Yet, the exclusiveness of these two religions required and guaranteed a high commitment from those who identified with the system. This in turn generated a strong internal organization and greater survival capacity. Non-exclusive religious systems were at the same time weakened by excessive pluralism and "lack of public reverence".[111] In other words, Judaism and Christianity had expansion capacity while other religious systems seem to decline.[112]

In light of the fact that it may have been an earthquake that triggered the need for a renovation of the synagogue, the *chronological* coincidence with Constantine's erection of a basilica has become somewhat less weighty. Considering the fact that already the earliest construction of the synagogue was monumental, I would also wish to replace the term "monumentalization" for the fourth century with "embellishment with religious symbolism." That the embellishment was part of a reaction against Christianity's ascent to the status of official state religion, however, appears a plausible conclusion. What was happening in Ostia was not a singular event. The embellishment of synagogues with religious symbols and the installation of fixed Torah shrines from the third century onwards has been documented also for other older syna-

---

[109] Mitternacht, "Recipient-oriented," 430–3.
[110] Cf. Zetterholm, "Struggle," e.g. 99–136, 238–42.
[111] Stark, *Rise of Christianity*, 200–4.
[112] Ibid., 199.

gogues.[113] S. Schwartz has devoted a whole chapter to the phenomenon, labeling it "Judaization."[114] "Judaization" may not characterize all of what is going on, however. One also needs to consider that the addition of two doors flanking the main entrance on either side may be less reminiscent of Palestinian synagogues[115] or the temple and more of what is the standard scheme for Early Christian basilicas. Nevertheless, I think it holds true that in the "struggle among brothers" the older brother decided to display his own religious identity, demonstrating to the formerly little brother that he could not subdue that which had a strength of its own.

Worship in Action

In her contribution to *SAOJR,* Irene von Görtz-Wrisberg makes it her objective to construct a worship service in the ancient synagogue on the Sabbath or a holiday. Beginning with a discussion of the pros and cons for public prayer as part of the synagogue service before 200 C.E., she then provides a general description of the ancient Sabbath service, and ventures finally to construct a Sabbath service in a Diaspora synagogue, namely Ostia.

The Theodotos inscription, the New Testament, Philo and Josephus all agree that the reading of the law and the teaching of the commandments were functions of the synagogue (e.g. Mark 1:21, Acts 13:15–41, Philo, e.g. *Leg.* 23.156, Josephus, *C. Ap.* 2.175). But none of the

---

[113] Dura Europos, Ḥammath Tiberias B, e.g. (Hachlili, *Ancient Jewish Art,* 166–92). The same tendency is apparent from the Jewish catacombs of Rome and even in the Beth (Shearim cemetery in the Land of Israel (Hachlili, *Menorah,* 247–9).

[114] Schwartz, *Imperialism,* 240–74. Already in 1976 Nahman Avigad had maintained that the Diaspora Jews, more than Jews in the Land of Israel, used religious emblems to emphasize their identity (Avigad, *Beth Shearim, III,* 273).

[115] Some synagogues of Palestine had three door entrances but far from all. Among the earliest buildings Masada and Qiriat Sefer have one, Gamla two and Herodium three. In the Late Roman period (70–fourth century C.E.), to name but a selection, Chorazim, Gush Ḥalav, Qatzrin had only one entrance, Meiron and Baram had three. The issue of temple resemblance is also problematic. "Rabbinic Judaism on the rise" may have contributed to the removal of the washing basin at the entrance towards the Via Severiana. But the Rabbis may or may not have supported a reconstruction of the synagogue entrance in order for it to resemble the temple entrance. The rabbis were divided in that regard (for references and discussion cf. Levine, *Ancient Synagogue,* 188–90). For the influence of Christian church buildings on Byzantine synagogue architecture, cf. Levine, *Ancient Synagogue,* 582–5.

sources prior to 200 C.E. mention prayer in synagogues *on the Sabbath*. McKay has concluded from that, that neither in Palestine nor in the Diaspora did the Sabbath service prior to 200 C.E. include public prayer.[116] Conversely, S. Fine had argued that prayer in a synagogue was taken for granted. If one calls a meeting house a *preseuche* as is the case with the Diaspora synagogue, the presence of prayer is self-evident.[117] In other words, prayer is not mentioned simply because there was no need to mention it.

According to L. I. Levine, the distance to the temple and the use of hymns and prayers in Hellenistic religious associations led to an early introduction of prayer in synagogue services in the Diaspora.[118] In Palestine *public* prayer became part of synagogue services only after 70 C.E., since up till then it was associated primarily with the liturgical activity of the temple. Even *private* prayer confirms the close association, as one would turn one's eyes to the temple mount in prayer (c.f. Dan 6.11).

For further evidence of pre-200 C.E. public prayer in Diaspora situations, Görtz-Wrisberg points out that the Jews worshipping in the streets of Alexandria and by the sea (Philo, *Flacc.* 120–4) testify by their very action to being accustomed to praying together. In addition, their march to the beach and their prayers at the shore may indicate an awareness that locations close to water where considered to imply purity. The sea shore would thus function as a synagogue substitute.[119] Further, in the decree of Sardis (Josephus, *A.J.* 14.259–61) Jews are explicitly permitted to perform their ancestral prayers (εὐχάς) and sacrifices (θυσίας), and the record of the incident in the synagogue of Tiberias is accompanied by the reference: "we were proceeding with the ordinary service (tav novmina) and engaged in prayer (εὐχάς)," (Josephus, *Vita* 280–303).

Finally Görtz-Wrisberg argues that *m. Meg.* 4.3 not only reflects earlier traditions but that the coincidence of the order in which *public* prayer (the presence of a *minyan* being presumed[120]), Torah and *haftarah* are referred to in *m. Meg* 4.1–3 with the order of the main parts of the later synagogal services implicates that—contrary to McKay's asser-

---

[116] McKay, *Sabbath and Synagogue*, 128–31, 173–5, 199–200, 246–51.
[117] Fine, "Meeting House,"22–3.
[118] Levine, "Formative Years," 22, idem, "Nature and Origin," 444–5.
[119] Görtz-Wrisberg, "Service," 171.
[120] Cf. Levine, *Ancient Synagogue*, 526–7.

tions—public prayer was part of synagogue services prior to 200 C.E., particularly in the Diaspora.[121]

One might wish to add a reference from Josephus, *C. Ap.* 1:209, where Agatharchides of Cnidos (ca 200–130 B.C.E.) is cited to have said that on every seventh day the Jews abstain from work and "pray with outstretched hands in their sanctuaries until the evening." Here Sabbath service and prayer are linked and the plural of sanctuaries would seem to refer to synagogues rather than the temple.[122]

While being aware of inevitable uncertainties, Görtz-Wrisberg ventures a glimpse of a Sabbath service at Ostia—I will conclude by summing up the gist of her glimpse in the following narrative.

As worshippers enter the synagogue compound from the Via Severiana on a Sabbath morning some time in the middle of the fourth century C.E. in order to celebrate the *Shaharit* they stop at the water basin outside the eastern wall. They wash their hands and feet in order to purify themselves.[123] Entering the synagogue atrium, a mosaic on the floor depicting a cup and a loaf of bread[124] reminds them of the previous evening: the Qiddush, the benediction of the wine and the sanctification of the Sabbath.

As both women and men[125] are passing through the opening to the right of the columns in order to assemble in the main hall of the building, they are welcomed by the *archisynagogos*. He and some other esteemed persons sit on the benches on either side of the bimah along the curved wall at the far west end of the room. The *archisynagogos* assigns prayer recitals and scripture readings to some of the elders and priests

---

[121] Görtz-Wrisberg, "Service," 174.
[122] Horst, "Sabbath Worship," 28, n. 51. Runesson, *Origins*, 346–7. For further arguments in support of the inclusion of prayer in Sabbath meetings in synagogues before 200 C.E., see Horst, "Sabbath Worship," 30–4. The importance of the name *proseuche* as indicating function has been strongly affirmed by Schwartz, *Imperialism*, 217, 220. His assertion that "the word *proseuché* also provides the *only* hint of what went on in the buildings" (italics mine) in ptolemaic Egypt is an overstatement to be sure (cf. the references in Runesson, *Origins*, 191, n. 91).
[123] Philo, *Spec.* 1.261, 3.205–6.
[124] Floriani Squarciapino, "La sinagoga di Ostia," 335.
[125] John Chrysostom, *Adv. Jud.* 1:2–3; Philo, *Contempl.* 32–3; *m. Ber.* 3.3, *y. Ber.* (3d); *b. Sot.* 22a; *b. ᶜAbod. Zar.* 38a–b). Cf. Sanders, *Judaism*, 223–30, 37.

that are present[126] and the psalm-singer gets ready to lead the congregation in worship.[127]

The Greek readings and recitals that will soon begin are conflated with a few Hebrew expressions like shalom or amen and a Latin phrase here and there. The assembly will recite the Shema and the Tefillah and a newcomer from Jerusalem will quote a scripture passage in Hebrew. The occasion of listening to the scriptures in the language of the home land, just like the odd Hebrew letter or word on the epitaphs, serves the worshipping community as a reminder of their descent and kinship. Roman visitors who are present in the synagogue would have benefited more from hearing the Shema and the Tefillah in Greek. But among the regulars Hebrew recitation is preferred.[128]

As the service starts the whole congregation turns towards the east facing the impressive Torah *aedicula* in the north-east corner of the assembly hall. Two columns, with architraves and a roof fries on top, flank the staircase that leads up to the ark where the Torah scrolls are stored. The corbels of the architraves facing the audience are decorated with a shofar, a *menorah*, a *lulav* and an *ethrog*—all reminders of the lost temple. Their eyes glance through the entrances towards the holy land, and as they meet the horizon of the twinkling ocean their minds wander up to the holy city.

The assembly hall has no chairs and the benches that once ran along the walls have been removed. Thus, the worshippers sit down on the ground and recite the Shema, but rise again to recite the Tefillah together. Now the Torah scrolls are taken from the aedicula and carried to the bimah. As the worshippers follow the procession of the scrolls, "the embodiment of the divine presence"[129] with their eyes, they turn towards the bimah from whence the scripture reading is to proceed. Now a sage rises and delivers a learned sermon to the assembly that has been seated again.

---

[126] Both before and after 70 C.E. priests served often as teachers of the law in the synagogue (Theodotos inscription, Philo, *Hypoth.* 7.12–13). This may explain why the priestly blessing was one of the earliest prayers transferred to the synagogue (*m.Ber.* 5.4).

[127] Cf. the funerary inscription found in the Villa Torlonia which tells of Gaianos, a γραμματεὺς ψαλμῳδὸς φιλονόμος, *JIWE*, 399.

[128] Levine, "Sages and Synagogue," 217–18.

[129] Fine, "Meeting House," 271.

In conclusion of the Shaharit the congregation stands for the Musaf prayer, reciting the Tefillah once more and closing with a quotation from the Psalms.

Conclusions

The explorations of the situation, organization and language skills of the Jews of Rome and Ostia and the ancient synagogue building and its surroundings have shown that we are in the middle of a dynamic process of research. A few years have passed and the research published in *SAOJR* has already had an impact on the scholarly debate. Yet also, some of that research needed to be updated or revised and some has even been outdated by new archeological data that have since become available.

Re-examinations of the textual evidence with regard to the Jews of the Diaspora are constantly forthcoming. The debate of the synagogue building's history has continued since *SAOJR*, the issues at stake have become clearer, resulting in renewed consensus in several regards. New archaeological finds and insights into the history of the Quarter outside the Porta Marina, the Tiber mouth harbor and suburban settling in the first century have brought—and are bringing—to light new insights on how and why the synagogue was placed where it is. Hopefully, the publication of the final excavation report on the synagogue building and new excavations in the Quarter will soon add further information and enrich our understanding.

The Jews of Rome

In terms of language, professions and trade, and even religious practices the Jews of Rome interacted readily with the surrounding environment. At the same time these communities of immigrants preserved devotion for the customs and traditions of the homeland, which at times may have been perceived as asocial isolationism by outsiders and may have contributed to the disdain that permeates much of the Roman writers' descriptions.

Persecution and violence against the Jews of Rome, however, was more often than not part of general retributions against foreign groups or religions. At times such acts of violence seem to have been part of a campaign to demonstrate the emperor's guardianship of Roman values; at times it may have been a way to quench detrimental rumors.

In the early years of Jewish settlement in Rome the Jews may have been ignorant of Roman religious policy, assuming conditions similar to those under Persian or Greek rule. Such ignorance may have led to unwanted confrontation and conflict and to persecution that was directed more pointedly at the Jews.

The Synagogue at Ancient Ostia

The evidence of the AAR/DAI excavation campaign 2001 confirms the assertions made by Floriani Squarciapino and affirmed by Runesson that the area surrounding the synagogue building at Ostia was not a wasteland where the undesirable were allowed to settle. Instead the impression of a well-situated community that emanated from the monumental and culturally adapted design of the earliest synagogue building is now confirmed by the *Villa suburbana* and several other both large and small edifices outside the city walls. Already in the middle of the first century we see a movement of affluent citizens away from the center to suburban areas of Ostia, often outside the city walls.

Due to observations of building peculiarities of the *Villa suburbana* together with the positioning of the synagogue building to the far south-east and the *insulae* right into the shore view of the villa, the conclusions drawn based on the synagogue's own building history were strengthened. The original synagogue building may stem from the early second half of the first century. It may have been erected immediately after or even concurrently with the villa.

Had the synagogue been built after the insulae there would have been no plausible cause to put it so far to the south, since the shore view was blocked already by the *insulae*. But then again, in order to make up one's mind, one would want to know more about the area to the north-west of the synagogue that has not yet been excavated.

With regard to the synagogue building itself, the roof construction requires further thought. Based on the floor erosion in C_2 I have ventured to suggest a roofless corridor for area C that separates and connects the synagogue hall of area D and a building consisting of areas B and G that contains the triclinium. The recognition of the earthquake that destroyed the *Villa suburbana* has led to an additional explanation (together with the socio-religious embellishment theory) for the reconstruction of the building in the third century which included wall reinforcements around much of area D.

The Jews of Ostia

We have seen numerous indications that the Jews of Ostia were culturally well integrated into Ostian society. The architecture of their synagogue building corresponded to that of the surrounding culture, they spoke the *lingua franca* and they moved to the city in a time of intense commerce, probably as traders and craftsmen. Especially during the first and second centuries they seem to have kept a low profile with regard to religious practice. They do not seem to wish to show off their religious symbols. They even adapted the practice from Gentile temples to put a washing basin at the entrance of the synagogue.

Ties between the Jews of Rome and the Jews of Ostia can be assumed to have existed not only because of the geographical proximity but also because of organizational similarity. Besides the fact that the first known settlement of Jews in Ostia coincides with a commercially expanding environment, it also coincides with the expulsion of Jews and other undesirable assemblages from Rome under Claudius. Some of the refugees from Rome may have found their way to Ostia and joined the new Jewish community (or even constituted it) that was planning to build their own sanctuary.

Knowing that there were Christ-believers among the Jews expelled, we may speculate that some also were among the refugees that came to Ostia. These refugees had many good reasons to accept the recognized Jewish boundaries and not to cause any disorder. For quite some time, they may have refrained from reaching out to Gentiles, which in turn may explain, partly at least, the lack of evidence of Christian presence in Ostia for so many decades, even though Christianity was on the rise everywhere else, so it seems. Maybe the Jewish Christ-believers faired well within a synagogue community that was culturally and economically well situated and may have been willing to accept confessions of faith in Jesus Messiah as one variety of Jewishness. At any rate, the earliest signs of a Christian presence are a few inscriptions that can be dated to the third century[130] and a tradition mentioned in sources from

---

[130] It must be remembered that no Jewish or Christian archeological traces have been discovered prior to the catacombs—none of which dates earlier than 200 C.E.—neither in Rome nor in Ostia.

around 700 C.E. that St. Aurea, the most famous but also the earliest known Christian martyr of Ostia was killed under Claudius Gothicus (268–270).

In the city of Rome things may have developed quite differently. Soon after the expulsion under Claudius, groups of Jews, including Christ-believers that were less cautious in terms of propagating their faith and activating separation processes, moved in, so that already during Nero's persecutions of Christians in Rome, the Jews do not seem to have been affected as a community by that measure.

As Christianity began to expand in Ostia and non-Jewish Christ-believers (who had long lost touch with the older "brother") moved into the city, antagonism and competition that had begun to divide Judaism and Christianity, may have caught up with ancient Ostia.

With the rapid expansion of Christianity in Ostia in the fourth century C.E. a shift of attitude among the Jews towards religious practice becomes palpable. The synagogue was embellished with religious symbols. This shift of attitude may be due to "rabbinic Judaism on the rise," it may also be a reaction against "Christianity on the rise." The brother who had ascended to the status of official state religion had become more than just a competitor and was to be informed that Judaism had a strength of its own.

Bibliography

Avigad, N., *Beth Shearim, III.* New Brunswick: Rutgers University Press, 1976.

Baltrusch, E., *Die Juden und das Römische Reich: Geschichte einer konfliktreichen Beziehung.* Darmstadt: Wissenschaftliche Buchgesellschaft, 2002.

Barclay, J. M. G., *Jews in the Mediterranean Diaspora: From Alexander to Trajan (323 B.C.E.–117 C.E.).* Edinburgh: T & T Clark, 1996.

Bauer, F. A., M. Heinzelmann, and A. Martin. "Ostia. Ein urbanistisches Forschungsprojekt in den unausgegrabenen Bereichen des Stadtgebietes." *MDAI. Römische Abteilung* 107 (2000): 375–415.

Becatti, G., *Scavi di Ostia II. I mitrei.* Roma, 1954.

Bengtsson, P. Å. "Semitic Inscriptions in Rome." Pages 151–66 in *The Synagogue of Ancient Ostia and the Jews of Rome: Interdisciplinary Studies*. Edited by B. Olsson, O. Brandt, and D. Mitternacht. Stockholm: Paul Åströms förlag, 2001.

Berger, P. L., and T. Luckman. *The Social Construction of Reality: A Treatise in the Sociology of Knowledge*. London: Penguin Books, 1966.

Boterman, H. *Das Judenedikt des Kaisers Claudius: Römischer Staat und Christiani im 1. Jahrhundert*. Stuttgart: Steiner, 1996.

Brandt, O. "The Quarter Surrounding the Syangogue at Ostia." Pages 19–28 in *The Synagogue of Ancient Ostia and the Jews of Rome: Interdisciplinary Studies*. Edited by B. Olsson, O. Brandt, and D. Mitternacht. Stockholm: Paul Åströms förlag, 2001.

Elbogen, I. *Jewish Liturgy. A Comprehensive History*. Translated by Raymond P. Scheindlin. Based on the original 1913 German ed. and the 1972 Hebrew ed. New York: Jewish Theological Seminary of America: Philadelphia: Jewish Publication Society, 1993.

Fine, S., "From Meeting House to Sacred Realm: Holiness and the Ancient Synagogue." Pages 21–47 in *Sacred Realm: The Emergence of the Synagogue in the Ancient World*. New York and Oxford: Yeshiva University Museum and Oxford University Press, 1996.

Floriani Squarciapino, M., "La sinagoga di Ostia." *Bollettino d'arte* 46 (1961): 326–37.

—, "Ebrei a Roma e ad Ostia." *Studi Romani* 11 (1963): 129–41.

—, "La sinagoga di Ostia: Seconda campagna di scavo." Pages 299–315 in *Atti del VI congresso internazionale di archeologia cristiana Ravenna 23-30 settembre 1962*. Città del Vaticano: Pontificio istituto di archeologia cristiana, 1965.

—, "Plotius Fortunatus archisynagogus." *La Rassegna Mensile di Israel* 36 (1970): 183–91.

—, "Synagogue d' Ostie." Pages 272–7 in *Ostia port et porte de la Rome antique*. Edited by J-P. Descoedres. Geneve: Musées d'art et d'histoire, 2001.

Gruen, E. S., *Diaspora. Jews amidst Greeks and Romans*. Cambridge: Harvard University Press, 2002.

Guidoboni, E., *Catalogue of Ancient Earthquakes in the Mediterranean Area up to the 10th Century.* Rome: Institutio Nazionale di Geofisica, 1994.

Görtz-Wrisberg, I. v., "What Do We Know about the Ancient Synagogal Service?" Pages 167–202 in *The Synagogue of Ancient Ostia and the Jews of Rome: Interdisciplinary Studies.* Edited by B. Olsson, O. Brandt, and D. Mitternacht. Stockholm: Paul Åströms förlag, 2001.

Hachlili, R., *Ancient Jewish Art and Archaeology in the Diaspora.* Vol. 1:35. Leiden, Boston, Köln: Brill, 1998.

—, *The Menorah, the Ancient Seven-Armed Candelarum: Origin, Form, Significance.* Leiden. Brill, 2001.

Hedner Zetterholm, K., "The Jewish Communities of Ancient Rome." Pages 131–40 in *The Synagogue of Ancient Ostia and the Jews of Rome: Interdisciplinary Studies.* Edited by B. Olsson, O. Brandt, and D. Mitternacht. Stockholm: Paul Åströms förlag, 2001.

Heinzelmann, M., "Ostia, Regio III. Untersuchungen in den unausgegrabenen Bereichen des Stadtgebietes." *MDAI. Römische Abteilung* 108 (2001): 313–28.

Hidal, S., "The Jews as the Romans saw them." Pages 141–4 in *The Synagogue of Ancient Ostia and the Jews of Rome: Interdisciplinary Studies.* Edited by B. Olsson, O. Brandt, and D. Mitternacht. Stockholm: Paul Åströms förlag, 2001.

Horst, P. W. v. d., "Was the Synagogue a Place of Sabbath Worship before 70 C.E.?" Pages 18–43 in *Jews Christians, and Polytheists in the Ancient Syangogue.* Edited by S. Fine. London: Routledge, 1999.

Kraabel, A. T. "The Diaspora Synagogue: Archaeological and Epigraphic Evidence since Sukenik." Pages 477–510 in *ANRW* II.19.1. Edited by H. Temporini and W. Haase Berlin, New York: de Gruyter, 1979.

Leon, H. J. *The Jews of Ancient Rome.* Peabody: Hendrickson, 1995 [1960].

—, *The Jews of Ancient Rome.* Philadelphia: The Jewish Publication Society of America, 1960.

Levine, L. I,. "The Second Temple Synagogue: The Formative Years." Pages 7–31 in *The Synagogue in Late Antiquity*. Edited by L. I. Levine Philadelphia: The American Schools of Oriental Research, 1987.

—, "The Sages and the Synagogue in Late Antiquity: The Evidence of the Galilee." Pages 201–22 in *The Galilee in Late Antiquity*. Edited by L. I. Levine New York: The Jewish Theological Seminary of America, 1992.

—, "The Nature and Origin of the Palestinian Synagogue Reconsidered." *JBL* 115 (1996): 425–48.

—, *The Ancient Synagogue: The First Thousand Years*. New Haven: Yale University Press, 2000.

Levinskaya, I. *The Book of Acts in Its Diaspora Setting*. Grand Rapids: Eerdmans, 1996.

Margaliot, M., *The Laws of Eretz Israel from the Geniza*. Jerusalem, 1973 (in Hebrew).

McKay, H. A., *Sabbath and Synagogue: The Question of Sabbath Worship in Ancient Judaism*. Leiden: Brill, 1994.

Meiggs, R., *Roman Ostia*. 2nd ed. Oxford: Clarendon Press, 1977.

Mitternacht, D., "Foolish Galatians? A Recipient-oriented Assessment of Paul's Letter." Pages 408–33 in *The Galatians Debate: Contemporary Issues in Rhetorical and Historical Interpretation*. Edited by M. D. Nanos. Peabody: Hendrickson, 2002.

Noy, D., *Jewish Inscriptions of Western Europe: Italy (Excluding the City of Rome) Spain and Gaul*. Vol. 1. Cambridge: Cambridge University Press, 1993.

—, *Jewish Inscriptions of Western Europe: The City of Rome*. Vol. 2. Cambridge, New York: Cambridge University Press, 1995.

Olsson, B., "Introduction." Pages 11–16 in *The Synagogue of Ancient Ostia and the Jews of Rome: Interdisciplinary Studies*. Edited by B. Olsson et al. Stockholm: Paul Åströms förlag, 2001.

Pavolini, C., "Ostia (Roma): Saggi Lungo la Via Severiana." *Notizie degli Scavi di Antichita* 35 (1981): 115–43.

Runesson, A., *The Origins of the Synagogue: A Socio-Historical Study*. Stockholm: Almqvist & Wiksell International, 2001.

—, "The Synagogue at Ancient Ostia: The Building and its History From the First to the Fifth Century." Pages 29-99 in *The Synagogue of Ancient Ostia and the Jews of Rome: Interdisciplinary Studies.* Edited by B. Olsson et al. Stockholm: Paul Åströms förlag, 2001.

—, "A Monumental Synagogue from the First Century: The Case of Ostia." *JSJ* 33 (2002): 171–220.

Rutgers, L. V., *The Jews in Late Ancient Rome: Evidence of Cultural Interaction in the Roman Diaspora.* Leiden: Brill, 1995.

Sanders, E. P., *Jewish Law from Jesus to de Mishnah: Five Studies.* London: SCM, 1990.

—, *Judaism: Practice and Belief 63 B.C.E 66 C.E.* London: SCM Press, 1992.

Schwartz, S., *Imperialism and Jewish Society, 200 B.C.E. to 640 C.E.* Princeton: Princeton University Press, 2001.

Stark, R., *The Rise of Christianity: How the Obscure, Marginal Jesus Movement Became the Dominant Religious Force in the Western World in a Few Centuries.* San Francisco: Harper Collins, 1997.

Stern, M., *Greek and Latin Authors on Jews and Judaism: From Herodotus to Plutarch.* Vol. 1. Jerusalem: The Israel Academy of Sciences and Humanities, 1974.

Walser, G., "The Greek of the Jews in Ancient Rome." Pages 145–50 in *The Synagogue of Ancient Ostia and the Jews of Rome: Interdisciplinary Studies.* Edited by B. Olsson et al. Stockholm: Paul Åströms förlag, 2001.

White, L. M., *The Social Origins of Christian Architecture. Building God's House in the Roman World: Architectural Adaptation Among Pagans, Jews, and Christians.* Vol. 1. Valley Forge: Trinity Press International, 1996.

—, "Synagogue and Society in Imperial Ostia: Archaeological and Epigraphic Evidence." *HTR* 90 (1997): 23–58.

—, "Synagogue and Society in Imperial Ostia: Archaeological and Epigraphic Evidence." Pages 30–68 in *Judaism and Christianity in First Century Rome* Grand Rapids: Eerdmans, 1998.

—, "Reading the Ostia Synagogue: A Reply to A. Runesson." *HTR* 92 (1999): 435–64.

Wright, B. G., "Jewish Ritual Baths–Interpreting the Digs and the Texts: Some Issues in the Social History of Second Temple Judaism." Pages 190–214 in *The Archaeology of Israel: Constructing the Past, Interpreting the Present*, edited by N. A. Silberman et al. Sheffield: Sheffield Academic Press, 1997.

Zappa, G. G., "Nuovi bolli laterizi di Ostia." Pages 257–89 in *Terza Miscellanea Greca e Romana*. Edited by G. Barbieri. Rome, 1971.

Zetterholm, M., "A Struggle Among Brothers: An Interpretation of the Relations Between Jews and Christians in Ostia." Pages 101–13 in *The Synagogue of Ancient Ostia and the Jews of Rome: Interdisciplinary Studies*. Edited by B. Olsson et al. Stockholm: Paul Åströms förlag, 2001.

Zevi, F., "La sinagoga di Ostia." *Rassegna mensile di Israel* 38 (1972): 131–45.

Conciectanea Biblica

New Testament Series

Present editors: Birger Olsson (Lund) and Kari Syreeni (Uppsala)

1. *Hartman, L.:* Prophecy Interpreted: The Formation of Some Jewish Apocalyptic Texts and of the Eschatological Discourse Mark 13 par. 1966.
2. *Gerhardsson, B.:* The Testing of God's Son (Matt 4: 1-11 & Par). An Analysis of an Early Christian Midrash.
   Fasc. I (chapters 1-4). 1966.
   Fasc. 2 in preparation.
3. *Kieffer, R.:* Au delà des recensions? L'évolution de la tradition textuelle dans Jean VI, 52-71. 1968.
4. *Kieffer, R.:* Essais de méthodologie neo-testamentaire. 1972.
5. *Forkman, C.:* The Limits of the Religious Community: Expulsion from the Religious Community within the Qumran Sect, within Rabbinic Judaism, and within Primitive Christianity. 1972.
6. *Olsson, B.:* Structure and Meaning in the Fourth Gospel: A Text-Linguistic Analysis of John 2:1-11 and 4:1-42. 1974.
7. *Cavallin, H. C. C.:* Life After Death: Paul's Argument for the Resurrection of the Dead in 1 Cor 15.
   Part 1. An Enquiry into the Jewish Background. 1974.
   Part 2 in preparation.
8. *Caragounis, C.:* The Ephesian *Mysterion*. Meaning and Content. 1977.
9. *Fornberg, T.:* An Early Church in a Pluralistic Society: A Study of 2 Peter. 1977.
10. *Westerholm, S.:* Jesus and Scribal Authority. 1978.
11. *Holmberg, B.:* Paul and Power: The Structure of Authority in the Primitive Church as Reflected in the Pauline Epistles. 1978.
12. *Hartman, L.:* Asking for a Meaning. A Study of I Enoch 1-5. 1979.
13. *Hellholm, D.:* Das Visionenbuch des Hermas als Apokalypse: Formgeschichtliche und texttheoretische Studien zu einer literarischen Gattung.
    Band 1. Methodologische Vorüberlegungen und makrostrukturelle Textanalyse. 1980.
    Band 2. Gattungs-bestimmung und Interpretation. In preparation.
14. *Franck, E.:* Revelation Taught: The Paraclete in the Gospel of John. 1985.
15. *Gerhardsson, B.:* The Gospel Tradition. 1986.
16. *Johansson, B. C.:* To All the Brethren: A Text-Linguistic and Rhetorical Approach to I Thessalonians. 1987.
17. *Enermalm-Ogawa, A.:* Un langage de prière juif en grec. Le témoignage des deux premiers livres des Maccabées. 1987.
18. *Hartman, L., Olsson. B.* (eds.): Aspects on the Johannine Literature: Papers Presented at a Conference of Scandinavian New Testament Exegetes at Uppsala, June 16-19, 1986. 1987.
19. *Strandenaes, T.:* Principles of Chinese Bible Translation as Expressed in Five Selected Versions of the New Testament and Exemplified by Mt 5:1-12 and Col 1. 1987.
20. *Portefaix, L.:* Sisters Rejoice: Paul's Letter to the Philippians and Luke-Acts as Seen by First Century Philippian Women. 1988.
21. *Übelacker, W. G.:* Der Hebräerbrief als Appell.
    Untersuchungen zu *exordium, narratio* und *postscriptum* (Hebr 1-2 und 13,22-25). 1989.
    Untersuchungen zu *argumentatio* und *peroratio* (3.1-13.21). In preparation.
22. *Ulfgard. H.:* Feast and Future: Revelation 7:9-17 and the Feast of Tabernacles. 1989.

23. *Christofferson, O.:* The Earnest Expectation of the Creature: The Flood-Tradition as Matrix of Romans 8:18-27. 1990.
24. *Byrskog, S.:* Jesus the Only Teacher: Didactic Authority and Transmission in Ancient Israel, Ancient Judaism and the Matthean Community. 1994.
25. *Lövestam, E.:* Jesus and 'This Generation': A New Testament Study. 1995.
26. *Winninge, M.:* Sinners and the Righteous: A Comparative Study of the Psalms of Solomon and Paul's Letters. 1995.
27. *Chow, S.:* The Sign of Jonah Reconsidered: A Study of Its Meaning in the Gospel Traditions. 1995.
28. *Holmstrand, J.:* Markers and Meanings in Paul: An Analysis of 1 Thessalonians, Philippians and Galatians. 1997.
29. *Eriksson, A.:* Traditions as Rhetorical Proof: Pauline Argumentation in 1 Corinthians. 1998.
30. *Mitternacht, D.:* Forum für Sprachlose: Eine kommunkationspsychologische und epistolär-rhetorische Untersuchung des Galaterbriefs. 1999.
31. *Hillert, S.:* Limited and Universal Salvation: A Text-Oriented and Hermeneutical Study of Two Perspectives in Paul. 2000.
32. *Svartvik, J.:* Mark and Mission: Mk 7:1-23 in its Narrative and Historical Contexts. 2000.
33. *Starr, J. M.:* Sharers in Divine Nature: 2 Peter 1:4 in Its Hellenistic Context. 2000.
34. *Tellbe, M.:* Paul between Synagogue and State: Christians, Jews, and Civic Authorities in 1 Thessalonians, Romans, and Philippians. 2001.
35. *Larsson, T.:* God in the Fourth Gospel: A Hermeneutical Study of the History of Interpretations. 2001.
36. *Gerdmar, A.:* Rethinking the Judaism – Hellenism Dichotomy: A Historiographical Case Study of Second Peter and Jude. 2001
37. *Runesson, A.:* The Origins of the Synagogue: A Socio-Historical Study. 2001
38. *Kazen, Th.*, Jesus and Purity Halakhah: Was Jesus Indifferent to Impurity? 2002.
39. *Olsson, B. and M. Zetterholm*, eds.: The Ancient Synagogue From Its Origins until 200 c.e.: Papers Presented at an International Conference at Lund University, October 14–17, 2001. 2003.

Distributed by:
Almqvist & Wiksell International
P.O. Box 7634
SE-103 94 STOCKHOLM
SWEDEN
Phone: +46 8 613 61 00
Fax: +46 8 24 25 43
E-mail: order@city.akademibokhandeln.se